DISINFECTION AND STERILIZATION
SECOND EDITION

Disinfection
and Sterilization

G. SYKES M.Sc. (Lond.), Hon. M.P.S., F.R.I.C.

With a Foreword by

SIR GRAHAM WILSON
M.D., F.R.C.P., D.P.H.
lately Director of the Public Health
Laboratory Service

SECOND EDITION
REVISED AND ENLARGED

CHAPMAN AND HALL LTD

First published 1958
by E. & F. N. Spon Ltd
Second edition 1965
Reprinted with corrections, 1967
Reprinted 1972
Published by Chapman and Hall Ltd,
11 New Fetter Lane, London, EC4P 4EE

Printed in Great Britain by
Redwood Press Limited,
Trowbridge, Wiltshire

SBN 412 11590 5

TO MY WIFE
whose patient tolerance
has made
this book possible

FOREWORD

by
SIR GRAHAM WILSON

IN my foreword to the first edition in 1958, I gave a brief review of the history of disinfectants during the last 100 years, and noted the comparatively recent introduction not only of new germicidal agents but of new ways of sterilization, disinfection and preservation of materials in common use. Because Mr. Sykes had fulfilled his task admirably, I had no hesitation in commending his book to those who, whether engaged in medicine, pharmacy, sanitary engineering, dairying, brewing or the food industry, wanted reliable and up-to-date information to help them in the multitude of problems that beset them in their various fields of activity. The fact that a second edition has been called for in so short a time leaves no doubt that the book is meeting a widespread need.

It would probably be true to say that more attention is being paid now to the use of physical than to chemical methods of removing, immobilizing, or destroying unwanted micro-organisms. Experience of chemical disinfectants, particularly in medicine and the dairy industry, has shown their inferiority to heat in the destruction of bacteria; and it is only right therefore that Mr. Sykes should expand, as he has done, the sections of his book dealing with such physical means of sterilization and disinfection as heat, filtration, and the various forms of irradiation and ultrasonic treatment now available.

He is wise too to set his face against the use of such imprecise terms as "Sterilant" and "Sanitization". The definitions that he has given of the terms he employs are ones that are etymologically correct and will be accepted by other scientific workers. To call a substance a sterilant that does not sterilize is misleading; and what the term sanitization means beyond mere cleansing it is impossible to say. It throws no light on the degree of bacterial destruction involved, if any, and it is but one more example of the use of a long, inexact word of Latin derivation to obscure the mental haziness of those who have never troubled to think what they mean.

Personally I welcome the publication of this new and enlarged version of Mr. Sykes's original book. It is an expression of his erudition and his literary ability to which all will pay tribute. It is doubtful whether anyone else in this country could have dealt so competently with so many controversial issues in so many different fields; and I hope the book will meet with the success that it deserves.

GRAHAM S. WILSON

PREFACE TO SECOND EDITION

ALTHOUGH it is less than six years since the first edition of this book appeared, investigation in nearly all of the fields has continued at an increasing rate and much new thinking has taken place. This second edition is, therefore, something more than the first edition "brought up to date". Most of the chapters, although retaining substantially the same titles and order of presentation, have been largely rewritten with emphasis on the revised outlooks and the newer evidences without sacrificing unduly the earlier foundational references.

In particular, attention is drawn to the changing attitudes towards the testing of disinfectants and antiseptics, as given in Chapters 3 and 4, and the substantial new information which has come to light concerning methods of sterilization, with special emphasis on several aspects of sterilization by heat and by radiations; new agents for gaseous sterilization have also been introduced.

In Part V dealing with Chemical Disinfectants the sections on 'germicidal' soaps and disinfectant fluids have been completely remoulded and new data have been added in other sections. Similarly in the chapter on surface active compounds a new section on amphoteric compounds has been added, together with some new information on quaternary ammonium compounds. The chapter on the heavy metals salts has also been extended.

Finally, a great deal more is now known about various aspects of preservation, particularly in relation to foods and pharmaceutical materials, and this has been mainly included in a rewritten chapter (17) on the subject.

Again I wish to thank my various colleagues and associates who have given valuable assistance and information. In particular I would commend Miss Barbara Hooton and Mr. R. Smart for their help in preparing the manuscript and in checking the proofs.

G. SYKES

Boots Pure Drug Co. Ltd.,
Microbiology Division,
Standards Department,
Nottingham.

July, 1964

PREFACE TO FIRST EDITION

WITH the many advances which are being made in the broad fields of hygiene, sanitation and medicine and the profound changes which are taking place in our everyday mode of living, more and more emphasis is being placed on the need for adequate and reliable methods for disinfection, preservation and sterilization. It is a matter which impinges on the social and economic welfare of the whole community and is seen in the continuous scientific and technical progress being made in the various sections of the food, pharmaceutical and chemical industries as well as in the several disciplines of medicine and public health.

The greatest advances have undoubtedly occurred during the last two or three decades and it is the purpose of this book to present a considered appraisal of these developments. In approaching the subject I have confined myself – if confined is still the right word to use in such a large field – to the chemical and physical aspects of disinfection and sterilization to the almost total exclusion of any discussion on chemotherapy or the role of antibiotics; these topics are now almost separate subjects in themselves and have already filled several volumes.

Perhaps it may appear that an unduly large proportion of the book is taken up with discussions on the theory and mode of action of disinfection, not only in the chapter bearing that title but also in other chapters; but this is deliberate, for this aspect of the subject is gradually assuming greater importance, and it seems that future developments are likely to take place from such considerations rather than from the erstwhile more empirical approach. It also seemed desirable to collect together as many as possible of the tried and proved methods of testing disinfectants and antiseptics, and this is done in Chapters 3 and 4; attention is also given in these chapters to some of the more historical methods of testing and to other potentially useful ones. With regard to the techniques available for disinfection, preservation and sterilization, I have endeavoured to cover the most recent developments in both the chemical and physical fields as completely as possible, devoting individual chapters to the important topics of radiation sterilization and the disinfection of viruses.

The usual abbreviations have been adopted for expressing units of time, volume, etc., and temperatures are quoted in degrees Centigrade except in the few places where they are specifically stated to be in degrees Fahrenheit. For bacterial nomenclature I have used the Topley and Wilson system, preferring *Pseudomonas pyocyanea* to *Pseudomonas aeruginosa*, *Chromobacterium prodigiosum* to *Serratia marsescens* and so on, but using *Escherichia coli* instead of *Bacterium coli*.

In preparing the text I have made frequent reference to the literature, and in this respect have greatly appreciated the facilities available through the libraries of Boots Pure Drug Co. Ltd. I wish to record thanks to Dr. R. S. Hannan and Dr. Margaret Thornley for their useful criticisms of the manuscript of the chapter on Radiation Sterilization, and to Dr. Löis Dickinson who has given similar help with the chapter on the Disinfection of Viruses. I am also indebted to several authors and publishers for permission to reproduce certain Tables and Figures, in particular to the editors of the *Proceedings of the Royal Society* for permission to reproduce Plate 1, to Dr. Harriette Chick and the editors of the *Journal of Hygiene* for Figure 1 and Table 1, to Dr. R. M. Savage and the editor of the *Journal of Pharmacy and Pharmacology* for Figure 6, to Dr. G. E. Stapleton, Dr. M. Levine and the editor of the *Journal of Bacteriology* for Figures 10, 15 and 16, and to the editors of the *Journal of Applied Bacteriology* for Figure 17 and Table 16. The help given by Mrs. Maureen Pole, Miss Pamela Chapman, Mr. D. V. Carter, Mr. H. M. Bunbury and other colleagues in assembling the manuscript and checking the proofs has been invaluable and I thank them all. Finally, I must mention Mr. C. E. Coulthard, under whose guidance I first began to learn something of the subjects about which I now venture to write.

G. SYKES

Boots Pure Drug Co. Ltd.,
Microbiology Division,
Standards Department,
Nottingham.

March, 1958.

CONTENTS

PART 1

Theory of Disinfection and Methods of Testing

PART II

Methods of Sterilization

PART III

Air Disinfection and Sterilization

PART IV

Disinfection of Viruses

PART V

Chemical Disinfectants

PART VI

Preservation and Preservatives

LIST OF LITERATURE ABBREVIATIONS

Acta microbiol., hung.	Acta microbiologica, Academicae Scientiarium Hungaricae
Acta path. microbiol. scand.	Acta pathologica et microbiologica scandinavica
Adv. appl. Microbiol.	Advances in Applied Microbiology
Adv. food Res.	Advances in Food Research
Amer. J. clin. Path.	American Journal of Clinical Pathology
Amer. J. Hyg.	American Journal of Hygiene
Amer. J. med. Sci.	American Journal of the Medical Sciences
Amer. J. Obstet. Gynec.	American Journal of Obstetrics and Gynecology
Amer. J. Ophthal.	American Journal of Ophthalmology
Amer. J. Path.	American Journal of Pathology
Amer. J. Pharm.	American Journal of Pharmacy
Amer. J. Physiol.	American Journal of Physiology
Amer. J. publ. Hlth	American Journal of Public Health
Amer. J. Surg.	American Journal of Surgery
Amer. Rev. Tuberc.	American Review of Tuberculosis
Analyst	The Analyst
Ann. appl. Biol.	Annals of Applied Biology
Ann. Inst. Pasteur	Annales de l'Institut Pasteur
Ann. N.Y. Acad. Sci.	Annals of the New York Academy of Sciences
Ann. Rev. Biochem.	Annual Review of Biochemistry
Ann. Rev. Microbiol.	Annual Review of Microbiology
Antonie van Leeuwenhoek J. Microbiol. Serol.	Antonie van Leeuwenhoek Journal of Microbiology and Serology
Antibiot. Chemoth.	Antibiotics and Chemotherapy
Appl. Microbiol.	Applied Microbiology
Arch. Biochem.	Archives of Biochemistry
Arch. Dermatol. Syphylol.	Archives of Dermatology and Syphylology
Arch. ind. Hyg.	Archives of Industrial Hygiene and Occupational Medicine
Arch. Mikrobiol.	Archiv für Mikrobiologie
Arch. Surg., Lond.	Archives of Surgery, London
Aust. J. exp. Biol. med. Sci.	Australian Journal of Experimental Biology and Medical Science
Bact. Rev.	Bacteriological Reviews
Biochem. J.	Biochemical Journal
Biochem. Z.	Biochemische Zeitschrift
Biodynamica	Biodynamica
Biol. Abs.	Biological Abstracts
Biometrics	Biometrics
Boll. Ist. sieroter. milan	Bollettino dell'Istituto sieroterapico milanese
Brit. J. exp. Path.	British Journal of Experimental Pathology
Brit. J. ind. Med.	British Journal of Industrial Medicine
Brit. med. J.	British Medical Journal
Brit. J. Pharmacol.	British Journal of Pharmacology and Chemotherapy

Brit. J. Urol.	British Journal of Urology
Brit. Vet. J.	British Veterinary Journal
Bull. Acad. méd., Paris	Bulletin de l'Académie de médecine
Bull. Hyg.	Bulletin of Hygiene, London
Canad. J. med. Sci.	Canadian Journal of Medical Sciences
Canad. J. Microbiol.	Canadian Journal of Microbiology
Chem. Abs.	Chemical Abstracts (American)
Chem. Fabrik	Chemische Fabrik
Chem. & Ind.	Chemistry and Industry
Compt. rend. Acad. sci.	Comptes rendus hebdomadaires des séances de l'Académie des sciences
Compt. rend. Soc. Biol.	Comptes rendus hebdomadaires des séances de la Société de biologie
Dansk Tidss. Farm.	Dansk Tidsskrift for Farmaci
Deut. med. Woch.	Deutsche medizinische Wochenschrift
Drug Stds	Drug Standards
Elect. Engng, N.Y.	Electrical Engineering, New York
Electronics	Electronics
Exp. cell Res.	Experimental Cell Research
Food Ind.	Food Industry
Food Mfg.	Food Manufacture
Food Res.	Food Research
Food Technol.	Food Technology
Gen. elec. Rev.	General Electrical Reviews
Gesund. Desinf.	Gesundheitswesen und Desinfektion
Heat. air Treat. Engr	Heating and Air Treatment Engineer
Heat. Pip. air Cond.	Heating, Piping and Air Conditioning
Heat. vent. Engng	Heating and Ventilating Engineering
Hosp. Engr	The Hospital Engineer
Ind. Chem.	Industrial Chemist
Ind. engng Chem.	Industrial and Engineering Chemistry
Ind. engng Chem. (Anal.)	Industrial and Engineering Chemistry (Analytical Edition)
Int. J. appl. Rad. Isot.	International Journal of Applied Radiation and Isotopes
Iowa engng exp. Sta. Bull.	Iowa Engineering Experimental Station Bulletin
Iowa State Coll. J. Sci.	Iowa State College Journal of Science
Johns Hopkins Hosp. Bull.	Johns Hopkins Hospital Bulletin
J. Amer. chem. Soc.	Journal of the American Chemical Society
J. Amer. diet. Ass.	Journal of the American Dietary Association
J. Amer. med. Ass.	Journal of the American Medical Association
J. Amer. pharm. Ass. (Pract.)	Journal of the American Pharmaceutical Association (Practical Edition)
J. Amer. pharm. Ass. (Sci.)	Journal of the American Pharmaceutical Association (Scientific Edition)
J. Amer. vet. med. Ass.	Journal of the American Veterinary Medical Association
J. Amer. Water Wks Ass.	Journal of the American Water Works Association
J. appl. Bact.	Journal of Applied Bacteriology
J. appl. Chem.	Journal of Applied Chemistry
J. appl. Phys.	Journal of Applied Physiology

J. Ass. off. agric. Chem.	Journal of the Association of Official Agricultural Chemists
J. Bact.	Journal of Bacteriology
J. biol. Chem.	Journal of Biological Chemistry
J. cell. comp. Physiol.	Journal of Cellular and Comparative Physiology
J. chem. Soc.	Journal of the Chemical Society
J. clin. Path.	Journal of Clinical Pathology
J. Dairy Res.	Journal of Dairy Research
J. Dairy Sci.	Journal of Dairy Science
J. exp. Med.	Journal of Experimental Medicine
J. gen. Microbiol.	Journal of General Microbiology
J. gen. Physiol.	Journal of General Physiology
J. Hyg., Camb.	Journal of Hygiene
J. Immunol.	Journal of Immunology
J. ind. Hyg.	Journal of Industrial Hygiene
J. infect. Dis.	Journal of Infectious Diseases
J. Inst. chem. Engrs	Journal of the Institution of Chemical Engineers
J. Inst. Water Engrs	Journal of the Institution of Water Engineers
J. invest. Dermatol.	Journal of Investigative Dermatology
J. lab. clin. Med.	Journal of Laboratory and Clinical Medicine
J. Milk Tech.	Journal of Milk (and Food) Technology
J. Obstet. Gynaec. Brit. Emp.	Journal of Obstetrics and Gynaecology of the British Empire
J. Nutrit.	Journal of Nutrition
J. oil col. Chem. Ass.	Journal of the Oil and Colour Chemists Association
J. Path. Bact.	Journal of Pathology and Bacteriology
J. Pharm. Pharmacol.	Journal of Pharmacy and Pharmacology
J. pharm. Sci.	Journal of Pharmaceutical Sciences
J. Pharmacol.	Journal of Pharmacology and Experimental Therapeutics
J. phys. Chem.	Journal of Physical Chemistry
J. roy. san. Inst.	Journal of the Royal Sanitary Institute
J. Sci. Food Agric.	Journal of the Science of Food and Agriculture
J. Text. Inst.	Journal of the Textile Institute, Manchester
Lancet	The Lancet
Med. norsk farm. Selsk.	Meddeleleser fra Norsk farmaceutisk Selskap
Mich. State Coll. Tech. Bull. Agr.	Michigan State College Technical Bulletin Agriculture
Milchwiss.	Milchwissenschaft
Nature, Lond.	Nature
Nord. hyg. Tids.	Nordisk hygienisk Tidskrift
Nucleonics	Nucleonics
Pharm. Acta Helv.	Pharmaceutica Acta Helvetiae
Pharm. J.	Pharmaceutical Journal
Pharm. Monat.	Pharmazeutische Monatshefte
Phil. Mag.	Philosophical Magazine
Physiol. Rev.	Physiological Reviews
Phytopath.	Phytopathology

Phytopath. Z.	Phytopathologische Zeitschrift
Practitioner	The Practitioner
Proc. nat. Acad. Sci.	Proceedings of the National Academy of Sciences, Washington
Proc. Roy. Soc.	Proceedings of the Royal Society
Proc. roy. Soc. Med.	Proceedings of the Royal Society of Medicine
Proc. Soc. agric. Bact.	Proceedings of the Society of Agricultural Bacteriologists
Proc. Soc. appl. Bact.	Proceedings of the Society for Applied Bacteriology
Proc. Soc. exp. Biol., N.Y.	Proceedings of the Society for Experimental Biology and Medicine
Publ. Hlth Rep., Wash.	Public Health Reports
Quart. J. Pharm.	Quarterly Journal of Pharmacy and Pharmacology
Radiology	Radiology
Rad. Res.	Radiation Research
Research, Lond.	Research
Rev. sci. Inst.	Review of Scientific Instruments
Science	Science
Soap	Soap and Sanitary Chemicals *later* Soap and Chemical Specialities
Soap, Perf. Cosm.	Soap, Perfumery and Cosmetics
Surgery	Surgery
Surg. Gynec. Obstet.	Surgery, Gynecology and Obstetrics
Trans. Faraday Soc.	Transactions of the Faraday Society
Trans. Inst. chem. Engrs, Lond.	Transactions of the Institution of Chemical Engineers
Tubercle	Tubercle
U.S. publ. Hlth Rep.	United States Public Health Report
Vet. Rec.	Veterinary Record
Virology	Virology
Yokohama Med. Bull.	Yokohama Medical Bulletin
Zent. Bakt.	Zentralblatt für Bakteriologie, Parasitekunde und Infektionskrankheiten
Z. ges. Hyg.	Zeitschrift fur die gesamte Hygiene und ihre Grenzgebiete
Z. Hyg. InfektKr.	Zeitschrift für Hygiene und Infektionskrankheiten
Z. physiol. Chem.	Hoppe-Seyler's Zeitschrift für physiologische Chemie

PART I

Theory of Disinfection and Methods of Testing

CHAPTER 1

INTRODUCTION

Historical

FROM the earliest days of recorded history we have evidence of the application of various forms of disinfection as a matter of regular routine. One is frequently surprised, in studying these early records, to find that a treatment of apparent novel modernity is in fact of considerable antiquity or is simply a recent development of a much older idea. Inevitably the methods used in the early days must have been empirical, based on experience, tradition and often superstition, and they must have been developed in entire ignorance of the theories of disinfection. Although some thousands of years later our approach to disinfection is much more rational, nevertheless our knowledge of the fundamental theories and processes remains far from complete in spite of considerable recent advances. Gale (1947) has written "Bacterial metabolism has been studied ever since the initial investigations of Pasteur, and as new techniques are devised our knowledge is continually increasing and accumulating, but it is still true to say that we understand only a very small part of the activities of bacteria, and there is immense scope for research in this field" – this was in connexion with the chemical activities of bacteria, but the same could be said of disinfection and sterilization.

In the early days processes of salting, smoking and drying and of treatment with wines and aromatic oils were widely known for food preservation and for preventing the spread of disease. The Hebrews, Greeks and Romans at various times employed sulphur for fumigation purposes as a religious rite; they burnt aromatic woods in the streets to ward off the plague and leprosy, and used essential oils for embalming. Records of these are to be found in the Bible, for example, in Leviticus, Judges and Jeremiah, which also include directions to burn the clothing of diseased persons. Persian law directed that drinking water shall be kept in bright copper vessels. Silver was also used for the same purpose, for we find in Herodotus' writings (Rawlinson's translation) "The Great King, when he goes to the wars, is always supplied with provisions carefully prepared at home, and with cattle of his own. Water too, from the river Choaspes, which flows by Susa, is taken with him for his drink, as that is the only water which the Kings of Persia taste. Wherever he travels, he is attended by a number of four-wheeled cars drawn by mules, in which the Choaspes water, ready boiled for use, and stored in flagons of silver, is moved with him from place to place."

In the Middle Ages, the burning of sulphur, of certain woods, notably juniper and cedar, and the restricted combustion of other substances was

3

practised as a means of combating the spread of bubonic plague. The vapours and gases often containing, as we now know, comparatively large amounts of formaldehyde were inhaled by patients, and were used to disinfect the air and to fumigate infected premises, thus reducing the dangers of cross-infection; bunches of aromatic herbs were also carried as a protective measure. We have reminders of this in certain traditional ceremonies carried out today in the City of London and elsewhere.

The real foundations of modern systems of disinfection and sterilization were firmly laid by a number of investigators during the nineteenth century, particularly in the latter half, and for a good historical review of the subject the reader is referred to the chapter by Bulloch (1930) in the Medical Research Council's publication *A System of Bacteriology in Relation to Medicine*. In 1827, Alcock drew special attention to the value of hypochlorites as disinfecting agents, claims which were supported by Lefevre. Chloride of lime was subsequently used with considerable success by a number of famous surgeons, including Semmelweis, as a means of preventing the spread of infection, particularly in cases of puerperal sepsis. The works of Spallanzani, of Semmelweis and the outstanding contributions of Pasteur on fermentation and on airborne infections, were all significant contributions to the proof of the germ theory of disease. As a direct result of Pasteur's work sprang Lister's concept of antiseptic surgery, involving the use of carbolic acid for dressings on wounds, for disinfecting instruments and for spraying the atmosphere before operations. It is of interest that Lister used a 1 in 20 solution for instruments and a 1 in 40 solution for skin disinfection, concentrations which are still widely employed for the same purposes. Later came proofs that carbolic acid destroyed the infectivity of anthrax blood, and the recommendations of various investigators for the use of potassium permanganate, iodine, eucalyptus oil, mercuric chloride and silver nitrate for the same purposes.

In spite of the anciently established practices of boiling and burning to prevent the spread of disease, the results of early studies on the effect of heat on fermentative and putrefactive processes were somewhat confused. This was mainly because many still held to the belief of spontaneous generation of micro-organisms. Heat treatment was, therefore, inevitably bound with the attempts to prove that the causative organisms, "animalculae" as they were then called, came from the air. In 1718, Joblot successfully sterilized a hay infusion by boiling for fifteen minutes and sealing the container before it cooled. Spallanzani later contributed to these studies by showing that not only the infusion but the air above it must be sterilized. But, because of the ignorance of the nature of the bodies concerned, and, therefore, the unsuspected complexity of the problem, these findings were not accepted; even after Pasteur's brilliant researches, published from 1860 onwards, there were still some disbelievers. Pasteur demonstrated clearly; first, that nutrient solutions of various types could be sterilized by boiling or by heating at temperatures somewhat above 100°; secondly, that sterile infusions could be re-contaminated from asbestos which had been heated and through which air had subsequently been passed; thirdly, that gun-cotton through which air had been filtered contained bodies like the spores of minute plants; and fourthly, that heated infusions could be kept sterile by storing them in hermetically sealed containers or in such a way that airborne organisms could not gain access. The various methods employed to prove the last point included passing the air through a red-hot platinum tube or through filters of gun-cotton or asbestos. Incidentally, cotton wool had first been used as an air filter by Schroeder and von Dusch in the early 1850s.

Some years later, Tyndall confirmed Pasteur's findings and went on to demonstrate the existence of bacteria in at least two forms, one which was easily killed by a short heating to 100° and another which withstood such heating for several hours. Elaborating this work further, he devised the method of fractional sterilization by discontinuous heating which we know today as tyndallization.

Heating at temperatures above 100° has been practised by different workers at different times. For example, a steam pressure vessel was used by Schroeder as early as 1859, and he also preserved egg yolk by pre-heating to 160° and meat by heating to 130°. Koch soon recognized the relative inefficiency of dry heat compared with moist heat as a sterilizing agent, but only very little work was done on the subject until quite recent years. Various contemporaries of Koch employed temperatures ranging from 140° to 160°, and Lister in 1878 specifically recommended the treatment of all glassware at 150° for 2 hours to ensure sterilization.

Filtration as a method of purifying water has been known since the first century A.D. It was employed by the Egyptians in treating their drinking water, and Aristotle refers to the use of unglazed porcelain filters for the same purpose. Subsequently, appreciation of the value of filtration seems to have been almost lost until the early nineteenth century when it was again introduced following a cholera epidemic in London. These filters were of the usual sand type but it was not until late in the nineteenth century that filters were produced for the specific purpose of removing bacteria. Several investigators from 1871 onwards successfully employed unburnt clay or plaster of Paris for removing anthrax bacilli and other organisms; asbestos was also used. In 1884, the Pasteur-Chamberland filter was described. It was made of a mixture of quartz and kaolin cast in the familiar candle-shaped body, and heated to a temperature just below sintering point. To it was fused a glazed nipple-shaped end piece. Seven years later the Berkefeld candle of similar shape but made from kieselguhr, or diatomaceous earth, made its appearance. Thereafter, several variants were produced, but the two original candles still remain the most popular of this type of filter. The asbestos pad, 'Seitz'-type filter, was not devised until a much later date and the sintered glass filter disc was not introduced until as late as 1937.

It is not surprising that, apart from drying and salting, and possibly a limited appreciation of sunlight, nothing was known in the early days of the various physical methods of disinfection such as treatment with ultraviolet radiations, X-rays or ultrasonics. Apart from these, it is of interest to realize how many of the principles and sterilization methods of today have been established for centuries past.

Terminology

Before attempting to discuss any subject in detail it is necessary to understand with some degree of clarity the special terms used in connexion with the subject. It is particularly important with the present subject because a good deal of confusion has arisen with some of the terms, partly because of incorrect, loose usage and partly because they are of somewhat old derivation. For example, the terms *antiseptic* and *disinfectant* were first introduced some two hundred years ago and, as is commonly found, their meanings have been rather modified with the passage of time.

Sterilization is an absolute term. It means in its proper sense the complete destruction or removal of all forms of life. The number of agents capable of achieving this is limited; it is confined to high temperatures, including fire, saturated steam under pressure and certain types of filter: only a few of the many chemicals employed, and possibly one or two of the radiation treatments suitably applied, are true sterilizing agents. *Sterilization* is often loosely and erroneously applied when disinfection is really implied. This is especially true in the medical field and with the food industries, where it is used to mean the destruction of micro-organisms undesirable under a particular set of circumstances. Thus, in the medical sense it is often intended to mean the destruction of pathogenic organisms only; in the food industry it may be applied primarily to the killing of micro-organisms causing spoilage, and in water purification it may simply involve the removal of water-borne disease germs. This abuse or misguided interpretation has often given rise to confusion in the past, and illustrates the need for proper care in always using the correct terminology. The Council on Pharmacy and Chemistry of the American Medical Association (1936) has recorded unequivocal opinion by registering its disapproval of "the use of the terms 'sterile', 'sterilize' and 'sterilization' in a bacteriological sense other than in their correct scientific significance; i.e. meaning the absence or destruction of all micro-organisms. These terms are not relative and to permit their use in a relative sense not only is incorrect, but opens the way to abuse and misunderstanding."

Disinfection may be defined as the process of eliminating or destroying infection; it is accomplished by the use of a *disinfectant*. The term was introduced before the establishment of the germ theory of infection, and so, because disease was always associated with foul odours, it tended to infer primarily the destruction or masking of these odours, although often the killing of bacteria was concomitant. On this account, the term *disinfectant* is frequently still confined to the strong smelling coal-tar fluids, and it is for this reason that *sterilant* is commonly used in the food industry. Nevertheless the term has a much wider application and meaning, although some authorities, with some justification, prefer to confine the use of the word to the treatment of inanimate objects. This is now the generally accepted context of *disinfection*. In spite of this we still talk quite properly about 'skin disinfection'.

Sanitization, an awkward word originating in the United States, means the process of rendering sanitary or of promoting health. It is akin to disinfection, but carries with it the inference of cleansing as well as removal of infection. It is not a term used to any extent in Great Britain.

Antiseptic is another very much misunderstood word. Literally interpreted from its Greek origin it means 'against putrefaction', but it has now been extended to include activity against bacterial sepsis or infection. By inference, the word conveys a meaning similar to that of 'disinfectant', and the tendency is to use the term specifically in relation to preparations for application to living tissues, especially in surgery and hygiene. It can also properly be used to denote a property of inhibiting or preventing the growth of micro-organisms under prescribed conditions of usage. Unfortunately, its significance has been belittled in recent years by the appearance on the market of so many preparations, mouth washes, tooth pastes, gargles, products for use on the hands and the like, which are barely able even to prevent the growth of micro-organisms in normal practice. This was felt to be so important in the United States that a paragraph defining the term *antiseptic* was included in the Federal Food, Drug and Cosmetic Act of 1938 which reads: "The representation of a drug, in its labelling, as an antiseptic, shall be considered to be a representation that it is a germicide, except in the case of a drug purporting to be, or represented as, an antiseptic for inhibitory use as a wet dressing, ointment, dusting powder, or such other use as involves prolonged contact with the body." There is no such parallel in English law, but it is evident that the same outlook is being established in this country by induction rather than by regulation. The subject is under active consideration in several quarters.

A *bactericide* kills bacteria, but not necessarily bacterial spores, whilst a *bacteriostat*, or *bacteriostatic agent*, prevents their growth and so gives rise to a state of *bacteriostasis*. Similarly, a *fungicide* kills fungi, and a *virucide* inactivates viruses.

A *germicide* kills all micro-organisms. The suffixes *-stat* and *-stasis* are not used in conjunction with this term.

By way of general explanation, it may be said that the suffix *-cide* always applies to any agent producing a killing effect on the micro-organisms concerned, whereas *-stat* means that the agent simply prevents or inhibits growth. *Stasis* is the state of suspended animation, or inhibition, produced by the latter type of agent.

REFERENCES

American Medical Association (1936). *Report of the Council on Pharmacy; J. Amer. med. Ass.*, **107**, 38.

BULLOCH, W. (1930). *History of Bacteriology*, from *A System of Bacteriology in Relation to Medicine;* Vol. 1: H.M.S.O., London.

GALE, E. F. (1947). *Chemical Activities of Bacteria:* Univ. Tutorial Press, London.

CHAPTER 2

THE THEORY AND MODE OF ACTION OF DISINFECTION

Microbial enzymes and their functions

Microbial enzymes and antimicrobial activity

Basically, the bacterial cell consists of a cell wall enclosing the cytoplasm which itself is enclosed in the cytoplasmic membrane. Under favourable conditions it is subject to growth and multiplication by simple asexual fission in a regular and orderly manner and this cycle is accomplished by virtue of its indigenous enzymic constitution. According to Gale (1943) "the enzymes with which the bacterial cell is equipped have at least four functions to fulfil: (*a*) to release energy for continued existence and division, (*b*) to provide essential metabolites and nutrilites, (*c*) to detoxicate toxic metabolic products, and (*d*) to stabilize the internal environment in a variable external environment." By these actions the organism is able to select suitable nutrient substances from the surrounding medium and modify them by appropriate synthetic and breakdown processes to make material for cell structure and for reproduction on a strictly genetic basis, giving rise to many end-products, nucleic acids, antigenic substances, polysaccharides, toxins and the like, all of which form the basis characteristics of the cell. The whole composite process comprises the metabolic cycle of the cell. The function of the enzymes is to act as catalysts for individual specific reactions, hence it is not difficult to imagine that a multiplicity of such agents with diverse properties must be present in any microbial cell, each one of which is carrying out its own specific function in the life-cycle of the cell.

Enzymes have the general structure and properties of proteins. They can be wholly protein in nature, but many are constituted of two main fractions, the larger being the protein moiety and the smaller, known as the 'prosthetic group', being of a simpler, non-protein composition. The link between the prosthetic group and protein molecule varies in strength in different enzymes. In some, it is so tight that separation can only be achieved with difficulty. In others it is sufficiently loose to allow the prosthetic groups apparently to wander from one protein moiety to another; such loose groups are known as 'co-enzymes'. Probably the differentiation between prosthetic groups and co-enzymes is an artificial one, since both carry out the same function in the enzymic reaction as a whole, the one as an integral part of the composite molecule, the other as a separate reactor or carrier. In either case, conjunction between the prosthetic group or co-enzyme and the protein molecule is essential for enzyme activity.

Because enzymes have, at least in part, a protein structure, it follows that they must possess the properties of proteins. They are, therefore, subject to inactivation through coagulation or denaturation by heat or other physical means, and by a wide range of chemicals, and herein lies a most probable explanation of the mechanism of antibacterial action. Any treatment which inactivates one or more of the essential enzymes of the microbial cell, or which so affects an essential metabolite that it is rendered unavailable to the enzyme, produces, in effect, a break in the life-cycle of the cell with the result that the cell is unable to reproduce and so by definition is presumed dead. But the situation is not quite as straightforward as this and there seem to be 'degrees' of inactivation according to whether the treatment is lethal or only inhibitory. These 'degrees' would appear to be associated not with the order of inactivation of an individual enzyme, but rather with its cellular function, whether it is essential, or somatic, or only ancillary to the life-cycle of the cell. Such a postulate implies, in fact, that the lethal and bacteriostatic phenomena are the results of two quite different processes, involving different reactions at different loci in the cell, and this has some support, as indicated by van Eseltine and Rahn (1949), in that the bactericidal effect of some disinfectants is known to increase with increasing temperature, but the bacteriostatic effect decreases. When the action is only bacteriostatic, it is such that the inactivation is reversible, or can be by-passed in some way so that when the organism is transferred to more favourable conditions it can resume its normal reproductive cycle. When the action is lethal, the damage to the enzyme system is so extensive, or alternatively the enzymes affected are so fundamental to the life of the cell, that restoration of viability is not possible under any circumstances.

There are many references in the literature to the inactivation of microbial enzymes by various germicidal treatments. To quote but one example, the energy-producing enzymes can be completely inactivated by bactericidal, but not by bacteriostatic, concentrations of phenol, mercuric chloride and a quaternary ammonium compound (Roberts and Rahn, 1946). Unfortunately, it has never been possible to establish a precise correlation between enzyme inactivation and lethal activity, although in several cases fairly close approximations have been found, and this lends support to the postulate that the process of disinfection may not be exclusively a function of enzyme inactivation but linked also with the interferences with the reproductive mechanisms of the cell (*see* Rahn, 1945). In the light of more recent discoveries it is almost certainly concerned with the nucleic acids, and in particular with the ribonucleic acids, of the cell, but at present it does not seem possible to go further, except that one can again ask: How far is this linked with enzymic activity?

Specificity of enzymes and selective antimicrobial activity

The life-cycle of the microbial cell consists, in effect, of a chain of enzyme-catalysed reactions, each cell bringing into action a succession of enzymes, each with its own specific characteristics, according to the stage of development of the cell and the sequence of availability of the necessary metabolites. Some of the reactions concerned are more fundamental to the life of the cell than are others, and so each enzyme must differ in its importance. Inevitably, each enzyme also differs in its sensitivity to any given treatment according to the intensity of the treatment, the conditions of its application and the nature of the enzyme. Therefore, it is quite feasible that many treatments could be such as would upset the enzyme system of the cell sufficiently to inhibit or restrict the normal growth of the cell, at least under the conditions prevailing, but not sufficiently to cause permanent damage and so destroy its viability completely. This, in effect, is the state of stasis in the cell, and the disfunction of the enzyme system has frequently been used to explain this phenomenon. Thus, MacDonald (1942) claimed that the esters of *p*-hydroxybenzoic acid are effective bacteriostats because they block an essential enzyme system and so prevent normal cell metabolism; Fildes (1940) showed that the mercury compounds block the cellular thiol receptors; the acridines are thought to close certain metabolic paths by interfering with the bacterial co-enzymes with which they appear to combine (Gale, 1947); quinones inhibit the respiratory enzymes (Hoffman-Ostenham, 1947); cationic detergents inhibit the metabolic enzymes (Knox *et al.*, 1949); phenols and quaternary ammonium compounds disrupt the enzymes of the energy yielding group (Stedman, Kravitz and King, 1957), and the triphenylmethane dyes prevent the essential metabolisms of glutamic acid within the cell (Gale and Mitchell, 1947).

Sulphanilamide provides yet another example, bacteriostasis in this case being due to inhibition of the enzyme action involved in the utilization of the essential cell metabolite, *p*-aminobenzoic acid (Woods, 1940). Here the interference can be overcome by adding small amounts of the latter compound, and the effect is so great that as little as one molecule of *p*-aminobenzoic acid will neutralize 5,000 or more molecules of sulphanilamide. By this means the enzyme blocking mechanism of the sulphanilamide is rendered nugatory and the cells are again free to develop normally. Other instances have since been found of substances of structure similar to those of other growth factors competing at foci in the cell for access to the particular enzymes.

Because of their chemotherapeutic significance, the subject has also received attention in the antibiotics field and here again the activities of most of these agents can be attributed to blocking or interference in the nutritional mechanisms of the cell. Thus, the cyclic peptide antibiotics, tyrocidin and the polymyxins, affect the permeability of the cell membrane and penicillin and griseofulvin impair cell wall synthesis, whilst novobiocin, bacitracin and vancomycin affect both cell wall synthesis and permeability. A numerically larger group, which includes the streptomycins, the tetracyclines, chloramphenicol and actidione, are effective by virtue of their ability to synthesize essential cell proteins, nucleic acids and purines. The subject has been reviewed most recently, and very completely, by Newton (1965).

Obviously not all micro-organisms can possess every possible enzyme, neither can they all be expected to have identical enzymic constitutions otherwise there would be no possible means of differentiation between genera, species, etc., for it is on this basis that such classification can be made. The fact that such groupings can be made indicates different enzyme structures, and from this emerges a possible explanation for at least some of the differences in resistance between types of micro-organisms. On account of their diverse chemical constitutions the constituent enzymes of each type are acted upon differently, both in rate and extent, by antibacterial agents. Moreover, the enzymes are sited in different parts of the cell, some in the surface and others in the cytoplasm. Hence it can be inferred that they are protected in varying degree from attack by an outside agent either because they are surrounded to a greater or less extent by other proteinaceous or fatty substances or because they are isolated by the barrier of the cell wall through which the agent must diffuse before gaining access. These factors all contribute to a varied rate of inactivation of the enzymes, hence a variable death-rate, between the many types of micro-organism.

By similar reasoning, the different resistances of individual cells of a single bacterial population can be explained. As in a given human population all the individuals are not identical, being at different stages of growth, virility and progress, so all of the cells of a pure culture are not identical. They have their likenesses in terms of general structure, metabolic characteristics and so on, but in many respects each retains its own individuality. For instance, because the cells are all of somewhat different age or maturity (*see*, for example, Wooldridge, Knox and Glass, 1936, and Gale, 1943), their 'virility' is at different levels and their constitutional enzyme balances may not be identical. Because of this, a disinfecting agent is bound to act unevenly on cell populations, resulting in a gradation of resistance from those readily susceptible to those, in diminishing numbers, of a more resistant nature. To illustrate this point, some work reported by Jacobs (1960) is of interest. In following the rate of death of *Escherichia coli* in the presence of different amounts of phenol, the curves followed the usual logarithmic form until reaching a certain lower range of concentration, when they became irregular and showed occasional transient increases in the viable population. No 'fully comprehensive explanation' was offered, but a simple and partial reason is based on two premises: (*i*) the inherent ability of a cell to withstand damage depends on the stage it has reached in its growth cycle, and from this is implied a phase of minimal resistance in the cycle, and (*ii*) the cells which are still able to divide under these conditions bring about their own destruction by virtue of the fact that the daughter cells after fission are much more susceptible than are the parents.

The indissoluble link between cell life and its enzyme activities has led some workers to investigate the relationship more closely with a view to assessing the survival of bacteria in terms of the function of one or more specific enzymes, in other words, to assess the value of disinfectants by measuring their effect on the enzyme. Thus, Sykes (1939), after examining the effects of alcohols and phenols on the dehydrogenases of *E. coli*, suggested that the succinic acid dehydrogenase activity might be used for this purpose; Sevag and Shelburne (1942) correlated closely the retardation of respiration and of growth of streptococci and pneumococci treated with sulphonamides; Knox, Auerbach, Zarudnaya and Spirtes (1949) showed that the death of *E. coli* in the presence of cationic detergents parallels the loss of certain metabolic functions through the inhibition of a number of enzymes, in particular, the lactic acid oxidase; and Robertson and Oliver (1954) similarly correlated loss of decarboxylase with loss of viability in certain organisms after treatment with heat or chemical disinfectants. In spite of these observations, there have been several publications denying such relationships, hence they would appear to be somewhat specific. Because of this, and because of the extreme variability in the modes of action of disinfectants, it seems unlikely that any enzyme-inhibition technique *per se* is likely to come to full fruition as a means of assessing disinfectants.

Enzyme adaptation and microbial resistance

Highly complex bodies carrying the multiplicity of activities of micro-organisms are obviously held in very delicate balance. Any upset in this balance can materially influence the characteristics of the organism, including its chances of survival. The life-cycle of the cell comprises numerous synthetic processes, involving amongst others the production of its own enzymes. According to Karström (1937) microbial enzymes can be considered in two groups; (*i*) constitutive enzymes, formed independently of the conditions of growth of the organism, and (*ii*) adaptive enzymes produced only as required when certain substrates are present. The former are essential to the life of the cell and cannot be substituted in any way. Some of the latter are now believed to be present always in the cell in a recessive role, only assuming significance when the specific conditions obtain to induce the change; others are believed to be synthesized from existing enzyme proteins in the cell by slight divergences from the normal path induced according to the substrates added. In either case, adaptive capacity is not a generalized function, it is severely limited to a few cellular activities. The subject has been dealt with extensively by Gale (1943) and by Stanier (1951).

Adaptation is one of the defence mechanisms which might be brought into action when an organism is subjected to adverse or unusual growth conditions, such as obtain in the presence of disinfecting agents. If, of course, the treatment is so severe that the essential constitutive enzymes are completely disrupted, then the metabolic functions of the cell cease and it dies. But if the conditions are less drastic, the organism may be able to accommodate itself to the new environment. The mechanisms by which this is accomplished are only little understood, but they are known to be diverse, involving simple adaptations, or the development of variants, to the more complex development of mutants. With simple adaptations, the organism brings into action the required recessive enzyme, thus accommodating itself to complete its metabolic cycles by alternative pathways. This type of adaptation usually takes place quite rapidly within a single cultivation, and it is characteristic with cultures grown under slightly different nutritive conditions, for example, in media of different composition; it is especially noticeable in their capacities to ferment carbohydrates. The extensive investigations into this aspect by numerous workers have been well summarized by Dubos (1940).

Typical also of this form of adaptation is the stimulus induced in organisms in the presence of antagonizing substances to produce excess of a particular enzyme in sufficient quantity to compete effectively with the antagonism and still have sufficient available to fulfil its role in cell metabolism. It is a purely defensive mechanism, and a good example is the production of penicillinase by many bacteria in the presence of penicillin. The existence of this enzyme was first demonstrated by Abraham and Chain (1940) to be markedly stimulated in production by adding penicillin to the growing cultures. Adaptations of this nature do not appear to be associated with many disinfection processes, but they can be of considerable significance in the recovery of organisms damaged by sub-lethal treatments, because such organisms may have more exacting nutritional requirements in the form of essential metabolites in order to overcome their enzyme deficiencies and so ensure survival (*see*, for example, Curran and Evans. 1937; Nelson, 1943).

It is difficult to differentiate between adaptation resulting from development of variants, described in disinfection studies by some authors as 'natural resistance', and that resulting from the development of mutants, often considered to be 'induced resistance'. Many so-called 'resistant variants' are really mutants of the original culture because the cells have also undergone a genetic change. That these cells are present in all pure cultures and account for many of the so-called 'adaptations' is now generally accepted. It is consistent with classical genetic theory and is supported strongly by many workers. Garrod (1952), for instance, is of the opinion that many examples of so-called acquired resistance are in effect only examples of selective breeding, and Wyss (1950), discussing bacterial resistance, has said "As we study adaptations, we find an increasing number of examples of this adaptation being a selection of pre-existing variants or mutants in the population." Pertinent examples are found in the antibiotics field, where, for instance, data published by Demerec (1948) "favour the assumption that resistance to certain concentrations of penicillin or streptomycin originates through mutation, and that resistant bacteria may be found in any large population, the proportion depending on the mutation rate", and where Barer (1951) showed the long lag phase of treated bacteria to be due both to enzymic adaptation and mutant selection. Barer inferred that adaptation is not a spontaneous mutation, but is induced by direct action of the drug on the enzyme system, whereas Sevag and Rosanoff (1952), investigating the increased resistance of *E. coli* to streptomycin, come to exactly the opposite conclusion, namely, that the resistance is due entirely to spontaneous mutation, to the exclusion of adaptation. Van der Meulen (1957) was also of the same opinion, but Eagle (1954), having made an extensive study of the problem, was rather more cautious. In his opinion there is considerable suggestive evidence in favour of adaptation, but it is not sufficiently clear cut to be decisive, since it is not practical entirely to eliminate the possibility of selective propagation resulting from interim multiplication of resistant mutants. Acquired resistance is not confined, of course, to the antibiotics field, but it can occur with nearly all types of antibacterial agents especially when they have substantial bacteriostatic properties. Thus, Thornley and Yudkin (1959) and Sinai and Yudkin (1959) produced evidence of mutation and selection occurring simultaneously with adaptation by induction in both *E. coli* and *Aerobacter aerogenes* when treated with proflavine. They were able to transform sensitive cells to resistant ones simply by adding deoxyribonucleic acid extracts from resistant cells—a clear example of adaptation. Similarly the resistance developed by *Staphylococcus aureus* to phenol is thought to be the result of "mutation with superimposed adaptation" (Berger and Wyss, 1953), although insufficient is known of the effect of phenol on bacterial enzymes to be certain of this. The last statement may, indeed, be true of far more systems than we at present imagine, so that it is perhaps wise at present not to be too dogmatic in either direction, for it seems highly probable that both factors could be operative, separately or together, depending on the system and conditions being considered.

Acquired resistances of the foregoing nature, whether they be by mutation or by adaptation, are in effect the products of modifications to the nutritional requirements of the organism, and these can vary greatly in their complexity. They may induce a simplification in the metabolic cycle of the organism, such as occurs with *E. coli* during its adaptation to streptomycin resistance when it dispenses with the oxalate-pyruvate stage in the citric acid metabolic cycle (Smith, Oginsky and Umbreit, 1949), or during its adaptation to hexachlorophane resistance when it by-passes the more sensitive oxidase systems through an alternative and more robust dehydrogenase system (Gould, Frigerio and Hovanesian, 1957). Alternatively, they may lead to an increase in the natural resistance of the cell by increasing its fat content or by reducing the permeability of its membrane. Penicillin is said to act by virtue of·its ability to reduce the permeability of the cell and so prevent the assimilation of the essential metabolite, glutamic acid (Gale and Taylor, 1947). Penicillin has also been shown to induce resistant organisms to become independent of pre-formed amino acids and to synthesize all of their requirements from ammonia and a carbon source (Gale and Rodwell, 1949).

Modifications in cell metabolism leading to increased lipid content are believed to account for the increased resistance of some organisms to quaternary ammonium compounds (Chaplin, 1952). This certainly appeared to be the case with cultures of *Chromobacterium prodigiosum* in which strains adapted to resist up to one thousand times the normal lethal dose of an alkyldimethylbenzylammonium chloride showed an increase from 5 per cent to 31 per cent in their content of ether-soluble, lipase-labile material. Moreover, the sensitivities of these cultures could be restored to normal simply by the action of lipase.

The presence of fatty substances was also thought to be the cause of abnormal resistance in several types of micro-organism, especially in the heat resistance of bacterial spores, the suggestion being (Curran, 1952) that this material present in large amounts in the cytoplasm and membrane of the spore protects the essential enzyme proteins from denaturation and so enhances the resistance of the cell. Further work has, however, shown the specific substances concerned to be dipicolinic acid and a range of amino acids. Dipicolinic acid is now known to be present in relatively large amounts in dormant or resting spores, and to be removeable only by somewhat vigorous treatments (Perry and Foster, 1955). From this, the acid is thought to be complexed in the cell, in the presence of calcium, with the amino acids (Young, 1959) which complex unites into larger structures with the essential enzymes, nucleic acids and other proteins. This renders the enzyme both inactive and resistant, hence the peculiar storage and resistance characteristics of the spore itself (Halvorson and Church, 1957).

Whether this is a true physico-chemical explanation remains to be seen, but quite definite evidence is now emerging concerning the unusual heat resistance of some of the spore enzymes. For example, during the early stages of sporulation in *Bacillus cereus* a heat-resistant glucose dehydrogenase appears which is identical with that of the vegetative cells in terms of its charge, chromatographic properties, reaction kinetics, etc., and differs only, as far as can be detected, in that it is fifteen times more resistant to heat (Bach and Sadoff, 1962). Similarly, Baillie and Norris (1962) have reported on the existence of catalase in two phases, the normal heat-labile one in vegetative cells and a heat-stable one as spores begin to develop.

Doubts have been expressed by some investigators whether enzyme inactivation is, in fact, a cause or an effect of the death of the cell. In certain cases it is a vexed question, but as the nutritional metabolism of micro-organisms is studied in greater detail the role of enzymes is becoming increasingly clear, and with it their indispensability in the life-cycle of the cell. It would be contrary, however, to known facts to assert that specific or group enzyme inactivation is the exclusive mechanism of all disinfection processes. Undoubtedly there are other mechanisms, amongst which are included lysis produced by surface tension reducing agents, and cell disruption brought about by various physical means.

The mechanism of acquired resistance in micro-organisms is at present a highly fertile field for speculation and investigation, especially in its chemotherapeutic and clinical contexts, and much fruitful work can be expected within the next few years.

Dynamics of disinfection

Logarithmic order of death

That disinfection does not take place instantaneously, but is a gradual process, was apparently first discovered by Abbott in 1891 as a result of his experiments examining the way in which *Staph. aureus* is killed by mercuric chloride. Subsequently, important contributions on the subject were made by Krönig and Paul in 1897 using their well-known garnet tests. The technqiue consisted in principle of drying organisms on the garnets, treating them under specified conditions with known concentrations of disinfectants and assessing the survivors by plating washings from the treated garnets. Not only did they assess the disinfecting power of various acids, alkalis and salts of mercury and silver against anthrax spores, but they also studied the effect of adding other electrolytes. Examining Krönig and Paul's results, Chick (1908) discovered that the logarithms of the numbers of bacteria surviving were directly related to the times of treatment so that, when one was plotted against the other, the points lay on a straight line. These observations were confirmed in her own experiments on the disinfection of anthrax spores with phenol and mercuric chloride, one typical result of which is quoted in Table 1, and illustrated in Fig. 1. Chick further stated "the curves appeared to be very similar in form to that expressing the course of a 'unimolecular reaction', and the equation

$$-\frac{dC}{dt} = KC,$$

or

$$\frac{1}{t_2 - t_1} \log \frac{C_1}{C_2} = K$$

was found to be applicable to the case of disinfection, if, in place of the terms C_1 and C_2 expressing concentration of reacting substance, numbers of surviving bacteria were inserted, thus:

$$\frac{1}{t_2 - t_1} \log \frac{n_1}{n_2} = K,$$

where n_1 and n_2 are the numbers of bacteria surviving after times t_1 and t_2 respectively." This concept of the logarithmic ratio of survivors against time is similar to that propounded in 1907 by Madsen and Nyman, but it is not entirely supported by other and later investigators. All agree in principle, but many instances àre cited in which this relationship could not hold. Chick herself found certain deviations. Sometimes the death-rate was initially slow but quickly accelerated to a constant value which was maintained until near the end of the process when the few remaining cells succumbed again at

TABLE 1

Disinfection of anthrax spores with 5 per cent phenol
(after Chick, 1908)

Time (min.)	Mean number of bacteria surviving in one drop of disinfection mixture	Log_{10} N
0	439	2·642
30	275·5	2·439
75	137·5	2·138
120	46	1·663
180	15·8	1·199
246	5·45	0·736
300	3·6	0·556
420	0·5	−0·301

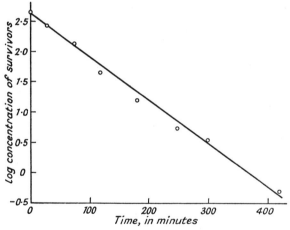

FIG. 1. *Disinfection of anthrax spores with 5 per cent phenol*
(after Chick, 1908)

comparatively slow rates. In these circumstances the graphs of logarithms of survivors plotted against time were of a sigmoid type rather than the straight line originally postulated. In other instances, as was found by Chick (1910) in treating *Salmonella paratyphi* with heat or phenol, the reverse was the case, death-rates being rapid at first but falling consistently as the disinfection proceeded. Other examples can be found in the literature of departures from the regular logarithmic response, but the most usual irregularity encountered is the sigmoid form.

Concentration of disinfectant and temperature of disinfection influence the rate of death and also alter the apparent shape of the time-survivor curves, but Jordan and Jacobs (1945*a*) assert that the latter is more apparent than real. This alteration was first noted by Henderson Smith (1921) whilst investigating the death rates of *Botrytis* spores in the presence of different concentrations of phenol. Typical results, illustrated in Fig. 2, suggest that

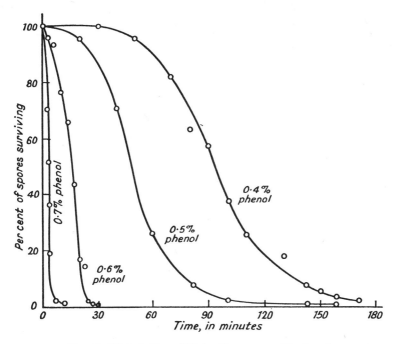

FIG. 2. *Disinfection of* Botrytis *spores with phenol*
(after Smith, 1921)

a curve of the sigmoid type is produced when the concentrations of phenol are low; when the death rate is increased by using higher concentrations of phenol the curve tends to become more of a logarithmic type. The overall effect seems to be that the initial lag is eliminated. The fact is, however, according to Henderson Smith (1923), that it is not eliminated but takes place so rapidly that it is not detected in ordinary tests. In proof of this, he carried out experiments in the higher range of phenol concentrations up to 1·25 per cent, but extended the time of disinfection by reducing the temperature and increasing the numbers of spores in the initial inocula. In every case the sigmoid character of the curve was restored.

Withell (1938, 1942*b*) also demonstrated a progression from a sigmoidal to an exponential curve by increasing the rate of disinfection and, like Henderson Smith, attributed the apparent change to the rapidity of the initial rate of kill which gave little opportunity to observe experimentally any lag phase. He also obtained different shaped curves with the same organism under ostensibly identical test conditions, and recognized three general types of response: (a) those which give sigmoid time-survivor curves, (b) those which give exponential time-survivor curves, and (c) those which give a lag phase followed by an exponential curve. Conversion of the graphs to a logarithmic survival-time basis yielded an approximately normal distribution of resistance and so revealed an initial lag phase under all circumstances. The normality was not absolute, however, and the deviations were attributed to slight differences in resistance consequent upon culture suspensions containing organisms of different age. Withell (1942a) concluded that "the 'fundamental' difference in shape of time-survivor curves obtained when arithmetic units are used is only apparent. All the shapes of curve found in the literature are due to variations in the way the resistances of the organisms are distributed."

In order to investigate the problem precisely it is obviously necessary to eliminate as far as possible external influences which may affect adversely the resistance of the organisms and their subsequent proliferation when damaged but not killed by the disinfectant. Age of the culture, change in environment and sudden changes in temperature can materially affect the apparent disinfection rate. Jordan and Jacobs (1944) recognized this and devised a justifiably elaborate testing technique to eliminate as many as possible of the adverse influences. They investigated in detail the effect of phenol on *E. coli*, and under the improved conditions obtained an initial lag phase of slow but increasing death-rate. This merged into a second phase of constant death-rate which continued until towards the end of the disinfection period when there was an indication of a decline in the death-rate. Skew distributions in resistance were obtained when high concentrations were employed, that is, when the disinfection rate was high, and Jordan and Jacobs (1944), like Withell and Henderson Smith, assumed these to be "artifacts due partly to technical difficulties in observing small mortalities when the death-rates are high." They also experienced difficulties in measuring accurately the survival rate when the mortality was over 95 per cent because of excessive variations occurring in replicate plate counts. Hobbs and Wilson (1942) also experienced the same difficulties in following the disinfecting rates of caustic soda solutions. The indication of a decline in death-rate towards the end of the disinfection period observed by Jordan and Jacobs has since been confirmed and extended by several workers, including Jacobs himself (1960). The extent of the decline depends on the concentration of the disinfectant, but it can reach a point, near to the critical lethal concentration, in which there is actually a recovery of some of the cells and an increase in their total and viable numbers, as can be shown with phenol-treated *E. coli*. The decline does not arise from a skew distribution of resistance, as is commonly thought, but from a change in the environment of the survivors consequent, as shown by Bean and Walters (1961), on the lysis of the killed cells and the release of nutrient material from them, which at least reduces the efficacy of the disinfectant and may in some conditions allow of some growth of the survivors.

Clearly Chick's original postulate of the reaction being truly monomolecular does not hold in all cases. In fact, it is only true in certain limited conditions, *i.e.*, when the disinfectant is present in excess and when the rate of disinfection is sufficiently rapid. The reasons for the divergencies are not difficult to see, for not only is there the factor of the variability in resistance of the individual cells of a given population but also the complexity of the mechanism of the disinfecting action involved. The latter is not a simple reaction such as between the disinfectant and a single cell or cell constituent; it includes a number of reactions embracing probably several constituents and involving osmosis, diffusion and other physicochemical phenomena. Each of these actions occurs at different phases of the disinfection process and there is an inevitable degree of overlap. Because of this, some investigators have suggested that the cumulative reaction is one approaching the seventh order.

It is considerations such as these which underline the difficulties of devising suitable and reliably reproducible disinfectant tests, particularly anent the choice of end-point. The standard tests all work to a point of total extinction, but this is not altogether satisfactory because (*a*) it is only a *virtual* total extinction as judged by the absence of growth from a very small sample, (*b*) when the survivor level has reached a certain value it is a matter of chance whether the particular sample carries a viable cell or not, and (*c*) the chances of proliferation of an occasional cell damaged by a disinfectant are unpredictable. Rahn (1945) has drawn attention to the wide spread of results by the conventional phenol coefficient methods consequent on these variables and it is because of such criticisms that tests embracing end-points of less than a virtual 100 per cent kill have been proposed. They are discussed in detail in Chapter 3.

Temperature coefficient

The temperature coefficient of disinfection may be defined as the measure of the change in velocity of disinfection per degree rise in temperature. It is a property of disinfectants which has not received much consideration because in practice most germicides are used either at blood heat or at normal room temperatures hence interest is confined to their activities at 37° and about 20°. Nevertheless it is important to be aware of the influence of temperature on disinfectant activity.

There is no simple way of estimating the temperature coefficient; it can only be assessed by direct measurement over the desired temperature range. This involves finding the times necessary to kill aliquots of a culture exposed to the same concentration of disinfectant at selected temperatures; usually a range of 10° is employed. Since the velocity of disinfection is related inversely to the time of disinfection then:

$$\text{temperature coefficient (per } 10° \text{ rise)} = \frac{\text{time to kill at } x°}{\text{time to kill at } (x+10)°}.$$

The coefficient is an exponential factor, therefore the relationship between the value for each degree rise in temperature and the experimental value obtained over the range of temperature employed is logarithmic and not one of direct proportion. High temperature coefficients are said to be characteristic of reactions involving denaturation or coagulation of proteins.

TABLE 2

Temperature coefficients of some phenols and alcohols
(after Tilley, 1942)

Substance	Coefficient with					
	E. coli			*Staph. aureus*		
	10–20°	20–30°	30–40°	10–20°	20–30°	30–40°
Phenol . . .	5·8	8·3	8·4	5·1	3·9	4·0
o-Cresol . . .	6·6	5·1	6·9	5·4	4·2	4·3
p-Cresol . . .	6·1	5·8	5·6	4·3	4·1	4·4
o-Butylphenol . .	5·2	4·1	5·2	5·4	3·9	3·1
Resorcinol .	7·1	7·1	8·8	3·1	3·2	4·4
Ethyl alcohol . .		43·0	54·0		13·0	9·0
n-Butyl alcohol .		31·0	40·0		11·0	9·0

According to Cooper and Haines (1928), they are particularly associated with oxidizing reactions, whereas low coefficients are associated with reducing reactions.

The activities of most disinfectants increase as the temperature is increased, but there are exceptions. Some reducing agents are unaffected by changes in temperature – hydrazine hydrate is an example – and occasionally an increase in temperature may decrease antibacterial activity – sodium hydroxide solution is an example, which, according to McCulloch (1933), has a lower disinfecting activity at 15° than at 5°. In many cases, the rise is two- to four-fold for each 10° elevation in temperature, but for phenols it may be much higher. The actual values recorded by different workers are far from consistent.

Some relationship is thought to exist between the temperature coefficient and the dilution coefficient of a disinfectant. Numerous formulae have been devised connecting the two, but according to McCulloch (1945) "such formulae have not proved entirely reliable, probably because of the complicated nature of the phenomenon of disinfection, including as it does the result of many diverse influences not readily expressed by simple equations."

Tilley (1942) investigated the subject in some detail by measuring the killing rates of various concentrations of a number of phenols and alcohols at 10° intervals of temperature. Considerable fluctuations in values of the coefficients were recorded, but they were obviously due to experimental errors, as shown by replicate observations. Allowing for these errors, the coefficient for phenol over the same 10° difference in temperature was the same over a range of concentrations; the coefficient was greater, however, at higher temperatures. The same was also encountered with other compounds examined, but it was by no means a general rule, as is clear from Table 2.

Jordan and Jacobs (1945b) also found none of the formulae hitherto proposed, formulae such as $t \times \theta^T = A$, $t(T - \alpha)^b = a$, and $C^n \times t = K$, suitable over an adequate wide range of temperatures. A plot of log (killing time − 10) against temperature for a number of phenol concentrations gave a sigmoid curve. The curve as found fitted exactly that obtained from the Pearl–Verhaulst logarithmic equation (Pearl, 1930), and so this equation was proposed as the most suitable means of calculating the temperature coefficient over the complete range from observations made over a smaller range.

Dilution coefficient

Change in concentration of a disinfectant always results in a change in rate of disinfection, the relationship, as with the temperature coefficient, being an exponential one. The nature of the relationship was apparently first discovered by Ikeda in 1897 following Krönig and Paul's work, but it was Watson (1908) who, working on Chick's (1908) findings, found that it could be expressed through the equation

$$tc^n = \text{a constant,}$$

or, more simply,

$$n \log c + \log t = \text{a constant}$$

when t = time of disinfection, c = concentration of disinfectant and n = the concentration exponent, or dilution coefficient, of the particular disinfectant.

In practice, the actual dilution coefficient is rarely calculated although its practical implications are of considerable importance. One must know, for instance, how dilution affects the efficiency of a disinfectant and it is virtually through the n value that this can be obtained. If the coefficient is high then the disinfectant can only be diluted a small amount before it loses its germicidal power, but if the coefficient is low it will remain active over a fair range of dilutions. To illustrate: phenol has an n value of about 5 and mercuric chloride about 1; thus halving the concentration of a mercuric chloride solution will only double its disinfecting time, but halving the concentration of a phenol solution will increase its disinfecting time by 2^5, *i.e.* 32 times.

According to Jordan and Jacobs (1944) the equation as given above only fits observed facts when *t* is the virtual sterilization time; if 90 or 99·9 per cent mortality times are used different values for *n* are obtained. Similarly, Tilley (1939) found that *n* varied with a given disinfectant according to the organism used.

It is considerations such as the foregoing which expose some of the weaknesses of the techniques as used at present for testing disinfectants and which underline the importance of devising proper evaluation methods.

Effect of organic matter

The influence of organic matter on the efficacy of a disinfectant is of the utmost practical importance. Occasionally a preparation is required to act in a purely inorganic menstruum, but more often there is present organic matter in the form of serum, blood, pus, milk, food residues, faecal material or suspended solids, all of which, even if there in only small amounts, reduce the efficacy of all disinfectants to a varying degree. It arises both as a result of the inactivation of the disinfectant and also through the protection of the organisms from attack. The mechanism of protection may be purely physical, or it may be of a more competitive, non-selective nature consequent on the similarity of many of the constituent substances of the bacterial cell— proteins, amino acids and the like—to those found in 'natural' organic matter. Thus, the types of action that may take place are:

(*i*) the disinfectant may react chemically with the organic material giving rise to a complex which is almost certainly non-germicidal. Competitive reactions are thereby set up between the disinfectant and the organic matter on the one hand and between the disinfectant and bacteria on the other, resulting in the total amount of germicide available for destruction of the cell being much reduced, possibly, as with chlorine, below its lethal concentration;

(*ii*) the disinfectant may form an insoluble compound with the organic matter, thus removing it from the sphere of activity. In some cases, the insoluble particulate matter may precipitate on the surface of the cell and so form a protective layer;

(*iii*) particulate and colloidal matter in suspension may adsorb the antibacterial agent so that it is substantially, if not totally, removed from solution;

(*iv*) naturally occurring fats, phospholipids, etc., in serum, milk or faeces may dissolve or absorb preferentially the germicide and so render it virtually inactive. This is especially so in the case of the cationic detergent type of disinfectants;

(*v*) organic and finely suspended matter forming a coating on the cell may render the fluid in the immediate vicinity rather more viscous, and so tend to prevent the ready access of the germicide to the cell. This, together with one of the reaction phenomena already suggested, may sufficiently delay the action of the germicide to allow the organism to adapt itself to resist.

From the foregoing observations, the role of organic matter in its various forms on the action of disinfectants is seen to be of primary importance in practice. Hence, in evaluating any germicidal substance, due account must be taken of the conditions under which it is likely to be used, especially the nature of the organic material it may encounter. Any testing system which does not include this aspect is incomplete.

Mode of action of disinfectants

Bactericidal action and bacteriostasis

The lethal action of a disinfectant is due in the main to its capacity to react with the protein, and, in particular, the essential enzymes, of micro-organisms. Any agent, therefore, which will coagulate, precipitate, or other-wise denature proteins will act as a general disinfectant. Amongst such agents are heat, phenols, alcohols, acids, halogen-releasing compounds and the salts of heavy metals, as well as certain radiations. A common phenomenon with all disinfectants is that at progressively weaker concentrations their lethal activities become more and more attenuated so that at last they give place to inhibitory action, and finally cease to exert any adverse influence at all. As is shown below, the mechanisms of the lethal action and of inhibition are probably quite different, but obviously the latter is the more persistent, since it can continue when all lethal activity has ceased. Hence, it would appear that even when killing is actually taking place the phenomenon of inhibition is also present although masked by the more potent action.

The ranges of concentrations over which these actions take place differ considerably and vary with the agent employed and the state of the culture. They cannot be divided into clearly defined stages; there is an inevitable transition and overlap, resulting in all three being manifest under some circumstances. This position arises because each cell in a bacterial population is an individual entity and as such its reaction characteristics are individual and can apparently be quite different from those of the population taken as a whole. Thus, at selected concentrations of a germicide the more sensitive cells are easily killed; others, being more resistant, may be held in a state of suspended animation, or inhibited, whilst a few of high resistance may be almost unaffected. In many instances, therefore, the processes of bacteri-cidal and bacteriostatic action take place simultaneously.

The transition brought about simply by reducing the concentration of disinfectant is a phenomenon of which our knowledge is limited. We do know, however, that before any antimicrobial activity can take place the disinfect-ant, whatever type it may be, must first be absorbed into each individual cell membrane and then react with one or more of the cell constituents. The amount absorbed, and consequently available for reaction, is related, amongst other factors, to its concentration. These points are well illustrated in some studies on the uptake of phenolic substances by bacteria by Bean and Walters (1955) and Beckett and colleagues (1958, 1959). The former working with benzylchlorophenol and the latter with hexylresorcinol both showed the uptake to be complete within about five minutes, and the amount of uptake to be directly proportional to the initial concentration of the phenol. In addition, the observations of Beckett *et al.* led them to postulate the site of absorption and interaction to be the cytoplasmic membrane and possibly also the cytoplasm, the initial effect being localized damage to the membrane with consequent release of cell exudate. From these observations it is seen that when the concentration of a disinfectant is progressively weakened a stage must be reached when it is not available in sufficient quantity to react with the sensitive foci of the cell and so becomes less effective in delivering a lethal blow. It is still able to exert some effect, however, and so the pheno-menon of inhibition occurs, the activities of the cell being partially sus-pended. If this stage is prolonged and the cell is unable to adapt itself to the new conditions, it does not reproduce and so it becomes moribund and dies. On the other hand, the cells can be restored to their normal reproductive activity if the period of inhibition is of shorter duration and the proper and complete cultural conditions are supplied.

The foregoing is probably an over-simplified version of what happens when a disinfectant acts upon an organism. Bactericidal and bacteriostatic actions are highly complex mechanisms depending on many factors, some quite delicately balanced. Their accompanying phenomena are in the main quite inadequately explained, and we are only beginning to learn why there are differences in susceptibilities between the individual cells of a bacterial population. We are also beginning to understand the reason why the various genera of bacteria exhibit marked differences in resistance to a given germi-cide, but we have no rationale as yet to explain why a given culture varies so much in its behaviour against different types of disinfectant or why the different bacterial species show a complete lack of consistency in their orders of resistance.

The relationship, if any, between bacteriostasis and bactericidal action is still unsolved and much of the difference of opinion on the subject would seem to arise from the natures of the different systems studied by the investigators concerned. It would appear at the outset, however, that bacteriostasis and bactericidal action are two quite separate and unrelated phenomena except in so far as by definition the former must always precede the latter. Roberts and Rahn (1946) observed complete inactivation of en-zymes at bactericidal concentrations of several germicides, but not at bacteriostatic levels, and thereby inferred differences in the two modes of action. There are numerous other examples of substances, such as the sul-phonamides, penicillin and some quaternary ammonium compounds, which are bacteriostatic at quite low concentrations but show little bactericidal action. In the opinion of Rahn and van Eseltine (1947) the two phenomena are different in their mechanisms and "Bacteriostasis may be due either to reversible inactivation of enzymes, or to reversible disruption of semi-permeable membranes, or to reversible interferences with the mechanisms of synthesis or cell division." In this hypothesis, reversibility of reaction is the key-note. This may be true, but in a complex system such as that of a bacterial cell, reversibility must be a delicately balanced phenomenon. If this balance is upset, it can only result in an apparent lethal action on the cell.

The ultimate effect of any antiseptic—bactericidal or bacteriostatic—is determined by a large number of factors, and two of them are concentration and time of contact. Bactericidal action is not instantaneous, therefore a short period contact with a germicide may give the impression of bacterio-stasis only, whereas a longer contact will prove lethal. Moreover, during bacteriostasis, certain changes can take place in the cell which render it incapable of proliferation, *ergo* the cell must be assumed dead; such is the case with some antibiotics. On premises such as these, Dubos (1945) wrote: "It appears, therefore, that the difference between bacteriostatic and bactericidal effect is often of a quantitative rather than of a qualitative nature." Price (1950) came to a similar conclusion as indicated in his state-ments that "between the time of first contact with the disinfectant and the time of death, there is a period of inhibition," and later, "sensitivity to inhibition and sensitivity to death cannot be separated. . . . Indeed, it may be questioned whether one often sees inhibition free from death, except in so far as one precedes the other." These conclusions were later supported on a quantitative basis by Cook (1954) as a result of his evaluations of the bacteriostatic activities of phenol against several types of organism.

Chemical disinfectants

The manner in which chemical disinfectants exert their germicidal activities varies with the type of compound. The hypochlorites, chloramines, and halogens generally depend on their intense reactivity with proteins and similar substances. Because of this they are highly sensitive to organic matter, which has the effect of reducing considerably their germicidal power. Their sensitivities are so great that even the organic matter contained in a normal broth inoculum significantly reduces the killing rate compared with that for washed bacterial cells. Depending for their activities on oxidizing reactions, the concentration exponents of this group of compounds are high and frequently their death-rate curves do not follow the normal logarithmic form.

Other oxidizing agents, hydrogen peroxide and the permanganates, also react vigorously with cell proteins. The mechanisms are various and irre-versible, but they all have the effect of destroying the basic molecular structure of the proteins. Formaldehyde is almost equally reactive, in this case with the amino groups of the cell proteins, with the same destructive effect. Certain also of the heterocyclic three-ringed compounds such as ethylene oxide, ethylene imine and ethylene sulphide, as well as methyl bromide and some lactones, notably β-propiolactone, are effective bactericides. They are all active alkylating agents and presumably act on the bacterial cell in this role.

Mineral acids and alkalis are active mainly through their hydrogen and hydroxyl ions respectively, although the characteristic ions also contribute. Their disinfecting action is related to the concentration of the ions concerned, and acids are more effective than alkalis because, at equal concentrations, the hydrogen ion is more effective than the hydroxyl ion. In contrast to the mineral acids, organic acids owe their activities to the undissociated molecules (Rahn and Conn, 1944).

Metallic salts prevent the normal development of the cell because they are protein precipitants. Mercury and silver salts are the most potent and mercury salts in particular are strongly bacteriostatic. There is little doubt that this is because they are first adsorbed on the surface of the cell and then form an insoluble complex with the surface proteins, thus retarding the diffusion inwards of more toxic ions and protecting the interior mechanisms of the cell. Proof of this lies in the fact that bacterial cells treated with weak solutions of mercuric chloride for suitably short times are inhibited in growth, even though the cells may be repeatedly water-washed. If, however, a soluble sulphide is added, the cells may recover their viability. A quantitative relationship has been demonstrated between the adsorption of mercury salts and their germicidal action on yeast cells, and the activities of mercury and silver ions can be enhanced by combining them in compounds with lipoid-soluble groups.

The general group of phenols also act as protein denaturants, but in a somewhat different manner from that of the metals. The action in this case (Reichel, 1909) is by absorption of the phenol by reason of its greater solubility into the protein phase yielding a complex which may ultimately be coagulated. The formation of the phenol-protein complex is a prerequisite for disinfecting activity. This theory also suggests an explanation of the selective germicidal action of phenols, the phenomenon being determined by the concentrations of phenol at which the various specific bacterial proteins react. According to Cooper and Sanders (1927, 1928), proteins in general are precipitated by 1 to 2 per cent phenol, but some can be precipitated by concentrations as low as 0·1 per cent.

It is the general belief that the bactericidal properties of the surface active compounds are also due to their ability to form complexes with proteins, and there is some experimental evidence for this. Thus, quaternary ammonium compounds are reactive in this way, but only at pH values above the isoelectric point of the protein, and it is in this range that the quaternaries exhibit their greatest activities. On the other hand both the amino and the ampholytic compounds can also form protein complexes, but the former are relatively inactive and the latter only do so at low pH values yet they are most active at higher pH levels. The protein reaction explanation is, therefore, at least an incomplete one, and some more recent work (Gilby and Few, 1960) has indicated that the site of reaction is not in fact with the proteins of the bacterial membrane, but with their phospholipids. This is an equally feasible explanation, and it remains to be seen whether it can be verified.

Factors influencing chemical disinfectant activity

Three basic phenomena are of importance for disinfecting action by chemical means: (*i*) adsorption of the compound by the cell wall, (*ii*) penetration into the cell protoplasm, and finally (*iii*) reaction of the compound with one or more of the cell constituents. The properties of adsorption and penetration of a substance in relation to the cell are not exclusive to the substance itself; they can be influenced by other constituents in the immediate environment, for instance those affecting surface tension and other physicochemical properties. Examples of these are the enhancement of the tuberculocidal activities of streptomycin (Fisher, 1948) and of certain other compounds (Youmans and Youmans, 1948) by nonionic surface-active agents, notably Tween 80, and the potentiation by sodium chloride and the suppression by cetomacrogol of the action of phenol and hexylresorcinol, the former being thought to act by virtue of its ability to facilitate the release of cellular constituents and the latter by virtue of its ability to form a complex with the hexylresorcinol and thus prevent its penetration into the cell wall (Beckett *et al.*, 1959). The most important factor, however, must be in the chemical constitution and configuration of the germicide. Thus Tilley and Schaffer (1926) found the activities of alcohols and phenols in homologous series to increase proportionately with their molecular weights up to the limits of their solubilities; Coulthard, Marshall and Pyman (1930) demonstrated bactericidal activity in the *n*-amyl series of the alkyl substituted phenols and cresols; Coates *et al.* (1957) made a similar discovery in examining the antifungal properties of alkoxy-substituted salicylamides; Albert and his co-workers (1945) associated bacteriostatic activity very closely with the degree of ionization and the dimensional structure of the molecule in over one hundred acridine compounds, and it is well known that substitution of halogen atoms, particularly chlorine, in many phenolic-type molecules considerably enhances their activities. These aspects are discussed in more detail in their appropriate sections in later chapters.

Solvents and solubilizers. The nature of the solvent is also important in that it affects the partition coefficient of the germicide. Chemical disinfectants can most readily gain access to the cell *via* the aqueous phase natural to the organism, hence they are most active in aqueous solution. Any solvent therefore which reduces the concentration of the germicide in the aqueous phase has the consequent effect of reducing the activity of the germicide. Oils, fats and alcohols behave thus with phenol, and so depress its activity with these solvents. In contrast, a germicide of high oil/water partition solubility is easily adsorbed by the lipoid fraction of the cell, hence such compounds might be expected to be more effective against those organisms of high fat content.

Emulsification of phenols in soap solution and even in tragacanth mucilage appreciably enhances their activities. As long ago as 1903, Rideal and Walker found that such an emulsion of Tricresol, a mixture of *o*-, *m*- and *p*-cresols, is equal in germicidal power to an aqueous solution three times the strength. This characteristic is made use of today in preparations such as lysol and the various 'Disinfectant Fluids'. The enhanced activity was said to be due to the increased absorption by the organism, with the effect of increasing the local concentration of disinfectant. This was demonstrated by Chick and Martin (1908) in their investigations into the absorption of tar acids from emulsions of different strengths, in which they showed a direct relationship between amount absorbed and concentration. The relationship held over the lower range of concentrations, but at higher levels the ratio fell away, indicating ultimately complete saturation of the organisms. A somewhat different explanation was put forward by Bean and Berry (1950, 1951, 1953) following their detailed investigation into the properties of chloroxylenol and benzylchlorophenol in potassium laurate solutions. This is based on the fact that all soaps in aqueous solution form into micelles, and these act as centres for solubilizing substances which are otherwise relatively insoluble. They have the property, therefore, of increasing the effective concentration of the germicide in the immediate vicinity of the cell, and so its apparent activity, and Bean and Berry showed this by relating the bactericidal activities of such solutions to the concentration of the phenol in the micelles, but not to the overall concentration in the system as a whole.

Other solutes. The presence of various inorganic salts in suitable concentrations also enhances the power of disinfectants. That this is due to the increased absorption of the phenol by the organism was proved by Reichel (1909) who showed that the salts increased the partition coefficient of the phenol in favour of the protein phase. These effects are part of the phenomenon of osmosis associated with the cytoplasmic membrane of the cell. The nature of this barrier, its functions and its permeability, along with its breakdown by surface-active agents, have been notably summarized by Mitchell (1949) and more recently by Work (1957), and Beckett *et al.* (1958, 1959) and Malchenkoff (1963) have shown how frequently cell disruption and the release of cellular exudate is the cause of death by antibacterial agents and how this can be affected by the presence of sodium chloride and other substances.

Different anions and cations exert independent effects on both the permeabilities of cell membranes, and the partition coefficients of disinfectants. In general, trivalent ions produce a greater effect than divalent, and divalent ions than univalent (Lundy, 1938); there are also differences between ions of the same valency.

Osmosis and surface tension. Most organisms have their optimum tonicity for growth, and they differ considerably in their response to osmotic changes. Some can suffer great changes without any apparent harm, but others, *e.g. Vibrio cholerae, Salmonella typhi,* are highly sensitive. Reduction of tonicity of the environment of such organisms by transfer to distilled water will cause the membrane to swell and even to burst, whereas increase of tonicity gives rise to the reverse phenomenon of plasmolysis. Thus, on the one hand, many organisms tend to die out in water; on the other hand, growth of certain organisms can be prevented in media of high osmotic value, and so bacterial spoilage of meats can be prevented by 'curing' in strong brines, with or without the addition of sodium nitrate and sodium nitrite. Even normal saline is deleterious for some organisms, and as a diluent for counting purposes or for the recovery of treated organisms quarter-strength Ringer's solution or 0·1 per cent peptone solution is now much preferred.

In terms of a structure such as the microbial cell with its membrane surface, osmosis is inseparable from surface tension, because any change in surface tension inevitably affects the local effective concentration of substances in the environment (sometimes known as their "fugacity") and hence the local osmotic pressure. Reduction of surface tension would appear, therefore, always to increase the activity, beneficial or deleterious, of a solute. Thus, the disinfecting power of a substance may be expected to depend in part on its surface tension in solution, and this is well illustrated with the hydroxybenzene compounds, phenol, resorcinol, quinol, thymol and hexylresorcinol, in which germicidal activity is distinctly related to lowering of surface tension. It is true also of many other substances, but the relationship cannot be generalized by any means. Moreover, it is not a rule that surface tension reducers have the effect of increasing the activity of all germicides; the efficiency of phenol is only increased by the addition of certain wetting agents (Ordal, Wilson and Borg, 1941); the activity of *p*-chloro-*m*-cresol is stimulated by only a few saturated fatty acid soaps (Roelcke and Reichel, 1944), and, as already stated, the action of hexylresorcinol and other phenolic substances is abolished by some nonionic surface-active agents, notably cetomacrogol (Beckett *et al.*, 1959).

Low surface tension is a characteristic of solutions of all the cationic detergent disinfectants but it contributes little, if anything, to their antibacterial activities. With this type of compound, killing of bacteria is always associated with some degree of cytolytic damage, which results in leakage of growth material from the cell. This phenomenon has been described in relation to cetrimide (Salton, 1951; Salton, Horne and Cosslett, 1951) and to dodecylammonium chloride (Eggenberger *et al.*, 1950) but it is not unique to these compounds, as shown in a review of the subject by Newton (1958). It is, however, a secondary effect and not a primary cause of death, as demonstrated by Stedman, Kravitz and King (1957) who produced equally clear evidence that with quaternary ammonium compounds lysis lags far behind the death of the cell in terms of both time and concentration, and they state "drastic changes in survival rate and enzyme inhibition occur when no significant change in the degree of lysis is observed, showing that the contribution of lysis to kill is of secondary importance under the conditions tested." In further confirmation, there is good evidence by Gilby and Few (1957, 1960) of a very close relationship between bactericidal action and lysis of the inner cellular protoplast, the lethal concentration of a number of quaternaries being only slightly greater than that required to lyse 90 per cent of the protoplasts.

The discovery of the many antibiotics and other chemotherapeutic agents in recent years has opened up a wide field of investigation into the mode of action of anti-bacterial agents. The information already available would provide enough material for several books. It must suffice, therefore, to refer the reader interested in this aspect to the several reviews and symposia on the subject (Julius, 1952; *Bacteriological Reviews*, 1953; Hugo, 1957; Society for General Microbiology, 1958; Reynolds, 1962) and to the work of Gale and colleagues (Gale, 1947; Gale and Mitchell, 1947, 1949; Gale and Folkes, 1953), of Albert and colleagues (Albert *et al.*, 1945; Albert and Goldacre, 1948) and of McIlwain (1941).

Selective action of disinfectants

The well recognized property of many compounds in their capacity to exert a selective influence on the growths of mixed bacterial populations has been made use of in various media devised for diagnostic purposes in bacteriology. The selection depends on the suppression of growth of the majority of organisms in favour of development of a limited few types. The same effects are found in the field of disinfection where certain compounds may kill or inhibit some groups of organisms and leave others to survive apparently unharmed. The mechanism of such selection is probably the least understood of all disinfection processes. The characteristic is associated more with the antiseptic group of compounds rather than with the strong disinfectants of the phenolic types whose killing rates are practically the same for all types of bacteria.

Numerous suggestions have been put forward from time to time in explanation. All appear to be valid, insomuch as they fit the facts in specific circumstances. But it is evident that a multiplicity of phenomena must come into action according to the disinfectant substance employed, the type of organisms involved and the conditions of application.

All types, species and varieties of micro-organisms have their own morphological, cultural, metabolic, and catabolic characteristics. It is reasonable to expect, therefore, that their responses to substances generally, and to disinfectants in particular, would not be the same. The interesting point is the way in which they can often be grouped in their responses. The most commonly claimed differentiation with disinfectants is between the Gram-positive and Gram-negative groups, and this must be due to their varying chemical constitutions. Salton (1956) has shown, for example, that although the cell walls of Gram-positive and Gram-negative bacteria have many amino acids and amino sugars in common, the walls of the Gram-negative bacteria carry a more complex structure. On such a difference alone some variation in resistance may thus be expected, but detailed examination shows that it can only be considered as a generalization with many exceptions. There are always the enigmas of the abnormal behaviour of certain types of organism within the group, such as the greater resistance to many chemical disinfectants of *Pseudomonas pyocyanea* within the Gram-negative group, and of *Staph. aureus* within the Gram-positive group. Moreover, there are many known cases of organisms which change their Gram-staining response with age. There is no complete explanation of this as yet, but Henry and Stacey (1943, 1946) have shown that differences in the staining affinities of bacteria are due to their ribonucleic acids content. These acids can be stripped from Gram-positive organisms through the agency of surface-active compounds such as bile salts to render them Gram-negative, and the positive response can be restored by treating the cells with magnesium ribonucleate. In this connexion it is claimed (Dufrenoy and Pratt, 1947) that bacteriostatic levels of penicillin effect changes in the distribution of the amino acid vacuola material of the cell, involving the nucleoprotein synthetic processes and these in turn cause loss of the positive reaction to the Gram stain.

There are several other known cellular constitutional differences which contribute to selectivity. Every protein has its own specific isoelectric point, therefore each will respond characteristically to changes in pH value. On this basis, one might readily envisage micro-organisms varying in their sensitivities to acid or alkaline conditions according to their constitutional protein types. The presence, and dominance, of acid-tolerant proteins in yeasts and moulds probably accounts for their ability to survive, and even to grow, at pH values as low as 2. The same argument can also be extended to germicidal substances containing acidic or basic groups, on the assumption that the specific group exhibits a greater selectivity, or reactivity, for one type of cellular group than for another.

Turning to another aspect of the cellular constituent influence, we know that the lipoid content of the different micro-organisms varies considerably —in some types it is quite low, whereas in others, such as the acid-fast bacteria and the mould spores, the level is comparatively high. We know also that the nature of the fatty substances concerned is quite different between the types, and this can act in one of two ways: a high lipoid content will attract more readily a lipophilic moiety in a disinfectant substance, thus increasing the concentration of the agent within the cell and so increasing its germicidal effectiveness; contrariwise, it will repel a hydrophilic substance and so prevent its access to the cell and reduce its apparent efficacy.

Disinfection by physical means

Heat, cold, agitation and treatment by ultraviolet, X- and high energy ionizing radiations constitute the possible physical means of disinfection. Heat treatment of the cell brings about a progressive coagulation of its vital proteins, resulting in disorganization of the cell and loss of viability. The exceptional heat resistance of bacterial spores has been attributed to their high lipoid content, and in particular dipicolinic acid, which complexes with the cellular protein and so prevents it from coagulation (*see* page 16). The particular nature of the lipoid in the bacterial spore differentiates it from that of the mycobacteria and mould spores which do not exhibit this protection and are susceptible to the same order of heat as are the vegetative bacteria.

Freezing is regarded by many as a killing process for micro-organisms, but this is quite erroneous. It is in fact a process of preserving them, so much so that freeze drying is now the classical method of preserving bacteria of all types. By this means they retain for many years their characteristic biochemical properties and antigenic structures without further attention. But freezing and thawing of cultures always results in some loss in viability, hence, if carried out sufficiently frequently or rapidly, virtual sterilization may be achieved. The percentage loss at each stage depends on the method of carrying out the process. The rate of freezing and thawing is important, and a protein- or sugar-containing medium exerts a protective effect on bacterial cells. The lethal action appears to be due to physical disruption. The same effect is observed when bacteria are subjected to ultrasonic waves, although the efficacy of this treatment is only of a low order.

Ultraviolet radiations, high energy electron radiations and ionizing radiations have all been used with varying degrees of success. They are the forms of treatment known as 'cold' sterilization. Each one depends for its efficacy on conveying a lethal quantum of energy. The death rate of organisms under such radiations indicates a target theory in which killing is brought about by a 'hit' on one or more of the susceptible areas of the cell. Such a theory is quite acceptable and workable in many cases, but in others it is evidently incomplete.

Discussing the efficacy of ionizing radiations, Hannan (1953) states "The main effect appears to be on the cell nucleus to produce a high frequency of mutations, a proportion of which lead to a failure to reproduce. Whether or not this is the sole explanation of the lethal effects, the fact remains that most of the cells affected are not killed instantly but rather die after a definite lapse of time." In line with this thought, Pollard (1955), Kelner (1955) and Bellamy (1955) are also of the opinion that the primary reaction is one of exciting ionization, resulting in the expulsion of one electron from an amino acid, enzyme or other molecule in the cell nucleus. This leads to a serial ejection of electrons from a line of molecules, the electrons passing in turn from one molecule to the next. Thus, each molecule in turn is left with a positive charge which upsets the energy balance and sets up a thermal agitation within the molecule. This gives rise to a chain of intracellular reactions which goes far beyond that of simple enzyme inactivation—in fact, the enzymes in the bacterial cell appear to be much less sensitive than are other essential cellular constituents. The many reactions set off by the initial ionizing process must each contribute to the disruption of the cell metabolism, hence the significance, as will be seen in more detail in Chapter 6, of oxygen, sulphydryl compounds and various environmental conditions in the lethal process.

All of the ionizing radiations have substantial powers of penetration, their capacity in this direction depending on their energies. For this reason the 'induced' electromagnetic radiations, cathode rays, X-rays and gamma rays, are more potent than are the high velocity 'electronic' radiations, alpha rays and beta rays. In general smaller doses are required to kill vegetative cells than to kill spore-formers, although there is one notable exception in *Micrococcus radiodurans* which can exhibit an inordinate degree of resistance.

Ultraviolet radiations also show the same selectivity, the differentiation in this case being somewhat more marked. Their lethal efficiency depends on the particular wave length employed and on the state of the organism concerned. They have no penetrative power into solids and only very little into liquids, hence all micro-organisms can be easily protected with coatings of organic material such as serum or saliva.

High-frequency voltage fields of varying intensity have also been investigated, but it has been found that any sterilizing effects arise not from the voltages applied, but from the local increases in temperature resulting from the treatment (Jacobs, Thornley and Maurice, 1950; Ingram and Page, 1953).

REFERENCES

ABBOTT, A. C. (1891). *Johns Hopkins Hosp. Bull.*, ii, 50.
ABRAHAM, E. P. and CHAIN, E. (1940). *Nature, Lond.*, 146, 837.
ALBERT, A. and GOLDACRE, R. J. (1948). *Nature, Lond.*, 161, 95.
ALBERT, A., RUBBO, S. D., GOLDACRE, R. J., DAVEY, M. E. and STONE, J. D. (1945). *Brit. J. exp. Path.*, 26, 160.
BACH, J. A. and SADOFF, H. L. (1962). *J. Bact.*, 83, 699.
Bacteriological Reviews (1953). 17, 17.
BAILLIE, ANN and NORRIS, J. R. (1962). *J. appl. Bact.*, 25, vii.
BARER, GWENDA R. (1951). *J. gen. Microbiol.*, 5, 1.
BEAN, H. S. and BERRY, H. (1950). *J. Pharm. Pharmacol.*, 2, 473, 484.
BEAN, H. S. and BERRY, H. (1951). *J. Pharm. Pharmacol.*, 3, 639.
BEAN, H. S. and BERRY, H. (1953). *J. Pharm. Pharmacol.*, 5, 632.
BEAN, H. S. and WALTERS, V. (1955). *J. Pharm. Pharmacol.*, 7, 661.
BEAN, H. S. and WALTERS, V. (1961). *J. Pharm. Pharmacol.*, 13, 183T.
BECKETT, A. H., PATKI, S. J. and ROBINSON, ANN E. (1958). *Nature, Lond.*, 181, 712.
BECKETT, A. H., PATKI, S. J. and ROBINSON, ANN E. (1959). *J. Pharm. Pharmacol.*, 11, 360, 367.

BELLAMY, W. D. (1955). *Bact. Rev.*, **19**, 23.
BERGER, H. and WYSS, O. (1953). *J. Bact.*, **65**, 103.
CHAPLIN, C. E. (1952). *J. Bact.*, **63**, 453.
CHICK, HARRIETTE (1908). *J. Hyg., Camb.*, **8**, 92.
CHICK, HARRIETTE (1910). *J. Hyg., Camb.*, **10**, 237.
CHICK, HARRIETTE and MARTIN, C. J. (1908). *J. Hyg., Camb.*, **8**, 698.
COATES, L. V., DRAIN, D. J., MACRAE, F. J. and TATTERSALL, K. (1959). *J. Pharm. Pharmacol.*, **11**, 240T.
COOK, A. M. (1954). *J. Pharm. Pharmacol.*, **6**, 629.
COOPER, E. A. and HAINES, R. B. (1928). *J. Hyg., Camb.*, **28**, 163.
COOPER, E. A. and SANDERS, E. (1927). *J. phys. Chem.*, **31**, 1.
COOPER, E. A. and SANDERS, E. (1928). *J. phys. Chem.*, **32**, 868.
COULTHARD, C. E., MARSHALL, J. and PYMAN, F. L. (1930). *J. chem. Soc.*, p. 280.
CURRAN, H. R. (1952). *Bact. Rev.*, **16**, 111.
CURRAN, H. R. and EVANS, F. R. (1937). *J. Bact.*, **34**, 179.
DEMEREC, M. (1948). *J. Bact.*, **56**, 63.
DUBOS, R. J. (1940). *Bact. Rev.*, **4**, 1.
DUBOS, R. J. (1945). *The Bacterial Cell*, p. 290: Harvard University Press, Cambridge, Mass.
DUFRENOY, JEAN and PRATT, R. (1947). *J. Bact.*, **54**, 283.
EAGLE, H. (1954). *Ann. N.Y. Acad. Sci.*, **59**, 243.
EGGENBERGER, D. N., HARRIMAN, L. A., MCCLORY, M. J., NOEL, D. and HARWOOD, N. J. (1950). *Ann. N.Y. Acad. Sci.*, **53**, 105.
ESELTINE, W. P. VAN and RAHN, O. (1949). *J. Bact.*, **57**, 547.
FILDES, P. (1940). *Brit. J. exp. Path.*, **21**, 67.
FISHER, M. W. (1948). *Amer. Rev. Tuberc.*, **57**, 58.
GALE, E. F. (1943). *Bact. Rev.*, **7**, 139.
GALE, E. F. (1947). *The Chemical Activities of Bacteria:* Univ. Tutorial Press, London.
GALE, E. F. (1948). *J. gen. Microbiol.*, **2**, iv.
GALE, E. F. and FOLKES, J. P. (1953). *Biochem. J.*, **53**, 493.
GALE, E. F. and MITCHELL, P. D. (1947). *J. gen. Microbiol.*, **1**, 299.
GALE, E. F. and MITCHELL, P. D. (1949). *J. gen. Microbiol.*, **3**, 369.
GALE, E. F. and RODWELL, A. W. (1949). *J. gen. Microbiol.*, **3**, 127.
GALE, E. F. and TAYLOR, E. SHIRLEY (1947). *J. gen. Microbiol.*, **1**, 314.
GARROD, L. P. (1952). *Proc. roy. Soc. Med.*, **45**, 321.
GILBY, A. R. and FEW, A. V. (1957). *Nature, Lond.*, **179**, 422.
GILBY, A. R. and FEW, A. V. (1960). *J. gen. Microbiol.*, **23**, 19.
GOULD, B. S., FRIGERIO, N. A. and HOVANESIAN, J. (1957). *Antibiot. Chemotherap.*, **7**, 457.
HALVORSON, H. and CHURCH, B. D. (1957). *Bact. Rev.*, **21**, 112.
HANNAN, R. S. (1953). *Proc. Soc. appl. Bact.*, **16**, 88.
HENRY, H. and STACEY, M. (1943). *Nature, Lond.*, **151**, 671.
HENRY, H. and STACEY, M. (1946). *Proc. Roy. Soc. B.*, **133**, 391.
HOBBS, BETTY C. and WILSON, G. S. (1942). *J. Hyg., Camb.*, **42**, 436.
HOFFMAN-OSTENHAM, O. (1947). *Science*, **105**, 549.
HOTCHKISS, R. D. (1946). *Ann. N.Y. Acad. Sci.*, **46**, 479.
HUGO, W. B. (1957). *J. Pharm. Pharmacol.*, **9**, 145.
INGRAM, M. and PAGE, L. J. (1953). *Proc. Soc. appl. Bact.*, **16**, 69.
JACOBS, S. E., (1960). *J. Pharm. Pharmacol.*, **12**, 9T.
JACOBS, S. E., THORNLEY, MARGARET J. and MAURICE, P. (1950). *Proc. Soc. appl. Bact.*, **13**, 161.
JORDAN, R. C. and JACOBS, S. E. (1944). *J. Hyg., Camb.*, **43**, 275, 363.
JORDAN, R. C. and JACOBS, S. E. (1945a). *J. Hyg., Camb.*, **44**, 210.
JORDAN, R. C. and JACOBS, S. E. (1945b). *J. Hyg., Camb.*, **44**, 243, 249, 421.
JULIUS, H. W. (1952). *Ann. Rev. Microbiol.*, **6**, 411.
KARSTRÖM, H. (1937). *Proc. 2nd Int. Cong. Microbiol., Lond.*, p. 473.
KELNER, A. (1955). *Bact. Rev.*, **19**, 22.
KNOX, W. E., AUERBACH, V. H., ZARUDNAYA, K. and SPIRTES, M. (1949). *J. Bact.*, **58**, 443.

Krönig, B. and Paul, T. (1897). *Z. Hyg. InfektKr.*, **25**, 1.
Lundy, H. W. (1938). *J. Bact.*, **35**, 633.
McCulloch, E. C. (1933). *J. Bact.*, **33**, 40.
McCulloch, E. C. (1945). *Disinfection and Sterilization:* Kimpton, London.
MacDonald, Etta M. (1942). *J. Amer. pharm. Assoc.* (*Pract.*), **3**, 181.
McIlwain, H. (1941). *Biochem. J.*, **35**, 1311.
Madsen, T. and Nyman, M. (1907). *Z. Hyg. InfektKr.*, **57**, 388.
Malchenkoff, A. R. (1963). A translation of *Microbiology*, **32**, 65.
Meulen, J. van der (1957). *Acta path. microbiol. scand.*, **41**, 411.
Mitchell, P. D. (1949). *The Nature of the Bacterial Surface*, p. 55: Blackwell Scientific
    Publications, Oxford.
Nelson, F. E. (1943). *J. Bact.*, **45**, 395.
Newton, B. A. (1958). *The Strategy of Chemotherapy*, 8th Symposium of the Society for
    General Microbiology; University Press, Cambridge.
Newton, B. A. (1965). *Amm. Rev. Microbiol.*, **19**, 109.
Ordal, E. J., Wilson, J. L. and Borg, A. F. (1941). *J. Bact.*, **42**, 117.
Pearl, R. (1930). *Medical Biometry and Statistics:* Saunders, London.
Perry, J. J. and Foster, J. W. (1955). *J. Bact.*, **69**, 337.
Pollard, E. (1955). *Radiobiology Symposium:* Butterworths Scientific Publications,
    London.
Price, P. B. (1950). *Ann. N.Y. Acad. Sci.*, **53**, 76.
Rahn, O. (1945). *Biodynamica*, **5**, 1.
Rahn, O. and Conn, J. E. (1944). *Ind. engng Chem.*, **36**, 185.
Rahn, O. and Eseltine, W. P. van (1947). *Ann. Rev. Microbiol.*, **1**, 173.
Reichel, H. P. (1909). *Biochem. Z.*, **22**, 149, 201.
Reynolds, B. L. (1962). *Austral. J. Pharm.*, **76**, 209.
Roberts, Martha H. and Rahn, O. (1946). *J. Bact.*, **52**, 639.
Robertson, P. S. and Oliver, W. H. (1954). *J. gen. Microbiol.*, **11**, 130.
Roelcke, K. and Reichel, H. P. (1944). *Z. Hyg. InfektKr.*, **125**, 666.
Salton, M. R. J. (1951). *J. gen. Microbiol.*, **5**, 391.
Salton, M. R. J. (1956). *Bacterial Anatomy*, 6th Symposium of the Society for General
    Microbiology: University Press, Cambridge.
Salton, M. R. J., Horne, R. W. and Cosslett, V. E. (1951). *J. gen. Microbiol.*, **5**, 405.
Sevag, M. G., Richardson, Ruth A. and Henry, Jane (1945). *J. Bact.*, **49**, 79.
Sevag, M. G. and Rosanoff, E. I. (1952). *J. Bact.*, **63**, 243.
Sevag, M. G. and Shelburn, Myrtle (1942). *J. Bact.*, **43**, 421, 447.
Sinai, J. and Yudkin, J. (1959). *J. gen. Microbiol.*, **20**, 373, 384, 400.
Smith, J. H. (1921). *Ann. app. Biol.*, **8**, 27.
Smith, J. H. (1923). *Ann. app. Biol.*, **10**, 335.
Smith, Patricia H., Oginsky, Evelyn L. and Umbreit, W. W. (1949). *J. Bact.*, **58**, 761.
Society for General Microbiology (1958). 8th Symposium: *The Strategy of Chemotherapy:*
    University Press, Cambridge.
Stanier, R. Y. (1951). *Ann. Rev. Microbiol.*, **5**, 35.
Stedman, R. L., Kravitz, E. and King, J. D. (1957). *J. Bact.*, **73**, 655.
Sykes, G. (1939). *J. Hyg., Camb.*, **39**, 463.
Thornley, Margaret J. and Yudkin, J. (1959). *J. gen. Microbiol.*, **20**, 355, 365.
Tilley, F. W. (1939). *J. Bact.*, **38**, 499.
Tilley, F. W. (1942). *J. Bact.*, **43**, 521.
Tilley, F. W. and Schaffer, J. M. (1926). *J. Bact.*, **12**, 303.
Watson, H. E. (1908). *J. Hyg., Camb.*, **8**, 536.
Withell, E. R. (1938). *Quart. J. Pharm.*, **9**, 736.
Withell, E. R. (1942a). *J. Hyg., Camb.*, **42**, 124.
Withell, E. R. (1942b). *J. Hyg., Camb.*, **42**, 339.
Woods, D. D. (1940). *Brit. J. exp. Path.*, **21**, 74.
Wooldridge, W. R., Knox, R. and Glass, V. (1936). *Biochem. J.*, **30**, 926.
Work, T. S. (1957). *Nature, Lond.*, **179**, 841.
Wyss, O. (1950). *Ann N.Y. Acad. Sci.*, **53**, 183.
Youmans, Ann S. and Youmans, G. P. (1948). *J. Bact.*, **56**, 245.
Young, I. Elizabeth (1959). *Canad. J. Microbiol.*, **5**, 197.

CHAPTER 3

METHODS OF TESTING DISINFECTANTS

BEFORE discussing the methods available for testing disinfectants, it is necessary to have the purpose of such testing clearly in mind. The function of a disinfectant is to kill contaminating micro-organisms and so prevent the spread of infection, and to this end a microbiological assessment is necessary. It may appear simpler and more precise in some cases to substitute a chemical assay of one or more of the constituents but such information unfortunately gives only an incomplete picture. Formulation is important in determining the activities and properties of any disinfectant or antiseptic, and these cannot be assessed by straightforward chemical means, hence the need for a microbiological control.

Unlike a sterilization treatment, in which the response is virtually all or nothing, the result from a disinfectant test is always conditional. Disinfectants are rarely called upon to act in an absolute capacity; more often than not they are required to deal with certain types of organisms in a given time under a given set of conditions, and so the principle of all such testing is to assess the degree of efficiency as measured by the rate of kill of a chosen range of organisms in specified circumstances, a principle which also applies in antiseptic testing as is shown in Chapter 4. Disinfectants are used in so many and diverse conditions—against organisms in suspension, on the surfaces of inanimate objects, on the skin and other living tissues, and having sometimes differing periods in which to act—that a single overall test to assess their performance characteristics is an impossibility. Because of this, a wide range of tests to meet these different conditions has been devised, many of which are in constant use and some of which have been adopted officially.

All disinfectant tests can be classified into one of two categories. There are those which are of a purely routine control nature and are suitable for the batch-to-batch control of a standard formulation, and there are those which can be used for the proper evaluation or assessment of a disinfectant under practical conditions. The former is typified by the Rideal-Walker and other phenol coefficient tests, in which the conditions are rigidly specified, whilst in the latter falls a large group of other methods ranging from those allowing different times of contact with various organic materials in suspension to those employing organisms on different types of surfaces including the skin of animals and humans. These tests are generally more exacting and difficult to carry out so that hitherto the phenol coefficient type of test has always been applied as a first action. Unfortunately there has been a tendency to read too much into the results of such tests. Undoubtedly they can be of considerable value, but their scope is strictly limited and they must not be interpreted too broadly, otherwise some quite misleading deductions may be formed. There seems to be no reason, however, why a relatively simple evaluation-type test, or group of tests, should not be devised which could cover both categories, and the present tendency is to think in this direction.

Most of the published developments in the field of disinfectant testing have come from the United States, but this does not mean that the subject has been neglected in Great Britain. Although the publications from this country are certainly not as prolific, many unpublished methods are in regular use in different laboratories, but with the exception of the Rideal-Walker and Chick-Martin techniques and a more recent method for the laboratory evaluation of quaternary ammonium compounds they are unofficial in so far as they do not feature in any Regulation or British Standard. This represents a basic difference between the English and American outlooks: in the United States the Department of Health, Education and Welfare and the Department of Agriculture specify in detail a series of tests which shall be applied according to the nature of the disinfectant and its probable use (and similar regulations also exist in Western Germany and other European countries) whereas in Britain the policy has been to avoid any such specifications and limitations. There is a tendency, however, for certain type tests and 'minimum performance' requirements to be specified, notably by Local Authorities and by hospital boards where large quantities of disinfectants are concerned.

Development of disinfectant testing

The techniques developed over the years for testing disinfectants and antiseptics have all stemmed from those devised about the turn of the last century by Koch, by Krönig and Paul, by Rideal and Walker, and by Chick and Martin, although as early as 1750 Sir John Pringle had attempted to assess the 'coefficients' of a number of compounds in terms of their capacities to prevent the putrefaction of raw lean beef. The present techniques have all been evolved as a result of experience, and sometimes of necessity, and they cover not only the assessment of the lethal properties of disinfectants against bacteria and fungi but also their inhibitory effects under certain conditions when used as antiseptics.

The first test to be recorded was the silk thread technique of Koch (1881). In this, the threads were impregnated with anthrax spores, immersed in the disinfectant dilution for a given time and then transferred to a nutrient medium, or sometimes planted in test animals, to find the point at which the organisms were just killed. The method was adapted by Delepine (1907) for testing the germicidal activities of disinfectants against non-sporing bacteria such as *Escherichia coli* and *Salmonella typhi*. Some few years after Koch's work, Krönig and Paul (1897) published their findings also on the disinfection of anthrax spores. Their technique was basically the same as that of Koch, but differed in that the bacterial spores were dried on garnets instead of silk threads, and the garnets were rinsed after treatment before putting them into broth. As a result of their work Krönig and Paul made the important observation, fundamental to all subsequent disinfection and sterilization

TABLE 3

Some of the more important disinfectant testing techniques

Date	Suspension techniques	Surface film techniques
1881		Koch (silk thread)
1887		Krönig and Paul (garnets)
1903	Rideal and Walker (standardized phenol coefficient method)	
1908	Chick and Martin (faeces added)	
1912	U.S. Hygienic Lab. method	
1931	Ruehle and Brewer (U.S.F.D.A. method)	
1933		Jensen and Jensen (cover slips)
1934	British Standard No. 541: Rideal-Walker test	
1938	British Standard No. 808: Chick-Martin test	
1941	Baker *et al.* (inactivator introduced)	
1945		Mallmann and Hanes (glass cylinders with inactivator)
1946	Quisno *et al.* (Lecithin-Tween inactivation for Q.A.C.)	Johns (glass slides and milk)
1947		Neave and Hoy (metal trays and milk)
1948	Weber and Black (inactivator and plate counts)	
1949	Davies (Lubrol W inactivator for Q.A.C.)	
1950		Goetchius and Botwright (rubber and milk)
1952	Cousins (milk with inactivator for Q.A.C.)	
1953		Hoy and Clegg (milk cans with plate counts) Stuart, Ortenzio and Friedl ('Use-Dilution Confirmation' test)
1954	Berry and Bean (extinction-time)	
1955	A.O.A.C. method (phenol coefficient)	
1960	British Standard No. 3286: Laboratory evaluation of Q.A.C.	
1961	British Standard No. 2462: Phenol coefficient with *Staph. aureus*	

This table gives the authors of the methods and the principal points of development. Details are given in the text.

Q.A.C. = quaternary ammonium compounds

work, that bacteria are not killed instantaneously, but are destroyed at a measurable and orderly rate: they also observed that the temperature and concentration of the disinfectant is significant. Unfortunately, both methods, although well advanced in technique insofar as they employed highly resistant organisms in contact with a surface, were lacking because the test conditions were somewhat arbitrary and uncontrolled. Moreover, they did not take into account the persistent bacteriostatic carryover of the disinfectant into the culture medium, a factor which was not appreciated until many years later.

Realizing the need for greater standardization of the testing conditions in order to obtain reproducible results, and realizing also other imperfections in the existing techniques, Rideal and Walker (1903) devised a method of testing which at that time was entirely novel. It was the first to standardize the conditions of testing; it used a culture of vegetative organisms suspended in broth in the place of spores dried on a surface and it included a reference germicide, phenol, from which the activity of the disinfection in relation to phenol could be calculated, hence the 'phenol coefficient.' Chick and Martin (1908) used a similar technique to the Rideal-Walker method, but, appreciating the significance of organic matter in practical disinfection, they included dried faeces in the disinfectant dilutions. The method also gives a phenol coefficient, but it is generally a much lower value than that given by the Rideal-Walker test.

For a number of years after the basic work of Koch, Krönig and Paul, Rideal and Walker, and Chick and Martin a *status quo* seems to have been established. The fundamental phenol coefficient test seems to have been accepted as the best means for assessing germicides and little attempt seems to have been made to improve on them or to devise new tests until about 1928, since when progress has been rapid and has gathered momentum. Developments have been on two main lines: (*i*) suspension type tests in which liquid cultures are used, and (*ii*) surface tests in which the organisms are treated on surfaces. For greater clarity in following these developments the various techniques proposed from time to time are set out in chronological order in Table 3. Only those tests which appear to mark a major advance are recorded and several of them are concerned primarily with testing quaternary ammonium compounds; these are dealt with specifically in Chapter 14.

Principles of testing

It is a principle of all biological testing, and not the least of disinfectant testing, that the greatest accuracy and reproducibility is obtained when (*i*) 'like' is compared with 'like', that is, when the test sample and the control material are as identical as possible, (*ii*) the test is designed to give a measurable response in relation to the dose employed, and (*iii*) an adequate number of replicates are used. Even under the best of conditions, there is always a natural biological variation to be contended with and it is not unusual to find on occasion that a test has gone completely awry. Here statistics can be of value in determining from experimental results the degree of variation which might be expected and the amount and type of replication necessary to give results within certain limits. Statistics cannot, however, adjust results which are obviously different, nor do they provide an excuse for not paying careful attention to accuracy of technique in carrying out any prescribed test; to this end the simpler the method the better. It is no use approximating a technique in any way and hoping to get 'the right figure'; equally so it is vain to expect a greater accuracy from a test than that of which it is capable, and abortive to use a method which is so sensitive that it does not allow of reasonable reproduction. These aspects will be discussed in more detail in subsequent pages.

Culture selection and maintenance

In deciding upon the type of organism to be used in any disinfectant test, due attention is always given to the purpose for which the germicide is required. Frequently the need is met by using one or more of the established strains obtainable from the various National Collections, but in other cases special cultures of recent isolation may be required. In phenol coefficient tests in particular, the right strain of organism is of utmost importance as was clearly demonstrated by Ostrolenk and Brewer (1949)—but it shows at the same time the artificiality of such tests.

Having selected a culture for a particular purpose, it should be immediately preserved by freeze-drying. By this means, a reference standard culture is always available. If kept in continuous culture, it is not unknown for an organism to change its characteristics somewhat and for its resistance to vary. This is liable to occur even under the most carefully controlled cultural conditions, and in such circumstances the only solution is to revert to the original freeze-dried master culture.

The conditions of daily maintenance of the organism can affect greatly the results of any disinfectant test. For this reason, incubation of the culture in the proper medium at the correct temperature and for the right length of time are essential. Even so, fluctuations still occur, and variations in the resistance of *Salm. typhi* to phenol at dilutions ranging between 1 in 65 and 1 in 100 have been recorded (Ortenzio *et al.*, 1949).

All bacteria have an optimum growth temperature and they will grow over a reasonably wide range either side of this temperature. But it is self-evident that changes in temperature must affect the metabolic and growth rates of the organism and might even cause some change in the mode of metabolism. This would inevitably lead to an alteration in the resistance of the culture and so affect the levels of response in a test. Marked changes of this nature have been recorded by differences as little as 1° in the temperature of incubation. Sudden changes in temperature can also affect viability quite seriously. As early as 1934, Sherman and Cameron observed a 95 per cent loss in the viability of a growing culture of *E. coli* by reducing the temperature from 45° to 10°, and more recently this action has been shown to be associated not only with the temperature change but also with the phase of growth (stationary phase cells are not affected) and with the diluent. In this respect *E. coli* (Meynell, 1958) and *Pseudomonas pyocyanea* (Gorrill and McNeil, 1960) are most susceptible when diluted in water. 0·3M sucrose is one of the best diluents, and others include nutrient broth and ¼-strength Ringer's solution; full strength Ringer, normal saline, and water alone are undesirable because they all bring about a certain death rate in many cultures. Curiously enough, staphylococcus cultures do not seem to be affected in this way.

The age of the culture is of equal significance. Young actively growing cells are often more susceptible than their maturer relatives, and sometimes it appears that quite small differences in the age of the culture can give rise to large variations in its resistance. Great variations have been found between cultures of different age of *Streptococcus faecalis* (White, 1951) and *E. coli* (Elliker and Frazier, 1938) in their resistance to heat, and also to phenol (Lemke, 1955).

Two notes, published independently in 1955 (Cook and Steel; Hugo), indicate that suspensions of *E. coli* of concentrations of the order of 10^9 organisms per ml can be kept viable and constant for periods up to 40 days. If this is proved, and especially if it applies to other bacterial species, one of the problems in disinfectant testing, namely, that of ensuring that the test organism has a standard resistance, may be nearer to being solved, since it will be possible to prepare a bulk of the culture suspension, and then check it, and know that it will remain constant for a reasonable period.

Choice of culture media

Probably the most important single factor in influencing the characteristics of an organism is the culture medium in which it is grown. In disinfectant testing it plays a dual role, first in maintaining the culture prior to its use in the test, and secondly in providing the means of recovery and growth after treatment in the test. The high significance of the peptone source, for instance, is well illustrated in the widely divergent phenol coefficients obtained by Hampil (1928) on a homologous series of alkyl resorcinols. In an otherwise standard medium, but using Witte and Difco peptones, she recorded coefficients of 40·9 and 50 respectively for the isoamyl compound, 40·9 and 75 for the isohexyl compound and 49 and 127 for the heptyl compound. Even different batches of the same brand of peptone are subject to the same difficulties, and variations in phenol coefficient have been attributed to this (Brewer, 1943). Unfortunately, the nutrient characteristics of peptones cannot be judged from their chemical analyses alone; they can only be assessed by actual cultural tests (Society for General Microbiology, 1950, 1956; Meyer, 1954).

Different sources of meat extract have also been shown to cause fluctuations in the resistance of *Salm. typhi* to quaternaries as well as to standard phenol, resulting in coefficients for the same compound varying between 155 and over 500 (Goetchius, 1950). Not only were there marked differences between the different extracts, but they also influenced the day-to-day variations. In order to overcome some of these variations, a number of synthetic or semi-synthetic media have been suggested (*e.g.* Klarmann and Wright, 1945; Pelczar, 1952, 1953). Even the distilled water used may have some influence. Depending on its source and system of distillation it can contain varying amounts of trace elements and these almost certainly affect the virility of the resultant cultures.

Interpretation of results

The majority of the methods established for testing the germicidal activities of disinfectants, as well as of some types of antiseptic, employ phenol as the reference standard, and so a phenol coefficient is regularly quoted for these preparations. Through much publicity, this value has attained a certain magical charm in many quarters, but no meaning can or should be read into it other than the simple fact that it indicates that in terms of dilution a preparation is so many times more active than phenol *under the strictly defined conditions of the test*. Any assumption beyond this is unwarrantable, because even under slightly altered conditions the relationship may be quite different.

Phenol coefficient tests are undoubtedly useful in assessing disinfectant activities, but in most cases they must be regarded as no more than a first performance test. They are valuable tools in the routine examination of established products, in the preliminary determination of the antibacterial properties of germicides for screening purposes and in research on new compounds or new formulations, but many words of warning have been written over the years on the pitfalls and dangers of applying the results of such tests directly to field or clinical use (*e.g.* Browning, 1934; Hunter, 1943; Slocum, 1950). It does not need much imagination to realize, for instance, that to quote the Rideal-Walker coefficient of a preparation as a measure of its activity as a skin disinfectant means nothing. But even if a test has been devised to simulate more closely the conditions as found in practice, we have only made a *laboratory* evaluation. There may still be unknown factors which can only be discovered as a result of actual field trials. Such trials, however, are often difficult to plan with any degree of certainty, or to execute in such a manner that the results can be assessed satisfactorily to the exclusion of other interfering factors; hence we may be left with no choice but to make use of the best resources and facilities available and to trust that the laboratory evidence so obtained will have the desired effect in practice.

Sometimes it is possible to interpret laboratory results by means of a factor derived from information gained from actual field experience. Such is the case with phenolic disinfectants. In Great Britain, twenty times the Chick-Martin coefficient, after a minor adjustment, is the authorized dilution factor under the Diseases of Animals Act, 1950, and in the United States 20 times the phenol coefficient is considered to be satisfactory, subject to that dilution passing the Use-Dilution Confirmation test (*see* below).

Phenol coefficient tests

In spite of their severe shortcomings, phenol coefficient tests in one form or another have been, and still are, applied to all types of disinfectant, and coefficient values are awarded. Several such tests are official in different parts of the world, the principal ones being the Rideal-Walker, the Chick-Martin and the United States Association of Official Agricultural Chemists (A.O.A.C.) methods. The primary purpose of a phenol coefficient test is to compare the efficacy of phenolic coal-tar disinfectants against a standard phenol, and as such it is useful as a buying-and-selling test for disinfectant fluids. It can also be used within limitations for selecting the most active of a series of similar preparations or of homologous compounds, but to attempt to assess by it the relative values of, say, a quaternary ammonium compound and a slow-acting acridine can only give false and misleading information. It is by using the tests in this way and by interpreting the results obtained beyond their intended limits that phenol coefficient techniques have been much maligned and brought into disrepute in recent years. The conditions of the tests are admittedly artificial in many respects, but they still have a valuable function if handled properly.

The Rideal-Walker test

The Rideal-Walker test is not only of historical importance, it is used extensively today in all parts of the world; it therefore justifies consideration in some detail. In its original form, as published by Rideal and Walker (1903), the test represented the first real attempt at putting the assay of disinfectants on a quantitative basis; in its present form it is a valuable tool in the routine assessment of standard disinfectants. Although over sixty years old, it is today the same in principle as it was originally, but a number of modifying refinements have been made, all with the object of improving the precision of the test. When first produced, it represented an entirely new departure in testing techniques in that it specified standardized cultural and other conditions and, most important, it used a standard substance, pure phenol, against which the disinfectant under examination was compared.

The test specifies the species and age of the culture, the culture medium employed, the amount of inoculum used, the temperature and time of medication, the period of incubation of the subcultures, and the resistance of the test organism in terms of the phenol control. The organism used in the original test was the Rawlings strain of *Salm. typhi*, chosen because the authors were only interested in examining disinfectants used for general purposes, therefore, an organism of the intestinal typhoid-colon group seemed most suitable and this particular strain was believed to be more stable and reproducible in its growth characteristics than, say, *E. coli*. For the same reason, Liebig's meat extract and Witte's peptone were specified, on the assumption that they would ensure reproducibility in the nutrient properties of the culture medium and, therefore, in the growth characteristics of the organism. A deliberately short disinfection time of about five minutes was chosen because, to use Rideal's words "any lengthening of the time of the test is open to the objection that we want disinfectants to act in the shortest possible time," and phenol was the natural choice for a standard because in those days disinfectants of a phenolic type were the only concern and phenol itself had been the well established and well tried antiseptic since Lister's day.

In subsequent years, the authors made various modifications which they later published as an "approved technique" (Rideal and Walker, 1921). The preface contained the admonition that to avoid discrepancies "strict observance of the conditions laid down by the authors cannot be too strongly emphasized." The new technique included modifications to the volumes of disinfectant dilutions and of culture medium employed, the time of medication, the test temperature, and it substituted Witte's peptone by Allen and Hanbury's Eupeptone.

Later, further modifications were published by various workers, with the result that a number of variants of the method were at one time in simultaneous use. This gave rise to so much confusion that the whole technique was again reviewed in detail, mainly under the aegis of the British Disinfectant Manufacturers' Association, and a standard technique was published by the British Standards Institution (1934). With three minor modifications made at subsequent dates, this technique stands today. For the exact details of procedure the reader should consult this approved technique, but in outline the main items are:

THE CULTURE MEDIUM. Prepare a medium containing 20 gm of Lab-Lemco (Oxo), 20 gm of Eupeptone No. 1 (Allen and Hanbury) and 10 gm of sodium chloride in 1,000 ml of distilled water. Boil or heat in the steamer for 30 minutes, cool and make up to volume. Titrate a 25 ml aliquot at 37° with $0.1N$ sodium hydroxide using phenolphthalein indicator and by calculation from this adjust the bulk of the broth with N sodium hydroxide. Bring to the boil, or steam for half-an-hour, and remove the precipitated phosphates by hot filtration. Adjust to pH 7·6 and sterilize the bulk in steam at 121° (15 lb steam pressure) for 20 minutes. When required, filter if necessary, fill in 5 ml amounts into 5 in. by ¾ in. hard glass test tubes, plug with cotton wool and sterilize in steam at 121° for 10 minutes. No other sterilization is permitted. The medium has a final pH value between 7·3 and 7·6 and it keeps indefinitely in bulk but is liable to evaporate if kept more than a few days in tubes.

A solid medium is also required to maintain the current stock culture. To prepare this dissolve a suitable amount (1·2 to 2 per cent) of agar powder in the standard broth, distribute into small bottles or tubes, sterilize in steam at 121° for 10 minutes and allow to solidify in the 'slope' position.

THE CULTURE. The test organism is *Salmonella typhi* (*Bacterium typhosum*), culture number NCTC 786, obtainable from the National Collection of Type Cultures, London. It is supplied in the freeze-dried state and for current use can be maintained by weekly subculture on a Rideal-Walker agar slope, incubating for the first 24 hours at 37° and then keeping it at room temperature.

Resort should be made at intervals to a new freeze-dried culture to ensure that the standard strain is always used.

For test purposes, use a 24-hour growth in the standard broth, initiated from a stock agar slope culture. Transfer a little of the growth from the slope to a 5 ml tube of the broth and incubate for 24 hours at 37°; this is the first generation. For subsequent generations, transfer one standard 4 mm bacteriological loopful to a fresh 5 ml tube of broth and incubate at 37° as before.

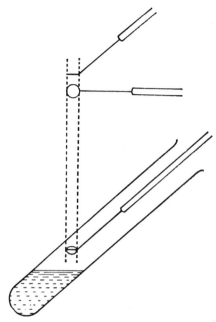

FIG. 3. *The platinum subculture loop in use*
Note the loop bent at an angle to the shaft to allow it to be withdrawn vertically from the surface of the liquid.

Only cultures which are 22 to 26 hours old and only those between the third and fourteenth generations may be used.

DISINFECTANT DILUTIONS. For the standard phenol prepare a stock 5 per cent (w/v) solution of pure phenol in distilled water and from this make further dilutions containing 1 gm of phenol in 95, 100, 105, 110 and 115 ml of solution.

For the test disinfectant measure 5 ml in a capacity pipette and discharge it into about 480 ml of sterile distilled water in a 500 ml cylinder. Rinse the pipette in the clear liquid, make up to volume, mix thoroughly by a corkscrew motion. In the case of solids, prepare a similar solution by weight instead of by volume. Substances of low solubility may require a small amount of alcohol or other solvent to assist solution. To prepare the final dilutions, make up 5 ml or 20 ml amounts of the stock dilution up to the appropriate volume with sterile distilled water. For each test four dilutions are required arranged in arithmetic series with spacings generally being in units of 50, *i.e.* 1 in 200, 1 in 250, 1 in 300, 1 in 350 and 1 in 400, after which they are in units of 100.

PROCEDURE. Measure 5 ml of each of four chosen dilutions into each of four sterile 5 in. by ¾ in. tubes, and place them alongside the 24-hour broth culture in a rack in a water bath held between 17° and 18°; a fifth tube contains 5 ml of one of the standard phenol dilutions.

After allowing the contents of the tubes and the culture to reach the required temperature add 0·2 ml of the culture by means of a dropping pipette to the first tube in the rack and shake it gently. Thirty seconds later inoculate the second tube in a similar manner and repeat the operation until the fifth tube has been inoculated. Thirty seconds after the last inoculation, *i.e.* 2½ minutes after inoculating the first tube, remove the tube from the rack, shake it gently, transfer one standard loopful to a 5 ml tube of broth and return the tube to the rack. (Make sure that the amount removed is a full loopful droplet and not just a 'film' within the loop—*see* Fig. 3.) Repeat this procedure at 30 seconds' intervals with each tube in turn until the whole cycle has been repeated four times, *i.e.* until each medication tube has been subcultured after intervals of 2½, 5, 7½ and 10 minutes. Incubate the broth tubes at 37° for not less than 48 hours and not more than 72 hours and record the presence or absence of growth in each tube.

In order to obtain a satisfactory end-point, it may be necessary to test more than one group of four disinfectant dilutions: in such cases a standard phenol dilution should be included in each group examined.

CALCULATION OF THE COEFFICIENT. The Rideal-Walker coefficient is calculated by dividing the dilution of disinfectant which shows life after 2½ and 5 minutes, but not after 7½ and 10 minutes, by that dilution of phenol which shows the same end-point.

A typical test result is as follows:

Disinfectant	Dilution	Time (*min.*) culture exposed to action of disinfectant			
		2½	5	7½	10
A	1 in 1,000	−	−	−	−
A	1 in 1,100	+	−	−	−
A	1 in 1,200	+	+	−	−
A	1 in 1,300	+	+	+	−
Control phenol	1 in 105	+	+	−	−

(+ = growth; − = no growth)

$$\text{Rideal-Walker coefficient} = \frac{1200}{105} = 11\cdot4 \text{ (approximately)}$$

Comments on the test. Here it will be of interest to record some of the findings which led to the adoption of the approved technique in 1934, and also to discuss some of the experiences of various groups of workers in their subsequent investigations.

The culture deposited with the National Collection of Type Cultures was a mixture of the Hopkins and Rawlings strains of *Salm. typhi.* The mixture was chosen in the then belief, since shown to be misguided, that it would give a growth of more constant resistance than the Rawlings strain first prescribed. It was maintained for many years by regular subculture on agar until 1951 when it was freeze-dried and subsequently issued in this form. There is no doubt that the culture today cannot be the same mixture as that originally set up, but fortunately, it still retains its standard phenol resistance.

In the earlier techniques the temperature at which the test was carried out ranged between 15° and 20°. This spread was found to allow too much variation, and so in the 1934 approved technique the limit of 17° to 18° was set. The reason for this was that the rather lower temperature level appeared to be more realistic where disinfection with coal-tar preparations was concerned.

With regard to the inoculating loop, the size of the droplet picked up obviously affects the number of organisms transferred to the subculture medium, and consequently may influence the test result. For this reason the droplet must be as uniform in size as possible. It must be big enough on the one hand to ensure a reasonable uniformity in volume, whilst on the other hand it must be small enough to avoid a carry-over of a bacteriostatic concentration of the disinfectant dilution. It is for this reason that pipette transfers are not made. Both spiral and single-turn loops of different size were tried during the investigation, but in no case was any improvement in test results noted. Reddish (1927) had already found this in his investigation of the United States Hygenic Laboratory test when he wrote "the spiral H.L. method is an unnecessary refinement . . . [it] does not increase the accuracy of the test to any appreciable extent." Even so, care and experience are necessary to minimize undue errors from this source. It is an easy matter to pick up loopsful varying between the more usual hanging drop size and a mere film of liquid simply by altering the angle and speed at which the loop breaks through the surface of the liquid; surface tension will also play some part in this respect. The personal element in this can be very great, for in the author's experience skilled workers regularly picked up loopsful which although apparently normal and standard differed by as much as 30 to 40 per cent. Moreover, there were considerable variations in each case in the sizes of the individual droplets. With one worker, for example, the variation for a 1 in 100 solution of phenol was between 8·3 and 14·2 mgm and for a 1 in 250 dilution of lysol between 7·3 and 13·0 mgm, with averages of 10·4 and 9·3 mgm respectively. These ranges and variations are substantial and point to a weakness in the testing technique; they also show that the surface tension of the solution has some effect, lysol having a lower surface tension than phenol, but this is apparently much less significant.

Finally, it goes without saying that because of its fundamental importance, the choice of culture medium merits careful consideration both in the nature and amounts of constituents used and the way in which it is handled. For these reasons, Lab-Lemco and Eupeptone No. 1 were specified in the 1934 technique in the belief that they were more suitably standardized for the purpose of the test. Likewise the pH value and the amount of heat treatment during sterilization were carefully specified. Each of these can obviously affect appreciably the nutrient properties of the medium. Some workers consider that much more attention should be paid to the total solids of the final medium, others are equally concerned about the inorganic salts content, whilst yet others believe that the 'titration value' (*sic*) of the peptone is important. There is not sufficient evidence to pin-point any of these as a major cause of variation.

In spite of the carefully considered attempts to eliminate many variables in the test, it is quite plain that several still remain either undetected or uncontrolled. In the face of this it is difficult to assess the significance of any one known variable or to appreciate the nature of the unknown ones. To illustrate: in one series of comparative tests between different laboratories, coefficients were obtained, under ostensibly standardized conditions, varying between 15·7 and 21·5 for one fluid, 18·5 and 26·0 for a second fluid and 8·0 and 13·6 for a third. The discrepancies were reduced, but by no means eliminated, when the same workers carried out the tests side by side in one laboratory. This indicates a significant human element as one of the variables of the test.

The Chick-Martin test

One of the weaknesses of the Rideal-Walker test is that the disinfectant dilutions are made in distilled water, hence the practical value of a result obtained from such a test is very limited. Disinfectants are almost invariably required to act in the presence of organic or suspended matter of some sort, and Chick and Martin (1908) believed that this should be taken into account in any testing technique, particularly in the light of their experience that such material exerts an unpredictable influence in reducing the efficacy of all disinfectants. They also believed that a disinfecting period of only 10 minutes, such as it used in the Rideal-Walker test, places many preparations at a disadvantage, and so on the basis of these arguments, they proposed a test "the essential features of which are those of the Rideal-Walker process, but a constant time, 30 minutes, is allowed for the disinfectant to act." The disinfectant and phenol dilutions contained 3 per cent of sterilized human faeces, previously dried and ground, the culture was a *Salm. typhi*, but different from the Rideal-Walker strain, and subcultures were made in duplicate into a peptone-meat extract-glucose medium.

From the outset, the authors were not enamoured of the use of dried faeces – they were unpleasant to use – but they did simulate some of the conditions in which disinfectants are required to act. Later, Garrod (1934, 1935) suggested a yeast suspension as being more suitable and giving less variable results. This view was accepted by a panel of the British Standards Institution then considering the test, and the use of yeast, along with other minor alterations, was incorporated in the British Standard Specification, B.S.808 : 1938.

As with the Rideal-Walker test the reader should consult this Standard for the exact details, but in principle they are:

THE CULTURE MEDIUM. Prepare a medium containing 10 gm of Lab-Lemco (Oxo), 10 gm of Eupeptone No. 1 (Allen and Hanbury) and 5 gm of sodium chloride in 1,000 ml of distilled water. Boil or heat in steam for 30 minutes, cool and make up to volume. Titrate a 25 ml aliquot with 0·1N sodium hydroxide using phenolphthalein indicator and by calculation from this adjust the bulk of the broth with N sodium hydroxide. Bring to the boil, or steam for half-an-hour, and remove the precipitated phosphates by hot filtration. Adjust to pH 7·6 and sterilize the bulk in steam at 121° (15 lb steam pressure) for 20 minutes. When required, adjust the broth if necessary to pH 7·5, fill in 10 ml amounts into 5 in. by ¾ in. hard glass tubes, plug with cotton wool and sterilize in steam at 121° for 10 minutes. No other sterilization is permitted. The medium has a final pH value between 7·3 and 7·6.

A solid medium is also required to maintain the current stock culture. To prepare this dissolve a suitable amount (1·2 to 2 per cent) of agar powder in the standard broth, distribute into small bottles or tubes, sterilize in steam at 121° for 10 minutes and allow to solidify in the 'slope' position.

THE CULTURE. The test organism is the 'S' strain of *Salm. typhi* (*Bact. typhosum*), obtainable from the National Collection of Type Cultures, London. It is supplied in the freeze-dried state and for current use can be maintained by weekly subculture on a nutrient agar slope, incubating for the first 24 hours at 37° and then keeping it at room temperature. Resort should be made at intervals to a new freeze-dried culture to ensure that the standard strain is always used.

For test purposes, use a 23- to 25-hours' growth in the standard broth, initiated from a stock agar slope culture. Transfer a little of the growth from the slope to a 10 ml tube of the broth and incubate for 24 hours at 37°; this is the first generation. For subsequent generations, transfer one standard 4 mm loopful to a fresh 10 ml tube of broth and incubate as before. Only cultures between the third and fourteenth generations may be used.

THE YEAST SUSPENSION. A special moist yeast, "Yeast for B.S.I. C/10 tests" obtainable from the Distillers Co. Ltd., Bristol, England, is used in 5 per cent dry weight suspension in distilled water. Cream the yeast with water to give about a 40 per cent suspension, pass it through a 100-mesh sieve to remove large particles, dilute with an equal volume of water and sterilize in 100 ml amounts in screw-capped bottles in steam at 121° for 15 minutes. Determine the total dry solids of the suspension and the amount of alkali necessary to bring the pH value to 7·0, and use these values to adjust each bottle as required to give a 5 per cent dry weight suspension at pH 7·0.

DISINFECTANT DILUTIONS. A series of dilutions is required in regular diminishing stages of 10 per cent.

For the standard phenol prepare a stock 5 per cent (w/v) solution of pure phenol in distilled water and from this make further dilutions to contain 2·0, 1·8, 1·62 and 1·46 per cent of phenol.

For the test disinfectant, prepare an initial 2 per cent dilution in distilled water (5 ml in a capacity pipette made up to 250 ml and thoroughly mixed) and from this prepare in a graduated cylinder 100 ml of the strongest concentration required. Remove 10 ml of this, put 2·5 ml into a sterile 5 in. by ¾ in. tube and reject the remaining 7·5 ml. Make the volume in the cylinder up to 100 ml and again remove 10 ml, using 2·5 ml for the second test dilution. Repeat the process until the required range of dilutions has been obtained.

PROCEDURE. Mix 2 ml of the 24-hour *Salm. typhi* culture with 48 ml of the diluted yeast suspension in a suitable tube or bottle and place in a water bath at 20° along with the tubes containing the phenol and disinfectant dilutions.

After allowing time for the temperature to become uniform, add 2·5 ml of the yeast-culture mixture to the first medication tube and shake well. Inoculate the remainder of the tubes similarly at half-minute intervals. Exactly 30 minutes after inoculation, subculture each tube in duplicate by transferring one standard loopful to each of two 10 ml tubes of medium. Incubate the broth tubes at 37° for 48 hours and record the growths.

CALCULATING THE COEFFICIENT. The Chick-Martin coefficient is calculated "by dividing the mean of the highest concentration of phenol permitting growth in both cultures and the lowest concentration showing absence of growth in both cultures by the corresponding mean concentration of the disinfectant." For example, a test showing results:

Phenol %				Disinfectant %			
2·00	—	—		0·457	—	—	
1·80	—	—	} mean = 1·71	0·411	—	—	} mean = 0·390
1·62	+	+		0·370	+	+	
1·46	+	+		0·333	+	+	

gives a coefficient of $\dfrac{1\cdot71}{0\cdot39} = 4\cdot4$;

and a test showing results:

Phenol %				Disinfectant %			
2·00	—	—		0·457	—	—	
1·80	—	—	} mean = 1·62	0·411	—	—	} mean = 0·390
1·62	+	—		0·370	+	+	
1·46	+	+		0·333	+	+	

gives a coefficient of $\dfrac{1\cdot62}{0\cdot39} = 4\cdot15$.

It is recommended in the technique that in reporting results it should be indicated that the value is subject to an error of ± 10 per cent.

Use is made of the Chick-Martin coefficient for approving disinfectants under the Diseases of Animals Act, 1950. By this authority, a dilution award is made which is the germicidal value plus 10 per cent of the germicidal value rounded off to the nearest 0·5 and then multiplied by 20. The coefficient is also recommended by the Medical Research Council (1951) as a guide to the selection of disinfectants for certain hospital uses.

The 'Lancet' Commission test

In 1909, the *Lancet* appointed a commission of inquiry into the chemical and bacteriological standardization of disinfectants. Their report was published the same year (*Lancet*, 1909), and in it was described a new testing technique. It differed from the Rideal-Walker test in the following respects: (*i*) it used *Bact. coli communis* as the test organism, stating that the use of *Salm. typhi* was a fetish; (*ii*) it employed MacConkey's medium; (*iii*) sampling was done with platinum spoons of three times the capacity of the normal loop; (*iv*) killing dilutions of phenol and the test disinfectant were found after 2½ minutes and 30 minutes contact and the phenol coefficient calculated from the means of the two killing dilutions.

The test does not appear to have received much acknowledgement.

The United States Hygienic Laboratory method

For several years the Rideal-Walker test was used in the United States. But in 1911 Anderson and McClintic endeavoured to overcome some of its recognized defects and published a modified technique which became the Hygienic Laboratory Method (1912, 1921). It differed from the Rideal-Walker test in that a more dilute peptone-meat extract medium was used, the medication temperature was raised to 20°, a spiral inoculating loop was introduced and the method of calculating the phenol coefficient was altered.

Although eliminating certain faults in the Rideal-Walker test, the new method introduced others. For example, the pH of the medium was not defined, there was no specified range of resistance of the test organism to phenol and the test was carried out in open tubes. Because of these faults, the test soon fell into disrepute.

The United States Food and Drug Administration (F.D.A.) method

Taking advantage of the virtues of the Rideal-Walker test and the Hygienic Laboratory method, Shippen, followed by Reddish, produced a new technique which was later adopted as the official F.D.A. method (Ruehle and Brewer, 1931). Generally speaking, the Rideal-Walker, the Hygienic Laboratory and the F.D.A. methods give almost identical coefficients for phenolic disinfectants, the principal exceptions being with the more powerful preparations which tend to yield higher coefficients by the Rideal-Walker method than by the F.D.A. method.

The test organism used in the F.D.A. method is a 22 to 26 hour culture of *Salm. typhi* (Hopkins strain) grown in nutrient broth at 37°. The broth contains 10 gm of Armour's peptone, 5 gm of Liebig's beef extract and 5 gm of pure sodium chloride in 1,000 ml of distilled water and has a final pH value of 6·5. The culture is maintained in the same way as that for the Rideal-Walker test and the inoculating loop and phenol standard are the same. The test is run at 20° instead of 17–18° and the exposure times are 5, 10 and 15 minutes. The phenol dilutions specified are 1 in 90 and 1 in 100.

Only tests giving phenol culture readings *within* the following limits are considered satisfactory:

		Phenol	5 *min*	Growth after 10 *min*	15 *min*
	(a)	1–90	+	+	0
		1–100	+	+	+
or					
	(b)	1–90	0	0	0
		1–100	+	+	0

The phenol coefficient is "a figure obtained by dividing the numerical value of the greatest dilution of the disinfectant capable of killing *Eberthella typhi* (*Salm. typhi*) in 10 minutes but not in 5 minutes, by the greatest dilution of phenol showing the same results; that is, by the phenol control." When none of the test dilutions shows this actual response, it is permitted to interpolate the result, but not to extrapolate.

The published technique takes into account substances such as the mercury compounds which are highly inhibitory. In such cases, a second subculture into broth is made. It also warns against the misuse of the phenol coefficient so obtained for oxidizing agents whose activities are materially affected by organic matter.

The technique recognizes that it is desirable to know the performance of disinfectants against other test organisms, and, indeed, makes provision for a similar test using *Staph. aureus*. It expresses the opinion that for disinfectants "the *Eberthella typhi* and *S. aureus* phenol coefficients give, in general, sufficient information to render tests with other organisms unnecessary, except in special instances." The *Staph. aureus* method is the same as that using *Salm. typhi* except that the phenol dilutions must be changed. When the disinfectant is for external use the test is carried out at 20°, and the resistance of the *Staph. aureus* must be such that it survives a 1 in 60 dilution of phenol for 5 minutes and a 1 in 70 dilution for 15 minutes. For disinfectants for personal use, or for application to wounds, the test temperature is 37°, and the organism must survive a 1 in 80 dilution of phenol for 5 minutes and a 1 in 90 dilution for 10 or 15 minutes.

The United States Association of Official Agricultural Chemists (A.O.A.C.) Phenol Coefficient method

In recent years, the F.D.A. has been officially superseded in many directions by the A.O.A.C. method as described in the Official Methods of Analysis published by the Association (A.O.A.C., 1960). In principle it differs little from the F.D.A. method, the main points of departure being that (a) it permits a choice from three subculture media to eliminate the carry-over of bacteriostatic effects and (b) it specifies the use of two test organisms, a *Salm. typhi* and a *Staph. aureus*. The subculture medium is chosen according to the type of disinfectant being examined. The principal points of the method are:

> THE CULTURE MEDIA. Use either (a) a medium containing 5 gm of Difco beef extract, 10 gm of Armour peptone (special grade) and 5 gm of sodium chloride made up to 1,000 ml with water and adjusted to pH 6·8, (b) the thioglycollate medium of the U.S.P. XVI containing 0·75 gm of l-cystine, 0·75 gm of agar, 15 gm of pancreatic digest of casein, 5 gm of yeast extract, 2·5 gm of sodium chloride and 0·5 gm of sodium thioglycollate made up to 1,000 ml with water and adjusted to pH 7·0, or (c) a 'Letheen' medium containing the same ingredients as in (a) but with the addition of 0·7 gm of lecithin (Azolectin) and 5 gm of Tween 80 (a sorbitan mono-oleate). In each case, distribute the medium in 10 ml amounts in cotton wool plugged tubes and sterilize at 121° (15 lb steam pressure) for 20 minutes. Medium (a) is intended for phenolic-type disinfectants, medium (b) is for those containing mercury and other heavy metals, and medium (c) for tests with cationic surface-active substances.

THE CULTURE. The cultures specified are *Salm. typhosa (typhi)* (Hopkins strain 26, ATCC 6539) and *Micrococcus pyogenes* var. *aureus* (F.D.A. 209, ATCC 6538). They are maintained on nutrient agar slopes by monthly subculture, and for use in the test are grown for at least four consecutive daily transfers at 37° in the nutrient broth described. They must be between 22 and 26 hours old.

DISINFECTANT DILUTIONS. Prepare a stock 5 per cent (w/v) solution of pure phenol in distilled water, and for the tests with *Salm. typhi* prepare from this two dilutions of 1 in 90 and 1 in 100; for the *Staph. aureus* test the dilutions required are 1 in 60 and 1 in 70.

For the disinfectant, prepare a 1 per cent dilution in water, and from this a further series of dilutions, each in 5 ml amounts in sterile medication tubes, which "should cover killing limits of disinfectant in 5–15 min. and should at the same time be close enough for accuracy."

PROCEDURE. Place the tubes of phenol and disinfectant dilutions and that containing the test culture in a water bath at 20°. At half-minute intervals inoculate 0·5 ml of the culture by means of a graduated pipette into each of the dilutions. At the end of 5, 10 and 15 minutes' disinfection time transfer one standard 4 mm loopful to a 10 ml tube of the chosen culture medium, and read the results after 48 hours' incubation at 37°.

CALCULATION OF RESULTS. The results are assessed "in terms of phenol coefficient number, or highest diln killing test organism in 10 min, but not in 5 min., whichever most accurately reflects germicidal value of disinfectant." The tests are only valid if the responses obtained are:

		Phenol	5 *min*	10 *min*	15 *min*
For *Salm. typhi*	. .	1 in 90	+ or 0	+ or 0	0
		1 in 100	+	+	+ or 0
For *Staph. aureus*	. .	1 in 60	+	0	0
		1 in 70	+	+	+

Interpolation of results is permitted where none of the disinfectant dilutions show growth in 5 minutes and killing in 10 minutes, and coefficients are quoted to the nearest first decimal place.

The 'Use-Dilution Confirmation' test

According to the A.O.A.C. (1960) it is a "commonly accepted criterion" that disinfectants in use shall be at least as efficient as 5 per cent phenol and it is considered that a dilution of twenty times the phenol coefficient meets this requirement. This is recognized as the highest possible dilution which might be used, and in order to confirm it the Use-Dilution method is applied. It is not strictly a phenol coefficient test but it follows quite naturally as the next action after the A.O.A.C. first test. The results will either confirm the use-dilution derived from the phenol coefficient test or give a correction figure. Mallmann and Hanes (1945) proposed this system of testing disinfectants and it was subsequently adopted by the A.O.A.C. as an official test.

The details are given in the A.O.A.C. Official Methods (1960), but the salient features of the test are: cleaned and polished stainless steel cylinders, 8 mm diameter and 10 mm long and called in the test 'carriers', are sterilized in groups of 10 immersed in a 0·1 per cent solution of asparagine. Twenty such carriers are placed in 20 ml of a culture of the test organism, either *Salmonella choleraesuis* (ATCC 10708) grown in broth for 48 to 54 hours or *Staph. aureus* grown for 24 hours. After 15 minutes' immersion the carriers are transferred to a petri-dish and stood vertically on a filter paper to drain. The dish is then placed in an incubator to allow the carriers to dry for not more than 60 minutes. One infected carrier is dropped into each of ten tubes containing 10 ml of the chosen disinfectant dilution. After exactly 10 minutes, each carrier is transferred to a 10 ml tube of subculture broth and incubated at 37° for 48 hours. Dilutions of 1 in 90 and 1 in 100 of pure phenol are used to confirm that the *Salm. choleraesuis* has a standard resistance (the 48 hour culture is said to have the same resistance as a 24 hour culture of *Salm. typhi*); similarly dilutions of 1 in 60 and 1 in 70 are used with the *Staph. aureus*. The subculture media are the same as those given in the A.O.A.C. phenol coefficient method above, the choice being the one giving the lowest result with the particular disinfectant under test.

The phenol coefficient dilution number is satisfactory if all 10 carriers show no growth in the test. Growth from any of the 10 carriers means that the dilution is not satisfactory for use in practice and an appropriate adjustment should be made.

Results from the Use-Dilution test have been compared with phenol coefficient values over a period of several years in the United States and the general conclusion is that it is much more reliable in indicating safe practical dilutions for all types of disinfectant. This applies particularly to those used in hospitals where the control of cross-infections due to staphylococci is so important. Thus, the test shows clearly the inefficiency of the pine oil disinfectant in this respect, and it frequently exposes the deficiencies of the "low challenge phenol coefficient test" when applied to white disinfectant fluids (Klarmann, 1959), and to phenolic formulations containing excess of alkali and therefore of phenate ions (Ortenzio, Opalsky and Stuart, 1961).

An adaptation of this technique for assessing virucidal activity has been suggested (*see* Chapter 11).

Defects in phenol coefficient tests

Comments have already been made on the Rideal-Walker test drawing attention to several defects in the technique. It must not be imagined, however, that they are unique to the Rideal-Walker test; far from it. Indeed, these and many other criticisms can be levelled against all phenol coefficient type tests, and feeling is so strong in some quarters that they would have them abandoned completely. This attitude is a somewhat academic one because at present there is no adequate substitute. It stems in part from the known misuse and sometimes commercial exploitation of the results obtained from such a test. It must be remembered, however, that the methods were devised primarily for the control of phenolic disinfectants and as such they are adequate. They can even be extended within limits to other types of disinfectant *for purely routine control* purposes, and it is only when they are applied indiscriminately to any formulation, or when attempts are made to determine performance characteristics from them that trouble is encountered and the tests are brought into disrepute.

Nevertheless, they carry and perpetuate a number of defects, some of which the significance is not fully appreciated. One of the principal criticisms revolves around the choice of phenol as a standard. Traditionally, since Lister's day, phenol has been recognized as the standard antiseptic for surgical use, but in the light of present knowledge a more unfortunate choice could not have been made. It is a water-soluble compound of small molecular size whereas many of the preparations it is intended to control contain higher and more complex phenols in an emulsified or solubilized form. On these grounds alone, one might expect to find differences in the bactericidal characteristics of such preparations, and this is the case. They are manifest in their different dilution coefficients (phenol has an unusually high value) and, more important, in the way in which their actual killing concentrations can quite independently fluctuate from day to day. Largely because of this latter point, some authorities would dispense with phenol as a means of calculating the coefficient value, even though retaining other details of the test, and use it only to check the resistance of the culture.

Another defect in the tests is the choice of a total kill as the end-point and the attempt to use a single 'all-or-nothing' response to assess it. This inevitably leads to a variability in results which cannot be avoided and which derives from the fact that bacteria under the influence of a disinfectant are in a dynamic state with their cells losing viability at a controlled rate. In such a system a stage will be reached, towards the end of the process, when the numbers of cells surviving average some four or five per loopful. At this point the response will nearly always be positive, but as the numbers further decline it becomes more and more a matter of chance whether or not small volumes, such as a loopful, may contain a viable cell, a fact the implications of which have taken some time to become properly appreciated. It was actually suspected and demonstrated nearly thirty years ago by Thaysen (1938) in a series of Rideal-Walker-type tests using direct plate counts and different transfer volumes from phenol dilutions after varying times of contact. When standard loopful transfers were made survivors were found regularly up to 15 minutes contact, but never beyond, whereas when the transfer volume was increased to 2·8 ml they occurred up to 45 minutes. This chance can be calculated statistically and some figures supplied by Dodd (pers. comm.) based on Mather (1949), are as follows:

Average no. survivors per loopful	*% chance of failure*	*success*
4	1·8	98·2
3	5·0	95·0
2	13·4	86·6
1	36·8	63·2
0·5	60·7	39·3

These figures represent the chances of picking up a surviving cell when the *average* numbers per loopful range from 0·5 to 4.

Small variations in the density or amount of the original inoculum do not affect the situation significantly; it is only when it is varied tenfold or more that a noticeable change occurs.

Rahn (1945) approached the problem from a somewhat different angle, basing his argument on the fluctuations in response permitted in the F.D.A. test and associating them with the death rates of the test organism and the concentration exponents of phenol and other disinfectants. According to his calculations, a test is acceptable if the control phenol kills at a 1·11 per cent concentration in 14 minutes or at a 1·0 per cent concentration in 11 minutes. Using the equation $K_1 t_1 c_1^n = K_2 t_2 c_2^n$ and using a value of 6 for n (the concentration exponent of phenol), he computed that the death-rate constant can vary by a factor of 2·4 and still remain within the limits of tolerance of the test. On the same basis, the factor for a disinfectant might be 1·5, therefore the total fluctuation in the death-rate constant might be as high as $2·4 \times 1·5 = 3·6$. This represents a 360 per cent variation in the phenol coefficient value, and "this is the error which the specified conditions present and to which must be added the personal error of the experiments." From his observations Rahn concluded "If we consider phenol coefficients more accurate than the death-rate constant we are merely fooling ourselves. They appear more accurate only because the larger deviations are not published." There is certainly a tendency to reject results which 'look wrong' but frequently they are not wrong, they are simply an expression of the hazard of the test! The figures given by Rahn, of course, represent maxima and as such they are only occasionally encountered. The majority of the day-to-day variations are generally of a much smaller order, in fact, Ortenzio, Friedl and Stuart (1949) estimated 95 per cent confidence limits for phenol alone of $\pm 13·2$ per cent and later, working on the A.O.A.C. method with two operators in the same laboratory and correcting the results for 'wild plus' and 'wild minus' readings, they concluded that "a ± 12 per cent tolerance for a label phenol coefficient claim would have to be acknowledged." (Stuart, Ortenzio and Friedl, 1958).

Frequently also a recovery incubation temperature below the optimum for normal untreated organisms is favoured, but this is not universal. In effect, as stated by Harris (1963), the conditions "optimal for the recovery of damaged cells . . . cannot be selected on the basis of conceptions derived from established information with undamaged cells"; each form of treatment, theoretically, requires its own individual consideration, as will be seen from examples given in later sections and chapters.

Closely associated with the stability and level of resistance of the culture are the media used both for growing the initial inoculum and for recovering the treated organisms and the temperature of incubation at both stages. Departure from the specified media formulae, even to changes in the brand

and source of individual constituents, and variations in the method of sterilization can have a marked influence on resistance, and on this account several synthetic or semi-synthetic media have been proposed. A medium containing acid-hydrolysed casein (as the sole source of amino acids) and uracil was claimed (Wolf, 1945) to be superior for maintaining the resistance of both *Salm. typhi* and *Staph. aureus*, likewise, a medium containing prescribed inorganic salts, amino acids and growth factors gave a remarkably consistent level of resistance with *Salm. typhi* (Klarmann and Wright, 1945). Extending this, and imputing all of the variations to the peptones used Wright and Mundy (1960) devised a medium containing inorganic salts, cystine, thiamine, nicotinamide and seventeen amino-acids which they claimed to be superior for both *Salm. typhi* and *Staph. aureus*. This medium is not as good for the recovery of treated organisms but, according to the authors, this is not important because the test is essentially a comparative one. Such an opinion is contrary to the general, the tendency being for efforts to be directed more and more towards obtaining maximum recoveries of 'insulted' organisms. Increased survival rates of cells treated with phenols, for instance, are obtained when charcoal or ferric chloride is added to a normal liquid medium (Flett *et al.*, 1945; Jacobs and Harris, 1954), or when the peptone is pre-extracted with pyridine (Jacobs and Harris, 1960), a phenomenon attributed to the removal of unknown toxic substances from the medium.

Finally, a disinfecting period of only some few minutes, such as is allowed in most of the tests, is probably much too short. It results in the medication mixture being sampled and subcultured at times when the death rate of the organism is high. This inevitably reduces the precision of the end-point determination, and an extension to the period of some 20 or 30 minutes would be beneficial.

The foregoing observations serve to underline the sensitivity and inherent variability of phenol coefficient-type tests, and indeed to some extent of all laboratory tests. They not only indicate the unreliability of single test results, but also pose the larger problem, without giving an answer, of how any laboratory evaluation can be correlated with in-use requirements.

Other tests

General observations

Because of criticisms levelled against the phenol coefficient methods of testing, and, indeed, against the principle of using a phenol coefficient value at all in assessing disinfectants, many attempts have been made to devise tests which are entirely divorced from these established, and now almost traditional, techniques. The approach has been in two main directions: (*i*) in devising tests giving end-points of less than a total kill of the organism, and (*ii*) in attempts to evaluate germicidal activities more realistically and less relatively – that is, under conditions more akin to those in which the disinfectant is likely to be used, and in terms of its actual, rather than relative, performance.

Choice and use of standards. Disinfectants of all types are examined for one of three reasons: (*a*) to ensure that the standard of a routine manufactured product is maintained at the proper level, (*b*) as a help in producing a new preparation which is at least equal, and preferably superior, to existing preparations, or (*c*) in eliminating from the market preparations for which bogus performance claims are made. By inference, a standard of some sort is requisite under each of these headings, but the standard need not be phenol. It has been argued that the adoption of any other standard would give rise to many problems, including that of stability of the standard. This must be admitted where work involving several laboratories is concerned, but the position is quite different within one laboratory or organization. In this case, each standard can be treated purely domestically and can be set up according to the particular interests of the laboratory.

Another aspect of the question concerning the proper place of a standard in the test involves the culture employed. As has been stated earlier, there is an inevitable fluctuation from day to day in the resistance of any culture. It is usually fairly small, but there are the occasions when it becomes large and throws the test responses awry. The only way in which this can be detected is by using a standard germicide against which the resistance can be checked on each occasion. Again, it is not essential, and often not desirable, always to fall back on phenol for this purpose: a broader outlook is necessary, especially when compounds other than phenolic types are being examined. The use of phenol can, in fact, lead to a false sense of security, for behind it is implicit the hypothesis that fluctuations in the susceptibilities of a culture to phenol exactly parallel those to every other type of germicide: and this is not so.

Choice of end-point. There is a sharp division of opinion on the most suitable end-point for any germicidal test. On one side, there is the school which plumps for the total kill; on the other side, there are increasing numbers who believe that on scientific grounds a kill of the order of 99·9 per cent is more desirable. It is argued by those of the first group that proper disinfection infers a total kill of all of the offending organisms, and therefore this should be demonstrable in laboratory tests—added to which is the psychological advantage of recording a total kill. But these are specious arguments. They assume *nolens volens* that the conditions which hold in the laboratory also obtain in daily practice, whereas some adjustment and allowance is always necessary, hence the 'use-dilution' correction factor. A change to a percentage kill would, therefore, only be a matter of using another factor on a result which has been determined more reliably. Moreover, a so-called total kill is, in fact, a kill only of something over 99·99 per cent, the exact value depending on the test sample volume examined and the ability of the culture medium to resuscitate moribund cells. As Withell (1942) put it: "The 'end-point' is not necessarily sterility, but absence of viable organisms in the sample removed and diluted with broth. The sample is small, and a varying percentage of viable organisms may still be alive when the broth yields a negative result."

If any further argument is needed against the total kill end-point, it can be found in evidence which has recently come to light and which has been referred to in Chapter 2. It has long been recognized that the end-points in all of the present tests depend not on the average resistance, but on the most resistant cells, of a culture. But these cells may not be typical in several respects, and they can, in some circumstances, apparently reverse the disinfection process and actually begin to grow again in the so-called lethal environment. Moreover, they do not always follow the normal logarithmic or sigmoidal survivor-time curve but produce an extended 'tail' to the curve. These may both be phenomena associated with adaptations, and they could easily explain the occurrence of indeterminate end-points under the present conditions of testing. In most biological assays a 50 per cent response is accepted as the most satisfactory end-point, but in bacteriology, and particularly in disinfectant tests, there are several reasons against it. First, in dealing with the large numbers of cells used in this type of work it only adds to the complexity of the test to attempt to assess such a high survival level; second, a reduction in a bacterial population of only 50 per cent is of no practical significance; third, the dilution coefficients of the different types of disinfectant vary so greatly that results obtained at this level can be misleading; fourth, and probably most important, the rate of loss of viability at this point is near the maximum and is therefore subject to the greatest error. The final choice end-point must, therefore, rest on a killing level lying between 50 and 100 per cent, with a strong bias towards the latter. From all considerations, a choice of 99·9 per cent or greater seems to be the most reasonable, for, as Jordan and Jacobs (1944) pointed out, at least a linear response is being maintained in this range.

In spite of these arguments, an extinction-time method has been devised (*see* below) which depends for its end-point on the total kill of a given small inoculum. Its authors (Berry and Bean, 1954) claim that it gives results at least as reproducible as by other methods.

The post-disinfection handling of surviving organisms. Inseparably connected with the choice of end-point is the way in which the surviving organisms are handled immediately after their disinfection treatment. Most of the survivors will be in a near-moribund state and so require the gentlest of treatments if they are to recover and proliferate: any further strain due even to temporary adverse conditions may easily cause their inadvertent death, and thus lead to a false test result. In this context, apart from the constitution of the recovery medium which is discussed elsewhere in this chapter, the two major factors are the nature of any intermediate diluent which may be used and the extent and rate of change in temperature to which the survivors may be subjected.

It is common practice to use either plate counts or subcultures into liquid media to assess survivors, but in spite of the fact that the latter gives only a qualitative plus or minus response it is the preferred method, if only because 'insulted' or damaged cells would seem to have a better chance of recovery if cultured direct into a medium at about the same temperature as that of the test than if subjected to a further shock treatment by having their temperature raised instantaneously to 40° or more on being transferred to molten agar when a plate is poured. If a plating method is chosen then the Miles and Mizra drop technique should be employed because this at least eliminates the violent changes in temperature associated with the more traditional plating methods. But even here much care is needed because, as shown by Wills (1957), heat-treated cultures of *E. coli* give much higher recoveries if the plates are placed in the incubator immediately after inoculation than if they are first left for a period at room temperature. Other workers, including Harris and Whitefield (1963), have also expressed similar opinions.

A further disadvantage of plating techniques is that they inevitably involve a dilution stage with a so-called 'inert' diluent. But this in itself is a complex problem as illustrated in a recent symposium on the survival of bacteria in which this very topic was discussed in relation both to disinfectant testing and in other fields (Jayne-Williams, 1963). In this, the dangers of diluents such as water, saline and Ringer's solution, hitherto considered safe, were underlined, and various preferences for dilute media and certain buffer solutions expressed.

Clearly from the two foregoing sections there is still much research to be pursued before some of the fundamental problems of disinfectant testing can be eliminated and the present opposing opinions reconciled. In the next few pages the various attempts made towards these goals are described.

A nephelometric end-point test

A method of evaluating disinfectant performances by nephelometric means has been proposed by Needham (1947). It embraces two particular features. First, it employs a triple end-point, representing survivor levels of 3, 2 and 0·75 per cent, and disinfectants are compared by their mean performances at these three levels; secondly, it uses a subculture volume of 0·5 ml, instead of the usual loopful, in order to overcome some of the sampling irregularities; thirdly, the amount of medium in each tube is raised proportionately to 50 ml. The medium is a simple nutrient broth containing 1 per cent of Oxoid peptone and 0·5 per cent of sodium chloride, chosen because the author claimed it to give more reproducible results than do other more complex media. *Salm. typhi* is the test organism.

Equal volumes of the broth culture and disinfectant dilution are mixed and the disinfection allowed to proceed at 20°. After ten minutes' contact time, 0·5 ml is transferred to 50 ml of broth, previously brought to 37°, and immediately placed in a water bath at 37° for exactly 5 hours. Immediately at the end of this period, the opacities developed from the proliferation of the surviving viable cells are measured in a compensated photometric nephelometer, the apparatus having previously been adjusted to give standard opacity readings equivalent to survivor levels of 0·75, 2 and 3 per cent of the control culture. The slope of dilution against percentage survivors gives a measure of the disinfectant activity of the preparation, and the relative efficiencies of two disinfectants can be obtained by comparing the means of the three dilutions giving the chosen responses. By including phenol in the series, a 'phenol ratio' can be obtained if required.

The method employs a principle which ought to be capable of being developed for routine control purposes, but as it stands it appears to be too sensitive. It has proved valuable as a research tool in several fields.

An extinction-time test

An extinction-time test for measuring bactericidal activity was devised by Berry and Bean (1954) partly to overcome the difficulties of the indeterminate end-point of the traditional methods. It was put forward as a more suitable and acceptable test because it is easy to carry out, the results are rapidly read, the calculations are relatively simple and, according to Cook and Wills (1954), it has a reproducibility at least equal to other methods in common use. The chief features of the method are the use of extensive replication, short sampling intervals and constant sampling volumes withdrawn immediately after inoculation of the bactericide. It requires the chosen test organism (*E. coli*) to be grown for 24 hours on a simple agar medium containing 1 per cent of Oxoid peptone and 0·5 per cent of sodium chloride. The growth is washed several times and finally suspended in quarter-strength Ringer's solution. 0·2 ml of this suspension is added to 5 ml volumes of the test dilutions of the disinfectant at 20° and immediately after mixing one drop is transferred to each of six test tubes. After a predetermined time interval, 5 ml of sterilized broth are added to each tube, which is then placed in a water bath at 37° and examined for growth after 3 days. The immediate transfer to the more favourable growth environment at 37° is claimed to allow damaged organisms to make good their recovery before death supervenes.

In spite of the six-fold replication in each test, there are still fluctuations in the apparent extinction point. To meet this, the authors suggest taking the mean of several repeat determinations.

Tests involving enzyme inhibition

Because the activities of certain enzymes are associated fundamentally with the life of the bacterial cell, it is natural that attempts should have been made from time to time to correlate loss of viability of the cell with the inhibition, or cessation, of its enzyme activities. The primary objective in most cases has been to find the mode of action of germicidal substances, particularly those of chemotherapeutic value, but out of such investigations have emerged several observations which might form the basis of assessing certain disinfectants. It must be stated at the outset that none of the originators has made any strong claims in this direction, indeed, it seems unlikely that any such method could be adopted as a universal means of evaluating disinfectants. One pertinent reason is that germicidal substances are so diverse in their chemical constitution that their modes of action, although producing the same ultimate effect on the cell, may be quite different, one type of compound affecting one group of enzymes, another type a second group, and so on. Another reason is that specific enzyme inactivation does not necessarily parallel loss of viability in all types of bacteria. All the same, these approaches are of interest in that they indicate some new lines of thought in the assessment of disinfectants.

The respiratory rate of a bacterial population, as measured by its rate of oxygen uptake, has been found to be proportional to the viable cell content, and this forms the basis of several of the methods. Bactericidal, but not bacteriostatic, concentrations of various germicides have been shown to inhibit completely the respiration of bacterial suspensions (Ely, 1939; Roberts and Rahn, 1946), and inhibition of the normal increase in oxygen uptake of a growing bacterial culture treated with substances such as phenol, sulphanilamide and mercuric chloride has been related to a corresponding inhibition of growth (Greig and Hoogerheide, 1941); similarly, the respiration of streptococci and pneumococci is suppressed by treatment with sulphanilamide and hydroxylamine (Sevag and Shelburne, 1942). With cultures of *E. coli* and *Staph. aureus*, Bronfenbrenner, Hershey and Doubly (1938, 1939) were able to correlate germicidal activity precisely with inhibition of respiration by taking as the end-point the concentration causing 50 per cent reduction in oxygen uptake between the fifteenth and twentieth minute after treatment.

Complete inactivation of the dehydrogenases of *E. coli* has been associated with their total, or almost total, loss of viability (Quastel and Wooldridge, 1927), but the action is not uniform amongst this group of enzymes. According to Bach and Lambert (1937) the succinic, formic, pyruvic and glutamic acid dehydrogenases are the most sensitive and their inhibition follows most closely the death curve. Sykes (1939) also made a similar observation in his examination of the actions of several phenols and alcohols on *E. coli* suspensions, from which he suggested that loss of succinic acid dehydrogenase activity might be used as a means of assessing disinfectant activity. Similar effects were found when *E. coli* was treated with certain cationic detergents (Knox *et al.*, 1949) but in these cases loss of lactic oxidase activity paralleled most closely the loss in viability.

In spite of these observations, it cannot be said that opinions on the correlation of inhibition of cellular enzyme activity with loss of viability are unanimous. To many the idea of such an association is quite untenable (*see* Rahn, 1945), and there are numerous records of enzyme activities surviving long after the death of the cells (Yudkin, 1927; Mellon and Bambas, 1937; Kohn and Harris, 1941; Bucca, 1943), and even of their activities increasing under certain circumstances (Hugo, 1952).

Miscellaneous tests

Although not likely to prove of any great value in testing disinfectants generally, a number of techniques based on a miscellany of reactions have been put forward from time to time. They are generally acknowledged to be more useful as research tools rather than in routine disinfectant testing, but they are mentioned here because of their novelty of interest and approach to the testing problem. All are of quite recent date.

One of the techniques applicable to water-soluble substances is based on a correlation established between the bactericidal activities of such substances and their affinity for wool (Fischer and Larose, 1952; Larose and Fischer, 1952). The correlation appears to be due to a common α-keratin structure found in both wool and the cytoplasmic membrane of bacteria. The test replaces bacteria by wool, and simply measures affinity in terms of the amount taken up by 1 gm of wool when the latter is immersed in an aqueous solution of the bactericide.

Again, according to Mandels and Darby (1953), when microbial cells are freshly inoculated into a nutrient medium an increase in cell volume occurs within about three hours, and the increase is proportional to the total viability of the cell population. On this basis the authors devised a test intended primarily for testing fungicidal or fungistatic agents, but which they claimed was equally applicable for testing bactericides. The method consists of treating washed fungal spores or bacterial cells with the chosen germicide dilutions for a given time and then centrifuging and washing them. After resuspending the cells in a sugar-yeast extract, they are incubated for 3 hours and the total cell volumes measured and compared with control suspensions.

An improved test design

From what has been written in the preceding pages there are two distinct approaches to the testing of disinfectants: first, there is their evaluation, or assessment of their performance characteristics under different conditions; secondly, there is the routine, batch-to-batch control. Ideally one basic test structure should be suitable for both of these requirements, the former being simply an elaboration of the latter, but to the present such a goal has not been reached, largely because of the place occupied by the phenol coefficient type of test. There is, however, no need to retain such a test, neither is there any need to perpetuate the defects accompanying them—defects which have already been discussed in some detail.

By inference, any 'improved design' should allow for:

(*i*) a more definitive end-point representing a kill of something less than the pseudo-100 per cent;

(*ii*) a wider choice of test organisms;

(*iii*) adequate quenching systems to avoid bacteriostatic carry-over;

(*iv*) the facility to include organic matter;

(*v*) a reasonably long disinfecting period,

and a structure covering these requirements in relation to the quaternary ammonium germicides, but which is readily adaptable to other disinfectants, is already in existence in the British Standard Specification BS 3286 (1960).

The end-point. The two basic requirements for obtaining a more reliable end-point are (1) replication of the observations made and (2) adjusting the conditions in the test so that a kill of 99·99 per cent or greater is recorded. As indicated on pages 62 to 65 the various attempts to circumvent the traditional methods of determining the amount of kill, such as by enzyme inactivation or nephelometric procedures, have not met with any success, and so it is still necessary to rely on direct cultural methods. There are several ways in which these objectives might be achieved but the choice is either (*a*) to prepare and inoculate replicates at each level of a series of dilutions of the disinfectant and subculture each one individually, or (*b*) to prepare single dilutions at each level and make replicate subcultures from each.

At least 10 replicates are desirable and the range of disinfectant dilutions chosen should be such that the subcultures from at least one of them give some positive and some negative responses, so that the actual numbers of survivors can be calculated according to a method of statistical analysis devised by Mather (1949).

Whichever method may be adopted, it is usual to add 1 ml of a suitably diluted culture of the test organism to each 10 ml of disinfectant dilution and then at the end of the disinfection period either to culture a single drop, or other convenient small volume, of the mixture direct to 10 ml or more of nutrient broth, or to deal with larger volumes, transferring 1 ml to 100 ml of a selected diluting fluid (thus quenching the action of the disinfectant) and culturing 1 ml or more of this. In the latter case, by using an appropriate amount of the initial culture and adjusting the subsequent dilution levels it is possible to obtain nominal percentage kill end-points of 99·99 per cent and greater.

It remains to be seen which of the procedures just described will prove to be the most suitable and acceptable in everyday practice.

For the routine control of a disinfectant of known formulation it should be possible to obtain a result using not more than three dilutions, hence the amount of work and material involved in handling either method, including the necessary replication, is only a little more than by the present methods employing a range of dilutions with subcultures at several different time intervals.

Choice of organisms. Hitherto most of the tests described, with the notable exception of the American A.O.A.C. method, have specified only one organism, *Salm. typhi*, but this is entirely inadequate for assessing the practical efficacy of any disinfectant; at least two different types are needed. The choice is a wide one, but in the first place we need only be interested in those infective types which are highly resistant and persistent—any treatment which deals with these will automatically deal with the less resistant ones—and so the field is immediately restricted.

In the past, *Salm. typhi* was a natural choice because of its public health significance, but latterly there has been a shift of emphasis from the intestinal contaminants to the Gram-positive cocci, particularly *Staph. aureus*, which has loomed so large in hospital cross-infections, and the pseudomonads, especially *Ps. pyocyanea*, which is so highly resistant and still a source of trouble in wound infections. For these reasons alone these two organisms should be included in any selection, and, in fact, they could be adequate in themselves without further additions. There is no point in extending the range unduly, but a member of the *Proteus* group or if a representative of the intestinal group is desired a strain of *Salm. typhi* or of *E. coli*, could be included.

Neutralization of bacteriostatic carry-over. Whichever cultural method may be used, it is frequently not sufficient to rely on simple dilution to eliminate the residual antibacterial activity: something more positive is required otherwise grossly misleading results may be obtained. Notorious in this respect are the quaternary ammonium compounds and the mercurials. For the quaternaries the 'inactivator' most commonly used is either a solution of lecithin in Tween 80 or a solution of the non-ionic substance Lubrol W; details of the procedures recommended and of other suitable agents are given in the chapter on the quaternary ammonium compounds (Chapter 14). Similarly, for the organic mercurials, a 0·25 per cent solution of sodium thioglycollate is recommended. Some workers would also use a Tween 80 solution with the phenolic disinfectants, but usually a straightforward dilution into a large volume of dilute broth or of quarter-strength Ringer's solution is adequate. Water alone or saline should be avoided because, in the author's experience, both can cause further damage to cells already affected by the disinfectant and so give a lower recovery rate (*see* also p. 62).

Addition of organic matter. Only rarely is a disinfectant required to be used in a plain aqueous medium, hence the inclusion of organic matter in some form seems fundamental. The exact choice of such material may not be significant, but it is important to realize that it can be present in solution or as suspended matter. In practice those most likely to be encountered are blood or serum, milk and faecal or urinary matter. Garrod successfully replaced dried faeces with a killed yeast suspension in the Chick-Martin test, hence the choice might well be serum or milk, with or without added yeast cells.

Disinfection time. The Rideal-Walker test depends in effect for its result on a kill after only 5 minutes' contact time, likewise the Americans depend on a 10 minutes' contact time. During these short periods, however, the state of viability of the organisms is changing at such a rapid rate that large errors in finding the end-point must be inevitable; hence a longer period is desirable. Thirty minutes seems to be a reasonable optimum for general purposes; anything beyond this is unduly prolonged. There will, of course, always be specific cases where much shorter killing times are needed.

Supplementary tests

The foregoing improved design is, of course, only an outlined test procedure, the details remain to be filled in as a result of further experience, and it is only a suspension-type test using non-sporing bacteria. Further tests are needed to support and extend the preliminary findings, and these might include tests for sporicidal and fungicidal efficacies as well as the effects of different surfaces.

Sporicidal tests

Both the A.O.A.C. (1960) and the German Society for Hygiene and Microbiology (1959) describe methods for assessing the sporicidal activities of disinfectants. The A.O.A.C. method employs "Any species of *Clostridia* or *Bacilli*", and suggests *Bacillus subtilis* and *Cl. sporogenes* as typical: but it is strictly a surface disinfection test and so is described in more detail on p. 55. The German method employs a saline suspension of spores of *B. subtilis* or *B. mesentericus* which has been heated to 60° for 60 minutes.

A test for available chlorine

Because the disinfectants depending on available chlorine for their activities are rapid in action and have variable chlorine capacities (according to the nature of the materials to be disinfected), the A.O.A.C. (1960) prescribes a special test for this type of formulation. The organisms specified are a *Salm. typhi* (ATCC 6539) and a *Staph. aureus* (ATCC 6538) and the principle of the test is as follows: Starting with 10 ml volumes of a series of dilutions containing 200, 100 and 50 ppm of available chlorine, add 0·05 ml of the culture and one minute later subculture a 4 mm loopful into a liquid culture medium. Half-a-minute later add another 0·05 ml of culture and after a lapse of a further minute subculture again. Repeat the operations until 10 increments have been added. The preparation is satisfactory if it shows absence of growth in as many consecutive subculture tubes as does a standard sodium hypochlorite solution. Normally, the standard will be effective at 200 ppm of available chlorine up to the fifth addition, at 100 ppm up to the third addition, and at 50 ppm up to the second only.

A tuberculocidal test

Occasionally information is required on the tuberculocidal activity of a disinfectant in contrast to its general antibacterial activity, which can be quite different, and to this end Wright and Shternov (1958) have described a simple adaptation of the A.O.A.C. phenol coefficient method. The strain used is H37Rv grown for 3 weeks at 37° in a medium containing asparagine, glycerol, magnesium sulphate, potassium phosphate and sodium citrate. The contact time is 10 minutes and the subculture amount is two loopfuls into the above medium with 1 per cent of serum added; incubation is for 8 weeks. There is no need to include phenol in such a test, but if used as a control the killing concentration ranges between 1 in 50 and 1 in 80. The test can also be adapted to a use-dilution type, injecting 1 ml of the mixture after 10 minutes' disinfection time into guinea pigs and observing them over a three months period.

Surface disinfection tests

The expanding use of germicides, particularly those of the cationic detergent group, for disinfecting glass, metal, rubber and wood surfaces such as are used in hospitals, in dairying and in the catering industry has led to the development of many tests in which the disinfectant is allowed to act on infected, soiled surfaces rather than on organisms in suspension. Some of the tests were designed for general disinfecting purposes, whilst others were devised with a specific use in mind, especially dairying. As might be expected porous, irregular, or pitted surfaces are usually more difficult to disinfect than are hard, smooth ones because the organisms are less accessible and tend to be more protected by the soiling material. This, however, depends to a large extent on the nature of the surface itself and its degree of irregularity. Frequently also the disinfecting agent is more readily retained in a porous or fibrous material and it may, as in the case of rubber and some plastics, even dissolve in it. Textiles are particular examples of highly porous and absorptive materials, and advantage is sometimes taken of this property, especially with the quaternary ammonium compounds, to provide self-disinfecting surfaces.

General tests

The idea of testing the efficacy of disinfectants on infected surfaces is not new. Both Koch and Krönig and Paul used it in their classical investigations, but it was not until some thirty years ago, when Jensen and Jensen (1933) published their cover-slip technique, that interest was again stimulated. In the Jensen and Jensen technique a culture of *Staph. aureus* grown on agar is suspended in saline and a loopful of the suspension is spread on each of a number of cover glasses. After drying for 30 minutes at 37°, the glasses are immersed one in each of a series of suitable dilutions of the disinfectant. After 2 minutes' contact, each glass is removed, rinsed twice in sterile water and incubated in 10 ml of nutrient broth. If desired the process is repeated with phenol in the dilution range 1 in 55 to 1 in 70 so that a phenol coefficient can be obtained. The test is carried out at 20°, and *Staph. aureus* is the chosen test organism because of its high resistance to disinfectants. A relatively short disinfecting period of only 2 minutes was selected presumably because it approximates the actual time taken to wash and rinse in practice, but it introduces certain experimental hazards and errors.

Several years later, the glass cylinder method of Mallmann and Hanes (1945) appeared. A particular feature of this method is that precautions are taken to eliminate the carry-over of disinfectant, particularly of quaternary ammonium compounds, by using appropriate neutralizers in the subculture media. The technique, after slight modification, was adopted for the official United States 'Use-Dilution Confirmation' test (*see* p. 55). Subsequent studies of the technique (Litchfield and Ordal, 1955) have shown the recommended test organism, *Salm. choleraesuis*, to be sometimes more resistant than the *Salm. typhi* strain originally used, and this results, rather unexpectedly, in the official phenol coefficient method giving satisfactory use dilutions with quaternary ammonium germicides, but not with phenolic or pine oil germicides.

A further modification to the technique was proposed by Stedman, Kravitz and Bell (1954*a*, 1954*b*) in which 1 in. squares of test material—metal, glass, or other surface—replace the glass cylinders. They are inoculated with a mixture of *Staph. aureus*, *Salmonella schottmuelleri* and a *Trichophyton* and dried for a short period. The inoculum may or may not contain serum. The squares are immersed in the disinfectant dilution for 10 minutes and then removed, shaken and rinsed in an 'Azolectin' neutralizing medium. The squares are discarded and the rinsing fluid plated. Results are calculated on the basis of a 99·9 to 99·99 per cent mill, and replicates up to eight in number are recommended.

In the course of their investigations the authors found a rinsing method with subsequent colony counts preferable to swabbing techniques, which were "markedly inferior" for assessing survivors, and several other workers have made the same observations, *e.g.* Hirsch and Muras (1955), Whitt (1958) and Rogers, Maher and Kaplan (1961). Not all, however, agreed on the detail of the rinsing technique, some carrying out plate counts on samples of the rinse itself, whilst others reject the rinse and immerse the test strip in agar, thus obtaining colony counts of the organisms remaining on the surface after the rinse. Hirsch and Muras (1955) devised a novel variation by immersing their treated metal strips in a liquid medium and measuring the pH value after a given incubation period: this is tantamount to a plate count, the change in pH value depending on the amount of growth of the surviving cells.

The general preparation and disinfection procedures adopted by the various workers differ only little from that originally used by Jensen and Jensen. Stainless steel strips or glass slides are the surfaces most commonly used, and others include tinned mild steel, painted wood, glazed or unglazed tiles, lino and rubber, usually in about 1 in. squares. Apart from its porosity the nature of the material itself can influence greatly the efficacy of a disinfectant, as shown by Rogers, Maher and Kaplan (1961), who found a forty-fold difference in the concentration of a phenolic germicide required to disinfect a glazed or waxed tile on the one hand and a rubber tile on the other. Earlier, Stedman, Kravitz and Bell (1954c) had observed that, in general, higher concentrations of all disinfectants are required to treat porous surfaces than non-porous ones, but subsequently claimed "the practice of waxing surfaces daily does not alter markedly the pattern of disinfectant efficiency." The explanation for this may lie in the fact that on waxed surfaces the inoculum does not spread evenly, but tends to run together into droplets, thus leaving areas with high concentrations of cells, and therefore mutually protected, which presumably balances the protection afforded by uneven porous surfaces.

Having selected a suitable material, the strips or squares are inoculated either by dipping them in a culture of the test organism or by spreading it evenly over the surfaces with a loop, then air-drying them for periods ranging from 15 minutes to 24 hours. Hirsch and Muras (1955) devised a special apparatus for this purpose consisting of a circular carrier on which six inoculated strips can be hung at a time, and which rotates at about 450 rpm thus effecting drying in only 10 minutes. Some care is necessary in cleaning the surfaces so that they will take the inoculum evenly, and in the case of stainless steel it is recommended that they be pretreated by immersion in sour milk for two days (Neave and Hoy, 1947; Garvie and Clark, 1955). Actual disinfecting times vary between 1 minute and 10 minutes, depending on the concentration of the disinfectant under test and its intended use, after which the strips are transferred to a neutralizing rinse solution and the survivors estimated as indicated above. The test organisms used includes *Strep. faecalis*, *Salm. choleraesuis*, *Salm. schottmulleri*, *E. coli* and *Staph. aureus*, the last two being favoured by those concerned with dairy disinfection.

A variation of this procedure, devised by Hare, Raik and Gash (1963), is to use an impress technique. Initially the flat bottoms of round tablet tubes, about 2·5 cm in diameter, are inoculated with a broth culture and air-dried. They are then immersed for as long as required (periods ranging from 0·5 to 15 minutes are the most usual), rinsed under the tap and finally pressed on an agar plate surface and incubated. There seems, however, to be a weakness in the method, as well there might also be in other similar methods, because it showed *Pseudomonas* strains as being too sensitive to chloroxylenol preparations, a 1 per cent solution killing 14 strains in a matter of minutes.

Scant attention seems to have been paid to the survival rate of organisms during the preparatory drying period. Most workers use direct broth cultures for inoculating the surfaces and Whitt (1958) points out that there is a substantial loss of viability from such cultures during the first 10 minutes of drying after which the rate of loss becomes small. In the author's experience this initial loss can be 99 per cent or greater, but the original inoculum is usually so great that the number of viable cells remaining is still sufficiently large to make the test valid.

Some loss in viability during drying is inevitable, but in order to reduce it to a minimum, and at the same time to simulate more closely conditions as found in practice, several variations on nutrient broth or saline have been tried as suspending media. Hoffman, Yeager and Kaye (1955), in describing a method for examining self-disinfecting surfaces, preferred to spray their organisms on surfaces and noted how much less stable are organisms sprayed from a broth suspension than those from dilute milk; Hirsch and Muras (1955) tried adding various thickening agents and finally selected cornflour, and in an extreme case Guiteras and Shapiro (1946) used a mixture of raw egg, milk, butter and other fats.

All of these additions, of course, afford protection to the organisms and so tend to lower the efficacy of the disinfectant. So much so that when, for example, blood is added to a sprayed culture a disinfecting paint surface becomes practically ineffective (Morris and Darlow, 1959).

Spray disinfectants. Because of the introduction in the past few years of spray and pressurized spray methods for disinfecting surfaces, the Association of Official Agricultural Chemists (1960) has produced a tentative test to cover such preparations. It is at present being studied collaboratively, and first reports (Stuart, 1963) are promising. The method consists briefly of inoculating a 1 × 1 inch non-corrodible microscope slide with a culture of either *Staph. aureus* or *Salm. choleraesuis*, the same strains as in the Use-Dilution method, air-drying them for a period, and then spraying on the disinfectant, allowing it to act for 10 minutes and finally culturing it in 20 ml of the appropriate subculture medium.

Detergent disinfectant tests. With most disinfectants, and particularly those containing the quaternary ammonium compounds, Weber and Black (1948) were not convinced of the necessity to use deliberately infected surfaces, having obtained results by a suspension method identical with those by the 'Use-Dilution' method. They considered the wall of the medication tube to provide an adequate surface and so put forward a suspension test method for assessing preparations intended for disinfecting food utensils. The test has attained some popularity in the United States mainly because preparations passing the test have been found completely satisfactory in field use, and with certain adaptations has become an official A.O.A.C. method

(1960). In the official method, as in the original, *Staph. aureus* and *E. coli* are the two chosen test organisms and they are used at a concentration of about 10×10^9 organisms per ml, 1 ml of the suspensions being added to 99 ml of the disinfectant dilution. The test is specially designed to deal with "germicidal and detergent sanitizers", in other words, those mainly containing quaternary ammonium compounds, and so, because of its influence on the activities of these compounds the prescribed diluting fluid for the disinfectant is a synthetic hard water. The test is carried out at 25° and subcultures are made after 30 and 60 seconds' contact, 1 ml volumes being removed into an appropriate quenching solution which is then plated to count the survivors. Weber and Black considered that a complete kill was the only acceptable end-point, because of the asymptotic nature of the death-rate curve, but in spite of this the official method uses a kill of 99·999 per cent as the end-point, which a disinfectant must achieve in 30 seconds to be satisfactory.

A similar technique, described by the authors as the "speed reaction" test, was earlier devised by Mallmann, Kivela and Turner (1946), who claimed it to be particularly applicable for assessing disinfectants, especially those of the cationic group, used for 'sanitizing' beverage glasses. The claim is made on the basis of comparative field trials, in spite of the fact that the laboratory test is made in the absence of organic matter. One ml of a saline suspension of *Staph. aureus* or *E. coli* is added to 10 ml amounts of various concentrations of the disinfectant and 1 ml samples are taken at 5, 10 and 15 seconds' intervals. These are placed in saline containing an appropriate neutralizer and subsequently plated in agar to determine the surviving bacteria. An effective concentration is lethal in 5 to 10 seconds, and the end-point in relation to the serial dilutions employed seems to be fairly sharply defined. Other workers are not as sanguine as Mallman *et al.* and believe that the only reliable test is the functional test; hence the reason for using metal trays (Neave and Hoy, 1947), 10-gallon milk churns (Hoy and Clegg, 1953), (see below), or small drinking glasses (Gilcreas and O'Brien, 1941).

Tests on textiles

Because of the special position of textiles in relation to disinfection, special techniques have been devised using such materials as test surfaces. Those concerned with hospital disinfection variously use cotton sheet and wool blanket, always being aware of the radically different characteristics of these two materials. The German Society for Hygiene (1959) specifies pieces of linen each about 1 cm square. About 100 such pieces are placed in 15 ml of a culture of the test organism which can be *Staph. aureus, E. coli, Ps. pyocyanea* or even *Mycobacterium tuberculosis*. After soaking for 15 minutes they are transferred to a dish and flooded over with a chosen dilution of the disinfectant. After specified time intervals several of the squares are rinsed in a neutralizing solution and transferred to a culture medium, one square to each 10 ml tube, and incubated at 37°.

Tests on dairy disinfectants

In dairy disinfection the principal requirement is to kill bacteria protected to a greater or less extent by milk solids and fats on mainly metal or rubber surfaces. All tests under this heading incorporate one or more of these essential features, and in fact several of those described in the previous section are easily adaptable to dairying conditions. In particular, attention is drawn to the available chlorine test for assessing hypochlorites and other chlorine-bearing compounds (*see* p. 68). Clegg (1955), however, expressed himself strongly in favour of surface film tests, believing that they simulate most nearly the conditions of farm trials, and noting also that they take some account of the effects of detergency: evidence produced later by Cousins (1961) supports this view.

Johns (1946) devised a glass slide method, in which 10 per cent of skimmed milk in water is inoculated with a test organism, spread on microscope slides, and partially dried. The disinfection time is very short, 1 to 20 seconds only, and the end-point is that dilution showing a kill of 99·9 per cent or greater as compared with control untreated slides. The survivors are assessed by rinsing the slides after treament, then flooding them with agar in petri dishes and incubating.

A somewhat similar procedure was put forward by Goetchius and Botwright (1950) the differences being that glass slides are replaced by rubber strips of the same size. The strips are immersed in a heavy suspension of the chosen test organism in sterile whole milk, drained, and dried for 10 minutes. They are then immersed in the disinfectant dilution for 3 minutes, rinsed, and plated in a glucose agar containing a neutralizer if necessary. Test organisms recommended are *E. coli*, *Strep. faecalis* and *Ps. pyocyanea*, and a 99 per cent reduction in the bacterial count is considered satisfactory for use. High activity against the last-mentioned organism is an especially favourable criterion.

Another method using stainless metal strips has been described more recently by Garvie and Clarke (1955), in whose opinion, "the percentage of survivors was higher when the organisms were in a surface film than when they were inoculated directly into the disinfectant." These investigators used both *E. coli* and *Staph. aureus* as the test organisms, the cultures being suspended in 10 per cent of sterile whole milk. The strips were inoculated with this suspension and then dried at constant humidity. This was found necessary because of the significant effect of humidity on the survival of the inoculated bacteria (*see also* p. 72). Agitation during the disinfection period increased the rate of kill.

Neave and Hoy (1947) attempted to approach nearer to reality by using tinned trays infected with *Staph. aureus* suspended in diluted milk and subsequently dried, and later Hoy and Clegg (1953) went even further by producing the 'Hoy Can' test which uses 10-gallon milk churns. The cans are soiled with a poor quality milk and allowed to drain and stand overnight. The cans are then treated with the disinfectant in a specified manner and the reaction stopped after a fixed time by a neutralizer. The inside of the cans is next rinsed and squeegeed with Ringer's solution, some portions of which are plated to determine surviving bacteria and others added to fresh raw milk to observe the depression in keeping quality. This test has been found valuable for determining the field performance of dairy disinfectants, and it is tending to be used more for this purpose.

Not everyone, however, has the facilities to handle 10-gallon milk churns, and a method using short lengths of stainless steel tube is claimed (Lisboa, 1959) to be equally effective in grading different disinfectant formulations. In this method, lengths of steel tubing, 33 cm by 3·25 cm external diameter and closed at both ends with removable rubber caps, are 'soiled' with a raw milk having a low methylene blue reduction time of 1 to 2 hours, and then sealed and incubated for 4 hours at 30°. Fifty ml of a warmed disinfectant dilution are added, the tube is recapped and rolled horizontally so that the whole of the inside surfaces are treated. After exactly 1 minute's contact, the tube is quickly drained, 25 ml of neutralizing solution are added, the residual milk film removed by means of a special fitting squeegee disc and the resultant solution plated for surviving organisms. Various comments on the method and suggestions for its improvement have been made (Mitchell, 1964), but they may not be as significant as claimed by the author. The method is likely to be adopted as official.

Antifungal tests

The lower fungi, and the moulds in particular, are responsible for the loss of vast sums of money annually through their spoilage of materials such as textiles, wood, paints, building materials, pharmaceutical products and foods, as well as others of domestic and industrial importance. Reliable methods for assessing the antifungal activity of any preparation used for this purpose are therefore essential. Basically they are the same as those used for testing for antibacterial activity, although the tendency is to use techniques which give direct rather than comparative results, so that phenol coefficient tests as such do not apply. Frequently resort is made to field assessments, because the conditions here found are liable to such large variations that it is almost impossible to simulate them in the laboratory. In spite of this, valuable information can be obtained by the judicious selection of a number of laboratory tests. Inevitably such tests, whether field or laboratory, must be of long duration; one cannot obtain reliable results from only short-term trials.

Not infrequently there has been obvious confusion in the literature between fungicidal and fungistatic activities, any form of antifungal activity being classed as fungicidal. This has resulted in many assessments being made and reported in terms only of inhibitory and not of lethal capacity, in spite of the suggestion made from more than one source that fungicidal activity should be demonstrable in laboratory tests for a preparation to be of practical value.

Laboratory tests

Fungicidal tests. Both fungicidal and fungistatic tests in their simplest form can be applied to compounds in just the same ways as can the various antibacterial tests. For assessing fungicidal activity, suitable serial dilutions of the compound are made in a chosen diluting fluid, and inoculated with a spore suspension of one or more cultures of the commoner moulds. After appropriate intervals, subcultures are made into a nutrient medium and incubated at 25°. The medium can be either liquid or solid, and it can be of a simple synthetic nature such as Czapek's medium, or it can be more complex such as is found in Sabouraud's medium or the various wort and malt media. The basic requirements are that there shall be carbohydrate and inorganic salts present and that the pH value is slightly on the acid side at about pH 6 to 6·5. The choice of mould types is a wide one, but it is usual to include examples of *Penicillium, Aspergillus, Mucor* and *Cladosporium.* One problem to be considered is the wettability of such spores. It is obviously desirable for the sake of reproducibility to use an evenly dispersed spore suspension but this is not always easily done. For some purposes a small amount of a wetting agent can be added to the suspension fluid, but this naturally gives some advantage to the compound under test, since it renders the compound more easily accessible to the spore. A method devised by Marsh (1938) consists of spraying microscope slides with solutions of the disinfectant, drying them, and then applying single drops of a mould spore suspension. The slides are incubated moist and the percentage spore survivors assessed at chosen intervals. This method has the limitation that it does not take into account any concentration factor for the disinfectant, and so it can only be applied on a 'use-dilution' basis, nevertheless, it has been adopted by the American Phytopathological Society as a standard test for fungicides.

The Association of Official Agricultural Chemists (1960) prescribes a test which employs the fungus *Trichophyton interdigitale* and which is, therefore, designed primarily for dealing with pathogenic infections. It is applicable to water-miscible substances intended for disinfecting inanimate objects. The culture must sporulate readily 'and the conidia are required to survive treatment with a 1 in 60 dilution of phenol, but not a 1 in 45 dilution, for 10 minutes at 20°. The conidial suspension is prepared by scraping the growth from a 10 to 15 day culture on an agar surface and suspending it in saline to give a concentration of 5 million conidia per ml, and the test is carried out in a similar manner to the A.O.A.C. phenol coefficient method, subculturing at 5, 10 and 15 minutes and incubating the subcultures at 25° to 30° for 10 days. The culture medium is a dextrose-Neopeptone liquid medium at pH 5·6–5·8.

Fungistatic tests. The simplest way of carrying out a fungistatic test is to prepare serial dilutions of the compound in a liquid or solid nutrient medium, inoculate with the spores of selected mould cultures, incubate for several days at 25° and observe the dilution at which growth is just prevented. This type of test is suitable for determining straightforward inhibitory concentrations, but it does not take into account penetrability, which may be an important factor. Such a test, which is claimed to be a quantitative one, was devised by Blank (1952). In this test, plates of a yeast extract–maltose medium are inoculated with spores from a chosen mould culture and strips of paper soaked in a solution of the disinfectant preparation are laid on the surface. The plates are incubated at 30° up to five days, and the zones of inhibition of growth measured (*see* Plate 1). A similar technique has also been used for testing antifungal agents for paper and board (Howard, 1954).

Manten, Klöpping and van der Kerk (1950) discussed the various methods used for investigating antifungal substances in the laboratory and compared four of them, a slide germination method, a plate-dilution method, a gravimetric and a roll-tube method. The first mentioned method was rather less exacting than the other three, the difference being attributed to the absence of an organic substrate in the slide test. The three remaining tests all gave similar responses with a variety of disinfectants, and the roll-tube method was preferred because of its convenience in handling. The procedure used in this test was to add 0·3 ml volumes of a series of dilutions of the disinfectant to 1·5 ml amounts of melted malt agar in test tubes, inoculate each tube with 200 to 300 mould spores, roll in the usual way until set, and incubate. The end-points chosen by the authors were the dilutions giving 50 per cent and 95 per cent so-called lethal levels. In fact they are only levels of inhibition and not of killing.

Practical tests

Having determined the activity of a preparation by one or other of the foregoing laboratory tests, the next stage is to carry out tests using as nearly as possible the materials and conditions which will be encountered in practice. These can be so diverse that it is only possible to indicate here some general principles to be followed. It is usual and most effective to employ the particular types of mould likely to cause spoilage trouble, and the fungicide should be applied in a similar way to that used in practice. It may be necessary to run tests for periods as long as several months before a definitive result is obtained, but in some cases accelerated tests can be applied such as in the examination of paints (Galloway, 1954). One essential is that the humidity must be kept high, because moulds will cease to grow if the relative humidity falls below about 70 or 80 per cent. An example of such a test with paints containing bifferent antifungal agents is illustrated in Plate 2.

REFERENCES

Association of Official Agricultural Chemists (1960). *Official Methods of Analysis of the A.O.A.C.*, 9th Ed., Washington, D.C.

BACH, D. and LAMBERT, J. (1937). *Compt. rend. Soc. Biol.*, **126**, 298, 300.

BERRY, H. and BEAN, H. S. (1954), *J. Pharm. Pharmacol.*, **7**, 224.

BLANK, F. (1952). *Canad. J. med. Sci.*, **30**, 113.

BREWER, C. M. (1943). *Amer. J. publ. Hlth*, **33**, 261.

British Standard Method for the Laboratory Evaluation of Disinfectant Activity of Quaternary Ammonium Compounds by Suspension Test Procedures. British Standards Institution, B.S. 3286: 1960.

British Standard Technique for Determining the Rideal-Walker Coefficient of Disinfectants, British Standards Institution, B.S. 541: 1934.

British Standard Specification for the Modified Technique of the Chick-Martin Test for Disinfectants, British Standards Institution, B.S. 808: 1938.

BRONFENBRENNER, J., HERSHEY, A. D. and DOUBLY, J. (1938). *Proc.Soc.exp. Biol.,N.Y.*, **38**, 210.

BRONFENBRENNER, J., HERSHEY, A. D. and DOUBLY, J. (1939). *J. Bact.*, **37**, 583.

BROWNING, C. H. (1934). *Brit. med. J.*, ii, 579.

BUCCA, M. A. (1943). *J. Bact.*, **46**, 151.

CHICK, HARRIETTE and MARTIN, C. J. (1908). *J. Hyg., Camb.*, **8**, 654.

CLEGG, L. F. L. (1955). *J. appl. Bact.*, **18**, 358.

COOK, A. M. and STEEL, K. J. (1955). *J. Pharm. Pharmacol.*, **7**, 224.

COOK, A. M. and WILLS, B. A. (1954). *J. Pharm. Pharmacol.*, **6**, 638.

COUSINS, CHRISTINA M. (1961). Ph.D. Thesis: University of Reading.

DAVIES, G. E. (1949). *J. Hyg. Camb.*, **47**, 271.

DELEPINE, A. S. (1907). *J. roy. san. Inst.*, **28**, 1.

ELLICKER, P. R. and FRAZIER, W. C. (1938). *J. Bact.*, **36**, 83.

ELY, J. C. (1939). *J. Bact.*, **38**, 391.

FISCHER, R. and LAROSE, P. (1952). *Canad. J. med. Sci.*, **30**, 86.

FLETT, L. H., HARING, R. C., GUITERAS, A. F. and SHAPIRO, REBECCA L. (1945). *J. Bact.*, **50**, 591.

GALLOWAY, L. D. (1954). *J. appl. Bact.*, **17**, 207.

GARROD, L. P. (1934). *J. Hyg., Camb.*, **34**, 322.

GARROD, L. P. (1935). *J. Hyg., Camb.*, **35**, 219.

GARVIE, ELLEN I. and CLARKE, PAMELA M. (1955). *J. appl. Bact.*, **18**, 90.

German Society for Hygiene and Microbiology (1959). *Instructions for Testing Chemical Disinfectants:* Fischer, Stuttgart.

GILCREAS, F. W. and O'BRIEN, J. E. (1941). *Amer. J. publ. Hlth*, **31**, 143.

GOETCHIUS, G. R. (1950). *Soap*, **26(9)**, 131.

GOETCHIUS, G. R. and BOTWRIGHT, W. E. (1950). *J. Milk Technol.*, **13**, 63.

GORRILL, R. H. and McNEIL, EVELYN M. (1960). *J. gen. Microbiol.*, **22**, 437.

GREIG, MARGARET E. and HOOGERHEIDE, J. C. (1941). *J. Bact.*, **41**, 557.

GUITERAS, A. F. and SHAPIRO, REBECCA L. (1946). *J. Bact.*, **52**, 635.

HAMPIL, BETTYLEE (1928). *J. infect. Dis.*, **43**, 25.

HARE, R., RAIK, EVA and GASH, SARAH. (1963). *Brit. med. J.*, **1**, 496.

HARRIS, N. D. (1963). *J. appl. Bact.*, **26**, 387.

HARRIS, N. D. and WHITFIELD, M. (1963). *Nature, Lond.*, **200**, 606.

HIRSCH, A. and MURAS, ROSEMARY E. (1955). *J. appl. Bact.*, **18**, 425.

HOFFMAN, R. K., YEAGER, S. B. and KAYE, S. (1955). *Soap*, **31(8)**, 135.

HOWARD, E. (1954). *J. appl. Bact.*, **17**, 219.

HOY, W. A. and CLEGG, L. F. L. (1953). *Proc. Soc. appl. Bact.*, **16**, i.

HUGO, W. B. (1952). *Proc. Soc. appl. Bact.*, **15**, 29.

HUGO, W. B. (1955). *J. Pharm., Pharmacol.*, **7**, 360.

HUNTER, A. C. (1943). *J. Amer. med. Ass.*, **121**, 25.

Hygienic Laboratory Method (1912). Hygienic Lab. Bulletin, No. 82.

Hygienic Laboratory Method, Disinfectant testing by (1921). *Publ. Hlth Rep., Wash.* **36(27)**, 1559.

JACOBS, S. E. and HARRIS, N. D. (1954) *J. Pharm. Pharmacol.*, **6**, 877.

JACOBS, S. E. and HARRIS, N. D. (1960). *J. appl. Bact.*, **23**, 294.
JAYNE-WILLIAMS, D. J. (1963). *J. appl. Bact.*, **26**, 398.
JENSEN, V. and JENSEN, E. (1933). *Dansk. Tidss. Farm.*, **7**, 77.
JOHNS, C. K. (1946). *Amer. J. publ. Hlth*, **37**, 1322.
JORDAN, R. C. and JACOBS, S. E. (1944). *J. Hyg.*, *Camb.*, **43**, 363.
KLARMANN, E. G. and WRIGHT, ELEANOR S. (1945). *Soap*, **21**(1), 113.
KLARMANN, E. G. (1959). *Soap*, **35**(3), 101.
KNOX, W. E., AUERBACH, V. H., ZARUDNAYA, K. and SPIRTES, M. (1949). *J. Bact.*, **58**, 443.
KOCH, R. (1881), cited by CHICK, HARRIETTE (1908). *J. Hyg.*, *Camb.*, **8**, 92.
KOHN, H. I. and HARRIS, J. S. (1941). *J. Pharmacol.*, **73**, 343.
KRÖNIG, B. and PAUL, T. (1897). *Z. Hyg. InfektKr.*, **25**, 1.
Lancet (1909), pp. 177, 1495, 1516, 1612.
LAROSE, P. and FISCHER, R. (1952). *Research, Lond.*, **5**, 419.
LEMKE. RUTH M. (1955). *J. appl. Bact.*, **18**, xi.
LISBOA, N. P. (1959). *Proc. XV internat. dairy Cong.*, **3**, 1816.
LITCHFIELD, J. and ORDAL, E. J. (1955). *Appl. Microbiol.*, **3**, 67.
MALLMANN, W. L. and HANES, MARJORY (1945). *J. Bact.*, **49**, 526.
MALLMANN, W. L., KIVELA, E. W. and TURNER, G. (1946). *Soap*, **2**(8), 130.
MANDELS, G. R. and DARBY, R. T. (1953). *J. Bact.*, **65**, 16.
MANTEN, A., KLÖPPING, H. L. and KERK, G. J. M. VAN DER (1950). *Antonie van Leeuwenhoek J. Microbiol. Serol.*, **16**, 282.
MARSH, R. W. (1938). *Ann. appl. Biol.*, **25**, 583.
MATHER, R. L. (1949). *Biometrics*, **5**, 127.
Medical Research Council (1951). Memorandum No. 11, *The Control of Cross Infection in Hospitals:* H.M.S.O., London.
MELLON, R. R. and BAMBAS, L. L. (1937). *Proc. Soc. exp. Biol., N.Y.*, **36**, 682.
MEYER, R. (1954). *Z. Hyg. InfektKr.*, **138**, 382, via *Chem. Abs.* (1954). **48**, 5922.
MEYNELL, G. G. (1958). *J. gen. Microbiol.*, **19**, 380.
MITCHELL, T. G. (1964). *J. appl. Bact.*, **27**, 45.
MORRIS, E. J. and DARLOW, H. M. (1959). *J. appl. Bact.*, **22**, 64.
NEAVE, F. K. and HOY, W. A. (1947). *J. dairy Res.*, **15**, 24.
NEEDHAM, N. V. (1947). *J. Hyg.*, *Camb.*, **45**, 1.
ORTENZIO, L. F., FRIEDL, J. L. and STUART, L. S. (1949). *J. Ass. off. agric. Chem.*, **32** 401.
ORTENZIO, L. F., OPALSKY, C. D. and STUART, L. S. (1961). *Appl. Microbiol.*, **9**, 562
OSTROLENK, M. and BREWER, C. M. (1949). *J. Amer. pharm. Ass. (Sci.)*, **38**, 95.
PELCZAR, M. (1952). *J. Ass. off. agric. Chem.*, **25**, 394.
PELCZAR, M. (1953). *J. Ass. off. agric. Chem.*, **36**, 364.
QUASTEL, J. H. and WOOLDRIDGE, W. R. (1927). *Biochem. J.*, **21**, 148.
QUISNO, R. A., GIBBY, I. W. and FOTER, M. J. (1946). *Amer. J. Pharm.*, **118**, 320.
RAHN, O. (1945). *Biodynamica*, **5**, 1.
REDDISH, G. F. (1927). *Amer. J. publ. Hlth*, **17**, 230.
RIDEAL, S. and WALKER, J. T. A. (1903). *J. roy. san. Inst.*, **24**, 424.
RIDEAL, S. and WALKER, J. T. A. (1921). *An Approved Technique of the Rideal-Walker Test:* H. K. Lewis, London.
ROBERTS, MARTHA H. and RAHN, O. (1946). *J. Bact.*, **52**, 639.
ROGERS, M. R., MATHER, J. J. and KAPLAN, A. M. (1961). *Appl. Microbiol.* **9**, 497.
RUEHLE, G. L. A. and BREWER, C. M. (1931). *United States Food and Drug Administration, Methods of Testing Antiseptics and Disinfectants.* U.S. Dept. of Agric., Circular 198.
SEVAG, M. G. and SHELBURNE, MYRTLE (1942). *J. Bact.*, **43**, 421, 427.
SHERMAN, J. M. and CAMERON, G. M. (1934). *J. Bact.*, **27**, 341.
SLOCUM, G. G. (1950). *Ann. N.Y. Acad. Sci.*, **53**, 147.
Society for General Microbiology (1950): Preliminary Report of the Standardization Subcommittee; private publication.
Society for General Microbiology (1956). *Constituents of Bacteriological Culture Media:* Univ. Press, Cambridge.
STEDMAN, R. L., KRAVITZ, E and BELL, H. (1954a). *Appl. Microbiol.*, **2**, 119.
STEDMAN, R. L., KRAVITZ, E. and BELL, H. (1954b). *Soap*, **30**(11), 132.

STEDMAN, R. L., KRAVITZ, E. and BELL, H. (1954c). *Appl. Microbiol.*, **2**, 322.
STUART, L. S. (1963). *J. Ass. off. agric. Chem.*, **46**, 1.
STUART, L. S., ORTENZIO, L. F. and FRIEDL, J. L. (1953). *J. Ass. off. agric. Chem.*, **36**, 466.
SYKES, G. (1939). *J. Hyg., Camb.*, **39**, 463.
THAYSEN, A. C. (1938). *J. Hyg., Camb.*, **38**, 588.
WEBER, G. R. and BLACK, L. A. (1948). *Amer. J. publ. Hlth*, **38**, 1405.
WHITE, HELEN R. (1951). *Nature, Lond.*, **168**, 828.
WHITT, EUNICE W. (1958). *J. appl. Bact.*, **21**, 272.
WILLS, B. A. (1957). *J. Pharm. Pharmacol.*, **9**, 864.
WITHELL, E. R. (1942). *J. Hyg., Camb.*, **42**, 339.
WOLF, P. A. (1945). *J. Bact.*, **49**, 463.
WRIGHT, ELEANOR S. and SHTERNOV, V. A. (1958). *Soap*, **34**(9), 95.
WRIGHT, ELEANOR S. and MUNDY, R. A. (1960). *J. Bact.*, **80**, 279.
YUDKIN, J. (1927). *Biochem. J.*, **31**, 1065.

CHAPTER 4

METHODS OF TESTING ANTISEPTICS

THE testing of antiseptics presents a number of problems quite different from those associated with the testing of disinfectants because of their different modes of application. By definition, antiseptics are preparations possessing antibacterial or antifungal activities which are suitable for application to living tissues of the human or animal body, hence in assessing their activities a certain amount of *in vitro/in vivo* testing is necessary, but not to the same extent as would be applied to chemotherapeutic agents.

The ideal antiseptic, whilst being effective against microbial infections, must not be unduly irritant to the skin and it must not destroy the body tissues and cells; it should not be toxic to the leucocytes of the blood when applied to an open wound, and it should not interfere in any way with the natural resistances of the body. All of these attributes need not be embodied in one single antiseptic preparation – the ideal antiseptic possessing all of the desired properties is not likely ever to be realized – but their significance must be judged according to the application for which each preparation is intended. Some are employed for disinfecting the unbroken skin of the hands, others are used on the more sensitive membranes of the body cavities, and a third group is used for the treatment of wounds. Opinions differ as to whether their activities must be lethal in every case, and some authorities would say that this is only essential for skin disinfectants and oral antisepsis. Obviously a good formulation must be reliably inhibitory to the growth of micro-organisms and it must retain its activities in contact with the skin or in the presence of blood, pus, serum, mucus or saliva. With some preparations, such as mouthwashes and gargles, the application can only be of short duration, hence the action must be rapid; with others, such as ointments and dressings, the contact period is much longer, often extending into days, and so the action may be more prolonged.

On the basis of the foregoing considerations, a diversity of tests has been developed over the years, all of which are designed to evaluate some particular performance characteristic. They differ from many of the tests applied to disinfectants in that the majority approximate much more closely to the actual conditions of use.

Profile evaluations

In considering any approach to the assessment of an antiseptic preparation, it is first desirable to obtain an evaluation of the potentialities of the compound, or compounds, constituting the active principle of the preparation, and so the compound must be submitted to a series of tests with the object of assessing its performance under a variety of different conditions. The information required from such an assessment includes:

(*i*) the minimum lethal concentrations of the compound against infective organisms such as *Staphylococcus aureus, Streptococcus pyogenes, Escherichia coli, Pseudomonas pyocyanea* and the pathogenic fungi;

(*ii*) its bacteriostatic and/or fungistatic concentrations;

(*iii*) the effect of organic matter on these values;

(*iv*) the speed of action;

(*v*) its penetrability, and

(*vi*) its toxicity.

Such a system of evaluation, consisting in effect of a number of individual tests, many of them well known and established over many years, collected into a logical group, was put forward by Salle and Catlin (1947). There is much to be commended in the system, because each test reveals a specific property of the substance, and from this it is possible to predict to a large extent its practical applications. But to leave the situation at this stage is incomplete, for having incorporated the substance in an appropriate pharmaceutical formulation it is necessary to confirm with further tests that the antiseptic activity as predicted is still there, because other constituents of the formulation might unexpectedly affect it either antagonistically or synergistically. The preparation has been devised with a specific purpose or purposes in mind; it is possible now to extend the range of tests and at the same time to concentrate on those with a greater bearing on practical applications. Thus, they might include an appropriate selection from the following:

(*i*) inhibitory and lethal tests against a range of bacteria and/or fungi;

(*ii*) similar tests to (*i*), but in the presence of whole blood, serum or other body fluids;

(*iii*) *in vivo* type tests, including toxicity assessments (although these are pharmacological in nature);

and for specific purposes:

(*iv*) tests for activity and retention of activity on the skin;

(*v*) diffusion or penetration tests, for assessing germicidal ointments and similar preparations;

(*vi*) short period contact tests for oral antiseptics.

Within the compass of these individual groups many techniques have been proposed, most of which are little more than variations on a theme. Obviously it is not necessary to put every preparation through tests in every group, in fact it is more than likely that a selection of some two or three will be quite adequate.

In the next few pages, some of the standard techniques and proposed methods will be discussed.

Bacteriostatic and bactericidal tests

Bacteriostatic and bactericidal tests are designed for the purpose of determining the minimum concentrations at which a germicide inhibits the growth of, or is lethal to, bacteria. As such, their primary function and purpose is to assess antiseptic properties in general terms; they can also provide useful indications of chemotherapeutic activity, but such considerations are outside the scope of this book.

In order to obtain the maximum information from bacteriostatic or bactericidal tests, observations should not be confined to one type of organism. There is a tendency to concentrate attention on responses with *Staph. aureus*, since this ranks amongst the most resistant of the pathogenic non-sporing organisms, but the information so gained can be very misleading. Ostrolenk and Brewer (1949), for example, tested a representative collection of germicides, including phenols, alcohols, mercury compounds and quaternary ammonium compounds, and demonstrated wide variations in resistance not only between types but also between species of the same organisms. The same is the author's experience. Thus, whilst agreeing that *Staph. aureus* is often amongst the most resistant of the non-sporing organisms there are many instances when Gram-negative bacteria, and sometimes the streptococci, may be more resistant. It is desirable, therefore, to include at the minimum selected strains of *Staph. aureus, E. coli, Ps. pyocyanea* and a *Proteus* species, the last two because of their significance in wound infections.

Bacteriostatic tests

Tests of this type are amongst the simplest to carry out. They consist essentially of preparing appropriate serial dilutions of the germicide, inoculating with the chosen test organism and observing the weakest concentration which just prevents growth after incubation. Ideally, the dilutions in the first tests should be made in water or saline, but growth does not normally take place in such substrates, hence it is more usual to employ a nutrient medium.

The amount of inoculum can naturally influence the result of the test, and quite commonly one loopful of a diluted 24-hour culture in broth is inoculated into 10 ml of each test dilution. An incubation period of not less than 72 hours at 37° is desirable to allow resistant cells to overcome the prolonged lag-phase and develop into a visible turbidity. This 72-hour period should be a very minimum; Rahn (1945) has suggested that the lag-phase of 'damaged' cells may be extended to at least 100 hours.

Organic matter. It is desirable to repeat the tests in the presence of added organic matter such as serum because of the influence, sometimes profound, of such material on antibacterial activity. The concentration of organic matter may significantly alter the end-point of the test: 10 or 20 per cent is the usual amount of serum added although sometimes as much as 50 per cent may be used.

Bactericidal tests

In general, the principles of the phenol coefficient tests can be applied to the assessment of the lethal properties of antiseptics, but with several modifications in detail. In the first place a 'coefficient' is not being sought, hence there is no need to include a standard phenol. Then there is a greater flexibility of choice of organisms, of temperature and of disinfection time. As discussed in an earlier paragraph the range of organisms selected should include *Staph.*, *aureus*, *Ps. pyocyanea* and a *Proteus* strain along with any other types specially required. *Salm. typhi* is not a good choice. Many workers advocate that only freshly isolated strains from natural sources should be employed in order to ensure a high level of resistance, and for the same reason others advocate using several strains of each type; as many as ten strains have been suggested for some purposes. The temperature of disinfection is also subject to adjustment; in many cases 37° is the obvious choice, but in others, ambient temperatures of about 20° are suitable. Actually for many purposes a temperature of 30–32° is probably better than 37°, because this is nearer the temperature level of the skin and other outer membranes of the body, and, in fact, several workers use this range. Finally, there is the permitted time of disinfection. Sometimes, as with oral antiseptics, the period must be of short duration measured in minutes or even in seconds, but for most purposes much longer periods can be used. Frequently the time can be measured in hours rather than minutes, and a killing time of 24 hours is often used.

Organic matter. In view again of the significance of organic matter, tests should also be carried out in the presence of blood or serum, and this applies particularly to wound antiseptics. As well as the immediate effect, it is often desirable to know something of the effect of prolonged contact on the activity of the antiseptic and for this purpose tests on immediate contact and after one hour contact can be made. A suggested method is to prepare serial dilutions of the germicide and mix with an equal volume of defibrinated blood previously infected with *Staph. aureus*. After 5 or 10 minutes' contact subcultures are made to determine the survival of the organism. One hour later, the blood-germicide mixture is again inoculated with the culture and the survivors again determined after 5 or 10 minutes' contact. Many germicides, including those of the chloroxylenol type, show some loss of activity after contact with blood, a point which is not without significance in practice.

Wet and dry filter-paper tests

These two tests figure in the United States F.D.A. Methods of Testing (Ruehle and Brewer, 1931). They are identical in that both use small squares of sterile Whatman filter paper No. 2 impregnated with a 24-hour broth culture of *Staph. aureus*, but in the one the squares are treated immediately whilst in the other they are dried for two days at 37° before treatment. The infected paper squares are dipped or otherwise immersed in the test material and after a chosen period of contact, such as 5, 15 or 60 minutes, hooked out and placed in a tube of broth. After removing as much of the medicament as possible they are transferred to a second tube of broth and incubated at 37°. Both methods have a number of disadvantages and are now little used.

Antifungal tests

The antifungal and antibacterial characteristics of most substances are quite different and so in considering antiseptics for use against fungal infections specific tests must be used. The types of infection which are subject to topical treatment are the superficial skin mycoses such as ringworm and athlete's foot. The organisms causing such infections include *Trichophyton*, *Microsporon*, *Epidermophyton* and *Monilia* species, and so should comprise the organisms used in any testing scheme. They are generally less resistant in culture than are the common saprophytic moulds, but their occurrence in skin infections, sited as they are in the folds and intradermal layers, makes their treatment in practice difficult. For this reason it is generally considered that an effective preparation should show fungicidal, rather than fungistatic, activities *in vitro*. In spite of this, fungistatic tests are still widely employed.

In clinical practice, an antiseptic will have to deal with an established infection in all stages of growth and there will always be protein and other adventitious material present. These are important aspects which should be borne in mind in assessing any testing technique.

Fungistatic tests

The simplest test for determining the fungistatic activity of a substance is to prepare serial dilutions in a suitable liquid or solid nutrient medium, inoculate with an active culture of the test fungus and incubate for several days to ascertain the point at which growth is prevented. The liquid medium can be an ordinary nutrient broth containing carbohydrate and adjusted to about pH 6·5, and the solid can be a simple glucose agar or Sabouraud agar; in either case, sterile serum should be added.

An alternative technique is an adaptation of the agar cup or ditch-plate method, described on page 90. A prepared serum agar plate is inoculated on the surface with one or more of the test fungi. A cup or ditch is cut out of the agar, filled with the antiseptic preparation and the plate incubated. During incubation the antiseptic diffuses out and a zone of inhibition of growth is formed at the periphery of the cup or ditch. By standardizing the test conditions, the method can be given a quantitative aspect (Oster and Golden, 1947).

Another simple method was described by Blank (1952). It can be used both for testing pure substances and also the same active ingredients incorporated in pharmaceutical preparations. Plates of a suitable peptone-maltose-serum agar are inoculated with suspensions of whole cultures, including spores and mycelium, of different fungi. The suspensions are rendered uniform by adding one or two drops of a wetting agent, Tween 80, to each 200 ml. The antiseptic is applied on strips of filter paper by soaking them in solutions of the substance under test, or by spreading them with thin layers of the preparation if it is in the form of an ointment or cream. The strips are then laid on the agar surface and the whole incubated at 30° to obtain the zones of penetration and inhibition.

Fungicidal tests

Lethal activity is most easily assessed by preparing serial dilutions of the substance in a suitable diluting fluid, inoculating with an actively growing culture of the organism and subculturing at appropriate intervals into a nutrient medium to obtain the point of elimination of viability. A fungicidal test using *Trichophyton interdigitale*, as recommended by the Association of Official Agricultural Chemists, has already been described in Chapter 3 (p. 76), but it has a disadvantage in that the killing period is limited to 15 minutes only.

In a test devised specifically for evaluating fungicides for treating athlete's foot, Klarmann, Shternov and Costigan (1941) experimented with several fungi and finally chose a 10-day culture of *Trichophyton rosaceum* as the most suitable. It was grown in a maltose-peptone medium in screw-capped bottles containing a large number of beads; these were added to facilitate breaking up of the culture just before use. The shaken suspension was diluted with saline to give a spore concentration of $1\cdot5 \times 10^6$ per ml, and 0·5 ml of this in each 5 ml of the fungicide dilutions constituted the inoculum. The tests were carried out at 20° and subcultures were made at 1, 5 and 10 minutes. The dilution producing a complete kill in 1 minute was considered satisfactory for use in antiseptic foot baths.

Objections raised to such a test are that it does not give any measure of penetrability and it does not test a natural hyphal mat of the fungal growth such as occurs in practice. These were overcome to a large extent by Burlingame and Reddish (1939) in an adaptation of a technique originally proposed by Smyth and Smyth (1932). They employed five cultures, three of *Trichophyton* and two of *Epidermophyton*, grown for 5 days on the surface of Sabouraud agar plates. The surfaces were flooded with the fungicide solutions, and after 5, 15 and 30 minute intervals small discs or squares measuring about 1 cm were cut out and transferred to broth. After shaking lightly to wash out the fungicide, the plug of growth was transferred to a Sabouraud agar slope and incubated. Such a washing technique would not be suitable for an ointment preparation, but this has been overcome(*sic*) by imposing a rinse in 30 per cent acetone in water followed by a second wash in broth (Golden and Oster, 1947).

A semi-in vivo *test*. Obviously the ideal method of testing for antimycotic activity is by *in vivo* techniques, but results from such methods are usually not clear cut, they are expensive and are subject to other external influences such as the susceptibility of the animal to the infection and its sensitivity to the test material. For this reason Dolan and colleagues (1957) proposed a semi-*in vivo* method which employs the epidermal scales taken from the abdominal areas of guinea pigs infected locally some 8 or 9 days before with a culture of *T. mentagrophytes*. Approximately 30 scale particles measuring 0·5 to 1 mm are placed in stainless steel gauze capsules and immersed in the disinfectant. At intervals of 5, 15, 30 and 60 minutes one capsule is removed and rinsed in a suitable neutralizing solution. The capsule is opened and the scales plated on Sabouraud agar and incubated for 10 days at 30°. If required human scales or hair, or other organisms, can be substituted.

From results quoted by the authors, only a few of the many preparations active *in vitro* are effective in this test, hence its value as a second stage screening method, but not necessarily a replacement for clinical evaluation.

In vitro-in vivo antibacterial evaluations

It is not sufficient to assess an antiseptic simply on its *in vitro* performance against a range of micro-organisms. Other factors such as odour, skin irritation, tissue toxicity, and haemolytic activity may be of equal importance. Much useful information can be gained on these points by combined *in vitro-in vivo* tests using tissue culture techniques and tests involving the leucocytes of living blood. Moreover, by combining these with normal bactericidal tests a 'toxicity index', or a measure of the relative toxicities to body cells and to bacteria, can be obtained. Such an assessment is important in certain aspects of surgical disinfection and it is especially significant in chemotherapy.

Toxicity indexes have been determined by observing the comparative inhibitions of the oxygen uptake of mouse liver cells and of the growth of *Staph. aureus* in the presence of horse serum (Bronfenbrenner, Hershey and Doubly, 1939). A rather more complex technique was earlier described by Salle, McOmie and Sechmeister (1937) in which suspensions of chick embryo heart tissue and of bacteria in serum are treated with serial dilutions of disinfectant for 10 minutes at 37°. After treatment, the tissues and bacteria are transferred to fresh nutrient solutions and incubated to ascertain their viability—the tissue fragments to a plasma-Tyrode solution for 72 hours at 37° to observe cell proliferation, and the bacteria to nutrient broth also for 72 hours to observe growth—and the ratio of the concentration of disinfectant just killing the bacteria to the concentration just preventing proliferation of the tissue cells gives the toxicity index. Indexes quoted by the authors (Salle *et al.*, 1939) using *Staph. aureus* and *Salm. typhi* were 2·0 and 1·2 respectively for phenol, 0·9 and 0·8 for hexylresorcinol, 0·2 and 0·2 for iodine, 0·3 and 0·08 for azochloramide, 7·2 and 0·6 for mercurochrome, and 1·8 and 0·11 for silver nitrate. From these values it is seen that the halogens emerge best, followed by hexylresorcinol and other phenols; the silver and mercury compounds score well against *Salm. typhi* but not against *Staph. aureus*. This test, although requiring an exacting manipulative technique, has the virtue, according to the authors, of approaching practical *in vivo* conditions, but it has been criticized in that there is no similarity between chicken heart muscle and human tissues, neither are the disinfectant dilutions used in the test at all like those used in practice.

Tests in living blood

The slide-cell test. One of the natural defence mechanisms of the human body has long been known to rest with the leucocytes of the blood which are phagocytic to invading bacteria. Destruction of leucocyte activity is, therefore, undesirable in surgical disinfection. Fleming (1924) early recognized this and adapted the Wright 'slide-cell' as a means of assessing both germicidal and leucocytic inactivating property in the presence of whole blood. The test is carried out in slide-cells prepared by dipping narrow strips of sterile paper in hot soft paraffin wax and laying them on a sterilized microscopic slide to give four equal 'cells' on the slide. The whole is then covered by a second sterile slide. Defibrinated blood is infected with a pyogenic *Staphylococcus* culture to a level of about 2,500 organisms per ml and mixed with equal volumes of serial dilutions of the germicide. About 50 cu mm of each of the mixtures is then placed in each cell, and the slide is incubated overnight. The following day the number of colonies can easily be counted.

One of Fleming's own observations with phenol serves as an example of the type of result obtainable by this test. Of 56 organisms originally inoculated into each cell all but one were inhibited by the leucocyte activity of the blood itself; this is the control cell. As the concentration of phenol was increased from 1 in 20,000 so the leucocytes were inactivated and consequently the number of surviving organisms increased until at the 1 in 640 dilution there was a total survival. At this stage the natural bactericidal power of the blood had evidently been destroyed by the action of the phenol, but the phenol concentration of itself was still not adequate to kill the bacteria. As the concentration was increased still further its antibacterial action became more manifest until at 1 in 320 it was wholly effective. Fleming (1931) later evaluated a number of antiseptics then in common use, and pointed out, amongst other items, the almost complete absence of leucocyte toxicity of the flavines, and the total unsuitability of mercuric chloride and mercurochrome.

In its time, the test was valuable in sorting out the miscellany of compounds which had come into popular use as antiseptics, but it has been criticized (Garrod, 1955) on the grounds that "even if an effective application does kill some leucocytes it probably matters little; plenty more will take their place." In any case, there now seems to be little need for a test of this type, because the present trends in testing chemotherapeutic agents are leading more towards direct animal tests.

Phagocyte toxicity tests. A test for inhibition of phagocytosis was included in a four-stage composite test suggested by Nye (1937). At the first stage, the highest dilution killing *Staph. aureus* in 5 minutes is assessed using a modified U.S.F.D.A. technique; at the second stage, a similar determination is made in the presence of 50 per cent serum; the third stage comprises a measure of the diffusibility of the disinfectant through 'Parlodion' sacs, and the fourth stage is the test for combined leucocytic toxicity and bactericidal activity in 50 per cent whole blood. For this last stage, the inhibition of phagocytosis in fresh human blood diluted with Locke's solution is first measured by assessing the degree of damage to the leucocyte function after contact with the disinfectant for 20 minutes at 37°, and the bactericidal activity is measured in the same blood mixture after 10 minutes at 37°. The whole test seems to be rather lengthy to carry out and unnecessarily cumbersome.

A somewhat similar two-stage test was put forward by Welch and Hunter (1940), the first stage of which measured the phagocytic level of the disinfectant and the second the bactericidal level, thus still allowing a bactericidal-leucocidal toxicity index to be calculated. But to Greenberg and Ingalls (1957) the method still seemed to be unduly complex, involving the preparation of artificially opsonized staphylococci, special apparatus and also an excessively long disinfection period (30 minutes at 37°), and so they devised a simpler procedure. Their bactericidal level was measured with a broth culture of *Staph. aureus* after only 10 minutes' contact at 37° and their leucocidal level by means of fresh rat blood, 0·2 ml of the blood being mixed with 1 ml of the disinfectant dilution and the survival of the leucocytes being measured, again after 10 minutes' contact, by their ability to phagocytize a bacterial suspension in rat serum. With several disinfectants examined, the indexes obtained by this type of test agreed closely with those computed by Salle and co-workers (*vide supra*) from their tissue toxicity test method.

Tests on egg membranes

Another *in vivo* method employs the chorio-allantoic membranes of hen eggs, and two very similar techniques have been described by independent authors, Green and Birkeland (1944) and Murphy *et al.* (1951), both of whom claimed them to be improvements over the standard *in vitro* procedures for the evaluation of wound antiseptics and at the same time easy to follow and reasonably reproducible. The membrane of an 11- or 12-day-old chick embryo is infected with a *Staph. aureus* by putting a drop of a diluted culture on the exposed membrane. Having allowed the culture to establish itself overnight, small volumes of the test antiseptic are dropped on the membrane at intervals as required up to 5 days, the eggs being kept at incubator temperature throughout. On the day following the last treatment the membrane is swabbed and the approximate number of surviving organisms estimated. The technique affords a means of ascertaining not only the influence of the disinfectant on the infecting organisms but also its toxicity to the growing tissues, the latter by observing the condition of the embryo at the end of the test. The test is considered valid because it shows phenol to be therapeutically inactive, and penicillin highly active, but the same criticism holds against this as against other tissue culture tests, namely, the dissimilarity of chick embryo membranes and human tissues.

Agar diffusion and surface contact tests

An antiseptic ointment, cream, dusting powder, or similar preparation, must always allow its active constituents to diffuse from its base to exert its antimicrobial properties effectively. These properties can be measured by several variants of a simple agar diffusion method. Such tests are mainly qualitative, but they can be used semi-quantitatively.

The tests all have the advantage of being relatively easy to carry out, but the results so obtained may need to be interpreted with some discretion because of the possible influence the agar itself may have. This arises from the presence of trace contaminants some of which are extractable by solvents such as ethyl alcohol. These naturally vary with the source of the agar, and can have varying effects on different types of antimicrobial agents. Such interferences may not be characteristic for whole groups or related compounds—they may be applicable only to certain members of a group—or be applicable to all types of organism. In the majority of cases, agar causes a reduction in apparent activity and examples quoted by Bennett (1963) include certain acridine compounds, crystal violet, phenol, mercurials and quaternary ammonium compounds. He suggests, therefore, that "To avoid errors in screening . . . agar should be added to media only after careful evaluation of its effects upon the inhibitory activity of the test compound". This is a salutary warning, but in spite of the unpromising prognosis, such tests are always likely to have a place in any screening programme. Fortunately the results so obtained are likely to be weighted against the antiseptic preparation, so that better responses are likely under more favourable conditions.

Agar cup diffusion tests

The agar cup diffusion type of test is applicable to solid, semi-solid and liquid preparations, and its modification, the surface diffusion test, is applicable only to solid or semi-solid preparations, but excluding those which become fluid in the incubator and so flow over and flood the agar surface. Two variants of the tests are used, one which employs one organism per plate or petri dish and the other which allows several organisms to be tested together. Since the preparations will always be used on the skin and often in contact with wounds, it is advisable to include serum in the agar medium – 10 per cent of inactivated ox or horse serum is satisfactory.

In the first procedure, 20 to 25 ml of molten agar containing serum are inoculated at 40°–45° with a loopful of a 24-hour broth culture of the test organism, usually *Staph. aureus,* and poured into a petri plate. When the agar has set, a cup about 1·5 cm in diameter is cut with a sterile cork borer and the disc of agar removed. The bottom of the cup may be sealed with one or two drops of molten agar and then the test sample filled into the cup. Air pockets must be avoided. After 24 hours' incubation at 37° the extent of the zone of inhibition is measured. A typical test response is shown in Plate 3. The test is essentially a qualitative one, but it can be put on a more quantitative basis by carefully standardizing each stage of the test and always using the same culture, agar medium, cup size, incubator temperature, etc., as suggested by Rose and Miller (1939).

In the second procedure, six or eight cultures can be used in one test. A sterile agar plate is prepared containing 20 to 25 ml of serum agar, and a single cup is cut out in the centre of the plate. One loopful of a broth culture of each of the chosen organisms is streaked radially from the cup to the edge of the plate, each organism representing in effect the spoke of a wheel. Immediately after inoculating all of the cultures, the test preparation is filled into the cup, and the plate is then incubated at 37° for 24 hours. If the preparation is active, clear zones of inhibition of different size will show at the periphery of the test sample along each line of inoculum, the width of each zone being a measure of the activity of the preparation against the particular organism. A typical result from such a test is illustrated in Plate 4. If the preparation is for treating fungal infections, a selection of pathogenic fungi can be used as the test organisms.

Ditch plate tests. This type of test is, in effect, a variation on the agar cup test, and it is particularly suitable for testing antiseptic substances themselves rather than their preparations, the 'ditch' usually being filled with known dilutions of the substance in agar. A sterile serum agar plate is prepared containing 25 ml of medium. When the agar has set, a ditch 1 cm wide is cut across a diameter of the plate, and a solution or suspension of the material is filled into the ditch. A loopful of a culture of each test organism is then streaked across the plate at right angles to the ditch, and after incubating for 24 hours the extent of inhibition of growth of each organism is noted. A typical plate is shown in Plate 5.

Surface contact tests

Surface contact and diffusion tests are made in a similar manner to those described for agar cup tests, except that the antiseptic preparation is applied to the surface of the agar instead of being introduced into cups. By such means it is possible to obtain a measure of the rate of release of an antibacterial agent from, say, an ointment base and also to ascertain its lethal activities. A surface inoculum only is required and this is obtained either by flooding the surface of the agar with a suspension of the test organism and draining off the excess or by using the streak technique to spread it as evenly as possible.

Surface inhibition tests. For this type of test the simplest procedure is to place small amounts of the material under examination on specified areas of the inoculated agar, incubate overnight and observe if there has been any inhibition of growth at the periphery of the samples. A more clear-cut result can be obtained by using a serum agar plate containing 0·5 per cent of glucose and 0·5 per cent of sterile calcium carbonate in even suspension. Provided an organism is used which will ferment glucose, *e.g. Staph. aureus*, the result after incubation will be a clear plate with small residual white areas of undissolved calcium carbonate under the test material where inhibition has taken place.

If the test material is a powder the procedure is to dust it over specified areas of the plate, using a metal or card shield with 10 mm diameter holes in it, shake off the excess powder and incubate. Brewer (1939) claimed this technique to be much more realistic than others because it tests only the amount of powder which adheres naturally to a moist agar surface and so is directly applicable to skin treatment.

Diffusion tests. In order to get a measure of the rate of release of an antibacterial agent from its base it is usual to interpose a cellophane membrane, thus causing the substance first to diffuse through the cellophane before coming into contact with the agar. Clark and Davies (1949) laid small squares on the surface of an inoculated agar plate, incubated for 45 minutes to allow the cellophane to lie evenly on the agar and then applied the ointment or other preparation at the centre of each square. At given time intervals from 5 minutes onwards the squares were removed, the plate incubated and the minimum time to cause complete inhibition of growth over that area was recorded. A similar idea was used by Conter (1957), the only difference being that he filled his test materials into small tubes covered at one end with cellophane, and stood them on the agar surface. Fiedler and Sperandio (1957) also used a similar method to ascertain the retention of activity and availability over prolonged periods. In this case, the cellophane-covered tubes were transferred every 24 hours to a fresh agar plate and the order of inhibition noted at each stage. The transfers can be continued for as long as is required.

Surface contact lethal tests. With some antiseptic preparations, information may be required on their lethal action in contrast to their inhibitory powers. To obtain this it is necessary to have a test organism already grown on the nutrient medium. A culture of *Staph. aureus*, or of any other chosen organism, is streaked on an agar slope or on the surface of a poured agar plate and incubated. After 16 hours at 37°, the antiseptic preparation is poured or spread in a thick layer over the cultured surface and the incubation is continued. At chosen intervals of time a scraping of the culture mass on the agar surface is taken with a stiff platinum needle and inoculated into nutrient broth. If a petri dish culture method is used the subculturing can be more usually done by cutting out a small disc of the agar, transferring it *in toto* to nutrient broth and incubating at 32° or 37°, or plating aliquots and incubating to count the survivors.

To measure the combined diffusibility and lethal activity of preparations, again the cellophane membrane is introduced. Conter (1957), for example, laid the cellophane over the whole surface of the plate and then spread the ointment over it. At intervals up to 6 hours small discs were cut out of the agar and the survivors counted. This procedure in some ways is preferable to that described in the previous paragraph because it is cleaner to handle and avoids carry-over of excess of the medicament to the plating medium.

An agar 'replicate' test. In 1932, Lederberg and Lederberg devised a labour-saving method for selecting culture mutants by a rapid replica plating technique. In this method the pile of a piece of velvet serves as a multi-needle inoculating device in place of the tedious platinum needle procedure. The velvet, stretched over a block of wood or cork, is pressed lightly on the surface of the initial agar culture and then on to a succession of sterile agar plates, thus transferring impressions, or 'replicates', of the original. Substituting small agar 'tops' for the velvet, Parry (1961) adapted the method for testing the bactericidal activities of antiseptic creams and ointments. The agar tops are prepared by filling metal bottle-caps, 3 cm diameter, with nutrient agar so that on setting the agar stands proud of the rim of the cap. An agar plate is inoculated with the test organism and a small piece of sterile tissue paper laid on the surface. A small amount of the cream or ointment is placed on the centre of the paper. After a given contact time the paper is removed and an agar top pressed lightly on the same area, removed and incubated. Bactericidal action is indicated by absence of growth in the centre of the top but growth at the peripheral areas where the medicament did not come in contact with the organisms. Check tests are necessary to ensure the absence of bacteriostatic carry-over which might be significant and produce misleading results. The method is more easy to manipulate than is that using velvet pads, and comparative tests with the two yielded almost identical results.

Tests on the skin

A bewildering number of tests has appeared, and continues to appear, in which the actual skin of animals or humans is employed. Most of them use the intact or an abraded skin but a few use excised portions, and for convenience of presentation and discussion they can be classified into three groups:

(*i*) skin infection tests designed to measure the efficacies of antiseptics for wound dressing;

(*ii*) skin disinfection tests to assess the value of preparations, particularly of soaps, for surgical and similar purposes;

(*iii*) skin penetration and absorption tests to determine retention of activity.

Skin infection tests

The purpose of this type of test is to assess the efficacies of preparations intended for use as wound antiseptics and for this reason the wounded or abraded skin of experimental living animals is employed. One criterion of such tests is that the observed effects are assumed to be due to bacterial proliferation and development of toxins in the animal and not to any form of systemic toxicity of the test substance, sometimes a dangerous assumption. One of the earliest of this type of test was proposed by Browning (1934). It comprised inoculating skin wounds in guinea-pigs with a virulent strain of *Corynebacterium diphtheriae*, allowing some 3 or 4 hours for the infection to become established and then treating it with a solution of the disinfectant. The organism being lethal to the test animal, the survival level gives a measure of the actual *in vivo* activity of the disinfectant. Virulent streptococci have also been used in the same technique.

A modification of the Browning test uses the method of infecting the abraded skin of mice with a non-lethal test organism, treating it with the disinfectant for a specified period of time, and then planting pieces of the skin into the peritoneal cavity and observing the extent of development of peritonitis. Yet another modification (Hunt, 1937) involves observing the extent of necrotic lesions developing in test animals after inoculating them subcutaneously first with a non-lethal organism, such as a *Staph. aureus*, and then with the test disinfectant in the same site.

All of the organisms mentioned above are subject to marked fluctuations in their virulence to experimental animals and some do not cause death until a generalized septicaemia is established. To overcome these disadvantages, Brewer and McLaughlin (1951) proposed a test with *Clostridium tetani* spores. It is a two-fold test designed to test the ability of an antiseptic not only to destroy or prevent the growth of pathogens in a wound, but also to prevent subsequent infection over a period. Two essential features of the test are; first, the spores are introduced subcutaneously in a necrotizing solution (6 per cent calcium chloride in water) to ensure the untreated infection being fatal, and secondly, the organisms and germicide are inoculated at exactly the same site. By this test, the authors showed iodine, benzalkonium chloride, and mercurochrome to give good protection, a protection which, in the case of mercurochrome, was retained for several hours after administration.

Skin disinfection tests

Normal skin carries a resident bacterial population, mainly of the *Staphylococcus* group, buried deep in the pores and protected by the sebum, and also a smaller proportion of a transient population variable both in numbers and types on the immediate surface. The latter is relatively easy to deal with, in fact many organisms of this group die naturally in a fairly short space of time because of the fatty acids and other substances naturally present on the skin, but the former being much less readily accessible are far more problematical. Nevertheless, it is essential in surgery and for some other purposes to reduce the total bacterial population of the skin as far as possible and to keep it so for an appreciable length of time.

Complete sterilization seems from the outset impossible because the treatment necessary may be so drastic as to lead to the destruction not only of the organisms but also of the skin and tissues, hence the only method of containing these inaccessible organisms is to impose a bactericidal barrier through which no viable organisms can penetrate. Several different techniques have been used for such assessments, all of which involve either hand-washing procedures with bacterial counts made on the rinse waters, or the treatment of deliberately infected small areas of the skin, with subsequent quantitative assessments of the organisms surviving. Although some of the methods were devised particularly for testing soaps, they can be applied to other disinfectants, and they can also be adapted to measuring the retention of activity, an important aspect of skin disinfection.

Direct swabbing techniques

The following direct swabbing test, which is both simple and less time consuming than the washing methods, has been found highly satisfactory by the author over a number of years. It was designed for testing the retention of activity of disinfectants other than soaps and is an adaptation of that originally described by Colebrook and Maxted (1933). The procedure is:

Two loopfuls of each of a set of serial dilutions of the germicide are spread evenly on an area of about half-an-inch square on the basal internodes of the backs of the fingers, and allowed to dry. After a fixed time, usually 2 hours, during which the operator has gone about his normal activities, excluding washing or wetting the hands, a loopful of a diluted culture of *Staph. aureus* is spread within each area. After 10 minutes' contact, the area is thoroughly swabbed and the swab shaken in a 10 ml tube of broth. One ml of the broth is plated on nutrient agar and the colonies counted after incubating for 48 hours. By including a parallel series of dilutions from a known standard germicide, a measure of the relative activity of the preparation can be obtained. A typical result is shown in Table 4.

A similar technique was proposed by Story (1952). In this, small circles on the forearm are infected with one drop of a chosen culture. After drying, the disinfectant is applied with a throat swab, and the areas sampled at intervals up to 5 minutes. Sampling is carried out by means of glass cylinders held over each area. Five ml of water are placed in each cylinder, the skin inside the cylinder is rubbed over for 15 seconds with a glass rod, and then

1 ml of the water plated. The method as described is only one of a short period contact, but could easily be lengthened according to requirements.

Relying on the natural flora of the skin, Reid, Black and Dean (1958) used large areas of the abdomens of patients being prepared for surgical treatment. Broad strips were painted with tinctures of the different substances under examination and the areas covered with a sterile towel. After an interval two swabs were taken from each strip and cultured into broth. The efficacy of the preparation was judged according to the numbers of positive cultures obtained from the test strips compared with those from the

TABLE 4

Results of a skin disinfectant test

Concentration of sample applied %	Plate counts			
	Sample 1		Sample 2	
	A	B	A	B
10	52	26	0	0
7·5	176	308	12	3
5	+ +	+ +	26	34
3·5	+ +	+ +	74	96
2·5	+ +	+ +	236	218
1·0	+ +	+ +	+ +	+ +

+ + = count over 500

Sample 1 was a pine oil disinfectant.
Sample 2 was a chloroxylenol preparation.
A and B were duplicate tests carried out on different days.

control areas. The method as reported seems to be rather insensitive, largely because for some reason the control areas did not always yield positive growths.

The 'mouse tail' test. This test was originally proposed by Christiansen (1918) as an *in vitro-in vivo* test but was later modified into an *in vivo* test by Nungester and Kempf (1942). It does not resort to swabbing or similar techniques for the recovery of organisms but relies on their direct culture *in vivo*. In the modified technique, the tips of the tails of mice are infected by swabbing with a culture of the chosen test organism. They are then dipped into a dilution of the disinfectant and after 2 minutes' contact the tail tip is snipped off and planted in the peritoneal cavity of the mouse. The method is said to overcome entirely any carry-over of residual bacteriostatic activity. It is also said to be easily carried out, but its application is limited in that it can only employ those organisms which are lethal to mice by the peritoneal route, and this in effect limits it to the pneumococci and the streptococci. The usefulness of the test is thereby severely restricted because these organisms are amongst the most susceptible of the pathogens. By its nature, it is not applicable for measuring retention of activity.

'*Hand-basin-washing*' *tests.* Many hand-washing techniques have been published from time to time by various workers, all of which stem from that originally devised by Price (1938). Most of them were produced with the primary purpose of testing antiseptic soaps but they are readily adaptable for other skin disinfectants. The Cade (1950) modification is now the method most generally used. The original Price technique requires ten basins each containing 2 litres of water. The hands and arms are scrubbed with a control soap for 35 seconds and rinsed in the first basin. The scrubbing and rinsing is repeated in the remaining nine basins and the bacterial content of each basin obtained by plate counts. The whole procedure is repeated later with the test disinfectant. The number of organisms washed off at each stage is progressively smaller, and a graph of the number of bacteria removed at each rinsing produces a logarithmic curve, the slope of which is the measure of the bactericidal activity of the preparation.

The method is a very tedious one, and Cade's (1950) modification is a simplified version in that it uses the equivalent of only five basins. Briefly, the procedure is to scrub the hands with an ordinary soap for 60 seconds and then rinse for 15 seconds in the first basin. The rinsing is repeated twice 'under the tap' without collecting the rinsings, and then twice more in two further basins; these are the equivalents of Price's basins 4 and 5. Plate counts on these three rinsings constitute the controls. The next day, the test disinfectant is applied and the scrubbing and rinsing techniques are repeated, using the control ordinary soap for this purpose. This test can be turned into one for assessing retention of activity by adjusting the timing between applying the disinfectant and the first washing process, and the washings can be repeated at daily intervals if desired.

Even this procedure is still rather tedious, particularly when it is borne in mind that to obtain reliable results several subjects are needed for each assessment; Cade suggested at least six but in the author's experience even twice this number is barely sufficient, each requiring his own separate series of counts. In order to overcome this to some extent and to provide the test with self-contained controls, Quinn, Voss and Whitehouse (1954) proposed a method for examining soaps in which one hand of the subject is used as the control and the other for the test. It is described as the "split-use procedure", and has been favoured by several subsequent investigators. With the right hand gloved, the left hand is washed with ordinary soap in a basin of water, lathering in a prescribed manner for 95 seconds and then rinsing for 20 seconds. The glove is then removed, a fresh one put on the left hand and the washing procedure repeated on the right hand with the test soap. Colony counts are made on each basin within 5 minutes of completing the washings. A somewhat complicated routine is set forth covering a five-day test period. The procedure is to wash both hands separately in the morning and afternoon on the first day in order to obtain a control count. The test soap is then applied three times each day to the right hand and the control soap to the left hand. On the third and fifth days, counts are taken with a single ordinary soap wash, as on the first day. The results, expressed as percentage reductions in viable counts, can be calculated in various ways.

One of the attributes claimed for medicated soaps is that if used regularly there is a build-up of activity during the first two or three days due to the gradual adsorption of the antiseptic by the skin, after which it is maintained at a high bactericidal level, hence tests with this type of preparation are inevitably lengthy and the variations in procedure and of calculating the bactericidal efficiency are legion. Two examples illustrate this. Using the Cade technique, Hurst, Stuttard and Woodroffe (1960) caused each of twelve subjects to wash three times a day for a week with a control toilet soap and then during the second week to repeat the procedure with the test soap. The bactericidal efficiency was calculated by comparing the mean log count for the last three days with the test soap with that for the last three days with the control soap.

Quite different was the method used by Frisch, Davies and Krippaehne (1958), which is applicable to other types of skin disinfectant as well as soaps. Their procedure is:

(*a*) wash for 1 minute in toilet soap;

(*b*) rinse in a prescribed fashion for 1 minute in 2 litres of water—*control* 1;

(*c*) repeat the rinse in another 2 litres of water—*control* 2;

(*d*) disinfect the hands as instructed for 5 minutes and rinse in tap water with inactivator if necessary;

(*e*) wash for 1 minute in toilet soap;

(*f*) repeat the rinse as in (*b*) in four successive 2 litre amounts of water—*tests* 3, 4, 5 *and* 6;

(*g*) take the average bacterial count per ml for controls 1 and 2 and the sum of the counts for tests 3, 4, 5 and 6 and from these obtain a ratio which gives an index of the efficiency of the disinfectant.

A pig skin-respiratory method. All hand-washing techniques are of necessity tedious and time-consuming, and, in a search for a screening method which would eliminate the multiple washing and plating procedures, Woodroffe (1963) lighted on a novel *in vitro* method which used pig skin as the test surface and depended for its responses on the change in respiration of the bacteria naturally found there. He chose pig skin, in the form of thin strips taken from the trotters of animals immediately after killing, because both its structure and its bacterial population are similar to those of human skin. Likewise a respiratory response was selected because it could be measured while the bacteria and germicide were still in contact.

Unfortunately, as with nearly all enzyme inhibition techniques (*see* chapter 3) no correlation was found between changes in respiration of the skin bacteria and the activities of various preparations as measured by the more orthodox methods. The differences were attributed to the different modes of action of the various germicides tested, as well as the difficulties or correlating several treatments at short intervals with cumulative *in vivo* effect, as measured by the washing techniques, which occurs over several days.

Tests for penetration and retention of activity

As indicated earlier mere disinfection or degerming of the surface of the skin is not adequate for most purposes; some degree of penetration and of retention of activity is necessary. One such test has already been described on p. 95 and hand-washing tests of the types discussed in the preceding section can also be adapted for the purpose, but apart from these, several

TABLE 5

Results of various antiseptic treatments on the flora of hands
(after Lowbury and Lilly, 1960)

Treatment	Pin-hole washings			Glove rinses		
	No. samples	Treated (orgs./ml)	Control (orgs./ml)	No. samples	Treated (orgs./ml)	Control (orgs./ml)
Spirit swab .	10	79·5±36	392±140	20	24·2±4·1	63·2±14
70% alcohol for 3 minutes .	18/19	7·5±5·4	81·0±12	10	3·0±0·7	62·5±18
70% alcohol with 0·5% chlor-hexidine .	19/20	3·2±2·1	69·9±14	10	3·1±0·7	151±48
Hexachloro-phane soap (after 1 week) .	20	7·3±2·8	51·2±8·7	10	14·9±6	169±66
Neomycin and bacitracin in glove powder .	10	0·6±1·1	332±120	20	3·7±3·1	73·6±17

other tests have been devised with the specific objective of assessing penetration and retention of activity. They can be considered in two categories, glove tests and those involving skin biopsy.

Glove tests. The principle of these tests is that after treatment with the disinfectant, rubber gloves are put on the hands and the organisms secreted in the sweat enumerated. Bowers (1950) for instance devised a 'single wash—glove juice' test in which the hands are first washed with a control soap and then sterile gloves are put on. After 2 hours the gloves are carefully pulled off without turning them inside out and 100 ml of water poured in and shaken. Plate counts are made on 1 ml amounts of the water. The next day the procedure is repeated with the disinfectant, and the counts compared. There are always wide fluctuations in the counts, but the reductions are always significant when an effective germicide is used.

In a rather more elaborate test devised by Lowbury and Lilly (1960) one glove of each pair is punctured several times at each finger-tip with a hypodermic needle. After the disinfection treatment, the gloves are put on and one hour later are washed *in situ* with soap and dried. Then the tip of each finger is inserted in a small tube containing Ringer solution and small glass beads and rubbed round with the beads for 3 minutes. After this the gloves are removed and rinsed out with 100 ml of Ringer solution. Both the finger-tip washings and the glove rinses are plated on a nutrient agar containing an appropriate neutralizer where necessary, from which an estimate is obtained of the efficacy of the disinfectant treatment in reducing the numbers of viable bacteria emerging from the pin holes in the gloves and of those deposited in the gloves. Typical results obtained by Lowbury and Lilly are given in Table 5.

Penetration tests. Most of the tests which give a measure of the penetration of disinfectants into the dermal layers involve skin biopsies, the object being to recover surviving organisms which still remain in the hair follicles, sebaceous glands and the lower layers of the skin generally. Both human and animal subjects have been used, and the principle of the tests is that small full-thickness pieces of skin are taken from the abdomen, chest or flanks of the subject, ground in a broth culture tube with sterile sand and incubated. The first of such tests was described by Walter (1938), and in a later modification Murphy *et al.* (1951) used 5 pieces of skin measuring 2 mm by 1 mm for each test and rated the efficacy of the disinfectant by the growths recorded after 24, 48 and 72 hours incubation. Reid, Black and Dean (1958) used rather larger pieces each about 5 mm square and incubated overnight. With an effective germicide they found the numbers of positive cultures from the 5 pieces of skin reduced to about 2.

Some skin disinfectants in common use

During the normal course of investigation, many different types of skin disinfectant have been examined and for those directly interested in the subject a list is given in Table 6. References quoted in this Table are far from complete, being based on those in which a testing technique is described; they serve therefore simply as an introduction to the literature. No mention is made of antiseptic dusting powders, which in these days can include a range of antibiotics as well as many other bactericidal agents; neither is it possible to give an opinion as to the efficacies of the preparations listed largely because the results reported by the different workers have frequently been contradictory probably because each one has used his own preferred method of assessment.

Tests on oral antiseptics

The principal requirements for an effective oral antiseptic, apart from its taste and odour, are that it shall be active in the presence of saliva, it shall kill organisms of the Gram-positive non-sporing types (Gram-negative organisms are of little concern in the mouth) and it shall be fairly rapid in its action. A reliable bacteriological test on such a preparation should, there-

TABLE 6

Some recent references to skin disinfectants

Reference	Substances
	Aqueous solutions and tinctures
Frisch *et al.* (1958) . .	Alcohol; benzalkonium chloride; hexachlorophane; 'pHisoHex' (a hexachlorophane formulation); 'Virac' (an iodophore); 'Zephiran' (a quaternary formulation).
Gardner (1948) . . .	Alcohol; iodine; cetrimide; 'Chloros'; chloroxylenol ('Dettol'); mercurials; 'Zephiran'.
Henderson, R. J. (1961) .	Alcohol; cetrimide; euflavine; iodine.
Lowbury (1957) . . .	Chlorhexidine.
Lowbury and Lilly (1960) .	Alcohol; chlorhexidine; 'pHisoHex'.
Lowbury *et al.* (1960) .	Alcohol; iodine; chlorhexidine; 'Virac'; cetrimide; 'Penotrane'.
Murphy *et al.* (1951) . .	Iodine; hexachlorophane; 'Zephiran'; 'Acrizane' (an acridine derivative).
Myers *et al.* (1956) . .	Chlorhexidine.
Price (1951) . . .	Alcohol; mercurials; iodine; hexachlorophane; 'Zephiran'.
Reid *et al.* (1958) . .	Alcohol; iodine; 'Penotrane' (a phenylmercuric compound).
Smylie *et al.* (1959) . .	Hexachlorophane; 'pHisoHex'.
Story (1952) . . .	Iodine; cetrimide; 'Bradosol' (a quaternary formulation); 'Zephiran'.
	Soaps
Frisch *et al.* (1958) . .	Hexachlorophane.
Hurst *et al.* (1960) . .	Dichloro-*m*-xylenol; hexachlorophane (G11); tribromosalicylanilide (T.B.S.); tetrachlorosalicylanilide (T.C.S.); Bithionol (a thio-bisdichlorophenol); tetramethylthiuram disulphide (T.M.T.D.); trichlorocarbanilide (T.C.C.).
Lowbury and Lilly (1960) .	Hexachlorophane.
Quinn *et al.* (1954) .	Bithionol; hexachlorophane.
Vinson *et al.* (1961) . .	Hexachlorophane; T.B.S.; T.C.C.; T.M.T.D.

fore, be able to assess such features, and it should be carried out at body temperature.

Oral antiseptics can be divided into two groups, the mouthwashes and gargles, in which the period of contact for disinfection is measured in seconds, and the sweets and lozenges, in which the effective period of contact is over several minutes, that is, during the time taken to dissolve the sweet normally in the mouth. Thus, two types of test are needed, one with very short disinfecting times and the other with somewhat longer ones. Oral antiseptics are not called upon to deal with Gram-negative bacteria, and so the organisms used in the tests can be confined to the typical Gram-positive types, the staphylococci and the streptococci. The use of saliva in the tests automatically introduces the normal bacterial flora of the mouth, but other cultures should also be included.

Testing techniques

In vitro *tests*. Bearing in mind the points enumerated above, a typical test procedure for sweets or lozenges might be as follows: collect an adequate volume of saliva from several subjects and inoculate with a resistant culture of *Staph. aureus* or *Strep. pyogenes* in the ratio of 1 ml of culture to 10 ml of saliva. Dissolve one sweet or lozenge in 5 ml of water at 37° and at zero time inoculate this with 0·5 ml of the saliva mixture. At intervals ranging between about 2 minutes and 10 minutes subculture one loopful into nutrient broth and incubate to determine the point of extinction of the viable bacteria. In this form it is an 'all-or-nothing' test, but it could be made more quantitative by introducing plate count procedures.

In the case of mouthwashes and gargles the tests can be carried out in a similar way, using suitable dilutions of the preparation, but the contact times should be much shorter; 15, 30 and 60 seconds are appropriate.

In vivo *tests*. *In vivo* tests of this type are difficult to carry out and interpret because of the extreme fluctuations in the bacterial content of the mouth at different periods of the day. Nevertheless, such tests have been described. Ostrolenk *et al.* (1953) devised a test in which mouth rinses with 20 ml of saline are taken from each subject at hourly intervals for 4 hours and the bacterial content is estimated by plate counts. At the half-hour interval between the second and third hour, 20 ml of the mouthwash is introduced for 30 seconds, and the fall in subsequent rinse counts is compared with the untreated controls. When this method was used on seven preparations shown to be satisfactory in an *in vitro*-30 second contact test, three reduced the counts after the first half-hour to 10, 11 and 14 per cent of the original and two reduced them to 43 and 49 per cent.

In remarkable contrast to these findings and underlining the uncertainty of the methods and of the results of any one investigator in this field, Wolf and Brown (1946) had earlier examined eight preparations and found even with the best of them an immediate reduction in count of only 50 per cent, with the numbers recovering after a space of only 10 minutes and back to normal within one hour. They observed that a mouth rinse taken 1½ to 2 hours after a meal tended to yield constant bacterial counts and so carried out their tests between 9.30 and 10 o'clock every morning. Each of 24 volunteers rinsed his mouth 'vigorously' for 1 minute on alternate mornings with either 18 ml of Ringer solution or 18 ml of the mouthwash diluted according to instructions. Immediately on ejection 1 ml of the rinse was diluted with 99 ml of Ringer solution and counts made with blood agar.

Similar tests have been made with antiseptic lozenges, using one rinse before and one after allowing the lozenge to dissolve, and reductions in counts of the order of 90 per cent could be obtained with the most active preparations (Benjafield and Benjafield, 1955). Substantial, though transitional, reductions were also obtained by Schuster and Iannarone (1955) with antibiotic lozenges. Their procedure was first to take two control rinses with 10 ml of saline, and then dissolve the lozenges in the mouth in the usual way and take further rinses at appropriate intervals up to 2 hours. By this means a maximum reduction in bacterial count of about 90 per cent occurred after 5 minutes, after which the count rose steadily to 66 per cent of its original at the end of the test. A mouth wash was more effective, but again there was a gradual restoration in numbers of viable organisms as the test proceeded. The test is not a good one because of the wide variations in the control counts.

This extreme variation in saliva counts had been appreciated even in the early 1920's and in order to by-pass it Bloomfield (1922) proposed a buccal swab test. This has since been modified in several ways and out of it Vinson and Bennett (1958) developed a dual "buccal tissue count" and "buccal epithelial substantivity" test. This employs the buccal epithelial scrapings taken by each subject before and after the antiseptic treatment by drawing a small curette gently over the inside of each cheek until the curette is filled with mucus-epithelial detritus. For the first part of the test, the scrapings are simply shaken in 10 ml of sterile peptone water and the viable bacteria enumerated. For the second part, the substantivity test, the contents of a curette are transferred to the centre of a small filter-paper disc, 12 mm diameter, allowed to dry for one hour at 55° and then placed tissue downwards on an agar plate seeded with either *Staph. aureus* or *Lactobacillus casei* and incubated. The next day the discs are removed and the zones examined with a low-power microscope for evidence of bacterial growth. The authors used this test particularly to examine mouthwashes and dentifrices and always found substantial reductions in counts with preparations already proved effective by *in vitro* tests.

This brief review of the techniques used for testing antiseptics illustrates some of the attempts made to reproduce in the laboratory actual conditions of usage. It is clearly within the competence of any bacteriologist to develop many variations on such methods to suit specific requirements, and even to devise others with a modicum of novelty in them. But the final criterion must always lie in the answer to the question: does the preparation work in practice? Laboratory tests are indispensable for development and control work, and a variety of simple and well-tried tests is in continuous use. Such tests give useful information on the relative activities of different preparations but there is still room for the development of methods which are more directly applicable to practical usage without the need of further interpretation.

REFERENCES

BENJAFIELD, N. B. and BENJAFIELD, J. D. (1955). Lancet, 269, 1301.
BENNETT, E. D. (1963). Soap, 39(10), 87.
BLANK, F. (1952). Canad. J. med. Sci., 30, 113.
BLOOMFIELD, A. L. (1922) Johns Hopkins Hosp. Bull., 33, 145.
BOWERS, A. G. (1950). Soap, 26(8), 36.
BREWER, J. H. (1939). J. Bact., 37, 411.
BREWER, J. H. and McLAUGHLIN, C. B. (1951). J. Amer. med. Ass., 146, 729.
BRONFENBRENNER, J., HERSHEY, A. D. and DOUBLY, J. (1939). J. Bact., 37, 583.
BROWNING, C. H. (1934). Brit. med. J., ii, 579.
BURLINGAME, ELLA M. and REDDISH, G. F. (1939). J. lab. clin. Med., 24, 765.
CADE, A. R. (1950). Soap, 26(7), 35.
CHRISTIANSEN, J. (1918). Z. physiol. Chem., 102, 275, quoted in Lancet (1935), 228, 114.
CLARK, G. H. and DAVIES, G. E. (1949). J. Pharm. Pharmacol., 1, 521.
COLEBROOK, L. and MAXTED, W. R. (1933). J. Obstet. Gynaec., Brit. Emp., p. 966.
CONTER, J. (1957). J. Pharm. Belg., 12, 101.
DOLAN, M. M., EBELHARE, J. S., KLIGMAN, A. M. and BARD, R. C. (1957). J. invest.
    Dermatol., 28, 359.
FIEDLER, W. C. and SPERANDIO, G. J. (1957). J. Amer. pharm. Ass. (Sci.), 46, 4.
FLEMING, A. (1924). Proc. Roy. Soc., B, 96, 171.
FLEMING, A. (1931). Proc. roy. Soc. Med., 24, 808.
FRISCH, A. W., DAVIES, G. H. and KRIPPENHAENE, W. (1958). Surg. Gynec. Obstet., 107,
    442.
GARDNER, A. D. (1948). Lancet, 255, 760.
GARROD, L. P. (1955). Proc. roy. Soc. Med., 48, 21.
GOLDEN, M. J. and OSTER, K. A. (1947). J. Amer. pharm. Ass. (Sci.), 36, 350.
GREEN, T. W. and BIRKELAND, J. M. (1944). J. infect. Dis., 74, 32.
GREENBERG, L. and INGALLS, J. W. (1958). J. Amer. pharm. Ass. (Sci.), 47, 531.
HENDERSON, R. J. (1961). Brit. J. Surg., 48, 362.
HUNT, G. A. (1937). J. infect. Dis., 60, 232.
HURST, A., STUTTARD, L. W. and WOODROFFE, R. C. S. (1960). J. Hyg., 58, 199.
KLARMANN, E. G., SHTERNOV, V. A. and COSTIGAN, STELLA M. (1941). J. Bact., 42, 225;
    Soap, 17(12), 129.
LEDERBERG, J. and LEDERBERG, ESTER M. (1932). J. Bact., 63, 399.
LOWBURY, E. J. L. (1957). Practitioner, 179, 489.
LOWBURY, E. J. L. and LILLY, H. A. (1960). Brit. med. J., i, 1445.
LOWBURY, E. J. L., LILLY, H. A. and BULL, J. P. (1960). Brit. med. J., ii, 1039.
MURPHY, J. J. and seven others (1951). Surg. Gynec. Obstet., 93, 581.
MYERS, G. E., McKENZIE, W. C. and WARD, K. A. (1956). Canad. J. Pharmacol., 2, 87.
NUNGESTER, W. J. and KEMPF, A. H. (1942). J. infect. Dis., 71, 174.
NYE, R. N. (1937). J. Amer. med. Ass., 108, 280.
OSTER, K. A. and GOLDEN, M. J. (1947). J. Amer. pharm. Ass. (Sci.), 36, 283.
OSTROLENK, M. and BREWER, J. H. (1949). J. Amer. pharm. Ass. (Sci.), 38, 95.
OSTROLENK, M., WEISS, W., EDELSON, H. and FRIEDBERG, S. (1953). J. Amer. pharm
    Ass. (Sci.), 42, 200.
PARRY, JOY (1961). J. appl. Bact., 24, 218.
PRICE, P. B. (1938). J. infect. Dis., 63, 301.
PRICE, P. B. (1951). Drug. Stds, 19, 161.
QUINN, H., VOSS, J. G. and WHITEHOUSE, H. S. (1954). Appl. Microbiol., 2, 202.
RAHN, O. (1945). Biodynamica, 5, 1.
REID, H., BLACK, T. and DEAN, DOROTHY (1958). Practitioner, 180, 707.
ROSE, S. B. and MILLER, RUTH E. (1939). J. Bact., 38, 525.
RUEHLE, G. L. A. and BREWER, C. M. (1931). United States Food and Drug Administration
    Methods of Testing Antiseptics and Disinfectants: Circ. No. 198. U.S. Dept. Agric.,
    Washington.
SALLE, A. J. and CATLIN, B. W. (1947). J. Amer. pharm. Ass. (Sci.), 36, 129.
SALLE, A. J., McOMIE, W. A. and SECHMEISTER, I. L. (1937). J. Bact., 34, 267.

SALLE, A. J., MCOMIE, W. A., SECHMEISTER, I. L. and FOORD, D. C. (1939). *J. Bact.*, **37**, 639.

SCHUSTER, F. and IANNARONE, M. (1955). *Drug Stds*, **23**, 190.

SMYLIE, H. G., WEBSTER, C. V. and BRUCE, MARIAN L. (1959). *Brit. med. J.*, ii, 606.

SMYTH, H. F. and SMYTH, H. P. (1932). *Arch. Dermatol. Syphylol.*, **26**, 1079.

STORY, P. (1952). *Brit. med. J.*, ii, 1128.

VINSON, L. J. and BENNETT, A. G. (1958). *J. Amer. pharm. Ass. (Sci.)*, **47**, 635.

VINSON, L. J., AMBYE, E. L., BENNETT, A. G., SCHNEIDER, W. C. and TRAVERS, J. J. (1961). *J. pharm. Sci.*, **50**, 827.

WALTER, C. W. (1938). *Surg. Gynec. Obstet.*, **67**, 683.

WELCH, H. and HUNTER, A. C. (1940). *Amer. J. publ. Hlth*, **30**, 129.

WOLF, J. and BROWN, JEAN (1946). *Proc. Soc. appl. Bact.*, **9**(2), 99.

WOODROFFE, R. C. S. (1963). *J. Hyg., Camb.*, **61**, 283.

PART II

Methods of Sterilization

CHAPTER 5

STERILIZATION BY HEAT

EXPERIENCE over many years has shown that of all the methods available
for sterilization, heat, and particularly moist steam under pressure, has
proved to be the most reliable and universally applicable. The only occasions
when heat cannot be used are when the material to be sterilized is heat-labile
or when it is otherwise adversely affected by elevated temperature or by
moisture. The efficiency of heat in the form of fire has, of course, been
known as a means of preventing the spread of disease for many centuries
and the policy of boiling water for drinking was advocated by Aristotle for
Alexander the Great's armies on the march. Steam heat was not used
scientifically, however, until the time of Koch and Pasteur when bacteriological techniques were being developed. A steam pressure vessel was
described as early as 1859.

Reiterating the definition of the term 'sterilization', it is an absolute
term, and means the total destruction of all micro-organisms, including
the most resistant bacterial spores. This disposes of a popular fallacy which
has grown up through the years that sterilization can be effected simply by
boiling, an idea devolving from medical practice where it is often intended
to infer no more than the destruction of certain pathogenic organisms. The
term is also used commercially, mainly in the food industries, but here again
not often in its absolute sense; in this case it indicates rather the destruction
of spoilage organisms. It is true, of course, that quite frequently boiling will
effect sterilization, but this can only be due to the fortuitous absence of
bacterial spores of sufficient resistance, and its acceptance on any other
terms must inevitably lead to difficulties.

Mechanism of thermal destruction

Thermal death of micro-organisms takes place as the result of the inactivation
of essential cellular proteins or enzymes, and there is ample proof of this in
the high temperature coefficient of the death process and in the close correlation of cell destruction and protein inactivation under a variety of
conditions. But in considering methods of heat sterilization it is important
to differentiate between dry and moist heat, a differentiation recognized by
Koch, who, as early as 1881, pointed out the relative inefficiency of dry heat.
It is evident that the conditions and mechanisms of the two lethal processes
are not the same, and the greater resistance to dry heat is generally attributed
to the greater heat stability of proteins in the dry state. Some data on the
coagulation of egg albumen illustrate this point:

albumen containing 50 per cent of water coagulates at 56°

,,   ,,   18   ,,   ,,   ,,   80°–90°

,,   ,,   6   ,,   ,,   ,,   145°

,,   ,,   no added water coagulates at   160°–170°

As early as 1945 Rahn (1945) stated "The cause of death in moist heating is quite different from that in dry heating, and the rules applying to the one method do not fit the other", and then went on "Death by dry heat is primarily an oxidation process; death by moist heat is due to coagulation of some protein in the cell." This concept is still accepted in principle, but naturally more is now known of the detail of the mechanism. According to Precht and colleagues, as explained by Hansen and Riemann (1963), when wet proteins are heated they release free SH groups and give rise to smaller peptide chains. These chains are mobile and so have the capacity to establish new bonds between themselves, thus forming new complexes different from the original protein molecules. In the absence of water, the polar groups in the peptide chains are less active, by virtue of the lack of water dipoles, so that their mobility is much reduced. It requires, therefore, more energy to open the peptide molecules, hence the increased apparent resistance of the protein in the dry state.

Much care is needed in carrying out any heat sterilization process to ensure that the whole of the material reaches the required temperature for a sufficient length of time, and any breakdown in the process can almost invariably be attributed to lack of care in this direction. The British Pharmacopoeia recognizes two procedures, namely, saturated steam at 115° (10 lb pressure per sq. in.) for 30 minutes and dry heat at 160° (or in certain cases at 150°) for 1 hour; the United States Pharmacopeia quotes the use of steam under pressure at 121° (15 lb per sq. in.) for 20 minutes (30 minutes for dressings) and dry heat at 170° for 2 hours. This last recommendation seems to be excessive both in temperature and time, because experience over many years has confirmed that only in certain exceptional cases can organisms be found which survive even 150° for 1 hour. Until recently the British Pharmacopoeia also allowed dry heat at 140° for 4 hours, and even 125° for 15 hours has been used successfully with some substances which are damaged at higher temperatures. Other treatments now in use, particularly for sterilizing dressings, include 126° for 10 minutes and 134° for 3 minutes; a 'flash' heating at about 150° has also been suggested, but this is of dubious reliability.

Thermal death measurements and heat resistance

Thermal death time

The commonly used term 'thermal death point' is generally defined as the lowest temperature at which a suspension of bacteria in an aqueous medium is killed in 10 minutes. It is an unfortunate term, because it disregards entirely any temperature coefficient and, although it gives some indication of the relative susceptibilities of different organisms, it takes no count of their physiological state or of the influence of the nature of the environment, and so for sterilization purposes it is valueless and can be misleading. Heat resistance is a far from constant characteristic, and out of the many varied cultural conditions emerge the oft-encountered organism of apparent exceptional resistance which would upset all calculations based on the premise of a fixed thermal death point. A much more practical term is that of 'thermal death time', which by inference is the time required to kill a culture at any predetermined temperature. It is a more flexible term and can include some assessment of the temperature coefficient, but again it takes no account of the cultural state of the organism.

Amongst the non-sporing bacteria, the thermal death times range from a few minutes at 47° to 60 minutes at 60° or 5 minutes at 70°. None is able to withstand more than a few minutes at 80°, and it is safe to state that heating at this temperature under wet or moist conditions for 10 minutes will kill all such organisms; some of the most susceptible bacterial spores will also succumb, but in the majority of cases the proportion killed is relatively small. The mould spores are all fairly easily killed, and few survive heat at 80°. Amongst the resistant types are certain strains of *Byssochlamys fulva* which in the ascospore state are said to resist 86–88° for 30 minutes (Brown and Smith, 1957).

The wide variations in the recorded thermal death times for the non-sporing bacteria are undoubtedly due to strain differences and differing cultural and recovery conditions. These are discussed in detail later, but as an example of the significance of recovery conditions some findings by Busta and Jezeki (1963) can be quoted. In investigating the heat senstivities of several strains of staphylococci in milk they obtained much lower recoveries in Difco S110 medium, containing 7·5 per cent of sodium chloride and used for the selective detection of these organisms, than in media with lower sodium chloride contents. Thus, in one experiment, the apparent thermal death time at 60° with S110 was 18 minutes, but with normal nutrient agar as the recovery medium it was as long as 40 minutes: in another experiment the respective times were 8 and 28 minutes.

Some of the viruses are probably more resistant to heat than might at first be imagined. The majority are inactivated in periods up to about 20 minutes at temperatures of 50° to 60°, but there are a few notable exceptions. The poliomyelitis virus is said to vary so much in its resistance that on some occasions it requires treatment for 30 minutes at 75° to effect complete inactivation (Bergey, 1948). Likewise the causative agent of Q fever in milk has survived for 40 minutes at 63° (Ransom and Huebner, 1951), and the bacteriophage of *Escherichia coli* has survived for 5 minutes at 70° (Chang, Willner and Tegarden, 1950); a virus associated with infantile diarrhoea has resisted heating at 70° for 1 hour (Light and Hodes, 1943) and the causative agent of infective hepatitis when suspended in human serum is said to require 10 hours at 60° for inactivation.

Thermal death rate

The death rate of any micro-organism subjected to lethal heat always approximates to a logarithmic form, but there are many examples of the curve deviating from a straight line. The slope of the curve varies very much between different organisms and according to the temperature applied, and there is also some evidence that the rate of death at a given temperature may vary according to the speed at which the temperature is reached, a 'shock' treatment being more effective than a gradual rise to the acquired level. Whatever the slope of the curve, however, the fact that it is approximately logarithmic indicates that the lethal process follows the order of a unimolecular reaction and thus suggests that death is due to the inactivation of a single molecule in the cell. Rahn and Schroeder (1941) go further and suggest that it must be "a very rare molecule, *e.g.* a gene or an equally important molecule of the cell division mechanisms." Be that as it may, there are certain exceptions to the rule of logarithmic death which cannot be explained simply as deviations from the normal due to experimental error, and there is often a parallelism between the rates of death of organisms by heat and by chemical disinfectants, many of which, as explained earlier (Chapter 3) conform to a sigmoidal response curve. Reynolds and Lichtenstein (1952) for instance, showed that the death rates of an anaerobic organism, designated PA 3679, increase during the first intervals of exposure until half or more of the spores are killed, then the rate becomes exponential until the final phase is reached when the last few spores exhibit abnormal resistance. Reed, Bohrer and Cameron (1951) also found abnormal responses with a number of food spoilage organisms, including *Clostridium botulinum*, and another case is that of the sclerotia of a *Penicillium* species which can withstand heat at 90·5° for some 20 minutes and then die off quite rapidly within the next 5 or 10 minutes. For those directly concerned with the problem, Humphrey and Nickerson (1961) and Hansen and Riemann (1963) quote other references to this same sort of non-logarithmic behaviour.

Thermal destruction of bacterial spores

Because their resistance is far in excess of that of any other group of micro-organism and because they include some of the pathogens, the killing of bacterial spores constitutes the principal problem in any sterilization process, not excluding that by heat. The protective mechanism by which spores develop such resistance is not known with any certainty, but one explanation put forward by some workers is that the envelope around the spore is so thick and rendered so impervious that when subjected to steam treatment access of moisture to the vital part of the cell is retarded. There seems to be no justification for retaining the idea that the thickness of the cell wall retards heat penetration – the size of the cell makes this argument untenable – but the thesis of impermeability seems eminently reasonable, and a theory that bacterial death is due to the destruction of a "heat-induced, heat-labile reproduction initiator" is being studied by Humphrey and Nickerson (1961). They postulate that the initiator can be thought of at the outset as being tied up in a less heat-labile and inactive state which is freed by a certain amount of heat but destroyed by further heat. Such a premise also impinges on the problem of the recovery of heat-treated spores, a matter which is discussed later. Resistance is also thought to be related to the gravity of the spores, or in other words, to the densities of the protein in the cells (Yesair and Cameron, 1936), and this suggestion, inferring a difference between the protein structures of spores and of vegetative cells, has, in fact, been taken further by the finding that the water contents of the two types of cell differ significantly (Friedman and Henry, 1938), the amount in the spores being so low that the protein present must be in a dehydrated form (Ross and Billing, 1957).

Destruction by moist heat. Since the original studies of Burke (1919), Bigelow and Esty (1920) and Esty and Meyer (1922), there have been numerous investigations into the resistances of many species of spores to moist heat at different temperatures. Rahn (1945) has calculated that the temperature coefficients per 10° increase (Q_{10}) lie for most spores between 8 and 10 over the range 100° to 135°. On this basis, the equivalent sterilizing times are as follows (Thiel, Burton and McClemont, 1952):

Temperature (°C)	*Time* hr min
100	20
110	2 30
115	51
121	15
125	6·4
130	2·4

But this can only be a generalization, because each species of spore has its own specific resistance characteristics, and they can vary over a broad range according to cultural conditions. Because of such variations there have been many diverse opinions expressed in the literature for practically every organism studied, as indicated in Table 7. Topley and Wilson (1955) have illustrated the complexity of the problem by stating, in relation to the genus *Bacillus*, "All are killed by steam under pressure at 120° in 40 minutes", and later quoting *B. megatherium* as able to withstand 18 lb steam pressure (124°) for 1 hour and *B. mycoides* 15 lb steam pressure (121°) for 1 hour. These diversities are undoubtedly attributable to three controlling factors: (*a*) the initial concentrations of organisms in the test samples, a point first brought out by Bigelow and Esty (1920); (*b*) the nature of the environment in which the spores were treated; and (*c*) variation in experimental techniques used by different workers.

It seems very doubtful whether it is possible to breed a more heat-resistant culture of any organism by selection—any cells surviving a heat treatment always produce progeny with a normal spread of resistance—neither is there any doubt that organisms as found in nature, on foods, in packing materials, in soil and dust, are far more resistant than are those cultivated on laboratory media, even though they may be freshly isolated from their natural state. Thus, in trying to find a suitable spore preparation to use for the routine testing of sterilizers, Kelsey (1958) examined a number of cultures of reputedly high heat resistance, but found that none of them survived beyond 2 minutes at 110°, neither could they stand up for this time

TABLE 7

Some quoted destruction times of bacterial spores by moist heat

Organism	Destruction times (minutes) at:							
	100°	105°	110°	115°	120°	125°	130°	134°
B. anthracis .	2–15	5–10						
B. subtilis .	many hours			40				
A putrefactive anaerobe .	780	170	41	15	5·6			
Cl. tetani .	5–90	5–25						
Cl. welchii .	5–45	5–27	10–15	4	1			
Cl. botulinum .	300–530	40–120	32–90	10–40	4–20			
Soil bacteria .	many hours	420	120	15	6–30	4		1·5–10
Thermophilic bacteria .		400	100–300	40–110	11–35	3·9–8·0	3·5	1
Cl. sporogenes .	150	45	12					

at 121°. Similarly, Cameron, Esty and Williams (1936) isolated a spore-forming organism from canned beets, which, from heat-penetration data, should have been killed at 116° in 10 minutes; under laboratory culture conditions it did not survive 5 minutes at 110°. There is also the case of the Loch Maree outbreak of *Cl. botulinum* infection originating from potted duck. This infection initially survived the incredibly long period of 2 hours at 115°, but in subsequent culture it was much less resistant (Topley and Wilson, 1955).

Most of the organisms of reputedly high resistance have been isolated from heat-treated foodstuffs but there seems to be little doubt that in several instances insufficient allowance was made for heat to penetrate through the sample, and so the resistances reported are exaggerated. On the other hand, some of the examples must be accepted as authentic because the spores were heated in buffer solutions. Such is the case with a strain of *Clostridium sporogenes* isolated by Baumgartner and Wallace (1936) which required heating at 115° for 40 minutes, and with a 'flat-sour' thermophilic organism, "No. 1518", which had maximum survival times of 110 minutes at 115° and

35 minutes at 120° (Williams, Merrill and Cameron, 1937). The author himself encountered some years ago an unidentified organism in meat which caused trouble in media sterilization by resisting flowing steam treatment for 1 hour followed by steam pressure at 115° for 45 minutes; it was killed by extending the time to 90 minutes or by treating at 121° for 60 minutes.

In face of these observations, treatment with steam under pressure at 115° for only 30 minutes, as given in the British Pharmacopoeia, may seem unreliable as a sterilization process, but it must be borne in mind that in practice two quite different sets of conditions obtain. Highly resistant organisms are mainly encountered in certain foods and similar materials where especially favourable conditions exist for protecting the organisms.

TABLE 8

Some quoted killing times of bacterial spores by dry heat

Organism	Destruction times (minutes) at:						
	120°	130°	140°	150°	160°	170°	180°
B. anthracis			up to 180	60–120	9–90		3
Cl. botulinum	120	60	15–60	25	20–25	10–15	5–10
Cl. welchii	50	15–35	5				
Cl. tetani		20–40	5–15	30	12	5	1
Soil spores				180	30–90	15–60	15

These are special cases and allowances are made for such eventualities by applying more intensive heat treatments. On the other hand, pharmaceutical preparations, the only other group of materials which are subjected to heat sterilization, are generally much less heavily infected numerically, and they do not carry organisms of the most resistant types; moreover they do not provide any appreciable protection for those which may be present. On these premises, therefore, a less severe heat treatment is permissible, and the apparently short pharmacopoeial sterilizing period is completely reliable. In fact, a period as short as 15 minutes will often prove satisfactory.

Destruction by dry heat. The position with regard to resistance to dry heat sterilization is much the same as that with moist heat, although because of its more limited applications it has attracted much less attention. In terms of killing times at different temperatures, Table 8 gives the range of some of those recorded for different organisms.

These figures are no more consistent than those quoted in the previous Table for moist heat, and again the variations are probably largely due to the different degrees of protection of the organisms or to unevenness of heating in the sterilizing oven. Nevertheless, they do suggest that the occasional organism with abnormal resistance undoubtedly occurs. One such example was encountered by the author in a soil sample which was able to withstand heating to 170°, as checked by a thermocouple, but not 180°, for 1 hour: similar findings have also been reported by Darmady, Hughes and Jones (1958). Curran (1952) has even gone so far as to state that "Some spores may survive heating at 300° for 30 minutes," but in the light of wider experience this is an evident exaggeration.

Again, as with moist heat, the officially recommended dry heat steriliza-tion procedures would appear to be inadequate, but it must be reiterated that much practical experience has proved temperatures of 150° or 160° satisfactory under normal circumstances. In special cases where abnormally resistant organisms are expected or known to occur, it is only reasonable for a more rigorous treatment to be given.

Factors influencing thermal resistance

As has already been indicated, the nature of the environment influences to a marked degree the heat resistance of both vegetative and sporing organisms, and the first differentiation can be made between organisms found in nature and those grown in laboratory culture. The process of natural selection undoubtedly has a bearing on this, and sometimes the natural environment seems to confer a resistance factor on the organism. This is particularly noticeable with soils, and can be demonstrated by growing cultures in media containing soil or soil extract, when often a greater heat resistance is obtained compared with the same cultures grown in ordinary media. Many other factors can affect the heat resistance of micro-organisms, the more important of which are discussed in the next paragraphs.

Concentration and age of cells. Perhaps the first item to be mentioned should be the concentration of cells in the material to be sterilized. From the logarithmic order of death it follows that the higher the initial number of organisms the longer is the time required to effect their complete destruction. But this holds only for cells from identical suspensions. If different suspen-sions are used, other factors will mask the relationship, even though the suspensions are made under the same conditions.

Resistance is also bound up with the age of the culture, but unfortunately there is no uniformity of opinion amongst those who have examined the subject. Some favour the theory that young spores of a few days old are more resistant than older ones, and this has been demonstrated with certain strains of *Cl. botulinum* (Esty and Meyer, 1922) and *Cl. sporogenes* (Sommer, 1930; Bashford, 1942). Contrariwise, there are some who have shown continuously increasing resistance with age (*e.g.* Curran, 1934) and still others who could find no correlation (*e.g.* Williams, 1936). All of these investigators worked with different cultures, and undoubtedly their experimental conditions must have varied. It seems, therefore, that the only general conclusion to be drawn is that, with some organisms at least, heat resistance varies with age.

Cultural environment. The environment in which an organism finds itself either immediately prior to, or during, a heat treatment can influence profoundly its resistance, and such factors as the organic make-up of the environment, its protein content, fat content and inorganic salts content, as well as its physical properties, all contribute significantly. A high organic content in a medium during heating exerts generally a protective influence on the spores. Such is particularly the case when they are held in solid suspension, as in coagulated serum media or in muscle fibres, although under such circumstances it is difficult to assess how much is due to fat protection and lack of heat penetration. Spores grown in digest media, except casein digest, or media containing vegetable extracts and gelatin usually exhibit enhanced resistance (Williams, 1929), and it is said that the use of different brands of peptone can result in differing resistances. More recently, however, Williams and Harper (1951) have grown *Bacillus cereus* on a number of chemically defined media with varied luxuriance in growth and sporulation but with no correlation in resistance.

Sugars, syrups, starch, nucleic acids, albumin, gelatin and glycerol all protect spores, as well as vegetative organisms, from the destructive effects of heat (Baumgartner and Wallace, 1934; Baumgartner, 1938; Anderson, Esselen and Fellers, 1949; Sugiyama, 1951; Amaha and Sakaguchi, 1954) and oils and fats undoubtedly act in the same way. The effect of the latter is most marked with moist heat, and arises presumably because the fats prevent access of moisture to the cell and so create local conditions approaching those of dry heat treatment.

From the work of Sugiyama (1951), fatty acids in the sporulation medium enhance resistance, the extent of which depends on the chain length of the acid. *Per contra*, extraction of the medium with ether or chloroform results in reduced resistance.

It might be expected that the presence of antibacterial agents would automatically reduce heat resistance, but in a survey of 650 such compounds, Michener, Thompson and Lewis (1959*a*, *b*) found only 26 to be really effective. Using as a yardstick a reduction in thermal death time at 113° of 45 per cent or more with a *Clostridium* sp. (PA 3679) as the test organism, the most effective substances included subtilin, nisin, formaldehyde, cetrimide, vitamin K and tetrachlorohydroquinone. Activity occurred most frequently amongst the mutagenic agents and the organic sulphur compounds.

Inorganic salts. Many inorganic salts exert their independent influences on heat resistance, and often concentration is a governing factor. Sodium chloride, for instance, in concentrations of 2 to 4 per cent confer protection against heat, but concentrations above about 8 per cent effect a diminution in resistance (Esty and Meyer, 1922; Headlee, 1931; Anderson, Esselen and Fellers, 1949). Magnesium ions increase the resistance of *Cl. botulinum*, whereas the elimination of iron or calcium can lower its resistance (Sugiyama,

1951). This may be because the calcium ions are capable of linking various groups in a peptide chain thus yielding a protein more resistant to denaturation; some credence may be attached to this idea because excess of phosphate in the medium, which would remove the calcium present, leads to a reduction in resistance (El-Bisi and Ordal, 1956a).

pH value. pH value is, of course, of fundamental importance. A sufficiently acid or alkaline medium itself can be lethal without applied heat. Greatest resistances amongst the bacterial spores occur in the pH range 6·0 to 8·0 whereas for the moulds and yeasts they are somewhat on the acid side. With most organisms there appears to be an almost critical lower pH value below which the resistance falls away rapidly; thus *B. subtilis* suffers a marked reduction in resistance at pH 6·6 (Nichols, 1940), and a similar change is said to take place with *Cl. botulinum* at pH 6·9.

Temperature. The effect of temperature on thermal resistance has been examined from two aspects, namely, the incubation of cultures prior to heating and the selection and propagation of cultures from survivors from moderate heat treatment. In terms of incubation temperature the greatest resistances are developed in individual cultures propagated at or just above their optimum growth temperatures. This has been demonstrated in a number of organisms of the *Bacillus* group (Curran, 1934; Lamanna, 1942; El-Bisi and Ordal, 1956b), in ten strains of *Bacillus stearothermophilus* with optimum growth temperatures of 45° or 55° (Williams and Robertson, 1954), and in *Cl. botulinum* which exhibits greater resistance when grown at 37° than at 29° or 41° (Sugiyama, 1951). Generally speaking, the most resistant organisms are found amongst those with the highest optimum growth temperatures.

Turning to the aspect of induced resistance by selection of survivors from heat treatment, the evidence is contradictory. Sommer (1930), Morrison and Rettger (1930a), Williams (1936) and Desrosier and Esselen (1951) were all unable to demonstrate any significant increases with several cultures of the *Bacillus* and *Clostridium* groups, whereas Bigelow and Esty (1920), Magoon (1926), Williams (1929) and Davis and Williams (1948) working with a variety of spore-forming aerobes, including *B. subtilis, B. mycoides, B. globigii* and thermophils, all claim to have obtained more resistant cultures by this means. In some instances the increases were only of a qualitative nature, that is, the *proportions* of survivors at given elevated temperatures were greater, but the ultimate resistance remained unchanged. In other cases, the change was certainly quantitative and the actual lethal level was increased. Rahn (1943), however, has criticized the evidences presented, on the basis that the last survivors are not really more resistant than the average, having simply survived the heating period by the normal statistical chance, and in this argument he is supported by Knaysi (1948) who draws attention to the inconsistencies of bacterial cultures in producing spores with identical characteristics even under apparently constant conditions.

There is, of course, the possibility of mutation occurring by adaptation to growth at higher temperatures than normal, which might yield cells of greater resistance, but this is at present speculation.

Recovery of treated organisms

Cultures which have survived drastic treatment of any sort are much more exacting in their nutritional requirements than the less resistant individuals comprising the bulk of the original population, and this applies no less significantly to heat-treated spores. Therefore, unless suitable conditions are provided for their recovery, falsely low estimates of their resistance are obtained. Knaysi (1948) has listed some of the many environmental factors influencing the germination of spores, amongst which he includes incubation temperature, 'heat-shock' treatment, types and concentrations of nutrients in the medium, and such physical attributes as osmotic pressure, surface tension and oxidation-reduction potential.

Media enriched with tomato juice, yeast extract (Morrison and Rettger, 1930*b*), blood, milk, or even glucose (Curran and Evans, 1937) give appreciably larger recoveries of survivors in a variety of sporing and non-sporing bacteria than do plain media, and beef-infusion agar is said to be superior to "ordinary nutrient" agar or a synthetic medium (Nelson, 1943). Wynn and Foster (1948) preferred a pork infusion medium, but this according to Frank and Campbell (1955) is not as good as a yeast extract medium containing 0·1 per cent of starch. The idea of including starch in the medium to enhance recoveries of organisms originated from Olsen and Scott (1946) who used it successfully with several strains of *Bacillus* and *Clostridium*. The reason for this enhancement is not clear, but presumably it is associated with the removal of some antagonizing factor by adsorption, because charcoal will do the same. Probably the best all-round medium is one based on the Krebs cycle and containing peptone, alanine, asparagine, histidine, acetate, citrate, glutaric acid, glutamic acid and inorganic salts.

Not a great deal of work has been done on the optimum incubation temperature for recovery of heat-treated organisms, but such information as is available suggests that a level below the normal optimum is the most suitable. For instance, greater recoveries of *Cl. botulinum* were obtained in the range 24° to 31° than at 37° (Williams and Reed, 1942), but there does not seem to be any parallel information for the genus *Bacillus*. What is known is that, with the thermophils at least, growth at different temperatures is closely linked with their nutritive requirements, some requiring additional metabolites as the incubation temperature is increased and others as it is decreased (Campbell and Williams, 1953), so much so that certain so-called "obligate" themophils are said to grow quite happily at 37° provided a highly nutrient "tryptose basamin glucose" medium is used in place of ordinary nutrient broth (Long and Williams, 1959).

With the non-sporing bacteria there can actually be a prolonged fall in the number of viable organisms during incubation under so-called optimum conditions. This has certainly occurred with *Staph. aureus* (Jackson and Woodbine, 1962) and with faecal streptococci after heating in foods (Hansen and Riemann, 1963), and there is no reason to believe that these are isolated instances. Similarly, some organisms are not recoverable from pasteurized milk until it has been kept for a period at 5° (Macauley and James, 1963).

One other interesting observation is that a mild 'heat shock' treatment after a sub-lethal heating encourages the germination of spores. The exact relationship of temperature with degree of heat activation seems to be a variable characteristic, but treatments such as heating at 96° for 10 minutes (Curran and Evans, 1945), or at 100° for 20 minutes (Reynolds and Lichtenstein, 1952) have been used. The same phenomenon has been observed in dairying where it is recommended that samples be pre-heated to at least 50° for 10 minutes (Mattick and Hiscox, 1945), and even as high as 85° (Evans and Curran, 1943), to avoid false-negative results from so-called sterilized milk. In some cases observed viable spore counts have been increased ten- or twenty-fold by such treatment. The role of endogenous dipicolinic acid in maintaining the dormancy of spores has already been discussed in Chapter 3, and the function of the heat-shock treatment would seem to be to release this acid more readily from the cell, thus allowing the cell to germinate freely, the differing amounts of heating advocated by various workers depending on the amounts of dipicolinic acid in the organisms used (Keynan, Murrell and Halvorson, 1961).

Even though apparently suitable conditions for growth recovery are established there is still often a dormancy or delayed germination of heated spores, and this can run into periods of years. The reason is still a matter for conjecture, but Topley and Wilson (1955) suggest that it is the result of cell injury sustained from the heating, which interferes with the normal reproductive mechanism, and to which the cell has to adapt itself. It is quite common for surviving spores to take some two to three weeks to germinate completely, and Kurzweil (1954) has said that it takes up to five weeks at 37°. Spoilage in foods occurs frequently up to 100 days after treatment, and Esty and Meyer (1922) found *Cl. botulinum* to remain dormant for periods up to nearly 400 days; Dickson (1928) went further and extended it to as long as six years. Jones and Pearce (1954) have given several examples of organisms remaining dormant in canned foods for periods up to several years, and there is the celebrated case, quoted by them, of six strains of sporing organisms being isolated from wholesome canned roast veal 113 years old.

The phenomenon is not confined to anaerobic organisms. It has been observed with *B. subtilis*, *B. megatherium* and even with *E. coli* (Burke, Sprague and Barnes, 1923).

Sterilization by steam

Basic principles

Sterilization by steam under pressure is so fundamental and yet is so taken for granted in many quarters that it is worth while considering for a brief period the mechanics involved in the process.

The basic essentials for sterilization in the autoclave are that the whole of the material, whether liquid or solid, shall be treated with saturated steam at the required temperature for the necessary length of time. The pressure of itself contributes nothing to the lethal process, but serves solely as a convenient means of attaining moist heat temperatures higher than those otherwise obtainable. Sterilization is achieved exclusively through the combined action of heat and moisture.

When steam is brought into contact with any material or body cooler than itself, it gives up its latent heat and in so doing condenses on the material concerned and raises its temperature. This action goes on until a temperature equilibrium has been reached, after which there is no more heat exchange and no further condensation. It can be seen then, that whatever the nature of the material being sterilized, whether it be liquid or solid, the sterilization takes place in virtually an aqueous medium.

Two corollaries arise from this premise: first, that superheated steam must be avoided, and secondly, that all air must be excluded. Superheated steam, or steam heated above its normal temperature in relation to its pressure, must be avoided because although condensation takes place during the initial heating stages in the usual way, later it is re-vaporized and the sterilization procedure becomes a dry heat one, for which the conditions are quite different and the sterilizing temperature much higher. Air must be excluded completely otherwise it collects in pockets or layers and so prevents adequate steam penetration and heat transfer.

The process of heating is never an instantaneous one, and the time taken to reach equilibrium at the required temperature will vary with the size of the autoclave, the size of the load and its heat capacity and the rate of steam penetration. With bulk liquids and materials such as glassware, where the heat capacity is high, or with rubber or fabrics where penetration is difficult, the time factor may be considerable and due allowance must be made in the treatment cycle. This preliminary heating period may be of quite long duration compared with the actual sterilization time, but with dressings and instruments it can be substantially reduced by using the pre-vacuum technique (see later).

The autoclave

Design and operation. The basic function of a steam autoclave is to provide a means of treating the whole of the material to be sterilized with saturated steam at a given temperature for a specified length of time, and every sterilizer should be constructed to fulfil these requirements with the maximum efficiency. Whether the autoclave be a self-contained unit generating its own steam by gas or electricity or a unit connected to a steam mains supply, or whether it be manually operated or fully automatic on a timed cycle of operations, the basic design and technique of handling remains the same.

The smallest autoclaves in use are adaptations of the domestic gas-heated pressure cooker. They are just as efficient as any larger and more

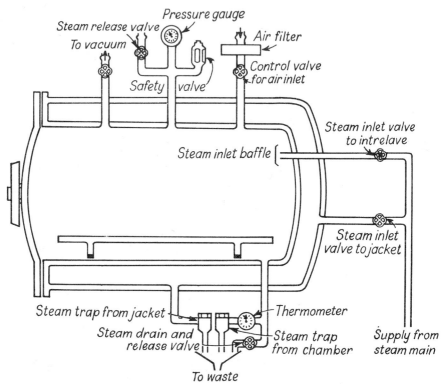

Fig. 4. *Basic design for a sterilizer operated from a steam main*

orthodox installation and are very useful for sterilizing small quantities of materials. The largest autoclaves may measure some 20 ft long by 6 ft square, and, because of the amount of steam required, are essentially operated from a mains boiler supply. The larger models are always horizontal in design, but those up to about 18 in. diameter and 30 in. long can be either vertical or horizontal, and this is about the limiting size for self-contained gas or electrically heated models. A rectangular design is obviously the most economical in terms of usable space in the chamber, but it is much more expensive to produce than a cylindrical one because it requires a heavier gauge metal and additional reinforcements to be able to withstand the pressures used. Incidentally, all steam sterilizers, being pressure vessels, are subject to regular inspection under Board of Trade regulations.

The basic design of a mains-operated model for universal use in sterilizing dressings and other hospital equipment, as well as aqueous solutions, is illustrated diagrammatically in Fig. 4. It can, of course, be varied within certain limitations but the main features to be observed are:

(*i*) the steam supply to the chamber and to the jacket is controlled by separate valves;

(*ii*) the steam as it reaches the chamber must be saturated with water and not superheated to any degree;

(*iii*) the steam may enter the chamber either centrally or towards the top, but in any case it must be baffled or sparged on entry;

(*iv*) the autoclave must be sited so that the drain is at the lowest point of the chamber;

(*v*) there must be valves in the top and bottom of the sterilizer to allow the free exit of air and steam as required;

(*vi*) a safety valve is essential;

(*vii*) the ports for air inlet and to vacuum must carry an air filter;

(*viii*) a thermometer or other temperature recording device should be sited in the steam drain on the chamber-side of the steam trap and non-return valve;

(*ix*) all joints and seals, especially the door gasket, must be airtight. These and other details are incorporated in three British Standard Specifications (1960) for different types of hospital sterilizers. In addition, Thiel, Burton and McClemont (1952) have drawn up model specifications for the design, construction and operation of vertical, gas-heated laboratory sterilizers. This design, and any other which generates its own steam, is always a single-chamber instrument without an outer steam jacket.

Sterilization indicators and controls. The efficacy of steam sterilization can be controlled and assured by using indicators judiciously placed in each autoclave load. Every autoclave should be fitted with a thermometer to indicate the temperature in the chamber, preferably in the steam exhaust line, but in addition there should be other indicators either in the form of a thermocouple inserted in the load, a chemical indicator or a preparation containing resistant bacterial spores. A fundamental necessity with all such indicators, if they are to be used successfully and reliably, is that they must be properly placed in the load to be sterilized. It is of no avail to pack all the material into the chamber and then just pop in an indicator. It must be placed in the most critical position in the sterilizer, that is, towards the centre and bottom of the load where the steam heat can least easily penetrate.

Since the object of steam sterilization is to kill off bacteria, the obvious choice of indicator is that of bacterial spores. Whilst this might be the ideal choice in some respects, it has a number of disadvantages. First, there is the question of obtaining cultures of adequate resistance; secondly, a culture test takes some days to complete and the sterilized material may be required for immediate use; thirdly, it is difficult, as shown earlier, to fix cultural conditions suitable for the rapid recovery of heat-damaged organisms. In spite of these drawbacks, the cultural control method is widely used. The simplest procedure is to use a garden soil to which has been added a number of sporing cultures of known resistant laboratory strains. To make an auto-clave test, a small packet or cotton-wool plugged tube containing about 0·5 gm of the mixture is inserted at a critical point in each sterilizer load, and afterwards cultured in the usual way. Unfortunately not all such mixtures have the right degree of resistance and several batches of material may have to be made before a suitable one is found. Kelsey (1958) has shown how unreliable laboratory control cultures can be, but both the Nuffield Provincial Hospitals Trust (1958) and the M.R.C. Working Party (1959) consider that suitable preparations can be made by impregnating small pieces of filter paper with the spores of *Bacillus stearothermophilus*, and Kelsey (1961) has confirmed it; papers of this type are available commercially. However they may be prepared, they should survive steam under pressure at 121° for at least 5 minutes or 130° for 1 minute (Kelsey, 1958). In the United States, survival for at least 5 minutes in constant-boiling hydrochloric acid (Ortenzio, Stuart and Friedl, 1953) is accepted as the official standard. Because they do not give an immediately readable result spore tests are not of great value for day-to-day routine control, and the use of such controls is best confined to the testing of new techniques or equipment or for special investigational occasions.

Of the other methods of control, the thermocouple is the most direct. It gives a direct reading, and provided again that it is inserted at the most critical point in the load, the sterilization period can be timed from the point when the couple-reading reaches the required temperature.

Pure chemicals of known and well-defined melting points are also employed, and an entirely novel device incorporating such compounds has been described by Brewer and McLaughlin (1954). It is based on the hour-glass principle, and depends on the flow time of a fixed amount of a selected substance in the molten state through the capillary constriction of the glass. The substance selected must be one which melts just below the required sterilizing temperature, so that at that temperature it is sufficiently liquid to give an easy flow. By this means it can be established that a minimum time as well as temperature for each operation has been attained. For sterilizations at 121° succinic anhydride (m.p. 120°) is recommended, and for sterilizations at 115° sulphur (m.p. 115°) or acetanilide (m.p. 116°). The device is somewhat limited in its use because its size prevents it from being inserted easily in packaged materials.

Quite different types of chemical indicators are those which change colour after a sterilization treatment. In this country Browne's tubes are the most favoured, but in the United States coloured papers or strips are the more popular. Browne's tubes (available from A. Browne Ltd., Leicester) are small sealed glass tubes containing a red fluid which changes colour through amber to green on heating and they are available in three types: Type I which responds to sterilizations at 115° for 25 minutes or 121° for 15 minutes, Type II at 115° for 15 minutes and Type III for dry heat sterilizations at 160° for 1 hour. They have been reported upon favourably by several investigators (Howie and Timbury, 1956; Scott, 1957; Alder and Gillespie, 1957; Nuffield Provincial Hospitals Trust, 1958) but in the opinion of the author, and of others (Kelsey, 1958, 1959; Medical Research Council Working Party, 1959), they are not entirely reliable because they do not provide an adequate safety margin at the lower temperature ranges and will, in fact, change colour if heated below the desired sterilizing temperature for a longer time, *e.g.* 100° for about 2 hours: these are certainly undesirable weaknesses. But if used intelligently and stored properly they are probably the best for routine control. The strip or patch indicators which also change colour, or rather in some cases develop a greater intensity of contrast between two colours, *i.e.* from a light grey on a fawn background to an almost black on the same fawn background, include the 'Klintex' paper (Robert Whitelaw Ltd., Newcastle-upon-Tyne), reported upon favourably in the Nuffield Report (1958), a Scotch tape (Minnesota Mining and Manufacturing Co. Ltd.) and also 'Diacks', 'Tempilpellets' and 'Tempilstiks' all made in the United States. Several of these have been examined comparatively by Brown and Ridout (1960), who found the Browne tubes, in spite of their storage instability, to be the most suitable. For greater precision they suggested comparing the colours of the processed tubes with a standard colour.

Such a test is quite satisfactory for determining whether the proper temperature has been reached and held for the requisite time at a given point in the sterilizer, but in the case of dressing sterilizations it is equally important to know whether the treatment has been uniform throughout a load of, say, towels or sheeting. For this purpose, the Minnesota Mining and Manufacturing Co. tape "type 1222" is considered to be the most satisfactory (Bowie, Kelsey and Thompson, 1963) because the strips can be stuck diagonally across each package if necessary and the uniformity of colour change observed. The responses of the strips agreed well with thermocouple readings but, like the Browne tubes, they also respond to lower temperatures if held for longer times. A time control system is, therefore, essential.

Some common operational faults. Sterilization failures occur either through faults in the design or instrumentation of the autoclave or through faulty manipulation due to ignorance or carelessness on the part of the operator. Such occurrences are far from infrequent and have been traced as the cause of many post-operative infections as well as of the failure of batches of injection products to pass the test for sterility. Until recently faults in construction seemed to be rife in hospital sterilizers, but thanks largely to the efforts of the Nuffield Hospitals Trust, the Medical Research Council Working

Party, and several individual investigators, the situation today is entirely different. Age of itself does not, of course, affect the performance of an auto-clave, but the design and methods of control of such an apparatus may well be at fault. Bowie (1955), Howie and Timbury (1956), Scott (1957) and Alder and Gillespie (1957) have all quoted examples of many hospital sterilizers falling far short of their expected standards of efficiency, and the authorities quoted above, along with others such as Bowie (1959, 1961), Kelsey (1958, 1959), Wells and Whitwell (1960) and Wilkinson, Peacock and Robins (1960) have shown how the faults could fairly easily and inexpensively be overcome and controlled in the future.

The matter is so important that at the risk of repeating information given in other pages the possible causes of failure in a steam sterilization are listed below. They include:

(1) a general lack of cleanliness;

(2) reliance on faulty instruments, through not checking them regularly, to measure temperature, vacuum and steam pressure;

(3) reliance on the pressure in the sterilizer as an indicator of the temperature of the contents;

(4) incorrect packing or loading so that steam does not have ready access to all the material to be sterilized;

(5) failure to remove air from the chamber;

(6) not allowing sufficient time for the whole of the load to be heated to the required temperature, and consequently allowing too short a holding time;

(7) the presence of rare organisms of unexpectedly high resistance;

(8) attempts to sterilize materials wrapped or sealed to exclude the ready access of steam;

(9) attempts to sterilize materials such as powders and oils which are impervious to steam;

(10) recontamination of the sterilized material during drying and cooling, or during storage, due to faulty wrapping or sealing and the consequent ingress of contaminated air.

All of these points are important and it is only with constant skilled super-vision that they can be avoided.

The sterilization cycle

Consideration of the mechanisms of steam sterilization shows that the process can be conveniently divided into four stages:

(1) loading and packing the autoclave;

(2) raising the load to the required temperature and pressure;

(3) holding at this level for a specified time;

(4) cooling and unloading.

These stages apply both to aqueous fluids and to dressings and instruments, but the detailed procedures with the two are somewhat different; the latter is therefore treated separately on p. 133. The paragraphs immediately following apply mainly to aqueous solutions, but many of the points have some bearing on dressings sterilizations.

Loading and packing the autoclave. The first requirement is that steam should have direct and ready access to all parts of the material to be sterilized. The packing must, therefore, be loose and ordered in such a way that a free flow of steam is possible throughout the sterilizer. Dead areas must be eliminated, and it must be possible to sweep out all of the air without leaving pockets. This means that solid trays must be avoided, and so must deep containers with no bottom vent. Dressing drums should have their side vents open, but the lids can be sealed, and when large numbers of small tubes or ampoules are being handled they must not be piled haphazard in boxes or crates, but arranged so that there is no undue inhibition of steam flow. Details of the precautions necessary in the wrapping and packing of dressings and rubber gloves are given on p. 133.

The preliminary heating period. When once the autoclave is sealed, the only means of conveying heat to the material to be sterilized is by the steam first giving up its latent heat and condensing on all accessible surfaces. Thereafter the penetration and heat transfer is by conduction and convection. All this takes time, and it is of primary importance in arranging a time-cycle of operations to allow ample time at this stage. At this stage also, the air in the autoclave must be replaced by steam so that the later treatment is in saturated steam and the correct steam pressure-temperature ratio is obtained.

The heating is usually carried out in two phases, the first with flowing steam at normal atmospheric pressure, and the second with the autoclave sealed and the steam pressure rising slowly. During the first phase the load is raised from ambient temperature to nearly 100°, and in the second stage the load temperature is raised from 100° to that required for sterilizing. The heating can also be carried out in one phase, which saves a little heating time and so may be useful with heat-sensitive materials, but it adds to the hazards of the process. In this case, steam is admitted into the sealed and preferably evacuated chamber at the normal rate and the pressure gradually allowed to build up. Provided the steam enters in a turbulent fashion through the usual baffle it condenses uniformly on the cold containers and as the temperature rises the air is gradually removed. No pressure develops, in fact, until all of the air has been removed, so that if the temperature is recorded at the chamber drain and the sterilization period timed from when it reaches the required level of 115° or 121° a satisfactory treatment will result. This process is used successfully in the author's laboratory and it has been advocated by Wilkinson and Peacock (1961a).

As stated earlier, the actual time required to complete the preliminary heating stage depends very much on the size of the individual items constituting the load. To illustrate this point and draw attention to the marked differences which actually occur in practice, some tests were made with a normal-flow sterilization with (*a*) small containers treated individually and in large numbers packed in crates, and (*b*) single containers of different size, all filled with water. In each case they were sealed in the autoclave and steamed under identical conditions, and the rates of heating were measured by taking thermocouple readings at regular short intervals during the heating process. The results obtained are recorded graphically in Figs. 5 and 6. They

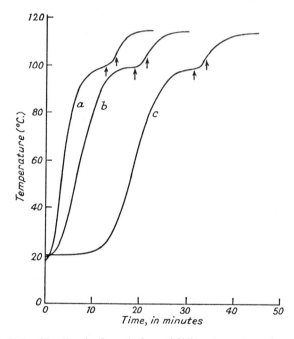

FIG. 5. *Rate of heating in the autoclave of different numbers of containers*
$a = 1 \times 100$ ml bottle; $b = 1$ crate of 100 ml bottles; $c =$ two stacked crates of 100 ml bottles. The arrows indicate the times at which steam pressure was applied and at which the pressure in the autoclave reached 10 lb per sq in. (115°)

need little comment, but perhaps special attention might be drawn to the lag in heating when stacked crates are used (Fig. 5).

Another phenomenon encountered with large containers is that of heat layering. This is illustrated by some experiments on the rate of heating of an 8 litre pyrex flask of water, which required 30 minutes longer for the upper layers, and 55 minutes longer for the lower layers, to reach 121° than did the autoclave chamber itself (Brewer and McLaughlin, 1954). Many sterilization failures can be attributed to lack of appreciation of these two important aspects of rate of heating.

Effect of air. It is of primary importance to remove the air from the sterilizer and replace it with steam, and the reasons are threefold: (*a*) admixture of air with steam reduces the partial pressure of the steam in the atmosphere and so the temperatures of air-steam mixtures are always lower than those of pure steam at the same pressure; (*b*) in a jacketed autoclave with the jacket temperature maintained at the normal sterilizing level an admixture of air in the chamber will lead to superheating, and (*c*) a local atmosphere of air or even a residual air pocket acts as an insulator against steam penetration and heating.

Admixture of air with steam shows its effects in two ways: first, it influences significantly the temperature of the steam at all pressures; secondly,

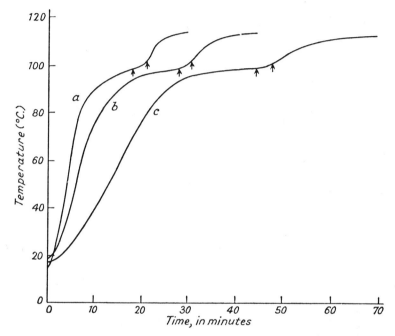

FIG. 6. *Rate of heating in the autoclave of containers of different sizes*
a = 160 ml bottle; *b* = 1 pint bottle; *c* = 5 litre flask. The arrows indicate the times at which steam pressure was applied and at which the pressure in the autoclave reached 10 lb per sq in. (115°)

it does not mix readily with steam, and, being the heavier fraction, tends to layer at the bottom of the chamber and so give rise to a temperature gradient at different levels. The significance of the former is illustrated in some figures recording the maximum temperatures obtainable with different steam-air mixtures in a sealed chamber at various pressures:

| | | Temperature with: | |
Pressure gauge reading (*lb per sq in.*)	pure steam (°C)	half air discharged (°C)	no air discharged (°C)
5	109	94	72
10	115	105	90
15	121	112	100

These figures need no comment, and serve to underline the importance of eliminating air from the autoclave.

The second phenomenon associated with steam-air mixtures, that of lack of mixing, also affects temperatures, but in a different way. This time, the layering effect gives rise to lower temperatures in the bottom of the sterilizer, and the differences recorded can be substantial. Walter (1940), for instance, found that in a sealed autoclave from which no air had been allowed to discharge, a nominal temperature of 115° at the top of the chamber gave a level of only about 70° at the bottom. He showed, moreover, by means of temperature diagrams taken at various points in an autoclave with and without a mixing fan in operation, that, although there may be adequate initial mixing, separation and layering can quickly take place. The phenomenon has also been described graphically and commented upon by Savage (1959), and it underlines the importance of temperature readings taken at strategic points in the sterilizer in contrast to reliance simply on pressure gauge readings. It also illustrates the need of having a bleed valve in the bottom of the chamber to allow accumulated residual air to be discharged during the sterilization process.

The usual method of removing air during the initial heating process is by sweeping it out with a good flow of steam by downward displacement with the escape cocks fully open. The time necessary for this operation will vary with the load, and it can be judged best from the temperature of the steam outflow at the bottom drain. Where dressings and other dry packages are concerned it is advisable to use a vacuum system as a more positive means of preventing layering and pocketing, although normal gravity downward displacement can be used equally effectively provided the packing is suitably arranged.

An anomalous position might seem to present itself where sealed bottles or ampoules containing aqueous solutions are being sterilized, because of the fact that air cannot be removed from inside the container. Savage (1944), however, has shown that air does not exert any specific effect, and that mixtures of air and steam can be as effective as pure steam, *provided the physical state of the steam can be controlled*. This situation does not, therefore, raise any problem because, as was stated earlier in this chapter, it is the temperature of the treatment which is important. In such cases, the correct temperature level is reached, because it is that of the autoclave chamber itself, and the atmosphere inside the container must be saturated with water vapour because of the presence of water in the container. In effect, a normal sterilization takes place at the correct temperature but at a somewhat elevated relative pressure.

Effect of superheated steam. The essence of steam sterilization is that it shall be carried out in the presence of moisture, and the use of superheated steam, by its very nature, would turn the process into virtually a dry heat sterilization. Such conditions can only lead to sterilization failures.

In practice, it is not possible to produce superheating in an autoclave generating its own steam, and obviously it cannot occur when aqueous solutions are being sterilized. It is most likely to arise in a jacketed autoclave through the jacket being maintained at a pressure, and consequently temperature, above that of the chamber, or through the incomplete removal of the air. Superheating in the first manner is a direct process, but as pointed out by Savage (1959), that by air mixture is more varied and subtle. It will occur if the steam supply contains entrained air, or if air is left in the chamber, both because, as Savage puts it, the air "carries part of the load, with the result that the pressure of the steam is reduced" and some of the water vapour is taken up by the air. It will also occur when the materials to be sterilized themselves tend to absorb water, and quite large increases in temperature consequent on this have been reported. The phenomenon can occur readily in powders, and the author himself has found temperature elevations of up to 25° above that of the sterilizing chamber when bulks of Fullers earth were sterilized after they had been substantially dried; with a normal moisture content of about 10 per cent the standard sterilizing temperature was maintained throughout.

Fortunately there is a margin of safety within the range of superheating where satisfactory sterilizations can be assured (Savage, 1937). This margin is narrow at the lower sterilizing temperatures, but it widens as the temperature of the initial saturated steam increases, until ultimately the steam temperature reaches that of a dry heat sterilization and the two processes merge into one. The position is illustrated diagrammatically in Fig. 7. Normal steam at the temperature indicated on the abscissa is assumed to be heated, in the absence of additional water and at a constant pressure, to the temperature levels indicated on the ordinate, and the margin of safety, as found by experimental observation, is found to be that described by the area between the "steam line" and the "safety line". The area above the "safety line" is the area of sterilization failures, and the broken line indicates the merger of the dry heat and steam processes.

The holding time. It has been said that no living cell can survive 10 minutes' direct exposure to saturated steam at 121° or 15 minutes at 115°, and this, although perhaps not absolutely correct, is a good basis from which to work. Tubes of culture media in 5 or 10 ml volumes can always be sterilized by holding for 10 minutes at 121°, and 20 minutes' treatment at 115° was used successfully by the author for a number of years for media volumes up to 50 ml. In the light of experience, recommended holding times might therefore range between 10 and 45 minutes at 121°, or 15 and 60 minutes at 115°, depending upon whether the autoclave load is light and consists of small items, or whether it contains dressing drums and large items. For many purposes fixed times and temperatures are specified, and the various pharmacopoeias each have their own standards: one should always be aware of these.

There is no point in using temperatures above 121°, *i.e.* pressures above 15 lb per sq in. for most sterilizations, because they would not significantly shorten the sterilizing time, although a notable exception is made to this with dressings, instruments and rubber gloves (see later). Excessive holding times should be avoided on account of the destructive effect of unnecessary

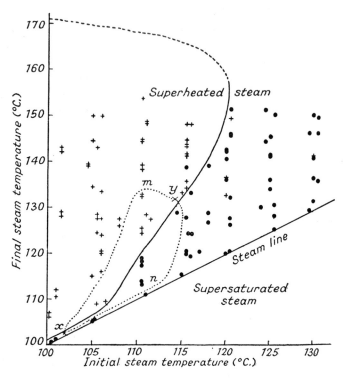

Fɪɢ. 7. *The relationship between the degree of superheating of steam and its sterilizing efficiency*
(Savage, 1937)

● successful sterilization
+ sterilization failing

heat on materials in general and on fabrics, rubber and culture media in particular.

The cooling process. When materials such as dressings, rubber and instruments are being sterilized, the steam pressure can be released immediately at the end of the holding period without any further ado, in fact, the quicker the better in many cases, but to treat aqueous solutions in the same way would be courting disaster. If the release of steam is too rapid, the rate of loss of pressure far exceeds the rate of reduction in temperature and this causes the solutions to boil vigorously. To avoid this, the rate of fall of steam pressure must be steady and slow, taking between about 7 and 30 minutes, according to the load, to reach the atmospheric pressure.

A safer way of avoiding boiling is to replace the steam with air at the same pressure, or higher, taking care during the exchange not to allow the total pressure at any time to fall. Cooling can then be allowed to proceed at normal rates. Even better is the spray-cooling method, in which pressure is maintained in the chamber by compressed air and in addition water is sprayed uniformly over the containers, thus accelerating the rate of cooling of the contents by virtue of the evaporation of the water on the outer surfaces of the containers. It is only applicable, of course, to ampoules, sealed vials or closed bottles etc. where there is no danger of the water leaking inwards and thus spoiling the contents, and it is particularly useful with large volume containers such as transfusion bottles. Bowie (1959) pointed out the necessity to spray the water slowly enough to prevent breakage of the bottles due to thermal shock, and Wilkinson, Peacock and Robins (1960) overcame this difficulty by using a fine, non-wetting water spray delivered from a whirling nozzle so that the droplet size did not exceed a mean of 80 microns. In the author's experience it can be overcome even more easily by using a coarse hot-water spray, the water being collected from the condensate during the sterilization and circulated through the spray as rapidly as possible.

When the contents need to be dry they can be finished off by immediately applying a high vacuum and holding for several minutes. By this means, the residual water is evaporated under the reduced pressure. When air is let into the chamber at the end of the process it must always be through a pre-sterilized air filter thus avoiding recontamination of the freshly sterilized load with air-borne organisms.

Sterilization of dressings

For the sterilization of dressings, rubber gloves and surgical instruments there is an increasing trend towards the use of the prevacuum-high temperature-short time process as advocated by the Medical Research Council Working Party (1959, 1960). It cannot be over-emphasized, however, how much care is needed if the process is to be carried through satisfactorily.

One of the most important factors is the removal of air from the materials and its complete replacement by steam. This can be done by the traditional 'downward displacement' method with free-flowing steam or by a pre-vacuum treatment. The former is satisfactory but is a slow process and requires, amongst other things, that (*a*) the dressings must not be wrapped, folded or rolled too tightly, (*b*) the packets must not be too big, (*c*) the external wrapping must not be impervious to steam (if paper or a heavy-weave fabric is used it is advisable to leave vents which must be sealed at the end of the process), (*d*) rubber gloves must be arranged loosely in their packages or containers so that the steam can get not only to the outer surfaces but also to the inner ones—the same applies to syringes, needles, etc., but to a rather less extent because here the situation can be materially helped by first rinsing them with water and leaving them wet, (e) the drum or casket should lie on its side with the vents open so that the air can escape downwards and outwards and not remain as a pool in the bottom of the container.

For the pre-vacuum method an efficient pump is essential so that the residual pressure in the chamber can be reduced below 20 mm absolute. According to most workers who have studied this subject, *e.g.* Perkins (1956), Bowie (1958, 1959, 1961), Knox and Penikett (1958) and Wilkinson and Peacock (1961b), this is an important threshold value. The reason is that air and steam do not mix easily so that the residual air in a package after a partial evacuation will subsequently act in a concertina fashion expanding and contracting according to the pressure applied but never diffusing into the chamber generally.

A further point to be noted is that there is an optimum time for which the vacuum should be held in the chamber. If not held long enough the occluded air in the cotton or other fibrous material is not removed, and if held too long it tends to extract the natural moisture of the fibres and so leads to super-heating, as explained on p. 131. Although not absolutely confirmed, the general conclusion seems to be that the holding time should be about 8 minutes. Unless, however, the seals on the sterilizer, and particularly those on the door gasket, are virtually leak-proof, so that no air can gain re-entry, the vacuum holding time and the evacuation residual pressures are meaningless. Were it otherwise, the leaking air during and at the end of the evacuation period would ultimately leave a residual pressure of greater than 20 mm and so cause a breakdown in the sterilization conditions.

The question of superheating of dressings during sterilization seems enigmatic at present, but one certain cause is the use of excessively dried materials. Cotton naturally has a water content of about 8 per cent held in a physico-chemical combination, and if dried below this level it will pick up moisture as soon as it comes into contact with it. This causes some elevation of temperature which, if sufficiently great, leads to superheating in a bulk of material. Bowie (1961) found, for instance, that if a packet of 29 huckaback towels were dehydrated to a water content of 3·6 per cent the resultant superheating was only 2°, but if the residual water was reduced to 0·1 per cent it rose by 12°; likewise, Knox, Penikett and Duncan (1960) found superheating to the extent of 8–9° if the water content were reduced below 1 per cent, and these levels are outside the margin of safety. Similar occurrences had been reported earlier (Savage, 1937, 1959; Walter, 1948; Henry, 1959) and various means have been proposed to eliminate them. The simplest, of course, is to equilibrate the dressings for a period with the normal atmosphere immediately before putting them in the sterilizer, thus allowing them to pick up their quota of moisture (Knox, Penikett and Duncan, 1960), but others (Henfrey, 1961; Wilkinson and Peacock, 1961b) have recommended a steam injection into the load in the sterilizer, the process being to evacuate to 20 mm pressure, let in steam to raise the pressure by a few inches and then re-evacuate. This procedure also deals with another difficulty, that of sterilizing small loads, which rather incongruously are less readily sterilized than are large loads. The problem here is one of superheating, arising from the presumption that when steam is let into the evacuated sterilizer and begins to condense on the dressing material it pulls with it the remaining small amount of residual air in the chamber and so fills a small package with air: the effect is not noticed with larger loads which fill the chamber more, and therefore distribute more widely the entrained air. The occurence is known as the 'small package' effect, and along with the possible methods of overcoming it (as indicated above), has been described fully by Henry and Scott (1963).

Having prepared the load satisfactorily thus far, the steam is let into the evacuated chamber and immediately put up to the required pressure and held there for the prescribed time. All the evidence available (Bowie, 1961; Henfrey, 1961; Wilkinson and Peacock, 1961b) shows the heat penetration to be almost instantaneous, certainly within seconds, so there is virtually no preliminary heating period and the sterilization can pass to its holding period.

The holding time depends, of course, on the temperature chosen, and for high temperature sterilizations Perkins (1956) has made certain suggestions which have been adapted by the Medical Research Council Working Party (1959) by adding a 'safety period'. They are:

Perkins	*M.R.C.*
2 min at 132°	3 min at 134° (30 lb per sq in.)
8 min at 125°	10 min at 126° (20 lb per sq in.)
12 min at 121°	15 min at 121° (15 lb per sq in.)

Control indicator tubes, 'Vac Control' (Smith and Underwood, Michigan, U.S.A.), are available for the higher temperature process.

Having completed the sterilization period the steam pressure is released as quickly as possible and a vacuum applied so that the dressings will emerge as dry as they went in. If the sterilization cycle has been run properly and dry steam used, the simple application of the vacuum to 50 mm residual pressure will be adequate (Penikett, Rowe and Robson, 1959), but in any case it need only be of short duration.

The foregoing cycle of operations is complicated and subject to considerable human error. For these reasons a fully automatic control is recommended with or without a time-temperature integrator for the holding period. Some such machines incorporate a 'rubber glove cycle' as well as a normal dressings one, but experience is proving that no special treatment for them is necessary. If handled properly they can be sterilized in the normal cycle many times without deteriorating.

The rubber glove cycle, which is usually at a lower temperature than that set for cotton dressings and instruments, was introduced under the misguided conception that heat in itself is the exclusive damaging factor to rubber.

Recent experiments, (Fallon and Pyne, 1963), however, have shown that air is the main culprit, so that under a proper pre-vacuum cycle the damage caused by sterilizing at 134° for 3 minutes is no greater than at 126° for 10 minutes or 121° for 15 minutes. If the air removal is incomplete, or, worse still, if the gloves are 'aired' in the sterilizer to dry them off whilst still hot, then considerable damage can result, and in this respect dipped gloves are more sensitive than Latex ones. The same is also true of cotton goods when subjected to repeated sterilizations (Henry, 1964).

To illustrate the value of these high speed sterilizers, Wells and Whitwell (1960) have carried out 53 dressings and 2 glove sterilizations in a $3\frac{1}{2}$ cu ft fully automatic and integrated machine in the space of 12 hours.

Sterilization by dry heat

Compared with moist heat, sterilization by dry heat has limited application, mainly because of the necessity of using much higher temperatures for much longer times which may well be destructive to the materials being handled. Dry heat is used mainly for sterilizing oils, petroleum jellies, surgical catguts, surgical instruments and glassware. It is not suitable for sterilizing dressings because of the damage to the cotton fibres, and care must be used in handling powders, because many of them are discoloured or decomposed at such high temperatures; similarly it cannot be used when water, including water of crystallization, is present.

The manipulations of dry heat sterilization are much less complicated than with moist heat, in fact, the only requisite is that the *whole* of the material to be sterilized shall be treated for a sufficient length of time at the specified temperature. The only possible reasons for failure, therefore, are (a) incorrect measurement of temperature, (b) lack of heat penetration, or (c) the presence of organisms of abnormal resistance.

Apart from the usual bacteriological spore control, there seems to be only one simple chemical indicator for dry heat sterilization, namely, the Browne tube, Type III. It changes colour dependably after 1 hour at 160° (Brown and Ridout, 1960).

The hot air oven. Heating of the contents of a normal hot air oven takes place mainly by radiation from the walls and floor, and its distribution will not be even and uniform throughout the load unless steps are taken to make it so. This means that the oven must not be overloaded and ample air spaces should be left between individual items; a forced air circulation within the oven by means of an enclosed fan is also advantageous. A British Standard is now in existence (1961) for the performance of hot air sterilizing ovens, the specifications for which include (i) temperature control in the range 140° to 180°, (ii) a maximum heating up time for a given load, and (iii) after reaching the required temperature, a variation within the load of not more than 5°. It also warns against overloading which impedes the free flow of air. The possible extent of the unevenness of heating which can occur is illustrated from the author's experience with one particular oven. This was an electrically heated model with the elements in the base only and its walls were lined with asbestos. The rates of heating in different parts of the oven were followed by means of thermocouples fixed 1 inch or so above each shelf. The control thermometer took 1 hour to reach 160°, whereas the thermocouples ranged

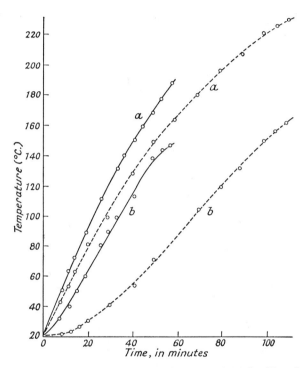

FIG. 8. *Rate of heating in a hot air oven not fitted with a fan*
a = temperatures taken on lower shelf; b = temperatures taken on upper shelf. Continuous lines indicate temperatures in empty oven and broken lines those in loaded oven.

from 148·5° to 189° after the same time, the higher temperatures being recorded on the bottom shelf. These results are similar to those quoted by Darmady and Brock (1954) who also obtained temperature differences up to 40° in two ovens heated by gas to a nominal 160° level. In this respect, electrically heated ovens are said to give more uniform temperatures than gas-heated ones, probably because their heating elements are built in the base and three walls, whereas the source of heat in gas ovens is from the base only.

The consequences of overloading are equally significant, as illustrated in some experiments obtained with a laboratory oven by a student of the

School of Pharmacy of the University of London; they are quoted by permission. The oven was heated from its base only, and its load consisted of petri dishes packed on the lower shelf and bottles and flasks on the upper shelf. Temperatures were measured in different parts of the load by means of several thermocouples. The findings, illustrated graphically in Fig. 8, show clearly the marked lack of uniformity in rates of heating and in the final temperatures reached.

Another point to be remembered is that the size and nature of the individual items in a load are more significant in terms of heat penetration than they are with moist heat sterilization. Even comparatively small bulks take a considerable time to heat through, so much so that a 4-oz jar of powder can take up to 55 minutes longer to reach 160° than the same material spread in thin layers in petri dishes. For reliable dry heat sterilization, therefore, the greatest area possible should be exposed to direct heating, and attempts to sterilize containers holding more than an ounce or two of a solid should be discouraged. Oils, petroleum jellies and the like also have a lag in rate of heating, but because they are liquid at elevated temperatures the lag should be rather smaller than with fixed solids. The same rule also applies to wrapped instruments and syringes, particularly if sterilized in individual containers, and due time allowances must be made in all of these cases for the sterilizing temperature to be reached.

A novel means for sterilizing small numbers of syringes and instruments has been described by Darmady *et al.* (1958). It depends on heating by conduction rather than by radiation, and consists of a thermostatically controlled hot plate on which an aluminium block is fixed. In the block are holes to take different sized syringes, and a shallow flat tray on the top takes the cutting instruments, the whole being covered by an insulating cover. By this means the temperature is so carefully controlled that the maximum variation is only 2°. In practice, the hot plate is set at 190° at which level a syringe in its container can be sterilized in 22 minutes.

Infrared radiations. Infrared radiations from electrical sources are becoming popular for space heating generally and they also have their applications in the sterilization sphere. The system must obviously be confined to relatively small units of apparatus and it has been used with considerable success for sterilizing up to 600 syringes per day for a central supply service (Darmady, Hughes and Tuke, 1957). The syringes are passed on a slowly moving belt through a tunnel in which are mounted the heater units. By varying the surface of the syringe containers from a polished aluminium to a black anodyzed one the rate of heating can be varied so that ultimately syringes of all sizes get the same sterilization treatment. Under these conditions, even the most resistant spores do not survive heating at 180° for more than 15 minutes, the total heating time on the belt being $22\frac{1}{2}$ minutes.

For sterilizing instruments for theatre use when a suitable steam supply is not available, Darmady *et al.* (1961) have described an elaborate high vacuum apparatus which reaches a maximum temperature of 280° and requires only a 15 minutes' sterilization time (apart from the cooling period). The advantage claimed is that because a high vacuum is used (2 mm residual pressure only) there is practically no damage to cutting edges or other surfaces.

Other heat sterilization processes

As well as treatment by dry heat at 150° or 160° and by saturated steam under pressure, there are other methods of heat sterilization which employ either dry heat at temperatures above 160° or moist heat at temperatures of 100° or lower. In the latter case, some of the processes rely on the combined effect of moderate heat plus that of a mild bactericidal agent. These methods are described below.

Heat-plus-bactericide. It is a general characteristic of chemical antimicrobial agents that their activities increase with increases in temperature, and this is made use of in the heat-plus-bactericide process. The first investigations on this subject were published by Coulthard (1936), who showed that aqueous suspensions of resistant bacterial spores can be sterilized by adding small amounts of substances such as brilliant green, formaldehyde and mercuric chloride. These observations were confirmed independently by Berry, Jensen and Siller (1938), whilst Coulthard (1939) extended them to include *p*-chloro-*m*-cresol and phenylmercuric nitrate. The method was immediately accepted by the British Pharmacopoeia in which it has featured since 1941 as a means of sterilizing certain injections, the process being to heat the sealed containers to 98°–100° for 30 minutes in the presence of either 0·2 per cent of *p*-chloro-*m*-cresol or 0·002 per cent of phenylmercuric nitrate. It is perfectly satisfactory under normal conditions, but it has been shown to fail with a resistant organism of the *B. cereus* type (Davison, 1951). The author states, however, "It still remains to be established whether the pathogenicity of the organisms has been reduced by contact with the bactericide." An answer to this has been supplied by Coulthard and Chantrill (1951, unpublished) in which aqueous suspensions of spores of *Clostridium septique* were treated at 80° and then inoculated into groups of five mice. To one portion of the suspension was added 0·1 per cent of chlorocresol, to a second was added 0·002 per cent of phenylmercuric nitrate, and the third was the control. The results given in Table 9 show clearly the advantage of the bactericide in the heat process and prove that the action is actually bactericidal and not simply bacteriostatic.

Weak acids and alkalis also act in the same way (Davis, 1934; Coulthard, 1939) so that many injections having a pH value of about 4·5 or lower can be sterilized by mild heat without adding any bactericide. This action is due to the effect of the hydrogen ions; hydroxyl ions also act in the same way, and it has been suggested that the simplest and most rapid way of sterilizing surgical instruments is to boil them for 5 minutes in water containing 2 per cent of sodium carbonate (*Brit. med. J.*, 1943). This treatment certainly kills off all bacterial spores, but it might at the same time cause rusting of some plated instruments or spoil their cutting edges. These defects do not seem to be as serious, however, as with the various forms of 'cold' sterilization, in which the instruments are immersed in aqueous solutions for prolonged periods; in any case they can be arrested by including anti-rust compounds (Malloch, 1951).

The process has, in effect, been used for many years in the canning industry in the preservation of fruits and fruit juices, and more recently it has

TABLE 9

The effectiveness of the heat-plus-bactericide method as shown by animal experiment

Suspension	No. mice surviving after inoculation with suspensions heated at 80° for		
	5 min	15 min	30 min
Control	0	1	0
With 0·1 per cent chlorocresol .	0	1	4
With 0·002 per cent P.M.N.* .	1	4	5

*Phenylmercuric nitrate

been extended for other foods to include the addition of certain antibiotics. The acidity of some fruits is sufficiently great for practical sterilization to be achieved by holding for a short time at 75° to 80°, but in other cases, such as tomato juice which is susceptible to spoilage by spore-forming bacteria, or certain fruit juices containing resistant mould spores (Brown and Smith, 1957), a boiling water treatment is necessary. Uniformity of heat penetration is again a matter of importance and various types of rotary or agitation cookers are now being developed for this purpose. Often, of course, with whole-skinned fruits the contamination is only on the surface and it can be easily dealt with. This accounts for the success of home bottling methods which can rely on a combination of the heat capacity of the syrup used in bottling plus the acidity of the fruit.

The methods do not apply to meats or pastes, where heat penetration is difficult, neither can they apply to vegetables such as peas, beans and potatoes, because their acidity is not sufficiently great to contribute to the sterilization process. With these products attempts have been made to overcome the difficulty by adding small amounts of the more stable antibiotics. Successes have been claimed with subtilin (Andersen and Michener, 1950) and to a limited extent with nisin (Hirsch, 1953), but evidence to the contrary has also been produced (Cameron and Bohrer, 1951; Williams and Fleming,

1952). Differences in resistance between the various species and strains of organism used appear to be the straightforward explanation of these contradictory opinions. In spite of this, however, active research is still proceeding because of the potential value of such a treatment in all branches of the food industry.

The low temperature stream-formaldehyde vapour method of Alder, Brown and Gillespie (1966) (see p. 211) is also worthy of note.

Tyndallization. This method of treatment, named after its discoverer Tyndall, was devised many years ago as a means of sterilizing materials which would be damaged at temperatures above 80°. It is a fractional method of sterilization, the procedure being to heat at 80° for 30 minutes on three successive days, the material being kept at normal temperatures between the heatings. It now has a number of variants, including heating to 100° by boiling or in flowing steam instead of at 80°, and a range of heating times up to 1 hour.

The theory of the treatment is that at the first heating all organisms but the resistant spores are killed. In the intervening period between the first and second heating these spores are able to grow out into vegetative forms and they are caught by the second heating; the third heating is a safeguard against any organisms missed at the first two stages. The method is properly applicable only to conditions in which bacterial spores surviving the first heating have a chance to develop during the next 24 hours, and so it should be limited to the sterilization of nutrient solutions in which germination can take place. It was used for a number of years as a means of sterilizing solutions for injection but it was proved quite unreliable when resistant spores were present (Burke, 1919; Coulthard, 1933; Davis, 1934; O'Brien and Parish, 1935) and was replaced by the heat-plus-bactericide method.

Aseptic technique followed by heating. It is perhaps useful to refer briefly to this method since it has a number of applications in both pharmacy and the food industry. It consists of sterilizing the material in bulk form, filling it under aseptic conditions into pre-sterilized containers, sealing them and then heating for a relatively short time at 80° or 100° to destroy contaminations accidentally introduced during the filling procedures. It is suitable for materials which for various reasons are more easily sterilized in bulk or cannot be sterilized in the final containers, and depends on the assumption that an occasional contamination gaining access during filling can be easily dealt with by the subsequent mild heating.

Dry heat above 150°. It has been shown earlier in this chapter that there is a time-temperature relationship for all heat sterilization processes, shorter times being required at higher temperatures. From this it follows that a point must be reached when sterilization is almost instantaneous, or at least takes place whilst the particular temperature is being reached. Comparatively little work has been done on sterilization at high temperatures, but from the evidence produced by Bourdillon, Lidwell and Raymond (1948) aerosols of bacterial spores passing through an externally heated furnace can be sterilized in 0·4 to 0·6 second at 225°, and in about 8 seconds at 272° in an internally heated one. Bearing in mind the difficulties attendant on such experiments these figures are not different from those quoted by Decker *et al.* (1954) of 24 seconds at 218°, 10 seconds at 246° and 3 seconds at 302°.

These observations were made with bacterial aerosols, in which the organisms would be single and unprotected and, therefore, most easily susceptible; in larger agglomerates or with a protein coating they might be expected to be more resistant, as evidenced from figures quoted by Oag (1940). He cited sterilization times for anthrax spores coated on glass slides of 9 minutes at 160°, 3 minutes at 185°, 2 minutes at 288°, and 20 seconds at 400°. Other organisms were killed at about the same rates, although some required 30 seconds at 400°. Unfortunately, he made the unwarrantable assumption that when put in the furnace the slides "reached the temperature of the furnace almost instantaneously", therefore due allowance must be made for this and the sterilizing times reduced appropriately.

The application of high temperatures to air sterilization is dealt with more fully in Chapter 10.

Flaming. Flame sterilization is common practice in the bacteriology laboratory for sterilizing platinum loops and for 'burning off' cotton wool plugs, but it is doubtful whether some of the flaming of the necks of tubes, etc., which one frequently sees practised in the laboratory, can have any really salutary effect; it undoubtedly has some psychological value.

Flaming is also used in preparing certain instruments for minor surgery by dentists and medical practitioners, but it cannot have wide application because of its obvious limitations. Often the procedure is to swab the surfaces with alcohol and then burn it off, but direct heating by holding in a naked flame is the safest method because it also effects the oxidation of any destructible organic matter. Unfortunately, it often leaves a layer of oxidized metal and must inevitably dull the edges of any cutting instrument. The alcohol swabbing and burning off method is really a treatment by indirect heating. The heat is derived from the burning vapour, and not from the liquid in contact with the surface and so any heating of the surface comes from the heat of combustion being conducted through the thin liquid layer.

REFERENCES

ALDER, V. G. and GILLESPIE, W. A. (1957). *J. clin. Path.*, **10**, 299.
ALDER, V. G., BROWN, ANNE M. and GILLESPIE, W. A. (1966). *J. clin. Path.*, **19**, 83.
AMAHA, M. and SAKAGUCHI, K. (1954). *J. Bact.*, **68**, 338.
ANDERSON, E. E., ESSELEN, W. B. and FELLERS, C. R. (1949). *Food Res.*, **14**, 499.
ANDERSEN, A. A. and MICHENER, H. D. (1950). *Food Technol.*, **4**, 188.
BASHFORD, T. E. (1942). *Proc. Soc. agric. Bact.*, p. 37.
BAUMGARTNER, J. G. (1938). *J. Bact.*, **36**, 369.
BAUMGARTNER, J. G. and WALLACE, M. D. (1934). *J. Soc. chem. Ind.*, **53**, 294 T.

BAUMGARTNER, J. G. and WALLACE, M. D. (1936). *Food Mfg*, **10,** 11.
Bergey's *Manual of Determinative Bacteriology* (1948). BREED, R. S., MURRAY, E. G D.
and HITCHENS, A. P., 6th Ed: Baillière, London.
BERRY H., JENSEN, E. and SILLER, E. K. (1938). *Quart. J. Pharm.*, **11,** 729.
BIGELOW, W. D. and ESTY, J. R. (1920). *J. infect. Dis.*, **27,** 602.
BOURDILLON, R. B., LIDWELL, O. M. and RAYMOND, W. F. (1948). *Studies in Air
Hygiene*, Med. Res. Counc. Spec. Rep. Ser. No. 262: H.M.S.O., London.
BOWIE, J. H. (1955). *Pharm. J.*, **174,** 473, 489.
BOWIE, J. H. (1959). *The Operation of Sterilizing Autoclaves*—Report of a Symposium,
p. 28; Pharmaceutical Press, London.
BOWIE, J. H. (1961). *Sterilization of Surgical Materials*—Report of a Symposium, p. 109:
Pharmaceutical Press, London.
BOWIE, J. H., KELSEY, J. C. and THOMPSON, G. R. (1963). *Lancet*, **1,** 586.
BREWER, J. H. and MCLAUGHLIN, C. B. (1954). *Science*, **120,** 501.
British Standards Institution: Horizontal Cylindrical Hospital Sterilizers, B.S.
3219:1960; Horizontal Rectangular Hospital Sterilizers, B.S. 3220:1960; Pressure
Steam Sterilizers of Small Size, B.S. 3233:1960.
British Standard Specification for Performance of Electrically Heated Sterilizing Ovens.
British Standards Institution B.S. 3421:1961.
Brit. med. J. (1943). p. 633.
BROWN, AGNES H. S. and SMITH, G. (1957). *Trans. Brit. mycol. Soc.*, **40,** 17.
BROWN, W. R. L. and RIDOUT, C. W. (1960). *Pharm. J.*, **184,** 5.
BURKE, A. (1919). *J. Amer. med. Ass.*, **1,** 88.
BURKE, V., SPRAGUE, A. and BARNES, L. V. (1923). *J. infect. Dis.*, **36,** 555.
BUSTA, F. F. and JEZEKI, J. J. (1963). *Appl. Microbiol.*, **11,** 404.
CAMERON, E. J. and BOHRER, C. W. (1951). *Food Technol.*, **5,** 340.
CAMERON, E. J., ESTY, J. R. and WILLIAMS, C. C. (1936). *Food Res.*, **1,** 73.
CAMPBELL, L. L. and WILLIAMS, O. B. (1953). *J. Bact.*, **65,** 141.
CHANG, S. L., WILLNER, M. and TEGARDEN, L. (1950). *Amer J. Hyg.*, **52,** 192.
COULTHARD, C. E. (1933). *Pharm. J.*, **130,** 266.
COULTHARD, C. E. (1936). *Quart. J. Pharm.*, **9,** 174.
COULTHARD, C. E. (1939). *Pharm. J.*, **142,** 79.
CURRAN, H. R. (1934). *J. Bact.*, **27,** 26.
CURRAN, H. R. (1952). *Bact. Rev.*, **16,** 111.
CURRAN, H. R. and EVANS, F. R. (1937). *J. Bact.*, **34,** 179.
CURRAN, H. R. and EVANS, F. R. (1945). *J. Bact.*, **49,** 335.
DARMADY, E. M. and BROCK, R. B. (1954). *J. clin. Path.*, **7,** 290.
DARMADY, E. M., HUGHES, K. E. A. and JONES, J. D. (1958). *Lancet*, **2,** 766.
DARMADY, E. M., HUGHES, K. E. A., JONES, J. D., PRINCE, D. and TUKE, WINIFRED
(1961). *J. clin. Path.*, **14,** 39.
DARMADY, E. M., HUGHES, K. E. A., JONES, J. D. and TUKE, WINIFRED (1958). *Lancet*,
2, 769.
DARMADY, E. M., HUGHES, K. E. A. and TUKE, W. (1957). *J. clin. Path.*, **10,** 291.
DAVIS, F. L. and WILLIAMS, O. B. (1948). *J. Bact.*, **56,** 555.
DAVIS, H. (1934). *Quart. J. Pharm.*, **7,** 379.
DAVISON, J. E. (1951). *Pharm. J.*, **167,** 190.
DECKER, H. M., CITEK, F. J., HARSTAD, J. B., GROSS, N. H. and PIPER, F. J. (1954).
Appl. Microbiol., **2,** 33.
DESROSIER, N. W. and ESSELEN, W. B. (1951). *J. Bact.*, **61,** 541.
DICKSON, E. C. (1928). *Proc. Soc. exp. Biol., N.Y.*, **25,** 426.
EL-BISI, H. M. and ORDAL, Z. J. (1956a). *J. Bact.*, **71,** 1.
EL-BISI, H. M. and ORDAL, Z. J. (1956b). *J. Bact.*, **71,** 10.
ESTY, J. R. and MEYER, K. F. (1922). *J. infect. Dis.*, **31,** 650.
EVANS, F. R. and CURRAN, H. R. (1943). *J. Bact.*, **45,** 47.
FALLON, R. J. and PYNE, J. R. (1963). *Lancet*, **1,** 1200.
FRANK, H. A. and CAMPBELL, L. L. (1955). *Appl. Microbiol.*, **3,** 300.
FRIEDMAN, C. A. and HENRY, B. S. (1938). *J. Bact.*, **36,** 99.
HANSEN, N.-H. and RIEMANN, H. (1963). *J. appl. Bact.*, **26,** 314.
HEADLEE, M. R. (1931). *J. infect. Dis.*, **48,** 328.

144   Disinfection and sterilization

HENFREY, K. M. (1961). *Hosp. Engr*, **15**, 260.
HENRY, P. S. H. (1959). *J. appl. Bact.*, **22**, 159.
HENRY, P. S. H. (1964). *J. appl. Bact.*, **27**.
HENRY, P. S. H. and SCOTT, E. (1963). *J. appl. Bact.*, **26**, 234.
HIRSCH, A. (1953). *Proc. Soc. appl. Bact.*, **16**, 100.
HOWIE, J. W. and TIMBURY, M. C. (1956). *Lancet*, **271**, 669.
HUMPHREY, A. E. and NICKERSON, J. T. P. (1961). *Appl. Microbiol.*, **9**, 282.
JACKSON, H. and WOODBINE, M. (1962). *J. appl. Bact.*, **25**, viii.
JONES, O. and PEARCE, EVELYN (1954). *J. appl. Bact.*, **17**, 272.
KELSEY, J. C. (1958). *Lancet*, **1**, 306.
KELSEY, J. C. (1959). *The Operation of Sterilizing Autoclaves:* Report of a Symposium, p. 22: Pharmaceutical Press, London.
KELSEY, J. C. (1961). *J. clin. Path.*, **14**, 313.
KEYNAN, A., MURRELL, W. G. and HALVORSON, H. O. (1961). *Nature, Lond.*, **192**, 1211.
KNAYSI, G. (1948). *Bact. Rev.*, **12**, 19.
KNOX, R., PENICKETT, E. J. K. and DUNCAN, MARY E. (1960). *J. appl. Bact.*, **23**, 21.
KNOX, R. and PENICKETT, E. J. K. (1958). *Brit. med. J.*, **1**, 680.
KURZWEIL, H. (1954). *Z. Hyg. InfektKr.*, **140**, 29.
LAMANNA, C. (1942). *J. Bact.*, **44**, 29.
LIGHT, J. S. and HODES, F. L. (1943). *Amer. J. publ. Hlth*, **33**, 1451.
LONG, S. K. and WILLIAMS, O. B. (1959). *J. Bact.*, **77**, 545.
MACAULEY, D. M. and JAMES, N. (1963). *Appl. Microbiol.*, **11**, 90.
MAGOON, C. A. (1926). *J. infect. Dis.*, **38**, 429.
MALLOCH, M. McG. (1951). *Pharm. J.*, **167**, 49.
MATTICK, A. T. R. and HISCOX, EDITH R. (1945). *Proc. Soc. appl. Bact.*, p. 78.
Medical Research Council, Report by Working Party on Pressure—Steam Sterilizers (1959). *Lancet*, **1**, 425.
Medical Research Council, Report by Working Party on Pressure—Steam Sterilizers (2nd communication) (1960). *Lancet*, **2**, 1243.
MICHENER, H. D., THOMPSON, P. A. and LEWIS, J. C. (1959a). Report No. ARS 74-11: U.S. Dept. of Agriculture, Western Utilization Research Division, Washington.
MICHENER, H. D., THOMPSON, P. A. and LEWIS, J. C. (1959b). *Appl. Microbiol.*, **7**, 166.
MORRISON, E. W. and RETTGER, L. F. (1930a). *J. Bact.*, **20**, 299.
MORRISON, E. W. and RETTGER, L. F. (1930b). *J. Bact.*, **20**, 313.
NELSON, F. E. (1943). *J. Bact.*, **45**, 395.
NICHOLS, AGNES A. (1940). *J. dairy Res.*, **11**, 274.
Nuffield Provincial Hospitals Trust (1958). *Present Sterilizing Practice in Six Hospitals*, N.P.H.T., London.
OAG, R. K. (1940). *J. Path. Bact.*, **51**, 137.
O'BRIEN, R. H. and PARISH, H. J. (1935). *Quart. J. Pharm.*, **8**, 94.
OLSEN, A. M. and SCOTT, W. J. (1946). *Nature, Lond.*, **157**, 337.
ORTENZIO, L. F., STUART, L. S. and FRIEDL, J. L. (1953). *J. Ass. off. agric. Chem.*, **36**, 480.
PENIKETT, E. J. K., ROWE, T. W. and ROBSON, EVELYN (1959). *J. appl. Bact.*, **21**, 282.
PERKINS, J. J. (1956). *Principles and Methods of Sterilization:* Thomas, Springfield, Illinois.
RAHN, O. (1943). *Biodynamica*, **4**, 86.
RAHN, O. (1945). *Bact. Rev.*, **9**, 1.
RAHN, O. and SCHROEDER, W. R. (1941). *Biodynamica*, **3**, 199.
RANSOM, S. E. and HUEBNER, R. J. (1951). *Amer. J. Hyg.*, **53**, 110.
REED, J. M., BOHRER, C. W. and CAMERON, E. J. (1951). *Food Res.*, **16**, 383.
REYNOLDS, H. and LICHTENSTEIN, H. (1952). *Bact. Rev.*, **16**, 126.
ROSS, K. F. A. and BILLING, EVE (1957). *J. gen. Microbiol.*, **16**, 418.
SAVAGE, R. M. (1937). *Quart. J. Pharm.*, **10**, 459.
SAVAGE, R. M. (1944). *Quart. J. Pharm.*, **17**, 165.
SAVAGE, R. M. (1959). *The Operation of Sterilizing Autoclaves*—Report of a Symposium, p. 1: Pharmaceutical Press, London.
SCOTT, A. C. (1957). *Lancet*, **273**, 633.
SOMMER, E. W. (1930). *J. infect. Dis.*, **46**, 85.
SUGIYAMA, H. (1951). *J. Bact.*, **62**, 81.
THIEL, C. C., BURTON, H. and McCLEMONT, J. (1952). *Proc. Soc. appl. Bact.*, **15**, 53.

TOPLEY and WILSON's *Principles of Bacteriology and Immunity* (1955). Revised by
MILES, A. A. and WILSON, G. S.; 4th Ed: Arnold, London.
WALTER, C. W. (1940). *Surg. Gynec. Obstet.*, **71**, 414.
WALTER, C. W. (1948). *Aseptic Treatment of Wounds:* Macmillan, New York.
WELLS, C. and WHITWELL, F. R. (1960). *Lancet*, **2**, 643.
WILKINSON, G. R. and PEACOCK, F. G. (1961). *J. Pharm. Pharmacol.*, **13**, 72T.
WILKINSON, G. R., PEACOCK, F. G. and ROBINS, E. L. (1960). *J. Pharm. Pharmacol.*,
12, 197T.
WILLIAMS, C. C., MERRILL, C. M. and CAMERON, E. J. (1937). *Food Res.*, **2**, 369.
WILLIAMS, O. B. (1929). *J. infect. Dis.*, **44**, 421.
WILLIAMS, O. B. and FLEMING, F. R. (1952). *Antibiot. Chemoth.*, **2**, 75.
WILLIAMS, O. B. and HARPER, O. F. (1951). *J. Bact.*, **61**, 551.
WILLIAMS, O. B. and REED, J. M. (1942). *J. infect. Dis.*, **71**, 225.
WILLIAMS, O. B. and ROBERTSON, W. J. (1954). *J. Bact.*, **67**, 377.
WILLIAMS, T. F. (1936). *J. Bact.*, **32**, 589.
WYNN, E. S. and FOSTER, J. W. (1948). *J. Bact.*, **55**, 61.
YESAIR, J. and CAMERON, E. J. (1936). *J. Bact.*, **31**, 2.

CHAPTER 6

RADIATION STERILIZATION

THE range of radiations which have been used for killing micro-organisms fall into two groups: (a) the ionizing radiations comprising X-rays, gamma rays, cathode rays, beta rays and the relatively heavy particulate neutrons, protons, etc., and (b) the longer electromagnetic and ultrasonic waves comprising ultraviolet rays of wavelength 2,000 to 4,000 Angstrom (A) (1A = 1/10,000 micron), infrared, and radiofrequency radiations, and ultrasonic waves of very high frequency. The terms 'radiation sterilization', 'cold sterilization' and 'electronic sterilization', terms which have become quite commonplace in present-day parlance, apply exclusively to the various forms of ionizing radiations; they do not include ultraviolet irradiations, and they represent the field in which the greatest advances have been made in the most recent years. Infrared radiations can be dismissed immediately as having no antibacterial activity apart from the heat effect.

The salutary influence of sunlight in preventing the spread of disease has been known for centuries, but it was only towards the end of the last century that it was realized that the radiations primarily responsible lie in the ultraviolet range of wavelengths. This discovery coincided approximately with Roentgen's discovery in 1895 of X-rays, the potentialities of which were immediately recognized as lethal agents to pathogenic organisms, and therefore of value in biology and in therapy. In later years, other electromagnetic and ionizing radiations were discovered, as well as supersonic vibrations, and many advances were made subsequently in the knowledge of their physical properties, in methods of generating and harnessing them and, particularly for present interests, in assessing their characteristics as microbicidal agents.

In terms of ionizing sterilization, the most spectacular and rapid advances have been made only within the last two decades, and accelerated under the stimulus of the more recent developments of the various atomic research projects.

The ensuing pages give a summary of the characteristics, limitations and practical applications of each of the various types of radiation, but it can be stated at the outset that the ionizing radiations hold the greatest promise for general sterilizing purposes, especially in the pharmaceutical and food industries. Ultraviolet irradiation has now been fairly accurately assessed as a vector in air hygiene in the prevention of cross-infection and more recently as a means of disinfecting water supplies, and ultrasonics are still in the development phase, offering some possibilities for treating liquids. The last

146

are somewhat different in character from the other forms of radiation, being mainly associated with physical disruption, and so they are dealt with in Chapter 9.

Mechanisms of disinfecting actions

The mechanisms of the disinfecting actions of the various radiations are not wholly understood, but broadly speaking they result from interferences in the cellular metabolism. Such interferences are all of a molecular nature and can be caused by the breakdown, or changes in the structure, of essential cell metabolites such as amino-acids, nucleic acids and the protein complexes, including the cellular enzymes. Wyckoff (1930) has calculated that "the sensitive cell constituents whose destruction leads to cell death must have a volume which is less than 0·06 of the bacterium itself." If this is true then it seems reasonable that interference with a single molecule in the sensitive 'target' volume of a vegetative bacterial cell could suffice to render it non-viable (Lea, Haines and Bretscher, 1941) or that with viruses a single ionization in the nucleoprotein complex could render it inactive (Lea and Salaman, 1946).

It follows that such interferences cannot be confined to those molecules constituting the microbial cell but must include all similar molecules in the environment. Thus in the case of foods, milk and certain pharmaceutical preparations, molecular changes may be induced by the radiations which, as well as sterilizing them, also affect their palatability, their safe storage period or their nutritive or therapeutic value, and this constitutes one of the main disadvantages of radiation treatment. Some of the more important aspects of this will be mentioned in later sections.

Death rate of micro-organisms

In common with other killing processes, the death rate of organisms under the influence of most lethal radiations follows an exponential form, although there are some cases where this simple relationship does not hold and where the relationship tends to follow the more sigmoidal rule. In general, the exponential form is indicative of a reaction of a unimolecular type, whereas the sigmoidal form suggests a bi- or poly-molecular reaction, and in terms of bactericidal activity they can be accounted for by assuming that each cell possesses certain vulnerable 'targets' in which one or more 'hits', that is, ionizations or molecular disruptions, must be registered to bring about its inactivation. For those cells requiring only one 'hit' the exponential form of response is obtained, whereas for those requiring two or more 'hits' the more complex sigmoidal form is found. These different forms of response are well illustrated with the haploid and diploid yeasts, the former of which require only one 'hit' per cell and the latter two 'hits'. With the bacteria, the position is not quite as clearly defined; most of them appear to comply with the 'one hit' mechanism, but some, *e.g.* certain strains of *Escherichia coli*, indicate a 'two hit' mechanism (Gunter and Kohn, 1956). Amongst the spores, there seem to be both types, the differentiation being based apparently on the dipicolinic acid content (Woese, 1958, 1959). The 'multi-hit' spores give rise to 'two hit' vegetative cells, and the 'single hits' to 'single hits', and one might wonder if this might be associated with calcium dipicolinate- and L-alanine-induced germination (Keynan and Halvorson, 1962).

This 'target' theory of radiation disinfection was discussed in detail by Lea (1946) and it was supported subsequently by Pollard and Forro (1951), Epstein (1953), and Spear (1953). Kelner (1955), however, believes that it cannot hold in all cases because many of the effects have been shown to be reversible and preventable. The theory is based primarily on physical considerations, but this does not preclude the possibility of it also having chemical implications, because one of the results of the primary activation of the single molecule target is to disrupt the physical structure of the molecule and so probably set up a chain of chemical reactions.

When the death-rate is exponential, the plot is fully defined by the expression

$$N_1/N_0 = e^{-Lt}$$

(where N_0 is the initial number of organisms, N_1 is the number of survivors at time, t, and L is the death-rate constant). Wyckoff (1930) has defined L in terms of the average number of quanta of energy absorbed per second, a, and so has written the expression thus:

$$\frac{N_1}{N_0} = e^{-0.06at}$$

Being exponential, the complete death-rate curve can be drawn from measurements of the percentage inactivation produced by a specific radiation dose or time of exposure, and, since the expression contains a natural logarithm, the survival level of 36·8 per cent (or 37 per cent) is usually taken. This is known as the *mean lethal dose*, often misleadingly abbreviated simply to *lethal dose*. It is naturally of quite a different order of magnitude from the true lethal dose, or *sterilizing dose*, which is, of course, the dose of greater practical importance.

The total dose of any irradiation can be varied by adjusting either the intensity of emission or the duration of exposure to a fixed radiation. Within certain broad limits the choice is immaterial, because in radiation sterilization the efficacy depends on the *total* dose received and is, therefore, independent of time. It follows, however, that in any comparative quantitative work there must be a means of measuring the amount of radiation falling on the test subject. Such standards exist, and they will be discussed in their appropriate sections.

High energy ionizing radiations

Although their lethal effects on micro-organisms and other living cells have been long known, it is only within the last 20 years or so really serious and vigorous attention has been given to the possibilities of using X-rays and other ionizing radiations for sterilizing purposes. The main reasons for this sudden stimulation of activity appear to be three-fold: (a) the development of powerful electron generators and accelerators in the form of the Capacitron, the Van de Graaff accelerator, the linear accelerator and the like; (b) the increasingly abundant supplies of radioactive isotopes, notably Cobalt 60 and Caesium 137 as by-products of atomic fission reactions, and (c) advances in the knowledge of the control and harnessing of these radiations, together with the protection of personnel from their ill-effects. The major contributions in this field have originated mainly from the Isotope Division of the British Atomic Energy Research Establishment, the Food Investigation organization of the Department of Scientific and Industrial Research (Hannan, Ingram and colleagues), the United States Atomic Energy Commission, the Massachusetts Institute of Technology (Proctor and Goldblith), the Electronized Chemicals Corporation (Brasch and Huber) and the General Electric Research Laboratories (Bellamy and Lawton), but other substantial contributions have been made by the Quartermasters Corps of the U.S. Army, as well as by several other industrial organizations and British and American universities. For further information on many of the publications from these sources the reader is referred to the monograph by Hannan (1955) on food preservation, to several books written in the last seven years on the subject and especially to the various international conferences held since 1956, notably the United Nations' *Peaceful Uses of Atomic Energy* and those on the *Preservation of Foods by Ionizing Radiations*.

Types and sources of ionizing radiations

The most important types of ionizing radiations are listed in Table 10. It would be out of place and irrelevant in the context of this book to describe the methods available for the production of these radiations – that is the province of the physicist and the electronic engineer – but it is desirable to know something of their nature, hence a few short paragraphs on this aspect are here inserted.

When a high voltage potential is established between a cathode and anode, or series of anodes, in an evacuated tube, the cathode emits beams of electrons known as *cathode rays*. Under the influence of the electrostatic forces present, the electrons so emitted are not only accelerated, and thereby their kinetic energy and penetrability increased, but they can also be formed into a narrow beam and extracted from the tube through a 'window'. This in effect is the principle behind the construction of the various generators and accelerators now available. The energy gained by an electron moving through a potential difference of 1 volt is 1 *electron volt* (eV), and the common unit of reference is the 'million electron volts' (MeV), this being the order of voltage required for sterilization purposes.

Beta rays are similar in character to cathode rays and, like gamma rays, are emitted naturally by radioactive elements. Their average energy is of a lower order than that of cathode rays from modern generators, and so their powers of penetration are lower.

When a cathode beam strikes a metal target, preferably one of high atomic number, the electrons are absorbed and the absorbed energy is converted into electromagnetic radiations of short wavelength known as *X-rays*.

TABLE 10

Some well-known ionizing radiations
(after Hannan, 1955)

Radiation	Nature	Main source
Electromagnetic waves		
X-rays	wavelength approximately	Electrical generators
Gamma rays	10A–10⁻⁴A	radioactive elements
Particulate radiations		
Cathode rays	Fast electrons	Electrical generators
Beta rays	Fast electrons	Radioactive elements
Fast protons	Mass 1, +ve charge	Electrical generators and
Fast neutrons	Mass 1, no charge	nuclear reactions
Fast deuterons	Mass 2, +ve charge	Electrical generators
Alpha rays	Mass 4, 2 +ve charges	Radioactive elements
Nuclear fission fragments	Heavy atomic particles	Nuclear reactions

Only a small percentage of the energy of an initial electron beam emerges in the X-ray beam, the remainder being dissipated and lost in the target area. Various types of generator are available, but generally the cathode beam is produced in an accelerating tube and the resultant X-rays escape through the walls of the tube or through a specially constructed window. The spectrum of an X-ray emission can vary in wavelength between about 10A and 10⁻⁴A, the actual range depending on the voltage and the angle of the incident beam on the target, the nature of the target material and the nature of the window. The longer wavelength group, or 'soft' rays, are produced at voltages up to about 100 kilovolts and have relatively low penetrating power, whereas the shorter wavelength group, or 'hard' rays, are produced at higher voltages and have greater penetrating power.

Gamma rays resemble X-rays of short wavelength and therefore are akin to hard X-rays. They are emitted by both natural and artificial radioactive elements and their main difference from X-rays is that they are emitted from a given element at one or two fixed wavelengths instead of in a continuous spectrum.

The remaining forms of ionizing radiations are all relatively heavy and particulate and have the property of bringing about nuclear transformations and of inducing radioactivity. Whilst this may be of no concern in treating micro-organisms it can most certainly be disadvantageous and deleterious in the products being sterilized, therefore these radiations are not at present regarded as having any value for practical sterilization.

Penetrating power

Powers of penetration into liquids and solids of all types are amongst the important practical attributes of all ionizing radiations. Of the electron radiations, cathode rays have the greatest energies and therefore the

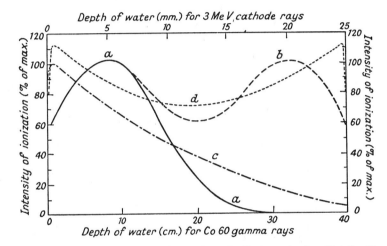

Fɪɢ. 9. *Intensity of ionization at various depths in water irradiated with 3 MeV cathode rays and Co 60 gamma rays*

——————— = curve for cathode rays irradiated from one side
— — — — = curve for cathode rays irradiated from opposite sides
—·——·——· = curve for gamma rays irradiated from one side
— — — — — = curve for gamma rays irradiated from opposite sides

greatest penetrating power, but X- and gamma rays, being electromagnetic radiations, have much greater relative powers of penetration. The actual penetrating power of the electromagnetic radiations depends on their wavelength and, since the shorter waves are produced by higher energy primary electron beams, it follows that hard X-rays penetrate deeper than do soft X-rays. In terms of effective penetrating distance cathode rays may only go to a maximum of 1 cm in water for each 2 million volts of energy, whereas the intensity of a similar powered X-ray beam diminishes by only one-half for each 10 cm depth (Lea, 1946).

Because of the different nature of cathode and X- radiations, there may well be certain differences in the distribution of ionization in a medium, as well as in the rate of fall in intensity of ionization through the medium. To illustrate these points, Fig. 9, compiled from diagrams given by Hannan (1955), shows the variations in intensity of ionization produced in water at various depths when irradiated: (a) from one side and from both sides of a cell by cathode rays at 3 MeV, and (b) by gamma rays from a Cobalt 60 source at photon energies of 1·17 and 1·33 MeV. With cathode rays the intensity of ionization increases initially with depth of penetration to a maximum at one-third of the total range and then falls to zero as the ionizing electrons lose their energy and become progressively more scattered, whereas with a beam of gamma rays the photons of energy are scattered and absorbed more regularly through the medium so that the intensity of ionization falls exponentially. The actual shape of the penetration diagram can be varied somewhat depending on whether the irradiating beam is broad or narrow, and so on.

Penetrating power is usually measured in relation to water. With materials other than water, it is found for cathode rays to be in inverse proportion to their densities. Since it is also related directly to the energy of the irradiating beam, the simple relationship is established:

$$\text{Penetration} \propto \frac{\text{Electron energy}}{\text{Density}}$$

With gamma rays the situation is somewhat similar, although more complex in detail.

Mechanism of the lethal action

As has been indicated earlier, the mechanism of the lethal action of high energy radiations results, as with other lethal processes, from interferences in the metabolism of the cell. The action cannot be one of general breakdown of the cell because the cell after treatment remains morphologically the same, apart sometimes from an increase in size (Lea, Haines and Coulson, 1937), it continues its normal enzyme respiratory activity (Billen, Stapleton and Hollaender, 1953), and it retains its motility at least for a short time (Lea, Haines and Bretscher, 1941; Grainger, 1947). Since, however, it is unable to reproduce normally its respiration fairly rapidly falls away. This form of lethal action suggests something quite specific and indicates that one particular compound or enzyme, fundamental to the life of the cell and therefore probably resident in the nucleus, is involved. Scholes and Weiss (1953a, 1953b, 1954) have shown that nucleic acids are readily degraded by X-rays by fragmentation through ring fission, liberation of ammonia and dephosphorylation, and Epstein (1953) has expressed the firm conviction that it is the breakdown of these acids which is the principal cause of cell inactivation, the nucleoproteins and amino acids playing only a secondary role. Errera (1955) has further pin-pointed it specifically to the disturbance of the deoxyribonucleic acid metabolism, a disturbance which apparently continues for some time after irradiation, the actual duration depending on the conditions prevailing (Conway, 1954). These points are extremely difficult to confirm because isolated substances of this nature rarely behave in the same manner as they do in nature, but some support is found in the work of Emmerson *et al.* (1960) who concluded that deoxyribonucleic acid is much more susceptible than its equivalent nucleoprotein in calf thymus extract, the difference being due to the protection afforded by the protein in the complex. The same occurred in synthetic mixtures.

In spite of these evidences there still remain some objections to the DNA-damage theory, and an alternative, proposed by Bacq and Alexander (1961), is based on the disorganization of the enzyme system of the cell consequent on the rupture of its internal membranes: this is a different concept from one of direct enzyme inactivation. It is likely, of course, that both theories may have a place, but there is some support for the later one in two groups of findings (as yet incomplete) reported by Thornley (1963). In the first place, she and her colleagues were able to correlate inversely the penicillin and radiation resistances of 15 strains of the *Achromobacter-Alkaligenes* group, and penicillin is known to act on the synthesis of cell wall material; secondly, *Micrococcus radiodurans*, a culture with exceptional radiation resistance, has an unusual multi-layered cell wall structure.

That any form of irradiation produces changes in the proteins and nucleic acids, as well as in many other compounds has been known for some time, but the mechanisms involved still remain somewhat obscure. It is quite certain, however, that they can occur either by direct action, when the radiation beam attacks directly the sensitive molecular foci of the compounds, or by indirect action, when the changes are produced through a chain of energized chemical reactions. But whether the ultimate effect be direct or indirect, the first result of any radiation energy bombardment is to cause the intercepting molecules to be elevated into a state of agitation and disruption, the degree of which depends on the energy of the particles or photons of the irradiating beam. At low energies, the effect is to induce the outer electrons into wider orbits of higher energy, thus leaving the molecule in an excited, and therefore more reactive, state; this is similar to that which occurs with ultraviolet irradiation. At higher energies, one or more electrons is actually ejected from the molecule. This leaves it as a positively charged ion, with the electron free to attach itself to another molecule thus giving rise to a negative ion. By this means, 'ion pairs' are formed. At even higher energies the electron is ejected at increased velocity and so it attacks a number of molecules before it comes to rest, thus leaving clusters of ion pairs. Finally, at energies above about 4 MeV, the atomic nucleus begins to be attacked with the result that the material itself tends to become radioactive. The generally accepted threshold level for induced activity is 5 MeV above which more and more elements become active but below which there is no danger of such an occurrence.

These effects at the different energy levels are not, of course, definitive in themselves but they lead to other energy transfers amongst which are the redistribution of the ionizing forces within the molecule and the transformation of active ions into more stable free radical forms. Moreover, they are not confined to the individual molecules, but can be transmitted to adjacent molecules. The net effect, therefore, is that some molecules in the system are disrupted, many others are unbalanced through losing or gaining electron charges and the whole is left in a high state of activity.

On these premises, direct action changes can be seen to be brought about by the transfer of the radiation beam energies to receptive molecules in their path. The effect on the receptive molecule varies considerably with its structure and size, but often it causes cleavage at weak bond linkages, the elimination of groups such as halogen atoms and the fission of certain ring structures. Frequently also free radicals are set up as a result of the cleavage and these can initiate and take part in a complex series of secondary reactions.

Indirect action changes are brought about in the same way as direct action changes, except that the molecules initially excited and disrupted are those of water. The basic effect of irradiation on the molecules of water is to produce hydroxyl radicals and free hydrogen, and these trigger off a chain of reactions, not only with other molecules of water to produce entities such as hydroxyl ions, hydrogen ions, hydroperoxide radicals ($\cdot HO_2$) and hydrogen peroxide (Weiss, 1944, 1947), but also with other molecules in the immediate vicinity. In terms of the substances most concerned with the life of the microbial cell, that is the nucleic acids and their complexes, these reactions induce deamination, dephosphorylation and other degradations, and this results in the elimination of substances required by the cell as essential metabolites.

Clearly, the detailed mechanism of the lethal actions must be highly complex and involve a number of subtle chemical changes. It is therefore useful that Kelner (1955) has presented a condensed version of the overall picture which for the sake of simplicity is worth recording here. He has suggested that the events leading to a lethal irradiation occur in three main steps: the first stage being that of the primary ionizing reaction; the second, the "middle period" of variable duration in which the secondary reactions take place; and the third involving the final alterations in the make-up and constitution of the cell consequent upon the reactions of the second stage.

This may be an oversimplified version of what occurs, nevertheless it provides a reasonable basis for the consideration of some of the fundamental aspects of the mechanisms of radiation sterilization. For example, it is probably because of the chain-form of the lethal mechanism and because of the specificity of the reactions concerned that irradiation does not necessarily cause the immediate death of the cell and that certain of its metabolic functions may continue after it has ceased to be viable. There is some evidence that death does not occur until after the first or second cell division (Lea,

Haines and Bretscher, 1941), but undoubtedly this must depend to some extent on the intensity of the lethal radiation.

It is probably not surprising that these reactions, whatever their detailed mechanisms and ultimate significance in the life of the cell, do not occur as readily in the natural cellular surroundings as they do with the free isolated substances, and that consequently the efficacy of a given irradiation dose will vary according to the local conditions prevailing. This is because in the natural state with many other compounds present in the cellular complex, the whole of the irradiation is not available for the reaction of specific interest but is dissipated between other reactions of only secondary moment. The particular target molecules are thus virtually protected by other substances constituting the protoplasm of the cell. Several examples of this type of protection both in the cell and in other milieu are given later.

Measurement of radiation and lethal doses

Radiation dose units. Since the primary effect of any high energy radiation is to produce ionizations, it is natural that the unit of dosage should be defined and measured in such terms. This, however, is a far from easy matter, because apart from the physical problems involved there is the difficult question of the loss of the incident energy through its dissipation into thermal and other secondary channels, so that measurement of any of the end-effects, such as chemical, heat and electrical changes produced in a body cannot give a true assessment of the total energy originally absorbed by the body. However, with the development of the electronic valve, the position has radically changed and now the small electrical charges associated with the ionization phenomenon can be measured with fair accuracy.

The fundamental unit used in the measurement of radiation doses is the *roentgen* (r) which is defined in terms of the number of ionizations produced per unit volume of air. It is equivalent to an energy absorption of about 83 ergs per gm of air, but the exact value is not precisely agreed. It is also a variable value depending on the nature of the absorbing material (for water it is 93 ergs per gm) and with the radiation wavelength. Two other units in common use are: (1) the *rad*, which represents an energy absorption of 100 ergs per gm of material and (2) the *rep* (roentgen-equivalent-physical) which appears to be the same as the roentgen, although opinions do not seem to be quite clear on this. For all practical purposes each of these units can be taken as equivalents, the error introduced by their interchange being comparatively small. There is now a leaning towards the use of the *rad* as the most suitable unit, although the *rep* is still frequently used. For sterilization purposes the term *Mrad*, or 1×10^6 rad, is the more practicable.

Measurement of doses. There are various methods available for measuring radiation doses, but it is not proposed to go into any technical details on this point, except to state that they are either electrometric, calorimetric or chemical. Electrometric methods involve collecting the radiation on a suitable small metal receiver and assessing the energy collected by measuring the current produced: it can be converted to a calorimetric method by assessing the energy in terms of the amount of heat generated. Electrostatic methods can also be used, and these involve passing the radiation between charged plates and measuring the change in charge so induced. Chemical methods are based mainly on oxidative changes such as the oxidation of ferrous to ferric sulphate in solution, and these methods are probably the most promising and useful.

Lethal doses. With such diverse systems of irradiation it would not be surprising to find marked differences in the doses found necessary to kill various cultures of micro-organisms. In fact, however, there is a remarkable

TABLE 11

Lethal doses of different radiations

Type of organism	Lethal doses (Mrad) from			
	Cathode rays (a)	(b)	Gamma rays (c)	X-rays (d)
Vegetative, non-pathogenic .	0·1–0·25	0·1–0·25	0·15–0·25	0·03–0·5
Vegetative, pathogenic .	0·45–0·55			
Bacterial spores . . .	0·5–2·1	0·2–0·4	c 1·5	0·5–2·0
Moulds	0·25–1·15	0·35–0·4	0·2–0·3	0·25–1·0
Yeasts	0·5–1·0	—	0·3	0·25–1·5

(a) From van de Graaff accelerators (various authors).
(b) From Capacitron pulsed beam (Huber and colleagues, quoted by Hannan, 1955).
(c) From Cobalt 60 (Lawrence, Brownell and Graikoski, 1953).
(d) From 3 MeV source (Dunn *et al.*, 1948).

degree of agreement on the subject, and a summary of the figures quoted by various investigators is given in Table 11. The rather lower values of Huber and colleagues may be explained by the fact that they used a Capacitron with a pulsated radiation, and it is possible that high doses given over a very small duration of time (it may be of the order of 1×10^6 rad per micro-second) may act differently from doses administered more continuously and evenly at a lower level.

The resistances of bacteria as they occur in the natural state are always apparently greater than when cultured in laboratory media, and the differences can be quite considerable. It is not, however a difference in actual resistance of the organism but a difference in the level of protection afforded by the natural conditions, and this is most noticeable in foods. Even so, the range of resistance between the different bacterial types is extremely large, the factor between the doses required to inactivate 90 per cent of a sensitive pseudomonad and the most resistant *Clostridium botulinum* being about 50 (Thornley, 1963). Broadly speaking, the vegetative organisms are more susceptible than are the spores, and the Gram-positive organisms tend to be more resistant than the Gram-negative ones, although there is a considerable overlap. Thus, the times found by Goldblith *et al.* (1953) to deliver a mean lethal dose from a kilocurie Cobalt-60 source were 7 minutes for *E. coli* and the pseudomonads and 13 to 39 minutes for *Staphylococcus, Streptococcus* and other species. Similarly Koh, Morehouse and Chandler (1956) reported lethal doses for the Gram-negative bacteria ranging from 0·025 to 0·25 Mrad, with a *Pseudomonas* sp., a *Salmonella* and the *Bacteroides* showing least resistance, and 0·05 to 0·5 Mrad for the Gram-positive group, with several strains of *Diplococcus pneumoniae* showing the greatest resistances. Certain *Achromobacter* species isolated from chicken meat can also exhibit high resistance

TABLE 12

Percentage kills of various micro-organisms with different doses

| | Percentage kill by | | |
	35,000 rad	100,000 rad	500,000 rad
E. coli	92·86	99·97	100
Ps. fluorescens . . .	99·97	99·999	100
Staph. aureus , . .	94·6	99·998	100
B. stearothermophilus . .	—	99·0	99·99
B. thermoacidurans . .	—	95·41	99·997
Torulopsis rosea . . .	67·3	97·98	99·999

(Thornley, 1962), but outstanding in this sphere is the organism aptly named *Micrococcus radiodurans*, a red-pigmented coccus found in minced beef and pork which can withstand, even in isolated culture, up to 6 × 10⁶ rad (Anderson *et al.*, 1956). From Table 11 it is also clear that the bacterial spores comprise the most resistant group, and in particular the high resistance of *Clostridium botulinum* (Proctor and Goldblith, 1951; O'Meara, 1952; Thornley, 1963) needs special emphasis because of its importance in food canning. They were the most resistant of a series of spore-forming and thermophilic food-spoilage organisms examined by Morgan and Reed (1954), requiring something over 2 × 10⁶ rad to effect sterilization. Amongst the foods, beef, pork and peas appear to offer the most protection, doses as high as 4 Mrad being necessary to prevent spoilage (Pratt *et al.*, 1959). The toxins are denatured about the same rate as are their corresponding spores (Wagenaar, Dack and Murrell, 1959), but spoilage enzymes can survive much greater doses. These might require doses up to 10 × 10⁶ rad to inactivate them.

The figures quoted in Table 11 give the range of doses necessary to effect complete destruction of the organisms concerned, but the doses necessary to effect a near-total kill of the order of 99 per cent, bearing in mind the logarithmic order of death, are much less. Often, for instance, a dose of 100,000 rad will bring about a kill of over 99·9 per cent whereas 500,000 rad are necessary to finish off the remaining 0·1 per cent. Some figures given by Dunn *et al.* (1948) illustrate this (Table 12).

Similar information is available from Goldblith *et al.* (1953) who demonstrated that the dose necessary to produce a complete kill might be anything from 7 to 200 times the exposure required to effect a 63 per cent kill. These doses do not vary with the concentrations of the organisms, provided they are initially high, as under these circumstances the fraction of a population killed by a given dose is independent of the number initially present (Lea, 1946; Morgan and Reed, 1954). There is some evidence, however, that at high concentrations there is a mutual protective effect (Koh, Morehouse and Chandler, 1956) and this may well be due to the rapid removal of oxygen from the suspension consequent on the respiration of the large numbers of cells in the suspension (Gunter and Kohn, 1956). In dilute suspensions the percentage inactivation seems to vary with the initial concentration (Hollaender, Stapleton and Martin, 1951; Biagini, 1953; Edwards, Petersen and Cumming, 1954).

Dried organisms, of course, show a different order of sensitivity from those in aqueous suspension, but here the system is quite different. It is discussed in more detail later.

There is no relationship between heat resistance and resistance to radiation.

A great deal of work has been done on the viruses, mainly with small doses with a view to determining the mode of the lethal action. Their sensitivities appear to be of the same order as those of the bacterial spores, although there are notable and significant exceptions. Jordan and Kempe (1956) examined the effect of gamma radiations on several types and found an inverse relationship between particle size and lethal dose, the smaller viruses in crude suspensions requiring the higher doses. Thus, the vaccinia virus was inactivated by doses of 2–2·5 Mrad, Lansing polio virus by 3·5–4 Mrad and the encephalitis viruses by 4–4·5 Mrad. With pulsed radiations from a Capacitron machine the inactivating doses are lower, 0·85 Mrad being adequate for rabies virus (Traub *et al.*, 1951), 2·5 Mrad for polio (Dick *et al.*, 1951) and 0·8 Mrad for vaccinia (Kaplan, 1960). Hannan (1955) has stated, however, that doses as high as 5×10^6 rad may be needed in some cases, and Kaplan (1960) has quoted one such case in which vaccinia virus freeze-dried from 5 per cent peptone solution was mainly killed by 3–4 Mrad but a few viable particles remained even with doses as high as 11 Mrad.

Factors affecting lethal activity

In common with other disinfection processes, the cultural conditions of the organism before irradiation treatment, the conditions of actual treatment and the conditions for recovery of the treated organisms can each affect the lethal activity, real or apparent, of ionizing radiations.

The 'oxygen' effect. Undoubtedly the most significant factor affecting sterilization rate is the oxygen tension during irradiation, the significant concentration lying between 1 and 10 mg per litre. Below 1 mg per litre there is little observable effect, and above the 10 mg level there is no enhancement of its activity. According to the authors concerned (Hollaender and Stapleton, 1953) these findings show the importance of radical formation and the consequent oxidative changes involved in the lethal process. The phenomenon has been demonstrated with yeasts and with larger living cells as well as with the bacteria. Quantitative tests with washed cells of *E. coli* have shown them to be three times more sensitive in the presence of oxygen than in its absence (Hollaender, Stapleton and Martin, 1951), and with some strains of *Pseudomonas* the factor is as high as four (Thornley, 1962). Anaerobic organisms are said to require 10 to 12 times the dose needed to kill aerobic ones (Hollaender and Stapleton, 1953) and bacterial spores are also said to manifest the effect but to a much smaller degree, although comparatively little work seems to have been done with them. With a spray-dried powder containing *Bacillus subtilis* spores, Tallentire (1958) found a substantial difference in the death-rates between the normally dried material and the same powder subsequently hard-dried and sealed in air or in high vacuum, the factor between the last two being about 100-fold with the air-dried material lying in between.

It also appears possible for post-irradiation conditions to affect the survival level, for these same hard-dried powders sealed in air and subjected to a dose of 5 Mrad showed a rapid decline during the 24 hours immediately following irradiation and tailing off in about 70 hours, whereas those sealed in vacuum showed a constant survivor level (Tallentire and Davies, 1961). The total depression in the survivor count was about 99 per cent.

From the evidence available it seems that the 'oxygen effect' arises from the formation of the oxidized radicals of water, namely ˙OH and ˙HO$_2$, and also from the formation of peroxides. If this is so, then any substance in a suspension of organisms capable of reacting competitively with the free radicals will reduce the lethal efficacy of the radiation. Thus, amino acids, proteins and nutrient broth all give protection (Hollaender, Stapleton and Martin, 1951; Moos, 1952; Biagini, 1953) and quite low concentrations of gelatin also act in a similar manner.

Huber, Brasch and Waly (1953) claim that there is no oxygen effect with pulsed radiations from a Capacitron. They have not published their detailed findings to support such a claim, but it seems likely that under irradiating doses at such high intensities for such short periods the water radicals produced do not react with oxygen and other external chemical entities but rather react with themselves, and so preclude the possibility of an oxygen effect. There is evidence in other fields of chemical irradiation treatment that this may be the case.

Sulphydryl and other protecting compounds. Besides the protection afforded naturally by amino acids, proteins and other cellular constituents (Bellamy, 1955), several other groups of substances including sulphydryl compounds such as cysteine and glutathione, thiourea, hydrosulphites, metabisulphite and other reducing agents are also active in a similar manner (Burnett *et al.*, 1952). Their modes of action differ, however, with the type of compound. Thus, the reducing compounds are effective simply by their ability to combine with free oxygen, and the sulphydryl compounds probably act as acceptors of free radicals (Burnett *et al.*, 1951), although Hollaender and Stapleton (1953) think it may also be due to their removal of oxygen. That this is the more likely explanation appears from the observed effect of hydrogen sulphide on the lethal efficacy of X-rays on bacterial spores. If irradiated in the presence of the gas there is a 75 per cent loss in killing power, but if it is introduced after the irradiation the loss is 50 per cent (Powers and Kaleta, 1960). The reason given for the lower killing power in the first instance is that the hydrogen sulphide prevents the formation of radicals which are toxic when combined with oxygen, and in the second instance such radicals produced by the irradiation react with the gas and are thereby removed.

Nitrites and several hydroxy compounds including alcohols and glycols also decrease the efficacy of irradiation and this is thought to be due to their capacity to modify the metabolic processes of the organisms. In this connexion it should be realized that any substance which can act as a stimulant to metabolic respiration will automatically reduce the oxygen tension and thus assume the role of a protective agent. The concentrations at which these compounds become effective vary somewhat, but Hollaender and Stapleton (1953) quote levels of $0\cdot0001M$ for reducing compounds, up to $0\cdot04$ per cent for sulphydryl compounds and up to $3\cdot5$ per cent for the hydroxy compounds. In passing, it might also be mentioned that catalase is also a protective agent by virtue of its reactivity with the hydrogen peroxide generated during irradiation (Chance, 1952).

Resistance can also be induced by subjecting cultures to near-lethal radiation doses (Erdman, Thatcher and MacQueen, 1961). To do this it is necessary to allow a survivor level of only $0\cdot01$ per cent or less, and then the irradiation dose is immediately increased up to two-fold. It does not occur with all strains, and at the same time often gives rise to mutants with different antigenic structures.

Sensitizing agents. There is no real evidence of substances other than oxygen being able to sensitize micro-organisms, although several have been thought to do so. There are, of course, many compounds, including the antibiotics, which contribute their own toxicities, but this is not sensitization in its proper sense. In this category also come the mineral salts.

One way of surmounting the problem of high resistance amongst the spore-formers is to induce germination by adding compounds such as L-alanine and adenosine, and this is certainly successful with aqueous suspensions of *Bacillus cereus* (Kan, Goldblith and Proctor, 1958).

Age and pH of cultures. Stapleton (1955) has observed that variations in X-ray sensitivity occur with the growth phase of the organisms. The changes take place in three stages and are illustrated in Fig. 10. The first stage is a continuous increase in resistance during the lag phase of growth until the end of that phase; the second is a rapid fall during the log-growth phase reaching a minimum at the end of the phase; the third is a steady return to the original resistance during the 'stationary' phase.

Changes in pH value over the range 2 to 10 appear to affect the susceptibilities of vegetative organisms and spores but little, although there is

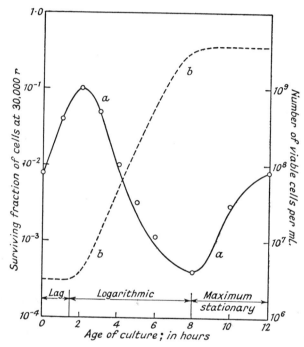

Fig. 10. *Survival at a constant dose of X-rays as a function of age of culture*
(after Stapleton, 1955)

——— = surviving fraction at 30,000 rep for cells at ages indicated
– – – – – = growth curve

sometimes evidence of a rather higher resistance in the neutral zone at a pH value of 7 down to about 5.

Freezing. In the normally accepted sense of the term there is no temperature coefficient for radiation sterilization, but from some evidence available there seems to be a marked reduction in sensitivity as suspensions of bacteria change from the liquid state to the frozen solid state. According to Denny *et al.* (1959) the factor between freezing and room temperature is about 50 per cent. Originally it had been thought that the sensitivities of spores at least remained the same down to −20° (Lea, Haines and Coulson, 1936), but subsequent work has shown the reverse to be the case with yeasts (Wood, 1954), *E. coli* (Field, Proctor and Goldblith, 1957), *Staph. aureus* and *B. subtilis* spores (Lawton and Bellamy, 1954) and *Cl. botulinum* spores in phosphate buffer (Denny *et al.*, 1959). On the other hand Kempe *et al.* (1956) found no variation in the range $-80°$ to $+80°$, apart from a curiously high resistance at $25°$, neither did Field, Proctor and Goldblith (1957) with *B. thermoacidurans* or *Cl. sporogenes*, although they did with *B. subtilis*. The reason for these differences could lie in species differences, in the variable irradiation doses applied or in the type of recovery medium used, of which the last two would result in different survivor levels being measured. The most likely explanation however is to be found in the present imprecision of such work, for, as Ingram and Thornley (1961) have put it, "it has become apparent that, because of limitations inherent in this method of approach, such experiments would be incapable of establishing appreciable differences . . ., if any existed."

If such a state does exist, it might be attributed to the loss of mobility of the free active radicals with a consequent reduction in the efficacy of the indirect lethal action, the direct lethal action being unaltered; alternatively if the effect is selective with different types of organism it may be associated with a particular physiological state immediately before or after the irradiation, a view which links with the findings of Tallentire and Davies (1961) as quoted on page 159.

Moisture. The removal of water from a system inevitably increases the resistance of the organisms concerned, and the main reasons for this are threefold: first, the indirect action changes induced by the $H^{\cdot}$ and $^{\cdot}OH$ radical formation are largely eliminated; secondly, the mobility of any free radicals formed is naturally reduced in the absence of a continuous water phase, and, thirdly, organisms in the dry state are more intensively protected by the surrounding menstruum. Examples include the spores of *B. subtilis* dried on kaolin (Tallentire, 1958), the protracted survival of vaccinia virus freeze-dried from peptone solution (Kaplan, 1960), both of which have been discussed in more detail on earlier pages, and the extension of the median lethal dose for *E. coli* from 0·36 Mrad in the wet state to a maximum of 1·24 Mrad 24 hours after freeze-drying (Bhattacharjee, 1961).

From Tallentire's subsequent work (Tallentire, Dickinson and Collett, 1963) the change in resistance of *B. megaterium* spores takes place comparatively suddenly as the moisture content passes through the critical range equivalent to a partial pressure of 8 to 5 torr, on either side of which it has a constant value. The critical range undoubtedly varies with the bacterial species and with their physical and cultural conditions.

Heat sensitization. Although, apart from the freezing effect, temperature does not seem to influence the rate of kill during irradiation, it plays an important part in pre- and post-irradiation treatment. The cells of *E. coli* and of yeasts can be sensitized by heating to sub-lethal temperatures before irradiation and it is claimed that milk can likewise be more easily sterilized by flash-heating to 74·5° (Huber, Brasch and Waly, 1953). That this heat treatment gives rise to a sensitization within the cell is evidenced by the fact that heat-resistant organisms, that is, bacterial spores, are not so affected (Morgan and Reed, 1954; Kempe, 1955).

However, pre-irradiation renders bacterial spores much more sensitive to subsequent heat treatment (Morgan and Reed, 1954; Kempe, 1955), and this is important in relation to food processing although it has been stated that such a process would be impracticable commercially. Cook and Roberts (1963) for instance, in a short series of experiments with *Bacillus subtilis* spores, showed a small increase in the apparent survivor count after heating at 60° for 15 minutes but a decrease by up to 34 per cent when the heating was at 90° for 5 minutes, in contrast to a normal 'heat-activation' increase of 82 per cent with unirradiated cells. The actual degree of heat sensitization increased with the irradiation dose, as had earlier been found by Kempe (1955) who subsequently discovered a log relationship between the F_0 value (the number of minutes required to sterilize at 250°F) and the radiation dose (Kempe, Graikoski and Bonventre, 1959). In minced beef inoculated with anaerobic spores, the F_0 fell from 7–8 to about 4·5 after 1 Mrad pre-treatment and to 2·5–3 after 1·5 Mrad. A dose of 1·8 Mrad reduced the heating time to about one-quarter of the original. The suspending medium is important in this respect because spores are more resistant and less easily sensitized in a ham medium containing 3·5 per cent of solids than in water, and the protection is even greater in a ham purée with 22 per cent solids (Kan, Goldblith and Proctor, 1957).

Recovery conditions. In terms of post-irradiation treatment, the greatest influence on the recovery of organisms may be expected from the nutritive properties of the culture medium and the temperature of incubation. In this respect *E. coli*, particularly strain B, seems to behave quite differently from other organisms in that it requires suboptimal conditions for optimal growth. With this organism, there is maximum apparent survival after treatment with X- or gamma rays at incubation temperatures well below normal (Hollaender, Stapleton and Billen, 1953). The actual temperature varies for the different strains of this organism and ranges between 12° and 21° with a mean at about 8°. By incubating irradiated organisms for 24 hours at this suboptimal temperature recoveries of up to one hundred times those at 37° have been recorded (Hollaender and Stapleton, 1953).

No reactivation is found by exposure to visible light rays, such as occurs after ultraviolet irradiation (see below).

In terms of the recovery culture medium the best results are obtained with rich medium containing yeast extract, meat extract and even blood, although often there is little to choose between them (Freeman and Bridges, 1960). Detailed investigation (Stapleton, Sbarra and Hollaender, 1955) has shown this to be due to the presence of ribonucleic acid metabolites such as glutamic acid, serine, methionine and tryptophane, along with guanine and uracil, and this can be taken as further proof that the lethal action of ionizing radiations is fundamentally one of interference in the ribonucleic acid metabolism. The exception to this is *E. coli* B which is extremely sensitive to an unknown factor present in Oxoid but not in Difco peptone and to the chloride balance in the medium, and this can give rise to quite different recovery curves (Alper and Gillies, 1958).

Applications of ionizing radiation sterilization

Their powers of penetration and the absence of any thermal effect makes the high energy ionizing radiations of particular potential value in the sterilization of materials which are difficult to treat by the more orthodox heating methods. Thus, any material which has low heat conductivity or is adversely affected by heat is especially suited to treatment by radiations provided there are no adverse side effects, and for this reason investigations have been largely centred on the preservation of foods and the sterilization of pharmaceutical products. One characteristic of the treatment is that it is virtually devoid of any thermal reaction, the maximum recorded rise in temperature being only some 3 or 4 degrees.

Foods. One of the most important applications of radiation treatments is in the preservation of foods. Large sums have been spent on the various projects involved, and the United States in particular has two major programmes, one under the Army Quartermaster Corps dealing with sterilized foods for military defence purposes and the other for the preservation of foods by low doses for civilian economy. In Great Britain much of the work is undertaken at the Low Temperature Research Station at Cambridge and is concerned with investigating mainly the treatment of meats and meat products. Several other European countries also have their individual programmes.

Because of the intense interest in the subject the literature is now extensive and voluminous and is to be found in a wide range of books, journals, official reports and reports of national and international conferences. For this reason it is difficult to make a true appraisal of progress and the present position.

Much of the earliest work was carried out at the Massachusetts Institute of Technology by Proctor and his colleagues who demonstrated that X-rays could destroy quite heavy contaminations. Sterilizing doses for a number of foods reported at various times by the Massachusetts team include:

Milk . . . . $7 \cdot 5 \times 10^5$ and 1×10^6 rad
Frozen milk . . . 1×10^6 rad
Minced beef . . . $1 \cdot 5 \times 10^6$ rad
Sausage skins . . . $1 \cdot 5 \times 10^6$ rad
Haddock . . . 9×10^5 and $1 \cdot 5 \times 10^6$ rad
Orange juice . . . 1×10^6 rad.

Thus, 2 Mrad would appear to be a reliable sterilizing dose, but there are occasions, as pointed out by Hannan (1955), such as when the material is free of oxygen and frozen to $-70°$, in which much higher doses are required. They may also be associated with the high initial bacterial content or the particularly high resistance of the organisms present in the material. For example, Kempe and Graikoski (1962) have confirmed their earlier observation (1954), as well as that of Pratt *et al.* (1959), that doses as high as 4 Mrad may be necessary to sterilize cooked meat deliberately infected with *Cl. botulinum* and other anaerobic spores, and several other instances have been quoted where doses of 2·5 to 5 Mrad are needed to effect a reduction in the contamination level by the safe factor of 10^{12}.

Of particular interest in this context is the organism *M. radiodurans*, originally isolated from irradiated meat (Anderson *et al.*, 1956). It is not a pathogen, but has an abnormally high resistance to gamma radiation and also to ultraviolet irradiation. Even in buffer solution a dose of 3 Mrad is needed to reduce the viable count by 10^{-5}, and in order to reduce it by 10^{-9} 4 Mrad are required: there is some strain variation in resistance. In meats the equivalent lethal doses are higher, raw beef and chicken giving the greatest protection. Freezing also enhances its resistance, but because of its low heat resistance, a mild pre-heating has the reverse effect (Duggan, Anderson and Elliker, 1963). It would appear from preliminary observations (Thornley, 1963) that the high resistance to radiation can be attributed to the unusual cell structure of this organism.

One of the great problems, at present insuperable, is the wholesomeness and acceptability of some foods organoleptically, nutritionally and from appearance after irradiation. As has already been indicated, the chemical changes brought about during a radiation sterilization are not confined to the micro-organisms alone but take place throughout the bulk of the material being treated. The amount of chemical change is often quite small, but as is well known it only requires a very small change in a food to affect its palatability seriously. Red meats will change colour on irradiation at room temperature, vitamins can be destroyed, fats may develop rancidity, carbohydrates can be degraded and some bleaching may take place; furthermore, certain fruits and vegetables may lose their characteristic flavours, and frequently an 'irradiation' flavour with a tallow odour may appear. Some of these disadvantages can be controlled to the point of elimination by reducing the temperature substantially and by removing oxygen, but such precautions are often not practicable or they may not be applicable to all foods; for instance, fruits and vegetables cannot withstand freezing without some tissue damage and adverse effect on their texture. High dose rates are said to be advantageous, and the use of the Capacitron with its ultra-short, high-intensity pulsed radiations has been commended in this context because it reduces to a minimum the occurrence of undesirable side effects (Huber, 1948).

With canned meat products substantial 'sterilization' is essential for safe storage purposes, and this is generally taken to mean that the most resistant organisms, usually *Cl. botulinum*, must be reduced by a factor of at least 10^{12}. For this purpose a high radiation dose is inevitable unless it can be combined with a heat process or with an antibiotic treatment. But for fresh meats and fish lower 'pasteurizing' doses can be applied simply to extend the safe storage time; and this can have considerable economic advantages. Thus doses as low as $2 \cdot 5 \times 10^4$ to 10×10^4 rad will retard the spoilage of meats (Lea, MacFarlane and Parr, 1960), but even at these levels there can be a detectable change in flavour and odour which make the authors wonder if the margin between acceptability and satisfactory treatment is too narrow for practical consideration. Similarly, doses of $2 \cdot 5 \times 10^5$ rad will substantially pasteurize raw milk and $2 \cdot 5 \times 10^5$ to 5×10^5 rad will extend the storage life of minced chicken (Thornley, 1957) and of fatty fish such as salmon (Larke, Farber and Huber, 1961).

Salmonella infections in frozen whole eggs have attracted much attention in recent years, and Thornley (1957) has indicated that they could be adequately dealt with by a dose of 2×10^5 rad. Subsequent investigations, however, have proved this to be on the low side, and it has now been established that doses in the range $3 \cdot 6 – 5 \cdot 4 \times 10^5$ rad are needed to reduce the infection level by a factor of 10^{-7} (Comer, Anderson and Garrard, 1963). This range represents the variation in resistance between the different *Salmonella* species, the highest dose being that required to inactivate *Salm. typhi-murium*, the species which always exhibits the highest resistance in all foods (Ley, Freeman and Hobbs, 1963). Comparable inactivation doses in other foods are: in meat, $6 \cdot 5 \times 10^5$ rad to effect a reduction of 10^{-5}; in bone meal, $5 \cdot 0 – 7 \cdot 5 \times 10^5$ rad to reduce by 10^{-5} to 10^{-8}, and in desiccated coconut, $4 \cdot 5 \times 10^5$ rad to reduce by 10^{-3}. These figures illustrate the point made earlier concerning the effect of environment on the apparent resistance of micro-organisms. A radiation dose of 5×10^5 or greater induces off-flavours in egg, but these are said to disappear on storage (Comer, Anderson and Garrard, 1963).

The principal organisms causing spoilage in normal meats are the pseudo-monads, but since they are comparatively sensitive to radiations they are easily eliminated by such treatments with the result that the *Achromobacter* types along with the Gram-positives tend to take over. Certain strains of *Achromobacter* are particularly resistant to radiation, as shown by Thornley (1962), and they produce a somewhat different spoilage from the pseudo-monads. In some cases, however, as when eviscerated chickens (Thornley, Ingram and Barnes, 1960) or fish (Shewan, 1959) are chilled in ice-slush, which might be heavily contaminated, the pseudomonads are substantially, but not totally, eliminated, with the result that they are the ultimate cause of spoilage. In some foods 'aseptic autolysis' takes place due to the survival of autolytic enzymes which may require up to fifteen times the normal sterilizing dose before they are inactivated (Brasch and Huber, 1947). This autolysis is the partial cause of red meats becoming unacceptable after irradiation; it can be eliminated by heat.

Chilling, of course, will stay the growth of micro-organisms and this is a common means of retarding spoilage in 'radiopasteurized' meats. But more important from the acceptability angle is the temperature during treatment, and it is now established with a fair degree of certainty that although the lethal efficiency of the radiation is not reduced at temperatures of $-75°$ or lower the side effects are much reduced, thus resulting in a better finished product (Coleby *et al.*, 1961). Likewise acid conditions will aid the sterilizing dose, so much so that it has been stated that foods with pH values below 4·5 do not require such a high level of kill to render them safe even when contaminated with *Cl. botulinum*.

Promising results have also been obtained by combining an antibiotic treatment with the radiation (Shewan, 1959; Thornley, 1958; Thornley, Ingram and Barnes, 1960). The principle here is to dip the chicken or fish in a solution of 10 ppm of chlortetracycline (Aureomycin) which reduces preferentially the *Achromobacter* organisms, and then irradiate with a sub-sterilizing dose. At a level of $2·5 \times 10^5$ rad this will extend the storage life of chickens, for example, two-and-a-half times.

In some instances, treatment has been limited to sterilizing the surface layers only (Huber, 1948), a procedure which has been used effectively in extending the storage life of eggs and of thick- and tough-skinned fruits such as melons, apples, pears, corn and nuts, as well as of meats, fish and cheese. A certain amount of caution is necessary because, as has been pointed out by Nehemias, Brownell and Harlin (1954), sub-lethal doses can actually increase the rate of mould infection, particularly in fruits.

The position is not as yet sufficiently stable to move into large-scale radiation handling of foods and the outlook would be greatly improved if means could be devised for 'sterilizing' with doses not exceeding about 5×10^5 rad. But radiation knowledge is still very much in its infancy, and as one writer has said, even "the science of canning is still being improved 50 years after Appert's primary discovery."

Pharmaceutical and medical products. In the pharmaceutical field, it is now accepted that a dose of 2·5 Mrad is adequate to achieve sterility. The Association of British Pharmaceutical Industry (1960) has reported on the suitability of this treatment for a range of materials, mainly injection products in terms of their colour change, loss of activity, etc., with the following conclusions:

Satisfactory	*Not satisfactory*
Benzylpenicillin	Neomycin sulphate
Streptomycin sulphate	Polymyxin-Bacitracin Ointment
Dihydrostreptomycin sulphate	Morphine sulphate Injection
Polymyxin sulphate	Atropine sulphate Injection

Satisfactory	*Not satisfactory*
Zinc bacitracin	Ergometrine Sulphate Injection
Ergometrine maleate	Progesterone
Atropine sulphate	Mersalyl Injection
Procaine hydrochloride	Stibophen Injection
Sulphapyridine	Cyanocobalamin Injection
Sulphathiazole	Sulphapyridine sodium
Lactose	Sulphathiazole sodium
Ascorbic acid	Glucose
Soft paraffin	Thiopentone
Talc	Pentobarbitone
	Insulin
	Heparin
	Hyaluronidase

Other reports have been made, however, on the discolouration of some samples of streptomycin, chloramphenicol, penicillin, polymyxin sulphate and zinc bacitracin (*see* Powell and Bridges, 1960). In addition, Tarpley *et al.* (1954) have treated cortisone and pregnenolone acetates with only a small lowering in melting points and Colovos and Churchill (1957) have reported on the stability of cortisone up to 10 Mrad, of penicillin and multivitamin preparations after 2 Mrad but on the instability of serum and plasma due to large changes in their globulin fractions. According to a Japanese source (*Chem. Abs.*, 1958) hormones are unstable, oxytocin and vasopressin losing over 40 per cent and insulin 93 per cent of their activities following a 2 Mrad irradiation. Carbohydrate solutions can develop cytotoxic properties (Berry, Hills and Trillwood, 1965).

Dry enzyme preparations are generally stable, and pyrogens are particularly resistant requiring up to 20 Mrad before they are destroyed (Whittet and Hutchinson, 1957).

In the medical sphere, package irradiation at dose levels of 2·5 Mrad is becoming increasingly popular and even greater numbers of disposable syringes, needles and catheters are being handled successfully this way (Darmady *et al.*, 1961). Rubber gloves and tubing can also be sterilized satisfactorily with the same dosage, there being no loss of tensile strength until a total dose of 8 Mrad has been administered, a level which is increased to 30 Mrad if the rubber is in a vacuum pack (Oliver and Tomlinson, 1960). Sutures likewise are most reliably treated in this way, there being no denaturation of the animal protein and no consequent loss of strength provided they are adequately dehydrated before the tubing fluid is added. Cotton dressings, gauzes and bandages, along with adhesive dressings, need careful handling because of the damage which can occur to the fibres: petri dishes and instruments present no difficulties. A high standard of packaging is needed to avoid subsequent contamination.

Irradiations have been applied to inactivate suspensions of the viruses of nfluenza, vaccinia, poliomyelitis and rabies for use as vaccines (Dick *et al.*, 1951; Traub *et al.*, 1951), and they have been used successfully for sterilizing kin grafts and bone transplants (Meeker and Gross, 1951; Brunnen, 953).

Economic considerations. Radiation sterilization equipment cannot be nstalled without a considerable capital outlay. Electron generators of the an de Graaff type can cost anything up to £250,000 depending on their utput capacity, and this does not include installation. On the other hand, ubstantial quantities of Caesium-137 are now becoming available from tomic energy plants, and this element, which has a half-life of 37 years, is onsidered to be an ideal source of gamma-radiation for industrial purposes. ts present cost is something under £2 per curie, but this will be substantially educed as supplies become more plentiful. An additional outlay is necessary or concrete shielding and this may be of the order of £20,000 for a 10,000 urie source. The maintenance costs of such a source are, of course, nil, but here is always the necessary upkeep of the mechanical equipment needed to onvey the materials to be sterilized to and from the area of irradiation, and uch an installation will always require highly trained and skilled staff in ontrol.

The question of the safety of all of the personnel engaged in such work is a natter needing constant attention. The amount of irradiation dose which a uman can withstand is small, and the danger lies more in the cumulative ffect of minute doses rather than from single larger doses, therefore strin-ent safety precautions are indispensable. The symptoms of damage do not sually appear until some long time after exposure, therefore careful medical ontrol is essential, and this at the minimum should include routine blood ounts together with a regular assessment of the general well-being of the ndividual.

In considering the installation of any irradiation sterilization unit, all of hese factors, the economic and the personnel considerations, need to be veighed against the advantages likely to accrue, and they must be compared gainst the efficiencies of the existing and more traditional methods of treat-nent. In some cases, there are undoubted advantages to be gained, but in nany others irradiation treatment is simply another method of sterilization, he use of which would not justify the initial capital outlay.

Ultraviolet radiations

The action of ultraviolet radiations

The amount of microbial destruction by sunlight is enormous and con-titutes one of Nature's ways of maintaining the balance of life and so of roviding a degree of protection from invasion and infection with pathogenic nicro-organisms. Its efficacy is mainly attributable to the ultraviolet range of wavelenths, although visible light up to 5,800 A can be slowly lethal to air-borne organisms (Webb, 1961), and it is readily demonstrated by exposing a freshly inoculated agar plate for a few minutes to its direct rays and observing the reduction, or even total elimination, of viable cells.

Ultraviolet radiations have wavelengths ranging between about 3,280 and 2,100A but the most effective bactericidal range is much narrower, between about 2,800 and 2,400A. The sensitivities of micro-organisms vary with the wavelength of the radiation, and optimum sensitivities of different types do not occur at the same wavelength, although they all occur within a reasonably short range. According to Gärtner (1947) the optimum lethal wavelength for all types of bacteria is at 2,540A, but Gates (1929) states that 2,652A is the optimum for staphylococci, and Duggar and Hollaender (1934a) give figures ranging between 2,652A and 2,804A for bacterial spores. In practice the radiation wavelength of 2,537A is always used, in spite of its lower efficiency against many organisms, for the essentially practical reason that most commercially produced lamps are now of the quartz tube, low pressure, mercury vapour type, and they emit over 95 per cent of their total radiation at 2,537A. The intensity of emission of such lamps is reasonably constant, their performance is reliable over periods measured in thousands of hours although there is a gradual and continuous decline with age, and they are little affected by temperature changes.

As might be expected, because its wavelength range is near to that of visible light, the quantum of energy radiated by ultraviolet light is not large and so its lethal activity is of a relatively low order and its powers of penetration are much smaller than those of other radiations. The lethal action falls short of ionization, being rather one of excitement of receptive molecules motivated by conveying additional energy to their orbital electrons and thus leaving them in a state of unbalance and of greater reactivity. The molecules most readily affected are the larger ones of the size of proteins, and it has been suggested that bactericidal action is associated entirely with the nucleic acids, and particularly the deoxyribonucleic acid, structure of the cell, the reason being that these compounds have strong absorption bands in the ultraviolet wavelength range. The initial action is probably that of preventing deoxyribonucleic acid formation, resulting in lysis and breakdown of the functions of the cell. Supporting this line of thought, Pratt, Dufrenoy and Gardner (1950) have suggested that the main reaction is an oxidizing one in which the sulphydryl reaction, $-SH \rightleftharpoons S-S$, is shifted to the right and this has the effect of inactivating the nucleotidases. Not dissimilar to this are the results of Aldous and Stewart's (1952) study of the irradiation of baker's yeast, in which certain of the cellular enzymes were inactivated to approximately the same extent as was the viability of the culture. The enzymes so inactivated included hexokinase, carboxylase, and the zymase complex, but others such as catalase and the dehydrogenases were unaffected.

Measurement of radiation intensity and lethal dose

The energy outputs of the many different types of ultraviolet lamps vary according to their individual characteristics. Their wattage, whether they are of the hot or cold cathode type, and their age, all influence their performance. It is desirable, therefore, to be able to assess their radiation energy at any time, and such measurements are made in terms of ergs, micro-watts or watts per sq cm or sq ft.

There are various methods of measuring radiation intensity. In one, the intense fluorescence of zinc silicate is used, the fluorescence being measured with an ordinary light meter (Luckiesh and Taylor, 1940), but most methods employ special ultraviolet-sensitive photocells. Such a method is Rentschler's 'click-meter' device (Rentschler, Nagy and Mouromseff, 1941), in which current from a photocell is allowed to charge a condenser across which is connected a neon discharge tube. At each discharge a mechanical counter is operated through a valve amplifier. Each click of the counter represents a definite amount of radiation falling in the photocell. An improved device, described by Mellors (1952), is in the form of a portable direct-reading instrument. With this instrument, the initial radiation falls on an ordinary gas-filled ultraviolet photocell at low voltage, and the impulses arising therefrom pass through a balanced electrometer amplifier to give a linear response recorded on a micro-ammeter. By varying the resistances in the circuit, the total coverage of the instrument can range between 0 and 1,000 microwatts (μW) of radiation per sq cm.

The unit of lethal radiation has been described by Wells (1955) as the number of "watt-minutes per square foot of uniform intensity, or foot-watt-minutes per cubic foot of uniform radiation, which . . . reduce standard test organisms 1 lethe in dry air." The "lethe" he defines as the amount of radiation giving a survivor level of 37 per cent, this level being chosen because of the logarithmic ratio of death rate against exposure (*see* p. 147). Beyond the fact that it enables irradiation efficacy to be related to equivalent ventilation efficacy, the lethe seems to have little value. On the other hand, the measurement of lethal radiation intensity in terms of total energy per unit area irradiated is of practical significance, and on this basis several estimates have been made of the amounts of energy necessary to kill varying proportions of bacterial cultures. Some idea of the order of such doses is given in the following figures (Rentschler and Nagy, 1942):

Percentage kill	Irradiation dose ($\mu W/sec/sq\ cm$)	
	E. coli	*Staph. aureus*
50	500	1,450
63	660	1,750
90	1,450	2,640
99	> 2,500	> 4,500

Broadly speaking, the doses necessary to inhibit the growth of most organisms to the extent of 90 per cent fall in the range 2,000 to 5,000 micro-watts per second per sq cm (Hollaender, 1942). Since the radiation intensity from even a 15-watt lamp at 30 cm (approx. 12 in.) distance is of the order of 400 microwatts per sq cm (Coblenz, 1942), it follows that exposures up to a maximum of about 13 seconds should be adequate to effect 90 per cent kills in most cases, but from some experiments conducted by the author in 1949 these values would seem to be substantially underestimated (see below).

Lethal efficiency

Against bacteria. Not all organisms have the same susceptibilities to ultraviolet radiation. In general, the Gram-negative bacteria are the most sensitive, the Gram-positive cocci occupy an intermediate position and the bacterial and mould spores exhibit the greatest resistance. Such divisions, however, can only be taken as approximations on account of the great variations found between strains of the same species, and even between cultures or generations of the same organism, and this is illustrated in Table 13 which shows the relative susceptibilities of some of the commoner types

TABLE 13

Relative susceptibilities of micro-organisms to ultraviolet irradiation

Type of organism	Relative susceptibilities after Wells (1955)	after Sharp (1939)
Staph. aureus	1·0	1·0
Staph. albus	0·88	1·41
Strep. pyogenes	0·71	1·20
C. diphtheriae	0·86	0·77
B. subtilis (vegetative)	1·25	—
B. subtilis (spores)	0·16	—
B. anthracis (mixed spores and vegetative cells)	—	0·58
E. coli	—	1·06
Salm. typhi	—	1·22
Chr. prodigiosum	0·99	1·18
Pneumococcus (type I)	1·44	—

(*Note*. The larger numbers indicate greater susceptibilities.)

of bacteria as found by two independent observers. These values might be compared also with the lethal-dose ranges quoted by Hollaender (1942):

Staph. aureus	2,180–4,950 μW/sec/sq cm
Staph. albus	1,840–3,300 ,, ,, ,,
Strep. pyogenes	2,160 ,, ,, ,,
E. coli	2,100–6,400 ,, ,, ,,
Salm. typhi	2,140 ,, ,, ,,
Chr. prodigiosum	830–2,420 ,, ,, ,,
Ps. pyocyanea	5,500 ,, ,, ,,

Some workers have declared that bacterial spores are only slightly more resistant than are vegetative cultures (*e.g.* Duggar and Hollaender, 1934*b*; Hercik, 1936) but the majority opinion is to the contrary. For example, McCulloch (1946) has stated that bacterial spores require about ten times the exposure of vegetative cultures to effect the same level of kill, and mould spores require about fifty times the exposure. Such ratios find support in Wells' observations (1955) that the spores of *B. subtilis* are about eight times more resistant than are the vegetative cells, and also in figures of the same order quoted by Mellors (1952). Likewise, Monaci (1952) found that a radiation intensity killing over 99·7 per cent of cultures of *Staph. aureus* and

TABLE 14

The bactericidal effect of ultraviolet light against vegetative and sporing organisms

Time of exposure (sec)	Percentage kill of		
	Chr. prodigiosum (aerosol)	*B. subtilis* spores (aerosol)	(dust suspension)
4·5	93	37	—
7·5	—	53	29
15	98·6	61	—
20	> 99·97	97	60
45	—	97·8	86
60	—	—	90
90	—	99·97	95

E. coli was only 84 per cent effective against *B. subtilis*, and Gundersen and Clausen (1954) in an examination of 33 different bacterial types found sporing strains always to be more resistant than non-sporing cultures.

The physical state of the organisms also plays some part in affecting their apparent resistance, as illustrated in the author's experiments referred to earlier. In these experiments, a cold cathode lamp, 3 ft long, was mounted coaxially in a pipe 6 in. in diameter, and bacteria dispersed either as an aerosol or mixed in a fine dust were passed through the pipe at a known mean velocity. By such an arrangement none of the cells could be more than 2½ in. from the lamp during their irradiation passage through the tube, and the percentage kills of *Chr. prodigiosum* and *B. subtilis* spores after various exposure times are given in Table 14. These figures confirm the much greater resistance of the sporing types and also the protective influence of dust particles, a matter of some significance in practice.

Also of interest is the work of Ramage and Nakamura (1962) relating the susceptibilities of cultures of *Shigella sonnei* to their phase of growth. Such cultures showed the greatest sensitivity in the early log phase, the resistance increasing as this phase merges into the static phase and reaching a maximum after about 7 hours. Thereafter there is a gradual decline in resistance until the culture is about 100 hours old when it again reaches a minimum. Sensitivities, or resistances, were assessed by exposing the washed cells to a given irradiation dose and counting the survivors, the range between the maxima and minima being from 5 per cent to 45 per cent. The explanation offered is that in the static phase of growth there is a longer lag phase than at any other stage, hence the cells have a longer time to adapt themselves to the effects of the radiation. This seems to be an eminently reasonable explanation and could well follow as a natural corollary to the varied resistances of the different species and types of micro-organisms.

Such differences are to be anticipated from a number of considerations. First, because the numbers and types of susceptible molecules functioning as cell metabolites are not the same in all types of strains; secondly, because the siting of such metabolites may be different both in relation to the cell membrane and in relation to other cellular compounds which could act as metabolite 'protectors'; thirdly, because the extent to which the radiations can penetrate the cell wall must again depend on the structure of each individual type of organism as well as on its age and possibly on its nutritional environment. In this connexion it is interesting to note that in a study of a large number of fungi Fulton and Coblenz (1929) observed greatest resistance in those having dark spore walls, that is, in those cells presumably having the greatest opacity to light.

In passing it is worth noting that resistance to ultraviolet radiation can be induced, at least in *E. coli*, by repeated exposure to sub-lethal doses. The increase is not great and reaches an apparent maximum after five such treatments when the increase in resistance is about twofold (Luckiesh and Knowles, 1948).

The relative resistances of different organisms to ultraviolet radiations are not necessarily the same as with other forms of disinfection. The reason for this is not difficult to see, it is simply that their modes of action are quite dissimilar.

Against viruses. It has been stated that the smaller the organism the more susceptible it is to ultraviolet radiation, and from theoretical considerations this would seem to be quite feasible. It is to be expected, therefore, that viruses can be rendered non-viable by irradiation, but as stated by Taylor *et al.* (1957) "A veritable horde of factors must be considered when it is utilized as an inactivating agent", hence the diverse findings reported in the literature, depending as they do on the type of virus, its concentration, the suspending agent and so on. This can be illustrated simply by some experimental results communicated privately by Dickinson in which she irradiated shallow layers, 1 mm deep, of suspensions of bacteriophage and of ectromelia in open petri dishes at about 15 in. distance from a 15-watt lamp. The suspensions of both viruses in Ringer's solution were inactivated in 15 to 20 minutes, but those in broth were still active after 1 hour. In the case of the bacteriophage *Ps. pyocyanea* Pe and Pz the titre had only fallen from 10^5 to 10^2 particles per ml after 2 hours' exposure.

Opinions differ as to the relative resistances of viruses and bacteria. Wells (1955) found influenza virus to have about the same order of susceptibility as vegetative bacteria, but McCulloch (1946) declared the filterable viruses to be extremely resistant, and Duggar and Hollaender (1934*b*) state "the energy values representing 100 per cent kill of the bacteria are far below the values having any measurable effect on the virus [tobacco mosaic]. The resistance ratio of virus to bacteria is about 200:1". This opinion was sustained by them four years later (Hollaender and Duggar, 1938) when they simply modified the ratios to 10 to 100:1.

Obviously thickness of the liquid film to be treated is significant, as pointed out by Taylor *et al.* (1957) and Oppenheimer, Benesi and Taylor (1959). Both used precision apparatus for obtaining suitable films of about 70 microns thickness, the former finding polio virus to be inactivated by a factor of 10^7 in doses varying from about 20,000 to about 28,000 microwatts per sq cm, and the latter finding hepatitis virus in serum and plasma to be inactivated by 34,000 microwatts per sq cm without altering the protein.

Working with bacteriophage particles sprayed in a small room, Czulak (1953) demonstrated substantial reductions in titre after 5 to 10 minutes' irradiation, and complete elimination in 25 minutes.

Factors affecting lethal activity

Power of penetration. Because the energy of any ultraviolet radiation is low, it follows that its powers of penetration into solids is negligible and its penetration into liquids can only be slight. By the same argument, any protective coating round a bacterial cell, or even a thick cell wall, must act as a deterrent to the efficacy of the lethal radiation. It is obvious, therefore, that if solids or opaque materials are subjected to such treatment, only their surfaces can be effectively disinfected, and even then with the provisos that the organisms are not protected by blood or other organic materials and the surfaces themselves are smooth. It follows also that air-borne organisms protected by mucous or other organic matter, and even by dust particles, must be less susceptible than the free, unprotected organisms, and this is a matter of some importance in air disinfection. This fact was evidently not anticipated by Wells and his colleagues (Wells, 1955) who retreated in alarm to the laboratory on finding that "irradiation of the air of a poliomyelitis clinic proved less effective against dust-borne organisms . . . than it has against atomized *E. coli* suspensions!" They should not have been so alarmed because they should have realized that they were dealing with natural air-borne organisms as against atomized laboratory cultures, and some years earlier it had been shown (*Studies in Air Hygiene*, 1949) that the rate of kill under these two conditions might differ by as much as forty-fold. Moreover, they were presumably trying to compare the lethal rate of the radiation against *E. coli* with that against a natural aerial contamination including dry bacterial spores. Some years ago the author made some tests on this very point and obtained the type of result which caused so much concern to Wells and his colleagues. In these tests, described in more detail on p. 173, the lethal efficiency from a standard ultraviolet lamp was compared against a sprayed aerosol of *Chr. prodigiosum*, a sprayed aerosol of bacterial spores and a fine dried dust mixture of the same spores, with the results quoted in Table 14.

It is not impossible, of course, that the differences in response between dry and moist bacterial spores may be partly due to their increased natural resistance on drying.

Humidity. From evidence given by Whistler (1940) there is an abrupt fall in the sensitivities of air-borne bacteria between relative humidities of 60 and 70 per cent. The variations above and below these levels are comparatively small, but he found a ten-fold difference within the range. Information from another source also suggests a large stepwise change between relative humidities of 35 and 68 per cent, but such differences do not seem to be universally agreed. Lidwell (1946), for instance, using salivary organisms obtained a ratio of only 2·7:1 for the humidity range 32 to 72 per cent, and Luckiesh and Holladay (1942) quoted an even lower value of 2·2:1 for the whole range of "dry air" to a "very moist atmosphere". More recently Wells (1955) has also quoted values indicating three-fold differences in sensitivities at 33 and 56 per cent relative humidities and also between air-borne organisms at 56 per cent humidity and organisms settled on moist plates.

According to Rentschler and Nagy (1942) there are no real differences in the vulnerabilities of organisms due to humidity, the apparent differences being attributed entirely to methods of sampling. The basis of this argument is that air samplers of the impingement type, such as the air centrifuge, are "selective in taking bacteria from the air", the larger particles being collected more readily than the smaller ones. The argument is quite acceptable if the correlative idea suggested by Bourdillon and Lidwell (1948) is accepted, namely, that there is an increase in the size of individual particles of a bacterial aerosol as the humidity is increased. This, however, would react in two ways. On one hand, the increased size of the particles would certainly increase the collecting efficiency of the sampler, and so result in an *apparent* reduction in bactericidal efficiency; on the other hand, the increased size would certainly reduce the penetration of the irradiation into the cell, and so give a *real* reduction in bactericidal efficiency.

Conditions of organisms. Closely allied to the humidity phenomenon is the question of the relative susceptibilities of air-borne organisms and those carried on surfaces. Again there are certain differences of opinion. The majority agree that air-borne organisms are more susceptible, and this appears to be the more logical deduction, because on a surface they might be expected to be more protected by virtue not only of one 'face' being presented to the irradiating beam, but also of the presence of solutes or solutions causing them to adhere to the surface. One fundamental factor in such studies is the variation in the physiological age of air-borne organisms and of those on moist nutrient surfaces, but Rentschler and Nagy (1942) claim to have met this, and from a carefully controlled series of experiments, they concluded that "a bacterium floating in air at high or low relative humidity requires the same amount of radiation as is needed to kill the same bacterium when seeded on the surface of agar". Unfortunately, the figures they quote do not entirely support this conclusion!

In general, antioxidants exert a protective action on organisms in suspension (Pratt, Dufrenoy and Gardner, 1950), and catalase has also been shown to act in the same way (Ogg, Adler and Zelle, 1956), both by virtue of the fact that they antagonize the formation of hydrogen peroxide.

Recovery of irradiated organisms

In addition to the factors affecting the lethal efficiency of ultraviolet irradiation there are others, probably of equal importance from the experimental point of view, affecting the recovery of treated organisms. From the fact that recovery can be effected only within certain radiation doses, cellular damage in this range must only be of a minor nature, and it has been suggested that the so-called injury is the result of the development of a metabolitic poison, possibly a substrate or enzyme degraded by a temporary stereochemical change, producing what might be described as a 'radiation sickness'. Little is known of the nature of this toxin but it is obviously associated with the mechanism of cell division and often manifests itself in the evolution of filamentous or 'snake' forms. It equally obviously renders the cell much more sensitive to its environment because, amongst other characteristics, recoveries are better in semi-solid than on conventional agar media. The make-up of the medium is highly significant and so are the temperature of recovery and the time lapsing between irradiation and the subsequent culturing for recovery (Roberts and Aldous, 1949). In general, the survivors appear to be least numerous on media which are optimal for the growth of normal bacteria, a point which lends support to the postulate of metabolic imbalance as the cause of 'sickness' (Alper and Gillies, 1958), as does the finding that improved recoveries can be obtained by adding extra nutrients in the form of supernatants from other irradiated bacterial suspensions (Whitehead, 1955). The extent of these phenomena varies with the irradiation dose, and so it must be assumed that the mechanism of poisoning must be complex and may involve more than one poison.

Improved recoveries might also be attained by adding an appropriate essential metabolite to bridge a gap in the synthetic processes of the cell created by the irradiation, and this has been proved with certain strains of bacteria which were protected by adding pyruvate to the suspension during irradiation (Thompson, Mefferd and Wyss, 1951). Metabolic reactivation of

E. coli has likewise been established by incorporating the same substance in the plating medium to enhance recovery rates by up to one-thousandfold (Heinmets, 1953) or by using several other metabolites of the citric acid cycle (Heinmets *et al.*, 1954). The acetate ion has been shown to act in a similar capacity (Ellison, Erlanger and Allen, 1955) and so has iodoacetate (Wainwright and Nevill, 1955). The phenomenon is not, however, as straightforward as would appear at first, because concentration, pH value, temperature and time of incubation all exert their independent influences. In terms of pH value, recoveries at pH 5 can be as much as 1,000 times those obtained at pH 8 (Weatherwax, 1956).

Reactivation can also be accomplished by heat or light treatment, but heat reactivation may not be as general a phenomenon as photoreactivation (Anderson, 1951). Photoreactivation was first discovered by Kelner (1949) who demonstrated that visible light of wave-lengths below 5,100A if applied immediately after irradiation, induced greater recoveries in several different types of bacteria. In line with this Nishiwaki (1954) found the optimum reactivation wavelength to lie between 4,520 and 4,900A, but Webb (1961) investigating the phenomenon in more detail found two "peaks in enhancement", one in the range 3,400–4,000A and the other in the range 5,500–5,800A, the former being the more active. The curious feature of this, as pointed out by Webb, is that these are the very wavelengths which in different conditions are actually slowly lethal to bacteria. The solution to the apparent enigma is that the visible wavelengths only act in their stimulatory and photoreactive role if applied immediately after irradiation. If the treatment is delayed it becomes ineffective, although some allowance can be made if the cells are chilled, the time limits being 3 hours at 37° as against 5 hours at 11° (Nishiwaki, 1954). Rather strangely, according to Linz and Lecoq (1961), the reactivation does not take place in frozen suspensions but will do so when they are thawed out. In terms of heat reactivation, Anderson (1951) has shown better recoveries of *E. coli* on incubating at 40° than at 30°, the degree of enhancement being of the same order as for light reactivation at 37°.

Ultraviolet irradiation in practice

The most useful practical application for ultraviolet radiation is in the field of air disinfection and there have been many publications on both its value and its limitations in this respect. Undoubtedly, if used in a sensible manner, it has a useful function in air hygiene, but it has been subject in many instances to much abuse through over-enthusiastic application, and this has tended to bring it into a certain amount of disrepute. In the first place, it should be realized that ultraviolet light is not a *sterilizing* agent except in exceptional circumstances – it can reduce substantially the content of airborne micro-organisms, but their total elimination is quite a different matter; secondly, it has a limited range of action, the efficacy of the radiation at a given point varying with the square root of its distance from the source;

thirdly, it is very easy to protect organisms from its direct action. It is, therefore, unreasonable to fit an array of ultraviolet lamps near the ceiling of a room and shield them so that only the upper areas of the room receive the direct rays and then expect them to affect significantly a bacterial population at normal working levels in the room. In fact, it has been shown (Air Hygiene Committee, 1954) that two 30-watt low-pressure lamps can irradiate the upper areas of a room at intensities of the order of 8·4 to 13·4 μW, but at desk level the intensity is only about 1 μW per sq cm. Greater disinfecting efficiency can be expected if a forced air circulation is used because all of the air is thereby brought in close contact with the lamp. By this means, claims for over a 99 per cent reduction in the air-borne bacteria in a normal room have been made, the installation being simply a portable air conditioner with one ultraviolet lamp fitted in it (Harstad, Decker and Wedum, 1954). However, using a similar portable apparatus with an air flow of about 45 cu ft per minute the author has not been quite as successful. Under normal conditions a reduction of only about 50 per cent was obtained, but if the air was continuously recirculated in a room of about 1,000 cu ft capacity the viable organisms were reduced to about 10 per cent of their original level in about 30 minutes.

In hospitals. Because of its efficiency against air-borne pathogens, ultraviolet irradiation has many potential uses in hospitals and elsewhere as a means of combating cross-infection and post-operative sepsis, and by its judicious introduction into operating theatres and surgical dressing-rooms Hart (1944) claims to have effected a reduction in "unexplained infections" of from one-twentieth to one-hundredth of the previous level. Others have recorded similar improvements, but rather significantly Colebrook (1955) omits it from his list of suggestions for reducing transmission of infections in hospitals. It is obvious that if such installations are made great care must be taken to see that the patients and staff are adequately protected from the deleterious effects of the radiations on the eyes and the skin. This, amongst many others, is one of the points raised by the American Council on Physical Medicine (1948) in their report on the acceptability of ultraviolet irradiations for disinfectant purposes in hospitals.

Of particular interest in preventing cross-infection is its use in maternity wards and baby clinics, where 'curtain irradiation' is often practised. The 'curtain' consists of a series of germicidal lamps placed in line over the entrance to each cubicle and 'focussed' so that the irradiation is concentrated into a narrow vertical beam covering the whole of the air entering or leaving the cubicle. By such means it has been claimed (Wells, Wells and Mudd, 1939) that as much as 99 per cent of test organisms are killed as they pass through the barrier, and Wells (1955) cites instances where it has proved of value in reducing respiratory cross-infection in several American hospitals.

It must not be thought, however, that ultraviolet irradiation is the be-all and end-all in eliminating the risks of cross-infection. An observation by Hobby and Lenert (1954) on the resistance of the tubercle bacillus is of some significance in this connexion. Working with the H37Rv strain, they found that cultures inoculated on agar plates required up to fifteen hours' exposure at 6 ft distance from a 'Hi Intensity' lamp to effect sterilization, although "a significant decrease in the number of viable cells occurred within one-half hour to three hours."

In schoolrooms. The present position with regard to ultraviolet irradiation in air hygiene has now been put in its proper perspective in two publications from the Medical Research Council. In the first monograph, *Studies in Air Hygiene* (1948), the difficulties of correlating practical working conditions with laboratory trial conditions are emphasized and it is shown by various calculations that the rate of kill in practice might be as low as one-fortieth of that found experimentally. In the second monograph (Air Hygiene Committee, 1954) the consequences of this in terms of the transmission of respiratory infections in schools is assessed. An example quoted in the first-mentioned monograph is that of a room of 3,500 cu ft capacity, fitted with ultraviolet lamps so that up to six could irradiate the upper areas of the room. The mean level of air-borne bacteria during irradiation over long periods was only 22·4 per cent below that of the normal room, a value far below that expected from laboratory tests. The second monograph deals with one extensive set of observations in London schools covering a period of three years, in which the reductions in total organisms were again only of the order of 20 per cent, but up to 80 per cent of the air-borne haemolytic streptococci were killed and up to 70 per cent of *Streptococcus salivarius*. This did not result in any change in the overall absence rate amongst the children, although the transmission rates of measles, mumps and chicken pox were reduced. These observations confirm the results of the earlier studies of Wells, Wells and Wilder (1942) over a four-year period in American schools, and of Wells and Holla (1950) in community centres and the like.

For industrial processes. As well as its surgical and clinical applications, ultraviolet irradiation also has certain uses in industry where bacterial invasion must be minimized. In particular it is frequently recommended where large-scale and continuous aseptic manipulations are involved, hence it is often installed in certain branches of the food industry and where sterile injections are being prepared. Such installations are acceptable and advantageous in their proper place, provided not too much reliance is placed on their performance with the consequent sacrifice of normal standards of cleanliness or asepsis. This was emphasized some years ago in a report by the American Council on Physical Medicine (1948) who underlined the dangers not only of incomplete disinfection but also of side effects due to ozone generation. Thus, low intensity lamps can be used effectively in the control of mould infections in bakeries and cheese factories, or even in barbers' shops (*J. Amer. med. Ass.*, 1953) but they should only be used as an adjunct to the usual cleaning and safety precautions.

To illustrate the point in pharmaceutical practice, the results of some experiments can be quoted in which rubber-capped vials were filled aseptically with sterile nutrient broth in a small screen fitted with a 15-watt ultraviolet lamp. The atmosphere of the screen was deliberately infected at intervals during the filling period by spraying in an aerosol suspension of *Staph. aureus*. In each experiment between 70 and 100 vials were filled and the following figures were obtained from two such groups:

| Bacterial aerosol | UV lamp | Average no. sterile | |
		First group (2 expts)	Second group (6 expts)
No	Off	99	97
Yes	Off	36	5·5
Yes	On	84	41

Such results give a good indication of the value of ultraviolet irradiation, but they show clearly that it is not absolute.

Frequently, exaggerated claims are made that air can be sterilized for commercial purposes by merely passing it at fairly high speed through ducting fitted with ultraviolet lamps. The fallacy with such claims is that the times of exposure are negligibly small compared with the actual lethal time. Sometimes only a fraction of a second of effective exposure is allowed, whereas experiments have shown that exposures of the order of 30 to 40 seconds are necessary to kill *Chr. prodigiosum* even in ducting of only 6 in. diameter (*see* p. 173). There may be something in the suggestion made by some workers that a multiplicity of lamps has an enhanced collective value, but this would appear to be simply the result of increased turbulence of air flow, and consequently of a longer and more intimate contact period.

In water treatment. Ultraviolet light also has been recommended as a means of disinfecting drinking water, but it does not seem at present to be an economic proposition. All of the equipment available commercially is some variant or other of a continuous flow system in which the water is passed through a tube with the irradiating lamp mounted coaxially. Because of the low penetration of the radiation into water, it is essential to use a fairly narrow tube and to induce a turbulent flow by baffling the water steam. The depth of effective penetration varies with the optical density of the water; for normal waters the intensity of irradiation at 2 in. depth may be only some 38 per cent of that at the surface (Cortelyou *et al.*, 1954a), whereas for polluted river waters it may be as low as 30 per cent at only 1 cm depth (Schmidt, Möller and Thiele, 1954). On this basis the indication made elsewhere that a 44-watt lamp will penetrate effectively into well waters at distances from 6 in. to 2 ft and only 1 in. into river water seems reasonable (Hoather, 1955). Artificial infections are always more readily killed than those occurring naturally, presumably because of the greater opacities of natural polluted waters, and so it is not surprising to find lower killing levels under these conditions. Thus, artificial infections of *E. coli* have been completely killed with mean exposure times of 1 minute from a lamp emitting 650 μW per sq ft at $2\frac{3}{4}$ in. distance (Cortelyou *et al.*, 1954*b*); *Salmonella* and *Staphylococcus* were equally susceptible, or more so, but *B. subtilis* was always more resistant. Cook and Saunders (1962) have also found spore-forming organisms of the *B. subtilis* type regularly to survive treatment in London tap water in a commercial irradiation unit.

The only liquid examined other than water is milk. It is clear at the outset that the greatest barrier is in the opacity of such a fluid, but curiously enough it is suggested that in this case disinfection results from absorption of the radiation by the milk. A layer only 0·003 in. thick absorbs 90 per cent of the energy; therefore the commercial practibility and reliability of the method seems remote.

In treating foods and food utensils. Ultraviolet light can be used for disinfecting surfaces and in this respect it is used for treating drinking glasses and similar equipment. Here again, exaggerated claims are made for its efficacy, claims which sometimes could not possibly be sustained in practice. It is of interest, however, to find that it can be used for prolonging the storage period of meat because it effectively reduces the surface contamination, but it does not affect those micro-organisms which have penetrated into the meat tissues. Similar observations have been made with custard pastries, in which *Salmonella* infections on the smooth surfaces of pies were substantially reduced, but not those on the irregular surfaces of custard puffs. Glucose powder and sand heavily infected with *B. subtilis* and other bacterial spores have been sterilized by the author by exposing them in thin layers at 2 in. distance from a 15-watt lamp for periods of 2 hours or so. It was necessary to keep them stirred continuously in order to expose all surfaces.

High-frequency electric fields

There are numerous accounts in the literature of the effects of high-frequency electric fields on micro-organisms, most of which describe attempts to prove that they have a specific lethal action *per se* apart from that produced by the heat generated in the medium during treatment. Summarizing the information available up to 1949, Burton (1949) said "There is no general consensus of opinion as to whether bacteria can be destroyed by the action of radio frequency waves, and in some cases it has been stated that they can be actually stimulated in growth at specific frequencies." He continued . . . "In the more recent papers a general destruction of the bacteria is often reported, and in these papers it is usually stated or implied that a high stress voltage is necessary". Two such papers have attracted some interest. In the first, Fleming (1944) exposed cultures of *E. coli* to frequencies in the range of 11 to 350 megacycles (Mc) per second, and obtained high mortalities for treatment periods of about one-half to three minutes. The maximum temperature reached did not exceed 30°, and the results obtained led to the conclusion that voltage gradient is the principal factor causing death. Current density was of little significance, because he used an output of only 10 watts and the effective energy was further reduced because the organisms were exposed in tubes between condenser plates. In the second paper a pulse-modulated field was used and it was generated from electrodes immersed in the suspensions. By this means even greater effective voltage stresses could be obtained and, using field strengths of 200 to 480 volts per cm, Nyrop (1946) confirmed Fleming's findings by inactivating *E. coli* and the virus of foot-and-mouth disease in a matter of seconds.

The striking nature of these results led Jacobs, Thornley and Maurice (1950) and Ingram and Page (1953) to investigate the systems further. Jacobs and colleagues used an electrode system external to the cell, after the style of Fleming, and worked with frequencies up to 66 Mc per second and exposure times up to 15 minutes. They reduced the heating effect by using dilute bacterial suspensions in a medium of low conductivity, and so were able to apply voltage gradients of up to 550 volts per cm. In spite of this they recorded at the best only a slight lethal action, and considered that this might well be attributed to the small residual thermal effect. Ingram and Page used electrodes immersed in the cell, after the style of Nyrop, and they worked with a "circulatory" and a "non-circulatory" cell system, both again being designed to eliminate as far as possible any internal thermal effects. Frequencies of 10 and 20 Mc per second with half-sine or rectangular pulse modulations were applied but no significant lethal effect was recorded with *E. coli*, yeast cells, tobacco mosaic virus or a bacteriophage. In confirmation of this, experiments conducted by Brown and Morrison (1954) with electrodes both internal and external to the cells again failed to demonstrate any destruction of bacteria that could not be accounted for by thermal effects.

It must be concluded, therefore, that high-frequency voltage fields *per se* have no bactericidal properties, and that any reported killing must be attributed entirely to internal thermal or other side effects.

REFERENCES

Air Hygiene Committee (1954). *Air Disinfection with Ultraviolet Irradiation and its Effect on Illness among School Children:* Med. Res. Counc. Spec. Rep. Ser. No. 283. H.M.S.O., London.
ALDOUS, J. G. and STEWART, D. K. R. (1952). *Canad. J. med. Sci.,* **30**, 56.
ALPER, TIKVAH and GILLIES, N. E. (1958). *J. gen. Microbiol.,* **18**, 461.
American Council on Physical Medicine (1948). *J. Amer. med. Ass.,* **137**, 1600.
ANDERSON, A. W., NORDAN, H. L., CAIN, R. F., PARRISH, G. and DUGGAN, D. E. (1956). *Food Technol.,* **10**, 575.
ANDERSON, E. H. (1951). *J. Bact.,* **61**, 389.
Association of British Pharmaceutical Industry (1960). *The Use of Gamma Radiation Sources for the Sterilization of Pharmaceutical Products:* A.B.P.I., London.
BACQ, Z. N. and ALEXANDER, P. (1961). *Fundamentals of Radiology,* 2nd edition: Pergamon Press, Oxford.
BELLAMY, W. D. (1955). *Bact. Rev.,* **19**, 23.
BERRY, R. J., HILLS, P. R. and TRILLWOOD, W. (1965). *Int. J. rad. Biol.,* **9**, 559.

184　　　Disinfection and sterilization

BHATTACHARJEE, S. B. (1961). *Rad. Res.*, **14**, 50.

BIAGINI, C. (1953). *Nature, Lond.*, **172**, 868.

BILLEN, D., STAPLETON, G. E. and HOLLAENDER, A. (1953). *J. Bact.*, **65**, 131.

BOURDILLON, R. B. and LIDWELL, O. M. (1948). *Studies in Air Hygiene:* Med. Res. Counc. Spec. Rep. Ser. No. 262, p. 173. H.M.S.O., London.

BRASCH, A. and HUBER, W. (1947). *Science*, **105**, 112.

BROWN, G. H. and MORRISON, W. C. (1954). *Food Tech.*, **8**, 361.

BRUNNEN, P. L. (1953). *Guy's Hospital Report*, **102**, 194.

BURNETT, W. T., MORSE, M. L., BURKE, A. W. and HOLLAENDER, A. (1952). *J. Bact.*, **63**, 591.

BURNETT, W. T., STAPLETON, G. E., MORSE, M. L. and HOLLAENDER, A. (1951). *Proc. Soc. exp. Biol.*, *N.Y.*, **77**, 636.

BURTON, H. (1949). *A Survey of the Literature on Bactericidal Effects of Short Electromagnetic Waves:* N.I.R.D. Paper No. 1041. Lamport Gilbert, Reading.

CHANCE, B. (1952). *Science*, **116**, 202.

Chem. Abs. (1958). Vol. **52**, p. 14077.

COBLENZ, W. W. (1942). *Aerobiology*, p. 138: Amer. Ass. Adv. Sci., Lancaster, Penn.

COLEBROOK, L. (1955). *Lancet*, **269**, 885.

COLEBY, B., INGRAM, M., SHEPHERD, H. J., THORNLEY, MARGARET J. and WILSON, G. M. (1961). *J. Sci. Food Agric.*, **12**, 483.

COLOVOS, G. C. and CHURCHILL, B. W. (1957). *J. Amer. pharm. Ass. (Sci.)*, **46**, 580.

COMER, A. G., ANDERSON, G. W. and GARRARD, E. H. (1963). *Canad. J. Microbiol.*, **9**, 321.

CONWAY, B. E. (1954). *Nature, Lond.*, **173**, 579.

COOK, A. M. and ROBERTS, T. A. (1963). *J. Pharm. Pharmacol.*, **15**, 345.

COOK, A. M. and SAUNDERS, L. (1962). *J. Pharm. Pharmacol.*, **14**, 83T.

CORTELYOU, J. R., McWHINNIE, M. A., RIDDIFORD, M. S. and SEMRAD, T. E. (1954a). *Appl. Microbiol.*, **2**, 227.

CORTELYOU, J. R., McWHINNIE, M. A., RIDDIFORD, M. S. and SEMRAD, T. E. (1954b). *Appl. Microbiol.*, **2**, 269.

CZULAK, J. (1953). *Proc. XIIIth Int. Dairy Cong.*, **3**, 1094.

DARMADY, E. M., HUGHES, K. E. A., BURT, MARGARET M., FREEMAN, BARBARA M. and POWELL, D. B. (1961). *J. clin. Path.*, **14**, 55.

DENNY, C. B., BORRER, C. W., PERKINS, W. E. and TOWNSEND, C. T. (1959). *Food Res.*, **24**, 44.

DICK, G. W. A., SCHWERDT, C. E., HUBER, W., SHARPLESS, G. R. and HOWE, H. A. (1951). *Amer. J. Hyg.*, **53**, 131.

DUGGAN, D. E., ANDERSON, G. W. and ELLIKER, P. R. (1963). *Appl. Microbiol.*, **11**, 398, 413.

DUGGAR, B. M. and HOLLAENDER, A. (1934a). *J. Bact.*, **27**, 241.

DUGGAR, B. M. and HOLLAENDER, A. (1934b). *J. Bact.*, **27**, 219.

DUNN, C. G., CAMPBELL, W. L., FRAM, H. and HUTCHINS, ADELIA (1948). *J. appl. Phys.*, **19**, 605.

EDWARDS, R. B., PETERSEN, L. J. and CUMMING, D. G. (1954). *Food Tech.*, **8**, 284.

ELLISON, S. M., ERLANGER, B. F. and ALLEN, P. (1955). *J. Bact.*, **69**, 536.

EMMERSON, P., SCHOLES, G., THOMSON, D. H., WARD, J. F. and WEISS, J. (1960). *Nature, Lond.*, **187**, 319.

EPSTEIN, H. T. (1953). *Nature, Lond.*, **171**, 394.

ERDMAN, I. E., THATCHER, F. S. and MacQUEEN, K. E. (1961). *Canad. J. Microbiol.*, **7**, 207.

ERRERA, M. (1955). *Radiobiology Symposium*, p. 93: Butterworths, London.

FIELD, G. J., PROCTOR, B. E. and GOLDBLITH, S. A. (1957). *Int. J. appl. Radiat.*, **2**, 35.

FLEMING, H. (1944). *Elect. Engng, N.Y.*, **63**, 18.

FREEMAN, BARBARA M. and BRIDGES, B. A. (1960). *Int. J. appl. Radiat.*, **8**, 136.

FULTON, H. R. and COBLENZ, W. W. (1929). *J. agric. Res.*, **38**, 3.

GÄRTNER, K. (1947). *Z. Hyg. InfektKr.*, **127**, 273.

GATES, F. L. (1929). *J. gen. Physiol.*, **13**, 231.

GOLDBLITH, S. A., PROCTOR, B. E., DAVISON, S., LANG, D. A., KARN, B., BATES, C. J. and KAREL, M. (1953). *Radiology*, **60**, 732.

GRAINGER, T. H. (1947). *J. Bact.*, **53,** 165.
GUNDERSEN, F. O. and CLAUSEN, O. G. (1954). *Med. Norsk. Farm. Sels.*, **11,** 127.
GUNDERSEN, F. O. and CLAUSEN, O. G. (1955). *Med. Norsk. Farm. Sels.*, **12,** 1.
GUNTER, SHIRLEY E. and KOHN, H. I. (1956). *J. Bact.*, **71,** 571.
GUNTER, SHIRLEY E. and KOHN, H. I. (1956). *J. Bact.*, **72,** 422.
HANNAN, R. S. (1955). *Scientific and Technological Problems Involved in using Ionizing Radiations for the Preservation of Food:* H.M.S.O., London.
HARSTAD, J. B., DECKER, H. M. and WEDUM, A. G. (1954). *Appl. Microbiol.*, **2,** 148.
HART, D. (1944). *Aerobiology*, p. 186: Amer. Ass. Adv. Sci., Lancaster, Penn.
HEINMETS, F. (1953). *J. Bact.*, **66,** 455.
HEINMETS, F., LEHMAN, J. J., TAYLOR, W. W. and KATHAN, R. H. (1954). *J. Bact.*, **67,** 511.
HERCIK, F. (1936). *J. gen. Physiol.*, **20,** 589.
HOATHER, R. C. (1955). *J. Inst. water Engrs*, **9,** 191.
HOBBY, GLADYS I. and LENERT, TULETA F. (1954). *Ann. Rev. Tuberc.*, **71,** 457.
HOLLAENDER, A. (1942). *Aerobiology*, p. 156: Amer. Ass. Adv. Sci., Lancaster, Penn.
HOLLAENDER, A. and DUGGAR, B. M. (1938). *J. Bact.*, **36,** 17.
HOLLAENDER, A. and STAPLETON, G. E. (1953). *Physiol. Rev.*, **33,** 77.
HOLLAENDER, A., STAPLETON, G. E. and BILLEN, D. (1953). *Science*, **117,** 468.
HOLLAENDER, A., STAPLETON, G. E. and MARTIN, F. L. (1951). *Nature, Lond.*, **167,** 103.
HUBER, W. (1948). *Electronics*, **21,** 74.
HUBER, W., BRASCH, A. and WALY, A. (1953). *Food Tech.*, **7,** 109.
INGRAM, M. and PAGE, L. J. (1953). *Proc. Soc. appl. Bact.*, **16,** 69.
INGRAM, M. and THORNLEY, MARGARET J. (1961). *J. appl. Bact.*, **24,** 94.
J. Amer. med. Ass. (1953). Vol. **153,** p. 775.
JACOBS, S. E., THORNLEY, MARGARET J. and MAURICE, P. (1950). *Proc. Soc. appl. Bact.*, **13,** 161.
JORDAN, R. T. and KEMPE, L. L. (1956). *Proc. Soc. exp. Biol. N.Y.*, **91,** 212.
KAN, B., GOLDBLITH, S. A. and PROCTOR, B. E. (1957). *Food Res.*, **22,** 509.
KAN, B., GOLDBLITH, S. A. and PROCTOR, B. E. (1958). *Food Res.*, **23,** 41.
KAPLAN, C. (1960). *J. Hyg., Camb.*, **58,** 391.
KELNER, A. (1949). *J. Bact.*, **58,** 511.
KELNER, A. (1955). *Bact. Rev.*, **19,** 22.
KEMPE, L. L. (1955). *Appl. Microbiol.*, **3,** 346.
KEMPE, L. L., BONVENTRE, P. F., GRAIKOSKI, J. T. and WILLIAMS, N. J. (1956). *Rep. U.S. Atomic Energy Commission*, TID-7512.
KEMPE, L. L. and GRAIKOSKI, J. T. (1962). *Appl. Microbiol.*, **10,** 31.
KEMPE, L. L., GRAIKOSKI, J. T. and BONVENTRE, P. F. (1959). *Appl. Microbiol.*, **7,** 131.
KEMPE, L. L., GRAIKOSKI, J. T. and GILLIES, R. A. (1954). *Appl. Microbiol.*, **2,** 330.
KEYNAN, A. and HALVORSON, H. O. (1962). *J. Bact.*, **83,** 100.
KOH, W. Y., MOREHOUSE, C. T. and CHANDLER, V. L. (1956). *Appl. Microbiol.*, **4,** 143.
LARKE, P. A., FARBER, L. and HUBER, W. (1961). *Food Technol.*, **15,** 145.
LAWRENCE, C. A., BROWNELL, L. E. and GRAIKOSKI, J. T. (1953). *Nucleonics*, **11(1),** 9.
LAWTON, E. J. and BELLAMY, W. D. (1954). *Nucleonics*, **12(4),** 54.
LEA, C. H., MACFARLANE, J. J. and PARR, L. J. (1960). *J. Sci. Food Agric.*, **11,** 678.
LEA, D. E. (1946). *Actions of Radiations on Living Cells:* Univ. Press, Cambridge.
LEA, D. E., HAINES, R. B. and BRETSCHER, E. (1941). *J. Hyg., Camb.*, **41,** 1.
LEA, D. E., HAINES, R. B. and COULSON, C. A. (1936). *Proc. Roy. Soc. B*, **120,** 47.
LEA, D. E., HAINES, R. B. and COULSON, C. A. (1937). *Proc. Roy. Soc. B*, **123,** 1.
LEA, D. E. and SALAMAN, M. H. (1946). *Proc. Roy. Soc. B*, **133,** 434.
LEY, F. J., FREEMAN, BARBARA, M. and HOBBS, BETTY, C. (1963). *J. Hyg. Camb.*, **61,** 525.
LIDWELL, O. M. (1946). *J. Hyg., Camb.*, **44,** 333.
LINZ, R. and LECOQ, E. (1961). *Ann. Inst. Pasteur*, **100,** 180.
LUCKIESH, M. and HOLLADAY, L. L. (1942). *Gen. elect. Rev.*, **45,** 223.
LUCKIESH, M. and KNOWLES, T. (1948). *J. Bact.*, **55,** 369.
LUCKIESH, M. and TAYLOR, A. H. (1940). *Rev. sci. Inst.*, **11,** 110.
MCCULLOCH, E. C. (1946). *Disinfection and Sterilization:* Kimpton, London.
MEEKER, I. A. and GROSS, R. E. (1951). *Science*, **114,** 283.

MELLORS, H. (1952). *J. appl. Chem.*, **2**, 68.

MONACI, V. (1952). *Boll. Inst. Sieroterap.*, *Milan*, **31**, 301.

MOOS, W. S. (1952). *J. Bact.*, **63**, 688.

MORGAN, B. H. and REED. J. M. (1954). *Food Res.*, **19**, 357.

NEHEMIAS .J .V., BROWNELL, L. E. and HARLIN, HARRIET A. (1954). *Food Mfg*, **29**, 431.

NISHIWAKI, Y. (1954). *Yokohama med. Bull.*, **5**, 21.

NYROP, J. E. (1946). *Nature, Lond.*, **157**, 51.

OGG, J. E., ADLER, H. I. and ZELLE, M. R. (1956). *J. Bact.*, **72**, 494.

OLIVER, R. and TOMLINSON, A. H. (1960). *J. Hyg.*, *Camb.*, **58**, 485.

O'MEARA, J. P. (1952). *Nucleonics*, **10**(2), 17.

OPPENHEIMER, F., BENESI, F. and TAYLOR, A. R. (1959). *Amer. J. publ. Hlth*, **49**, 903.

POLLARD, E. and FORRO, F. (1951). *Arch. Biochem. Biophys.*, **32**, 252.

POWELL, D. B. and BRIDGES, B. A. (1960). *Research*, **13**, 151.

POWERS, E. L. and KALETA, B. F. (1960). *Science*, **132**, 959.

PRATT, R., DUFRENOY, J. and GARDNER, GRACE (1950). *J. Amer. pharm. Ass. (Sci)*., **39**, 496.

PRATT, G. B., WHEATON, E., BOHRER, C. W. and DENNY, C. B. (1959). *Food Res.*, **24**, 51.

PROCTOR, B. E. and GOLDBLITH, S. A. (1951). *Food Tech.*, **5**, 376.

RAMAGE, CAROL M. and NAKAMURA, M. (1962). *Canad. J. Microbiol.*, **8**, 283.

RENTSCHLER, H. C. and NAGY, R. (1942). *J. Bact.*, **44**, 85.

RENTSCHLER, H. C., NAGY, R. and MOUROMSEFF, C. (1941). *J. Bact.*, **41**, 745.

ROBERTS, R. B. and ALDOUS, ELAINE (1949). *J. Bact.*, **57**, 363.

SCHMIDT, B., MÖLLER, I. and THIELE W. (1954). *Z. Hyg. InfektKr.*, **139**, 505.

SCHOLES, G. and WEISS, J. (1953a). *Biochem. J.*, **53**, 567.

SCHOLES, G. and WEISS, J. (1953b). *Nature, Lond.*, **171**, 920.

SCHOLES, G. and WEISS, J. (1954). *Biochem. J.*, **56**, 65.

SHARP, D. G. (1939). *J. Bact.*, **37**, 447.

SHEWAN, J. M. (1959). *Int. J. appl. Radiat.*, **6**, 143.

SPEAR, F. G. (1953). *Radiations and Living Cells:* Chapman & Hall, London.

STAPLETON, G. E. (1955). *J. Bact.*, **70**, 357.

STAPLETON, G. E., SBARRA, A. J. and HOLLAENDER, A. (1955). *J. Bact.*, **70**, 7.

Studies in Air Hygiene (1948). Med. Res. Counc. Spec. Rep. Ser. No. 262: H.M.S.O., London.

TALLENTIRE, A. (1958). *Nature, Lond.*, **182**, 1024.

TALLENTIRE, A. and DAVIES, D. J. G. (1961). *Exp. cell Res.*, **24**, 136.

TALLENTIRE, A., DICKINSON, N. H. and COLLETT, J. H. (1963). *J. Pharm. Parmacol.*, **15**, 180T.

TARPLEY, W., YUDIS, M., MANOWITZ, B., HORRIGAN, R. V. and WEISS, J. (1954). *Ind. engng Chem.*, **46**, 1458.

TAYLOR, A. R., KAY, W. W., McLEAN, I. W., OPPENHEIMER, F. and STIMPART, F. D. (1957). *J. Immunol.*, **78**, 45.

THOMPSON, T. L., MEFFERD, R. B. and WYSS, O. (1951). *J. Bact.*, **62**, 39.

THORNLEY, MARGARET J. (1957). *J. appl. Bact.*, **20**, 286.

THORNLEY, MARGARET J. (1958). *J. appl. Bact.*, **21**, i.

THORNLEY, MARGARET J. (1962). *J. appl. Bact.*, **25**, ii.

THORNLEY, MARGARET J. (1963). *J. appl. Bact.*, **26**, 334.

THORNLEY, MARGARET J., INGRAM, M. and BARNES, ELLA M. (1960). *J. appl. Bact,*, **23**, 487.

TRAUB, F. A., FRIEDEMANN, V., BRASCH, A. and HUBER, W. (1951). *J. Immunol.*, **67**, 379.

WAGENAAR, R. O., DACK, G. M. and MURRELL, L. B. (1959). *Food Res.*, **24**, 57.

WAINWRIGHT, S. D. and NEVILL, ANN (1955). *J. gen. Microbiol.*, **12**, 1.

WEATHERWAX, R. S. (1956). *J. Bact.*, **72**, 329.

WEBB, S. J. (1961). *Canad. J. Microbiol.*, **7**, 607.

WEISS, J. (1944). *Nature, Lond.*, **153**, 748.

WEISS, J. (1947). *Trans. Faraday Soc.*, **43**, 314.

WELLS, W. F. (1955). *Air-borne Contagion and Air Hygiene:* Harvard Univ. Press, Harvard, Mass.

WELLS, W. F. and HOLLA, W. A. (1950). *J. Amer. med. Ass.*, **142**, 1357.

WELLS, W. F., WELLS, MILDRED W. and MUDD, S. (1939). *Amer. J. publ. Hlth*, **29**, 863·
WELLS, W. F., WELLS, MILDRED W. and WILDER, T. S. (1942). *Amer. J. Hyg.*, **35**, 97.
WHISTLER, B. A. (1940). *Iowa State Coll. J. Sci.*, **14**, 215.
WHITEHEAD, H. A. (1955). *Canad. J. Microbiol.*, **1**, 266.
WHITTET, T. D. and HUTCHINSON, W. P. (1957). *J. Pharm. Pharmacol.*, **9**, 950.
WOESE, C. (1958). *Arch. Biochem. Biophys.*, **74**, 28.
WOESE, C. (1959). *J. Bact.*, **77**, 38.
WOOD, T. H. (1954). *Arch. Biochem. Biophys.*, **52**, 157.
WYCKOFF, R. W. G. (1930). *J. exp. Med.*, **52**, 435.

CHAPTER 7

STERILIZATION BY FILTRATION

FILTRATION occupies an important position in the armoury of the bacteriologist as a means of sterilization. It can be applied to both liquids and air, but only the filtration of liquids is considered here; air filtration is dealt with separately in Chapter 10.

Sterile filtration is used widely in the pharmaceutical industry where it is indispensable for sterilizing solutions which are heat-labile. It has the distinct advantage over other forms of sterilization in that it actually removes micro-organisms, but it does not of necessity remove their soluble products of metabolism such as toxins, pyrogens and the like. Under certain circumstances, therefore, it must be used with circumspection. It is also used extensively in the brewing industry both for clarifying the beers and for removing the yeasts at the end of the fermentation, for which purposes relatively coarse filters are adequate since the particles to be removed, including the yeasts, are rather larger than most bacteria.

Filtration is important in maintaining clean water supplies and is used in all public water undertakings. It is not strictly a sterilization procedure, as it does not claim to remove all micro-organisms; nevertheless it reduces the numbers to a sufficiently low level for the subsequent chlorine treatment to be effective. A short section on this aspect of filtration is included at the end of this chapter.

Sterile filtration

Types of filters

The types of filter available for sterilizing purposes are made with unglazed porcelain, diatomaceous earth (kieselguhr), asbestos or sintered glass. Porcelain and kieselguhr filters are available in disc or candle forms, but asbestos and sintered glass filters are made only in disc or sheet form. For the special purpose of ultrafiltration, that is for the removal of viruses and the larger protein molecules, collodion and similar membranes are used.

Porcelain filters. The first filters devised for the specific purpose of removing bacteria were produced by Pasteur and Chamberland in 1884. They were made by heating a mixture of quartz sand and kaolin to a temperature just below sintering point, and were fabricated in the shape of hollow unglazed candles. The English counterpart is now made by Doulton & Co. Ltd., and disc shapes as well as candles of various sizes and thicknesses are now available. The filters are obtainable in a number of grades of porosity, only one or two of which are made as sterilizing filters; the majority are used

188

mainly for clarification or for filtering the larger micro-organisms. They have the advantage that they can be used repeatedly and they are easily cleaned by scrubbing and then washing through with hot water. For a more thorough cleaning to eliminate absorbed materials they can be roasted in a muffle furnace or treated with strong hypochlorite solution; this removes organic matter accumulated in the body of the filters.

Diatomaceous earth filters. This type of candle filter was first produced in Germany by Nortmeyer and appeared shortly after the Pasteur-Chamberland filter. It is made with diatomaceous earth, or kieselguhr, and often there is a small admixture of asbestos and other materials. The process of manufacture is first to prepare a thick paste of the material and then cast it into the required shape. After it has dried and hardened sufficiently to handle, it is fired in a pottery kiln to give it rigidity and strength. This type of filter often goes under the popular name of the Berkefeld filter, but several types are made, under various trade names; the Mandler filter, for example, is an American equivalent.

As with the porcelain filter, this type of candle is available in a number of sizes and porosities, but only certain grades are suitable for sterile filtration. They are softer in texture than are porcelain filters, and so cannot withstand frequent scrubbing during cleaning. They can, however, be cleaned with hypochlorite solutions; acids must be avoided. Berkefeld candles are often sold for water sterilization, but the porosities of many of those now on the market are such that they are reliable for little more than clarifying purposes.

Both kieselguhr and porcelain candles have to be finished with suitable nozzle mounts, and this jointing is one of the weaknesses of such filters. Extreme care is necessary in handling them, especially during heat sterilization, to avoid the development of cracks and leaks, which are particularly liable to occur at the joints. Even with care, some distortion is inevitable and continuous tests are necessary to check this. They are most easily carried out by the bubble pressure method described later in this chapter.

Several 'improved' type candles have been produced in recent years, including an allegedly 'self-sterilizing' Berkefeld model under the name of Sterasyl. It is an ordinary candle of a rather coarse porosity with an 'antibacterial' coating, but experiments have shown it to be self-sterilizing only in terms of vegetative bacteria but not against bacterial spores or moulds. Another 'improved' type is a silicone-treated candle, but this seems to be self-defeating. It has the same porosity as the ordinary type but is slower in filtration due to the water-repellent properties of the silicones, and actually has a lower efficiency. This last point underlines the role of adsorption in such filters: the silicones undoubtedly reduce the charge on the interstitial surfaces of the candle and this leads to a reduced resistance or restriction on the passage of an organism through the filter.

Asbestos pad filters. The asbestos filter also had its origin in Germany, and it was universally known, and still is commonly known, as the Seitz filter. Now it is made by several manufacturers in different parts of the world; in this country the Sterimat is its popular equivalent. These filters are available in different grades and although described as asbestos pad filters contain, in fact, different admixtures of other fibrous or granular materials, mainly sulphited cellulose and cotton linter, which serve as binders and fillers (Webb, 1946). Those with the higher proportions of asbestos are of the finer grades and are suitable for sterile filtrations, whilst those with the lower amounts are the coarser ones and are suitable only for clarification or for removing the larger organisms such as yeasts from beers. They are manufactured in sheets and cut into discs or squares, and because of their softness and pliability are easily susceptible to distortion and cracking, especially if wet; for this reason they need to be handled carefully during sterilization. They will continue to filter even nutrient solutions satisfactorily for several hours, but eventually micro-organisms will grow through just as with candle filters. Each pad can be used only once.

The manner in which this type of filter removes bacteria is not properly known. Its efficiency cannot be related to pore size, as with the candle filters, because its structure does not lend itself to porosity measurements. It is, however, strongly adsorptive, and always carries a negative charge, therefore adsorption phenomena must play a significant part.

Frequently it is recommended that the filtration pressure, positive or negative, across a pad should not exceed 5 lb per sq in., otherwise the efficiency will fall. It is difficult to see the reason for this, but fluctuating or pulsating pressures are certainly undesirable.

One particular drawback with the asbestos filter is that on account of its chemical composition it yields alkali, alkaline earths and sometimes traces of iron, and it has even been suggested that filtrates can become progressively more alkaline during use if the asbestos is not properly treated during manufacture (Webb, Irish and Lydal, 1944). There have been many reports of alkaloids and substances in solution near their isoelectric points being precipitated on passing through a pad filter because of its alkalinity (Seiler, 1933; Eschenbrenner, 1933; Brown, 1942; Webb, 1946), and so care must be exercised in handling such solutions. The difficulty can largely be eliminated either by rejecting the first filtrate from a bulk of solution or by pre-washing the filter with a dilute acid.

Another difficulty encountered with this type of filter is that it tends to shed fibres continuously into the filtrate, a matter of some importance where final clarity, such as in solutions for injection, is concerned. There is, however, a resin-coated pad available, at least on the English market, which largely overcomes this problem and at the same time gives the pad more rigidity but does not reduce the rate of filtration.

Finally, there is the problem of adsorption. Asbestos, being negatively charged, is so strongly adsorptive that it can remove substantial amounts of therapeutically active substances from solution, and some enzymes, viruses and similar complex materials can be totally adsorbed if only small quantities are handled. One means of overcoming this, at least where virus particles are concerned, is to pretreat the pad with a dilute protein solution, thus coating and saturating all of the fibres and leaving subsequent materials a free flow. It is not possible to eliminate adsorption completely, but by using a dilute gelatin solution (0·006 per cent), or even better a 0·05 per cent solution of sodium alginate, the losses can be reduced from a factor of 10^5 to one of about 10^1 to 10^2 and can be as little as 2 or 3 per cent (Hyslop, 1961).

Sintered glass filters. The sintered glass disc filter is a comparatively recent innovation, having been first described only some thirty years ago (Bruce and Bent, 1931). Its application to bacteriological work was not reported until even later (Morton and Czarnetzky, 1937). The discs are made by heating pulverized glass in a suitable mould to a temperature just below fusion point, thus causing the particles to adhere together but leaving the disc porous. They are available in a range of porosities, the coarsest grade, 00, have pore sizes normally from 250 to 400 microns, and the finest, 5-on-3, from 1 to 1·5 microns (Smith, 1943).

Sintered glass filters carry a negative charge but in spite of this they do not adsorb solutes during filtration to the extent of other filters, neither do they yield any particulate or soluble matter to solution filtrates. Their porosity is not affected by heat sterilization, and they are easily cleaned with acids. As with other filters, micro-organisms will grow through if left in contact with a nutrient solution longer than about 18 hours (Morton, 1943).

Membrane filters and ultrafilters. These two types of filter are in principle the same, the only distinction between them being in terms of their porosities, ultrafilters having pore sizes of 100 millimicrons or less and membrane filters, pores of over 100 millimicrons. For this reason they have somewhat different functions in the bacteriological and biochemical fields, membrane filters being used for removing or collecting bacteria and the larger micro-organisms, and ultrafilters for filtering the viruses and other large-molecule proteins. The first ultrafilters were made, in fact, by Bechhold in the early 1900's for the purpose of separating crystalloids from colloids. Hardened gelatin or collodion (nitrocellulose in an ether-alcohol solvent) was first used, but later it was found that a solution of gun-cotton in glacial acetic acid was equally suitable. Subsequently cellulose esters were used and a patent on this was taken in 1922 by Zsigmody and Buchmann (U.S. Pat. 1,421,341). Polyvinyl sheets of different porosities were introduced for the same purpose in the late 1940s, but they do not seem to have received much recognition.

One of the characteristics of membrane and ultrafilters is that they can be made with various porosities, and several methods have been described to this end. One such method involves incorporating water-soluble, non-volatile swelling agents in a collodion solution, forming the membrane by evaporating the solvent in a dry atmosphere and then eluting the added soluble matter with water (Pierce, 1927). Elford (1931) has also described a technique which makes use of the antagonistic solvent action between amyl alcohol and acetone on nitrocellulose. By this means he has prepared a series of membranes with graded porosities ranging from 3 microns to 10 millimicrons. Zinc chloride solution dissolves nitrocellulose compounds selectively, and this also has been used for the same purpose (Seymour, 1940), Membranes made by several different methods are now available commercially, the main types being the Gradocol, the Millipore, and the German Membranfilter-Gesellschaft series in porosities ranging from 5 microns to 5 millimicrons; they are also available from Oxo Ltd. in one grade only.

Because of the nature and method of preparation, the finer ultrafilters need careful handling, and base formers of suitable shape and size must be used on which to precipitate the membranes; similarly they must be supported in use on a rigid mount. For this reason they are often prepared on porous paper or on thin porcelain cylinders. Such filters are used for filtering viruses and other large-molecule proteins, and by means of a series of graded porosity filters the relative sizes of such particles can be determined.

Membranes in the larger range of porosities, that is, over 100 millimicrons, are much more robust and of recent years have come into extensive use in the bacteriological examination of water supplies (Goetz and Tsuneishi, 1951; Taylor, Burman and Oliver, 1953), of ice cream (Nutting, Lomot and Barber, 1959), of air (Gohar and Eissa, 1957) and of clinical samples, as well as for examining small samples of liquids and for isolating specific organisms. They are also becoming increasingly valuable in testing the antibiotics and other materials for the presence of bacteria, their virtue being that they allow the antibacterial agent to be washed away completely whilst retaining any organisms which may be present (Holdowsky, 1957; Sykes and Hooper, 1959). The method is now adopted in the British Pharmacopoeia, 1963, for testing antibiotics for sterility. The technique in all cases is simply to filter the sample through a membrane mounted in a suitable holder and then culture it by laying it on the surface of a suitable nutrient agar and counting the colonies after incubation. Alternatively, the membrane can be cultured whole in a liqud medium, as is done in sterility testing, or the organisms enumerated directly by simple staining (Ehrlich, 1955).

Membranes can be sterilized either in steam or by ethylene oxide, and provided the porosity is correct—they act simply as mechanical sieves—will hold back all organisms for a limited time. They are, however, only about 150 microns thick, and so bacteria will ultimately penetrate through, the time depending somewhat on the nature and nutritive properties of the suspending liquid.

Other types of filter. From time to time other types of bacterial filter have been described, some of which are worth a passing reference. Filters made with plaster-of-Paris, and frequently with calcium carbonate and magnesium oxide added, have had a degree of popularity. They can easily be cast in the laboratory to any shape or size and have the particular property of carrying a positive charge (Kramer, 1927).

Other filters include the Imperator and Hansa makes which are variants of the Berkefeld type, and the Jenkins porous porcelain plug, but these now seem to have been displaced by other better known types. The Meta filter, consisting of a series of laminated plates of adjustable spacing and compressibility, is still in current use, but it is not a sterilizing filter; it is used for water-treatment and for clarifying purposes.

Mechanism of sterile filtration

The exact mechanism by which a bacterial filter is able to function with such a high degree of efficiency is as yet far from clearly understood. Several investigators have advanced their various 'theories' in explanation of the phenomenon, but unfortunately the majority seem to have been based on little more than guesswork or inconsequential thinking, and sometimes general conclusions have been drawn from specific observations or from incomplete experimental evidence. Such publications have therefore proved to be misleading rather than helpful and should be discounted. One difficulty seems to be that the three types of filter under discussion, candles, asbestos pad and membranes, apparently act in different ways.

It has long been recognized that the filtration of particles as small as bacteria involves properties associated with electrostatic phenomena, loosely referred to as "electrical adsorption", as well as simple mechanical sieving, and probably the former is the more significant. Hoek (1928) gave the first indication of this by demonstrating that the maximum pore size of any bacterial filter is always greater than the sizes of the particles it can remove.

Attention was first drawn to the possible significance of electrostasis by Mudd (1922) who demonstrated by means of the selective adsorption of basic against acidic dyes that most bacterial filters carry a negative charge. From this it was freely assumed that bacteria are adsorbed on the filter and held there by electrical attraction or 'adsorption'. But bacteria themselves are also negatively charged; therefore, any electrostatic effect must be one of repulsion rather than attraction, thus preventing a cell from passing through a pore rather larger than itself. On the other hand, proteins play a large part in the life of the cell, and they are amphoteric in nature. It is possible, therefore, that they may be adsorbed through their basic components and so cause the whole organism to be held.

In extension of this argument is the fact that the velocity of flow of water through a candle filter is only of the order of 0·1 cm per second (Ronca, pers. comm.), and so there is not a great flow pressure thrusting the organisms through. Under these circumstances quite small charges on the filter material and on the bacteria, whether of mutual attraction or repulsion, might exert a significant influence on the passage of a particle through the filter and so would affect considerably its efficiency. Such an occurrence does not seem beyond the bounds of possibility.

A further postulate to account for the 'adsorption' phenomena is based on purely mechanical considerations. The structure of a filter can be likened to a large number of thin porous diaphragms layered in intimate proximity, each layer carrying a multitude of holes or pores. These pores are not all of the same dimensions (their actual sizes and range of sizes depend on the nature of the filter material), and so the porous nature of the filter body is determined partly by the sizes of the individual pores and partly by their coincidence in the proximate layers. The chances of a series of large holes coinciding in more than a few successive layers, and so of forming a continuous uninterrupted pore over any appreciable length, must be very remote and the chances of such a pore extending through a filter of normal thickness are virtually non-existent. Therefore, the overall picture of the structure of a filter is one of an indeterminate number of pores or short passages all of varying size and tortuousness. Furthermore, the pores themselves, by reason of the nature of the filter material, must be entirely irregular in shape; they are neither circular in cross-section, nor have they any other constant dimensions. Thus, when an organism enters a filter it comes up against numerous hazards and restrictions all of which it must negotiate successfully if it is to pass through, and in any one of which it may become lodged and trapped. It is, therefore, these factors which determine the efficiency of a filter on mechanical considerations. The extent of this mechanical filtering effect may be judged from an estimate made by Ronca (pers. comm.) that in a normal porcelain candle half-an-inch thick there may be as many as two thousand such hazards to be negotiated.

With asbestos pad filters there is certainly a tortuous path for any particle to follow, but the thickness of the pad and its fibrous structure are such that one would expect particles of a fair size to pass through unhindered. In this case therefore it would appear that adsorption is the dominant factor. In this connexion some work by Wyllie (pers. comm.) is of interest. By means of a series of autoradiographs with yeasts grown on a P^{32}-enriched medium he was able to show their selective adsorption on the asbestos fibres, but not on the filler materials of the pad. A photomicrograph kindly supplied by Mr. D. M. Wyllie of T. B. Ford Ltd. and reproduced in Plate 6 illustrates the point.

The foregoing arguments are not so readily applicable to membrane filters, largely because of their thin construction. Here, experience shows that the efficiency of filtration is much more directly related to pore size—some of the smallest bacteria will pass through membranes with pore sizes of 0·5 micron—and so appears to depend on mechanical sieving rather than on adsorption processes.

Factors influencing filter efficiencies

Pore size. With candle filters, as with any other filter, pore size is the most obvious factor likely to affect efficiency, and it is perhaps worth mentioning that it is the maximum pore size, and not the mean, which governs the efficiency. It is difficult, if not impossible, to determine the true pore size of any filter medium of the type under discussion because of the irregularities of its pore structure, and so porosity can only be considered in relative terms. The common method of assessment is by the 'bubble pressure' test, and the measurements from this can be converted to pore diameter by means of the Bechhold formula. It is because of this close relationship between

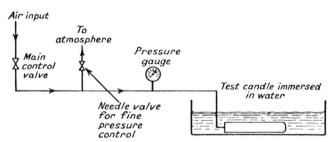

Fig. 11. *Diagram of apparatus for the bubble-pressure test*

porosity and bubble pressure that the two terms are often used interchangeably.

The bubble pressure test, first devised by Hoek (1930), is carried out by first soaking the candle in a liquid of low surface tension – water is most generally used, but sometimes ether is more suitable – until all of the air has been removed and all the pores filled with the liquid, and then applying a gradually increasing air pressure to the inner surface, observing the minimum pressure at which bubbles just break through the candle; the apparatus used for the test is illustrated diagrammatically in Fig. 11. This minimum pressure is known as the "bubble pressure" of the candle. The function of bubble-pressure against porosity is hyperbolic, and for cylindrical pores the following relationships hold:

Bubble pressure (lb per sq in.)	Estimated pore size (microns)
8	5·3
12	3·5
15	2·8
18	2·3

It has long been realized that the calculations employed are not strictly applicable to bacterial filters and some writers have even gone so far as to state that bubble pressure cannot be related to filtration efficiency. Nevertheless, others have taken a more optimistic view and have estimated critical porosities for candle filters capable of yielding sterile filtrates. Thus, by actual

Disinfection and sterilization

filtration tests, Hoek (1930) came to the conclusion that the critical porosity corresponds to a bubble pressure of 8 lb per sq in. Later Hunwicke (1932) quoted the rather higher value of 11 lb per sq in., and Berry (1937) indicated that 15 lb per sq in. is the minimum safe value.

When a filter is approaching an efficiency of 100 per cent, the number of organisms passing through it can only be small, but the passage of even a single organism through any bacterial filter at any stage constitutes the difference between efficiency and inefficiency. Therefore, to gain a correct appraisal of the ultimate efficiency of a filter, it is necessary to continue a

TABLE 15

Relationship between bubble pressure and efficiency of filtration of kieselguhr candles

Bubble pressure (lb per sq in.)	Period of filtration (min)	Fraction collected	Growths in: Whole filtrate	20 ml sample	1 ml sample
7–8	10	1st	+	+	−
	10	2nd	+	+	+
	10	3rd	+	+	+
10	10	1st	−	−	−
	10	2nd	+	−	−
	10	3rd	+	+	−
12	30	1st	+	−	−
14–15	30	1st	−	−	−
	30	2nd	+	−	−
17	c. 400	1st	−	−	−
18	c. 400	1st	−	−	−

+ = growth observed;   − = no growth

filtration for an appreciable length of time, if necessary to the breakdown point. This appears to have been one of the weaknesses of the earlier observations, and some investigators have even said, quite erroneously, that it is only the first small volume of filtrate which should be tested. Hoek (1941) went some distance towards correcting this by extending his filtration periods to several hours, but then he nullified the advantage so gained by testing only small volumes of the filtrate.

Each of these factors was taken into account in a detailed examination of the problem by Royce and Sykes (1950). These workers used a dilute suspension of *Chromobacterium prodigiosum* in nutrient broth and took the precaution of incubating the whole filtrate, as well as small samples, so that even a single organism passing through the filter had a chance of being detected. The results obtained are quoted in Table 15, from which it is seen that a bubble pressure of 15 lb per sq in. is about the threshold value, or critical pressure, for a reliable filtration for the particular type of candle under consideration. In practice, a slightly higher value is desirable to give a margin of safety.

Unfortunately this does not apply to all types of candle filters, as the same authors subsequently found. It applies certainly to Berkefeld and Doulton candles but not to certain others, notably the Aerox type, where bubble pressures as high as 45 lb per sq in. may be necessary to ensure a sterile filtration. This is a matter of considerable interest and points to a difference in the physical characteristics of the various types of filter, because

TABLE 16

The effect of wall thickness on efficiency of filtration

Candle	Bubble pressure (lb per sq in.)	Wall thickness (in.)	Period of filtration (hr)	Growth in filtrate
Kieselguhr	10–12	0·25	0·5	+
		0·5	0·5	+
		0·875	0·5 (a)	—
			0·5 (b)	—
			0·5 (c)	+
Kieselguhr	17	0·25	6–7	—
		0·5	6–7	—
Kieselguhr	19	0·25	6–7	—
		0·5	6–7	—
Porcelain	19	0·125	6–7	—

(a) = first, (b) = second, (c) = third period

in spite of the small pore size (high bubble pressure) required with Aerox filters the flow-rate of liquids is the same as with other lower bubble-pressure types.

Wall thickness. It might be inferred from the earlier discussion that wall thickness might be significant in determining the overall efficiency of a filter, but the experiments of Royce and Sykes (1950) show this not to be the case. The wall thicknesses of kieselguhr candles are normally one-quarter or one-half inch, depending on the size of the candle, and those of porcelain candles are usually thinner, and may be only about one-eighth of an inch thick. From the findings on such filters given in Table 16, wall thickness has no apparent influence with candles in the higher range of bubble pressure, and in the lower range the function seems simply to delay the penetration of organisms.

Positive and negative pressure filtration. It has been suggested by various investigators that sterile filtrations should always be carried out by vacuum and never under positive pressure, for the alleged reason that organisms can more readily be pushed than pulled through a filter. The argument is a specious one and is not backed by sound experimental evidence. Hurni (1948), for instance, made such a claim in relation to the filtration of oils, but oils are notoriously difficult to test for the presence of small numbers of organisms, and he further complicated matters by carrying out his filtration at 80°–90° and compared Seitz filters under pressure with candle filters under vacuum. Extensive practical experience has proved that both candle and Seitz-type filters can be used equally effectively with either pressure or vacuum, although some manufacturers of asbestos pads do not advocate using pressure differences across the filters of more than 5 lb per sq in. The only condition under which there might conceivably be a breakdown would be when a filter is at the threshold of critical porosity, in which case pressure on the filtering liquid might compress a bacterial cell slightly and so allow it to penetrate, whereas suction under reduced pressure would cause a slight swelling of the cell and so render it more easily trapped.

Nature of the filtering liquid. Because the electrical charge on the material of a filter is important in determining its efficiency, it might be expected that the nature of the liquid being filtered would exert some effect. The first indication of this came from Holman (1926), who coated filter candles with a mixture of petroleum jelly and paraffin oil and thereby apparently reduced their bubble-pressures and rendered them more permeable to bacteria. He did not give the porosity of the candles he used, but evidently they were not of high efficiency because he stated that the test bacteria, *Chr. prodigiosum*, "pass through the treated candles in a shorter time and are found in a smaller amount of filtrate than in the untreated candles." This idea was presumably pursued by the Pharmacopeia of the United States because the statement appears in the 13th edition "Liquid petrolatum and other oils are not to be sterilized by this method as they may increase the permeability of the filter to bacteria." It is not repeated in subsequent editions, and so presumably more reliable evidence to the contrary has come to light in the meantime.

Oils and oily solutions are frequently and reliably sterilized on both large and small scales by filtration – in many cases it is the only possible method – and in a carefully controlled series of experiments, Sykes and Royce (1950) showed that the rules applying to the sterile filtration of aqueous solutions apply equally to oily vehicles. They did find, however, one exception to this, namely, that asbestos filters can be made to break down by first 'insulating' them with oil and then filtering an aqueous suspension of bacteria. This is not a practical point because asbestos filters are only used once, and it does not seem to apply to candle filters of sufficiently fine pore size.

In addition to oils, there are several other agents which can render bacteria filterable through siliceous media, and these include a number of surface-tension reducing agents such as serum, bile and its component acids, soaps, turkey red oil, and sodium lauryl sulphate (Kramer, 1926, 1936, 1939; Varney and Bronfenbrenner, 1932). The author has also examined some silicone-treated candles which undoubtedly showed some increase in perme-ability, pore size for pore size. 'Insulation' of the charge on the surface of the filter by these agents is the reason put forward for the loss in efficiency, on the basis of the behaviour of basic dyes which are rendered filterable under these conditions.

Filterable forms of bacteria

One of the factors which sometimes might upset a sterile filtration is the occasional occurrence of filterable elements in bacterial cultures. Numerous authors have reported the existence of such forms, but it has not proved possible to repeat such observations with any regularity, and con-sequently interest has gradually subsided. The filterable elements are viable and they are said to be sufficiently small to pass through filters which hold back the normal bacteria. They are reported to occur amongst the spiro-chaetes, and Tilden (1937) has used kieselguhr candles and membranes with pore sizes down to 0·36 micron to obtain pure cultures of *Treponema pallidum* and *T. novyi*. According to several investigators (*see* Klieneberger-Nobel, 1951*a*), the filterable stage is a natural phase in the form of small granules. This granular phase is also said to occur in cultures of the acid-fast organisms, and Fraenkel and Pulvertaft (1935) claim to have obtained particles of these organisms as small as 0·1 micron. There are many reports of positive filtration results being obtained with these granular, non-acid-fast forms, and there is an almost equal number of negative ones, but, as Klieneberger-Nobel (1951*b*) says, "the negative results by no means disprove the existence of a filterable phase."

Other organisms can also apparently go through a filterable phase in their life cycle. Thus there is the well-known L phase of *Streptobacillus moniliformis* so carefully investigated by Klieneberger-Nobel (1936, 1949, 1951*a*, *b*) as well as the filterable forms of *Salmonella typhi*, *Shigella* and *Pasteurella*. These latter forms are now believed (Houduroy, 1954) to occur during the course of lysis by bacteriophage. The author has also encountered a waterborne organism which under some circumstances most certainly has a filterable form. It is apparently of the *Streptomyces* group but grows only slowly and with difficulty, producing filaments which are less than 0·5 micron in diameter.

Water filtration for public supplies

In terms of the treatment of water, filtration is not a sterilization process but one of purification. Its function is to remove suspended matter and the majority of micro-organisms, and so render the water suitable for human consumption. Filtration is not a new discovery for water purification. A process for treating drinking water by this means was used as early as the first century A.D. by the Egyptians, and a type of unglazed porcelain filter employed for the same purpose is referred to by Aristotle. The method seems to have been lost sight of in later years and it was not until the eighteenth century, following a series of epidemics, that interest was revived. After the disastrous cholera epidemic in London in 1839, the use of sand filters for purifying public water supplies became compulsory.

Types of filter

Sand filtration is an adaptation of the most effective and natural form of water filtration, namely, deep percolation through the soil. Water taken from a deep well is always of good bacteriological quality, the reason being that the time taken and the distance travelled during the course of percolation through the soil make it almost certain that all pathogenic bacteria and many of the saprophytes either die off or are otherwise removed. The same does not apply to shallow wells or to wells where the lining is incomplete, because the percolation distance and times are not adequate to remove all organisms, and surface or near-surface water, carrying with it natural organic matter in suspension, can gain easy access and thereby induce pollution in the supply.

Sand filtration through prepared filter beds is used in all public water supply undertakings, and two systems are employed, the slow filtration process and the rapid one. The slow filtering which can have an efficiency as high as 99 per cent, is suitable for supplies which are reasonably clear and free from suspended matter. The sand is not really used in this case for the purpose of mechanical straining but for supporting a protozoal growth which absorbs the bacteria. For this reason, a newly made filter always has a low efficiency and it remains low until the growth is established. Continuous usage renders the filter gradually more impervious until the flow rate diminishes below a useful level. At this stage the filter has to be renewed. This means that each filter has a limited life and a duplicate unit is necessary to maintain a public supply system.

The rapid filter is used where the water supply is turbid, and it depends for its efficacy on the action of an added coagulant. Aluminium hydroxide is often used for this purpose, the mechanism being that when it is precipitated *in situ* it carries with it bacteria and other suspended matter which are then easily removed on the sand filter. The efficiency of this type of filter is lower than that of the slow filter; at the best it is about 95 per cent and often lower than 90 per cent.

Because sand filtration is not wholly effective in removing all microorganisms – in particular it does not eliminate the viruses – it is never used alone, but is always followed by chlorination. The function of the sand is therefore mainly one of clarification with the removal of some of the microorganisms down to a level which can be easily dealt with by the chlorine added.

REFERENCES

BERRY, H. (1937). *Pharm. J.*, **139**, 267.
BROWN, H. H. (1942). *J. Bact.*, **42**, 315.
BRUCE, W. F. and BENT, H. E. (1931). *J. Amer. chem. Soc.*, **53**, 990.
EHRLICH, R. (1955). *J. Bact.*, **70**, 265.
ELFORD, W. J. (1931). *J. Path. Bact.*, **34**, 505.
ESCHENBRENNER, H. (1933). *Pharm. Monat.*, **8**, 169.
FRAENKEL, E. M. and PULVERTAFT, R. J. V. (1935). *Tubercle*, **17**, 97.
GOETZ, A. and TSUNEISHI, N. (1951). *J. Amer. Water Wks Ass.*, **43**, 373.
GOHAR, M. A. and EISSA, A. A. (1957). *Z. f. Hyg.*, **143**, 364.
HOEK, H. (1928). *Chem. Fabrik.*, **24**, 649.
HOEK, H. (1930). *Chem. Fabrik.*, **26**, 249.
HOEK, H. (1941). *Z. Hyg. InfektKr.*, **123**, 355.
HOLDOWSKY, S. (1957). *Antibiot. and Chemoth.*, **7**, 49.
HOLMAN, W. L. (1926). *Amer. J. Path.*, **2**, 483.
HOUDUROY, P. (1954). *Ann. Inst. Pasteur*, **86**, 395.
HUNWICKE, R. (1932). *Pharm. J.*, **130**, 350.
HURNI, VAN H. (1948). *Pharm. Acta. Helv.*, **23**, 283. ·
HYSLOP, N. ST. G. (1961). *Nature, Lond.*, **191**, 305.
KLIENEBERGER-NOBEL, E. (1936). *J. Path. Bact.*, **42**, 587.
KLIENEBERGER-NOBEL, E. (1949). *J. Hyg., Camb.*, **47**, 393; *J. gen. Microbiol.*, **3**, 434.
KLIENEBERGER-NOBEL, E. (1951a). *Bact. Rev.*, **15**, 77.
KLIENEBERGER-NOBEL, E. (1951b). *J. gen. Microbiol.*, **5**, 525.
KRAMER, S. P. (1926). *J. gen. Physiol.*, **9**, 811.
KRAMER, S. P. (1927). *J. infect. Dis.*, **40**, 343.
KRAMER, S. P. (1936). *J. Soc. chem. Ind.*, p. 260 T.
KRAMER, S. P. (1939). *Proc. Soc. exp. Biol.*, *N.Y.*, **42**, 448; *Science*, **68**, 88.
MORTON, H. E. (1943). *J. Bact.*, **46**, 312.
MORTON, H. E. and CZARNETZKY, E. J. (1937). *J. Bact.*, **34**, 461.
MUDD, S. (1922). *Amer. J. Physiol.*, **63-64**, 429.
NUTTING, L. A., LOMOT, P. C. and BARBER, F. W. (1959). *Appl. Microbiol.*, **7**, 196.
PIERCE, H. F. (1927). *J. biol. Chem.*, **75**, 795.
ROYCE, A. and SYKES, G. (1950). *Proc. Soc. appl. Bact.*, **13**, 146.
SEILER, K. (1933). *Quart. J. Pharm.*, **6**, 130.
SEYMOUR, W. B. (1940). *J. biol. Chem.*, **134**, 701.
SMITH, I. C. P. (1943). *Ind. Chem.*, **19**, 317.
SYKES, G. and HOOPER, MARGARET C. (1959). *J. Pharm. Pharmacol.*, **11**, 235T.
SYKES, G. and ROYCE, A. (1950). *J. Pharm. Pharmacol.*, **2**, 639.
TAYLOR, E. W., BURMAN, N. P. and OLIVER, C. W. (1953). *J. appl. Chem.*, **3**, 233.
TILDEN, EVELYN B. (1937). *J. Bact.*, **33**, 307.
VARNEY, J. L. and BRONFENBRENNER, J. (1932). *Proc. Soc. exp. Biol.*, *N.Y.*, **29**, 804.
WEBB, H. B. (1946). *Amer. J. clin. Path.*, **16**, 442.
WEBB, H. B., IRISH, O. J. and LYDAL, V. I. (1944). *J. Bact.*, **48**, 429.

CHAPTER 8

STERILIZATION BY GASES AND VAPOURS

NOWADAYS an increasing range of materials and medicaments is employed in pharmacy and medicine and in the food and allied industries, many of which, because of their heat-sensitivities, cannot be sterilized by the traditional methods, and it is in such cases that gaseous sterilization methods can be, and are being, successfully applied. Hence the reason why gaseous sterilization has come into greater prominence in recent years. Such treatments in general can only effect surface sterilization, but in dealing with surgical dressings, apparatus and other equipment, and even solid medicaments, this is practically all that is necessary. Sometimes a certain degree of penetration or diffusion is necessary, as when the material is porous or in a fine crystal or powder form, but the method of application can usually be adjusted to meet this. Two particular advantages with gaseous sterilization are that it can be carried out at normal or only slightly elevated temperatures, and that the vapour or gas can be completely removed from the treated material at the end of the sterilizing operation.

Certain spices, herbs and smokes have been used since time immemorial for preventing the spread of disease, and, although some of the treatments used in the past can only have exerted their effects through occult influences, others have subsequently been proved to have some scientific foundation. This form of treatment developed in the latter half of the nineteenth century into the practice of terminal disinfection of sick rooms after they had been occupied by persons suffering from any contagious disease, the procedure being to seal up the room with all its contents and then to admit the germicidal gas, vapour or smoke and leave it for some time to complete the disinfection. It was a very empirical method of disinfection and fell largely into disuse because of the destructive effects of the substances then used, namely, chlorine, sulphur dioxide or formaldehyde, and also because of the development of newer and more effective means of treatment. Although terminal disinfection as such has practically disappeared in these days, there is still the need to sterilize enclosed spaces, large and small, for other purposes, and this is one of the important functions of gaseous disinfectants.

One characteristic to be considered, apart from bactericidal efficiency of such agents, is the reactivity of the chosen gas or vapour. No gaseous disinfectant is chemically inert – it would not be germicidal if it were so – but certain of them, such as sulphur dioxide and chlorine, are much too reactive for practical consideration. Of the substances which are more acceptable from this point of view, ozone, formaldehyde, ethylene oxide, propylene oxide and β-propiolactone, and to a less extent some of the essential oils, have received most attention. But even these have their limitations; they are all toxic to humans above certain levels of concentration and they exhibit other unpleasant or undesirable side-effects.

Ozone

General Properties

Ozone is a pleasant smelling, but irritant and toxic gas which is fairly stable in dry air, but decomposes spontaneously in the presence of moisture. Elford and van den Ende (1942) state that it is twice as persistent in air at 50 per cent relative humidity than in air at 80 per cent humidity. It is highly toxic to all animal life in quite low concentrations, and from the various estimates made under different conditions Elford and van den Ende accepted a tolerance limit for humans of 0·04 parts per million in air. Ozone is generated by a continuous high voltage discharge through air between metal electrodes, and air treated in this way can contain up to 1 per cent of ozone. The purity of the product, and the concentration so achieved, depend on the actual high tension voltage employed, because at the higher voltage levels other oxidations are brought about. The most significant of these is the production of varying amounts of the oxides of nitrogen. These oxides are themselves highly bactericidal and more toxic than ozone and so can influence to a marked degree the apparent activity of ozone. This phenomenon can go a long way towards explaining the lack of agreement between different workers on the actual efficacy of ozone.

Bactericidal properties

Sensitivities of organisms. Ozone is an effective bactericide by virtue of its high reactivity with organic substances of all types, aldehydes, fats, amino acids, proteins and enzymes, hence it most probably acts as a general protoplasmic oxidant. Organisms differ in their sensitivities to ozone, and of the several common types examined Ingram and Haines (1949) found that *Bacillus subtilis*, *Bacillus mesentericus* and *Staphylococcus aureus* were amongst the most susceptible, *Proteus* and *Escherichia coli* were rather less susceptible, and *Achromobacter* and *Pseudomonas* species were the most resistant. The last group required about twice the concentration as did the first group to produce the same levels of kill, but this ratio is only a broad approximation. According to Fetner and Ingols (1956) the action in aqueous solution at least, is an all-or-nothing one and it is very rapid, being complete within a contact time of one minute: there is no effect below a certain critical concentration and above this concentration there are no detectable survivors. The mould fungi were found to be about as susceptible as bacteria, but later Ingram and Barnes (1954), in a review of the sterilizing action of ozone, commented that "The frequent contention that fungi are more resistant to ozone than bacteria appears to be justified, though there are occasional exceptions." In this review, the comparative sensitivities of several bacterial and fungal types as found by different workers under various conditions were listed, and this information is reproduced in Table 17. As is seen from the Table, the concentrations of ozone required depended very much on the conditions of application, and this combined with the state of growth of the organism, the protection afforded to the cells, and the temperature at which

TABLE 17

Comparative sensitivities of organisms to ozone
(Ingram and Barnes, 1954)

Action on suspensions of organisms in distilled water Rohrer (1952) 3 to 15 mg/l of water	Action on organisms on nutrient media (agar plates)	
	Kefford (1948) 5 µl/l in air at 5°	Ingram and Haines (1949) 200 to 1,000 µl/l in air applied from time of inoculation to cultures incubated at 20° to 25°

SENSITIVE

↑ Applied from time of inoculation

Ps. fluorescens	*Micrococcus*—no growth	*B. subtilis* (2 strains)
Sacch. cerevisiae	*Pseudomonas*—no growth	*B. mesentericus* (3)
(veg. cells)	*Candida*—retarded growth	*Staph. albus* (2)
Salm. paratyphi	*Achromobacter*—retarded	*Staph. aureus* (4)
Salm. typhi	growth	*Achromobacter* (1 slow grower)
Pr. vulgaris		*Micrococcus cinnebareus*
Mycob. tuberculosum	Applied to actively growing	*Pr. vulgaris* (3)
Pressed yeast	culture	*Bact. coli* (2)
Rhodotorula	*Micrococcus*—retarded	*Achromobacter* (7)
Sacch. cerevisiae	*Candida*—slightly retarded	*Pseudomonas* (4)
(spores)	*Pseudomonas* ⎱ no inhibition	*Achromobacter* (2)
Pen. brevicaule	*Achromobacter* ⎰	*Penicillium*
Oidium lactis		*Aspergillus*
		Cladosporium
		Thamnidium
		Mucor
↓		*Botrytis*

RESISTANT

the tests were made, affected somewhat the order of sensitivities of the organisms.

The influence of the state, or phase, of growth of bacteria on their sensitivities to ozone had been observed before Haines' investigations, but its significance had not apparently been appreciated. According to Ingram and Haines (1949) organisms in the logarithmic phase of growth require about ten times the amount of ozone to arrest growth than do the same cultures in the lag phase, and their suggested explanation is that it is not the organisms themselves which are responsible for these differences but the products of metabolism in the surrounding nutrient medium which absorb and react with the ozone preferentially.

Effect of organic matter. As indicated in the preceding paragraph, ozone is not exclusively active against bacteria, but it reacts readily with organic matter of all types, and so the protection afforded by any such material with which the organism is in contact may be considerable. This was demonstrated by Elford and van den Ende (1942) who obtained substantial kills of sprayed aerosols of *Streptococcus salivarius* and *Staph. albus* with gaseous concentrations of ozone as low as 0·04 part per million, whereas a level of 0·2 part per million was required for the same bacteria sprayed on plain glass surfaces, and an even higher level of 0·3 part per million was needed for those sneezed or absorbed on filter paper and wool serge. Cathcart, Wyberg and Merz (1942) on the other hand did not obtain any appreciable reduction in the numbers of airborne staphylococci and salmonellae with even 4 parts per million. These differences are attributable entirely to the varying degrees of protection afforded under the conditions described, a point which is further illustrated by the fact that Elford and van den Ende had to go as high as 330 parts per million before they could destroy bacteria inoculated on the surface of nutrient agar.

Quite naturally, the same protective influence can be exerted by the organic nature of any medium in which the organism may be suspended, as was plainly demonstrated in some experiments by Ingram and Haines (1949) in which increased amounts of ozone were needed for organisms in water, in synthetic media and in ordinary nutrient media. They found less than 7 parts per million in air to be effective when bubbled through suspensions in water, whereas 4 to 10 parts were needed for suspensions in a synthetic medium containing no amino acids, and 150 to 500 parts were needed with nutrient broth or nutrient agar. When the organisms had been allowed to grow in the synthetic medium, the required ozone level rose to 200 to 600 parts per million, and similarly in nutrient broth it rose to 500 to 4,000 parts per million.

Effect of humidity. Because of its instability in moist air, high humidities might be expected to affect adversely the bactericidal activity of ozone, but from the one source of information available, Elford and van den Ende (1942), the converse seems to be true. According to these workers, there is a threshold value at about 50 per cent relative humidity below which the disinfecting action is negligible, and the range for optimum activity appears to lie between about 60 and 80 per cent.

Effect of temperature. Temperature also exerts a significant influence, the general experience in practice being that treatments which are effective at reduced temperatures are ineffectual at normal temperatures. Haines, as reported by Ingram and Haines (1949), repeatedly found bacteria and moulds to be inhibited and killed by much lower concentrations of ozone at 0° than at 20°, and others have made similar observations (*see* Ingram and Barnes, 1954). Haines found, for example, that 150 parts of ozone per million of air were lethal to various *Achromobacter* and *Proteus* species inoculated on agar surfaces at 0°, whereas concentrations in the range 210 to 480 parts per million were necessary to kill the same organisms at 20°. The differences with various moulds were even wider, the respective values being 5 to 10 parts per million at 0° against 700 to 900 parts per million at 25°.

Ozone disinfection in practice

Ozone is used mainly for the disinfection of water and for the preservation of foods from spoilage during bulk storage. Its application to air disinfection is not practicable because of its relative inefficacy against sneezed organisms and those protected in other ways, and because of its high toxicity to humans.

In water treatment. In terms of water treatment – strictly not a form of gaseous disinfection although it is convenient to mention it here – it would be much too expensive to use ozone on the large scale in place of chlorine, but it has found some use for small-scale work, including the treatment of swimming-bath water. It has one particular advantage over chlorine in that it leaves no toxic residue in the water; it also has deodorant properties. Only quite low concentrations are necessary to effect practical disinfection in a relatively short time, but the amounts vary according to the amount of organic matter present. On this account, the actual levels recommended have ranged between 0·1 mg per litre and 4 gm per cubic metre, that is, between 0·1 and 4 parts per million (*see* Ingram and Barnes, 1954). In practice the concentration need not be limited to any particular upper value, because any excess ozone will rapidly disappear through its spontaneous decomposition in solution. Although this has its advantages it also has its disadvantages because it means that the disinfecting properties of the gas are only of short duration.

In food preservation. The value of ozone in food preservation lies exclusively in its ability to prevent surface growth; it is incapable of any deep penetration. Haines (Ingram and Haines, 1949) found 3 parts per million effective in preventing mould growth on the outside of eggs stored in an atmosphere of high humidity, but with meat even 10 parts per million did not delay bacterial growth. This difference was attributed to the fact that organisms on the surface of egg shells were dry and non-proliferating, whereas those on meat surfaces were in contact with reactive organic matter and also in a state of active growth, and under these conditions, as already stated, ozone is known to be less effective. In spite of this, claims have been made that as little as 1 part per million, and even less, was beneficial with stored foods, but in this case it must be assumed that other factors were operating synergistically (*see* Ingram and Barnes, 1954).

The natural reactivity of ozone with all types of organic materials raises certain difficulties in relation to food storage, for instance in the adequate distribution of the gas in a large storage chamber. This is particularly the case where carcase meats are present because they accelerate the rate of decomposition of ozone in the atmosphere (Kaess, 1956). Unless precautions are taken to ensure its full circulation throughout the chamber, the gas may be absorbed and lost in the immediate precincts of entry with the result that it never reaches the more remote areas, and Ingram and Barnes (*loc. cit.*) quote several examples of the consequences of this. One other important observation is that some foods are easily spoiled by ozone treatment. Fats in particular are rapidly turned rancid, and so it is unsuitable for treating butter in storage.

Formaldehyde

General properties

Formaldehyde gas has been known for many years as a bactericidal agent and it has long been used for fumigation purposes. It is a strongly reducing agent and is highly reactive with amino acids and proteins, and on these grounds it might be expected to have substantial antibacterial properties.

Formaldehyde gas can be generated either by vaporizing paraformaldehyde or by heating commercial formalin, that is a 37 per cent solution of formaldehyde in water stabilized with a small amount of methyl alcohol. It can also be generated by mixing about two parts of formalin with one part of potassium permanganate and allowing the heat of the oxidation reaction to volatilize the remainder of the formaldehyde gas.

One of the problems associated with formaldehyde sterilization arises from the spontaneous polymerization of the gas and its condensation on all available surfaces. This appears to take place, as evidenced by the occurrence of a thin white film over all of the surfaces affected, at normal room temperatures with both paraformaldehyde and with aqueous solutions, but it does not occur until the gaseous concentration exceeds about 3 mg per litre and there is insufficient water vapour to allow the formaldehyde to form a true solution. From these premises it would appear that condensation is most likely to occur in a closed atmosphere when there is excess of the gas present. If, therefore, the disinfection can be carried out in a stream of formaldehyde gas there is less chance of polymerization taking place, and this method was used by Nordgren (1939) and later by Bullock and Rawlins (1954) in their researches into the sterilizing properties of the gas.

Although formaldehyde has long been established as a disinfecting agent, the information available on its efficacy in the gaseous form under various conditions was singularly scant, and such as was available was extremely contradictory until Nordgren (1939) published his extensive investigations. As a result of his work, during which he used seventy different bacterial types, Nordgren showed that the rate of disinfection by formaldehyde gas is approximately the same as that of a solution giving the same formaldehyde vapour pressure. He established the relationship between gas concentration and rate of kill, its enhanced efficacy as the temperature increases and the fact that optimum activities are found when the relative humidity is over 50 per cent. He also showed that blood, sputum and similar material afford substantial protection to all organisms, a protection which can be largely overcome by the use of pre-vacuum, by increasing the temperature and extending the disinfection time. Many of these points were confirmed in a subsequent investigation by the Public Health Laboratory Service Committee on Formaldehyde Disinfection (*Report*, 1958).

One of the points unappreciated before Nordgren's time was the reversibility, within certain limitations, of the formaldehyde-protein reaction in the cell. Because of this, some workers were able to recover organisms after certain treatments, whereas others, using different cultural methods, were unable to do so, and this is the main reason for the contradictory and controversial opinions hitherto expressed. Two explanations of the reversibility phenomenon have been offered, one by Nash and Hirch (1954) based mainly on physiological considerations, and the other by Neely (1963) resulting from his more detailed examination of the chemical reactions taking place in the cell. The two explanations are complementary rather than contradictory. In the Nash and Hirch explanation, the proteins in the cell are presumed to be more protected than when in the free state, so that the formaldehyde-protein reaction takes place less readily. The effect of this is to produce a temporary state of suspended animation in the cell, not unlike that of a lag phase, during which revival can take place, provided the proper conditions of nutrition are presented. Beyond this stage of the reaction the cells become irreversibly moribund. Analysing the situation more detail, Neely conceived of a two-stage inhibition. In the first stage, cell division is stopped by virtue of the prevention of nuclear protein synthesis, and in the second stage homocysteine is removed from the field of biological action, with the formation of a thiazane-carboxylic acid, thus preventing its partaking in the formation of the essential amino acid, methionine. During both of these stages, the resting bacteria actually metabolize some of the formaldehyde, so that ultimately the concentration falls below its inhibitory level and the remaining cells can again start growth. The second stage can also be overcome by adding esters of methionine, but not methionine itself, to the recovery medium.

It is also necessary to have a rapid neutralizer for the formaldehyde in contact with the organism. Whilst Nordgren found the sulphite ion to be the most effective neutralizing agent and advocated adding 6 per cent of sodium sulphite to the inoculation medium, Nash and Hirch preferred a mixture of dimedone and morpholine. This gave optimum recoveries when used in equi-molecular mixtures at a concentration equivalent to 0·2 per cent of dimedone; higher concentrations were somewhat inhibitory. The mixture is said to act directly on either the formaldehyde or on the bacteria; it does not enhance the nutrient properties of the medium.

Bactericidal properties

Lethal concentrations. All bacteria, including spores, are fairly readily killed by formaldehyde gas and there is a linear relation between the speed of disinfection and the formaldehyde concentration (*Report*, 1958). But in order to obtain this rapidity of kill it is necessary for the gas to have easy access to the organisms, and this means that the organisms must have no protective coating. The protection afforded by even a thin coating of organic matter can sometimes be profound, and may increase the disinfection time substantially. Thus, Nordgren (1939), using bacteria dried on metal, glass or rubber tubing from suspension in distilled water, found that most organisms succumbed in an atmosphere containing 1 mg of formaldehyde per litre of air (equivalent to a partial pressure of 0·6 to 0·8 mm of mercury) within 20 to 50 minutes, the actual killing time depending on the type of organism used and the humidity. When the organisms were coated with blood or sputum or when they were dried on coarse soil, some spores survived the vapour of even neat formalin for 24 hours, but they succumbed within 2 hours if the temperature was raised to 55°. Similarly Bullock and Rawlings (1954) observed that up to 100 minutes were required to kill the spores of *B. subtilis* dried from peptone water, even though the formaldehyde concentration was as high as 2 mg per litre of air and the humidity was in the optimum range. Likewise, the Formaldehyde Committee (*Report*, 1958) found that cultures of *Staphylococcus albus* suspended in 90 per cent horse serum and then dried in short lengths of cotton thread were disinfected much more slowly than those suspended in 1 per cent gelatin solution, the time factor to give a similar level of kill being about tenfold. Tubercle bacilli suspended in serum or occurring naturally in sputum did not appear to be any more resistant than the cocci.

Bacterial spores are, of course, more resistant than vegetative types, but according to Phillips (1952) the ratio with formaldehyde and other alkylating agents is not as great as with other disinfectants. According to his statements, bacterial spores are usually "hundreds or thousands of times more resistant to chemical disinfectants than are vegetative bacteria", but "In this one class, however, no very great difference appears in the resistance of bacterial spores." The range of ratios he gave for formaldehyde was between 2 and 15, and for ethylene oxide between 2 and 6. These values were substantiated by the Formaldehyde Committee who in a limited number of experiments found ratios of about 2 or 3.

Because of its reactivity formaldehyde is an effective virucide in the gaseous form as well as in solution. The literature on this is sparse, but the Formaldehyde Committee reported that variola major impregnated on cotton threads was readily susceptible, provided the gas had ready access to the virus. If, however, variola or alastrim scabs in which the virus had some degree of protection were used it was ineffective.

This is similar to the position with regard to the tubercle bacilli. Under controlled experimental conditions these organisms, both avian and human can be killed within 2 hours, but under practical field conditions, that is, in large disinfectors with infected sputum smeared on fabric, the process is much less reliable.

Effect of humidity and temperature. Humidity is an important factor to be considered in relation to speed of disinfection of formaldehyde and this is one of the points on which there has been much difference of opinion in the past, largely because of the lack of precise definitions of the terms 'dry' and 'wet' by the various workers. This aspect was considered in much detail by Nordgren (1939), and from his investigations he concluded that the lowest activities are found at the lower humidities, with a maximum value at about 50 per cent relative humidity above which the enhancement was "relatively inconsiderable". The Formaldehyde Committee (*Report*, 1958) also investigated this aspect but with "somewhat equivocal" results. Their general conclusions were similar to those of Nordgren in that "there was no great difference over the range between 58 and 100% R.H.", "although the optimum appeared to be about 80–90% R.H." In a subsequent Note (1958), however, there is a much more definite statement to the effect that "the rate of killing . . . reaches a maximum at R.H. 80–90 per cent. Above this level it falls sharply, particularly if the objects are grossly wet."

In terms of temperature alone, little effect is found on the rate of disinfection between 0° and 37°. But under the conditions in which formaldehyde is normally used the effect of increasing the temperature is to increase the amount of formaldehyde in the vapour phase, to reduce its loss due to polymerization and also to reduce its adsorption on fabrics, hence the overall effect in practice of increasing the temperature is to increase the rate of disinfection. It is recommended the temperature should not be below 18° (*Note*, 1958).

Diffusibility. Several authors have commented on the low natural diffusibility of formaldehyde vapour into porous materials, a point of some importance where the disinfection of bedding, blankets and the like is concerned. The author himself has seen proof of this in a number of experimental results with organisms wrapped in a few layers of blanket, under which conditions even vegetative types were relatively unaffected after prolonged exposures. Nordgren (1939) investigated this aspect in some detail and found that the only way to sterilize small packets of soil was by using a pre-evacuation and heating technique. This aided the penetration of the gas in the material, after which exposures for 30 to 120 minutes at 60° were proved to be satisfactory. These findings tally with those of Coulthard, whose unpublished experiments showed that exposure to saturated formaldehyde vapour for as long as 48 hours at room temperature, or 24 hours at 37°, was necessary to sterilize spore-contaminated soil in small cotton wool plugged tubes.

Formaldehyde disinfection in practice

The uses of formaldehyde gas as a sterilizing agent in practice are limited by reason of certain of its physical properties such as lack of penetration, extreme pungency and the difficulty already referred to of removing the substance after treatment because of its polymerizing properties.

Formaldehyde gas is used mainly for disinfecting hospital bedding and for sterilizing certain types of medical and surgical equipment; it can also be used for sterilizing a limited few chemicals for pharmaceutical purposes provided it does not react with them. For these purposes large and small ovens are available commercially. Small units are also used in hairdressers' establishments for disinfecting scissors, combs and other equipment. In theory this is a useful application and in the interests of public health and hygiene is very desirable, but much depends on the way the apparatus is handled.

The Ministry of Health report (*Note*, 1958) states that small objects such as respirators and leather goods can be disinfected in a suitable chamber by boiling formalin into it at the rate of 50 ml to each 100 cu ft of space and holding for 3 hours or more at a temperature not less than 18°. On the other hand Dineen (1961) found paraformaldehyde tablets totally unsatisfactory for sterilizing instruments contaminated by immersing them in cultures of different organisms even though excessive numbers of tablets were used and the time of exposure extended to 20 hours. The difference here is probably to be found in the lack of control of humidity and the fact that one worker used formaldehyde solution and the other a polymer.

The lack of penetration and diffusion of formaldehyde gas is one of its main drawbacks, particularly where densely fibrous materials such as bedding and mattresses are concerned, and it is for this reason that the method is somewhat in disrepute and positive steps must always be taken to ensure that it reaches all of the surfaces to be disinfected. Nordgren drew particular attention to this hazard when considering the sterilization of rubber gloves, glassware, catheters and similar apparatus, and he recommended a pre-evacuation treatment to overcome the difficulty.

An alternative to vacuum pretreatment, which cannot always be readily applied on the large scale, is to use a heated chamber, and this has been found particularly useful when blankets or sheets cannot be hung individually or where bedding and pillows cannot be spread out so that all of the surfaces are accessible (*Note*, 1958). Formalin at the rate of 1 litre per 1,000 cu ft of air space is placed in the loaded chamber which after sealing is heated by steam coils to give an air temperature inside of 100°. After 3 hours the temperature of the interior of the bedding rises to not more than 60° and disinfection is complete. Bacterial spores and some other organisms will survive this treatment for 2 hours but not usually for 3 hours (Foter, 1960).

Mention should here be made of the use of low temperature steam with formaldehyde for sterilizing heat sensitive materials, clothing, etc. (Alder, Brown and Gillespie, 1966). Formaldehyde is vapourized into an evacuated sterilizing chamber at the rate of 5 ml of formalin per cu ft and then steam admitted at subatmospheric pressures to a controlled temperature of between 70 and 90°. Penetration is good, and a 2 hours treatment provides normally a margin of safety.

Rooms are still fumigated with formaldehyde gas either by boiling a 40 per cent solution or by treating it with potassium permanganate at the rate of 170 g to each 500 ml of formalin. The room must be emptied of fabrics and other absorbable surfaces, and if more than 500 ml of formalin is used to each 1,000 cu ft of air space trouble will be experienced due to the deposition of the polymer.

The position is probably best summarized by quoting the last paragraph of the Formaldehyde Committee report (*Report*, 1958) which reads: "It is concluded that disinfection by formaldehyde vapour should be used only when no other method is available. It certainly cannot be recommended for disinfection of fabric contaminated with smallpox virus or with anthrax spores, when complete destruction has to be ensured; and unless carried out with special care it is not really suitable for woollen garments and toys soiled with tubercle bacilli."

Ethylene oxide

General properties

Ethylene oxide has been in use for many years as a disinfesting agent, but its use as a gaseous disinfectant is a comparatively recent discovery. It is a three-membered ring epoxy compound, with the structural formula

$$CH_2\!\!-\!\!CH_2$$
$$\diagdown O \diagup$$

and as such it may be expected to be highly reactive. Its primary action is one of alkylation. Ethylene oxide boils at $10.8°$, and so at normal temperatures it is a gas. It is violently explosive in all mixtures with air ranging from 3 per cent to 80 per cent or even higher (Phillips and Kaye, 1949). The explosion hazard is eliminated if the gas is mixed with carbon dioxide, and a mixture containing 10 per cent of ethylene oxide is available commercially under the trade name of Carboxide; the explosiveness is also quenched if a sufficient quantity of nitrogen is admixed (Hess and Tilton, 1950). The mixture with carbon dioxide can be criticized in that a single cylinder does not yield constant proportions of the gases during its use, the first deliveries containing an excess, and therefore the last deliveries a deficiency, of ethylene oxide (Thomas, 1960). Other problems in handling ethylene oxide are concerned with its toxicity on inhalation—it is toxic at levels not detected by smell—and with the ease with which it produces erythema and oedema when in contact with the skin. Skin eruptions can result from direct contact with the substance in solution or with materials in which the vapour is absorbed (Phillips and Kaye, 1949; Moore and Royce, 1955), and hypersensitization may occur about three weeks after the first contact (Sexton and Henson, 1950). In this context rubber gloves sterilized with ethylene oxide need to be treated particularly carefully because of the high solubility of the substance in rubber. One gm of rubber immersed in liquid ethylene oxide will absorb as much as 0·6 gm, and in a 10 per cent gaseous atmosphere it will take up from 12 to 15 mg, and even this concentration is more than enough to cause a reaction in many subjects. The rate of loss of the gas is high, however, when suspended in free air, so that the concentration falls to 2 mg or less per 1 gm of rubber in the space of an hour or so, and this is safe for all but the most delicate skins (Moore and Royce, 1955).

Not only is ethylene oxide strongly absorbed by rubber but also to varying degrees by all sorts of other materials such as many of the plastics (excluding bakelite), wood, cardboard, hessian and certain powders (Royce and Bowler, 1959). This must be taken into account in some sterilization procedures.

Ethylene oxide is miscible with water, and it is said to be easily hydrolysed to ethylene glycol. This, however, applies only to solutions in acid conditions, because El Khishen (1950) has reported that the rate of hydrolysis at normal temperatures is very slow, and even at 80° it is not rapid. It reacts quantitatively with chlorides in acid solutions, and this forms the basis of a method for estimating ethylene oxide in small concentrations (El Khishen, 1950). It is also the basis of a method devised by Royce (Royce and Bowler, 1959) for controlling the efficacy of an ethylene oxide sterilization treatment, in which a small polythene sachet containing a magnesium chloride-hydrochloric acid solution with indicator just changes colour when the sterilization is complete. The reaction results from the slow diffusion of the gas through the polythene sheath, and the dimensions of the sachet and the volume of solution are such that the variations in reaction velocity due to changes in temperature, concentration and time, parallel very closely the equivalent variations in sterilization rate.

Bactericidal properties

Ethylene oxide was first quoted as a germicidal agent in 1936 when Schrader and Bossert (1936) patented the use of alkylene oxides for killing pests and germs. In the same year, Kirby, Atkins and Frey (1936) advocated its use in 10 per cent atmospheric concentration for controlling mould and 'rope' infections in bakeries. Later, other patents were taken out covering the use of ethylene oxide for sterilizing tobacco and for rendering sugar free from thermophils (Gross and Dixon, 1937), as well as for sterilizing organic materials and spices (Griffith and Hall, 1940, 1943). These patents specified that moisture must be present to effect proper treatment, but another patent (Baer, 1941), taken out to cover the treatment of organic products including foods, specifically excluded moisture. This is evidently a matter of definition, because it is now established that a certain minimal amount of moisture is necessary in the organism itself to allow the ethylene oxide to penetrate the cell and react with the appropriate protein cellular constituents. From Mayr's observations (1961) the most significant range of moisture content is from 5 to 15 per cent: below 5 per cent the fall-away in disinfection rate is rapid, and above 15 per cent there is little effect.

Disinfection and sterilization

According to Phillips (1949), the killing rate follows the usual logarithmic order throughout the whole sterilization period. He carried out most of his tests against *Bacillus globigii* dried on cotton material, having established this organism to be the most resistant of those examined which included *Staph. aureus*, *E. coli*, *Chromobacterium prodigiosum* and *Mycobacterium phlei*, and obtained killing times at different concentrations and temperatures as indicated in Table 18. From these and other data he deduced that "the

TABLE 18

Lethal action of ethylene oxide to B. globigii *spores*
(after Phillips, 1949)

Concentration of ethylene oxide		Time (in hours) required to kill	
mg/litre	% gaseous	99–99·9%	total
Temperature 37°			
22·1	1·1	4	8
44·2	2·2	2	6
88·4	4·4	1–2	6
442	22·0	$< \frac{1}{2}$	1
884	44·0	$< \frac{1}{2}$	$< \frac{1}{2}$
Temperature 25°			
22·1	1·1	10–24	> 24
44·2	2·2	8	24
88·4	4·4	4	10
442	22·0	1	4
884	44·0	1	2
Temperature 5°			
22·1	1·1	⩾ 72	
44·2	2·2	⩾ 72	
88·4	4·4	48	> 72
442	22·0	< 24	< 24
884	44·0	< 24	< 24

coefficient of dilution of the compound is close to unity and that the temperature coefficient, 2·74 for each 10-degree C rise, is not unusually high." This, however, is only true over a temperature range from 5° to 37° and for ethylene oxide concentrations up to about 884 mg per litre. Outside these limits the slope becomes steeper and at the higher temperatures coincides with that for the 1,500 mg per litre concentration, which is straight throughout (*see* Fig. 12) (Ernst and Shull, 1962).

Sometimes a degree of heterogeneity may be observed in the resistances of some organisms, *e.g.*, *B. cereus* and *B. polymyxa*, and this might be attributed to their varying lipid content, since the removal of fats reduces their resistance and the addition of fats has the reverse effect (Church *et al.*, 1956). In spite of this alleged fat effect the tubercle bacilli, either in culture or occurring naturally in sputum, seem to be killed at about the same rate as the staphylococci (Lammers and Tuncer, 1961).

The sterilizing action of ethylene oxide is not rapid, except where the organisms are free from any protective coating and the gas concentration is high, but it is certainly sporicidal the resistances of bacterial spores being only some 2 to 6 times greater than those of the vegetative cells (Phillips,

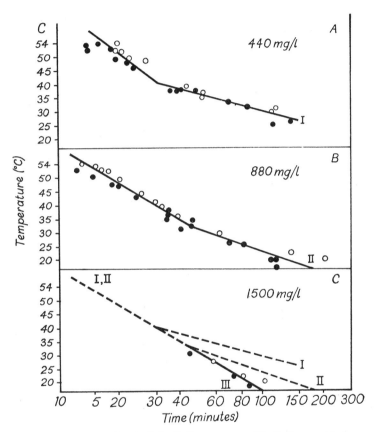

FIG. 12. *Thermochemical death time curves with ethylene oxide for spores of* Bacillus subtilis *var.* niger *dried on glass beads*
○, sterile sets; ●, sets not sterile

1952). An 80 per cent gaseous concentration in air has been reported to sterilize various soils in periods ranging from 2 hours to 6 hours (Roberts *et al.*, 1943), and 200 mg per litre of air (approximately 10 per cent in gaseous concentration) has killed off *Bacillus anthracoides* on glass, metal and paper surfaces and on dry or wet rags in 8 hours (Velu, Lepigre and Bellocq, 1942). From another report (Rauscher, Mayr and Kaemanver, 1957), clostridia and coliforms are easily killed, the most resistant organisms being the staphylococci and *B. anthracoides*, which are killed in ethylene oxide concentrations of from 500 to 750 mg per litre in 6 to 7 hours.

Although there is no disagreement as to the need for a minimal amount of moisture, opinions seem to differ concerning an optimum humidity level. According to Phillips (1961) this level occurs at about 33 per cent relative humidity, at which point the activity is about four times that at 65 per cent and ten times that at 97 per cent relative humidity (Kaye and Phillips, 1949). Perkins and Lloyd (1961), on the other hand, claim 55 to 60 per cent humidity as the optimum and Mayr (1961) has demonstrated a continual increase up to a relative humidity of 95 per cent. Although these figures are widely different they are not really at variance because they apply to organisms in different physical states. Phillips used washed, naked organisms and thus "made every effort to rule out that [physical protective] effect so that they could measure entirely separately the physiological status of the individual bacterium", whereas Mayr was using bacterial spores in a natural dry earth which were almost certainly protected by crystalloid and other substances. This difference was shown quite clearly by Royce and Bowler (1961) in their demonstrations of the greater susceptibilities of organisms dried on filter paper, and therefore exposed in the naked state, over those suspended in saline or serum and dried on glass surfaces. In summary, therefore, it can be said that with unprotected organisms it is necessary only to have sufficient moisture to allow the alkylating reaction to proceed, any excess merely using up ethylene oxide, but with naturally occurring protected organisms enough moisture is needed to allow also of absorption by the other materials present. The last point is important in practical sterilization and is discussed in more detail in the next section (p. 219).

Ethylene oxide is also a virucide, at least in terms of the larger elements of this group. The references on this aspect are sparse, but the indications are that herpes simplex, vaccinia and various infectious bovine respiratory viruses are no more resistant than are vegetative bacteria (Skeehan, 1959).

Ethylene oxide is also an aerial bactericide. When the washed spores of *B. globigii* were dispersed as an aerosol from a simple water suspension, a 90 per cent kill was obtained with a gaseous concentration of about 5 per cent in 84 minutes (Kaye, 1949).

Ethylene oxide sterilization in practice

Ethylene oxide treatment has now become an established method for sterilizing and disinfecting in the pharmaceutical and food industries and for these purposes a variety of equipment is available ranging from the small laboratory unit to the large-scale plant with a capacity of a thousand or more cubic feet. They can vary from the simple chamber into which the gas is pumped direct, with or without the application of a pre-vacuum—the latter increasing the rate of penetration (see below)—to the more complicated, and more expensive, fully automatic type which delivers a fixed amount of the gas from a canister and operates under pressure, thus increasing the effective gas concentration and so reducing the sterilization time: they may also include a means of heating, again with the object of reducing the time of treatment.

In treating foods. In the food industries, ethylene oxide is used for treating starch, desiccated coconut, spices, whey powders, cocoa powder and various other dry foods, but it has its limitations in that it reacts adversely with vitamins and their associated amino acids. In this category fall riboflavine, nicotinic acid, pyridoxine, folic acid and the essential amino acids, histidine, methionine, cysteine and lysine, both in the free state and in various dietary mixtures (Mickelson, 1957; Windmueller, Ackerman and Engel, 1956, 1959).

In pharmacy and medicine. In the pharmaceutical and medical fields the process can be applied successfully to the sterilization of the penicillins and other antibiotics in the solid state, but sometimes, as with the streptomycin-calcium chloride complex, some loss in activity may occur (Kaye, Irminger and Phillips, 1952). It will also effectively sterilize large bulks of powder such as french chalk and kaolin for pharmaceutical use, provided due allowance is made for the relatively large amount of the gas absorbed by the powder. This can be done either by using an excess of ethylene oxide over the normal sterilizing concentration or by employing an absorption pre-treatment. A further value in pharmacy is in the sterilization of small enclosed spaces for carrying out difficult aseptic manipulations, including tests for sterility on products for injection. For this purpose Royce and Sykes (1955) have described a 'sealed-screen' technique in which the sterilization is by a 12·5–15 per cent ethylene oxide concentration overnight.

In hospital practice it has been reported on favourably by several workers, including Phillips and Warshowski (1958), Thomas (1960), and Foter (1960), although several draw attention to the length of treatment needed. Surgical instruments, ophthalmoscopes, etc., can be sterilized by exposure to a gaseous concentration of about 500 mg per litre for 4 hours at room temperature (Skeehan, King and Kaye, 1956); plastic intravenous injection equipment has been similarly sterilized (Grundy *et al.*, 1957), and so have heart-lung machines, but this time using 10 per cent ethylene oxide for 24 hours at room temperature (Bracken, Wilton-Davis and Weale, 1960). One of the advantages of this form of treatment where plastics and rubber are concerned is that these materials absorb ethylene oxide and so the sterilization continues after the nominal treatment period until the gas has again been released into the atmosphere.

Mention has already been made of the fact that no special apparatus or equipment is really needed. The usual safety precautions must be followed, of course, and it is also necessary to be able to control the gaseous concentration, but this can be done by using one of the mixtures with carbon dioxide or one of the freons; it is necessary also to control the temperature and time within broad limits, but this again can be done quite simply. The author, in fact, has used for many years converted steam autoclaves of varying sizes to sterilize not only equipment but also a number of pharmaceutical materials in bulk. In this particular case a nominal sterilizing concentration of 10 per cent of ethylene oxide is used (due allowance being made for absorption, etc.) The treatment is for 18 hours at not less than 20°, and it has proved sucessful in the majority of instances, the exceptions being when the organisms were apparently protected in crystals and similar material. Winge-Hedén (1963) has also described an autoclave unit which can be used for both steam and ethylene oxide sterilizations. For the latter she used a pre-vacuum technique and a sterilizing time of 6 hours at 60° with a 10 per cent gaseous concentration of ethylene oxide. This was successful in sterilizing even the spores of *Bacillus brevis* dried on aluminium foil or on paper strips and wrapped in nylon foil, provided the humidity was appropriately adjusted by letting in a small amount of steam or by adding a drop of water to the test strips. In fact, this adapted sterilizer was considered to be superior in performance to a commercial high-pressure ethylene oxide sterilizer. As in the author's experience, Winge-Hedén found a pre-vacuum stage to be essential in order to help diffusion and penetration.

An alternative method applicable in some cases is to pack the materials to be sterilized in a gas-tight bag and then fill the bag with an ethylene oxide-carbon dioxide or -freon mixture, seal it and leave at room temperature for a given length of time. This has been proved successful by Lammers *et al.* (1960) for disinfecting bedding, blankets and pillows, the treatment being to expose them to a 17 per cent ethylene oxide concentration for a period of 48 hours. It is clearly important with this technique to use a material which is impervious to ethylene oxide so that the full concentration is maintained throughout the period of treatment. Winge-Hedén (1963) overcame this by using a "three-foil" laminate of paper, aluminium foil and polythene, and Bishop, Robertson and Williams (1964) used bags made of a Terylene fabric proofed with Neoprene, with the seams vulcanized; polyvinyl chloride is not satisfactory.

Other purposes to which ethylene oxide sterilization has been put are the sterilization of blankets, for which either a 10 per cent gaseous concentration overnight (Kaye, 1950) or 500 mg per litre for 4 hours or 1,000 mg per litre for 2 hours (Foter, 1960) have been found effective, and for sterilizing respirator and other ventilator filters (Bishop, Robertson and Williams, 1964), for which purpose the ventilator is enclosed in a Terylene-Neoprene bag (*see* above); the bag is then filled with the sterilizing gas which is cycled for 24 hours through the filter by means of a small pump. More topically it has been used for the safe rendering of space-travel vehicles for interplanetary flights (Phillips and Hoffman, 1960) concerning which at least one international conference has been held and reported on. Its particular value in the latter case is that it does not damage delicate electrical and electronic equipment.

In bacteriology. A further use for ethylene oxide, although strictly not a gaseous sterilization procedure, is in the sterilization of bacteriological culture media, particularly those containing carbohydrates which are sensitive to heat treatment (Wilson and Bruno, 1950; Judge and Pelczar, 1955). The material to be sterilized is chilled below 10°, one per cent by volume of liquid ethylene oxide is added and the container is lightly sealed. It is allowed to stand in this state for an hour or two, after which it is transferred to a warm place at 37° or 45° and kept there for a few hours, or overnight. During the first stage of the process the sterilization takes place and during the latter part the ethylene oxide is completely volatilized and removed. By this means, milk, serum and sugar-containing media are alleged to have been sterilized without impairing their nutrient properties, but the author has found several lots of serum and of other media treated in this way to be rather less capable of supporting bacterial growth. Vaccinia virus (Wilson and Bruno, 1950) and several other unrelated viruses (Ginsberg and Wilson, 1950) have also been substantially, but not totally inactivated by similar treatments.

Some limitations. Two points are implicit in any attempt at sterilizing with ethylene oxide, (*a*) the assumption that due account has been taken of the absorption of the gas by the materials being sterilized, and (*b*) that the organisms are accessible by the gas. As already indicated, powders, rubber and some plastics all absorb ethylene oxide to a greater or less extent—they also lose it equally rapidly on exposure to the air—so that unless allowances are made one can be under a false impression as to the concentrations of ethylene oxide actually used, hence the value of the Royce indicator sachet. The contingency can be met either by an absorption pretreatment, or by putting in a deliberate and calculated excess of the gas initially, or by topping up during the sterilizing period. All three methods have been used.

The question of the accessibility of the organism is a more difficult one and depends on two factors, its actual physical protection and the moisture present. The latter is of no significance if the organisms are brought from the moist state (which is rare), but if hard dried, or even if normally dried on hard surfaces a suitable equilibration or "dwell" period must be allowed for the cells to pick up the necessary moisture, the duration of which depends on the extent of the initial drying. For this reason, Perkins and Lloyd (1961) concluded that humidification to a level of 55–60 per cent must be established and they also showed that it must be maintained preferably for 60 minutes to allow the solid to absorb moisture and "thereby render the contaminants susceptible to ethylene oxide." Phillips (1961) was much less sanguine about the subject finding that with washed spores dried on cotton squares 'resistance' could be induced by drying for as little as one hour and that subsequent rehydration took as long as six days at 75 per cent, or four days at 98 per cent relative humidity.

The second aspect of the question, namely the physical protection of the organism, is in some ways bound up with the moisture aspect. It is known that some substances cannot be sterilized with ethylene oxide at any level of concentration or for any duration of time. This is because during manufacture organisms become occluded in their crystals and so are completely protected. This can occur with sodium chloride, glucose, procaine penicillin and the sulphonamides, as amply demonstrated by Royce and Bowler (1961), by precipitating the substances with bacterial spores present, by moistening the material with a concentrated suspension of spores and drying it, or, more naturally, by drying a suspension from saline or some other crystalloid solution. Contrary to expectation they found that serum offers a lower level of protection than does sodium chloride, and they were able to overcome the difficulty in some cases by raising the humidity to near saturation, thus rendering the protective coating more permeable and the organisms more accessible.

As might be expected, sterilization by ethylene oxide has many critics and adversaries, most of whom can produce evidence of the failure of the treatment in some particular circumstances. Sometimes the failure can be traced to leakages and loss of ethylene oxide; in other instances the organisms must have been inaccessible for one reason or another. Ethylene oxide sterilization is not a straightforward and easy method to employ and for this reason requires skilled and experienced workers to handle or supervise it.

β-Propiolactone

β-Propiolactone, frequently abbreviated to B.P.L., is another heterocyclic ring compound having the structure

$$CH_2—C{:}O$$
$$|\quad\quad|$$
$$CH_2—O$$

It boils at 155°, has a low vapour pressure, is a vesicant and lachrymator, polymerizes at elevated temperatures, is easily soluble in water and hydrolyses fairly readily at 25° and over. It is bactericidal, sporicidal, fungicidal and virucidal, and is reputed to be 4,000 times more active (presumably on a concentration basis) than ethylene oxide. In spite of this its development as a sterilizing agent has been restricted because of its allegedly carcinogenic and other physiologically undesirable properties (Wisely and Falk, 1960; Searle, 1961). It is probably because of these undesirable side-effects, which demand great caution in handling, that B.P.L. has not received the attention it merits as a sterilizing agent. Apart from these disadvantages it is particularly suitable for sterilizing large enclosed spaces but unsuitable for treating porous materials because of its low power of penetration (Hoffman and Warshowsky, 1958). It is used both in the vapour phase, when it has to be heated or atomized into the atmosphere because of its low volatility, and for sterilizing liquid preparations, having been first described as a bactericide and virucide under such conditions by Hartman, Piepes and Wallbank (1951). Like ethylene oxide it is nearly as effective against spores as against vegetative bacteria, the factor in this case being about 4 or 5.

Although its properties in liquid media have been known for some time it was not until 1958 that its properties as a gaseous sterilizing agent were described (Hoffman and Warshowsky, 1958), when it was likened more nearly to formaldehyde than to ethylene oxide in its germicidal properties, although the authors were careful to point out that it possesses a number of advantages over formaldehyde. Hoffman and Warshowsky's preliminary experiments were conducted with washed organisms dried on to small pieces

TABLE 19

The sporicidal action of β-propiolactone vapour
(after Hoffman and Warshowsky, 1958)

Concentration of vapour (mg/l)	Relative humidity (%)	Temperature	Time (in min) to kill 99·9% spores
0·1	80	27°	120
0·4	80	27°	30
1·5	80	27°	7–8
1·5	60	27°	360
1·5	50	27°	No kill
1·5	80	25°	10–15
1·5	80	15°	40
1·5	80	6°	80
1·6	80	−2°	140
1·5	80	−10°	300

Test organisms were spores of *B. subtilis* dried on cotto◀ squares.

of cloth and from their results they concluded that the activity of B.P.L. is directly dependent on its vapour concentration and on the relative humidity and temperature. They found the temperature coefficient for each 10° change over the range −10° to +25° to be 2 or 3, and the maximum death rate of spores to be at a humidity level of about 80 per cent. Below 70 per cent it fell away rapidly so that on reaching 45 per cent relative humidity the kill was almost negligible.

The vapour concentrations most commonly employed are about 1–1·5 mg of B.P.L. per litre of air (although amounts up to 4 or 5 mg per litre have been used in certain cases) and at this level a 90 per cent kill of spores is effected after 2 minutes at 25° and a 99 per cent kill after 10 minutes. The rate of kill of B.P.L. is, therefore, quite rapid compared with other gaseous agents. Some figures illustrating this are quoted in Table 19. This rapid death rate was subsequently confirmed by Spiner and Hoffman (1960) from which they concluded that for general disinfecting purposes a concentration of 2–4 mg of B.P.L. per litre of air should be used at a relative humidity of not less than

70 per cent and a temperature not below 24°, the disinfecting period being 2 hours. In a similar manner Bruch (1961) has used concentrations ranging from 3 to 5·3 mg per litre to disinfect operating theatres, maternity wards, laboratories, etc., and his results show that spore strips of *B. subtilis* and *B. stearothermophilus* are sterilized in a majority of cases in 2 to 4 hours under these conditions.

B.P.L. is also strongly virucidal. One to 2 mg per litre in air will inactivate completely the Venezuelan encephalomyelitis, smallpox, yellow fever, psittacosis and Q fever viruses dried on small cotton squares or pieces of filter paper in 30 minutes and often within 15 minutes (Dawson, Hearn and Hoffman, 1959; Dawson, Janssen and Hoffman, 1960). Because of this universal activity against all types of micro-organism and also because of its reported non-corrosiveness to metals, Allen and Murphy (1960) have suggested its use in the vapour state for sterilizing instruments. All that is needed is a suitable sealed box or other container in which to put the instruments and apparatus, including microscopes if necessary, and a means of dispersing the vapour either by heating the liquid in an air stream or by atomizing it. Sterilization is complete within one hour.

Turning to sterilization in aqueous media, B.P.L. was first used in this context by Hartman, Piepes and Wallbank (1951) for treating plasma and whole blood, again largely because of its sporicidal and virucidal activities and because of its non-toxic residue on hydrolysis. The concentration used was 1,500 mg per litre and it required up to 24 hours at 6–10°, 7–12 hours at 24–27° and 1–2 hours at 37°. Curran and Evans (1956) found it the most satisfactory of 400 compounds examined for the purpose, and for treating milk (if anyone would wish to do so)—a 0·3 per cent solution was rapidly lethal to bacterial spores at 25° and 37° but did not sterilize heavy infections presumably because of the concomitant hydrolysis—and Hartman, Kelly and LoGrippo (1955) found it the best of 550 compounds examined. Various other authors have described its use for sterilizing culture media for fermentations and the like containing carbohydrates (Himmelfarb, Read and Litsky, 1961), and in antibiotic fermentation work (Toplin and Gaden, 1961) by a continuous process (Toplin, 1962). Usually a 0·2–0·5 per cent solution is used and the residual B.P.L. is hydrolysed by heat at 80° for 15 minutes or 60° for 30 minutes. Unfortunately the hydrolysis reduces substantially the pH value of the medium to about 4, so that a subsequent adjustment is needed. This, however, is no disadvantage where mould culture is concerned, in which field it has been used for sterilizing various solids, such as bran and beet pulp, used for propagating fungi, the treatment being by a 1 per cent aqueous solution kept for 3 hours at 37° (Yulius and Bahzinov, 1963).

In the virus field it has been found effective against at least seventeen types and it has been described by LoGrippo (1960) as "the drug of choice" for sterilizing whole blood and plasma and freeing them particularly from the hepatitis infection. It can also be used for sterilizing tissue grafts and collagen sutures (Ball *et al.*, 1961) and on account of its speed of action for preparing vaccines quickly (LoGrippo and Hartman, 1955). A solution containing 10 mg of B.P.L. per ml will inactivate a suspension of the Venezuelan equine encephalitis virus in 5 minutes, and at one-tenth this concentration it takes 15 minutes: there is no action in 1 hour with a 0·1 mg per ml solution (Hearn and Dawson, 1961). The Eastern strain of this virus in plasma is inactivated by a 4 mg per ml solution at 37°, and at 4°, in about 15 minutes (LoGrippo, 1959), but it seems to take several hours if whole blood is present. There is frequently a tailing off in the rate of inactivation, and this, according to LoGrippo, can be overcome by combining the treatment with ultraviolet irradiation.

Other heterocyclic compounds

As well as ethylene oxide, other three-membered ring compounds have been examined for their activities as bactericides in the vapour phase. Although several of them are more effective than ethylene oxide, they have certain overriding disadvantages which make them unsuitable for use as practical disinfectants. Nevertheless, their bactericidal properties are worth recording.

Compounds of this group which have been examined (Phillips, 1949) include those containing oxygen in the ring, such as propylene oxide, epichlorohydrin, epibromohydrin, styrene oxide and glycidyl derivatives; those containing sulphur in the ring, such as ethylene sulphide and its chloromethyl homologue; and those containing nitrogen, such as ethylene imine and its homologues. All of these compounds are active alkylating agents and at the same time are bactericidal to a greater or less extent in the vapour state. Cyclopropane, on the other hand, is a stable substance and is devoid of antibacterial activity. Incidentally, methyl bromide, another alkylating agent, is also bactericidal, although it is most commonly used as a disinfesting and fumigating agent.

Of all of these compounds, Kaye (1949) found the nitrogen-substituted ring compounds, ethylene imine and some of its derivatives, to be the most effective bactericides, and these were followed by the sulphur-substituted ring compounds, ethylene sulphide and its homologues. They were all superior to the epoxy compounds. The outstanding compound, ethylene imine, was several hundred times more active on a concentration-killing time basis than ethylene oxide, but it is too unstable and too corrosive to be of practical value.

Another of this type of compound is glycidaldehyde. This compound boils at about 112° and so it must be dispersed in the vapour phase by spraying—a 50 per cent solution in water is used. At a concentration in air of 3–4 mg per litre it will kill *B. globigii* spores dried on paper strips in 4 hours at 28° but it only effects a 90 per cent reduction at 20° in 6 hours. For this order of activity the relative humidity must be high, over 75 per cent (Dawson, 1962).

Propylene oxide merits some attention, in view of the interest taken in it. It does not carry the same hazards as does ethylene oxide, but at best it is only about half as active and its other properties make it far less valuable as a sterilizing agent. Its boiling point is above room temperature—actually it is 35°—and so it is not readily dispersed or removed. Because of this, and of its low activity, its use is confined to the sterilization of powders, particularly those compounded in toilet and cosmetic preparations, for which purpose 1–2 per cent by weight of propylene oxide is added to the powder, the treatment being carried out in sealed containers. It is usual to raise the temperature to assist volatilization and also to increase the activity of the vapour. After 2–3 hours at 37° the total microbial count of cocoa powder has been reduced by 50–70 per cent and the moulds by 90–99 per cent (Bruch and Koesterer, 1961). In the presence of the necessary small amount of moisture propylene oxide hydrolyses slowly, hence there is no need to remove it after sterilization treatment.

Other vapours

Many other substances which are actively bactericidal in solution have been examined for their disinfecting powers in the vapour state, but only occasionally has any activity been manifest. Much more success has been obtained with the essential and perfume oils as can be seen from several reports in the literature dating from about 1920. Coulthard (1931) examined several such compounds by inoculating young cultures of organisms on the surface of nutrient agar in petri plates, inverting the plates and then putting small pieces of filter paper in the lids. Three drops of different concentrations of the test substance in acetone were placed on the papers and the plates incubated at 37°. Only acid-fast organisms were used, and under these conditions 4-*n*-amyl-*m*-cresol was the most active of the substances examined; thymol, oil of cassia, creosote and phenol were next in order, and guaiacol and eucalyptus oil were inactive. Subsequently several other workers have used similar methods to examine larger numbers of substances against bacteria and fungi but latterly Grubb (1959) developed a two-phase test, the first being described as a "static" test and involving the exposure of test organisms to the vapour for 18–24 hrs, and the second as a "dynamic" test with exposure times measured only in seconds if desired. In the static test, the organisms are inoculated in the surface of an agar plate, in the lid of which a small cup is sealed to take the volatile oil. The sealed plate is incubated at 37° overnight, after which the cupped lid is replaced by a fresh sterile lid and the incubation continued. Counts taken after the first incubation period can be considered to be "bacteriostatic" counts and those after the second incubation "bactericidal" ones.

In the second phase the vapour at a known concentration is drawn for given time over an agar slope freshly inoculated with the test organism after which the slope is incubated to assess survival and growth. Grubb was mainly interested in organisms causing respiratory infections, and so his range included *Staphylococcus*, *Streptococcus*, *Klebsiella* and *Pneumococcus* species, and, rather like Coulthard, found thymol, menthol and other drugs commonly used in inhalation therapy to be the most effectively bactericidal.

Some years earlier, Lebduška and Pidra (1940) tested 128 compounds for their activities against *Staph. aureus* and *E. coli* and found that only iodine, trichlorophenol and salicylaldehyde suppressed growth completely, whilst phenol, *o*-cresol, thymol and several others were partially inhibitory. Maruzzella and colleagues (1958*a*, 1958*b*, 1960) examined well over a hundred essential and perfume oils for their antibacterial and antifungal properties and found quite a surprisingly high proportion active, in many cases the vapour being actually lethal. The highest overall activities amongst the essential oils were with oil of thyme, cinnamon, savory and cassia. Other compounds which exhibited exceptional antifungal activities included several of the lower esters of benzoic, propionic, butyric, caproic and salicylic acids, several aldehydes, including the nonyl compound, heptyl and octyl formates, dipropyl and other ketones (Maruzzella, Chiaramonte and Garofalo, 1961).

With compounds of such low volatility treatment *in vacuo* and at elevated temperatures might be expected to enhance their activities, but even so only a few compounds show any appreciable activity. According to Coulthard (unpublished), bacterial spores under these conditions were killed only by phenol and iodine, but this required 14 days at 37°. If the temperature was raised to 70°, then sterilization took place within 24 hours. Guaiacol, creosote and several essential oils were ineffective.

REFERENCES

ALDER, V. G., BROWN, ANNE M. and GILLESPIE, W. A. (1966). *J. clin. Path.*, **19**, 83.
ALLEN, H. F. and MURPHY, J. T. (1960). *J. Amer. med. Ass.*, **172**, 1759.
BAER, J. M. (1941). U.S. Pat. 2,229,360.
BALL, E. L., DORNBUSH, A. C., SIEGER, G. M. and STIRN, F. E. (1961). *Appl. Microbiol.* **9**, 269.
BISHOP, C., ROBERTSON, D. S. and WILLIAMS, S. R. (1964). *Brit. J. Anaesth.*, **36**, 53.
BRACKEN, A., WILTON-DAVIES, C. C. and WEALE, F. E. (1960). *Guy's Hosp. Rep.*, **109** 75.
BRUCH, C. W. (1961). *Amer. J. Hyg.*, **73**, 1.
BRUCH, C. W. and KOESTERER, M. G. (1961). *J. food Sci.*, **26**, 428.
BULLOCK, K. and RAWLINS, E. A. (1954), *J. Pharm. Pharmacol.*, **6**, 859.
CATHCART, W. H., WYBERG, R. E. and MERZ, A. (1942). *Food Res.*, **7**, 1.
CHURCH, B. D., HALVORSON, H., RAMSEY, D. S. and HARTMAN, ROBERTA S. (1956) *J. Bact.*, **72**, 242.
COULTHARD, C. E. (1931). *Brit. J. exp. Path.*, **12**, 331.
CURRAN, H. R. and EVANS, F. R. (1956). *J. infect. Dis.*, **99**, 212.
DAWSON, F. W. (1962). *Amer. J. Hyg.*, **76**, 209.
DAWSON, F. W., HEARN, H. J. and HOFFMAN, R. K. (1959). *Appl. Microbiol.*, **7**, 199.
DAWSON, F. W., JANSSEN, R. J. and HOFFMAN, R. K. (1960). *Appl. Microbiol.*, **8**, 39.

DINEEN, P. (1961). *J. Amer. med. Ass.*, **176**, 772.
ELFORD, W. J. and VAN DEN ENDE, JOAN (1942). *J. Hyg., Camb.*, **42**, 240.
EL KHISHEN, S. A. E. (1950). *J. Sci. Food Agric.*, **1**, 71.
ERNST, R. R. and SHULL, J. J. (1962). *Appl. Microbiol.*, **10**, 337.
FETNER, R. H. and INGOLS, R. S. (1956). *J. gen. Microbiol.*, **15**, 381.
FOTER, M. J. (1960). *Soap*, **36**(4), 73.
GINSBERG, H. S. and WILSON, A. T. (1950). *Proc. Soc. exp. Biol.*, *N.Y.*, **73**, 614.
GRIFFITH, C. L. and HALL, L. A. (1940). U.S. Pat. 2,189,974 and 2,189,948.
GRIFFITH, C. L. and HALL, L. A. (1943). U.S. Pat. Re. 22,284.
GROSS, P. M. and DIXON, L. F. (1937). U.S. Pat. 2,075,845.
GRUBB, T. C. (1959). *J. Amer. pharm. Ass. (Sci.)*, **48**, 272.
GRUNDY, W. E., RDZOK, E. J., REMO, W. J., SAGEN, H. E. and SYLVESTER, J. C. (1957). *J. Amer. pharm. Ass. (Sci.)*, **46**, 439.
HARTMAN, F. W., KELLY, A. R. and LOGRIPPO, G. A. (1955). *Gastroenterology*, **28**, 244.
HARTMAN, F. W., PIEPES, S. L. and WALLBANK, A. M. (1951). *Fed. Proc.* **10**, 358.
HEARN, H. J. and DAWSON, F. W. (1961). *Appl. Microbiol.*, **9**, 278.
HESS, L. G. and TILTON, V. V. (1950). *Ind. engng Chem.*, **42**, 1251.
HOFFMAN, R. K. and WARSHOWSKY, B. (1958). *Appl. Microbiol.*, **6**, 358.
HIMMELFARB, P., READ, R. B. and LITSKY, W. (1961). *Appl. Microbiol.*, **9**, 534.
INGRAM, M. and BARNES, ELLA M. (1954). *J. appl. Bact.*, **17**, 246.
INGRAM, M. and HAINES, R. B. (1949). *J. Hyg., Camb.*, **47**, 146.
JUDGE, L. F. and PELCZAR, M. (1955). *Appl. Microbiol.*, **3**, 292.
KAESS, G. (1956). *Austral. J. appl. Sci.*, **7**, 242.
KAYE, S. (1949). *Amer. J. Hyg.*, **50**, 289.
KAYE, S. (1950). *J. lab. clin. Med.*, **35**, 823.
KAYE, S., IRMINGER, H. F. and PHILLIPS, C. R. (1952). *J. lab. clin. Med.*, **40**, 67.
KAYE, S. and PHILLIPS, C. R. (1949). *Amer. J. Hyg.*, **50**, 296.
KIRBY, G. W., ATKINS, L. and FREY, C. N. (1936). *Food Ind.*, **8**, 450, 470, 488.
LAMMERS, T., DAY, H., KÖRNLEIN, M. and SEIBEL, M. (1960). *Z. Hyg. InfektKr.*, **146**, 236.
LAMMERS, T. and TUNCER, U. (1961). *Gesund. Desinf.*, **53**, 1.
LEBDUŠKA, J. and PIDRA, J. (1940). *Zent. Bakt.*, **145**, 425.
LOGRIPPO, G. A. (1959). *Ann. N.Y. Acad. Sci.*, **83**, 578.
LOGRIPPO, G. A. and HARTMAN, F. W. (1955). *J. Immunol.*, **75**, 123.
MARUZZELLA, J. C., CHIARAMONTE, J. S. and GAROFALO, M. M. (1961). *J. pharm. Sci.*, **50**, 665.
MARUZZELLA, J. C. and HENRY, P. A. (1958a). *J. Amer. pharm. Ass. (Sci.)*, **47**, 250.
MARUZZELLA, J. C. and LIQUORI, L. (1958b). *J. Amer. pharm. Ass. (Sci.)*, **47**, 471.
MARUZZELLA, J. C. and SICURELLA, N. A. (1960). *J. Amer. pharm. Ass. (Sci.)*, **49**, 692.
MAYR, G. (1961). *Recent Developments in the Sterilization of Surgical Materials*, p. 90: Pharmaceutical Press, London.
MICKELSON, O. J. (1957). *J. Amer. diet. Ass.*, **33**, 341.
MOORE, W. K. S. and ROYCE, A. (1955). *Brit. J. ind. Med.*, **12**, 169.
MUSCI, J. N. (1957). U.S. Pat. 2,809,879.
NASH, T. and HIRCH, ANN (1954). *J. appl. Chem.*, **4**, 458.
NEELY, W. B. (1963), *J. Bact.*, **85**, 1028, 1420; **86**, 445.
NORDGREN, G. (1939). *Acta path. microbiol. scand.*, Suppl. 40.
Note on *The Practical Aspects of Formaldehyde Fumigation* (1958). *Month. Bull. Min. Hlth.*, **17**, 270.
PERKINS, J. J. and LLOYD, R. S. (1961). *Recent Developments in the Sterilization of Surgical Materials*, p. 76: Pharmaceutical Press, London.
PHILLIPS, C. R. (1949). *Amer. J. Hyg.*, **49**, 280.
PHILLIPS, C. R. (1952). *Bact. Rev.*, **16**, 135.
PHILLIPS, C. R. (1961). *Recent Developments in the Sterilization of Surgical Materials*, p. 59: Pharmaceutical Press, London.
PHILLIPS, C. R. and HOFFMAN, R. K. (1960). *Science*, **132**, 991.
PHILLIPS, C. R. and KAYE, S. (1949). *Amer. J. Hyg.*, **50**, 270.
PHILLIPS, C. R. and WARSHOWSKY, B. (1958). *Ann. Rev. Microbiol.*, **12**, 525.
RAUSCHER, H., MAYR, G. and KAEMANVER, H. (1957). *Food Mfg*, **32**, 169.

Report of the Committee on Formaldehyde Disinfection of the Public Health Laboratory Service (1958). *J. Hyg., Camb.*, **56**, 488.

ROBERTS, J. L., ALLISON, L. E., PRICHETT, P. S. and RIDDLE, K. B. (1943). *J. Bact.*, **45**, 40.

ROYCE, A. and BOWLER, C. (1959). *J. Pharm. Pharmacol.*, **11**, 294T.

ROYCE, A. and BOWLER, C. (1961). *J. Pharm. Pharmacol.*, **13**, 87T.

ROYCE, A. and SYKES, G. (1955). *J. Pharm. Pharmacol.*, **7**, 1046.

SALLE, A. J. and KORNEZOVSKY, M. (1942). *Proc. Soc. exp. Biol., N.Y.*, **50**, 12.

SCHRADER, H. and BOSSERT, E. (1936). U.S. Pat. 2,037,439.

SEARLE, C. E. (1961). *Brit. J. Cancer*, **15**, 804.

SEXTON, R. J. and HENSON, E. V. (1950). *Arch. ind. Hyg.*, **2**, 549.

SKEEHAN, R. A. (1959). *Amer. J. Ophthal.*, **47**, 86.

SKEEHAN, R. A., KING, J. H. and KAYE. S. (1956). *Amer. J. Ophthal.*, **42**, 424.

SPINER, D. R. and HOFFMAN, R. K. (1960). *Appl. Microbiol.*, **8**, 152.

THOMAS, C. G. A. (1960). *Guy's Hosp. Rep.*, **109**, 57.

TOPLIN, I. and GADEN, E. L. (1961). *J. biochem. microbiol. Technol. Engng*, **3**, 311.

TOPLIN, I. (1962). *Biotech. Bioengn.*, **4**, 331.

VELU, H., LEPIGRE, A. and BELLOCQ, P. (1942). *Bull. Acad. méd., Paris*, **126**, 62.

WILSON, A. T. and BRUNO, P. (1950). *J. exp. Med.*, **91**, 449.

WINDMUELLER, H. G., ACKERMAN, C. J. and ENGEL, R. W. (1956). *J. Nutrit.*, **60**, 527.

WINDMUELLER, H. G., ACKERMAN, C. J. and ENGEL, R. W. (1959). *J. biol. Chem.*, **234**, 895 (also p. 889).

WINGE-HEDÉN, KERSTIN (1963). *Acta path. microbiol. scand.*, **58**, 225.

WISELEY, D. V. and FALK, H. L. (1960). *J. Amer. med. Ass.*, **173**, 1161.

YULIUS, A. A. and BAHZINOV, A. G. (1963). Translation from the Russian of *Microbiology*, **32**, 122.

CHAPTER 9

TREATMENT BY COLD, DESICCATION AND CELLULAR DISINTEGRATION

As WELL AS the methods of sterilization by heat, by filtration and by radiation treatment, other physical methods have been tried with variable success. These comprise principally treatment with cold, by desiccation, by ultrasonics and other means of cellular disintegration. It can be said at the outset that none is wholly effective or practical; cold and desiccation, whilst being lethal to a certain extent, are means of preserving bacteria under some circumstances, and the various forms of cellular disintegration are severely limited in scope and application.

Cooling, chilling and freezing

Cooling to low temperatures, and the lower the better, is popularly considered to be fatal to all forms of life. Whilst this may be true in a measure for the larger forms of organized life, it is certainly not true for the smaller plant life, and especially that of micro-organisms. When bacterial cultures are chilled or frozen a proportion of the cells is nearly always rendered non-viable, the actual amount depending on the chilling or freezing procedure. It appears necessary, however, to differentiate between freezing and chilling without freezing, because different factors come into play with the change in physical state.

Cooling and chilling

The phenomenon of 'cold shock' produced by a sudden reduction in cell temperature is common to many types of micro-organisms; indeed some of the higher forms—some of the amoebae for instance—are quite unable to survive such treatment. With the bacteria, the death-level can be very high during the actual cooling process, but having been cooled the subsequent death-rate is much less rapid and may, in fact, become almost negligible. The amount of loss depends on several factors, the most important of which appear to be the rate of cooling, the nature of the suspending medium and the growth phase of the organism (Meynell, 1958).

The phenomenon is well illustrated with young cultures of *Escherichia coli* which if cooled rapidly from 45° to 10° (Sherman and Cameron, 1934) or from 37° to 4° (Meynell, 1958) can suffer losses in viability of 95 per cent or more. If, however, the temperature is reduced gradually over a period of 30 minutes there is practically no loss. A similar effect is noted with *Pseudomonas pyocyanea* and the salmonellae if chilled suddenly from 37° to 0°, in fact there is some loss at any chilling temperature below 18° (Gorrill and McNeill, 1960). The greatest losses occur, as might be expected, when the organisms exhibit their greatest activities, that is, when they are in the log phase of growth; in the lag or stationary phase losses are comparatively small. The phenomenon must not be construed to be universal; it depends very much on the interrelationship of organism and culture medium, as shown by Strange and Dark (1962) and Strange and Ness (1963).

Freezing

Mechanical and chemical considerations. When micro-organisms are subjected to freezing they are naturally susceptible to the phenomena associated with straight chilling, and in addition they suffer a further strain by virtue of the change in physical state associated with freezing.

In the absence of any real information on the subject, it was commonly believed that death by freezing is caused by the cells being crushed and ruptured by the ice crystals formed round them; in other words, the lethal process was assumed to be a purely mechanical action. This same mechanical action was also used to explain the observed fact that the death-rate is often higher at temperatures just below the freezing point than those much lower, the basis of this argument being that the larger ice crystals formed with a slow rate of freezing in the range −2° to about −20° exert a greater destructive pressure than do smaller crystals formed at lower temperatures.

Whilst, on the evidence now available, the hypothesis of mechanical destruction cannot be entirely ruled out, serious doubts were raised against the completeness of this explanation by the classical work of Haines (1938), which led him to express views based rather on physico-chemical considerations. Haines attributed death to changes in the cellular proteins ultimating in their denaturation and flocculation, and he established this by demonstration, showing that at the most critical lethal temperature, −2°, 50 per cent of the coagulable protein is precipitated within 8 days, whereas no precipitation occurs on freezing to −70°, neither does it occur on storage at −20°.

Based on these and other findings, several subsequent workers, notably Weiser and Osterud (1945), set forth a number of postulates most of which in the light of further experience have unfortunately been shown to be not wholly tenable. We are thus thrust back to a position in which we are aware of several facts and phenomena, but have as yet no conclusive explanation of them: mechanical damage by ice crystals undoubtedly takes place; there is obviously some metabolic damage, because frozen organisms frequently become progressively less able to recover on simple nutrient media and require much more nutritionally rich medium before they will grow out (Straka and Stokes, 1959; Nakamura and Dawson, 1961); dehydration of the cell protoplasm by the protective agent appears to be of some significance (Postgate and Hunter, 1961), and osmosis seems to play a role as yet undefined. All these are contributory factors.

For optimum survival at sub-freezing temperatures, a protective substance in the form of a non-electrolyte is essential. Opinions seem to differ as to which is the best material, but nutrient broth, peptone water, glucose (7·5 per cent), sucrose (6 to 10 per cent) and glycerol (10 per cent) rank high in the list. Sodium glutamate, lactate, malate, and pyruvate, certain buffer solutions, particularly Tris buffers, and culture supernatant fluids containing the products of cell lysis of the particular organism have also been

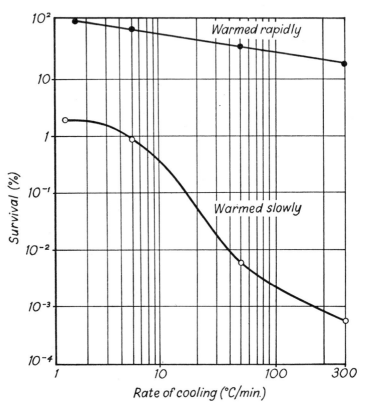

FIG. 13. *Survival of* Pasteurella tularensis *cells cooled at indicated rates to* $-75°$ *and warmed either rapidly or slowly*
(Taken from Mazur, 1960)

ased successfully, and more recently derivatives of urea have been suggested us well as some of the polymers of glucose, such as dextran, and polyethylene glycol. Saline, quarter-strength Ringer and water are to be avoided. They can be highly lethal and give survival rates of only a fraction of one per cent in contrast to 70 to 100 per cent for the other substances mentioned.

After freezing there can be a further fall in viability on storage, depending largely on the suspending medium employed. In some instances, as when erythritol is present, it can be quite rapid so that the culture becomes totally inactivated in a matter of minutes (Postgate and Hunter, 1961). On the other hand, dilute glycerol (5–10 per cent) has a considerable stabilizing influence and will maintain the viability of a culture for a year or more. In fact this method has been recommended for the preservation of assay organisms (Tanguay, 1959) because on thawing they are ready for immediate use without further manipulations or culturing. In yet a third group (*e.g.*, Clement, 1961) the situation appears to become stable after a short period. Again, opinions differ on the optimum storage temperature: some prefer an intermediate range of −20° to −30°, others a much lower level of −70° or less.

Susceptibilities of micro-organisms. The immediate death rate of bacteria from a single freezing and thawing varies considerably with the species and according to the suspending medium and the rapidity of the freezing. From data given by Haines (1938), and subsequently confirmed by Benedict *et al.* (1961), the greatest survival rates are to be expected when the organisms are frozen most rapidly, but in order to demonstrate this, rapid warming is also necessary (Mazur, 1960). If a rapidly cooled culture is allowed to warm only slowly then the advantage gained in the first stage is lost: this is most conveniently illustrated in Mazur's own example (Fig. 13) of the survival of *Pasteurella tularensis* frozen and warmed at different rates to and from −75°. Also of interest in this context is the effect of ultra-rapid freezing and thawing on different cultures. In Doebbler and Rinfret's (1963) experiments on this topic the organisms were grown in normal culture media and then frozen rapidly at the rate of several hundred degrees per second and finally warmed at the same rate (the former by spraying the culture on liquid nitrogen and the latter by putting the frozen droplets into saline solution at 37°). The survival rates thus obtained were:

Staphylococcus aureus	$91 \pm 11\%$
Escherichia coli	$100 \pm 4\%$
Aspergillus niger	$22 \pm 1\%$
Saccharomyces cerevisiae	$42 \pm 7\%$

Most of the data presented by different workers indicate that the most resistant bacteria, apart from the sporing forms, are to be found amongst those of the Gram-positive group, the micrococci, the lactobacilli, and the faecal streptococci. Proom (1951) also found this group to be the most resistant, for in an assessment of survival rates under different conditions he obtained values ranging "from nearly 100% in broth or saline with resistant species, *e.g.* Gram-positive cocci, to 20% in saline and 70% in broth with the intermediate species, *e.g.* Gram-negative rods, to 1% in saline and 15% in broth with susceptible species, *e.g.* the gonococcus." This is in contrast to the findings of others on the effects of chilling alone.

It has been frequently demonstrated that repeated freezing and thawing is much more effectively lethal than is a single treatment and according to

Harrison (1955) the plot of logarithm of survivors against numbers of freezings generally gives a sigmoidal curve. The configuration of the curve is influenced greatly by the period of storage between successive freezings, being much steeper when the intervals are as long as 24 hours than when they are as short as half an hour. It also tends to approach nearer to a straight line as the intervals are shortened. A remarkable, though incidental, finding was that the second freezing is generally more lethal than any other freezing!

Extremes of acidity increase the mortality rate, presumably due to the further concentration of the acid in the surrounding fluid when pure ice crystals are formed. On the other hand, as has already been indicated on p. 230, sugars and glycerol are amongst the best known agents for diminishing mortality.

Moulds and yeasts are generally more resistant than vegetative bacteria, but bacterial spores are in quite a different category. They are either completely unaffected by freezing or a small proportion only is rendered nonviable.

Many of the viruses are rapidly inactivated at low temperatures, but again some of them can be preserved in this way for quite long periods with only a slow rate of inactivation. In particular several bacteriophages from different hosts are known to survive freezing to ultralow temperatures ($-196°$) with recoveries ranging from 10 per cent to virtually 100 per cent, and with no loss in specificity or other properties (Clark, Horneland and Klein, 1962). In the experiments described the phages were only held frozen for two hours, but the temperature employed was so low, and the consequent energy of residual chemical or physical action so low, that they could probably be kept in this state indefinitely.

A limited few of the protozoa can also be preserved by freezing.

Preservation of foods

A sufficiently low temperature will arrest completely the growth of all micro-organisms, therefore, foods can be adequately preserved for long periods of freezing. The limiting temperature below which bacteria cease to grow appears to be about $-8°$ (Haines, 1934), but other organisms can pro-liferate at much lower levels. Thus, osmophilic yeasts can grow in orange juice as low as $-10°$ (Ingram, 1951), a "pink yeast" is said to grow on frozen oysters down to $-18°$, and a temperature of $-23°$ is said to be necessary to stop the growth of *Oospora lactis* in butter (Davis, 1951).

One important point to remember is that for successful food preservation the initial bacterial content must not be high. The organisms are not killed by freezing, neither are their toxins or other metabolic by-products des-troyed, therefore, when the temperature is restored to normal, growth is quickly resumed and spoilage can proceed. The majority of the enzymes remain intact, and it is clear from several reported observations (*see* Ingram, 1951) that some of them can even continue their activities in the frozen state. Therefore, in spite of the absence of microbial proliferation, a certain amount of spoilage can still take place affecting physical characteristics such as colour, consistency and, of course, taste. This emphasizes the fact that refrigeration cannot really take the place of good hygiene and correct handling of food.

In frozen foods there is a gradual death-rate of all vegetative organisms, but not of bacterial spores. The rate depends upon temperature, as already explained, and also on environmental conditions and it is roughly exponential with time.

Acids are less effective in the cold than at normal temperatures. It is not surprising, therefore, to find staphylococci and some salmonellae surviving in fruit juices for several months at −18° (McCleskey and Christopher, 1941) and other bacteria and yeasts for as long as 3 years (Tanner and Williamson, 1928; Tanner and Wallace, 1931).

Freeze-drying

Freeze-drying as a method for preserving bacteria and other micro-organisms has been known and practised for many years, and it has been extended beyond the field of microbiology to include a range of other biological materials. As such it has attracted much attention as witnessed by the number of reviews that have appeared (*e.g.* Greaves, 1946, 1962; Fry, 1954), and the number of symposia (*First International Symposium on Freezing and Drying*, 1951; Second International Symposium, 1960; Symposium, 1960) held on the subject.

Organisms treated in this way will certainly retain their viability almost indefinitely. It used to be thought that their antigenic structure remained completely inviolate, but more recently it has been shown that certain losses in this direction can occur. Davis (1963) for instance has kept 277 cultures of rhizobia, yeasts, actinomycetes and other bacteria and fungi for twenty-one years with a loss of only three cultures, two fungal and one bacterial. But of the 158 rhizobial strains so stored, 19 had lost their ability to produce nodules on their host plant, thus indicating a small change within the cells. *Chromobacterium prodigiosum* also undergoes a certain enzymic change as indicated by the different oxidative metabolism of glucose and ketogluconate (Wasserman and Hopkins, 1958). For this reason Tanguay (1959) prefers to preserve organisms used for assay purposes in the frozen state at −40° suspended in 15 per cent glycerol (see above).

The fundamental principle of the freeze-drying process is that the organisms shall be desiccated whilst still frozen, and two techniques are available for the purpose. The Swift technique (1937) employs the method of dehydration under high vacuum by means of a desiccating agent, and the Flosdorf and Mudd technique (1935) relies upon sublimation of the water through a manifold into a separate condenser: frequently the latter is carried out in two stages, the first to remove the majority of the water and the second, over a desiccant, to complete the process. These are the basic techniques around which all other methods have been constructed, methods which today have reached a certain degree of automation (Maister, Heger and Bogart, 1958) and certainly of mechanization, including a spray freeze-drying technique (Greaves, 1962).

A novel method of drying in a circulating gas system at atmospheric pressure has also been described. The principle of the method is that chilled air is continuously circulated first through frozen pellets or small rods of the culture (the latter prepared by freezing the suspension in small nitrocellulose tubes and then removing the tubes), where it picks up a certain amount of the water in vapour form, and then through a cold condensing chamber where the water vapour is removed. The method sounds to be more awkward and complicated than the more usual vacuum methods, but according to its originators, Wagman and Weneck (1963), it gives better survivals of organisms suspended in water.

Suspending media

As indicated in preceding paragraphs there is frequently some loss in viability during actual freezing and to this must be added a further small loss during drying. The extent of the lethal incidence at these stages depends mainly on the nature of the fluid in which the organisms are suspended immediately before drying and also to a less extent on the rate of freezing and drying. In the earlier years many different suspending media were reported satisfactory, amongst which the most favoured were nutrient broth, peptone water, serum, skimmed milk and gelatin. Various sugars, notably glucose, lactose and sucrose, as well as substances such as mucin and gum tragacanth, have since been added. For certain types of bacteria and viruses Hornibrook (1950) favoured a medium based on the product of dialysis of milk, and containing various inorganic salts and citrates plus 5 per cent of lactose. In a like vein, Benedict et al. (1958) grew their organisms in a medium containing 5 per cent of milk solids, 3 per cent of protopeptone and 2 per cent of glucose and found maximum survivals when the cells were dried as concentrates in their own supernatant fluid. The sodium salts of acids such as acetate, lactate, malate and pyruvate either singly or in admixtures, also acted as stabilizers and the level of protection was clearly linked with the cell concentration/stabilizer concentration ratio, maximum effects being obtained with cells at 200×10^9 per ml and stabilizer at 0·05–0·1M. Of all those listed probably the most popular, and certainly the most widely used, is the "Mist. desiccans" of Fry and Greaves (1951) which consists of one part of nutrient broth and three parts of serum, with 7·5 per cent of glucose added. Since its introduction it has been used successfully with many different types of organism, nevertheless experience has shown that it is not entirely satisfactory, particularly in relation to the preparation of freeze-dried vaccines and the long-term storage stability of organisms at elevated temperatures (a characteristic considered important by Greaves and others).

Besides the obvious fact that vaccines prepared in serum or broth cannot be safely injected into humans, the later investigations revealed two points of fundamental importance: (*i*) sodium glutamate greatly enhances the stability of BCG vaccine (Obayashi, 1960), and (*ii*) this protection is antago-nized by glucose, but not by sucrose or dextran (Muggleton, 1960). These findings led Scott (1960) to conclude that the instability of dried cultures is due to the presence of carbonyl groups which are contributed by the glucose but not by sucrose or other polysaccharides, and which are neutralized by amino acids; hence the value of broth and peptone. These findings also led Greaves (1960) to propose a new freeze-drying medium containing essentially (*a*) a glucose-free protective colloid, such as 5 per cent dextran, (*b*) a buffer to control the final moisture content (see below), *i.e.* sodium glutamate or sucrose in 5–10 per cent concentration, and (*c*) a neutralizer of adventitious carbonyl groups, *i.e.* broth or sodium glutamate. Subsequently (1962) he agreed with Obayshi, Ota and Shiro (1961) in substituting a polyvinylpyrrolidone of molecular weight about 45,000 in the place of dextran. The colloid is said to enhance the value of glutamate.

On the question of rate of freezing and drying there is little information available. The freezing itself should obviously be completed speedily to avoid separation and crystal damage whilst the temperature is being reduced, and equally obviously it is a matter of convenience to complete the drying as soon as possible, at the same time also avoiding overdrying (see below). Nevertheless there may be some advantage in not carrying the process through too rapidly because, according to Record, Taylor and Miller (1962), survival is "actually enhanced by avoiding the sharp decrease in temperature which accompanies evaporative freezing in high vacuum".

There seems to be no firm opinion about the optimum temperature of drying: some prefer to freeze at a very low temperature and then raise it to just below the eutectic level for the actual drying, others keep the mass at a constant low temperature all the time. On purely physical and mechanical grounds very low temperatures seem undesirable because they will retard the rate of sublimation of the water: on biochemical grounds there may well be an optimum temperature level because, according to Leach, Ohye and Scott (1959), there is a medium-temperature interaction which varies with the organisms and with the solutes being used, particularly the carbohydrates. The whole subject is still very empirical.

Storage conditions

It is becoming increasingly evident, in spite of earlier opinions to the contrary, that there is an *optimum* level of dryness for maximum survival and that overdrying can result in a relatively rapid death-rate. This observation was first made by Fry and Greaves (1949), who attributed the value of glucose in the drying medium to its buffering power in controlling the residual moisture content. The optimum value, according to Greaves (1962) is "around 1 per cent", and this is probably a reasonable all-round estimate although Scott (1958) has shown that it is not a constant value but varies according to the composition of the suspending medium and the presence or absence of air during storage. The suspending medium enters the argument because of its large bulk in relation to the bacteria being dried and its varying capacity to retain water. For this reason a total moisture content of the dried material cannot be accepted as a true measure of the water content of the bacteria, and on this basis Scott considered the a_w value (the "water activity" value, or the moisture level when equilibrated in an atmosphere at a definite relative humidity) to be a more satisfactory measure for comparative purposes.

Studying the effects of humidity, coupled in some cases with the influence of air, Scott found no consistent relationships. Frequently an increase in stability *in vacuo* occurred as the a_w was lowered, and frequently he found an optimum stability at an a_w value about 0·2, although sometimes it appeared nearer 0·4. Sucrose eliminated the a_w effect. On the occasions when stability continued to increase as the a_w was reduced to zero either glucose, arabinose whole serum or the dialysable serum fraction was always present, and this probably means that the agent in each case was able to retain sufficient water to prevent the cells from becoming absolutely dry. Such an argument fits Scott's own proffered explanation which he admitted is "by no means simple", but may be associated with "the removal of the most firmly held water molecules [which] results in some loss of stability especially in the presence of air".

With emphasis on the influence of *in vacuo* storage against storage in air Bateman *et al.* (1961) made a number of observations sometimes in contrast to those of Scott. They found, for example, an increasingly rapid decay in the stability of *Chr. prodigiosum* as the moisture content was reduced from 90 per cent to the "critical" level of 30 per cent (apparently equivalent to 94 per cent RH), but the rate of decay was lower in the presence of air, thus demonstrating air in a "protective" role. At lower moisture contents down to 10 per cent the stability *in vacuo* approaches that of wet cells, after which it remains steady; but in air there is a continuous decline in stability until below 1 per cent moisture the decay rate is approximately equal to that at the critical water level *in vacuo*, thus demonstrating air in a "toxic" role. These observations are more in line with the author's experience in which bacteria of many types dried in Mist. desiccans and sealed in air have become non-viable within a month or two, whereas the same organisms sealed in high vacuum have survived for many years. In one particular instance, a *Strepto-coccus pyogenes* culture was still viable after 13 years and had lost none of its original mouse-virulence.

In more systematic study of storage stability Harrison and Pelczar (1963) freeze-dried a wide range of bacteria, sealed them *in vacuo* with a residual air pressure equivalent to 70–100 microns of mercury and then stored them at 8°. They continued their observations for 10 years, after which *Vibrio* and *Acetobacter* cultures had become almost non-viable and the Bacteroides group of organisms had changed some of their functions. By extrapolation, other cultures, notably the Lactobacillaceae, would probably remain viable for centuries.

In passing, it is interesting to note that Benedict *et al.* (1961) found the unprotected cells of *Chr. prodigiosum* to be very susceptible to oxygenation after drying, so that even 10 minutes' exposure to air prior to rehydration could cause a 95 per cent loss in viability. Humidity was not a controlling factor, and the loss could be completely prevented by adding an antioxidant such as urea and related compounds, and even glucose or dextran.

Finally some comment is needed on certain aspects of the reconstitution of dried cultures. It is common practice simply to add a little water to resuspend the organisms and assume that all the viable cells will be thereby recovered. But unless carried out carefully this can be a highly lethal process. During rehydration, changes take place in the permeability of the cell membrane and this must have some influence on its subsequent viability. There is, for example, a high death rate amongst cells dried from sugars alone, due to the extreme osmotic effects during rehydration and the consequent formation of 'sterile' spheroplasts (Record, Taylor and Miller, 1962), an occurrence which can be partially offset by the presence of colloids; hence the further importance of proteins and similar materials in the drying medium. Extending the argument further it might be assumed that solutions of salts would give better recoveries than does water itself; and this is the case, 0·05M sodium malate being the best of a series tested by Wasserman and Hopkins (1957). Similar effects are also noted with the viruses.

This implication of cell permeability suggests that both the temperature and rate of rehydration may be of some significance, and there is experimental evidence to confirm this. Leach and Scott (1959), working with organisms dried from a peptone and sorbitol mixture, established that a rehydration rate of 0·01 to 0·1 mg of water per mg of dry matter per second was the most suitable. In everyday language this means the slow dropwise addition of the rehydration fluid over a period of 30 to 300 seconds. Other drying media might well require a different time factor.

The optimum temperature at which the rehydration is carried out varies with the organism. With some a low range of 0° to 15° is indicated; with others the best recoveries are at 30° to 37°.

Desiccation

In considering the effects of desiccation on bacteria under practical everyday conditions it should always be remembered that most of the findings reported in the literature are based on tests with laboratory cultures. Such cultures are notoriously more sensitive and less robust than their naturally occurring counterparts, and due allowances should be made for this. The findings in the following sections should not, therefore, be taken as absolute but simply as guides to what might happen when conditions are varied.

All micro-organisms subjected to drying under normal conditions, whether it be on surfaces, on fibrous materials, on dust particles or from aerosols, suffer some loss in viability. The least affected are the bacterial spores, with which the losses both during drying and on subsequent storage are small and frequently not significant. On the other hand the losses with all vegetative bacteria are rapid and substantial during the drying phase, and they continue on subsequent storage, although at a slower rate. Air drying is said to be more destructive than drying under vacuum, and organisms kept in air tend to fade out more rapidly than those kept in an inert atmosphere. The temperature of drying is also significant, but probably the most important factor for survival is the final moisture content. There is increasing evidence that the most destructive residual water content is about 30 to 40 per cent (Monk, McCaffray and Davis, 1957; Spicer, 1959; Bateman *et al.*, 1961). This points to two possible reasons: (*i*) the 'toxic' influence of one or other of the solutions, an influence not exerted when there is an excess of water, and (*ii*) a disturbance in the normal metabolic system whereby oxygen consumption and endogenous respiration still takes place but their reaction changes are suppressed.

Amongst the vegetative organisms, some of the more delicate pathogens can only survive an hour or two after natural drying, whereas others will remain viable for many months, especially if they are protected by serum protein or mucoid material and dried on a suitable material. One single infected hospital blanket, for instance, has served as a source of infection for aerial disinfectant tests for as long as eighteen months (Bourdillon, Lidwell and Lovelock, 1948).

Drying on hard surfaces

In a detailed examination of the survival of various cultures dried in thin films on glass cover slips, Lowbury and Fox (1953) found a sharp fall in the viabilities of all organisms during the first 100 minutes followed by a much more gradual fall during the next 60 hours. Many strains of *Staph. aureus*, *Strep. pyogenes*, *Ps. pyocyanea* and of the *Micrococcus* group were tested, and of these the micrococci and *Staph. aureus* were the most resistant, showing an immediate loss of only about 40 per cent, *Ps. pyocyanea* was the most sensitive, with average survivals of less than 5 per cent, and the *Streptococcus* culture fell by about 65 per cent. These figures were obtained with cultures suspended in distilled water; in serum suspensions, the proportions surviving were always higher. According to Garvie (1955) *E. coli* would appear to be much more sensitive than any of the organisms

ıentioned above. Examining the survival of two strains suspended in
) per cent whole milk and dried in thin films on stainless steel strips for
hours at 22°, she found with one strain survival levels ranging between
bout 0·1 and 22 per cent according to the conditions of the test, and with
ıe other strain only 0·01 to 3·3 per cent. The initial culture medium, the
ge of the culture and the number of daily subcultures were all significant.

For preservation purposes, good results have been obtained (Hunt,
ourevitch and Lein, 1958) by drying cultures on fish-spine beads under
acuum with silica gel or calcium chloride and then sealing the beads in
ıbes with the desiccant. By this means species of *Neisseria, Staphylococcus,
treptococcus, Klebsiella* and *Candida* have been kept for periods up to 10
ıonths with only little change, if any, in their antigenic structure and other
haracteristics.

)rying on textiles

The survival of organisms dried on textiles is of considerable importance,
specially in hospital practice where Rountree (1963) has found "some
ıegree of correlation between survival of staphylococci after 15 days and
mplication in epidemics of hospital infection". The general pattern, in terms
ıf sensitivity of organisms, the effect of drying medium and storage conditions,
ollows broadly that for organisms dried on other surfaces, the main difference

TABLE 20

Maximum survival times of Shigella *strains
dried on different surfaces*

Drying surfaces	Survival time (days) stored at				
	−20°	4°	15°	37°	45°
Glass	35	10	10	6	0
Metal	29	14	9	4	0
Cotton	36	32	27	12	0
Wood	46	24	23	13	1
Paper	57	40	28	10	2

)eing that the fibrous structure of the textile appears to afford a certain
ıegree of protection. Wood and paper also behave in the same way. This
vas confirmed by Nakamura (1962) who on examining ten strains of *Shigella
tonnei* found variations between individual strains, as might be expected,
vith *maximum* survival times as given in Table 20. The Table also shows
he significance of storage temperature, the results of which are in line with
hose of Spicer who also found much better survivals at 5–10° than at
!0–30°. No attempt was made to control the humidity, which on spot checks
·anged from 19 to 33 per cent.

Rountree (1963) made her observations with cultures of *Staph. aureus* dried on cotton lint, wool, cellular cotton, wood straw and other fibres and stored at 66–75°F and 42–50 per cent RH. Viabilities fell from initial counts of about 10^8 per gm to 10^3–10^6 per gm in 60–100 days, and the 38 strains she used could be divided into two groups: (1) those which showed a continuous fall during the first 14 days of storage, and (2) those which showed no significant loss in this period. Sunlight enhanced the death rate by as much as twenty-fold, and so did an increase in temperature or humidity.

Compared with freeze-drying methods the survival rates from ordinary drying are small. Spicer (1959), for instance, also working with the relatively delicate and sensitive *Shigella* species obtained survivals after drying on cotton for 24 hours only in the range of 10^{-2}–10^{-4}. These levels are typical for organisms dried from water or buffer solution, but if a protecting fluid is used the levels can be raised to nearer 50 per cent, at least with some organisms. Thus a fluid containing 2 per cent dextran and 0·5 per cent of each of ascorbic acid, thiourea and ammonium chloride will stabilize *E. coli* and *Chr. prodigiosum* but not *Saccharomyces cerevisiae*, *Micrococcus ureae* or *Streptococcus lactis* (Splittstoesser and Foster, 1957).

Again humidity plays an important part in storage survival, and Spicer (1959) obtained better results at 84 per cent RH than under completely dry conditions with his *Shigella* cultures. This finding is in contrast to that of Hunt, Gourevitch and Lein (1958), quoted above, for organisms dried on beads, but whether this is due to the different surfaces, the different cultures or the different methods employed is a matter of conjecture.

Drying on the skin

Normal unbroken skin has long been known to possess bactericidal properties against certain organisms, and the Gram-negative types are known to be more sensitive to drying on the skin than are the staphylococci or micrococci, which are normal residents. The skin is normally acid, and Burtenshaw (1938, 1942) was able to correlate lethal action against haemolytic streptococci with its acidity. He found the acids to be of the long-chain fatty acid group, and they have since been shown to be mainly oleic acid. The acidity explanation does not account for the rapid death of *Ps. pyocyanea* and other Gram-negative organisms, which can resist the normal skin acidity, but Lowbury and Fox (1953) remedied this by showing that *Ps. pyocyanea* is particularly sensitive to drying, and therefore the lethal effect in this particular case is due to the combined influences of acidity and drying.

Drying in oils

Bacterial spores can survive in the viable state for many years in oils, but only rarely is it possible to find vegetative bacteria. The reasons for this are two-fold: (*i*) the natural inability of organisms to survive for long periods n this state, and (*ii*) the difficulty of detecting organisms in any oily menstruum. The actual survival time would seem to depend to a large extent on the degree of protection of the individual cells, as well as on the type of organism.

Sykes and Royce (1950) were unable to prepare any oily suspension of relatively unprotected cells of *Chr. prodigiosum* which would remain viable for even a few hours, whereas Coulthard, Chantrill and Croshaw (1951) found that haemolytic streptococci protected with blood would survive for as long as 4 to 8 weeks in liquid paraffin or arachis oil at normal temperatures, and Bullock and Keepe (1951) recovered spray-dried *Streptococcus faecalis* from various oils after 6 months. These differences can only be attributed to culture differences and to different degrees of protection. It is interesting to note, however, that in some of Bullock and Keepe's experiments the organisms were spray-dried from suspensions containing stearin which would be expected to dissolve and disperse in the oil leaving the organisms uncoated and unprotected.

This survival, or otherwise, of bacteria suspended or dried in oils should not be confused with the preservation of cultures under oils, a procedure which has been known and practised for many years. The method employed is simply to grow the culture on a suitable agar slope and then to flood it with sterile white paraffin and store either in the cold or at room temperature. By this means it has been reported (Hartsell, 1956) that a range of yeasts and bacteria have remained viable for periods up to 14 years, and fungi, including *Candida*, *Rhodotorula* and *Torulopsis*, up to $3\frac{1}{2}$ years. There were, however, some changes in character in a few of the strains, and occasional ones actually metabolized the oil.

Spray-drying

It has been known for some time that spray-drying is not a means of sterilization, and good examples of this are found with milk and egg powders. Attention has, in fact, been drawn to many bacteriological problems associated with the spray-drying of milk (Hawley and Benjamin, 1955), not the least of which is the danger of bacterial growth during processing with the possible consequence of staphylococcal food poisoning (Hobbs, 1955).

In preparation for an investigation on certain gaseous disinfection processes, Bullock and his associates (Bullock and Lightbown, 1947; Bullock, Keepe and Rawlins, 1949; Bullock and Keepe, 1951) examined the effects of spray-drying on the viabilities of several organisms. The organisms they used were *Aerobacter aerogenes* (*Bacterium lactis aerogenes*), *Strep. faecalis*, and *Bacillus subtilis* suspended in 4 per cent peptone water. The *Aerobacter* strain was the most susceptible, showing losses in viability of the order of 99·9 per cent, and the surviving few cells were unevenly distributed and died off gradually during storage at a logarithmic rate. The *Streptococcus* culture suffered mortalities ranging from about 15 per cent to over 98 per cent, the latter value being recorded when the air inlet temperature in the system was raised to 150°, and *B. subtilis* spores were quite stable, showing at the worst losses of only about 10 or 12 per cent.

Ultrasonics

Interest in this aspect of sterilization dates from the descriptions by Wood and Loomis (1927) and Harvey and Loomis (1929) on the physical and biological effects of high frequency sound waves and their lethal properties against bacteria. Since that time, studies seem to have advanced spasmodically in three chronological periods, in the early 1930s, in the middle 1940s, and again in the last decade.

Two types of apparatus have been used in these investigations, the magnetostriction generator, which can produce vibrations within the sonic range and up to about 50 kilocyles (Kc) per second, and the quartz crystal generator, which has been used for frequencies up to 1·5 megacycles (Mc) per second. In this connexion a magnetostriction transducer described by Davies (1959) and a piezo-electric quartz apparatus with which the wave frequency and amplitude can be varied independently (Russell *et al.*, 1954) are of interest. Apart from these references it is not proposed to discuss the construction of these generators or to describe their uses in the biochemical field other than the disruption of microbial cells.

Mechanism of the lethal action

Ultrasound is only effective against organisms in liquid suspension and quite naturally the mechanism of the lethal action has attracted some attention. One of the difficulties in this field of work is that when the waves are passed through liquids there is always a rise in temperature. In one specific case, for example (Davies, 1959), the temperature of 4 ml of a yeast suspension subjected to a frequency of 26 Kc per second at a power of 500 watts rose from 0·05° to 18·7° in 5 minutes even though the steel transducer and cup assembly was surrounded by ice. Fortunately, all workers have been aware of the heating effects and have taken due care to exclude them in all of their reported experiments. Discounting, therefore, any local heating phenomena, the lethal action can be attributed almost entirely to the physical destruction of the cells with possibly the coagulation of cell proteins playing a minor role.

The physical destruction can readily be demonstrated microscopically. It is brought about exclusively through the phenomenon of cavitation, which arises through extreme fluctuations of mechanical pressure in the liquid. These pressure fluctuations, which are rhythmic and follow a wave form through the liquid, can amount to several hundred atmospheres (Rouyer and Grabar, 1947) and their effect is twofold. In the first place there is the purely mechanical strain put on the cell wall by the sudden application, and the equally sudden release, of pressure, creating minute cavities or vacuoles in the liquid; in the second place there is a 'gaseous' strain arising from the sudden extraction of the dissolved gases during the phases of reduced pressure. Evidence for this last point is obtained from the fact that the rate of cell destruction is much reduced by the prior removal of all dissolved gases from the cell suspension. The net result of these repeated wave treatments is the progressive collapse of the walls of the cells and the release of their contents into the liquid.

Physical considerations indicate that (*i*) the efficiency of the treatment should be related more to the intensity of the wave emission than to its

TABLE 21

Effect of intensity of ultrasonic waves on their lethal action

Power output (watts)	% viable cells after treatment for	
	20 min	40 min
274	76·8	55·7
765	25·3	0·36

frequency, and (*ii*) cavitation becomes more difficult and less intense as the frequency is increased, thus requiring a higher power input to produce any effect.

Proof of the first point is provided by Hamré (1949) who used a frequency of 700 Kc per second, and obtained a much greater killing rate against *Klebsiella pneumoniae* with a power absorption of 765 watts than with 274 watts (*see* Table 21). The validity of the second point is demonstrated in the relative rates of destruction of *E. coli* and *Strep. lactis* at 20 Kc per second and 1 Mc per second and in the clear evidence of a threshold of intensity at the higher frequency below which no cellular destruction is observed (Jacobs and Thornley, 1954).

Sensitivities of micro-organisms

All biological cellular forms are subject to destruction by ultrasound and there is ample evidence for it in relation to bacteria and yeasts but very little concerning moulds. Viruses come in a separate category. Because they are non-cellular, the treatment might be expected to be not very effective, but opinions differ on this. Some workers have found no action at all with exposures up to one hour at frequencies of 9 Kc per second or 550 Kc per second against the viruses (Hopwood, Salaman and McFarlane, 1939), whilst others, such as Takahashi and Christensen (1934) working with the tobacco mosaic virus, Rivers, Smadel and Chambers (1937) working with washed, but not unwashed, vaccinia virus suspensions, and Hamré (1949) with influenza A, have reported substantial activities. No indication of the intensity of the wave form is given in most of these papers, and it must be assumed that the different findings are due either to this factor or to the different natures of the suspending media.

The order of destruction of microbial and other cells follows the normal pattern of disinfection in that it is exponential, at least down to survivor levels of about 0·05 per cent, and according to Davies (1959) the rate of destruction is relatively independent of cell concentration. It is, however, inversely proportional to the volume of suspension, in terms of the length of

TABLE 22

Effect of ultrasound on different organisms

(after Davies, 1959)

Organism	Exposure time (min)	Effect
E. coli	1·0	90% of RNA'ase and 70% of protein non-sedimentable
	3·0	Complete breakage
Prot. vulgaris . . .	3·0	Complete breakage
Ps. aeruginosa . . .	2·0	Complete breakage
Staph. aureus H . . .	10·0	90% breakage
Staph. aureus D . . .	5·0	90% breakage
L. casei	5·0	Chains converted to single cells
	20·0	Complete breakage
B. megaterium . . .	2·0	Complete breakage
B. thuringiensis		
vegetative cells . . .	5·0	Complete breakage
spores	20·0	Slight breakage
Nocardia sp.	5·0	Complete breakage
Sacch. fragilis . . .	2·0	90% breakage
Bakers' yeast . . .	6·0	80% breakage
Aspergillus nidulans		
mycelium	20·0	No significant breakage
conidia	10·0	80–90% breakage
ascospores . . .	20·0	No breakage

All treatments were at a frequency of 26 Kc/sec and 500 W input. The densities of the various suspensions ranged from 10 to 90 mg/ml, and the volumes from 1·0 to 5·0 ml.

the volume being treated, and for each volume there is a maximum power input beyond which there is no increase in the rate of cell breakage.

In terms of relative sensitivities, Jacobs and Thornley (1954) have stated that, broadly speaking, the cocci or spherical organisms are more difficult to kill than the rod forms, a conclusion which is consistent with the idea that death is by cell destruction. This is perhaps a very broad conclusion, but it is in agreement with the general experiences of others. Yen and Liu (1934), for instance, found that the Gram-negative organisms were much more easy to kill than the staphylococci, streptococci, and *B. subtilis*. The spores of *Bacillus anthracis*, but not its vegetative cells, are practically unaffected, and the acid-fast organisms, *Mycobacterium tuberculosis* and *Mycobacterium phlei*. also exhibit exceptional resistance (Grabar and Rouyer, 1945; Skards, 1954),

Table 22, taken from a report by Davies (1959), indicates the type of result obtained with different organisms under various treatments.

The influence of age of the culture on disintegration rate would appear to vary with the type of organism. Hamré (1949), for instance, found no difference with cultures of *Kl. pneumoniae*, but Chambers and Gaines (1932) obtained increased resistance of *E. coli* with age. The suspending medium is also highly important. One example has already been quoted of the increased sensitivity of vaccinia virus when washed free from tissue matter, and Skards (1954) has shown that calcium ions, a decrease in temperature or a decrease in pH value acts in the same way. Fresh milk, skim milk, casein, gelatin, peptone, lactose and gum tragacanth all confer protection, the amount of protection depending on their concentration. In some cases they exert an almost complete protection (Jacobs and Thornley, 1954). A certain amount of this protection might be thought to arise from the different surface tensions or viscosities of the solutions, but such evidence as is available does not support this possibility.

Applications of ultrasonic disinfection

Although an interesting phenomenon in itself there does not seem to be a great future for ultrasonics as a practical means for sterilization, the great difficulty being the limitation in the amount of material that can be treated at any one time. It has been used to sterilize blood preparations and other biological solutions (Malkina, 1962) and also as a means for removing staphylococci from milking equipment surfaces (Masurovsky and Jordan, 1960). It is also used extensively for cleaning small pieces of surgical equipment such as needles and scissors, but its main value in bacteriology seems to lie in aiding the extraction of cellular contents, particularly enzymes and endotoxins.

Mechanical agitation

Cellular disintegration can also be brought about by violent mechanical agitation, especially when abrasives are present. This fact was noted before the end of the last century, but little notice was taken of it until some fifty years later when Curran and Evans (1942) again observed it whilst trying to break up small spore clusters in aqueous suspensions. The matter is not a straightforward one because Mattick (1951) noted that "lactobacilli shaken violently with carborundum powder do not disintegrate at all easily"—nevertheless it is a phenomenon which might play an important part and give misleading results in certain experimental investigations, and so it probably deserves more attention than it has hitherto been given.

Curran and Evans were apparently the first and only workers to carry out an organized investigation into some of the factors influencing the lethal efficiency of this treatment. Their experiments were made in a reciprocating shaker operating at between 330 and 570 oscillations per minute and they employed several abrasives of various particle sizes. Their results with the spores of *Bacillus cohaerens* and *Bacillus megatherium* using carborundum, sand and glass beads are quoted in Table 23. They demonstrate clearly the superiority of glass beads. Curran and Evans also obtained evidence showing: (a) the exponential rate of death with time over the whole range, thus indicating that the lethal action has the characteristics of a unimolecular reaction, and (b) the progressively increasing lethal efficiency with degree of agitation. Vegetative bacteria were more easily killed than

TABLE 23

The action of abrasives on bacterial spores

(Curran and Evans, 1942)

Material and particle size		Viable spores/ml after shaking 5 hr B. cohaerens B. megatherium	
Carborundum			
(abrasive no.)	Control	1,170,000	730,000
	20	290,000	—
	40	18,000	2,500
	60	4,850	250
	80*	3,850	150
	100	27,500	300
	120	83,000	11,100
Sand	Control	1,280,000	760,000
(sieve no.)	10	1,110,000	—
	10/20	500,000	350,000
	20/40	117,000	17,500
	40/60	17,000	1,100
	60/80	36,000	8,300
Glass beads	Control	1,280,000	760,000
(sieve no.)	20/40	131,000	2,320
	40/60	37	18
	60/80	13	1
	80/100	30	3

* equals about 80/100 sieve number

Shaking speed was 460 per min throughout

were spores, and foam-producing substances somewhat interfered with the lethal action.

Presses can also be used which depend for their action on the shearing force developed in a liquid suspension when pressure is suddenly applied and the liquid forced through a narrow orifice or groove. Two such units have been described (Hughes, 1951; Raper and Hyatt, 1963) in both of which the action depends on forcing the liquid at high pressure across the interspacing between two stainless steel faces, pressures up to 18,000 lb per sq in. being applied to the liquid by means of a closely fitting piston in a carefully machined cylindrical reservoir. The interspacing is only of the order of 0·25 mm and with the aid of finely divided abrasives such as powdered pyrex glass, emery powder or silica or zircon dusts disintegrations to the extent of 60–100 per cent are obtainable.

Vacuum and high pressure

Vacuum of itself is neither bactericidal nor bacteriostatic. Its only contribution to such activity is in depriving aerobic organisms of their necessary atmospheric oxygen or in allowing gaseous germicides to penetrate more readily.

Likewise, there is no real evidence to show that high pressure of itself can exert any adverse effect, even though pressures as high as 12,000 atmospheres have been applied (McCulloch, 1945). There is evidence, however, that the sudden local application of high pressure, such as occurs in ultrasonic treatment, can be effectively disruptive. This aspect is dealt with earlier in this Chapter (p. 242).

REFERENCES

BATEMAN, J. B., McCAFFREY, PATRICIA A., O'CONNOR, R. J. and MONK, G. W. (1961). *Appl. Microbiol.*, **9**, 567.
BENEDICT, R. G., GORMAN, J., SHARPE, E. S., KEMP, C. E., HALL, H. H. and JACKSON, C. W. (1958). *Appl. Microbiol.*, **6**, 401.
BENEDICT, R. G., SHARPE, E. S., CORMAN, J., MEYERS, G. B., BAER, E. F., HALL, H. H. and JACKSON, R. W. (1961). *Appl. Microbiol.*, **9**, 256.
BOURDILLON, R. B., LIDWELL, O. M. and LOVELOCK, J. E. (1948). *Studies in Air Hygiene.* Med. Res. Counc. Spec. Rep. Ser. No. 262, p. 54: H.M.S.O., London.
BULLOCK, K. and KEEFE, WINIFRED G. (1951). *J. Pharm. Pharmacol.*, **3**, 717.
BULLOCK, K., KEEPE, WINIFRED G. and RAWLINS, E. A. (1949). *J. Pharm. Pharmacol.*, **1**, 878.
BULLOCK, K. and LIGHTBOWN, J. W. (1947). *Quart. J. Pharm.*, **22**, 312.
BURTENSHAW, J. M. L. (1938). *J. Hyg., Camb.*, **38**, 575.
BURTENSHAW, J. M. L. (1942). *J. Hyg., Camb.*, **42**, 184.
CHAMBERS, L. A. and GAINES, N. (1932). *J. cell. comp. Physiol.*, **1**, 451.
CLARK, W. A., HORNELAND, WANDA and KLEIN, A. G. (1962). *Appl. Microbiol.*, **10**, 463.
CLEMENT, MARY T. (1961). *Canad. J. Microbiol.*, **7**, 99.
COULTHARD, C. E., CHANTRILL, B. H. and CROSHAW, BETTY (1951). *J. Pharm. Pharmacol.*, **3**, 215.
CURRAN, H. R. and EVANS, F. R. (1942). *J. Bact.*, **43**, 125.
DAVIES, R. (1959). *Biochem. Biophys. Acta*, **33**, 481.
DAVIS, J. G. (1951). *Proc. Soc. appl. Bact.*, **14**, 216.
DAVIS, R. J. (1963). *J. Bact.*, **86**, 486.
DOEBBLER, G. F. and RINFRET, A. P. (1963). *J. Bact.*, **85**, 486.
First International Symposium on Freezing and Drying (1951): Inst. Biol., London.
FLOSDORF, E. W. and MUDD, S. (1935). *J. Immunol.*, **29**, 389.
FRY, R. M. (1954). *Biological Applications of Freezing and Drying*, p. 215: Academic Press, New York.
FRY, R. M. and GREAVES, R. I. N. (1949). *J. Hyg. Camb.*, **49**, 220.
FRY, R. M. and GREAVES, R. I. N. (1951). *J. Hyg., Camb.*, **49**, 220.
GARVIE, ELLEN I. (1955). *J. appl. Bact.*, **18**, 78.
GRABAR, P. and ROUYER, M. (1945). *Ann. Inst. Pasteur*, **71**, 154.
GORRILL, R. H. and McNEILL, EVELYN M. (1960). *J. gen. Microbiol.*, **22**, 437.
GREAVES, R. I. N. (1946). *The Preservation of Proteins by Drying.* Med. Res. Counc. Spec. Rep. Ser. No. 258: H.M.S.O., London.

GREAVES, R. I. N. (1960). *Recent Research in Freezing and Drying*, p. 203: Blackwell, Oxford.
GREAVES, R. I. N. (1962). *J. Pharm. Pharmacol.*, **14**, 621.
HAINES, R. B. (1934). *J. Hyg., Camb.*, **34**, 277.
HAINES, R. B. (1938). *Proc. Roy. Soc., B*, **124**, 451.
HAMRÉ, DOROTHY (1949). *J. Bact.*, **57**, 279.
HARRISON, A. P. (1955). *J. Bact.*, **70**, 711.
HARRISON, A. P. and PELCZAR, M. J. (1963). *J. gen. Microbiol.*, **30**, 395.
HARTSELL, S. E. (1956). *Appl. Microbiol.*, **4**, 350.
HARVEY, E. N. and LOOMIS, A. L. (1929). *J. Bact.*, **17**, 376.
HAWLEY, H. B. and BENJAMIN, MARGARET I. W. (1955). *J. appl. Bact.*, **18**, 493.
HOBBS, BETTY C. (1955). *J. appl. Bact.*, **18**, 484.
HOPWOOD, F. L., SALAMAN, M. H. and McFARLANE, A. S. (1939). *Nature, Lond.*, **144**, 377.
HORNIBROOK, J. W. (1950). *J. lab. clin. Med.*, **35**, 788.
HUGHES, D. E. (1951). *Brit. J. exp. Path.*, **32**, 97.
HUNT, G. A., GOUREVITCH, A. and LEIN, J. (1958). *J. Bact.*, **76**, 453.
INGRAM, M. (1951). *Proc. Soc. appl. Bact.*, **14**, 243.
JACOBS, S. E. and THORNLEY, MARGARET J. (1954). *J. appl. Bact.*, **17**, 28.
LEACH, R. H., OHYE, D. F. and SCOTT, W. J. (1959). *J. gen. Microbiol.*, **21**, 658.
LEACH, R. H. and SCOTT, W. J. (1959). *J. gen. Microbiol.*, **21**, 295.
LOWBURY, E. J. L. and FOX, JEAN (1953). *J. Hyg., Camb.*, **51**, 203.
McCLESKY, C. S. and CHRISTOPHER, W. N. (1941). *J. Bact.*, **41**, 98.
McCULLOCH, E. C. (1945). *Disinfection and Sterilization:* Kimpton, London.
MAISTER, H. G., PFEIFOR, V. F., BOGART, W. M. and HEGAR, E. N. (1958). *Appl. Microbiol.*, **6**, 413.
MALKINA, V. M. (1962). via *Internat. Abs. Biol. Sci.*, **27**, 114 (original in Russian).
MASUROVSKY, E. B. and JORDAN, W. K. (1960). *J. dairy Sci.*, **43**, 1545.
MATTICK, A. T. R. (1951). *Proc. Soc. appl. Bact.*, **14**, 211.
MAZUR, P. (1960). *Ann. N.Y. Acad. Sci.*, **85**, 610.
MEYNELL, G. G. (1958). *J. gen. Microbiol.*, **19**, 380.
MONK, G. W., McCAFFREY, P. A. and DAVIS, M. S. (1957). *J. Bact.*, **73**, 85, 661.
MUGGLETON, P. W. (1960). *Recent Research in Freezing and Drying*, p. 229: Blackwell, Oxford.
NAKAMURA, M. (1962). *J. Hyg., Camb.*, **60**, 35.
NAKAMURA, M. and DAWSON, D. ANN (1962). *Appl. Microbiol.*, **10**, 40.
OBAYASHI, Y. (1960). *Recent Research in Freezing and Drying*, p. 221: Blackwell, Oxford.
OBAYASHI, Y. (1961). *J. Hyg. Camb.*, **59**, 77.
OBAYASHI, Y., OTA, S. and SHIRO, A. (1961). *J. Hyg., Camb.*, **59**, 77.
POSTGATE, J. R. and HUNTER, J. R. (1961). *J. gen. Microbiol.*, **26**, 367.
PROOM, H. (1951). *Proc. Soc. appl. Bact.*, **14**, 261.
RAPER, J. R. and HYATT, ELVA A. (1963). *J. Bact.*, **85**, 712.
RECORD, B. R., TAYLOR, R. and MILLER, D. S. (1962). *J. gen. Microbiol.*, **28**, 585.
ROUNTREE, PHYLLIS M. (1963). *J. Hyg., Camb.*, **61**, 265.
RIVERS, T. M., SMADEL, T. F. and CHAMBERS, L. A. (1937). *J. exp. Med.*, **65**, 67.
ROUYER, M. and GRABAR, P. (1947). *Ann. Inst. Pasteur*, **73**, 215.
RUSSELL, LILLIAN, A., BUSWELL, A. M., FRY, F. J. and WHITNEY, R. McL. (1954). *Ind. engng Chem.*, **16**, 1751.
SCOTT, W. J. (1958). *J. gen. Microbiol.*, **19**, 624.
SCOTT, W. J. (1960). *Recent Research in Freezing and Drying*, p. 188: Blackwell, Oxford.
Second International Symposium (1960). *Recent Research in Freezing and Drying:* Blackwell, Oxford.
SHERMAN, J. M. and CAMERON, G. M. (1934). *J. Bact.*, **27**, 341.
SKARDS, J. (1954). via *Chem. Abs.*, **48**, 12224 (original in Russian).
SPICER, C. C. (1959). *J. Hyg., Camb.*, **57**, 210.
SPLITTSTOESSER, D. F. and FOSTER, E. M. (1957). *Appl. Microbiol.*, **5**, 333.
STRAKA, R. P. and STOKES, J. L. (1959). *J. Bact.*, **78**, 181.
STRANGE, R. E. and DARK, F. A. (1962). *J. gen. Microbiol.*, **29**, 719.

STRANGE, R. E. and NESS, A. G. (1963). *Nature, Lond.*, **197**, 819.
SWIFT, H. F. (1937). *J. Bact.*, **33**, 411.
SYKES, G. and ROYCE, A. (1950). *J. Pharm. Pharmacol.*, **2**, 639.
Symposium (1960). *Freezing and Drying of Biological Materials: Ann. N.Y. Acad. Sci.*, **85**.
TAKAHASHI, W. N. and CHRISTENSEN, R. J. (1934). *Science*, **79**, 465.
TANGUAY, A. E. (1959). *Appl. Microbiol.*, **7**, 84.
TANNER, F. W. and WALLACE, G. I. (1931). *Proc. Soc. exp. Biol., N.Y.*, **29**, 32.
TANNER, F. W. and WILLIAMSON, C. S. (1928). *Proc. Soc. exp. Biol., N.Y.*, **25**, 377.
WAGMAN, J. and WENECK, E. J. (1963). *Appl. Microbiol.*, **11**, 244.
WASSERMAN, A. E. and HOPKINS, W. J. (1957). *Appl. Microbiol.*, **5**, 295.
WASSERMAN, A. E. and HOPKINS, W. J. (1958). *Appl. Microbiol.*, **6**, 49.
WEISER, R. S. and OSTERUD, C. M. (1945). *J. Bact.*, **50**, 413.
WOOD, R. W. and LOOMIS, A. L. (1927). *Phil. Mag., VII*, **4**, 417.
YEN, A. C. H. and LIU, S. (1934). *Proc. Soc. exp. Biol., N.Y.*, **31**, 1250.

PART III

Air Disinfection and Sterilization

CHAPTER 10

AIR DISINFECTION AND STERILIZATION

THE development of large-scale fermentation techniques in the manufacture of antibiotics and of aseptic methods for handling sterile solutions, as well as the increased consciousness of the role played by air-borne organisms in carrying cross-infections in hospitals, work-rooms, schoolrooms and elsewhere, have all underlined the increasing need for adequate means for air disinfection and sterilization. It became even more important to consider the question of air hygiene during the Second World War as a matter of urgency because of the dangers of serious epidemic infections arising from the enforced congregation of large numbers of people in confined spaces such as air-raid shelters and the like. It was this background which inspired the extensive work carried out by Bourdillon and his colleagues and published in the monograph *Studies in Air Hygiene*. Frequent reference will be made to this in the ensuing pages.

Investigations into methods of disinfection and sterilization can be classed under three main headings: (*i*) ultraviolet irradiation, (*ii*) chemical treatment, and (*iii*) filtration; heat and electrostatic precipitation have also received attention. Ultraviolet treatment is a useful adjunct in keeping the bacterial air contamination at a low level, it is not an air sterilizing agent; chemical disinfection can be highly efficient, depending on the substance used, but again is limited in its application because of the danger, direct or indirect, from many chemicals dispersed in vapour or aerosol form; filtration is the most efficient means of sterilization, provided the right type of filter material is chosen, and it has the additional advantage that it has none of the defects of ultraviolet or chemical treatment. Heat is an expensive method of air sterilization, and electrostatic precipitation methods, although showing considerable promise, are still in the process of development.

In considering any form of air disinfection, whether it be by filtration or by physical or chemical methods, it is important to remember that the physical state of naturally occuring organisms is nearly always quite different from that of artificially created aerosols. In rooms, offices and other occupied enclosed spaces micrococci and staphylococci constitute the main air-borne bacterial population. These organisms are mainly of human (or animal) origin, and so are carried on skin scales or hair particles or they are enclosed in dried saliva or mucus. In such a state their particle size can be considerably greater than that of the isolated cell, and Noble, Lidwell and Kingston (1963) actually estimated the majority to lie in the range of 4–20 microns. But more important than particle size is the protection afforded under such conditions, the consequences of which are discussed in detail in the following pages.

Air from the external atmosphere normally carries smaller numbers of micro-organisms than does air from enclosed spaces, and the types are somewhat different. Most of them are bacterial spores with a smaller proportion of mould spores, and they tend to be more free-floating with less debris attached, so that the particles are not much bigger than the spores themselves (Noble, Lidwell and Kingston, 1963). This is important when filtration is being considered.

Viability of air-borne organisms

Effect of humidity. On dispersal as an aerosol micro-organisms can be considered to be, momentarily at least, single cell or micro cultures in their original suspending fluid. But almost immediately their state is altered by reason of the evaporation of water from each droplet and the consequent drying of the cells, the speed and extent of which depends mainly on the relative humidity (RH) of the dispersal atmosphere and also on its temperature. And this can act in the present context in two ways: directly, by affecting the viabilities of the cells themselves, and indirectly, by affecting the efficacy of the germicidal aerosol.

The several investigations made into the direct effect of humidity on bacteria and viruses, mainly from the epidemiological aspect, have shown that on dispersal into the air, the decay in viability of bacteria takes place in two distinct stages (Dunklin and Puck, 1948), a rapid initial loss (K_0) which might be over in seconds (Ferry, Brown and Damon, 1958; Webb, 1959) and certainly within a minute or two (Morton, 1962) followed fairly abruptly by a much slower loss (K_1). At least two reactions are therefore responsible for the losses. The plot of log survivors/time for this latter stage usually results in a straight line, the slope of which represents the 'decay constant', a value frequently expressed in terms of percentage loss of viability per minute.

According to Webb the K_0 value becomes progessively smaller, that is the immediate survival level increases, as the RH is increased to 75 per cent, after which there is a sudden reversal. On the other hand the K_1 value measured at one hour remains fairly constant up to about 50 per cent RH and then it falls away quite rapidly. The net result is a gradual increase in the overall stability of the aerosol with increases in RH. Rather surprisingly this same trend occurred with all of the organisms tested, namely, *Staphylococcus aureus, Escherichia coli, Chromobacterium prodigiosum* and *Bacillus subtilis,* although the K_0 and K_1 values differed in each case. But it cannot be taken as universally applicable because Ferry, Brown and Damon (1958) had earlier made rather different observations, sometimes with the same organisms, finding that some were sensitive to drying and others were more or less indifferent to RH conditions. The differences may have been due to the suspending media used, Webb's cultures being sprayed from nutrient broth

nd Ferry's from a dilute buffer solution, but they are significant. Of the
ensitive ones, *E. coli* showed an abrupt change in the K_1 value at about 50
per cent RH, and similarly *Chr. prodigiosum* showed a gradual increase in
survival rate up to an RH of 65 per cent after which it fell away again. The
nsensitive organisms included *Micrococcus candidus*, *Mycobacterium phlei*
nd *Corynebacterium xerose* and they did not show any substantial reduction
n survival rate until the RH value was reduced below 30 per cent, or even

TABLE 24

Viabilities of aerosols of Brucella suis *and* Pasteurella tularensis

(Morton, 1962)

Organism and RH(%)	Viability (%) of aerosol at age (minutes)						Decay rate (%/min)
	0	5	30	120 ·	240	360	
Brucella suis							
87	106	91	100	95	82	56	0·16
60	66	63	67	56	43	41	0·13
50	76	78	76	62	54	47	0·13
Past. tularensis							
85	58	42	29	18	14		0·60
50	74	26	8·9	4·9	4		1·17
20	54	1·9	1·2	0·8	0·5		1·86

15 per cent sometimes. In like manner Morton (1962) found *Pasteurella
tularensis* to be sensitive in terms both of initial decay and subsequent
survival, but *Brucella suis* was relatively resistant in both stages. His actual
survival figures are quoted in Table 24.

Viruses are also sensitive to humidity conditions, but they exhibit no
regular pattern, some being more stable at high, and others at low, RH
values. Vaccinia, influenza (PR8) and Venezuelan equine encephalomyelitis
viruses, for instance, are much more stable at low humidities in the range
20–50 per cent, whereas the virus of poliomyelitis has optimum stability at
about 80 per cent RH: they all become less stable as the temperature is
raised from 10° to 32°. These facts were demonstrated by Harper (1961) in a
carefully controlled series of tests in which the virus aerosol was dispersed
under the conditions required and samples taken at intervals up to 23 hours.
The test chamber was a 75 litre drum rotating slowly to maintain even
conditions within the drum. In every case instability had become manifest
within half-an-hour, often less, and after 23 hours the survival rates ranged,
according to conditions, from 0 to 85 per cent. Similar observations had earlier
been made by Hemmes, Winkler and Kool (1960) with the influenza and
polio viruses, the change in stability with the 'flu type between RH 40 and
50 per cent being dramatic, and the decline with polio so great that below

45 per cent RH no virus could be detected 30 seconds after spraying. On the basis of these findings they suggested a correlation between the air-borne stabilities of these two viruses and their epidemiology. This confirmed that influenza is a winter disease, being more infective in the period when the relative humidity indoors is generally low, and offered an explanation for the increased polio morbidity in the summer when indoor conditions are optima. for the survival of the virus.

Other observations have shown the yellow fever virus to be fairly stable at 50 and 85 per cent RH, with initial recoveries of 65–70 per cent and a decay rate of about 6 per cent, but the Rift Valley virus to be relatively unstable initially (10–20 per cent recoveries) and rather more stable sub sequently, with a decay rate of 3–4 per cent (Miller *et al.*, 1963). Similarly the Rous sarcoma virus was stable at high RH values, 85 per cent recoveries being recorded at 80 per cent RH and nil at 30 per cent RH, but the pigeon pox virus gave recoveries of 70 per cent after 5 hours at 30 per cent RH and its stability was relatively constant at different humidities (Webb, Bather and Hodges, 1963).

The suspending medium must obviously influence considerably the stabilities of the aerosols of both bacteria and viruses, particularly in relation to those constituents which can control the moisture content of the cells. In this context, Webb (1960) found that the protective ability of a substance was connected with the presence of amino and secondary alcohol groups, either separately or in combination, and he concluded that, with certain exceptions, "the more able a compound is in displacing water, the less its protectiveness to air-borne cells". On this basis, he found inositol in 6 per cent solution to afford excellent protection both to bacteria, and to viruses at all RH values (Webb, Bather and Hodges, 1963).

Following the same line of argument, Webb also concluded that "Aerosol stability seems to be an intrinsic property of the structure of the natural proteins", loss of viability being associated with the loss of bonded water from these molecules and their consequent breakdown. The most obvious site of such damage would appear to be in the cellular membrane, thus causing loss of its differentiating structure.

Effect of temperature. Within the normal range of 'indoor' temperatures the change in the stability of aerosols is small, and certainly very small compared with the influence of humidity. Outside of this range there is very little recorded information, but within the range −40° to 35° Kethley, Fincher and Cown (1957) found *Chr. prodigiosum* to have a minimal death rate at 18° rising steeply as the temperature was increased and less steeply as it was decreased.

Testing techniques

The efficacy of any form of air treatment can be assessed either by measuring the death rate of an air-borne bacterial population under the influence of the germicidal agent or by measuring the percentage reduction in viable air-borne organisms after a given treatment. From this it follows that the techniques employed fall into two broad categories; (i) those employing a test chamber with a fixed volume of air and a known initial bacterial population, and (ii) those requiring a flowing air stream with a constant bacterial infection per unit volume of air. The former obtains mainly for testing chemical disinfectants and the latter for filtration, radiation and similar treatments.

Although these two techniques differ in their approach, they have certain aspects in common. Two of these are: (a) the methods of dispersal of the test organisms, and (b) the methods of sampling the air. It is appropriate, therefore, to consider these points at this stage.

Dispersal of bacteria

Dispersal from liquid suspension. The production of a bacterial aerosol of reasonable density and stability is a prerequisite for the study of any aspect of aerial disinfection. It can be generated either from liquid culture or from dried, infected dusts.

There are three basic designs of atomizer suitable for dispersing liquid cultures: (i) the direct spray, which operates by means of an air flow directed horizontally across the orifice of a vertical feed tube dipping into the culture; (ii) the nebulizer, or indirect spray, in which a spray is produced in a confined space and the coarser droplets removed by baffles; (iii) the peripheral jet atomizer, in which the liquid is drawn through a narrow central nozzle by means of a peripheral air jet and simultaneously nebulized into the surrounding atmosphere. The first type produces a coarse spray, consisting mainly of large rain droplets but with a high proportion of finer mist droplets. Typical examples of this type are the Flit spray and the hand scent spray. The second type, of which the Collison spray, the de Vilbiss spray and the Wells nebulizer are examples, gives a much more even aerosol of droplets which emerge slowly from the apparatus as a cloud and range from about one to several microns in size. With the third type, the peripheral jet atomizer, the droplet size depends largely on the size of the jet orifice and the peripheral air flow. The Chicago atomizer is probably the best known of this type. A variation on this method of dispersal is the spinning disc technique as first described by Walton and Prewett (1949) and used by Druett and May (1952) in their wind-tunnel devised for studying air-borne infections. It consists of a high-speed spinning disc, shaped as an inverted cone, with a flat polished top surface. It is kept spinning by means of an air blast passing up the fluted conical face of the disc. The suspension to be dispersed is introduced at the centre of the disc through a fine jet and it is immediately flung outwards on contact with the disc and dispersed with the aid of the air blast as a fine cloud. The droplet size can be varied by adjusting the flow of liquid and the speed of the spinning disc, and the apparatus can generate clouds with droplets of fairly uniform size down to about 1 micron.

The second and third types described are the most suitable for aerial disinfection work, the first being too coarse and wet to give a satisfactory aerosol, and the choice generally lies between the Collison type spray, as advocated by the Aerosols Panel (1949) and by Henderson (1952), and the Chicago atomizer, as preferred by Rosebury (1947).

Resistance of the test organism is highly important in air hygiene, and in this connexion it should always be borne in mind that organisms sprayed from the mouth by sneezing, or dispersed with a coating of serum or other organic matter, are always more resistant than those sprayed 'naked' from aqueous suspensions or cultures. To meet this point, Bourdillon and his team (1948) adopted the "spit spray" system, in which a bacterial aerosol is produced by actual spitting from the mouth. With a little practice this will give a good aerosol containing organisms 'naturally' protected with mucoid and similar material.

In contrast to the protective action of organic matter, inorganic salts exert a deleterious effect, so that organisms nebulized from saline suspension tend to die off rapidly. This is because the organisms are unable to withstand the high osmotic pressure which develops round the organism as a consequence of the natural air-drying of the dispersed droplets (*see* p. 254).

Dispersal of infected dusts. Frequently tests are required with dried dust-borne organisms, and here certain difficulties arise in their dispersal. An ordinary swept dust, or dust collected from a carpet sweeper, is not satisfactory and resort has to be made to other sources. One such source is from organisms dried on blanket or similar material. The infection can be natural or artificially planted, and in the dry state it can remain viable for several months. The organisms are released as fine particles either by beating or by blowing air through the material. An alternative method used successfully by the author employs an artificial mixture of bacterial spores, and other organisms as required, dried with a fine, easily dispersible powder such as French chalk or kaolin. The mixture is placed in a hopper and an air flow introduced through the bottom of the hopper. The air flow keeps the powder in a constant state of agitation and gradually carries away the finer particles. Evenness of dispersal is maintained with a mechanical beater constantly tapping the side of the hopper.

Methods of air sampling

Originally the 'falling plate' count was the only means available for estimating the bacterial population of the air, and it is still used by a number of experimenters. It is suitable for certain comparative work, but it is limited by the fact that it cannot measure the total air-borne population but only those which fall on the plate by gravity. The more modern methods of measurement depend on the collection of organisms from a known volume of air, and they use the systems of: (a) impingement on a solid agar medium (b) impingement in liquids from a flow of small air bubbles, (c) retention on suitable filter medium, (*d*) electrostatic precipitation, or (*e*) thermal precipitation. Of these, the first method only can detect any *change* in the bacterial content during sampling; the others assume uniform bacterial populations. Thermal collection was first mentioned in 1952 (Kethley, Gordon and Orr, 1952), but since then it has received only little attention: it has a theoretical efficiency of 100 per cent.

Impinger samplers. All of the impinger samplers are based on the principle of small air-borne particles moving at high velocities being thrust either against the surface of a solid nutrient agar medium and so being retained by the medium and developing into a visible colony on subsequent incubation, or into a suitable collecting liquid from which aliquots are then cultured. One of the first of these types was the Wells air centrifuge (Wells, 1933). This apparatus makes use of the centrifugal force exerted upon suspended bacterial particles when they are passed with a gentle air stream into a rapidly rotating cylindrical tube. The tube is lined with nutrient agar, and the bacteria under the influence of the centrifugal force are flung outwards and adhere to the agar surface; the tube is subsequently incubated. Its efficiency is low, and it is almost completely displaced by the Bourdillon slit sampler (Bourdillon, Lidwell and Thomas, 1941) and other more effective devices.

Impingement in the Bourdillon slit sampler results from passing the air at high velocity through a narrow slit and then immediately on the surface of a slowly rotating agar plate. The velocity of the air-borne particles causes them to impinge on and adhere to the agar surface. The efficiency of the apparatus varies with the rate of air flow, ano also on the width of the slit and the distance of the agar from the slit, but under optimum conditions, that is, with the slit 0·33 mm wide and 27·5 mm long and with the agar surface 1·5 to 2 mm from the slit, and an air flow rate of 1 cu ft per minute, the collection rate of particles down to about 1 micron can be as high as 99 per cent, but is usually rather lower.

Several variants of the original design of the slit sampler have been described but none departs from the basic principle. The purpose in producing the modified designs has been to measure more accurately small levels of aerial contamination by sampling larger air volumes (Bourdillon, Lidwell and Thomas, 1948), to cover longer periods of exposure (Schuster, 1948) or to give greater portability (Decker and Wilson, 1954). An interesting extension of this type of sampler is the Anderson model (1958) which employs the cascade principle, the air passing successively over six petri dishes assembled in a single column. The design of this model is interesting. Above each dish and at a distance of about 2·5 mm is a plate with 340 holes in it. The holes in each plate are progessively smaller, starting at 0·046 in. and finishing at 0·01 in. diameter, so that when air is drawn through the apparatus at a constant volume of 1 cu ft per minute successively smaller particles are collected according to their individual density and shape. Such an apparatus is useful for determining the distribution of bacteria carried on different sized dust and hair particles.

Normally, a nutrient agar is used as the collecting medium in all types of slit sampler, but if a gelatin medium is substituted it can also be used for estimating air-borne virus particles. Six to 12 per cent gelatin gels are used, the medium after collection being melted and cultured as for the specific viruses.

In collecting organisms by impingement in a liquid medium, the main points to observe are, (1) the air flow must be such that it attains the critical

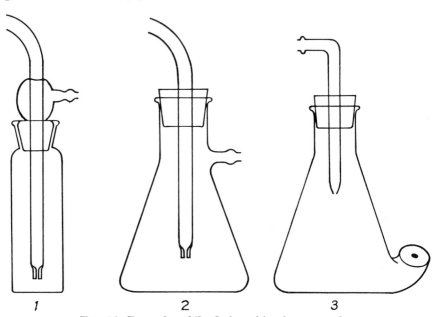

1   **2**   **3**

FIG. 14. *Examples of the design of impinger samplers*
1 is the all-glass model, 2 is the capillary impinger, 3 is the tangential
Shipe sampler

velocity for the particular orifice used, (2) the capillary should dip at least 5 mm into the liquid, and (3) the optimum distance of the orifice tip to bottom of the flask is about 4 mm. Several such devices have been described (*e.g.* Rosebury, 1947; Henderson, 1952; Cown, Kethley and Fincher, 1957; Tyler and Shipe, 1959; Shipe, Tyler and Chapman, 1959) their main differences being in the amount of air they can sample, the size and shape of the orifice jet, the distance of the orifice tip from the bottom of the collecting flask, and the type of collecting liquid. In these devices air is drawn rapidly through a critical orifice capillary and into a suitable collecting liquid. The velocity of the air-borne particles causes them to impinge on the surface of the liquid as they emerge from the capillary at sonic velocity, and so they are retained in the liquid. The collecting liquid may be water, broth or a weak gelatin medium, and a few drops of oil should be added to prevent frothing. According to Cown, Kethley and Fincher (1957) the best medium is a brain-heart digest broth or a proteose-peptone-yeast extract medium with 0·2 per cent of gelatin added. After the air has been sampled, the fluid is plated or cultured as desired.

Most of the samplers devised have fixed capillary sizes and therefore fixed air-flow rates. These range from 1·9 litres per minute for the Rosebury capillary impinger to 11 litres per minute for the Henderson standard 'Porton' model, and 12·5 litres per minute for the all-glass and "bulge" impingers described by Tyler and Shipe. In the Cown, Kethley and Fincher model the flow rate can be varied between 1 and 28 litres per minute according to the size of critical orifice employed, and the same applies to that described by Shipe, Tyler and Chapman.

One criticism levelled against all of these types of sampler, a criticism based more on induction than observation, is the possible destructive effects on vegetative bacteria when they are impinged at sonic velocities on the base of the receiver (Ray and Harper, 1957). For this reason the Shipe sampler was devised (*Report*, 1953; Shipe, Tyler and Chapman, 1959) in which the orifice tube enters the sampling liquid tangentially to the bottom of the flask. At the same time the long intake tube is eliminated by using a metal disc with a bored, sharp-edge orifice and introducing it near the base of the flask. By this means the possible losses of larger particles on the intake tube is minimized. Such a sampler does, in fact, give a greater sampling efficiency for particles greater than 3 microns, but for those less than 3 microns the collecting efficiency is marginally less than with a direct capillary impinger. The recovery rate is, however, marginally greater, thus giving some small support to the original criticism.

Also in this category of samplers can be placed the Moulton sampler (Moulton, Puck and Lemon, 1943) and its modification, the Lemon "aeroscope" (Lemon, 1943), although they are probably not so much impinger as bubbler samplers since neither employs a critical orifice. The original Moulton device had an air-flow capacity of about 3 litres per minute and in later models it was increased to 16 litres per minute. The Lemon modification is really a simplification of the original with an air-flow rate of 30 litres per minute. It consists basically of a Folin tube, the bubbler of which carries six holes, each 1 mm in diameter. The bulb dips into 20 ml of nutrient broth which serves as the collecting fluid. A small air-flow meter is attached to the intake of the tube and air is aspirated through the tube at a given rate and taken out through a Kjeldahl trap in which is fixed a small glass baffle. The collecting efficiencies of both the Moulton and the Lemon models are said to be over 90 per cent.

Filtration samplers. Filtration devices were amongst the earliest of the samplers. Sand was the first collecting material, but its efficiency is very low. Cotton wool is another obvious choice, but there is a large death-rate amongst vegetative organisms collected this way. The same losses do not occur with bacterial spores, and for this reason cotton wool is frequently used as the standard in assessing other samplers; and this in spite of the difficulty of removing all of the organisms from the fibres.

Another sampler of this type is the membrane filter. These are marketed by Oxo Ltd. in Britain, by the Millipore Filter Corporation in America and by the Membranfilter-Gesellschaft of Göttingen. They are available in different sizes and porosities and their advantages are that (i) the amount of sample examined can be adjusted at will according to the level of bacterial contamination expected, and (ii) the membrane can be cultured direct on the surface of an agar medium and the organisms estimated from the numbers of colonies formed. Filter papers (Whatman No. 40 or 42) have also been used in the same way (Torloni and Borzani, 1958).

Soluble filter materials in the form of alginate fibres are also used. Sodium alginate is particularly useful in this respect, because it is water soluble. Thus, the organisms can be collected by filtering the air through a plug of the alginate; this is then dissolved in water to give an even dispersal of the organisms suitable, aliquots of which are finally plated (Richards, 1955). Calcium alginate has likewise been used for swabbing the surfaces of dairy plant, the solvent in this case being a weak sodium hexametaphosphate solution. This material is reported to give higher recoveries of bacteria than do cotton wool swabs (Tredinnick and Tucker, 1951). Soluble foamed gelatin filters in the form of small cylinders have also been suggested, but they are very susceptible to changes in humidity, they are difficult to sterilize, and they allow small aerosol particles to pass so that they are not suitable for sampling bacterial aerosols (Noller and Spendlove, 1956).

Electrostatic and thermal precipitators. The electrostatic precipitators, as used in the disinfection of air (*see* p. 284), can also be used as air samplers, the only difference being that the collecting metal plate electrode is replaced by a conducting agar film or water layer. The agar collector, which forms the negative electrode of the system, consists of a glass cylinder which is coated internally with a thin layer of agar or lined with an agar-impregnated paper, or it can carry a small volume of water or liquid medium. The positive electrode to which the charge is applied is made of stainless steel and is sited along the axis of the cylinder. The cylinder is closed at each end with a metal cap suitably provided one with an air inlet and the other with an air outlet tube. The cylinder can either stand vertically or it can lie horizontally (as later described by Morris and colleagues) and be rotated slowly.

Such an apparatus was first described by Houwink and Rolvink (1957) and it was later modified by Morris *et al.* (1961) to make it more adaptable and more easily handled. In the Porton (Morris) model the cylinder measures 2 in. by 12 in. long, and charges between 5 Kv and 15 Kv can be applied, the usual level being 10 Kv. At the lower tensions the penetration of organisms through the system can range up to about 16 per cent, the actual amount depending on the type of aerosol being used and the air flow, but at the higher tensions of 10 Kv and greater and with air flows not exceeding 20 litres per minute this loss is almost totally eliminated. The apparatus has a collecting efficiency, therefore, of virtually 100 per cent. With liquid collection, however, other factors become operative and the recovery rate is not as consistent. Thus, Houwink and Rolvink reported recoveries of only about 75 per cent by this method, but Morris *et al.* did better than this and found substantial losses only at high humidities, presumably due to the generation of small amounts of ozone: higher tensions up to 15 Kv were necessary, however, to achieve this improved recovery. The Porton model can be used equally satisfactorily with phage and bacterial aerosols, in fact, it is sometimes superior to the impinger type of sampler because it avoids the destructive element associated with agitation; this is shown up very clearly with the T3 coliphage.

Thermal precipitators work on much the same principle as electrostatic ones, except that the "electrodes" consist of a hot and cold circular plate narrowly separated by only about 0·015 in. (Orr, Gordon and Kordecki, 1956). The hot plate is at a temperature of 125° and the cold surface, kept cool by circulating tap water on its underside, is covered with a filter paper dipped in a nutrient medium. Air is introduced at the centre of the plate and any particulate matter suspended in the air passing into the thermal field is forced and collected on the cooled surface. The air-flow rate is small, only 0·3 litres per minute, and under these conditions the collecting efficiency is about the same as the critical orifice impinger, that is approaching 100 per cent.

Comparative efficiencies of samplers. There is always considerable difficulty in assessing the efficiences of the various air samplers. Direct measures of efficiencies are not feasible because it is impossible to disperse a given volume of a suspension of bacteria and assume that each one of the cells is then available for collection from the aerosol so formed: there is always some loss, sometimes quite substantial, so that one can never have a "100 per cent" aerosol dispersal. In these circumstances all efficiency assessments must be comparative, using the best sampler available as the "after-control" for collecting any cells which might have escaped the sampler under investigation.

As might be expected, opinions differ somewhat on the relative merits of the different samplers, but all are agreed that for collecting small particles of 5 microns or less the impinger devices or the precipitators are the most selective. There seems to be no doubt, from the figures already quoted in the appropriate sections, that the precipitators and the critical orifice impingers give the best recoveries and so are the most efficient. Morris *et al.* (1961), for instance, found the performance of their electrostatic precipitator to be equal, if not slightly superior, to the orifice sampler, both giving recoveries approaching 100 per cent, and Orr, Gordon and Kordecki (1956) were of the same opinion regarding their thermal precipitator. But care is needed in selecting the standard for the critical orifice sampler: the all-glass and Porton standard models are good and are the devices normally referred to, but the so-called midget sampler, although operating on the same principle, for some reason has a low efficiency of about 80 per cent. Of the other impingers, Lemon (1943) found his aeroscope to be rather inferior to the Moulton sampler, which gave an efficiency of 96 per cent, but Bourdillon and Lidwell (1948) were of the opposite opinion. There was no equivocation by Wolfe (1961), however, who in a review on the characteristics of bacterial aerosols stated "If there is such a thing as a standard sampler for estimating the viable concentrations of organisms in aerosols it is the so-called Porton impinger. . . . The Porton impinger . . . is at present the most useful ampler we have for its particular purpose".

Testing chemical disinfectants

The testing of chemical formulations for their efficiencies as aerial germicides is a more difficult matter than testing the same materials in solution, on account of the various distribution and sampling problems associated with such tests. In the preceding sections methods for the dispersal of bacteria and of their subsequent sampling and counting have been discussed, but there is still the question of how to disperse the disinfectant as well as that of the choice of a suitable test chamber in which to carry out the experiments. A good deal of attention has been given to these questions by those interested in this aspect of disinfection.

The test chamber. For assessing the relative values of any chemical disinfectant a test chamber with a static volume of air is indispensable. The reason for this is that chemical disinfection of any type is a dynamic process and a fixed volume of air with a known initial inoculum is the only means by which the die-away of viable organisms during treatment can be measured. An air flow system would be far less adaptable for such an assessment.

Opinions vary on the optimum size for a test chamber. All are agreed that a space of only a few cubic feet capacity is unsuitable because of the impossibility of making uniform dispersals of disinfectants and of obtaining stable and reproducible bacterial suspensions in such small air volumes. Twort *et al.* (1940) found that a chamber of even 360 litres capacity was unsatisfactory and for their experiments used twin cylinders each of 3,050 litres. Most workers have preferred cube-shaped chambers with capacities between about 500 to 1,000 cu ft, although they have ranged as high as 16,000 cu ft (MacKay, 1952). After considering all the evidence available, the Aerosols Panel (1949) advocated a room of about 1,000 cu ft, shaped as near to a true cube as possible. Several workers, *e.g.* Pulvertaft and Walker (1939), Twort *et al.* (1940), Robertson *et al.* (1942*a*) and Puck, Robertson and Lemon (1943), have used twin chambers, the purpose of the second chamber being either to act as a control or to give greater experimental flexibility.

The chamber must be of plain construction with a minimum of equipment and it must be provided with a means for keeping the air mixed during the course of an experiment. There must also be facilities for ventilating the chamber before and after each experiment. The walls should be smooth and washable, and for this reason Robertson, Puck and Wise (1946) used a room constructed of glass.

Dispersing the germicide. The method used for dispersing a germicide must depend to a large extent on its properties. With gases there is no problem, but with liquids and solids volatility is a deciding factor. Certain compounds can be dispersed as vapours by dropping them on a hot plate or by similar heating methods, and such methods have been developed in the United States for large-scale use. Generally speaking they have limited applications, and the more usual method of dispersal is from solutions by means of one or other of the aerosol sprays, of which there are now many commercial models.

In practice, most of the aerial bactericides in common use have to be dispersed by spraying because they have only low vapour pressures and consequently low volatilities, but in some cases more natural methods can be used. Thus, resorcinol is sufficiently volatile to sterilize the atmosphere of a small chamber by simply painting the substance on the floor of the chamber (Twort, 1942). This idea was examined in some detail by Lovelock (1948b) who used it with several other substances such as lactic acid, α-hydroxy-α-methylbutyric acid, hexenoic acid and several esters of maleic acid. His method was simply to impregnate sheets of tissue paper with the test material at the rate of 0·5 gm per sq ft, and hang them in the test chamber. Volatilization can be assisted by using a small fan directed towards the paper surface.

Testing techniques. The efficiency of any air disinfection process is assessed either by measuring the death rate of a given air-borne bacterial population under the influence of the germicide or by measuring the percentage kill after a known interval of time. The technique is not a simple one because, in the first place, there is always a natural die-away of viable organisms due to their slow settling or adhesion to the walls of the test chamber, and secondly, the death process of organisms during disinfection is a dynamic reaction and so it is impossible to sample the air instantaneously at fixed time intervals such as is done with aqueous disinfectant mixtures. It is because of this that the slit sampler is an invaluable tool in testing aerial disinfectants, since it is the only device which allows the die-away rate to be estimated during a given test period. All other sampling devices can only give mean counts during the chosen sampling period.

Having fixed upon a convenient test chamber and appropriate dispersal and sampling systems, a typical test procedure might be as follows: (1) adjust the temperature and humidity conditions of the test chamber, allowing sufficient time for them to become stabilized; (2) disperse the bacterial aerosol and mix with the aid of a fan; (3) take a 30 seconds' sample with the slit sampler; (4) one minute later take a further 30 seconds' sample (this gives a measure of the stability of the bacterial aerosol); (5) disperse the bactericide rapidly; (6) at selected intervals, say of 2 minutes, take further 30 seconds' samples, and so obtain a death rate curve during the treatment. This gives a measure of the efficiency of the disinfectant.

It is advisable to include a standard germicide with each test series in order to check the conditions of the test, the resistance of the organisms, etc. This has the advantage, amongst others, of controlling the conditions of the test as well as allowing the performance of an unknown germicide to be assessed in terms of the standard.

The Aerosols Panel (1949) of the British Disinfectant Manufacturers' Association proposed a method based on the foregoing principles and it was subsequently incorporated in a British Standard Specification (1956) for the preliminary assessment of aerial bactericides. The standard germicide chosen is cyclopentanol-1-carboxylic acid, volatilized from a hot plate, and the test organism is a non-clumping *Staph. albus*. A bactericide is considered satisfactory if it effects a kill of not less than 85 per cent in 4–6 minutes at a relative humidity of 55–65 per cent and a temperature of about 20°. An alternative method for expressing the performance, since we are dealing with aerial disinfection, is in terms of ventilation rates. This is based on the assumption that the death-rate of bacteria during disinfection follows an exponential form the same as the rate of dilution of organisms in a given atmosphere by normal ventilation. By relating the killing rate of the disinfectant to the number of air changes in a given time producing the same reduction of viable bacteria, a killing constant (K) can be obtained. The time unit usually employed is one hour, and on this basis the K value is related to percentage kills as follows:

K value ($changes/hr$)	% kill after mean exposure time of 2 min	5 min
2	8	16
6	20	43
10	29	61
20	49	81
40	74	98

On this basis, the British Standard would specify a minimum K value of 22·5.

Kethley, Fincher and Cown (1956) were not enamoured of this static atmosphere technique and instead proposed a more dynamic test in which there is a constant flow of infected air and of the germicide through the system. In such a system all of the variables must be carefully controlled to ensure that the disinfection reaction proceeds constantly during the period of a test, and the authors paid much attention to this. Their test chamber was a cylinder, domed at each end, of 35 litres capacity and with a diameter of 12 in. and an overall length of 24 in. The test organism was a broth culture of *Chr. prodigiosum* aerolysed from a de Vilbiss spray and passed through a settling prechamber to remove the gross particles, the resultant aerosol being

90 per cent single cells. Tests were made at 25 and 80 per cent relative humidity and at normal temperature (20°) and the flow-rate through the system was such that the mean retention time in the cylinder was 3·5 minutes. Counts were taken on the air before and after treatment and from these the killing constant calculated from the expression

$$K = \frac{\log \text{input count} - \log \text{output count}}{3·5}$$

The standard used in the low humidity tests was triethylene glycol and in the high humidity tests 2-ethylhexane-1:3-diol.

Chemical disinfection

The primary requirement for an effective aerial germicide is that it must gain easy access to air-borne organisms. For this reason, disinfectants in the gaseous or vapour state are likely to be the most effective, but the less volatile substances can be equally effective provided they are dispersed in a sufficiently fine aerosol.

The substances which have attracted most attention in the past have been chlorine, or sodium hypochlorite, the glycols and hexylresorcinol. Many other substances, including the simpler phenols, cresols, phenyl-mercuric salts and quaternary ammonium compounds, have been used with some degree of success (*e.g.* Kliewe, 1946; Fulton *et al.*, 1948), but they have all been rejected as practical aerial germicides for reasons of odour, irritation and other unpleasant side effects. Formaldehyde gas and sulphur dioxide, although good bactericides are also eliminated for the same reasons. They are still used for terminal disinfection where there is no direct human contact, but this does not fall within the scope of aerial disinfection, since its primary purpose is to disinfect clothing, bedding and any other exposed surfaces.

Mechanism of chemical disinfection

Gaseous vs. *droplet disinfection.* There is no reason to suppose that chemical disinfectants should act differently on air-borne organisms than on those in aqueous suspension. But this should not be interpreted as meaning that substances active in solution are also active in aerosol form, for this is not the case. Many substances commonly accepted as effective antiseptics are of no value as air disinfectants. In aerial disinfection, other factors come into play, and the opinion has been expressed that physical behaviour is at least as important as germicidal action. One interesting feature of aerial disinfection is the comparatively low effective levels of concentration of practically all substances showing activity – a useful adjunct in considering the practical applications of aerial germicides from the aspect of toxicity to humans. Thus, as little as 0·025 mg of a 1 per cent solution of sodium hypochlorite dispersed in one litre of air, that is, 1 gm in 40,000 litres, is effectively bactericidal in a few minutes (Masterman, 1938, 1941). Similarly, some lethal action is observed with 0·02 mg of propylene glycol (Robertson *et al.*, 1941) and even with 0·001 mg of hexylresorcinol (Twort *et al.*, 1940).

The main divergence between the mechanisms of the disinfection processes on air-borne organisms and on organisms in aqueous suspension is the way in which the germicide gains access to the organisms, and in terms of aerial disinfection there are two schools of thought. In the first place, there is no contradicting the fact that the lethal action must result from the condensation of the germicide on the organism, but there were those on the one hand who believed that it followed the direct contact of the germicidal aerosol droplets with the bacterial particles (Trillat, 1938; Pulvertaft and Walker, 1939; Twort *et al.*, 1940), and those on the other hand who were equally convinced that it followed the volatilization of the droplets and so took place through the gaseous or vapour phase (Masterman, 1938, 1941; Elford and van den Ende, 1942; Lidwell and Lovelock, 1948*a*). These two theories were argued by their protagonists from various aspects and the droplet contact theory gradually lost ground. To say the least, there were still several points for which no adequate explanation seemed to be forthcoming and Puck (1947) went so far as to state that in some cases the theory was untenable. Nash (1951) was even more categorical, taking it as proved from the outset of his investigations that the vapour route is the only means of access of an aerial disinfectant to bacteria.

"Initial kill" phenomenon. A further insight into the mechanisms of aerial disinfection was provided by Darlow *et al.* (1958) consequent on their findings that much higher levels of kill are obtained if bacteria or viruses are sprayed into an established germicidal aerosol than if the normal practice is followed of introducing the germicide into the bacterial aerosol. This was attributed to an "initial kill" phenomenon, and although the report was concerned only with hexylresorcinol there is no reason why it should be confined to this substance. On spraying a variety of bacterial cultures, or the vaccinia virus, into an atmosphere containing only 0·1 μg of hexylresorcinol per litre of air there was an immediate apparent loss in viability of the cells or particles dispersed: there was no such loss if the bacteria were sprayed first. The losses ranged up to 90 per cent if a slit sampler was used but were rather smaller when samples were collected by an impinger. The difference is probably due to the fact that the impinger eliminates any residual bacteriostatic effect more rapidly by liquid dilution than does the slit sampler; in any case it certainly confirms that some quite intense bactericidal activity is taking place during this short initial phase. The explanation offered by Darlow and his colleagues for the phenomenon is that in an established germicidal atmosphere the agent is present to saturation in the vapour form so that on dispersing bacterial aerosol into it the momentarily wet droplets pick up some of the germicide, the relatively large droplets

aiding this, and then rapidly dry off leaving a high germicide content to act on the cell.

Effect of humidity. Because the germicidal action of a substance depends exclusively on its presence *in solution* around the individual bacteria, and because this in turn depends on the condensation of the vapour on each air-borne bacteria-carrying particle, humidity conditions might be expected to play an important part. On this account, optimum activities are generally found at fairly high humidities in the range 60–70 per cent RH, but there are exceptions, notably amongst the glycols. With most disinfectants there is not enough residual moisture on the bacterial particle at low humidities to dissolve an adequate amount of the germicide, hence their low activities, but with the glycols, which are only lethal in solution at high concentrations, the reverse is the case. Here the high humidities allow too much water to gather round the bacteria for an adequately lethal concentration to be reached.

On the basis of the foregoing arguments, there might be assumed to be some relationship between water solubility and activity. This idea was hinted at by Lovelock (1948a) and developed subsequently by Nash (1951) who conceived of two categories of aerial disinfectants; (*i*) the water-miscible substances which are bactericidal only at high concentrations *in vitro* and so are effective only at low humidities and (*ii*) those substances which are either partly soluble in water or are easily salted out of solution and therefore are limited in their activities at low humidities but are rapidly lethal at high humidities because of the lower overall concentrations needed for bactericidal action. The exceptions to these generalizations are to be found amongst the substances of low vapour pressure which, because they can only be present in the air in very small quantities, depend for their activities on their intrinsic germicidal properties; and these are not generally associated with high water solubilities. The same also applies to substances which are present in concentrations below their normal saturation vapour pressures.

The substances which remain active at low RH values have another interesting property—they can also protect living cells from lethal damage by freezing and thawing (Nash, 1962). It applies to the glycols and to dimethyl sulphoxide, pyridine N-oxide and possibly also to certain other Lewis bases, and is attributed to "the special solvent properties of these compounds, which come into play when most of the water usually present has been removed". This property prevents the lysis of cells by virtue of the increased salts concentration during freezing or drying and can be associated with the "S" value, or hydrophilic character, of the compound. This provides a new angle of approach in the search for aerial disinfectants which are active at low relative humidities.

Activities of some germicides

Hypochlorites. One of the first aerial disinfectants to be used was sodium hypochlorite. It had been in use for some years as a means of air purification before Douglas, Hill and Smith (1928) demonstrated its ability to reduce substantially the number of air-borne bacteria. Ten years later, Masterman (1938), and also Trillat (1938), confirmed the efficiency of hypochlorite sprays, showing that a 1 in 40,000,000 (weight in volume) dilution of a 1 per cent solution would sterilize infected air in a matter of minutes. In the course of his work Masterman conceived an elaborate theory to explain this high activity, but not all of his ideas were accepted. Some of his findings were challenged so seriously that he was led (1941) to a more intensive investigation of the subject to prove his earlier contentions. This subsequent work had a salutary effect, because it enabled him to reiterate and underline the importance of droplet size in relation to germicidal efficiency. Twort and Baker (1942) agreed with this, showing that a fine aerosol produced from an 'aerograph brush' spray might be some ten times more effective than a coarser one produced from a hand spray. They also showed that a 1 per cent solution of sodium hypochlorite is no more effective than a 0·2 per cent solution, both solutions killing approximately 98 per cent of the organisms in saliva within 30 minutes. Lidwell and Lovelock (1948a) supported this finding, with the proviso that the same *amount* of hypochlorite must be introduced into the air. In their particular experiments they sprayed 30 ml of a 1 per cent solution and 150 ml of a 0·2 per cent solution into a 4,500 cu ft test chamber, and obtained approximately 95 per cent kills of *Strep. salivarius* in serum broth within 5 minutes, and total destruction within 10 minutes. Earlier, Bourdillon, Lidwell and Lovelock (1942) had produced a complete kill of sneezed organisms within 3 or 4 minutes by treating the atmosphere with a 1 per cent solution atomized at the rate of 2·1 ml in each 1,000 cu ft of air. They also drew attention to the comparative inefficiency of the spray on infected dry dust, and the adverse influence of organic matter.

Hypochlorous acid is reported to be as effective against influenza A virus as it is against *Strep. salivarius* (Edward and Lidwell, 1943) and the source of the acid seems to be immaterial (Lidwell and Lovelock, 1948a).

A disadvantage with this form of disinfection is that the aerosol is only stable and effective for a few minutes. There is also the question of irritation, corrosion and possible attack on fabrics, although Masterman (1938), Challinor (1943), Lidwell and Lovelock (1948b) and others have used hypochlorite sprays satisfactorily in occupied rooms and in air-raid shelters.

Glycols. Propylene and triethylene glycols were first used in air disinfection as solvents for other germicidal substances, but they were later found to be effective *per se* (Robertson et al., 1941). Their action is quite rapid, but they are not persistent, and killing largely ceases when the vaporization is complete (Lidwell, Lovelock and Raymond, 1948a). They show maximum activities at low RH values. Above about 40 per cent RH they rapidly become less effective, the factor for ethylene glycol at 25 and 80 per cent RH, for instance, being about 30.

Some attention has been given to the method of generation and dispersal of the vapour, and the general preference, particularly amongst the American workers, is to use heating methods. Simple dropping on a hot plate has been used, but more complex devices have been invented to give continuous flows. These include an apparatus for vaporizing by boiling a mixture of glycol and water (Olson, Bigg and Jennings, 1947) using a 'glycostat' to control the concentration level (Puck, Wise and Robertson, 1944).

According to Lidwell, Lovelock and Raymond (1948b) the killing rate of propylene glycol is "very little dependent, if at all, on the amount of glycol vaporized or the vapour concentration attained." This applies to the range of concentrations examined, namely, 0·04 to 0·2 mg per litre, where approximately 90 per cent of organisms sprayed from saliva were killed in about 3 minutes. At a somewhat higher level of 0·5 mg per litre, there is evidence of a more rapid kill, Robertson *et al.* (1942b) finding it to be almost instantaneous.

Although much attention has been given to propylene glycol as an aerial disinfectant, triethylene glycol is in fact equally effective at about one-fortieth the concentration. Thus, pathogenic organisms, including influenza virus, sprayed from a saliva suspension have been killed within a few minutes (Robertson *et al.*, 1943), and they may sometimes succumb immediately (Bigg, Jennings and Fried, 1944), in a concentration of 1 part in 100 million parts of air. In the author's experiences, 125 μg of ethylene glycol per cu ft of air, *i.e.* 1 part in about 200 millions, will kill 90 per cent of staphylococci or spit-sprayed organisms in about 5 minutes.

In field practice it has been found by some to be of value in suppressing streptococcal cross-infections in wounds and of respiratory infections in army units (Hamburger, Puck and Robertson, 1945; Bigg, Jennings and Olson, 1945) but others have found it of little use as a schoolroom disinfectant. These differences are almost certainly due in a large measure to the different humidity conditions in which the trials were made. In no case, in fact, was the RH value mentioned.

Hexylresorcinol. Following extensive investigations on a number of phenolic derivatives in different solvents, Twort *et al.* (1940) selected hexylresorcinol in propylene glycol as the most promising of this group of compounds. Resorcinol had earlier been used by Trillat (1938) and by Pulvertaft, Lemon and Walker (1939) with some effect, but the hexyl derivative proved subsequently to be more effective. Twort and his colleagues obtained a 99·8 per cent kill of a selected *Staphylococcus* culture within 1 hour with only 1 part of a 10 per cent solution of hexylresorcinol in propylene glycol in 100 million parts of air, and the addition of small amounts of a wetting agent to the solution rendered it even more effective. Likewise, Pulvertaft (1944) obtained 90 per cent kills of sprayed *Streptococcus pyogenes* within one or two minutes by using a 0·25 per cent solution in propylene glycol. Hexylresorcinol was selected by Bourdillon (1948) as one of the outstanding aerial germicides, and by MacKay (1952) whose experiments showed it to be active in concentrations of 6 to 7 μg per cu ft (equivalent to 1 part by weight in several thousand-million parts of air by volume) against a variety of organisms, having obtained reductions in counts from millions to less than 10 per cu ft in about half-an-hour; it was not effective with *Bacillus subtilis* spores. Reference has already been made (p. 268) to the "initial kill" phenomenon as described by Darlow *et al.* (1958). Unfortunately, Lidwell and Williams (1954) found it quite ineffective when used as a continuous flow aerosol in clerical offices.

Smokes, notably cigarette smoke, interfere with the action of hexylresorcinol and all phenolic aerosols (Twort and Baker, 1942).

Hydroxy acids. The use of hydroxy acids for aerial disinfection was suggested by Lovelock, Lidwell and Raymond (1944), and they later studied the activities of lactic acid (Lidwell, Lovelock and Raymond, 1948*b*) and of several other hydroxy-carboxylic acids (Lovelock, 1948*a,b*).

Lactic acid is most effective at relative humidities in the range of about 60–80 per cent, depending on the state of the bacteria whether they are dispersed from liquid culture or in dry dust particles. With a reduction of even 10 per cent from the optimum humidity range there is a steep fall in activity. The killing rate also varies with the size of the bacteria-carrying particle, but with a sprayed culture of *Strep. salivarius* there is a 99 per cent kill in about 40 seconds at a concentration of 0·004 mg per litre of air. Below about 0·003 mg per litre the activity falls steeply, and at about 0·005 mg the aerosol becomes irritant, although it is not toxic. It has been used effectively in treating the air in a staff mess room, vaporization being from an aqueous solution dropped at regular intervals on a brass plate heated to 150°.

The other aliphatic α-hydroxycarboxylic acids are not quite as sensitive to RH conditions as lactic acid. Their optimum activities are still in the range 60–80 per cent, but several of them remain effective down to about 40 or 45 per cent RH, being able to reduce the numbers of air-borne organisms sprayed from the respiratory tract by 90 per cent in 5 minutes. They all show marked increases in activity as the aerial concentration is increased, and each has a maximum (saturation) concentration beyond which there is no further increase.

The two most interesting acids of the group are α-hydroxy-α-methylbutyric acid, which has about the same activity as lactic acid but is much less irritant, and α-hydroxy-*n*-decoic acid, which is about 35 times more active on a concentration basis, since about 0·07 μg per litre of air (2 μg per cu ft) is lethal in 6 minutes.

Miscellaneous compounds. Frequent claims have been made for the efficacy of ozone as an aerial disinfectant, but there appears to be only one record of any precise measurements (Elford and van den Ende, 1942). A tolerable, non-toxic concentration of ozone is 0·04 parts per million, and at this level it is active against sprayed bacterial cultures, but not against protected organisms as normally found in the atmosphere. Its optimum activity is in the 60–90 per cent range of relative humidity.

Iodine, vaporized by heat or from alcoholic solution, at a concentration of 0·003 μg per litre has also given good results. With sneezed organisms the optimum relative humidity is 50 per cent, but with dust-borne organisms it is 70 per cent (Raymond, 1946). Iodine had been used much earlier with some effect during the 1918 influenza epidemic (Plesch, 1941).

An aerosol of 2-chloro-4-phenylphenol is also claimed to be effective against staphylococci (Anderson, 1963). From his results, a concentration of 0·8 μg per litre of air killed 99 per cent of the organisms in about 20 minutes and 2·1 μg per litre was totally lethal in 2–3 minutes.

Several smokes have been tried with variable success. These include wood shavings, gear grease, cotton wool, incense and cardboard soaked in potassium nitrate (Twort and Baker, 1940). The last two mentioned were the most effective, 1 gm dispersed in 60 cu m of air giving about a 94 per cent kill of salivary organisms in 5 minutes, and a substantial kill at even lower concentrations within 30 minutes.

Formaldehyde, whilst being effective, is of no practical value because of its extreme irritant properties. Other aldehydes have proved of little value (Checcacci, 1947).

Filtration

Filtration as a means of sterilizing air achieved great prominence with the development of the antibiotics industry and its demands for large supplies of air entirely free from contaminating organisms for the fermentation stages. Filtration has proved to be the only feasible means of meeting such demands, other forms of treatment being ruled out because of their excessively high costs or because of their inefficiency. Filtration is also one of the most practicable means of supplying air to sterile filling rooms, operating theatres and similar premises, and indeed for many years it was the exclusive means for meeting the requirements for such areas. Latterly, electrostatic precipitation has also entered the field.

Many types of filter are available commercially. Some are made primarily for the purpose of eliminating dust from certain industrial processes, but even these will remove a proportion of air-borne bacteria; others are designed specifically for removing bacteria or even the smaller virus particles down to 0·1 micron, and as such are available in several grades Care is needed therefore in choosing the right type of filter for the job in hand. Some filters are also impregnated with a bactericide to give them added efficiency.

Of the materials used as filter media, cotton wool is the best known. It is well-tried for laboratory use, but it is not suitable on the large scale because of its lack of mechanical strength which causes it to pack down and so reduce the rate of air flow through the filter. Alumina and charcoal have attracted some attention, but the main interest has been centred on slag wool, glass wool and spun glass fibres, and on paper, asbestos and glass fibre mixtures. The last named have been developed for the finest filtration work where particles down to 0·1 micron have to be removed.

With the finer filters it is usual to have a coarser prefilter to remove the larger particles and thus prolong the life of the finer filter which is usually the more expensive one. Such a combination does not, of course, increase the efficiency of the system.

Needless to say, all filters must be kept dry if they are to perform efficiently. A wet filter merely acts as a vehicle for transmitting organisms, because, even though they may be collected in the filter bed, they can easily creep along the continuous wet film and so be carried through and away with the air stream.

Mechanism of air filtration

All bacterial air filters are made of either fibrous or granular materials, and it is obvious from a casual visual examination that the spacings of the fibres or particles of the coarser filters are such that mechanical sieving at best can take only a small part in the filtration process. As with bacterial filters for liquids, other physical phenomena must be involved, and it seems not unreasonable that the two filtration processes must have some characteristics in common.

Elegant, though somewhat complicated, mathematical theories have been expounded by Stairmand (1950), Thomas (1952) and Humphrey (1952) to account for the phenomena, and they have much in common. Each takes into account the fundamental observations that efficiency depends upon the size of the particles to be filtered, the diameter of the fibres or size of the granules constituting the filter material, the packing density of the filter, its thickness, and the rate of air flow through the filter. In summary, the theories state that filtration is the outcome of the retention of air-borne particles on the material of the filter, the degree of which must depend on the number of contacts the particle and filter can make. These chance contacts come about as a result of (*i*) direct interception or trapping of the air-borne particles, (*ii*) inertial impaction of the particles on the filter material, (*iii*) air flow turbulence, (*iv*) diffusion forces arising from Brownian movement, and (*v*) electrostatic attraction. Hence it is easily seen that the velocity, nature and size of the particles being filtered and the size and nature of the filter material all exert their independent influences.

In any one system, the direct interception and electrostatic effects are constant factors and are independent of outside influences; they differ only when the system is changed, that is, when the filter material or particles being filtered are changed. The remaining factors vary in their influence as the air velocity varies. The turbulence and inertial, or impingement, influences are negligibly small at low initial air velocities, but the effect of Brownian movement is significant. As the air flow increases, the Brownian influence diminishes, but the inertial and tubulence forces become increasingly dominant the extent of which depend on the sizes of the particles to be filtered. Thus, with any filter in which the efficiency is less than 100 per cent the overall effect of increasing the air flow rate is first to cause a decline in efficiency (corresponding with the decline in influence of the Brownian effect) followed by a continuous increase as the impingement forces become more effective.

Such a relationship can be shown to be operative with particles down to 1 micron and less, but with very small particles of about 0·05 micron, *i.e.*

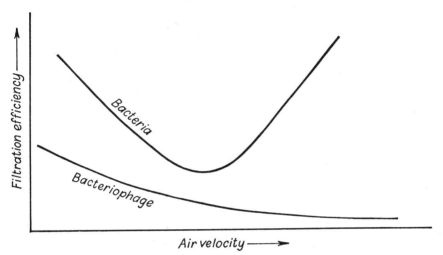

FIG. 15. *The relation between filtration efficiency and air flow rate for large (bacterial) and small (virus) particles*

bacteriophage and viruses, the inertial force ceases to be operative, and filtration efficiency depends entirely on Brownian movement and diffusional effects. The ordinary 'sterilizing' filters behave, therefore, quite differently in respect of bacteria on the one hand and phage and virus particles on the other, the general pattern being that the small particles are collected more efficiently at low velocities whereas for bacteria the efficiency increases as the air flow is increased. This is illustrated in Figure 15. The only way to overcome the difference and to make a filter behave with virus as with bacteria is to use fibres of much finer diameter, that is, of 2 microns or less instead of the usual 15 microns or more.

Stairmand (1950) states that the target efficiency of a single fibre is a function of the expression $\dfrac{Dg}{Vf}$ (where D is the diameter of the fibre, g is the gravitational constant, V is the velocity of approach of the particle and f is its free falling speed). From this he deduces that "very fine fibres and a high velocity of approach are essential if high target efficiencies are to be achieved" and this is entirely in line with the argument put forward in the preceding paragraph. He also emphasizes the not too obvious point that it is the fibre diameter and not the size of the interstices which gives a filter its efficiency. This would suggest that packing density is not important, but in this connexion the point must not be forgotten that at low packing densities there are smaller numbers of fibres, hence the number of opportunities for contact of filter with particles is reduced, and this also governs the filter efficiency.

No fibre or granular filter can have an efficiency of 100 per cent unless it is so fine that it acts purely as a mechanical sieve—and this is not usual with normal air filters. The normal penetration of micro-organisms is logarithmic in nature, therefore the efficiency of a filter varies with its depth or thickness, and the parameter of efficiency is given by the expression

$$k\mathrm{T} = \ln \frac{N_1}{N_2}$$

where k is a function embracing air velocity, fibre diameter, packing density and size of particles to be removed, T is the depth of the filter and N_1 and N_2 the number respectively of organisms entering and passing through the filter (Humphrey and Gordon, 1955).

A suggested testing technique

The principal requirements for testing air filter materials are a measured air flow, a means for introducing a regular and continuous inoculum of micro-organisms and a method for counting the number of organisms per unit volume of air before and after the filter. Such an apparatus was described by Terjesen and Cherry (1947); a similar one was used by the author in his work. It is illustrated diagrammatically in Fig. 16.

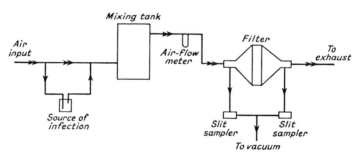

Fig. 16. *Diagram of apparatus for testing air filters*

Any organism can be used, depending on the purpose for which the filter is required, but it is usual to select either *B. subtilis* as representing a common dust-borne sporing organism, or one of the smaller vegetative types or even a virus or bacteriophage. *Chr. prodigiosum* is commonly chosen because of its size—it measures rather less than 1 micron—and because it is easily identified in culture by its pigmentation. The bacterial aerosol is generated from a dilute broth culture by spraying and baffling to remove the larger droplets and introduced into the main air stream through a Venturi throat system. For tests with infected dusts the dispersal system described on page 258 is used; in such tests *B. subtilis* spores must be used, as vegetative organisms are not sufficiently resistant to withstand drying.

The filter material to be examined can be used in the made-up form as supplied by the manufacturer, or it can be packed in small units of convenient experimental size. Much of the material examined by the author has been packed in tubes 2 in. diameter and up to 15 in. long.

In order to measure the rate of infection before and after the filter, an ordinary slit sampler is used. The initial infection rate should be such that a half-minute plate is easily countable, that is, half a cubic foot of air should contain between 100 and about 300 organisms. The air sample taken after the filter must be of much longer duration, especially if the filter is expected to have an efficiency approaching 100 per cent. A 15-minutes' plate exposure, for instance, will indicate efficiencies of the order of 99·98 per cent.

Another indirect method is by assessing the passage not of bacteria but of small particulate smokes through the filter. For this purpose, Rowley dust (a 100/200 mesh mixture of lamp black and fullers earth), a standard aerosol of methylene blue, dioctyl phthalate smoke or a sodium chloride aerosol are used. The methylene blue test is the present British Standard method; the dioctyl phthalate smoke method, which gives particles of size about 0·3 micron, is widely used in the United States; the sodium chloride flame test, devised at the Microbiology Research Establishment, Porton, uses a cloud of particles ranging from 0·01 to 1·5 micron the passage of which is detected by passing it through a hydrogen flame.

Efficiencies of some filter materials

Alumina and charcoal granules. The performances of all granular filter materials follow the general theory as regards granule size, depth of filter, air flow rate and so on. Coarse alumina granules of 8/16 mesh are much less efficient, as expected, than are finer granules of 16/32 mesh and the efficiencies of both increase with air flow rate (Sykes and Carter, 1954). These observations are shown clearly in Table 25.

McDaniel and Long (1954) made similar observations with carbon granules showing that spores of *Bacillus globigii* would pass through a column made with 10/20 mesh granules in 2 hours, but required 5 hours to pass through one made with 30/50 mesh granules. Kluyver and Visser (1950) also experimented with carbon granules of the grade "moist PK 0·5-1 mm" and found that a column at least 29 cm long was necessary to filter satisfactorily the spores of *Bacillus cereus*.

Carbon filters 6–9 ft in diameter and 6 ft deep have been used successfully in the fermentation industries, but possess several inherent dangers arising from their tendency to spontaneous ignition during sterilization by steam under pressure and when warm air is passing through them (Hastings, 1954). An interesting point in connexion with alumina granules is that sterilization by dry heat at 150° results in a slight, but only temporary, increase in efficiency. Kluyver and Visser (1950) made a similar observation with carbon

TABLE 25

The efficiencies of alumina granule air filters

Air velocity (ft/min)	Efficiency % with granules 8/16 mesh	16/32 mesh
80	—	92·0
240	88	99·4
480	98·7	99·9
720	99·96	—

Depth of filter—15 in.
Test organism—*Chr. prodigiosum* aerosol

granules and attributed it to activation by the heat treatment followed by de-activation during subsequent use.

Cotton wool. Cotton wool was the first material used in the laboratory for keeping infection away from sterilized media, and it is still invaluable for this purpose. It is, however, of little use for air filtration on the large scale, because

TABLE 26

Efficiencies of steel wool air filters

Air velocity (ft/min)	Percentage efficiencies of different filters of		
	Fibre diam (microns) 135	35	35
	Density (lb/cu ft) 35–40	15	35
	Length (in.) 11	4	11
80	68	90	99·8–99·9
160	—	91–95	99·8
240	75	97	99·7
320	—	99·2–99·8	—
480	96	—	—

Test organism—*Chr. prodigiosum* aerosol

it is easily wetted and so ceases to be an effective filter; it also packs down and tends to give an impermeable felt.

Such cotton filters as are available commercially vary somewhat in their performance. They are usually about one-quarter of an inch thick, mounted on a fine wire mesh frame, and their efficiencies are generally of the order of 90 per cent or greater against infected dusts, but much lower against bacterial aerosols (Sykes and Carter, 1953).

Steel wool. Experiment has shown that steel wools have appreciable filtration efficiencies, the actual values depending on their fibre diameters and on their packing densities. Some results under these different conditions are given in Table 26.

This information is probably of only academic interest, but it shows clearly that even quite coarse wools have some value in filtering air-borne bacteria, and once again the significance of air-flow rate is illustrated.

Glass wool and spun glass fibres. Glass wools are now available in fibre thicknesses ranging from some 200 to 300 microns down to about 0·5 micron,

TABLE 27

Efficiencies of some coarse fibre filters

| Air flow rate (ft/min) | Percentage filtration efficiency with | | | | | |
| | Coarse glass fibre filter | | Cotton fibre filter | | Wire gauze filter | |
	aerosol	dust	aerosol	dust	aerosol	dust
12	—	48	—	88	—	—
30	46	40	—	84	—	—
60	—	49	56	81	25	46
92	15	—	—	—	—	—
123	—	48	48	82	20	43
184	1	52	46	88	19	54
288	7	58	45	90	10	59
380	—	63	41	85	14	64
576	19	92	45	93	29	75

and a number of different types of assembled filters are available commercially, some of which are supplied as dust removers with no claim for their bacterial filtration efficiencies. Most of the coarser filters are bonded with a resin, this also renders them more adhesive for small particles.

As indicated in Table 27, some of the coarser fibre filters have very low efficiencies against bacterial aerosols, but they are much better against infected dusts when their efficiencies rise to 80 or 90 per cent at the normally recommended air flow rates. For higher efficiencies it is necessary to use finer glass fibres. The author's own experiments with different fibre thicknesses, packing densities and depths of filter, as summarized in Table 28, illustrate this point and show the superiority of the finer material.

These results are of the same order as those of Cherry, McCann and Parker (1951), who experimented with fibres of two grades. In both cases they used filters 3 in. thick and packed to a density of 16 or 17 lb per cu ft, and a single air-flow rate of 30 ft per minute. With these test conditions, they obtained efficiencies of at least 99·9 per cent with fibres up to 6 microns, and 99·86 per cent with fibres up to 12 microns in diameter.

Glass fibres are also available in resin-bonded, woven sheet form, and the author has experimented with samples of such material, employing different numbers of sheets in several filters to give different thicknesses. One such sample was made with glass fibres with an average diameter of 16 microns and layers of from 25 to 300 sheets were examined, representing thicknesses

TABLE 28

Efficiencies of glass fibre air filters

Filter details			Percentage efficiency at air velocities		
Fibre diameter (microns)	Packing density (lb/cu ft)	Filter depth (in.)	25 ft/min	50 ft/min	80 ft/min
200	4·5	2	—	—	22
18·5	14	2	—	—	97
18·5	14	4	—	—	99·3
18·5	14	6	—	—	99·97
"Pyrex coarse"	7·1	4	99·0	98·8	—
"Pyrex coarse"	9·6	7	99·4	99·55	—
"Pyrex fine top grade"	4	4	99·96	99·78	—
"Pyrex fine top grade"	4	7	99·99	99·99	—

Test organism—*Chr. prodigiosum* aerosol

TABLE 29

Filtration efficiencies of spun glass sheets

Number of layers	Thickness (in.)	Percentage efficiency
25	0·4	97·92
50	0·8	99·48
100	2·0	99·63
200	4·0	99·82
300	5·6	99·98

of from 0·4 to 5·6 in., all with air flows of 40 ft per minute, with the results given in Table 29.

Sheets of even finer fibres down to 0·5 micron are now available, and Smucker and Marlow (1954) examined the performance of a series of such sheets of different fibre diameter against Rowley dust and dioctyl phthalate smoke. Their findings are given in Table 30. The glass paper filters examined by the author are made of fine fibres of maximum diameter about 2·5 microns and are rather less than 1 mm thick. Their reported sodium chloride penetration values, at the recommended maximum air flow rate, range from 5 per cent to 0·005 per cent, and so the finest of them should give a sterile air, free from even virus particles. In practice efficiencies against bacteria of about

99·9 per cent, range 99·6 to 99·98 per cent, were found for the finer one, and 97 to 98 per cent for the coarser one.

Besides the various glass-fibre filters, asbestos-glass and asbestos-cotton filters are also available. Glass fibres of 1·5 micron diameter mixed with asbestos are reported to be 99·5 per cent efficient against 0·3 micron smoke particles (Silverman, 1955) and 99·99 per cent efficient in the methylene blue test against particles down to 0·2 micron (Stafford and Smith, 1951; Decker, Harstad *et al.*, 1954). The author has found asbestos-cotton filters, of thickness about 0·1 in. and with sodium chloride penetration values up to 0·05 per cent, to be 99·9 per cent efficient against bacteria.

Slag wool. Slag wool was first suggested as a filter medium by Terjesen and Cherry (1947), and its properties were investigated in greater detail by

TABLE 30

Filtration efficiencies of spun glass sheets

Fibre diameter (microns)	Percentage efficiency against	
	Rowley dust	0·3µ smoke
125 (2 in. thick)	80	—
20 (1 sheet)	90	—
4 (,,)	95–99	10
1 (,,)	100	80
0·5 (,,)	100	90

Cherry, McCann and Parker (1951). It is obtainable either as loose flock or in preformed slabs ready for fitting in a filter unit. The majority of its fibres are 6 microns or less in diameter, only some twenty to thirty per cent being greater than this. For reliable air sterilization Cherry and his colleagues specified that the filter bed should be not less than three inches thick, that it should be compressed to a packing density of about 16 lb per cu ft (later modified to 25 lb per cu ft), and that the air flow should not exceed a velocity of 30 ft per minute. The author's work (Sykes and Carter, 1954) agreed broadly with this, and confirmed the reliable efficacy of the lower packing density of 16 lb per cu ft. With infection rates of up to 3,000 cells of *Chr. prodigiosum* per cu ft, a 2 in. filter gave efficiencies of over 99·9 per cent and a 3 in. filter was virtually absolute; and these conditions were maintained successfully for continuous experimental periods up to sixteen days. One drawback with such a filter is the high resistance to air flows, especially at high velocities, and the consequent development of a substantial back pressure.

The lack of progressive penetration, regardless of the period of test, is an interesting phenomenon with all filters. With slag wool, for instance, penetration does not exceed more than about two inches. It has been suggested that this is due to the continuous die-off of filtered organisms during penetration, but there seems to be more to it than this, because Terjesen and Cherry (1947) observed the same thing with bacterial spores, which might be expected to be more resistant to such adverse conditions.

Impregnated filters. Various attempts have been made to improve the efficiency of fibrous filters by impregnating them with silver salts, organic tin compounds, surface active quaternary ammonium compounds and the like but with little success. Such a treatment may well deal more effectively with organisms once they have been collected on the fibres, but from the theories already stated, they cannot be expected to improve the collecting efficiency of the filter.

Heat

Heating is an obvious method for air sterilization, but on the large scale it is impracticable because of the high temperatures required and the consequent waste of energy. The treatment is by dry heat but at temperatures well above the usual 150° or so for the normal dry heat sterilization because the time of contact can only be of short duration.

Bourdillon, Lidwell and Raymond (1948) obtained sterility of the air passed through an externally heated furnace by treating at 225° for 0·4–0·6 second, but in an internally heated one, a somewhat higher temperature and longer heating time was necessary. They concluded from all of their work that the thermal death point, presumably the 'flash' level, of the organisms used must have been about 250°, and so recommended an air exit temperature of 300° to ensure complete freedom from all micro-organisms. Elsworth, Telling and Ford (1955) experimenting with two internally heated furnaces, one with an air capacity of 140 litres per minute and the other 1,700 litres per minute, estimated for the smaller model that "a minimum exposure time of 0·14 seconds at 300° gives a spore penetration of not more than one in 470 millions"; a longer time was necessary for the larger model. Later, Elsworth, Morris and East (1961) computed the penetration of spores (*B. globigii*) for a one second exposure to be 0·1 per cent at 210°, 3·6 × 10⁻³ per cent at 270° and 1·75 × 10⁻⁷ per cent at 330°. Using a proprietary heat sterilizer, Decker, Citek *et al.* (1954) quoted sterilizing times of 24 seconds at 218° (425°F), 10 seconds at 246° (475°F) and 3 seconds at 302° (575°F), with chances of survival of not more than one in a million. Bearing in mind the difficulties associated with carrying out such experiments and the short time intervals involved, these results by the different workers are remarkably consistent.

Some attempt has been made to operate at lower temperatures by combining a heat treatment with an admixture of steam, and this is covered by a French patent (Corblain, 1951). The procedure consists of heating the air to about 150°, introducing a small amount of steam at the rate of 150 gm to each cubic metre of air, holding in this condition for 1 minute and then cooling. The cooling causes the steam to condense, during which process it is alleged to carry with it all the particulate impurities and so leave a residual sterile air.

In the domestic field, a convection-type electric heater, with the air circulating over the elements at temperatures in the range of 600° to 800°, is reported to reduce the numbers of viable spores by 50–75 per cent, of vegetative bacteria by 90 per cent and of viruses by around 99 per cent (Clifton, 1955). The low values obtained in these experiments, compared with those quoted earlier, probably arise because most of the air does not pass sufficiently near to the elements to reach anything like the temperature indicated.

Air compression

Allied to the heat sterilization and filtration phenomena just described is the sterilizing effect of adiabatic compression such as occurs in reciprocating compressors. Stark and Pohler (1950) first drew attention to this in their experiments with a single-stage compressor working at 40–60 lb per sq in. They were able to produce sterile air in this apparatus provided the ingoing air had a temperature of not less than 21°. Turbo-compressors were not effective although giving higher discharge temperatures, and so the sterilizing action was thought to be due to the moisture content of the air and the presence of oil vapour. Similar findings were made by Sykes and Carter (1954). Their tests were carried out on a Broomwade compressor operating at 60 lb per sq in. The time of treatment in the Broomwade machine was calculated to be about one-twenty-fifth of a second, during which an air temperature of 150° was developed. Under these conditions the air was continuously sterilized, whereas under similar test conditions, the turbo-compressor gave efficienies of the order of 99–99·5 per cent. Estimations of efficiencies were made by passing volumes of 750 cu ft of air through 2-in. sterile plugs of cotton wool and then incubating them *in toto* in nutrient broth. On no occasion was any growth obtained in the tests with the Broomwade compressor.

Ultraviolet irradiation

Ultraviolet irradiation is dealt with at length in Chapter 6 on Radiation Sterilization, and so only the salient features will be mentioned here.

Ultraviolet irradiation is used in hospitals, mainly in surgical and maternity wards, and often by the 'curtain sterilization' method, as a means of reducing cross-infection. It is also used in industry where aseptic manipulations are involved, to keep down the level of bacterial contamination. It is often advocated for 'sterilizing' air flows into aseptic premises by putting a series of ultraviolet lamps in the air ducting, but the efficacy of this method of air treatment does not stand up to critical scrutiny. Such a treatment may be reasonably satisfactory for stationary or only slowly moving air inside a small enclosed space, but even so it does not sterilize the air completely; its efficiency with a moving air stream is described on page 181.

There are several disadvantages in the treatment of air by ultraviolet irradiation and they may be summarized as follows: (a) the time taken to disinfect even vegetative organisms is often too long to be of practical value; (b) often bacterial and mould spores are present which are highly resistant; (c) all organisms can be protected by thin layers of mucoid and other protein-containing materials, thus enhancing their apparent resistance, and (d) the efficiency of irradiation falls with the square of the distance from the source of the irradiation. Provided these limitations are appreciated, ultraviolet treatment can certainly be said to have a place in suppressing air-borne microbial infections.

Electrostatic precipitation

When small particles are caused to traverse an electric field with a high potential gradient they become ionized, so that if they are immediately passed between closely spaced plates, alternate ones of which carry a positive

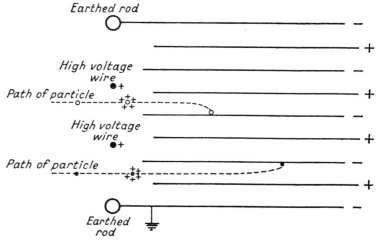

FIG. 17. *Operation of an electrostatic precipitator*

charge, they are attracted and held on the plate of opposite charge. This is the principle of one form of electrostatic precipitation, the process of which is illustrated diagrammatically in Fig. 17. One such model has been described by Penney (1937) in which the ionizing charge is developed from wires held at 14,000 volts (higher voltages are liable to cause sparking across the gaps) and the collecting plates are held at 7,000 volts. An alternative form involves using a honeycomb tube system with wires suspended in the middle of each tube to carry the positive charge. In this case the charging and collection are carried out in the single system. This model operates at the higher potential level of 20,000 volts (Munden, 1952).

Electrostatic precipitation was developed in the first place for removing pollens and other allergens from the atmosphere, and only recently has any attention been given to its performance with bacteria. In theory it should be completely effective, but from the scant information available it is not so found in practice. Undoubtedly its efficiency must vary with the size of the particles to be collected, the velocity of the air over the collecting plates and the length of the plates. A Precipitron machine, a model of the first type described above, has been reported to have a collecting efficiency of 98 to 99 per cent against dust and a rather lower value against bacterial spores (Munden, 1952), and similarly a Raytheon portable model examined in the author's laboratory gave efficiencies of the order of 99 per cent against air-borne mould spores and 96 per cent against bacteria.

A small free-standing model has been found of value in keeping the numbers of air-borne bacteria at a low level in small wards during bed making, changing dressings and other activities. With such a unit peak counts of about 50 organisms per cu ft were reduced to about 15 per cu ft in a surgical dressing room of 2,250 cu ft capacity and in a smaller side ward reductions up to 90 per cent were recorded (Steingold and Ashworth, 1960).

Air washing

A description of methods of air sterilization would be incomplete without some reference to washing and scrubbing techniques. These are usually practised for the purpose of air cleaning but they can be adapted to air disinfection. The air is either bubbled through a selected scrubbing liquor – sodium hydroxide or sodium carbonate solution is often used – or it is passed through a ring-packed column through which the liquor is trickling counter-currentwise; alternatively a spray washing system can be used. Such treatments are satisfactory for removing relatively large air-borne particles but with small ones of the size of individual bacteria there is the problem of wettability. Wetting agents, some of which are themselves bactericidal, have been added with some success, but, as with other disinfectants, there is always the possibility of carry over in the form of an aerosol and so contamination of the air stream (Hastings, 1954).

REFERENCES

Aerosols Panel, British Disinfectant Manufacturers' Association (1949). *Chem. & Ind.,* p. 115.
ANDERSEN, A. A. (1958). *J. Bact.,* **76**, 471.
ANDERSEN, A. A. (1963). *Appl. Microbiol.,* **11**, 239.
BIGG, E., JENNINGS, B. H. and FRIED, S. (1944). *Amer. J. med. Sci.,* **207**, 361.
BIGG, E., JENNINGS, B. H. and OLSON, F. C. W. (1945). *Amer. J. publ. Hlth,* **35**, 788.
BOURDILLON, R. B. (1948). *Studies in Air Hygiene,* Med. Res. Counc. Spec. Rep. Ser. No. 262, p. 311: H.M.S.O., London.
BOURDILLON, R. B. and LIDWELL, O. M. (1948). *Studies in Air Hygiene,* Med. Res. Counc. Spec. Rep. Ser. No. 262, pp. 27 and 50: H.M.S.O., London.

BOURDILLON, R. B., LIDWELL, O. M. and LOVELOCK, J. E. (1942). *Brit. med. J.*, i, 42.
BOURDILLON, R. B., LIDWELL, O. M. and LOVELOCK, J. E. and others (1948). *Studies in Air Hygiene*, Med. Res. Counc. Spec. Rep. Ser. No. 262: H.M.S.O., London.
BOURDILLON, R. B., LIDWELL, O. M. and RAYMOND, W. F. (1948). *Studies in Air Hygiene*, Med. Res. Counc. Spec. Rep. Ser. No. 262, p. 190: H.M.S.O., London.
BOURDILLON, R. B., LIDWELL, O. M. and THOMAS, J. C. (1941). *J. Hyg., Camb.*, 41, 197.
BOURDILLON, R. B., LIDWELL, O. M. and THOMAS, J. C. (1948). *Studies in Air Hygiene*, Med. Res. Counc. Spec. Rep. Ser. No. 262, p. 19: H.M.S.O., London.
British Standard Technique for the Preliminary Assessment of Aerial Bactericides British Standards Institution, 2796:1956.
CHALLINOR, S. W. (1943). *J. Hyg., Camb.*, 43, 16.
CHECCACCI, L. (1947). via *Chem. Abs.*, 1949, 43, 5083.
CHERRY, G. B., McCANN, E. P. and PARKER, A. (1951). *J. appl. Chem.*, 1, S103.
CLIFTON, C. E. (1955). *Science*, 122, 762.
CORBLAIN, H. (1951). Fr. Pat: 985,907.
COWN, W. B., KETHLEY, T. W. and FINCHER, E. L. (1957). *Appl. Microbiol.*, 5, 119.
DARLOW, H. M., POWELL, E. O., BALE, W. R. and MORRIS, E. J. (1958). *J. Hyg., Camb.*, 60, 108.
DECKER, H. M., CITEK, F. J., HARSTAD, J. B., GROSS, N. H. and PIPER, F. J. (1954). *Appl. Microbiol.*, 2, 33.
DECKER, H. M., HARSTAD, J. B., PIPER, F. J. and WILSON, M. E. (1954). *Heat. Pip. air Cond.*, 26(5), 155.
DECKER, H. M. and WILSON, M. E. (1954). *Appl. Microbiol.*, 2, 267.
DOUGLAS, S. R., HILL, L. and SMITH, W. (1928). *J. ind. Hyg.*, 10, 219.
DRUETT, H. A. and MAY, K. R. (1952). *J. Hyg., Camb.*, 50, 69.
DUNKLIN, E. W. and PUCK, T. T. (1948). *J. infect. Dis.*, 87, 87.
EDWARD, D. G. ff. and LIDWELL, O. M. (1943). *J. Hyg., Camb.*, 43, 196.
ELFORD, W. J. and VAN DEN ENDE, JOAN (1942). *J. Hyg., Camb.*, 42, 240.
ELSWORTH, R., MORRIS, E. J. and EAST, D. N. (1961). *Chem. Engr*, No. 137, p. A47.
ELSWORTH, R., TELLING, R. C. and FORD, J. W. F. (1955). *J. Hyg., Camb.*, 53, 445.
FERRY, R. M., BROWN, W. F. and DAMON, E. B. (1958). *J. Hyg., Camb.*, 56, 125.
FULTON, J. D., NICHOLS, M. E., WOEHLER, J. and SHREWSBURY, C. L. (1948). *Soap*, 24(5), 125.
HAMBURGER, M., PUCK, T. T. and ROBERTSON, O. H. (1945). *J. infect. Dis.*, 76, 208.
HARPER, G. J. (1961). *J. Hyg., Camb.*, 59, 479.
HASTINGS, J. J. H. (1954). *Trans. Inst. chem. Engrs, Lond.*, 32, 11.
HEMMES, J. H., WINKLER, K. C. and KOOL, S. M. (1960). *Nature, Lond.*, 188, 430.
HENDERSON, D. W. (1952). *J. Hyg., Camb.*, 50, 53.
HOUWINK, E. H. and ROLVINK, W. (1957) *J. Hyg., Camb.*, 55, 544.
HUMPHREY, A. E. (1952). *Studies of the Mechanisms of Bacterial Filtration from Air Streams.* Spec. Pub. No. 2, Chem. Engng Dept., Columbia Univ: Columbia Univ., New York.
HUMPHREY, A. E. and GORDON, E. L. (1955). *Ind. Engng Chem.*, 47, 924.
KETHLEY, T. W., FINCHER, E. L. and COWN, W. B. (1956). *Appl. Microbiol.*, 4.
KETHLEY, T. W., FINCHER, E. L. and COWN, W. B. (1957). *J. infect. Dis.*, 100, 97.
KETHLEY, T. W., GORDON, M. T. and ORR, C. (1952). *Science*, 116, 368.
KLIEWE, H. (1946). via *Chem. Abs.*, 1946, 40, 4478.
KLUYVER, A. J. and VISSER, J. (1950). *Antonie van Leeuwenhoek J. Microbiol. Serol.* 16, 299, 311.
LEMON, H. M. (1943). *Proc. Soc. exp. Biol., N.Y.*, 54, 298.
LIDWELL, O. M. and LOVELOCK, J. E. (1948a). *Studies in Air Hygiene*, Med. Res. Counc. Spec. Rep. Ser. No. 262, p. 68: H.M.S.O., London.
LIDWELL, O. M. and LOVELOCK, J. E. (1948b). *Studies in Air Hygiene*, Med. Res. Counc. Spec. Rep. Ser. No. 262, p. 165: H.M.S.O., London.
LIDWELL, O. M., LOVELOCK, J. E. and RAYMOND, W. F. (1948a). *Studies in Air Hygiene*, Med. Res. Counc. Spec. Rep. Ser. No. 262, p. 75: H.M.S.O., London.
LIDWELL, O. M., LOVELOCK, J. E. and RAYMOND, W. F. (1948b). *Studies in Air Hygiene*, Med. Res. Counc. Spec. Rep. Ser. No. 262, p. 82: H.M.S.O., London.
LIDWELL, O. M. and WILLIAMS, R. E. O. (1954). *Brit. med. J.*, ii, 959.

LOVELOCK, J. E. (1948a). *Studies in Air Hygiene*, Med. Res. Counc. Spec. Rep. Ser. No. 262, p. 89: H.M.S.O., London.
LOVELOCK, J. E. (1948b). *Studies in Air Hygiene*, Med. Res. Counc. Spec. Rep. Ser. No. 262, p. 130: H.M.S.O., London.
LOVELOCK, J. E., LIDWELL, O. M. and RAYMOND, W. F. (1944). *Nature, Lond.*, **153**, 20.
MCDANIEL, L. E. and LONG, R. A. (1954). *Appl. Microbiol.*, **2**, 240.
MACKAY, I. (1952). *J. Hyg., Camb.*, **50**, 82.
MASTERMAN, A. T. (1938). *J. ind. Hyg.*, **20**, 278.
MASTERMAN, A. T. (1941). *J. Hyg., Camb.*, **41**, 44.
MILLER, W. S., DEMCHAK, P., ROSENBERGER, C. R., DOMINIK, T. W. and BRADSHAW, J. L. (1963). *Amer. J. Hyg.*, **77**, 114.
MORRIS, E. J., DARLOW, H. M., PEEL, J. F. H. and WRIGHT, W. C. (1961). *J. Hyg., Camb.*, **59**, 487.
MORTON, J. D. (1962). *J. Hyg., Camb.*, **60**, 295.
MOULTON, S., PUCK, T. T. and LEMON, H. M. (1943). *Science*, **97**, 51.
MUNDEN, D. L. (1952). *J. appl. Chem.*, **2**, 65.
NASH, T. (1951). *J. Hyg., Camb.*, **49**, 382.
NASH, T. (1962). *J. Hyg., Camb.*, **60**, 353.
NOBLE, W. C., LIDWELL, O. M. and KINGSTON, D. (1963). *J. Hyg., Camb.*, **61**, 385.
NOLLER, E. and SPENDLOVE, J. C. (1956). *Appl. Microbiol.* **4**, 300.
OLSON, F. C. W., BIGG, E. and JENNINGS, B. H. (1947). *Science*, **105**, 23.
ORR, C., GORDON, M. T. and KORDECKI, MARGARET C. (1956). *Appl. Microbiol.*, **4**, 116.
PENNEY, G. W. (1937). *Elect. Engng, N.Y.*, **56**, 159.
PLESCH, J. (1941). *Brit. med. J.*, **1**, 798.
PUCK, T. T. (1947). *J. exp. Med.*, **85**, 729, 741.
PUCK, T. T., ROBERTSON, O. H. and LEMON, H. M. (1943). *J. exp. Med.*, **78**, 387.
PUCK, T. T., WISE, H. and ROBERTSON, O. H. (1944). *J. exp. Med.*, **80**, 377.
PULVERTAFT, R. J. V. (1944). *J. Hyg., Camb.*, **43**, 352.
PULVERTAFT, R. J. V., LEMON, E. C. and WALKER, J. W. (1939). *Lancet*, **236**, 443.
PULVERTAFT, R. J. V. and WALKER, J. W. (1939). *J. Hyg., Camb.*, **39**, 696.
RAYMOND, W. F. (1946). *J. Hyg., Camb.*, **44**, 359.
RAY, K. R. and HARPER, G. R. (1957). *Brit. J. ind. Med.*, **14**, 287.
Report No. 110, U.S. Chemical Corps (1953).
RICHARDS, M. (1955). *Nature, Lond.*, **176**, 559.
ROBERTSON, O. H., BIGG, E., MILLER, B. F. and BAKER, ZELMA (1941). *Science*, **93**, 213.
ROBERTSON, O. H., BIGG, E., PUCK, T. T. and MILLER, B. F. (1942a). *J. exp. Med.*, **75**, 593.
ROBERTSON, O. H., BIGG, E., PUCK, T. T., MILLER, B. F. and BAKER, ZELMA (1942b). *Aerobiology*, p. 271: Amer. Ass. Adv. Sci., Lancaster, Penn.
ROBERTSON, O. H., PUCK, T. T. and WISE, H. J. (1946). *J. exp. Med.*, **84**, 559.
ROBERTSON, O. H., PUCK, T. T., LEMON, H. F. and LOOSLI, L. G. (1943). *Science*, **97**, 142.
ROSEBURY, T. (1947). *Experimental Air-Borne Infection:* Williams and Wilkins, Baltimore, U.S.A.
SCHUSTER, E. (1948). *Studies in Air Hygiene*, Med. Res. Counc. Spec. Rep. Ser. No. 262, p. 24; H.M.S.O., London.
SHIPE, E. L., TYLER, M. E. and CHAPMAN, D. N. (1959). *Appl. Microbiol.*, **7**, 349.
SILVERMAN, L. (1955). *Heat. Air Treat. Engr*, **18**, 320.
SMUCKER, C. A. and MARLOW, W. C. (1954). *Ind. engng Chem.*, **46**, 176.
STAFFORD, E. and SMITH, W. J. (1951). *Ind. engng Chem.*, **43**, 1346.
STAIRMAND, C. J. (1950). *Trans. Inst. chem. Engrs, Lond.*, **28**, 130.
STARK, W. H. and POHLER, G. M. (1950). *Ind. engng Chem.*, **42**, 1789.
STEINGOLD, L. and ASHWORTH, L. (1960). *J. appl. Bact.*, **23**, 120.
SYKES, G. and CARTER, D. V. (1953). *J. Pharm. Pharmacol.*, **5**, 945.
SYKES, G. and CARTER, D. V. (1954). *J. appl. Bact.*, **17**, 286.
TERJESEN, S. G. and CHERRY, G. B. (1947). *Trans. Inst. chem. Engrs, Lond.*, **25**, 89.
THOMAS, D. J. (1952). *J. Inst. heat. vent. Engrs*, **20**, 35.
TORLONI, M. and BORZANI, W. (1958). *Appl. Microbiol.*, **6**, 252.
TREDINNICK, J. E. and TUCKER, J. (1951). *Proc. Soc. appl. Bact.*, **14**, 85.
TRILLAT, A. (1938). *Bull. Acad. Med.*, Paris, **119**, 64.

TWORT, C. C. (1942). *Brit. med. J.*, **ii**, 557.
TWORT, C. C. and BAKER, A. H. (1940). *Lancet*, **239**, 587.
TWORT, C. C. and BAKER, A. H. (1942). *J. Hyg., Camb.*, **42**, 266.
TWORT, C. C., BAKER, A. H., FINN, S. R. and POWELL, E. O. (1940). *J. Hyg., Camb.*, **40**, 253.
TYLER, M. E. and SHIPE, E. L. (1959). *Appl. Microbiol.*, **7**, 337.
WALTON, W. H. and PREWETT, W. C. (1949). *Proc. phys. Soc., Lond.*, **B**, **62**, 341.
WEBB, S. J. (1959). *Canad. J. Microbiol.*, **5**, 649.
WEBB, S. J. (1960). *Canad. J. Microbiol.*, **6**, 71, 89.
WEBB, S. J., BATHER, R. and HODGES, R. W. (1963). *Canad. J. Microbiol.*, **9**, 87.
WELLS, W. F. (1933). *Amer. J. publ. Hlth*, **23**, 58.
WOLFE, E. K. (1961). *Bact. Rev.*, **25**, 194.

PART IV

Disinfection of Viruses

CHAPTER 11

DISINFECTION OF VIRUSES

THE VIRUSES have been described as "exogenous submicroscopic units capable of multiplication only inside specific living cells" (Luria, 1950). They do not include the *Rickettsia* which are now considered to be a separate taxonomic group. They differ widely in their constitution and properties, in their size, general protein structure, infectivity and resistance to inactivation, and one outstanding characteristic is the lack of co-ordination between these properties in the different species. It is because of these differing characteristics, coupled with the increasing realization of the important role played by the viruses in medicine and in the economics of agriculture, that separate consideration of the sensitivities of these bodies to so-called adverse conditions and their responses to various disinfection procedures is merited. It is not the intention to repeat here the information already given in other chapters under the various special headings, although a certain overlap is inevitable.

The stabilities of the individual viruses under practically all environmental conditions vary considerably. Some, even when isolated from their hosts, will remain infective for several months at normal temperature, or even at 37°, but others may become inactive in a few hours (Eaton, Cheever and Levenson, 1951; Rasmussen and Stokes, 1951). Some remain infective for several hours after dispersal as an aerosol and a number of them resist drying on handkerchiefs, clothing, etc., for several weeks. There is every need, therefore, for adequate and reliable disinfection procedures.

Because of the dominant medical interest, attention has been focused mainly on the chemotherapeutic approach using *in vivo* testing methods. Much work has been done, however, on the *in vitro* disinfection of viruses, and it is this aspect which comes within the scope of this book. Such work is concerned only with the inactivation of extracellular virus divorced from its living host: it excludes their treatment in tissue culture, in eggs and, for bacteriophage, in the presence of living bacterial cells. It is nevertheless essential to resort to the appropriate living host because this is the only means by which the presence of viable virus particles can be ascertained.

Constitution and metabolism of viruses

The mechanisms by which viruses proliferate are obviously quite different from those associated with bacteria in that the viruses are essentially parasitic in nature, being dependent for their growth on the metabolic activities of their host cells. They have been reported to possess enzyme

291

activity, but the evidence, apart from the mucinase activity of influenza virus, is far from convincing. In a critical review of this topic, Bauer (1953) points out the difficulties in coming to any definitive conclusions because of the strongly adsorptive properties of the virus particles.

There is now substantial agreement that all viruses contain protein and nucleic acids, and in the case of the smaller viruses they may be the sole constituents (Bawden and Pirie, 1953; Knight, 1954). Most of the proteins, according to Knight (1954), are "rather ordinary in composition, being even, in some cases, quite acid in character", and the nucleic acids vary amongst the different types. In the plant viruses, only ribonucleic acid has been found (Stanley, 1935; Bawden and Pirie, 1937, 1938), whereas some of the bacteriophages contain only deoxyribonucleic acid (*see* Markham, 1953; Knight, 1954). The animal viruses may contain either or both types. Earlier reports on this topic may be subject to correction in the light of more recent work, but it seems certain that influenza and some of the smallest viruses contain only ribonucleic acid. Other constituents include lipoid substances, which seem to be present in all animal viruses in amounts ranging from nearly 50 per cent to 1·5 per cent (Beard, 1948). Polysaccharides are possible constituents of some viruses, and the vaccinia virus is said to contain riboflavine, biotin and copper (Hoagland *et al.*, 1940, 1941). These substances, however, may be present as contaminants from the host cells.

Mechanisms of virus inactivation

Much of the information on the inactivation of viruses is purely empirical and refers to their responses only under certain conditions, and these are not always well defined. Nevertheless, certain fundamental studies have been made, particularly in reference to vaccine production, and a few principles have been established.

In the first place, the rate of inactivation in most cases, but not all, has been shown to be exponential. It, therefore, follows the normal pattern of the death course of bacteria and, like bacteria, there is often a fall in the rate of inactivation towards the end of a disinfection process. A notable example of this, which has had its repercussions in practice, is the variable response of polyiomyelitis to formaldehyde. Here, the general exponential form is followed for the main part of the inactivation, but in some cases at least there remains a small nucleus of resistant particles. According to Scheele and Shannon (1955) this is to be expected because in high dilution "the residual live virus will probably consist of particulates of varying size and shape and in varying degrees of aggregation." In other words, the system becomes manifestly heterogeneous and, therefore, the regularity of the inactivation is disturbed. Moreover, the suspension contains other proteins coagulable by formaldehyde and this may result in virus particles being occluded in the protein precipitate and so becoming inaccessible to further action by the formaldehyde.

The general exponential form of the inactivation curve indicates that the amount of virus surviving at any given time is directly proportional to its initial concentration. This is important in considering the design, and reported results, of disinfection experiments. It also indicates that the inactivating reaction is one of the first order.

Other fundamental facts now well established are that antibacterial agents are not necessarily active against viruses, and that broadly speaking the bacteriophages are more resistant than most viruses.

Protein precipitants are generally effective but, on the other hand, several of the compounds which react readily with amino acids, and so might be expected to react with the virus proteins, are completely innocuous (Grubb, Miesse and Puetzer, 1947). Oxidizing agents are amongst the most effective inactivators, but reducing agents, with the exception of ascorbic acid, are practically without action (Knight and Stanley, 1944). Several of the sulphydryl compounds are also active.

Methods of testing for virucidal activity

The virucidal efficacy of any disinfection procedure can be determined simply by preparing a suspension of the virus, subjecting it to the prescribed treatment and then culturing the residue in the presence of the appropriate animal, plant or bacterial cells to assess the order of inactivation. For obvious practical reasons host cells should be present during testing but they often so complicate matters that tests are generally carried out with isolated and purified virus suspensions. The results so obtained are clearly somewhat empirical, and they are sometimes conflicting and misleading; moreover there is the possibility of auto-interference, that is, the inactivated virus interfering with the proliferation of the residual small amounts of viable virus (Groupé *et al.*, 1955).

Purified suspensions of viruses can be prepared by filtration or by washing and differential centrifuging techniques, but there is always a substantial loss of activity by such treatment and it is extremely difficult to remove the last traces of adsorbed foreign matter, hence a possible reason for the conflicting results often reported. The removal of the protective organic matter often reduces the stability of virus suspensions and it likewise affects their response to any disinfection process. For example, influenza virus is more stable in serum or broth than in saline or buffered saline (Foster, Love and Carson, 1947) and a broth suspension of the Pa bacteriophage of *Pseudomonas pyocyanea* is more resistant to hydrogen peroxide than is a suspension in a synthetic medium (Dickinson, 1948); other examples are given later. Therefore, in assessing the value of any *in vitro* test results, due attention must be paid not only to the nature and concentration of the virus suspension, but also to the suspending medium used in the test.

In a testing scheme proposed by Dickinson (1955, pers. comm.), a scheme designed primarily as an adjunct to chemotherapeutic testing, the selection of viruses included influenza A, vaccinia and one of the smallest viruses, such as Columbia-SK, as well as a bacteriophage, all chosen for their ease in laboratory handling and stability at 37° or room temperature (Dickinson, 1953). It is always useful to include a bacteriophage, particularly in preliminary testing, because results with it are obtained quickly and inexpensively, and they are generally more precise although not necessarily more accurate. The survival of the bacteriophage is assessed by the usual plaque count method, the influenza A is assessed by culture in the allantoic sac of chick embryos 9–10 days old, and the other viruses by culture in eggs or mice. High titre stocks of each virus, which need not be particularly purified, are kept in a refrigerator at −65°.

The first stage of the test is to determine the control slope of inactivation of each virus in a suitable chosen medium, which may or may not contain added protein material. It is then a simple matter to test the selected concentrations of the disinfectant by finding the residual titres of each virus after two intervals of exposure and thus compare the inactivation curve, or the half-life period, with that of the control. False impressions of the efficacy of a disinfectant are eliminated by this method.

A difficulty in titrating the surviving virus is that the disinfectant itself may prove toxic to the host. If this cannot be eliminated by direct inactivation it must be done by simple dilution. But in some cases the disinfectant may be so active that dilutions below the toxic limit may also take the virus below its titration end-point. In such cases, shorter intervals of exposure must be resorted to or lower concentrations of disinfectant used. so that points on the significant part of the inactivation curve can be obtained.

Besides the suspension methods for testing for *in vitro* virucidal activity, an adaptation of the Use-Dilution method for testing for disinfectant activity (*see* p. 55) has been proposed (Lorenz and Jann, 1964). It follows the same general principles of the technique as applied to bacteria, the only variations being in the cultural methods employed. In the first place, instead of a bacterial suspension, a suspension of Newcastle disease virus in allantoic fluid is used, and in the second place, each carrier ring after treatment is transferred to 10 ml of a nutrient broth and 0·1 ml of this is inoculated into each of six embryonated chicken eggs (10–12 days old). The death or survival of the total of 60 embryos thus inoculated is the criterion for judging the effectiveness of the disinfectant. Methods employing direct plaque formation can also be employed. This is a result of the discovery by Dulbecco (1952) that such formations are not confined to the bacteriophages but, because of their cytopathogenicity, can be induced with several of the animal viruses growing in tissue culture. The principle of the methods is that an established film of the host cells on a suitable agar medium is infected with the virus and then small discs of filter paper carrying the disinfectant are applied. After a suitable incubation period the discs are removed and the agar stained with a suitable dye to observe plaque suppression, and also possible toxicity to the host. In the method of Herrmann *et al.* (1960), trypsinized chick embryo cells are suspended in a calf serum-salts medium and incubated for 48 hours to obtain a confluent growth. The medium is then discarded and the cell film inoculated with virus and overlaid with a thin layer of serum agar. After this small paper discs carrying the disinfectant are put on the surface and the plates incubated for 3 days to allow plaque formation which is detected by staining in a tetrazolium agar and reading after 2–4 hours. Vaccinia, herpes, Newcastle disease and Nile disease viruses can be used and, as with antibiotic assay, a straight line ratio between log disinfectant concentration and zone of response is found. In a slight modification of this method, Siminoff (1961) grew the chick cells on a tris buffer-Earl's medium agar and stained with neutral red to observe plaque inhibition.

Methods of disinfection

Inactivation by physical agents

Because of the differing techniques employed by the various workers in his field, the differing concentrations of disinfectant, the differing times and conditions of exposure and above all the widely differing sensitivities of the viruses, it is not possible to prepare a concise summary of the situation. The best that can be done is to present a brief account of the various findings, drawing attention to some of the significant divergencies.

Heat. Heat is perhaps the best known and safest means of destroying the viruses. In general, a temperature of 60° is adequate but susceptibilities vary so much between the different species of virus and their origins, whether it is in experimental culture or in a natural habitat, that some are inactivated in a matter of seconds whilst others require up to 40 minutes. It is generally assumed that the rate of inactivation at any one temperature varies exponentially with the time of exposure, and this applies substantially over the majority of the killing range. But towards the end of the process there can remain a small residue of more resistant particles, the proportion depending somewhat on the temperature of inactivation. With the vaccinia virus it can vary from about 10^{-3} of the original particle count when the inactivation is carried out at 50° to about 10^{-7} at 60° (Kaplan, 1958). Moreover, the rapid initial inactivation is dependent on temperature, but the subsequent slow one seems to be independent of temperature, the slopes for the latter over the 10° range examined being parallel.

The viruses themselves do not necessarily behave in the same way as their infective ribonucleic acid moieties, a point which could be important in

practice. The inactivation of polio virus, for example, after 5 minutes at 60
is of the order of 10^{-7}, but that of its ribonucleic acid is of a much lower orde
(Norman and Veomett, 1960). The same occurs with bacteriophage and it
deoxyribonucleic acid (Pottinger and Bachofer, 1957), from which it can b
inferred that the mode of heat inactivation is by protein denaturation.

Normal serum and tissue material, unless they contain non-specifi
inhibitors, usually act in a protective manner, and so do some of the highl
ionizing inorganic salts, the explanation in the latter case being that meta
protein complexes are naturally more resistant to denaturation than ar
the free proteins. Adams (1949) restricted this property to the divalen
cations such as calcium, magnesium, copper and manganese, but Pottinge
and Bachofer (1957) also found a degree of protection with monovalen
cations; the anions also played a minor role, the sulphate and chloride ion
in particular being much more effective than nitrate or nitrite. The order o
efficacy was: magnesium sulphate (at $0.1M$ concentration), calcium chlorid
$(0.01M)$, sodium chloride, sodium sulphate, sodium nitrate and sodium nitrit
(all $3M$ or $4M$), the factor between the first and the last being about 10
This order of protection is almost exactly the reverse of that found by Kapla
(1963), who reported monovalent metals to be more protective than divalen
ones and the heavy metals to be rapidly destructive. It is also the revers
of the order of protection found with X-rays.

Low temperatures. Although some viruses are rapidly inactivated a
lowered temperatures, the majority can be preserved by freezing or b
freeze-drying. There is always some loss of activity during the process o
freezing and thawing. Once frozen, viruses retain their activities for lon
periods but the temperature of preservation is important. $-70°$, the tempera
ture of a solid carbon dioxide-alcohol mixture, is apparently satisfactory fo
all types, but intermediate temperatures are less reliable. Mouse pneumoniti
soon loses its activity at $-25°$, for example, whereas influenza A (PR8) wi
remain viable at this temperature for months, and the foot-and-mouth viru
is said to survive in meat as long as the meat remains frozen (Henderson an
Brooksby, 1948). The medium affects greatly the maintenance of viability a
low temperatures.

According to Piercy (1961) freeze-dried canine distemper virus can b
kept for several years at $-20°$, but its stability decreases progressively wit
increase in storage temperature, so that at $0°$ its life is reduced to 10 month
and at $28°$ to only two months.

Some viruses, including measles, influenza A, poliomyelitis, and en
cephalitis, will remain active at reduced temperatures without freezing fo
periods ranging from a few days to several months. In fact, a commo
method formerly employed for preserving certain viruses was storage in th
refrigerator in 50 per cent glycerol.

Desiccation. Under certain circumstances, some viruses dried unde
normal conditions will retain their activity for quite long periods. Th

actual survival time depends to a large extent on the presence or absence of protective substances. Serum and mucoid material always exert a protective effect, and under such conditions, influenza A, smallpox and vaccinia viruses have been recovered sometimes even several weeks after drying on cloth, inert powders such as talc, and glass (Edward, 1941; Parker and MacNeal, 1944). Smallpox and vaccinia virus are said to be exceptionally resistant to inactivation by desiccation.

Ultrasonics. The inactivation of viruses by ultrasonics is discussed in some detail in Chapter 9, therefore it will only be briefly mentioned here. Opinions are not unanimous on the efficacy of such treatment, but substantial results have been recorded. Hamré (1949), using a frequency of 700,000 cycles per second with a power input of 765 watts, was able to inactivate influenza A and the infective agent of feline pneumonitis. With the former, the survival level was 0·06 per cent after 60 minutes' treatment and with the latter, it ranged from 0·03 to 11·5 per cent after 40 minutes' treatment. Similarly, *Staphylococcus* bacteriophage has been inactivated with a frequency of only 9,300 cycles per second and an input of 320 watts (Krueger, Brown and Scribner, 1940). Other workers have been completely unsuccessful in obtaining any effective inactivation.

The reasons for these contrasting observations may be twofold. Either (a) too much attention has been given to the frequency of the emission and not enough to its energy, which is the more important factor in the lethal process, or (b) they arise because some have used purified suspensions, whereas others have used the naturally occurring ones which are always more resistant.

Ultraviolet irradiation. Opinions on the susceptibilities of the viruses to ultraviolet irradiation are widely divergent. Some workers have reported them to have the same susceptibilities as normal vegetative bacteria, whereas others believe them to be very much more resistant. Such wide divergencies must be attributed partly to species variations in both the bacteria and the viruses examined and partly to the test conditions and cultural environment. For a detailed discussion on the efficacy of ultraviolet irradiation the reader is referred to the appropriate section in the chapter on Radiation Sterilization.

According to Hollaender and Oliphant (1944) the viruses are divisible into two groups, those which have a maximum sensitivity to radiations at wavelengths of about 2,600A, and those which are highly sensitive at wavelengths of 2,300A and shorter. The first group includes influenza A, vaccinia and bacteriophage, and the second group tobacco mosaic and Rous sarcoma.

An interesting feature of ultraviolet irradiation is that the plot of the rate of inactivation against dose is frequently non-linear and tends to trail off. It occurs with both animal viruses and bacteriophage and is attributed (Taylor *et al.*, 1957) to differences in the energy absorptions of the virus and the suspending medium, which also contains its quota of protein material, as well as to the progressive increase in absorption by the virus particles themselves due to alterations in their structure. It is for this reason that irradiatic treatments cannot be considered reliable in rendering plasma safe from infective hepatitis (*Lancet*, 1950). Nevertheless, where practicable the addition of a small amount of virucidal agent such as formaldehyde or β-propio lactone will overcome the difficulty (Smolens and Stokes, 1954).

As with the bacteria, viruses are also subject to photoreactivatic provided the appropriate host is present. For the coliphage T4r the optimum reactivation wavelength is 4,047A; 4,440A and longer are without effec (Dulbecco, 1949). According to Fenner (1962) this reactivation can take pla by more than one route. It may occur genetically through the combinatio or co-operation of two or more particles which have been inactivated different ways but which together make a complete whole: it can also tal place by the cross-influence of one type of virus on another, such as betwee influenza and vaccinia, whereby the addition of viable particles of the or reactivates the non-viable particles of the other.

Ionizing radiations. From the many studies of the irradiation of virus and bacteriophage it can be concluded that their sensitivity is similar t or rather less than, that of the bacterial spores. According to Huber (195 the dose needed for total inactivation varies with the size of the virus, an he quoted a range of 4×10^5 rad for vaccinia and bacteriophage to one 1·4 $\times 10^6$ rad for poliomyelitis (Lansing). Others have quoted values as hig as 5×10^6 rad according to the particular virus and the conditions used.

The mode of attack was originally thought to be through the nucle protein, but Epstein (1953) has produced data showing that the radi sensitive portion of a virus is its nucleic acid, and this has been substantiate by Pottinger and Bachofer (1957) in the different rates of denaturation of th two fractions and the protective effect of certain inorganic salts. The broad exponential rate of inactivation of bacteriophage indicates the operation the 'one-hit' mechanism (Lea, 1946), although it is evidently not a simp and straightforward mechanism as at first thought. Alper (1948), for examp demonstrated experimentally that inactivation is due to a direct and a indirect action, the primary action being due to radicals ionized directly b the radiation and the secondary action arising indirectly from the productio of hydrogen peroxide. Doubts were also cast on the simplicity of the theor by Epstein (1953), as a result of his observations on the larger viruses, an by Bachofer (1953), who obtained different rates of inactivation of freez dried phage against vacuum-dried material. In both cases, the existence another controlling factor, which could be the size of the sensitive volume relation to the size of the whole particle, is indicated.

The nature and occurrence of viruses does not constitute them primar hazards in the food and similar industries, and therefore little work ha been done on their large-scale irradiation, but the problem in relation t serum and plasma for medical use is of great concern. In this connexion som promising results have been obtained on the inactivation of the virus of homologous serum jaundice in plasma (Huber, 1952). A dose of 1×10^6 rad from a Capacitron, whilst not unduly affecting the immunizing properties of the plasma, always eliminated all signs of living neurotropic virus, even when heavy artificial infections were present. This protection almost certainly arises from the histidine and *p*-aminohippurate naturally present, because these compounds have been shown to conserve the antigenicity, but not the viability, of the influenza B, influenza PR8 and mumps viruses (Polley, 1962).

Inactivation by chemical means

General investigations. It is natural that during the course of investigating means for inactivating the viruses, a vast number of chemicals with known antibacterial properties should be examined. These include not only those more commonly classed as disinfectants or antiseptics but also the wide range of compounds of chemotherapeutic interest. *In vitro* investigations on both types of compounds have been made but it is difficult to compare closely the results obtained because of the widely different test conditions used. Nevertheless the findings of each of these workers are significant. One important feature which seems to have emerged is the frequently superior resistance of the vaccinia virus.

Andrewes, King and van den Ende (1943) carried out their tests with 1 in 100 and 1 in 1,000 dilutions of a 10 per cent suspension of dried vaccinia virus having a titre of 10^6. They exposed the virus to the disinfectant for 2 hours at room temperature and determined the residual virucidal action by the response of rabbits to the reaction mixture when inoculated intradermally. Their main interest was in selecting compounds of potential chemotherapeutic value and so the concentrations of the substances used were never above the normal toxic levels. Some 74 substances, including alkaloids, essential oils, dyes, and compounds of heavy metals, as well as arsphenamines and sulphonamides, were examined but, although some gave positive responses, none was active "in such dilutions as to give promise of chemotherapeutic value."

Dunham and MacNeal (1943, 1944) in their tests used the comparatively short contact period of 3 minutes at room temperature and assessed inactivation by inoculating the reaction mixture either neat, or diluted ten or one-hundredfold according to the toxicity of the disinfectant, into egg embryos, and observing their subsequent survival. By this means they claimed 3 per cent of phenol, 1 per cent of tincture of iodine, 0·1 per cent of mercuric chloride, 90 per cent of propylene glycol and 2 per cent of lysol to be effective against viruses; but the value of their findings is somewhat vitiated by the absence of any clear information on the initial inoculating dose of virus. Such evidence as is available suggests that the inactivations recorded were of the order of 90 to 99·9 per cent. Groupé and colleagues (1955) were unable to evaluate some chosen preparations because of their toxicities to the host egg embryos, but, of those they were able to examine, the results obtained were not very different from those of Dunham and MacNeal. They used a 10 minutes' contact test at room temperature or at 37°, and their data indicated that both influenza A and vaccinia were completely inactivated by 2 per cent of phenol, 1 per cent of formaldehyde and 0·1 per cent of mercuric chloride, whilst 99·9 per cent inactivations were obtained with a 1·5 per cent or even a 0·6 per cent solution of sodium hypochlorite, a 1 per cent dilution of Lugol's iodine, 70 per cent of alcohol, 48·8 per cent of isopropyl alcohol and 1 per cent of crystal violet.

Knight and Stanley's investigations (1944) covered some twenty compounds, but again their test conditions were unusual. Their tests were carried out at 4° with washed suspensions of influenza A virus at high levels of infectivity and the times of contact were "0 days", and then at varying intervals from 1 day to 35 days. Under such conditions iodine and mercurochrome proved rapidly lethal at concentrations as low as 0·0005N. Similar rapid activity was also found with 0·05N solutions of salts of heavy metals, two quaternary ammonium compounds and formaldehyde, and with 0·5N phenol. Sodium sulphathiazole was of little value, and of the reducing agents only ascorbic acid showed any activity.

Horn (1960) conducted her experiments with four strains of influenza virus using suspension in allantoic fluid with and without egg albumen, as well as those dried on fabric. She used as her disinfectants 2 per cent phenol solution, 0·25 per cent chloramine, formalin and ethyl and propyl alcohols as well as some seventeen proprietaries of various types, of which all of the named compounds were effective, with the exception of phenol which was deficient in the fabric carrier test, and a few of the proprietaries. As might be expected the virus soaked in fabric was generally the most difficult to kill.

Inkley (1948, pers. comm.) used a bacteriophage of *Ps. pyocyanea* and so was able to determine the end-point of total inactivation more precisely by the plaque count method. His tests were carried out in nutrient broth, and his results with some commonly used disinfectants are given in Table 31. Compared with those quoted in the preceding paragraphs against other viruses, they indicate the greater resistance of the phage.

Phenols. Phenol itself inactivates viruses, but the concentration required to do so varies with the virus and condition of treatment, and the temperature coefficient is significant. According to Haseeb (1951) vaccinia lymph can be freed from bacterial contamination by adding phenol at a concentration of 0·5 per cent and storing at 0° for two weeks, whereas even a 5 per cent solution may not completely destroy the virus. Influenza A behaves in a similar manner at 4° (Knight and Stanley, 1944), but when the temperature is elevated to 25° a 2 per cent solution is effective in 10 minutes (Groupé et al., 1955; Horn, 1960). A *Ps. pyocyanea* bacteriophage is only slowly inactivated by a 1 per cent solution of phenol (Inkley, 1948, pers. comm.).

Of a number of common disinfectants examined, van Erven-Mok (1959) found only 5 per cent lysol to be consistently effective in inactivating several different viruses in 5 minutes, others taking 10 minutes and more. A variety of chlorinated phenols were also effective to a greater or less extent.

The effect of phenol on the rabies virus for vaccine preparations is indeterminate. There are numerous references in the literature and those

TABLE 31

Inactivation of Ps. pyocyanea *bacteriophage with antiseptics*
(after Inkley, 1948)

Compound	Percentage concentration in broth giving complete kill in				
	10 min	1 hr	6 hr	24 hr	48 hr
Formaldehyde . . .	4	1			0·4
Acetic acid	10			not 1*	
Lysol	10	6		not 1	
"Supersan" (a proprietary chloroxylenol preparation) .	10			not 1	
Sodium hypochlorite . .	10	6			not 1
Chloramine-T . . .	10				
Mercuric chloride . . .	1		not 0·1		
Proflavine	1		not 0·1		
Crystal violet . . .			1		
Brilliant green . . .			1		

Initial titre 2 × 10⁶/ml
* indicates not effective at concentration given.

particularly interested in this aspect are referred to a competent summary of the subject by van Rooyen (1948).

Alcohol. Ethyl alcohol, being a protein denaturant, is an effective virucidal agent, but its action depends upon its concentration and the absence of other protein-like substances. McCulloch (1945) found that a concentration as high as 70 per cent solution was effective in about 30 minutes and a 25 per cent solution was without action. These values are similar to those of Groupé et al. (1955) who found a 70 per cent concentration to be 99·9 per cent efficient and a 35 per cent concentration only weakly active in 10 minutes against influenza A and vaccinia. Evidently there was a strain difference in the influenza A used by Dunham and MacNeal (1943, 1944) because they found a 40 per cent solution effective in 3 minutes against this virus, but not against vaccinia. When large amounts of other protein are present inactivation is not complete, the reason being that the precipitated adventitious protein forms a protective coagulum round the virus particle and so inhibits the action of the alcohol (McCulloch, 1945).

Ether and chloroform. The viruses differ markedly in their susceptibilities to inactivation by ether. They are either wholly susceptible or wholly resistant, so much so that the ether response has been suggested as one means by which the viruses might be classified. Andrewes and Horstmann (1949) tested 25 viruses by treating them in serum broth suspension for 24 hours and found the sensitive group to include pneumonitis, herpes, influenza A and B, Newcastle disease, encephalitis, and louping ill, and the resistant group to include vaccinia, poliomyelitis, foot and mouth, ectromelia, papilloma and several bacteriophages. Somewhat earlier, Sulkin and Zaraufonetis (1947) had found three strains of encephalitis to be sensitive whilst rabies and poliomyelitis were resistant, and Stock and Francis (1940) had reported the inactivation of purified influenza virus within 90 minutes. The sarcomas, S13, Rous, R avian and Rubin's RIF, are also susceptible, inactivation in these cases being complete within 16 hours at 2° (Wallbank *et al.*, 1962; Wallbank and Stubbs, 1965).

In a like manner the chloroform response has also been suggested for classification purposes. Applying such a test, Feldman and Wang (1961) found several of the myxoviruses, including influenza and para-influenza, to be rapidly sensitive, but not others such as the polio ECHO, Coxsackie and adeno viruses. The S13, R avian and Rous sarcomas are also susceptible (Wallbank *et al.*, 1962; Wallbank and Stubbs, 1965).

Formaldehyde. Formaldehyde has the advantage that, whilst rendering viruses non-infective, it interferes little in their antigenic properties provided the conditions are carefully controlled. For this reason it is used extensively for preparing vaccines, the concentration employed being generally in the range of 0·2 to 0·4 per cent. Inkley (pers. comm.) found that a 1 per cent solution destroyed *Ps. pyocyanea* bacteriophage in a few hours and a 0·4 per cent solution in 48 hours; and a 0·1 per cent solution has rendered poliomyelitis non-infective to cotton rats within 24 hours (Schwerdt *et al.*, 1951).

Cotton threads dried from a suspension of variola major crusts in a serum fluid succumbed to the vapour of formaldehyde within 24 hours at 4°, but not so the crusts themselves (*Report*, 1958).

Salk (1953) used formaldehyde for preparing poliomyelitis vaccines for human use. As a result of his initial investigations, he fixed on a treatment with 0·4 per cent of neutralized formalin (a 37 per cent solution of formaldehyde) at the temperature of melting ice for at least 24 to 48 hours. Such a treatment yielded a non-infective virus vaccine, as proved by intracerebral inoculation into monkeys, but subsequently he (Salk, 1955) formed the opinion that a longer treatment up to nine days was necessary to ensure complete freedom from any demonstrably viable virus. This was due partly to the high resistance of a few of the virus particles in some batches of material and partly to the clumping and consequent protection of some of the particles as described earlier in this chapter.

Ethylene glycol. Ethylene glycol is an active virucide both in solution and as a vapour. A fairly high aqueous concentration of the order of 70 to 90 per cent is necessary for rapid inactivation within a few minutes (Dunham and MacNeal, 1944), weaker solutions being only partially effective.

For aerial disinfection, quite low vapour concentrations of 1 part or less per million of air are effective, and maximum activity is obtained at relative humidities in the range of about 40–65 per cent. Influenza virus is inactivated within ten minutes by a vapour concentration of 0·5 to 1 part per million Robertson *et al.*, 1943); meningopneumonitis and psittacosis are also susceptible (Rosebury *et al.*, 1947), and an aerosol at sub-saturation concentration has inactivated mumps and Newcastle disease viruses in a few minutes (Krugman and Sverdlow, 1949). Ethylene glycol is claimed to be of clinical value in reducing the spread of measles in children's hospital wards (Krugman and Ward, 1951).

Ethylene oxide. Ethylene oxide has come to the fore in recent years as a highly effective bactericidal and sporicidal agent. It is difficult material to handle because it boils at about 11° and is toxic and explosive (*see* Chapter 8). A 1 per cent liquid concentration is used for sterilizing culture media, and the same concentration has also proved virucidal. Ginsberg and Wilson (1950) destroyed the infectivity of influenza A and B, Newcastle disease, encephalomyelitis and vaccinia in serum suspensions by this means by introducing the substance in the liquid state at 4° into the suspensions, holding at this temperature for 1 hour and then placing them in the incubator at 35° for 24 hours during which time the ethylene oxide is volatilized away. The presence of serum somewhat reduces the efficacy of the treatment.

Ethylene oxide is also effective in the gaseous state, as demonstrated by Klarenbeek and van Tongeren (1954). Suspensions of vaccinia and Columbia-SK virus smeared on the insides of tubes and exposed to a 10 per cent gaseous concentration at room temperature were inactivated in 8 hours, but not in 6 hours.

Mustards. The sulphur and nitrogen mustards have attracted interest in recent years because of their many biological activities. Their capacity for inactivating viruses is greater than that for enzymes, as judged by the rates of inactivation, and the viruses containing deoxyribonucleic acid are more sensitive than those containing ribonucleic acid (Herriott, 1948).

Nitrogen mustard in twice, and sometimes half, saturation will inactivate rabies and encephalitis virus as quickly and effectively as formaldehyde (Tenbroeck and Herriott, 1946) and concentrations as low as $5 \times 10^{-4}M$ will reduce the infectivity of influenza A virus by 99·9 per cent in 30 minutes at 25° (Fong and Bernal, 1953). Large amounts of other biological materials such as blood cells and plasma interfere seriously in the reaction such that a 1 in 2,000 solution, whilst being effective against several other viruses, is ineffective against serum hepatitis in whole blood (Drake *et al.*, 1952).

Halogens. Solutions of iodine as weak as 0·0005N are effectively lethal to washed influenza virus (Knight and Stanley, 1944), but organic material in the suspension seriously reduces the action. Ten times the concentration may be necessary in undiluted allantoic fluid to produce the same inactivation as in diluted fluid (Dunham and MacNeal, 1944).

Iodine has been used for disinfecting drinking waters contaminated with viruses. A few parts per million will render them safe from poliomyelitis infection in 5–10 minutes (Chang and Morris, 1953) and concentrations ranging between 0·125 and 0·375 mg per ml, that is between 125 and 375 parts per million, are effective within 1 minute (Gershenfeld, 1955); for influenza infections only about 70 parts per million are necessary.

Chlorine at 50 parts per million in broth will easily kill fowl pox, foot-and-mouth and other viruses (McCulloch, 1945), but its only potential practical use in virus disinfection is in the treatment of water. From evidence available, however, it is not very effective at the concentrations normally used. Heinertz and Vahlne (1952) in Norway found it useless in preventing water-borne poliomyelitis infection, and there are similar evidences elsewhere (McCulloch, 1945). The reason for this failure most probably lies in the lack of appreciation of the normal chlorine demand of the system (Kabler *et al.*, 1961). Having done this, a *free* chlorine content as low as 0·2 parts per million will inactivate over 99·5 per cent of the enteric viruses, including hepatitis, polio, Coxsackie and ECHO, in 30 minutes at pH values ranging from 6·5 to 9·0. Chlorine-ammonia and azochloramide are not as effective.

Horn (1960) found 0·25 per cent chloramine-T consistently good against influenza virus, even when suspended in allantoic fluid and egg albumen and soaked on fabric. Likewise a 1 per cent solution was effective in 2 minutes against a polio fluid isolated from kidney tissue, but when cell detritus was added even a 2 per cent solution failed (Drees, 1958).

Antibiotics. Penicillin, streptomycin, tyrothricin and gliotoxin have all been shown to be ineffective against the pox viruses with contact periods of 2 hours at room temperature, but the impurities of a crude commercial penicillin (988 units per mg) manifested some activity against canary pox virus (Groupé and Rake, 1947). Aureomycin, likewise, has no activity *in vitro* against vaccinia, but impure material is effective through certain unidentified non-specific substances (Cabasso, Moore and Cox, 1952).

Phagolessin A50, an antibiotic isolated from a *Streptomyces* sp, is interesting in that it inhibits a number of free isolated bacterial viruses (Asheshov, Strelitz and Hall, 1952). It has not been tried against animal viruses and so no correlation is yet possible. The position is likely to be difficult in this respect, however, because of 60 phages examined, 37 were inactivated rapidly by 10 units per ml of the antibiotic, and there was no correlation between size and sensitivity. Moreover, of the coliphages, only 3 proved to be sensitive; this action was inhibited by adding nucleic acids (Hall and Asheshov, 1953).

Miscellaneous compounds. According to Parker and MacNeal (1944) soap increases rapidly the rate of inactivation of influenza virus on the hands, but this is not a general property of the surface active compounds. Of eighteen synthetic detergent compounds examined, comprising cationic, anionic and nonionic types, only seven were active *in vitro* against influenza A at dilutions greater than 1 in 1,000 in 10 minutes. These included cetyl pyridinium chloride, Phemerol, Zephiran and sodium lauryl sulphate, and they produced complete inactivation of the virus at dilutions ranging between 1 in 2,000 and 1 in 8,000; hexylresorcinol was also effective at 1 in 8,000 (Klein and Stevens, 1945). Subsequently Armstrong and Froelich (1964) confirmed the activity of Zephiran (benzalkonium chloride) finding it effective also in 10 minutes at either room temperature or 30° at concentrations ranging from 0·1 to 1·3 mg per ml against all viruses except those of the picorna group, *i.e.* the polio and encephalomyelitis viruses. Burnet and Lush (1940) also found sodium lauryl sulphate to be effective against a number of viruses in concentrations ranging between 0·005 and 0·2 per cent, and likewise saponin was effective between 0·002 and 0·2 per cent and sodium deoxy-cholate between 0·05 and 1 per cent.

In spite of the above observations, the surface active quaternary ammonium compounds are not considered to be particularly active against the viruses, and such activity as they possess is readily depleted in the presence of tissue and cellular material. Several of the quaternaries have, in fact, been used to free virus suspensions from bacterial contamination.

Amongst the metal compounds, silver nitrate destroys the infectivity of washed influenza A almost instantaneously (Knight and Stanley, 1944). Copper salts are only weakly active and mercuric chloride at a concentration of 0·1 per cent or less will inactivate influenza and vaccinia in a relatively short time, but it is not particularly active against *Ps. pyocyanea* phage. Care must be taken in interpreting the results with the mercury salts because their effects can be reversed in the presence of sulphydryl reagents, the extent of the 'reactivation' being approximately proportional to the amount of donor added. Thus, although a 1 in 10,000 solution of mercuric chloride will apparently totally inactivate vaccinia in 60 minutes at 37°, the addition of cysteine in a molecular ratio even as low as 2·5:1 gives a substantial recovery with an overall inactivation factor of only about 10^{-4} (Kaplan, 1959). Undoubtedly the activities of the mercury and silver salts are adversely affected by the presence of other materials in the virus suspensions.

Taken as a group organic mercury compounds do not show up well as virucides. The phenylmercuric compounds have variable activities; thiomer-salate (merthiolate) in solutions of 1 in 10,000 to 1 in 40,000 will slowly inactivate vaccinia over several days, the actual rate depending on the concentration (Micklem and Kaplan, 1958), and *p*-chloromercuribenzoate has about the same activity as mercuric chloride, effecting substantial inactivations in a few hours at 18° (Allison, 1962).

Iodoacetamide and *N*-ethylmaleimide, being thiol or sulphydryl reagents, will also reduce the titres of a range of viruses including the entero and pleuropneumonia groups (Philipson and Choppin, 1960; Allison, Buckland and Andrewes, 1962).

Tannic acid and other tannins are well-known protein precipitants and have been tested against viruses. Commercial tannic acid at a concentration of 0·1 mg per ml will inactivate a saline suspension of influenza A in allantoic fluid at least by a factor of 99·9 per cent in 10 minutes at 25° (Green, 1948), but it is inactive when other proteins are added. Chantrill *et al.* (1952) showed this in their investigation into the actions of many plant extracts on influenza A and bacteriophage. The activities of these extracts were believed to be due to their tannin content, and so several commercial tannins extracted from various plants were examined. They were highly active against *Ps. pyocyanea* bacteriophage in a simple defined medium, but completely inactive in broth. The activity against influenza A in eggs was shown to be due to inactivation of the virus in the almost protein free allantoic fluid; the extracts were inactivated by broth.

Summarizing this information, there are many compounds which can inactivate the viruses *in vitro*, the extent of the inactivation depending on the type of virus used and the conditions of application. But because of the way in which viruses occur in nature in close association with living cells, performance in the field will fall far short of that obtained with suspensions prepared in the laboratory, and so the methods available for practical, effective disinfection are strictly limited. In treating areas after foot-and-mouth disease, the official method still relies on a washing down process rather than on any proved virucidal agent, and simple washing soda is often used for this purpose.

REFERENCES

ADAMS, M. H. (1949). *J. gen. Physiol.*, **32**, 579.
ALLISON, A. C. (1962). *Virology*, **17**, 176.
ALLISON, A. C.. BUCKLAND, F. E. and ANDREWES, C. H. (1962). *Virology*, **17**, 171.
ALPER, TIKVAH (1948). *Nature, Lond.*, **162**, 615.
ANDREWES, C. H. and HORSTMANN, DOROTHY M. (1949). *J. gen. Microbiol.*, **3**, 290.
ANDREWES, C. H., KING, H. and VAN DEN ENDE, M. (1943). *J. Path. Bact.*, **55**, 173.
ARMSTRONG, J. A. and FROELICH, E. J. (1964). *Appl. Microbiol.*, **12**, 132.
ASHESHOV, I. N., STRELITZ, FREDA and HALL, ELIZABETH A. (1952). *Antibiot. Chemoth.*, **2**, 366.
BACHOFER, C. S. (1953). *Science*, **117**, 280.
BAUER, D. J. (1953). *The Nature of Virus Multiplication*, p 46.: Univ. Press, Cambridge.
BAWDEN, F. C. and PIRIE, N. W. (1937). *Proc. Roy. Soc., B.*, **123**, 274.
BAWDEN, F. C. and PIRIE, N. W. (1938). *Brit. J. exp. Path.*, **19**, 66, 251.
BAWDEN, F. C. and PIRIE, N. W. (1953). *The Nature of Virus Multiplication*, p. 21: Univ. Press, Cambridge.
BEARD, J. W. (1948). *Physiol. Rev.*, **28**, 349.
BURNET, F. M. and LUSH, D. (1940). *Austral. J. exp. biol. med. Sci.*, **18**, 141.
CABASSO, V. J., MOORE, IDA F. and COX, H. R. (1952). *J. infect. Dis.*, **91**, 79.
CHANG, S. L. and MORRIS, J. C. (1953). *Ind. engng Chem.*, **45**, 1009.
CHANTRILL, B. H., COULTHARD, C. E., DICKINSON, LÖIS, INKLEY, G. W., MORRIS, W. and PYLE, A. H. (1952). *J. gen. Microbiol.*, **6**, 74.
DICKINSON, LÖIS (1948). *J. gen. Microbiol.*, **2**, 154.

DICKINSON, LÖIS (1953). *Analyst.*, **78**, 283.
DRAKE, M. E., HAMPIL, BETTYLEE, PENNELL, R. B., SPIZIZEN, J., HENLE, W. and
STOKES, J. (1952). *Proc. Soc. exp. Biol., N.Y.*, **62**, 271.
DREES, O. (1958). *Z. f. Bakt.*, **173**, 539.
DULBECCO, R. (1949). *Nature, Lond.*, **163**, 949.
DULBECCO, R. (1952). *Proc. nat. Acad. Sci.*, **38**, 747.
DUNHAM, C. G. and MACNEAL, W. J. (1943). *J. lab. clin. Med.*, **28**, 947.
DUNHAM, C. G. and MACNEAL, W. J. (1944). *J. Immunol.*, **49**, 123.
EATON, M. D., CHEEVER, F. S. and LEVENSON, CHARLOTTE G. (1951). *J. Immunol.*, **66**,
463.
EDWARD, D. G. ff. (1941). *Lancet*, **241**, 664.
EPSTEIN, H. T. (1953). *Nature, Lond.*, **171**, 394.
ERVEN-NOK, D. J. VAN (1959). *Nederl. Tijdschr. Geneesk.*, **103**, 2048.
FELDMAN, H. A. and WANG, S. S. (1961). *Proc. Soc. exp. Biol., N.Y.*, **106**, 736.
FENNER, F. (1962). *Brit. med. J.*, **ii**, 135.
FONG, J. and BERNAL, E. (1953). *J. Immunol.*, **70**, 89.
FOSTER, G. F., LOVE, VENUS and CARSON, ESTHER (1947). *J. Bact.*, **53**, 380.
GERSHENFELD, L. (1955). *J. Amer. pharm. Ass. (Sci.)*, **44**, 177.
GINSBERG, H. S. and WILSON, A. T. (1950). *Proc. Soc. exp. Biol., N.Y.*, **73**, 614.
GREEN, R. H. (1948). *Proc. Soc. exp. Biol., N.Y.*, **67**, 483.
GROUPÉ, V., ENGLE, CLAIRE G., GAFFNEY, P. E. and MANAKER, R. A. (1955). *Appl.
Microbiol.*, **3**, 333.
GROUPÉ, V. and RAKE, G. (1947). *J. Immunol.*, **57**, 17.
GRUBB, T., MIESSE, MARIE L. and PUETZER, B. (1947). *J. Bact.*, **53**, 61.
HALL, ELIZABETH A. and ASHESHOV, I. N. (1953). *J. gen. Physiol.*, **37**, 217.
HAMRÉ, DOROTHY (1949). *J. Bact.*, **57**, 279.
HASEEB, M. A. (1951). *Lancet*, **260**, 114.
HEINERTZ, N.-O. and VAHLNE, G. (1952). *Nord. hyd. Tids.*, **33**(3), 65, via *Biol. Abs.*
1953, **27**, 676.
HENDERSON, W. M. and BROOKSBY, J. B. (1948). *J. Hyg., Camb.*, **48**, 394.
HERRIOTT, R. M. (1948). *J. gen. Physiol.*, **32**, 221.
HERRMANN, E. C., GABLIKS, JANIS, ENGLE, CLAIRE G. and PERLMAN, P. L. (1960).
Proc. Soc. exp. Biol. Med., **103**, 623.
HOAGLAND, C. L., WARD, S. M., SMADEL, J. W. and RIVERS, T. M. (1940). *Proc. Soc. exp.
Biol., N.Y.*, **45**, 669.
HOAGLAND, C. L., WARD, S. M., SMADEL, J. W. and RIVERS, T. M. (1941). *J. exp. Med.*,
74, 69, 133.
HOLLAENDER, A. and OLIPHANT, J. W. (1944). *J. Bact.*, **48**, 447.
HORN, ILSE M. (1960). *Z. f. Hyg. u. Grenz.*, **6**, 643.
HUBER, W. (1952). *Ann. N.Y. Acad. Sci.*, **55**, 536.
KABLER, P. W., CLARKE, N. A., BERG, G. and CHANG, S. L. (1961). *U.S. Publ. Hlth Rep.*,
76, 565.
KAPLAN, C. (1958). *J. gen. Microbiol.*, **18**, 58.
KAPLAN, C. (1959). *Nature, Lond.*, **184**, 1074.
KAPLAN, C. (1963). *J. gen. Microbiol.*, **31**, 311.
KLARENBEEK, A. and VAN TONGEREN, H. A. E. (1954). *J. Hyg., Camb.*, **52**, 525.
KLEIN, M. and STEVENS, D. A. (1945). *J. Immunol.*, **50**, 265.
KNIGHT, C. A. (1954). *Advances in Virus Research*, p. 153: Academic Press, New York.
KNIGHT, C. A. and STANLEY, W. M. (1944). *J. exp. Med.*, **79**, 291.
KRUEGER, A. P., BROWN, B. B. and SCRIBNER, E. J. (1940). *J. gen. Physiol.*, **24**, 691
KRUGMAN, S. and WARD, R. (1951). *J. Amer. med. Ass.*, **145**, 175.
KRUGMAN, S. and SVERDLOW, BERTHA (1949). *Proc. Soc. exp. Biol., N.Y.*, **71**, 680.
Lancet (editorial), (1950). **259**, 915.
LEA, D. E. (1946). *Actions of Radiations on Living Cells:* Univ. Press, Cambridge.
LORENZ, D. and JANN, G. J. (1964). *Appl. Microbiol.*, **12**, 34.
LURIA, S. E. (1950). *Science*, **111**, 507.
MCCULLOCH, E. C. (1945). *Disinfection and Sterilization:* Kimpton, London.
MARKHAM, R. (1953). *The Nature of Virus Multiplication*, p.85: Univ. Press, Cambridge;
Advances in Virus Research, p. 315: Academic Press, New York.

MICKLEM, L. R. and KAPLAN, C. (1958). *Virology,* **6,** 775.
NORMAN, A. and VEOMETT, R. C. (1960). *Virology,* **12,** 136.
PARKER, ERNESTINE R. and MACNEAL, W. J. (1944). *J. lab. clin. Med.,* **29,** 121.
PHILIPSON, L. and CHOPPIN, P. W. (1960). *J. Infect. Dis.,* **112,** 455.
PIERCY, S. E. (1961). *Vet. Rec.,* **73,** 898.
POLLEY, J. R. (1962). *Canad. J. Microbiol.,* **8,** 455.
POTTINGER, M. A. and BACHOFER, C. S. (1957). *Arch. Biochem. Biophys.,* **70,** 499.
RASMUSSEN, A. F. and STOKES, JULIA C. (1951). *J. Immunol.,* **66,** 237.
Report of the Committee on Formaldehyde Disinfection (1958). *J. Hyg., Camb.,* **56,** 488.
ROBERTSON, O. H., PUCK, T. T., LEMON, H. M. and LOOSLI, C. G. (1943). *Science,* **97,** 142.
ROOYEN, C. E. VAN (1948). *Virus Diseases of Man:* Nelson, New York.
ROSEBURY, T., MEIKLEJOHN, G., KINGSLAND, L. C. and BOLDT, M. H. (1947). *J. exp. Med.,* **85,** 65.
SALK, J. E. (1953). *J. Amer. med. Ass.,* **151,** 1081.
SALK, J. E. (1955). *J. Amer. med. Ass.,* **158,** 1239.
SCHEELE, L. A. and SHANNON, J. A. (1955). *J. Amer. med. Ass.,* **158,** 1249.
SCHWERDT, C. E., DICK, G. W. A., HERRIOTT, R. M. and HOWE, H. A. (1951). *Amer. J Hyg.,* **53,** 121.
SIMINOFF, P. (1961). *Appl. Microbiol.,* **9,** 66.
SMOLENS, J. and STOKES, J. (1954). *Proc. Soc. exp. Biol., N.Y.,* **86,** 538.
STANLEY, W. M. (1935). *Science,* **81,** 644.
STOCK, C. C. and FRANCIS, T. (1940). *J. exp. Med.,* **71,** 661.
SULKIN, S. E. and ZARAUFONETIS, C. (1947). *J. exp. Med.,* **85,** 559.
TAYLOR, A. R., KAY, N. W., MACLEAN, J. W., OPPENHEIMER, F. and STIMPERT, F. D. (1957). *J. Immunol.,* **78,** 45.
TENBROECK, C. and HERRIOTT, R. M. (1946). *Proc. Soc. exp. Biol., N.Y.,* **62,** 271.
WALLBANK, A. M., SPERLING, F. G., STUBBS, E. L. and HUBBEN, K. (1962). *Proc. Soc. exp. Biol., N.Y.,* **110,** 809.
WALLBANK, A. M. and STUBBS, E. L. (1965). *Proc. Soc. exp. Biol., N.Y.,* **120,** 754.

PART V

Chemical Disinfectants

CHAPTER 12

PHENOLS, SOAPS, ALCOHOLS AND RELATED COMPOUNDS

PHENOL and many of its derivatives, the phenol-soap preparations, the alcohols and the aldehydes are most important groups of disinfectants. They have filled much needed requirements both for general purposes and in their many applications in the fields of surgery and obstetrics as well as of chemotherapy, and they also have considerable commercial importance. The antimicrobial properties of these compounds have been examined many times in the past and the purpose of this chapter is to summarize the investigations and discoveries which have taken place mainly within the last twenty to thirty years.

Phenols

Although phenol has always occupied a prominent place in the field of disinfection since its discovery as a potential germicide by Lister in 1867, interest is now much more centred on the many derivatives of phenol as practical disinfectants. Probably more is known about the antimicrobial properties of phenol than of any other substance, and it is often used as the model for examining certain aspects of the theory of disinfection, but today its applications are virtually limited to that of the standard against which other germicides are compared and to that of a bacteriostat for use in preparations administered by injection. Little more will be said, therefore, about phenol; attention will be concentrated upon the many derivatives of phenol and their numerous preparations used in the various fields of disinfection.

Antimicrobial activities

All of the phenols can act either bactericidally or bacteriostatically depending upon their concentration, but the solubilities of some of the higher homologues and derivatives are so low that it is often difficult to demonstrate bactericidal action. Generally speaking the phenols are not sporicidal, but they are effectively tuberculocidal and they exhibit antifungal activities, some being more active against fungi than against bacteria; they are not particularly virucidal. They have relatively high concentration exponents, or dilution coefficients, so that small changes in concentration give rise to relatively large differences in killing rates, but they remain bacteriostatic over fairly wide ranges of concentration. This sensitivity in the case of phenol is one reason for its choice as a standard reference bactericide for testing purposes.

In terms of the influence of temperature, the phenols are always more effective as the temperature is increased, and a coefficient of about 2 has been found for phenol itself for each 20° rise between 2° and 40° (McCulloch and Costigan, 1936). For other phenols the observations appear to be mainly qualitative as no recorded values have been found.

In terms of the influence of pH value, alkaline solutions are always less active than acid ones. For phenol at pH 6 and pH 10 a coefficient of 2 has been quoted (Ordal, Wilson and Borg, 1941), but much greater values have been obtained for various other phenols (Ordal, 1941). Thus it is a proven fact that the sodium salts of the phenols are less active than the free phenols, and this is an important point in assessing their activities. Because of the greater solubilities of the sodium salts it is common practice to use small amounts of alkali to help the phenols into solution, but clearly only minimum amounts should be used so as not to depress activities unduly. Fortunately in this respect it is often not necessary to use even the stoichiometric amount of alkali, as the phenate ion acts as a solubilizer for the free phenol.

Mode of action. The phenols owe their antibacterial properties to their capacity to combine with and denature proteins. They are thus protoplasmic poisons. Quite early the parallelism between the protein denaturation and the bactericidal action of phenol was recorded, and more recently other aspects have been studied. These include its absorption by bacterial cells (Tezuka, 1940) and its effect on the permeability of the cells to amino acids (Gale and Taylor, 1947).

As evidenced by the low activities of the phenates compared with those of the free phenols, the attack on the cell must obviously take place through the undissociated molecule and not through its ionized form. This opinion has, in fact, never been disputed.

Effect of organic matter. The bactericidal power of the phenols is always reduced in the presence of organic matter, and the extent of the reduction depends on the particular phenol concerned and varies with the nature and amount of added organic matter. The various workers who have examined this have all made their tests under different conditions and so it is difficult to compare the way in which the various phenols are affected, but small amounts of milk, serum, faeces or similar matter can effect reductions of up to 90 per cent.

The many and varied phenolic disinfectant fluids now available do not all behave in the same way in this respect. With them it is an invariable rule that the higher the phenol coefficient the greater is the influence of organic matter. Thus, the cresols, including lysol, and the low coefficient cresylic acid preparations are only comparatively slightly affected, but a black fluid with a Rideal-Walker coefficient of over 20 may well have only a value of 3 or 4 when assessed by the Chick-Martin test.

Effect of other solutes and solvents. Several workers in the past have shown that phenol is more active in saline than in water, and some tests made recently by the author confirm this. These tests were made by inoculating 10 ml amounts of each phenol solution with 0·1 ml of a culture of *Escherichia coli* or of *Staphylococcus aureus* and subculturing one loopful after chosen intervals into nutrient broth to determine the point of total kill. The results so obtained are shown in Table 32. They parallel somewhat those of Agar and Alexander (1949) who found with soap and phenol-soap solutions that the addition of sodium or calcium chloride below the salting

TABLE 32

Germicidal activity of phenol in water and in saline

Time of contact	Survival of							
	E. coli in				*Staph. aureus* in			
	0·75% phenol in		0·5% phenol in		0·75% phenol in		0·5% phenol in	
	Water	Saline	Water	Saline	Water	Saline	Water	Saline
15 min	+	−	+	+	+	+	+	+
30 min	−	−	+	−	+	+	+	+
1 hr	−	−	+	−	+	+	+	+
2 hr	−	−	+	−	+	+	+	+
3 hr	−	−	−	−	+	+	+	+
6 hr	−	−	−	−	+	−	+	+
24 hr	−	−	−	−	−	−	+	−

out concentrations always caused an enhancement in activity. It occurred with both anionic and cationic soaps and was attributed to their greater ease of diffusion and penetration into the bacterial cells, induced by the lowering of their surface tension.

The activities of certain phenol solutions can also be enhanced substantially by adding certain definite proportions of metallic salts to give oxidation-reduction systems, and in particular a mixture of ferric and ferrous chlorides has proved highly effective and has increased the lethal dilutions of phenol, cresol and hexylresorcinol to *Staph. aureus* by as much as 45-fold (Salle and Guest, 1944, *see also* p. 425).

Because of the high oil-water partition coefficients of the phenols, the presence of oils is inimical to their antibacterial activities, and a solution of phenol in oil in contact with a nutrient surface will scarcely prevent the growth of organisms inoculated on that surface. Similarly, glycerol or ethylene glycol at concentrations of 30 per cent or greater will depress activities to the extent of some 20 to 40 per cent (Cooper, 1948). On the other hand, alcohol often enhances their activities.

Disinfection and sterilization

Homologues and derivatives of phenol

In considering the relative activities of the many derivatives of phenol, it would seem feasible to use the phenol coefficient as a basis for comparison, if only for the convenience and simplicity of the method. But such a comparison has its limitations and is not always valid. This is readily seen in the different patterns of the so-called phenol coefficients found in the homologous series of phenol, cresol and other derivatives when different test organisms are used. It is also seen in the varying concentration exponents of the different phenols – Withell (1942), for example, quoted values of 4·55 for phenol and

TABLE 33

Germicidal activities of alkyl phenols

Compound	Phenol coefficients against					
	Salm. typhi		*Staph. aureus*		*Myco. tuberculosis*	*Monilia albicans*
	(a)	(b)	(b)	(c)	(b)	(b)
Phenol	1·0	1·0	1·0	1·0	1·0	1·0
4-Methylphenol (*p*-cresol)	2·0	2·3	2·3	—	2·0	2·0
4-Ethylphenol	7·5	6·3	6·3	10	6·7	7·8
4-*n*-Propylphenol	20	18·3	16·3	14	17·8	17·8
4-*n*-Butylphenol	70	46·7	43·7	21	44·4	44·4
4-*n*-Amylphenol	104	53·3	125	20	133	156
4-*n*-Hexylphenol	90	33·3	313	—	389	333
4-*n*-Heptylphenol	20	16·7	625	21	667	556

(a) R.W. values at 18° (Coulthard, Marshall and Pyman, 1930).
(b) Coefficients measured at 37° (Klarmann, Shternov and Gates, 1934).
(c) Coefficients measured at 37° (Niederl *et al.*, 1937).

8·3 for *p*-chloro-*m*-cresol. Thus, a phenol coefficient assessment is suitable for a preliminary evaluation, but, as pointed out by Suter (1941), if too much reliance is placed on such a value, it only beclouds the issue of true activity.

Alkyl phenols. In the simple homologous series of the alkyl phenols and cresols, germicidal activity increases against all organisms as the alkyl chain is lengthened until the *n*-amyl compound is reached, and thereafter any further increase in chain length results in a decline in activity against *Salmonella typhi* (Tables 33 and 34). Against the Gram-positive and other organisms, however, there appears to be some uncertainty.

As is seen from Table 33, Klarmann, Shternov and Gates (1934) recorded very substantial increases in activity in both *n*-hexyl- and *n*-heptylphenol against *Staph. aureus*, *Mycobacterium tuberculosis*, and *Monilia albicans* – and this pattern occurs with other phenol derivatives – whereas Niederl *et al.* (1937) obtained a maximum value against *Staph. aureus* with the *n*-butyl compound, which was much lower than that of Klarmann, Shternov and Gates, and incidentally also of Read and Miller (1932), and which remained the same for the n-amyl and n-heptyl compounds. The reason for these gross differences in activity remain unexplained, but Suter (1941) has inferred that it may be due to the different methods employed in dissolving the phenols, a point earlier noted by Coulthard (1931). These compounds become progressively less soluble in water as the chain length is increased, so that solution-aids become indispensable. Sometimes a small amount of alkali is used and sometimes an initial organic solvent such as alcohol is preferred: with the former even a small excess will automatically reduce the

TABLE 34

Germicidal activities of alkyl cresols

(Coulthard, Marshall and Pyman, 1930)

Alkyl group	Rideal-Walker coefficients of		
	4-alkyl-*m*-cresol	3-alkyl-*p*-cresol	3-alkyl-*o*-cresol
Unsubstituted cresol . .	2·5	2·5	2·5
Ethyl	12·5	12·5	—
n-Propyl . . .	34	—	—
n-Butyl . . .	100	95	60
n-Amyl . . .	280	250	250
n-Hexyl . . .	275	175	180
n-Heptyl . . .	30	—	—

activity of the phenol, and with the latter the transition from organic to the final watery solution can be difficult and result in some loss of the phenol on the way by precipitation or oiling out.

Almost without exception straight chain primary alkyl phenols and cresols are more active than their secondary or tertiary isomers, and it has been suggested that a given number of carbon atoms in a single alkyl chain contributes more activity than when distributed between two or more chains. Whilst this may be true for the shorter length chains, it is not always true of the longer ones; n-hexylphenol, for example, is much less active than the n-amylcresols against *Salm. typhi*. The actual positioning of the alkyl group in relation to the hydroxy group of the molecule is of little significance and generally the three isomers have about the same activities. Thus, *o*-, *m*-, and *p*-cresol, all have phenol coefficients of about 2·2 (Schaffer and Tilley, 1927), the n-butylphenols have practically identical coefficients of about 50 (Read and Miller, 1932) and as seen in Table 34 the isomers of at least three of the alkyl-substituted cresols also have the same order of activities.

In the early 1930's, 4-n-amyl-*m*-cresol was the subject of detailed investigations (Coulthard, Marshall and Pyman, 1930; Coulthard, 1931). It is soluble in water only to the extent of about 1 in 20,000 but it is soluble in weak alkali, glycols and glycerol. It is fairly uniformly lethal to a wide range of organisms and is bacteriostatic in broth at dilutions between 1 in 20,000 and 1 in 100,000; it inhibits mould growth at 1 in 30,000. As might be expected the activity is reduced by serum and other organic matter and by excess of alkali and soaps. It is also lethal in the vapour phase to many organisms, including acid-fast types.

Of the dialkyl substituted phenols, the xylenol isomers all have phenol coefficients of about 4 or 5, but thymol and carvacrol, having longer chain substituent radicals, have coefficients of 28 against *Staph. aureus* (Schaffer

TABLE 35

Germicidal activities of halogenated phenols

Halogen compound	Phenol coefficients against			
	Salm. typhi		*Staph. aureus*	
	chloro	bromo	chloro	bromo
Phenol (unsubstituted)	1·0	1·0	1·0	1·0
o-Halophenol	3·6	3·8	3·8	3·7
p-Halophenol	3·9	5·4	4·0	4·6
2:4-Dihalophenol	13·3	19	12·7	22
2:4:6-Trihalophenol . . .	23	—	25	—
Resorcinol	0·4	0·4	0·4	0·4
4:6-Dihaloresorcinol . . .	3·2	4·0	3·9	4·5
2:4:6-Trihaloresorcinol . . .	5·0	6·4	4·3	6·4
3-Halo-4-hydroxydiphenylmethane . .	36	19	125	170
5-Halo-4-hydroxydiphenylmethane . .	74	26	215	295
5-Halo-2:4-dihydroxydiphenylmethane	48	37	37	45
4-Halo-2:4-dihydroxydiphenylmethane .	63	55	40	51

and Tilley, 1926) and about 25 against *Salm. typhi*. Thymol and carvacrol are also active against fungi, and dilutions of 1 in 2,000 to 1 in 3,000 have been found lethal to *Monilia, Cephalosporium* and *Sporotrichum* species within 30 minutes (Woodward, Kingery and Williams, 1934).

An interesting feature of the alkyl phenols as a class is their capacity mutually to potentiate antibacterial activity when mixed with certain other phenols, and this has been covered in at least two British patents (Lehn and Fink, Inc., 1932, 1936). These patents quote examples of combinations of *p-tert*-amylphenol and of *p-tert*-butylphenol with various other phenols and halogenated phenols which when dissolved in soap solutions have given increases in activity of from 30 to 300 per cent of those calculated for the individual compounds. An outstanding example was with equal mixtures of *p-tert*-amylphenol and *sym-m*-xylenol in castor oil soap which by calculation should have had a phenol coefficient of 6·9 but in fact gave a value of 20·0. Potentiations also occur with phenols mixed with terpene derivatives (see later).

Halogenated phenols. The introduction of a halogen into the molecule of any phenol always enhances its activity, and the extent of the enhancement depends upon the amount and nature of the halogenation. Two halogen atoms are always more effective than one, and the positions in which they are situated is significant. Summarizing the evidence available on this subject, Suter (1941) has stated "The effect of halogen substitution, in general, increases with increasing atomic weight of the halogen", and "This increase is less for the ortho-position than the para, perhaps owing to interaction between the hydroxyl groups and halogen atoms. Little evidence is available for meta-compounds." These points are illustrated in the phenol coefficients

TABLE 36

Germicidal activities of halogenated alkyl phenols

| Alkyl group | Phenol coefficients at 37° of | | | | | |
| | 2-alkyl-*p*-chlorophenol* | | 4-alkyl-*o*-chlorophenol* | | 2-alkyl-*p*-bromophenol** | |
	Salm. typhi	*Staph. aureus*	*Salm. typhi*	*Staph. aureus*	*Salm. typhi*	*Staph. aureus*
Unsubstituted compound .	4·3	4·3	2·5	2·9	6·0	5·0
Methyl-	12·5	12·5	6·3	7·5	12·5	11·3
Ethyl-	28·6	34·4	17·2	15·7	31·3	25·0
n-Propyl- . . .	93	93	40	32·1	62	62
n-Butyl- . . .	146	257	86	94	156	313
n-Amyl- . . .	156	500	80	286	62	571
n-Hexyl- . . .	(23)	1,250	23·3	500	—	1,250
n-Heptyl- . . .	(20)	1,500	16·7	375	—	—
n-Octyl- . . .	—	1,750	—	—	—	—

* Data from Klarmann, Shternov and Gates (1933).
** Data from Klarmann, Gates, Shternov and Cox (1933).

of the halogenated derivatives of several different phenols quoted in Tables 35 and 36. The data for these Tables are taken mainly from various publications of Klarmann and his collaborators, but they have been confirmed broadly by others. Blicke and Stockhaus (1933), for example, obtained similar results with the 4-alkyl-*o*-chlorophenols. An interesting point from these Tables is that bromination is not always superior to chlorination, in spite of Suter's postulation. This is seen in the 2-alkyl-*o*-halophenols (Table 36) and in the hydroxydiphenylmethanes (Table 35) when assessed against *Staph. aureus*.

Further examples of the effect of halogenation are seen with the cresols and xylenols. In the cresol series, the unsubstituted compounds all have phenol coefficients of about 2·5, whereas the monochloro derivatives have significantly higher values, *p*-chloro-*o*-cresol and its ortho-para isomer having values at 37° of 12·5 and 6·3 respectively and *p*-chloro-*m*-cresol having a Rideal-Walker coefficient of 13·3 (Rapps, 1933). The dichlorinated cresols are even more active, showing, according to a Japanese source quoted by Suter (1941), increases as much as ten-fold over the monochloro derivatives. The same is also true of the xylenols. The unsubstituted xylenols have Rideal-Walker coefficients of 4 or 5, whilst *p*-chloro-*sym*-*m*-xylenol has a coefficient of 36 (Rapps, 1933) with a similar activity against the Gram-positive organisms, and the 2:4-dichloro derivative has a Rideal-Walker coefficient of 250 and coefficients against *Staph. aureus* and *Streptococcus pyogenes* of 160 and 180 respectively (Gemmell, 1952).

In the case of phenol itself, trichlorination is even more advantageous (Klarmann, Shternov and von Wowern, 1929), but any further halogenation is retrograde. Tetrachlorophenol is only moderately active, and penta-chlorophenol is only a little better than its parent substance against bacteria although its fungistatic activity is enhanced. The trichloro isomers differ widely in their individual activities and they all appear to be highly sensitive to pH changes. However, according to Wolf and Westveer (1952) this may not be a true pH effect but is more likely to be associated with the low solubilities of the compounds.

Several other di- and tri-alkyl chlorophenols have also been examined, and some of them have higher phenol coefficients than the chloroxylenols, but the only one which has attracted any attention is chlorothymol. This compound has a Rideal-Walker coefficient of 160, and according to Wood-ward, Kingery and Williams (1934) has similar phenol coefficients against a range of fungi.

Polyhydric phenols. The three dihydric phenols, catechol, resorcinol and hydroquinone, and the two trihydric phenols, phloroglucinol and pyrogallol, have all comparatively low antibacterial activities, and in no case has a phenol coefficient of over 1 at normal temperatures been reported. Hydro-quinone, however, appears to have an exceptionally high temperature coefficient, so that at 37° it is alleged to have a coefficient of 12 against *Salm. typhi* (Klarmann, Gates and Shternov, 1932). It is also said to have high bacteriostatic activity against certain organisms.

The alkylated resorcinols follow more or less the pattern of activities exhibited by the alkyl phenols and cresols, except that the optimum occurs at the *n*-hexyl compound rather than at the *n*-amyl. This optimum is, of course, only for *Salm. typhi*; when assessed against *Staph. aureus*, activities continue to increase, as with the other phenols, at least up to the *o*-nonyl compound. Thus the hexyl compound, hexylresorcinol, has a coefficient of about 50 against *Salm. typhi* and 98 against *Staph. aureus*, whereas the coefficients for nonylresorcinol are 0 and 980 respectively (Schaffer and Tilley, 1926, 1927; Dohme, Cox and Miller, 1926). Again the positioning of the substituent radicals is significant, and generally the 5-*n*-alkyl derivatives exhibit less activity than do the 4-*n*-isomers. But this applies mainly with compounds tested against *Salm. typhi*; against *Staph. aureus* the difference does not show itself until the *n*-hexyl and higher homologues are reached

(Suter and Weston, 1939). It is because of its high general bactericidal activity combined with its low toxicity that 4-*n*-hexylresorcinol is an acknowledged general antiseptic for oral and topical use.

Homologues of the trihydric phenols have been prepared, but none of them has shown any outstanding bactericidal properties.

Chlorination of the alkyl resorcinols about doubles the bactericidal powers of the lower homologues (Suter, 1941), but in the case of the trihydric phenols there seems to be no information available.

Diphenyl derivatives. Investigations into the bactericidal properties of the phenols has naturally not been confined to the alkyl derivatives. A number of aryl derivatives has also been examined and several have proved sufficiently active as well as non-toxic and non-irritant to be recommended as clinical disinfectants. These compounds are all derivatives of phenylphenol, but they can be divided into two broad groups: those in which the two phenyl groups are linked directly and those in which they are bridged by linkages such as a straight or branched aliphatic carbon chain, a nitrogen group or a connecting sulphur or oxygen atom. The first group constitutes the diphenyls, and they have the general formula

The second group has the general formula

where R is an alkylene, nitrogen or sulphur group or an oxygen atom. Confusion has arisen in the past because of the different systems of nomenclature involving the numbering of the ring system. Being phenol derivatives, the numbering might be expected to start at the hydroxyl position in each nucleus, but the diphenyl configuration and nomenclature are now more generally adopted.

The antibacterial activities of the diphenylmethanes (where R = CH_2) were first observed by Ehrlich, but it was not until during the 1920s that interest was aroused in them, consequent upon their development in Germany mainly as mothproofing agents. The success of these investigations coupled with the knowledge of their antimicrobial properties stimulated further interest in these compounds, and so intensive searches were instituted, particularly in the United States, for other compounds of the group possessing enhanced bactericidal activities. Much of this work appeared in a stream of technical papers and of patents published from about 1929 onwards. The subject was not neglected in Great Britain, and it was again taken up in Germany after the Second World War.

As a result of these investigations the following broad, though not universal, principles emerged:

(*i*) for optimum activity, there should be a hydroxyl group in each phenyl nucleus, and they should be in the ortho, or 2:2', positions relative to the connecting carbon atom. 3:3' substituents are less effective, at least in the diphenylmethane series (Gump and Cade, 1952), and the 4:4' isomers are the least desirable, although an exception to this occurs with the stilbene derivatives, where the 4:4' compounds are apparently the most active (Faulkner, 1944). There is no point in introducing more than one hydroxyl in each ring;

(*ii*) halogenation always enhances activity, and it should preferably be effected in each phenol ring. The dichloro substituted compounds are the most active against the Gram-negative bacteria and the fungi, and the hexachloro derivatives are the most effective against the Gram-positive organisms (Cade, 1944; Marsh and Butler, 1946);

(*iii*) when there is a bridging group in the molecule, the phenol nuclei must not be too widely separated. Activities have been found to increase with the chain length of the bridge until the C_4 derivative is reached (Richardson and Reid, 1940), but after this they tend to become inactive against the Gram-negative organisms (Heinemann, 1944), although there are exceptions;

(*iv*) the sodium salts of these compounds are only a little less active than the compounds themselves, therefore the adverse affect of alkali is less than with the simpler phenols.

Of the straight diphenyl compounds many alkylated and halogenated derivatives have received patent cover as potential germicides, but in spite of this only o-phenylphenol (2-hydroxydiphenyl) has become established in the disinfectants field, and this is largely due to its low toxicity and lack of irritancy on the skin. It is the most active of the three hydroxydiphenyls against *Salm. typhi* but against *Staph. aureus* the 3-isomer is said to be more effective. o-Phenylphenol is lethal to *Salm. typhi* in 5 minutes at a dilution of 1 in 2,000 and to *Staph. aureus* at 1 in 800 (Harris and Christiansen, 1934) and it inhibits the growth of bacteria and moulds at dilutions of from 1 in 2,000 to 1 in 6,000. It is of course normally formulated in a soap base and this, as might be expected, somewhat alters its characteristics (*see* later).

Alkylation does not affect the diphenyl compounds in the same way as the simpler phenols. For instance, alkylation of o-phenylphenol in the 5-position itself gives enhanced activity against the staphylococci up to an optimum with the *n*-propyl derivative, but both the 3- and 5-alkyl homologues are less active against *Salm. typhi* than is the parent substance (Harris and Christiansen, 1934).

Turning to the diphenylalkane compounds, six of them, all of which are

2:2'-dihydroxychloro derivatives, have attracted most interest. Three are diphenylmethanes and three are the equivalent sulphides. The three diphenylmethanes are the 5:5'-dichloro, 3:5:3':5'-tetrachloro and 3:5:6:3':5':6'-hexachloro compounds, known by the short names of Dichlorophene, Tetrachlorophene and Hexachlorophane. They also have a variety of trade names of which the most popular are G-4, G-5 and G-11. The equivalent sulphides are known as G-4-S, G-5-S and G-11-S. In common with all of the diphenyl derivatives, these compounds have only very low solubilities in water but they can be dissolved with the aid of solubilizers such as alcohol, alkali or soap solutions, and these are the conditions under which they are always tested and used. Some of the solution aids, however, inevitably depress bactericidal efficiencies, and soaps in particular feature in this class. The Tweens are useful solubilizing agents, but they depress activities to such an extent that Tween 80 has been recommended as neutralizing agent in testing these compounds (Erlandson and Lawrence, 1953). As with most germicides, organic matter in the form of blood, serum, pus, milk, etc., markedly depresses the bactericidal efficiencies of the diphenyl derivatives, but it does not abolish their activities, and bacteriostasis can continue at very low levels of concentration. Thus, hexachlorophane will inhibit *Staph. aureus* to a greater or less extent at dilutions up to 1 in over 20,000,000 and tetrachlorophene at dilutions in the range 1 in 4,000,000 to 1 in 10,000,000 (Seastone, 1947; Price and Bonnett, 1948).

Because of this high degree of bacteriostasis the early assessments of the lethal activities of the diphenyl compounds were all much too high, and the introduction of antidotes of the proper type gave much lower values. Hexachlorophane, for example, was first thought to have a very high phenol coefficient against *Staph. aureus*, but Cade's (1944) later assessments for dichlorophene and hexachlorophane were:

	Dichlorophene	*Hexachlorophane*
against *Staph. aureus* at 37°	118 ± 18	125 ± 25
against *Staph. aureus* at 20°	111 ± 25	146 ± 36
against *Salm. typhi* at 37°	105 ± 15	about 20
against *Salm. typhi* at 20°	122 ± 12	about 20

Even lower values were obtained later, and now the accepted values for hexachlorophane are about 40 against *Staph. aureus* and 15 or less against *Salm. typhi*, but it is still confirmed that dichlorophene is the more effective against the Gram-negative organisms. According to a British Patent specification (Kunz and Gump, 1942), tetrachlorophene and hexachlorophane will kill *Staph. aureus* at 20° in periods ranging between 1 and 10 minutes at concentrations of the order of 1 in 1,000 to 1 in 5,000. These values, however, depend very much on the pH value for, according to Walter and Gump (1963), a solution of 5 mg per ml at 37° gives a total kill at pH 5, only a partial kill at pH 6, and is inactive at pH 7. On the other hand they found the inhibitory activity at pH 6 or 7 to be less than at pH 8 by a factor of

8 for the pseudomonads and 80 for the staphylococci. Tween 80 also has an adverse effect, the maximum effect being obtained by adding 8 parts of Tween to 1 of hexachlorophane. An emulsion containing 3 per cent of hexachlorophane, sometimes known under the trade name of "pHisoHex", has attained a wide popularity as a skin disinfectant in surgery. Opinions on its efficacy, however, are not uniformly favourable; it has been variously reported as better than, equal to, and inferior to a hexachlorophane soap (Traub, Newhall and Fuller, 1944; Smyllie *et al.*, 1959; Alexander, 1961; Lowbury and Lilly, 1960; Panzarella and Dexter, 1961).

Others of the many compounds of this type are a thiol compound, 2:2'-dihydroxy-3:5:3':5'-tetrachlorodiphenyl sulphide, or 2:2'-thiobis-(4:6-dichlorophenol), and also known as bithionol, Actamer or TBP,

and a urea derivative, 3:4:4'-trichlorocarbanilide, or TCC,

The first of these inhibits the growth of the Gram-positive bacteria at concentrations ranging from 1 in 100,000 to 1 in 10 millions and the Gram-negative bacteria and moulds from 1 in 1,000 to 1 in 100,000 (Shumard-Beaver and Hunter, 1953). TCC is also said to be bacteriostatic at concentrations ranging from 1 in 1 million to 1 in 10 millions (Roman, Barnett and Balske, 1958). No lethal tests seem to have been performed on these compounds because, along with many others of the group and type, they were thought of primarily as agents to add to soaps to give them germicidal properties (*see* later) and so only a cursory examination of the substance itself was made, or at least reported.

Taking a very great license and only because it is yet another substance which has been used in disinfectant soaps, a further bridged thiol compound can here be briefly mentioned. It is tetramethylthiuram disulphide, or TMTD,

a substance selected from a long series of dithiocarbamates because of its outstandingly high inhibitory properties (Miller and Elson, 1949). It will prevent the growth of *Staph. aureus* at a dilution of 1 in 160,000, *Strep.*

pyogenes at 1 in 1,280,000, *E. coli* at 1 in 20,000, *Ps. pyocyanea* at 1 in 5,000 and several of the pathogenic and saprophytic fungi generally at 1 in 80,000 to 1 in 160,000.

Phenylhydroxycarboxylic acids. Salicylic acid, or *o*-hydroxybenzoic acid, has been the subject of much investigation in the earlier days, and it has been variously estimated as one-tenth to thirteen times as powerful as phenol (Birkhaug, 1931; Woodward, Kingery and Williams, 1934). *m*-Hydroxybenzoic acid has also been subject to some scrutiny, but it is the esters of *p*-hydroxybenzoic acid which have attracted the most attention of more recent date, particularly because of their preservative properties in the pharmaceutical, cosmetic and industrial fields. *p*-Hydroxybenzoic acid itself, like *p*-aminobenzoic acid, is a known mould metabolite and it has been

TABLE 37

Antimicrobial activities of the esters of p-hydroxybenzoic acid

Organism	Inhibitive concentration % of the ester			
	Methyl	Ethyl	Propyl	Butyl
Gram-positive types . .	0·1–0·4	0·05–0·1	0·0125–0·05	0·0063–0·125
Gram-negative types . .	0·2	0·1	0·05–0·1	0·05–0·4
Aspergillus niger . .	0·1	0·04	0·02	0·02
Monilia albicans . .	0·1	0·1	0·0125	0·0125
Other pathogenic fungi .	0·016–0·05	0·008–0·025	0·004–0·0125	0·002–0·006

reported to be a bacterial vitamin in respect of a mutant of *E. coli* which is incapable of synthesizing aromatic acids (Davis, 1950): in contrast, its esters are all metabolite antagonists. Sabalitschka (1924) in Germany first discovered this and over a period of years published a series of papers lauding them not only as preservative but also as sterilizing agents. Some exaggerated claims were made in the first place for their sporicidal properties, but subsequently these have been amply disproved. A factor limiting the antimicrobial activities of the *p*-hydroxybenzoates, also known as parabens, is their low solubilities in water, and because of this they can only be considered to be mildly bactericidal. Their main virtues lie in their bacteriostatic and fungistatic properties and in the fact that, unlike benzoic and salicylic acids, they are relatively insensitive to pH changes, their activities at pH 8 being only slightly less than under more acid conditions. Because of their wide antimicrobial spectrum, their non-volatility, stability, compatibility with other medicaments, low toxicity and other attributes, some writers (*e.g.* Gershenfeld and Perlstein, 1939; MacDonald, 1942; Sokol, 1952; Aalto, Firman and Rigler, 1953) have gone so far as to describe them as the nearest approach to "the ideal pharmaceutical preservatives", but they are not so accepted in Great Britain.

According to Sokol (1952) the higher esters are always more active than the lower ones, but they also tend to be more selective in their activities. A summary of the inhibitory concentrations of the four aliphatic esters, as reported by Sokol, is given in Table 37. The tests were all made in nutrient media and the results with the bacteria were read after 24 hours' incubation, presumably at 37°, and with the fungi after 7 days at room temperature. They show the inhibitory concentrations of the methyl ester to be in the range 0·1–0·4 per cent, except for some of the fungi which are rather more sensitive, whereas the butyl ester inhibits the Gram-positive bacteria and most of the fungi at concentrations between about 0·006 and 0·02 per cent but requires 0·05–0·4 per cent to inhibit the Gram-negative types. Higher esters by and large seem to be rather less active.

These findings are broadly the same as those obtained earlier by the author, who also noted the effects of pH value on the lethal concentrations. At pH 5·0 the methyl ester was lethal in 24 hours, but not in 8 hours, to both *Staph. aureus* and *Ps. pyocyanea* at a concentration of 0·14 per cent, but at pH 7·0 a level of 0·2 per cent was necessary. The propyl ester was similarly lethal at a concentration of 0·02 per cent to both organisms at pH 5·0 but not to *Ps. pyocyanea* at pH 7·0. Serum, syrups and oils all reduce the activities of the esters so that four or five times the concentration may be required to give the same degree of protection to these fluids as to simpler aqueous solutions (Sokol, 1952) – but it is questionable whether such concentrations can in fact be obtained because of the limiting solubilities of the esters concerned.

Because of their different antibacterial and antifungal properties, mixtures of methyl and propyl parabens are frequently used as preservatives for pharmaceutical preparations, the more usual concentrations being 0·2 per cent of the methyl ester and 0·02 per cent of the propyl. These mixtures show no evidence of synergism.

Many derivatives of salicylic acid have antifungal properties and one group which has been investigated in some detail is the substituted salicylamides (Coates *et al.*, 1957). The substances were examined primarily for their potential chemotherapeutic values and so only pathogenic fungi were used. In summary, maximum activity was obtained in the alkoxy series, and occurred with the 2-*n*-amyloxy and 2-*n*-hexyloxy compounds; branched chains were less effective than unbranched ones. In these respects the salicylamides behave similarly to the alkyl substituted phenols (*see* p. 314). They differ, however, in that halogenation of the salicylamide nucleus confers no enhanced activity.

Mention must also be made of the antifungal and the antibacterial properties of salicylamide and some of its homologues. "Shirlan", the trade name for salicylanilide, is primarily an antifungal agent, and has been known for many years as a preservative for textiles. Interest in the homologues, which can be both antibacterial and antifungal, is centred on their use as additives to soaps for skin disinfection purposes, the compounds mainly concerned being the 3:4:5-tribromo, 2:3:3':5-tetrachloro and 3:3':4':5-tetrachloro derivatives, the last also being known as Irgasan BS 200. Their activities *per se* have been variously described in the literature, but as their interest is almost exclusively in the soap field, further discussion of them will be deferred until the appropriate section later in this chapter. It is of interest to note, however, that Irgasan is claimed to be inhibitory to staphylococci at 1 in 10 millions, to *Proteus* sp. at 1 in 100,000 and to *E. coli* and *Ps. pyocyanea* at 1 in 10,000. 125 parts per million (1 in 8,000) in water will kill staphylococci in 10 minutes, but with 10 per cent of serum or soap added it requires 250 parts per million (1 in 4,000) (Lennon, Furia and Zussman, 1960).

Other derivatives of phenol. The introduction of nitro groups into the molecule of phenol enhances its antimicrobial activities, the extent depending on the number of groups present, the particular isomer being examined and the organism used in testing them. According to some workers *m*-nitrophenol is the most generally active, but others believe the *p*-isomer to be the most active against some organisms and the *o*-isomer the most active against others. For the *o*-, *m*-, and *p*- isomers Woodward, Kingery and Williams (1934) found phenol coefficients with *Monilia tropicalis* of 6·6, 5·3 and 5·3 respectively.

Introduction of a second nitro group enhances activities still further, and of these isomers Lecoq, Landrin and Solomidès (1949) found the 2:5 compound to be the most generally efficient. This compound inhibited *E. coli* and *Strep. pyogenes* in serum broth at dilutions of 1 in 20,000 and 1 in 100,000 respectively, whereas the other isomers were effective only at about 1 in 10,000 or less; it was also about ten times more effective against *Myco. tuberculosis.*

Trinitrophenol, or picric acid, is about equally active against bacteria and moulds, having ascribed phenol coefficients in both cases of about 6.

The aminophenols vary in their activities compared with those of the equivalent phenols. *p*-Aminophenol is rather more effective than phenol itself, but in examining a series of *p*-alkyl derivatives of *o*-aminophenol Barber and Haslewood (1945) found that their activities were "not increased but may be decreased by simple nuclear substitution."

In the early days the naphthols were widely used as antiseptics but they have now been entirely displaced.

Uses of phenols in disinfection and antisepsis

Of the many derivatives of phenol prepared and examined over the years only a few have obtained any prominence as practical disinfectants. Some have achieved this because of their all-round usefulness, others have been found valuable for certain particular purposes whilst yet a third group has been pushed forward simply for commercial expediency and exploitation.

By far the greatest consumption of the phenols is in the manufacture of the coal tar disinfectant fluids and of the many soap-based preparations used for general and for surgical disinfection, and in this group are included the cresylic acids, the high-boiling tar acids, the chloroxylenols and the diphenyl derivatives. These are discussed in later sections of this chapter. Phenol, cresol, *p*-chloro-*m*-cresol and the *p*-hydroxybenzoate esters are also used as bacteriostats in preparations administered by injection, and many other derivatives are used industrially in the preservation of textiles, wood, paper, glues, paints and similar materials, as well as of certain foods. These applications are dealt with in the chapter on Preservatives and Preservation, Chapter 17.

Several of the alkyl and chlorinated phenols, cresols and xylenols have been used in the past in various branches of medicine, but they have now been largely displaced by other more suitable agents such as the sulpha drugs and the antibiotics. Amyl-*m*-cresol, chloro-*m*-xylenol and other halogenated phenols have been used successfully in treating urinary infections (Coulthard, Marshall and Pyman, 1930; Zondek, 1942), and chlorothymol dissolved in alcohol and glycerol has proved a useful skin disinfectant (Beck, 1933). Amyl-*m*-cresol and chlorothymol, amongst others, are still used orally by incorporating them in various antiseptic sweets, mouthwashes and gargles.

Reference will be made later in the chapter to the properties and uses as skin disinfectants of the various phenolic derivatives in different soap formulations, but apart from these another compound now claiming attention in the same field is chlorhexidine, also known as "Hibitane". This compound is a guanidino derivative, its full chemical name being 1:6-*di*-4'-chlorophenyl-guanidinohexane

$$Cl\langle\bigcirc\rangle\cdot NH\cdot C\cdot NH\cdot C\cdot NH\cdot[CH_2]_6\cdot NH\cdot C\cdot NH\cdot C\cdot NH\cdot\langle\bigcirc\rangle Cl$$
$$\qquad\quad NH\quad NH\qquad\qquad\qquad NH\quad NH$$

It was chosen by Davies *et al.* (1954), from a large number of bisguanidines which they examined, because of its good all round antibacterial properties and lack of toxic side-effects and also because of its efficacy in disinfecting artificial wounds. The compound itself has a very low solubility and so the diacetate is generally used. According to Davies and his colleagues it will inhibit the growth of *Staph. aureus* and *Streptococcus lactis* at dilutions as low as 1 in 2 millions, and at the other end of the scale *Ps. pyocyanea* at 1 in 50,000. These figures are similar to those reported by Lawrence (1960) who gave figures of 1 in 1 million for *Staph. aureus*, 1 in 100,000 to 1 in 200,000 for the clostridia, 1 in 800,000 for *E. coli*, 1 in 100,000 for *Ps. pyocyanea*, 1 in 80,000 for *Proteus vulgaris* and 1 in 80,000 to 1 in 100,000 for pathogenic fungi: he also found little difference, if any, between the lethal and inhibitory concentrations for these organisms. He did not, however, note the curious bactericidal action observed by Davies and his colleagues. At concentrations of 1 in 20,000 and weaker the initial kill is rapid and a very large proportion of the inoculum succumbs within 5 minutes; the action then tails off rapidly and the remaining few cells can persist for several hours: it requires a fairly high concentration to kill the whole population quickly and evenly. This phenomenon may have been missed by Lawrence by reason of the different experimental conditions employed and the different inactivator used; Davies found egg-yolk to be the best. The greatest activity is found in solutions at pH 8: below this level it falls fairly rapidly until at pH 5·2 it is almost non-existent. A 1 per cent solution is said to be sporicidal.

The general pharmacological properties of chlorhexidine, plus its known value in disinfecting artificial wounds, led to its introduction as a skin disinfectant and for use in urology and gynæcology, for which many favourable reports have appeared. It is applied as a 0·5 per cent solution in water or in alcohol, sometimes with cetrimide added, and with such a solution Myers, McKenzie and Ward (1956) found 76 per cent of treated skins, examined by biopsy, to be sterile after 3 minutes, and 95 per cent sterile after 4 minutes. Similarly, Scott (1961) could recover no organisms from 1,000 swabs taken during operational periods up to two hours, and the hands of the theatre staff remained sterile for up to 5 hours in 77·8 per cent of the cases. Recently, however, chlorhexidine has come under some criticism because of its low activity against some strains of *Pseudomonas* and *Proteus*, particularly *Ps. rettgeri*, against which it has been alleged to be active only at concentrations of 1 in 2,000 to 1 in 8,000, depending on the particular strains and media chosen (Lubsen, Boissevain and Fass, 1961). Whilst this is agreed in principle by several others in the field, it is not considered to be too serious a detraction from its value in the surgical field.

'Germicidal' soaps

Many attempts have been made to produce germicidal soaps simply by incorporating known bactericides into ordinary toilet soap. Originally interest was in formaldehyde, mercury compounds and silver salts, but it is now concentrated on the phenols and certain urea derivatives most of which have already been mentioned in the preceding pages. These formulations differ from the types of soap-based disinfectants discussed elsewhere in this chapter in the ratios of phenol and soap present, and consequently in their antibacterial properties. The soap-based disinfectants contain a large proportion of the phenol, and the soap is added mainly as a solubilizing agent, whereas the so-called 'germicidal' soaps are frankly ordinary toilet soaps with a small amount of phenol added, usually not more than 2 per cent. The soap formulations might, therefore, be expected to be less active than the other types of disinfectant, so much so that it is doubtful whether the designation 'germicidal' can ever be justified. They certainly possess antibacterial properties – and so do simple soaps – but their action is not rapid and is incomplete, especially against the staphylococci and some other organisms.

The maximum reduction obtainable under the most favourable circumstances is only about 95 per cent, and so it is not surprising that the term 'germicidal' as applied to soaps is not officially accepted in the United States, 'deodorant' being used in its place.

The reason for this lack of activity is not far to find. It follows as a natural consequence of the micellar theory of soap solution (p. 339), a theory which in the first place provides an explanation for the increased solubilities, hence the increased apparent activities, of phenols in the presence of soaps. It also infers that for optimum activity there is an optimum soap-phenol ratio and that this ratio will vary amongst the different soaps and phenols. For the cresols in lysol this ratio is said to be about 2:1, and this is very different from the 50:1 or even 100:1 ratio in the soap mixtures under discussion. From this it may be concluded that the excess of soap, or the deficiency of phenol, is such that a depleted activity is to be expected; and this idea is borne out in practice in that it is now recognized that 3 per cent of hexachlorophane in a liquid soap is more effective as a germicide than is the same amount in a solid soap, simply because, presumably, the soap-phenol ratio in the first example is more favourable.

The scientific, technical and trade literature for the last twenty years or so has abounded in papers and references on the subject, many of them lauding a given phenol as a soap antiseptic and expressing a preference for this over other phenols. It is not proposed to go into the details of even a proportion of these contributions, but only to summarize the general situation and to emphasize a few outstanding features.

References have already been made in pages 314–323 to most of the phenols and allied compounds used in this context, but for convenience they are given here together. The list is not complete but it includes – in alphabetical order, bithionol (Actamer), 2:4-dichloro-*m*-xylenol (DCMX), hexachlorophane, 3:4:5-tribromosalicylanilide (TBS), 3:4:4'-trichlorocarbanilide (TCC), 2:3:3':5- and 3:5:3':4-tetrachlorosalicylanilide (TCS) and tetramethylthiuram disulphide (TMTD). They are incorporated in soaps usually to a concentration of 2 per cent, but sometimes only 1 or even 0·5 per cent is used, and they possess in general three outstanding and important characteristics: first, they do not effect, even under the best of conditions, a total kill of the bacteria on the skin, the maximum reductions claimed being about 97 or 98 per cent with most of them in the range 75 to just over 90 per cent. Secondly, they are generally more effective against the Gram-positive bacteria, some more so than others. Thirdly, there is a gradual build up of activity on the skin with the continual and exclusive use of the soap so that the maximum effect is not observed until after several days of application; the value of one such treatment is negligible. Not all agree with this: Gemmell (1952, 1953), for instance, claims this to be a major difference between dichloroxylenol and hexachlorophane, but this and the relative efficacies of the two preparations have been strongly challenged by Gump and Cade

(1953b). And this sort of pro and con argument can be repeated *ad nauseam*.

Most of the arguments have been centred on hexachlorophane and amongst the claims and counterclaims made are:

(1) 2 per cent hexachlorophane in toilet soap reduces the numbers of bacteria on the skin by some 80–90 per cent, but only after 4 or 5 days application. The application must be continuous; if it is only intermittent, as, for instance, by nurses during their duty periods and not when off duty, it is valueless (Weatherall and Winner, 1963);

(2) 3 per cent bithionol reduces the count by 90 per cent within a week, whereas hexachlorophane only effects a 50 per cent reduction (Hopper and Wood, 1958);

TABLE 38

Minimum bacteriostatic concentrations of disinfectants used in soaps

Disinfectant	Bacteriostatic level* (ppm) against	
	Staph. aureus	*E. coli*
Bithionol	1·0	50·0
DCMX	2·5	50·0
Hexachlorophane . .	0·5	50·0
TBS	1·0	25·0
TCC	0·2	25·0
TCS	0·1	12·5
TMTD	0·25	25·0

* These values are for the substances themselves.

(3) tetrachlorosalicylanilide is superior to hexachlorophane (Frost, 1961);

(4) dichloroxylenol in 2·5 per cent concentration is at least equal to 2 per cent hexachlorophane, and much less costly (Gemmell, 1952);

(5) Irgasan reaches its near-maximum effect in 5 to 7 days, when a 1 per cent soap mixture reduces the counts by 10^3 or greater (Lennon, Furia and Zussman, 1960) – on the other hand I have found no advantage of a 0·5 per cent mixture over plain soap;

(6) there may be some synergism between certain of the salicylanilides.

Perhaps the situation is best summarized in the comprehensive investigations reported by Hurst, Stuttard and Woodroffe (1960) in which they examined several soaps by both *in vitro* diffusion and other methods and by *in vivo* hand washing tests. First they obtained the minimum bacteriostatic concentrations of the disinfectants themselves, with the results given in Table 38. As might be expected these values were all affected to a greater or less extent by scrum and skin dirt, and also by soaps. In particular, they found a considerable inactivation of dichloroxylenol and hexachlorophane by soap, as judged by the diffusion zones of inhibition on agar plates, some inactivation of bithionol, and some stimulation or potentiation of the tri-bromo- and trichloro-salicylanilides. The inactivation of hexachlorophane

TABLE 39

Effect of disinfectant soaps on the numbers of
bacteria on the skin

(after Hurst, Stuttard and Woodroffe, 1960)

Disinfectant	% Reduction in bacterial counts with soap + disinfectant (%)			
	2	1	0·5	0·2
Bithionol	77	64		
Hexachlorophane . . .	81			
Tetrachlorosalicylanilide . .			84	76
Tetramethylthiuram disulphide .		76		66
Tribromosalicylanilide . . .			65	56
Trichlorocarbanilide . . .	72			

Assessments were made after using the soaps for 7 days.

TABLE 40

Effect of disinfectant soaps on the numbers
of bacteria on the skin

(after Roman, Barnett and Balske, 1958)

Disinfectant	% Reduction in bacterial counts with soap + disinfectant (%)		
	2	1	0·5
Bithionol . . .	95·5	90·4	
Hexachlorophane . .	94·1	75·6	
TCC	97·8	91·7	88·5

Assessments were made after using the soaps for 12 days.

by soap was borne out in some work by Anderson (1962) in which *Ps. pyocyanea* spread on the surface of cakes of such a soap was still recoverable 36 hours later.

For the second phase of their investigations, Hurst, Stuttard and Woodroffe did a series of hand washing tests over a period of 7 days using a modification of the Cade method (*see* p. 97) with the results given in Table 39.

Rather different and somewhat higher responses were reported by Roman, Barnett and Balske (1958) – *see* Table 40. The differences may be due to the long period of treatment employed – 12 days against 7 – or more probably to the different testing techniques employed.

Coal tar disinfectants

After Lister's discovery of the value of phenol in his "new system of aseptic surgery" much work was put into investigating other phenolic fractions derived from coal tar, a direct outcome of which was the emergence of the groups of disinfectants known as the Black and the White Coal Tar Fluids, the traditional Disinfectant or Sanitary Fluids. These disinfectants still have a large market and are used extensively in domestic, hospital and other fields of general hygiene. As a group they are naturally more crude than the preparations made with pure synthetic phenols and, because of the natures of the phenols employed, they are all, with one known exception, toxic and irritant to the skin. Consequently they are only used for disinfecting inanimate objects; they are unsuitable for surgical and wound disinfection. Lysol, for instance, one of the mildest of the group, cannot be tolerated comfortably by normal skins at concentrations greater than about 1 per cent.

The black and white fluids

The active constituents of the black and the white fluids are derived from the various distillation fractions of coal tar, although latterly some chlorinated fractions and petroleum residues after cracking have sometimes been added. Being phenolic in nature they have only low solubilities in water, hence they must be either solubilized or emulsified in order to obtain an adequate concentration for disinfection processes. The solubilized types, the 'black' fluids, are solutions of colloidal electrolytes, usually soaps, in the chosen tar oil fractions, whilst the emulsified types; the 'white' fluids, are preparations in which the phenol is emulsified into a permanent suspension with the aid of gelatin, glue, casein or dextrins. The black fluids can vary in their phenols content from about 15 to 35 per cent and they usually have about 10 per cent of added water. They are quite stable in the concentrated form, but on dilution they form emulsions with stabilities varying according to the hardness of the water used, the extent of the dilution and, of course, the particular formulation. The white fluids contain from about 20 to about 40 per cent of phenols, and rarely contain less than 45 per cent of added water. They are naturally rather less stable than are the black fluids, but their particular characteristic is that on dilution even with seawater the emulsion remains much more stable. Requirements for the composition, stability, germicidal activity, odour and other properties for both types of fluid are laid down in the British Standard Specification B.S. 2462:1954.

Almost without exception a carrier in the form of a so-called "neutral oil" is added, the amount varying from 9 to 20 per cent and sometimes higher. These oils consist mainly of aromatic hydrocarbons of the naphthalene type besides certain organic bases, and they are devoid of any antibacterial activity in themselves. They were added in the first place to stabilize the fluids by preventing crystallization of the phenols, but they were quickly found to fill a much more important function in that they actually potentiate the activities of the phenols. They act in this way presumably because they alter the partition ratios of the phenols between the oil and water phases and also possibly because they reorientate some of the phenols. In any case there is always an optimum level for maximum potentiation beyond which some selectivity begins to show itself in favour of the Gram-negative bacteria by virtue of the continuous reduction in activity against the Gram-positive bacteria. Hence a sound reason for including more than one type of organism in any testing procedure as already expounded in Chapter 3.

The most important constituent affecting the germicidal properties of the black and white fluids is, of course, the phenol itself, of which various fractions distilling in the range 190° to about 300° are used. The lowest fraction, consisting mainly of the three cresol isomers, constitutes the basis for all of the lysols; the next higher boiling fraction, known as the 'cresylic acids' or 'middle oils' fraction and containing mainly cresol and xylenols, distills between 205° and 230° and is used for making fluids with phenol coefficients of the order of 8 to 10; the highest boiling fractions, distilling above 230° and containing the 'high boiling tar acids' along with naphthalenes and other hydrocarbons, form the basis of the high coefficient fluids with Rideal-Walker values up to 20 or more. Some indication of the make-up of these fractions in terms of their boiling ranges is given below (Gibson, 1936):

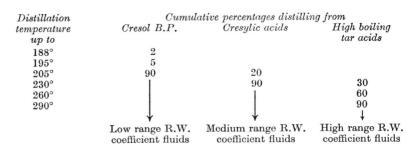

Distillation temperature up to	Cumulative percentages distilling from		
	Cresol B.P.	Cresylic acids	High boiling tar acids
188°	2		
195°	5		
205°	90	20	
230°		90	30
260°			60
290°			90
	↓	↓	↓
	Low range R.W. coefficient fluids	Medium range R.W. coefficient fluids	High range R.W. coefficient fluids

The higher boiling fractions, consisting mainly of the alkyl homologues of phenol, show increasingly divergent activities against the Gram-positive and Gram-negative bacteria. Thus, although the lysols made with the low boiling cresols are almost equally effective against *Staph. aureus* and *Salm. typhi*, the difference with the high coefficient black fluids can be as much as seven or eightfold, and even greater with certain formulations (Klarmann and Shternov, 1936). The author has also found that a certain black fluid had a critical lethal concentration against *Salm. typhi* in the standard Rideal-Walker test of 1 in 1,900, but the equivalent concentration against *E. coli* was only 1 in 900 and against *Staph. aureus* as low as 1 in 300. The situation is further complicated by the fact that sometimes certain substituted or 'irregular' phenols are used, that is, phenols which have been chlorinated to some extent, or fractions from which, for commercial expediency, certain constituents have been removed because of their greater value in other industrial fields. Either procedure is undesirable in the disinfectants field because it also results in an unbalanced fluid, thus further underlining the fallacy of placing too much reliance on standard phenol coefficient methods for assessing disinfectants.

The higher phenolic fractions are also more sensitive to the influence of organic matter – a point of considerable practical importance. Generally speaking the low boiling fractions, as represented by lysol, are only little affected in this way, so that their Chick-Martin coefficients are almost the same as their Rideal-Walker coefficients. But as the Rideal-Walker coefficient increases with the different phenol fractions so the gap widens such that fluids with coefficients of 20 or 25 have Chick-Martin values of only about 4. Much higher concentrations of these fluids, then, are needed for effective disinfection than is indicated from their Rideal-Walker coefficient.

Lysol

Lysol in its various formulations differs from the black disinfectant fluids in that, besides being made exclusively with the lowest boiling coal tar fractions, consisting mainly of a mixture of the *o*-, *m*- and *p*-cresols distilling between 195° and 205°, it also contains a much higher proportion of soap. As such it remains clear on dilution with all but the hardest of waters.

The amount and the type of soap influences considerably the activity of the final preparation. According to Tilley and Schaffer (1925, 1930) the optimum ratio with coconut oil, linseed oil and soya bean oil soaps is 2 parts of cresol to 1 part of soap, and this is the ratio most commonly used in the various preparations today. The Lysol, or Cresol and Soap Solution, of the British Pharmacopoeia, 1963, contains 50 per cent of cresols and about 22 per cent of linseed oil soap and the Saponated Cresol Solution of the U.S. National Formulary XI, 1960, the same amount of cresols but about 40 per cent of vegetable oil soap. If excess of soap is added the cresols may be deprived of most, if not all, of their activity. This point was early observed by Tilley and Schaffer (1930), but its explanation was not forthcoming until the theory of micelle formation in soap solutions was expounded (*see* p. 339).

The influence of different soaps has been recognized for many years, probably even before Tilley and Schaffer (1925) reported on the greater germicidal activity of cresol when dissolved in the right proportion in coconut oil soap than when dissolved in linseed oil soap. Subsequently, Berry and Stenlake (1942) examined the effects of a range of oils and fatty acids and also found that coconut oil soaps give the most active product. Their findings with the various soaps are given in Table 41. The author has also examined a number of formulations of lysol at different times and has obtained Rideal-Walker coefficients varying from 2·0 with oleic acid soap to 2·6 with linseed oil and 3·0 with castor oil and palm kernel oil soaps. These differences can most probably be attributed to the different sized micelles formed by the different soaps and the consequently greater or less availabilities of the cresols. As already stated, the British Pharmacopoeia specifies linseed oil only, but the U.S. National Formulary allows of corn oil, cottonseed oil,

TABLE 41

Germicidal activity of solutions of cresol in soaps
(after Berry and Stenlake, 1942)

Soap made with	% added	Phenol coefficient against	
		Salm. typhi (R.W.)	*Staph. aureus*
Arachis oil fatty acid . .	15·7	1·6	2·0
Olive oil	approx. 22	1·8	1·6
Oleic acid	17·5	1·6	1·3
Cottonseed fatty acid . .	16·6	1·7	1·9
Linseed oil . .	13·0	2·4	2·0
Soya bean fatty acid .	15·2	2·0	1·8
Palm oil fatty acid . .	17·6	2·1	2·1
Castor oil	35·0	2·2	1·3
Ricinoleic acid . .	33·0	2·3	1·3
Coconut oil fatty acid. .	16·0	2·9	2·4

linseed oil and soya bean oil to the exclusion of coconut and palm kernel oils. The lysols at present on the market vary in their phenol coefficients between about 1·9 and 3·5. The latter is obviously a formulation boosted in some way.

Sudol. A particular lysol-type formulation which has attracted some attention of recent years is the product marketed under the trade name of Sudol (Finch, 1953). Although it is basically a coal tar disinfectant it has none of the toxic and irritant properties normally associated with these products and so it can be used with good effect as a normal skin disinfectant: it is also advocated for instrument sterilization and other hospital uses. The reason for its lack of irritancy is that the phenol fraction is a carefully selected one distilling mainly in the range 216°–221°. It therefore contains practically no cresols, and other undesirable dihydric phenols, bases and sulphur compounds are reduced to a minimum: its constituents, in fact, are primarily xylenols with *m*- and *p*-ethyl phenols. It has a Rideal-Walker coefficient of 5·4 and a Chick-Martin coefficient of 3·3 and it is active against a wide range of bacteria, including the pathogens. Its phenol coefficient with *Staph. aureus* is 4·6. Other similar preparations are now on the market.

Synthetic phenolic disinfectants

The advent of the group of disinfectants containing synthetic phenols was in Germany in 1927 when a patent was taken out for a chloroxylenol disinfectant preparation, although their fore-runners, the soap-based pine oil disinfectants, had been known for some time before. The synthetic phenols now used are either a chloroxylenol, *o*-phenylphenol (2-hydroxydiphenyl) or one of the other diphenyl derivatives, and a characteristic of such preparations, in contrast to the cresylic or coal tar disinfectants, is their lack of toxicity and irritant properties. This, of course, is largely because they employ purer compounds selected with these properties in view. A further advantage is that they continue to exert their antibacterial action for prolonged periods after application to any surface.

Chloroxylenol and similar preparations. Following the 1927 German patent for a disinfectant containing 29 per cent of chloroxylenol (*p*-chloro-*sym-m*-xylenol), 10 per cent of alcohol and 57 per cent of castor oil soap, and the publication by Colebrook and Maxted (1933) of the first report of the examination of such a product in Britain, a new era in disinfection was opened. Colebrook and Maxted found this preparation not only to have excellent skin disinfecting properties, particularly against the streptococci, but also to retain its activity for some hours after application. They, therefore, strongly recommended it as of special value in obstetrics and midwifery in preventing puerperal sepsis. Hitherto the pine oil disinfectants had been popular for household and personal use because of their non-toxic and non-irritant characteristics, but the publication of these findings focused immediate attention on the superiority of this new type of disinfectant, so that it began to take a prominent place in hospital and surgical practice. Solution of Chloroxylenol was listed for the first time in the Sixth Addendum, 1943, to the British Pharmacopoeia of 1938. It contains 5 per cent of chloroxylenol, *5* 10 per cent of terpineol, 20 per cent of alcohol and about 7·5 per cent of castor oil soap, and this solution is recommended for use in surgical and obstetric practice at a dilution not weaker than 1 in 4.

The chloroxylenol disinfectants all contain added pine oil or other terpenes, and these are the substances which impart the pleasant odours. They may have been added in the first place for this reason, or alternatively to render the new disinfectants not so very 'different' from the then popular pine oil disinfectants, but in fact the presence of terpineol and various terpenes actually potentiates the activity of the xylenols. The terpenes are, in fact, carriers in just the same way as the hydrocarbons are carriers for the phenols, and most probably they are interchangeable.

Many different chloroxylenol preparations are now on the market under various trade names, of which probably the best known and most widely advertised is Dettol. Some of them contain other phenolic additives such as dichlorophenol or benzylcresol and they are made with any of a number of different soaps, so that within the general formulation of the chloroxylenol disinfectants wide variations are possible. As a consequence they exhibit marked differences in their bactericidal properties, although these are more of a quantitative than a qualitative nature. Compared with other disinfectants they have only moderate Rideal-Walker coefficients. The B.P. solution has a value of about 4·5 and others range between about 3 and 11. But this value is probably the least important characteristic of this type of disinfectant, designed as it is for personal and surgical use. Other properties such as sustained activity on the skin, in the presence of blood and the like, are much more important, and performance tests of this type are much more fundamental. The results obtained with one such preparation on the market will serve to illustrate the order of activity expected. This preparation had a Rideal-Walker coefficient of about 6 and a Chick-Martin coefficient of about 1·2. When subjected to the test for retention of activity on the skin as given on page 95, in which a series of dilutions are applied to the skin and 2 hours later their lethal action is assessed against a freshly inoculated *Staph. aureus*, a 3·5 per cent dilution was still lethal in 5 minutes. The preparation killed a variety of pathogenic organisms suspended in 50 per cent serum at dilutions of 1 in 33 to 1 in 55 within 5 minutes, and a dilution of 1 in 16 in whole blood was also lethal to *Staph. aureus* in the same time.

One or two points to be noted in connexion with these preparations are: (*i*) their activities are always depressed to some extent by prolonged contact with whole blood, so that a higher concentration is necessary to effect the same order of kill after a blood mixture has been standing for an hour than when freshly made; (*ii*) many of the formulations when diluted to 10 per cent concentration or less with water are incapable of preventing the growth of the *Pseudomonas* group of organism, including *Ps. pyocyanea*, so that such a dilution left standing overnight might show quite high counts of these organisms (Lowbury, 1951). This does not apply to all formulations – the nature of the soap here is apparently significant – and it is not exclusive to chloroxylenol disinfectants – cetrimide solution is equally susceptible.

Besides Chloroxylenol B.P. another chloroxylenol, 2:4-dichloro-*sym-m*-xylenol (D.C.M.X.) has also received publicity. As a chemical entity it was first described in 1923, but it was not until some years later that its bactericidal activities in soap solutions were recognized (Gemmell, 1952). A solution containing 1·5 per cent of D.C.M.X., 5 per cent of pine oil and 26 per cent of castor oil soap has a Rideal-Walker coefficient of 3·5 (Gemmell, 1953). It is now a basic active constituent of several disinfectant formulations.

o-Phenylphenol is also used in similar formulations, and its activities are like those of the chloroxylenols. It is more active against *Ps. pyocyanea* than are the chloroxylenols, and it is said to be lethal to *Myco. tuberculosis* at concentrations of about 0·5 to 1 per cent (Tilley, MacDonald and Schaffer, 1931). A 5 per cent solution in a castor oil soap base with added terpene has a Rideal-Walker coefficient of 3·7 and a 13 per cent solution has a value of about 7·0.

Pine oil disinfectants. The pine oil disinfectants, if properly constituted with the right terpene fractions and a suitable soap base, are reasonably active against many types of bacteria. They may have phenol coefficients as high as 8 or 9, but they tend to be selective in their action. At dilutions of 1 in 50 or less they will destroy Gram-negative organisms in a few minutes, but against the staphylococci they are practically without effect; neither are they particularly effective against *Myco. tuberculosis* (Wright and Shternov, 1958), although others have held the opposite opinion. For these reasons they cannot be considered to be particularly useful for general disinfection purposes, and on the same grounds Reddish (1941) advised against them in surgery and for skin disinfection. Attempts to overcome this defect have been made by adding up to 3 per cent of dichloroxylenol (Gemmell, 1953) but without a great deal of success.

A correctly formulated pine oil disinfectant contains at least 60 per cent of pine oil, but many of the preparations on the market contain lower proportions than this of oils of inferior quality, and consequently they merit being classed as little more than deodorants. According to Hogg and Little (1935) the most active fraction of pine oil is α-terpineol, whilst the terpenes and other hydrocarbons are rated amongst the least active and may in some cases actually depress the efficacy of the terpineol. Likewise, the most suitable solubilizing agent is rosin soap, and this is the one most commonly used. Other soaps in order of their effectiveness are the linoleates, oleates, laurates, palmitates and stearates, an order which follows a similar pattern as for the soaps alone (*see* p. 338).

Soaps

Much attention has been given in the preceding pages to the various phenol-soap formulations. It seems appropriate now to consider the antibacterial properties of soaps themselves.

The majority of the ordinary toilet and technical soaps on the market are not particularly germicidal. They will certainly kill the more delicate and sensitive of the bacteria but none justifies any of the descriptions 'disinfectant', 'antiseptic' or 'germicidal'. Equally certainly they can remove a large proportion of the bacteria on the skin but this is due to the detergent properties of the soap removing the bacteria along with the dirt and other debris by physical means: it is not a lethal action, as is readily proved on bacteriological examination of soap washings. Some bacteria are, in fact, remarkably soap-tolerant and are found frequently on sponges and face flannels – they are nearly all Gram-negative types. One such organism studied in detail by Billing (1955) would grow readily on a peptone agar containing 10 per cent of ivory soap: it was originally described as *Bacillus anitratum* but is now considered to belong to the genus *Achromobacterium*.

Fatty acid soaps. Bayliss and Halvorson (1935) and Bayliss (1936) examined a large number of soaps made with long chain fatty acids and found that amongst the aliphatic series the unsaturated soaps, sodium oleate, linoleate and ricinoleate, were the most active, followed by the saturated soaps, sodium myristate and laurate, and further down the line, sodium palmitate. The ratios of their activities varied according to the organisms used but always the pneumococci were the most sensitive, the lethal concentrations ranging from 0·04 to 0·004 per cent. *Streptococcus lactis* was from about 2 to 10 times more resistant, and *E. coli* was susceptible to sodium myristate and palmitate, and also stearate, but not to the oleate or linoleate. These observations are broadly in line with the earlier ones of Walker (1926) who found that sodium and potassium laurate "killed the pneumococci and streptococci in high dilutions, and at the same time had an appreciable effect upon typhoid bacilli", whereas the oleates, linoleates, and linolenates, the unsaturated acids, "seemed to be entirely inert against typhoid bacilli". Klarmann and Shternov (1941) examined a series of aliphatic soaps and found that against a range of organisms "Only salts of fatty acids with 8 to 10 carbon atoms evidenced a germicidal efficiency of some note", although their activities against *Salm. typhi* and other Gram-negative bacteria were maintained from the C_8 compound onwards.

Natural oil soaps. The variations in bactericidal properties found between the soaps of the different fatty acids suggest that similar variations are to be expected between those of the natural oils, and in practice this is so. Of the commoner fats and oils, coconut oil soap is the most effective and this is followed by linseed oil, castor oil and cottonseed oil soaps. The rosin soaps, although in some respects in a class separate from ordinary soaps because of their different physical characteristics, have been classed as superior to even coconut oil soap because of their greater efficacy against the staphylococci (Klarmann and Shternov, 1941; Stuart and Pohle, 1941). The main constituent of rosin is abietic acid, one of the unsaturated acids, and soaps of this acid are themselves bactericidal. According to Stuart and Pohle (1941) a 2 per cent solution will kill *E. coli*, *Salm. typhi* and the staphylococci within 2–5 minutes, and according to Bayliss (1936) a 0·2 per cent solution will kill *Strep. lactis* in 10 minutes, but Walker (1926) found that a 10 per cent solution was needed to kill *Salm. typhi* in 2½ minutes and a 2·5 per cent solution to kill both this organism and *Staph. aureus* in 15 minutes.

The action of soaps on phenols

Having discussed the phenol-soap disinfectants mainly from the performance angle, it is proper to consider some of the more theoretical aspects of the role of soaps in the phenolic germicides.

Normally, the phenols are only slightly soluble in water, but their solubilities can be considerably increased by adding soaps. The effect of this on their bacteriological properties is that their activities may sometimes be increased and sometimes decreased, depending largely on the nature of the soap and on the proportion of soap to phenol. Tilley and Schaffer (1925) were the first to observe this variation in activity, and Frobisher (1927) was the first to describe it as a function of the concentration of the soap.

The role played by soap in bringing about the various changes in activity is complex, and numerous attempts have been made to explain the phenomena, all of which are based on the theory of micelle formation in soap solutions. This theory is based on the various findings of McBain, Hartley, Lawrence and others, and summaries of it have been conveniently given in a review article by Berry and Bean (1950) and by Moilliet and Collie (1951) in their book *Surface Activity*. Briefly, the theory states that as the concentration of a soap solution is increased, a stage is reached when the fatty acid ions merge together into 'ionic micelles'. The concentration at which this occurs is known as the 'critical concentration'. With further increases in concentration the number of micelles increases until a second critical concentration is reached beyond which no more micelle formation occurs. This is known as the 'concentration for completion of micelle formation'. The micelles are liquid structures and spherical in shape, and they were thought at first to be formed suddenly at a particular level of soap concentration, but this now seems to be doubtful. There is no doubt, however, that at a particular concentration the conductivity and other physical characteristics undergo a sudden change. During these phases, the solubility of phenols, and indeed of other organic substances, increases. Below the first critical concentration there is no apparent change in direct solubility – although a concentrated solution diluted to below this level always manifests a greater solubility than in plain water (Bean and Berry, 1950) – but at this point the solubility increases rapidly and goes on increasing until the second critical concentration is reached. After this it remains constant. The effect of these changes on the bactericidal activities of the solution varies according to the solution system under consideration. If the system is one such as was studied by Bean and Berry (1951, 1953) in which there is a constant phenol-soap ratio and a continuously increasing soap concentration, the bactericidal activity shows an initial rapid increase until it reaches a maximum at the first critical concentration. After this there is a decline in activity until the second critical concentration is reached, when again a change occurs and the activity goes on increasing until saturation is reached. The order of these changes is illustrated in the death times quoted in Table 42 for two phenols, benzyl-chlorophenol (5-chloro-2-hydroxydiphenylmethane) and chloroxylenol (*p*-chloro-*sym*-*m*-xylenol), dissolved in potassium laurate solution, in which two ratios of phenol-soap concentration were used for both phenols, and the death times were measured at different levels of soap concentration.

The proffered physical explanation of these phenomena (Bean and Berry, 1951) is that when a phenol is dissolved in an aqueous solution of a soap the majority of the phenol goes into 'solution' in the micelles, and only a small proportion goes into the water phase, depending on the partition coefficient of the phenol. When bacteria are introduced into such a system, the soap micelles are immediately adsorbed on the bacterial surfaces and carry with them relatively large amounts of the phenol which immediately diffuses into the cells. Thus, the first increase in activity arises simply from the continuous rise in concentration of the phenol due to its increasing solubility as more soap is added to form micelle units; the subsequent decline in activity is attributed to the increasing number of micelles which preferentially absorb

TABLE 42

Death times of E. coli in solutions of benzylchlorophenol and chloroxylenol in potassium laurate

(Bean and Berry, 1951, 1953)

Molar concentration of potassium laurate	Death times of benzyl-chlorophenol solution with phenol/soap ratio		Death times of chloro-xylenol solution with phenol/soap ratio	
	0.0666	0.0778	0.046	0.061
	minutes	minutes	minutes	minutes
0.0065	> 480	> 480	—	—
0.0081	—	190	—	—
0.0093	31.6	3.8	—	—
0.0113	—	2.3	—	213
0.0130	11.0	2.2	> 240	55.8
0.0162	4.6	1.3	16.3	7.2
0.0194	3.6	2.8	5.3	3.3
0.0227	2.4	2.1	—	2.6
0.0259	4.6	8.6	3.6	1.9
0.0292	—	—	—	3.0
0.0324	13.3	13.3	7.8	4.2
0.0389	44.4	29.1	11.3	4.3
0.0520	28.3	19.6	15.0	5.6
0.0648	23.6	14.6	10.0	6.2
0.0778	22.6	10.3	6.0	5.6
0.0907	16.6	3.3	4.6	3.2
0.1037	9.0	3.2	—	3.3
0.1167	6.3	2.6	—	—
0.1296	4.2	—	—	—
0.1555	2.5	—	—	—

the phenol to the detriment of its bactericidal efficiency, and the further increase in activity after the second critical concentration has been passed results in the cessation of micelle formation and the consequent greater availability of the phenol in its disinfectant role.

The foregoing explanations account for one phenol-soap system only, namely, that in which the ratio of the two components remains constant. If other systems are examined in which one of the components is kept at a constant level of concentration whilst the other is varied then different orders of activity are found. Thus, if the soap concentration is kept constant and the phenol increased the result is a continuous increase in activity until the solution becomes saturated with respect to phenol. Conversely, if the phenol concentration is kept constant and the soap increased, there is likely to be an initial increase in activity due to the increased solubility of the phenol, followed by a continuous decline due to the progressive reduction in availability of the phenol (Alexander and Tomlinson, 1949).

From the findings described above, Bean and Berry (1953) came to the conclusion that the bactericidal activity of a phenol solubilized by soap is a function of the concentration of the phenol in the soap micelles and is independent of the total amount of phenol in the system. But Alexander and Tomlinson (1949) were not in entire agreement with this. They conducted a series of experiments with phenol and Aerosol MA (sodium dihexylsulpho-succinate) in which the phenol concentration was kept constant at 1 per cent and the soap concentration was varied, and obtained the same order of change in activity as did Bean and Berry. They agreed that the first increase results from the greater adsorption of the soap, by virtue of its greater surface activity, and postulated that it thereby "opened up or modified in some way" the bacterial membrane to allow the phenol to penetrate more readily. Their explanation of the subsequent decline in activity after the first critical concentration had been passed, however, was that it was due to the increasing number of micelles which "tend to pick up phenol molecules from the solution, thus reducing the concentration of *free* phenol and so leading to a diminution in bactericidal efficiency." On the face of it this explanation is as feasible under the conditions given as that of Bean and Berry, but it must be borne in mind that Alexander and Tomlinson were considering a substance which is easily soluble in water, whereas Bean and Berry were experimenting with phenols which have very low solubilities.

The importance of these findings is relation to the activities of 'germicidal' soaps is discussed in pages 327–331.

Alcohols

The alcohols as a group possess a number of interesting and desirable properties in the sphere of disinfection, but only a few have found any real practical applications. These are ethyl alcohol, isopropyl alcohol, benzyl alcohol and ethylene and propylene glycols.

The glycols are mainly active in the aerosol form and as virucidal agents, and they are considered in these contexts in Chapters 8 and 11. Likewise, the main use of benzyl alcohol is as a preservative, and as such it is discussed in the chapter on Preservation (Chapter 17); its chlorinated derivatives however, are of much wider interest and so are included here.

Mechanism of action

The action of the alcohols is bactericidal rather than bacteriostatic and they are only effective against vegetative or non-sporing cells; they are also fungicidal. The most feasible explanation of the mechanism of the lethal action is through their capacity to denature proteins. This finds considerable support in the parallel observations that proteins are less readily denatured in the absence of water than in its presence and that absolute alcohol is a less effective bactericide than alcohol containing water. Protein denaturation also fits in with the observations made by Sykes (1939) that alcohol destroys the bacterial dehydrogenases and by Dagley, Dawes and Morrison (1950) that the lag phase in the growth of *Aerobacter aerogenes*, prolonged by several antibacterial agents, including alcohol, can be reversed by adding certain amino acids.

The activities of the alcohols increase as their molecular weight and chain length increase, in much the same way as do the alkyl phenols, although their

TABLE 43

Phenol coefficients of alcohols

Alcohol	Phenol coefficient against	
	Salm. typhi	*Staph. aureus*
Methyl . . .	0·026	0·03
Ethyl . . .	0·04	0·039
n-Propyl . .	0·102	0·082
Isopropyl . .	0·064	0·054
n-Butyl. . .	0·273	0·22
n-Amyl. . .	0·78	0·63
n-Hexyl . .	2·3	—
n-Heptyl . .	6·8	—
n-Octyl . . .	21·0	0·63

actions against the Gram-negative and Gram-positive organisms run much more closely together. To illustrate this the phenol coefficients of several of the aliphatic alcohols as obtained by Tilley and Schaffer (1926) are quoted in Table 43. It is also found that in terms of chain structure, the order of activities is as follows: primary-normal > primary-iso > secondary > tertiary alcohols.

Against spores. Against bacterial spores the alcohols are practically non-lethal. Coulthard and Sykes (1936) quote several references in the earlier literature to the survival of spores for many months in ethyl alcohol of various concentrations, and several similar observations have been made subsequently. There is one record of the survival of anthrax spores in alcohol for 20 years and another one of *Bacillus subtilis* for 9 years. The lack of sporicidal action is not confined to ethyl alcohol, it applies to all of the alcohols (Tanner and Wilson, 1943). They can, however, be rendered sporicidal by adding 1 per cent of a mineral acid or of a caustic alkali or even by adding 10 per cent of amyl-*m*-cresol, and under these conditions even the most resistant spores are killed within 4 hours (Coulthard and Sykes, 1936).

Ethyl alcohol

The bactericidal activity of ethyl alcohol has been known since the time of Koch, and even as early as the 1890s it was stated that the optimum concentration was about 70 per cent. Whilst this has been accepted almost undisputed for many years, there is in fact little evidence to support it, and, as pointed out by Morton (1950) "it appears that too much emphasis has been placed on the importance of diluting 95 per cent alcohol to a lower concentration." It is often difficult to differentiate between the rate of kill of organisms in suspension with alcohol concentrations between about 50 per cent and 95 per cent by volume because it is always so rapid, but so far as can be judged there is a tendency for the death rate to increase as the concentration is raised from 60 to 95 per cent. Above 95 per cent, Archer (1945) found a significant decline in activity.

On surfaces, the differentiation seems to be much more clear-cut. Thus, with suspensions of organisms, Coulthard and Sykes (1936) and Morton (1950) found that alcohol concentrations between 60 per cent and 95 per cent by volume killed *Staph. aureus*, *Strep. pyogenes*, *E. coli* and other organisms within 10 seconds; similarly Price (1939) obtained kills of *E. coli* at 60 per cent and 80 per cent concentrations in 60 seconds and in less than 30 seconds respectively, and Smith (1947) observed that whereas 95 per cent alcohol killed tubercle bacilli in water in 15 seconds, 70 per cent killed in 60 seconds. On the other hand, the optimum rate of kill of *Staph. aureus* dried on threads occurs at concentrations of about 60–75 per cent, and Smith (1947) concluded that 50 per cent alcohol was best for disinfecting dry tubercle-infected surfaces and 70 per cent for moist surfaces. Likewise, Price (1951), as a result of a series of hand-washing tests, found 70 per cent alcohol more effective on the average than other concentrations and recommended it for routine surgical use.

Much lower concentrations are lethal to vegetative bacteria if longer periods of contact are allowed. Thus, in 24 hours a 5 per cent solution will kill *Pneumococcus* type I, an 8 per cent solution will kill *Strep. pyogenes*, and a 15 per cent solution will kill *Staph. albus* (Robertson *et al.*, 1948). Similarly a 20 per cent solution is slowly lethal to mould spores, although concentrations above about 5 per cent will inhibit the growth of most of them.

Against viruses, concentrations of alcohol above about 60 per cent appear to be active, but not rapidly so. The actual time of inactivation naturally varies with the particular type of virus, but at all levels it is measured in minutes if not in hours. This is because the viruses are almost invariably suspended in tissue or body fluid, the protein of which, when in contact with alcohol, is precipitated and so affords some protection to the virus. It is dangerous, therefore, to use alcohol for wiping instruments or for disinfecting syringes and needles which might be contaminated with blood carrying the virus of infective hepatitis.

Uses of alcohol. There is ample evidence to show that alcohol is effective in reducing the bacterial flora of the skin. It is also readily volatile and so leaves the skin dry almost immediately. For certain purposes this is an advantage, but for others it is a disadvantage because it means that there is no sustained antibacterial activity. According to Pillsbury, Livingood and Nichols (1942) concentrations over 70 per cent can be used safely for pre-operative skin preparations, and this was confirmed by Price (1951) and by Story (1950) who obtained a complete kill of all skin flora after a 30 seconds' swabbing.

A solution of 50 per cent alcohol and 10 per cent acetone is often used as the solvent for preparations intended for skin disinfection. This is undoubtedly a sound policy because of the efficacy of the solvent itself. In fact, as Morton (1950) states "it would be difficult to improve upon the germicidal action of a 50 per cent alcohol solution on organisms in a moist environment by the addition of another ingredient." There is the point, however, that the addition of a suitable non-volatile substance would ensure the continuance of the bactericidal action after the alcohol has evaporated.

Alcohol is not to be recommended for sterilizing instruments, partly because of its lack of sporicidal action and partly because of its lack of penetrability into blood and pus clots. But it can be used effectively for disinfecting clinical thermometers, provided the treatment is long enough. Smith (1947) asserted that they could be kept completely non-infectious, even from tubercle bacilli, by immersion in 70 per cent alcohol – a 50 per cent solution will not achieve this (Wright and Mundy, 1958) – and Gershenfeld, Greene and Witlin (1951) were likewise able to kill a variety of organisms by immersion for periods of a few seconds up to 10 minutes; Frobisher, Sommermeyer and Blackwell (1953) also found a 10-minute soak effective against the cocci, and the tubercle and diphtheria bacilli. In these tests the organisms were dried on the thermometer from sputum, and it was found advantageous to wipe the stems before immersing in the alcohol. McCulloch (1945) has suggested that only oral thermometers should be treated this way; rectal thermometers, being more highly contaminated, need a more rigorous and reliable treatment.

Isopropyl alcohol

In their investigations into the bactericidal properties of alcohols, Coulthard and Sykes (1936) found isopropyl alcohol to be slightly more effective than ethyl alcohol against vegetative organisms but completely inert against bacterial spores, and later investigations have broadly confirmed this. Against tubercle infections in dried sputum smears, Smith (1947) found isopropyl alcohol to be about as effective as alcohol in the upper levels of concentration, although more effective at lower levels, and Gershenfeld, Greene and Witlin (1951) and Frobisher, Sommermeyer and Blackwell (1953) confirmed this in disinfecting clinical thermometers.

Chlorinated benzyl alcohols

In common with many other compounds, halogenation of benzyl alcohol enhances its bactericidal properties, and several such derivatives have been examined by Carter *et al.* (1958). These included mono-, di- and tri-chloro substituents as well as several bromo and other derivatives, and they found the most active inhibitory member of the series to be 3:4:5-trichlorobenzyl alcohol; the 4:chloro-2:5-dimethyl, 2:4-dichloro and 3:4-dichloro compounds were, however, more rapidly bactericidal. 2:4-Dichlorobenzyl alcohol in particular is lethal at a concentration of 1 in 1,000 to a range of bacteria within one hour.

This compound, or one of its isomers, in 1 per cent solution was found to be a good skin disinfectant, reducing the bacterial count by 90–96 per cent (Grün, 1959).

Formaldehyde

Formaldehyde is an effective disinfectant both as a gas and in aqueous solution, and it has the particular advantage of being not only bactericidal but also sporicidal and fungicidal. Its properties in the gaseous form and its efficacy as a virucidal agent are dealt with in Chapters 8 and 11 respectively, so that here it is only necessary to mention briefly its activities in aqueous solution.

Germicidal activities

Lethal and bacteriostatic properties. The literature contains varied opinions concerning the sporicidal power of formaldehyde in solution. At one end of the scale we find a record of a 0·5 per cent solution said to be lethal to the spore-forming aerobes in 6–12 hours and at the other end of the scale a 5 per cent solution not killing the spores of *Bacillus anthracis* until after 32 hours' contact (Chick, 1908). These differences can be accounted for in the high degree of bacteriostasis exerted by formaldehyde and in its comparatively high temperature coefficient. The author has found that on some occasions *E. coli* and *Staph. aureus* are completely inhibited from growth in nutrient broth concentrations as low as 1 in 25,000 or even 1 in 50,000, and, therefore, unless special precautions are taken to neutralize the residual formaldehyde a false conception of its lethal activity could be obtained. Serum is not very effective because, even with a 20 per cent addition to nutrient broth, the inhibitory dilution is still of the order of 1 in 10,000. Nordgren (1939) has suggested adding up to 6 per cent of sodium sulphite to ordinary culture media, but Nash and Hirch (1954) found an equimolecular mixture of dimedone and morpholine to be more effective.

Effect of temperature. Chick's observation that a 5 per cent solution of formaldehyde was lethal to *B. anthracis* only after 32 hours refers to its efficacy at 20°; when the temperature was raised to 37° a complete kill was registered after only 90 minutes. Similarly, McCulloch and Costigan (1936) measured the concentration lethal to a suspension of *Salm. typhi* in 5 minutes and obtained total extinctions at 40° with dilutions down to 1 in 250, but only with dilutions down to 1 in 35 at 20° and down to 1 in 17·5 at 2°. These observations indicate a high temperature coefficient.

Antifungal activity. The common moulds are much more resistant than are the bacteria, and they are only inhibited in plain broth by dilutions of about 1 in 1,000. According to Emmons (1933) formaldehyde has a phenol coefficient of 2·5 against *M. albicans* and *Trichophyton gypseum*, and it appears to be the disinfectant of choice for treating footwear in cases of athlete's foot.

Uses

A formaldehyde-alcohol mixture is a more effective sterilizing agent than a plain aqueous solution of formaldehyde and the author has found that a 5 per cent solution of Formalin in alcohol will effectively sterilize all spores in 24 hours at 25°. Longer contact times are required at lower temperatures, but at 37° even a 1 per cent solution will kill in 24 hours. Various mixtures of this type, as well as those containing borax and Formalin, are used for the cold sterilization of instruments, and the addition of certain soaps is said to be even more advantageous. Some of these solutions are liable to cause corrosion and for this reason the formulations with borax are to be preferred. For some years the author used a mixture mainly of 11 per cent of Formalin, 0·1 per cent of borax and 1 per cent of terpineol in isopropyl alcohol for syringe sterilization, but it was unpleasant to handle because of the extreme pungency of the formaldehyde vapour. This is a disadvantage with all forms of formaldehyde sterilization.

A 10 per cent solution is a satisfactory disinfectant for thermometers (Wright and Mundy, 1958), and a water-in-oil emulsion containing 20 per cent of formaldehyde in white spirit has been advocated for disinfecting blankets, the advantage being that there is a residual germicidal activity for some time after treatment (Finch, 1958).

Glutaraldehyde

This compound was first selected as the most active of a series of dialdehydes (Pepper and Chandler, 1963).It is more active than glyoxal and substantially more active than formaldehyde, and does not have the toxic and irritant properties of the latter. It is necessary to 'activate' the solution by buffering it to pH 7·5 to 8·5 and adding a surface tension depressant (Stonehill, Krop and Borick, 1963), but according to Pepper and Chandler (1963) the necessary 'adjuvant' is 70 per cent isopropanol, in other words, the solvent must be 70 per cent isopropanol; even another alcohol is not suitable. A 2 per cent solution, thus activated, kills vegetative bacteria in 3 minutes, bacterial spores in 3 hours and tubercle bacilli and viruses in 10 minutes. The solution, available commercially as Cidex, is recommended for disinfecting instruments and hospital equipment which cannot be treated by heat; it is still active in the presence of blood (Stonehill, Krop and Borick, 1963; Rittenburg and Hench, 1965; Snyder and Cheatle, 1965).

REFERENCES

AALTO, T. R., FIRMAN, M. C. and RIGLER, N. E. (1953). *J. Amer. pharm. Ass. (Sci.)*, **42**, 449.
AGAR, ANNE and ALEXANDER, A. E. (1949). *Trans. Faraday Soc.*, **45**, 528.
ALEXANDER, A. E. and TOMLINSON, A. J. H. (1949). *Surface Activity*, p. 317: Butterworths, London.
ALEXANDER, J. C. (1961). *Lancet*, ii, 315.
ANDERSON, K. (1962). *Med. J. Austral.*, **2**, 463.
ARCHER, G. T. L. (1945). *Brit. med. J.*, ii, 148.
BARBER, MARY and HASLEWOOD, G. A. D. (1945). *Biochem. J.*, **39**, 285.
BAYLISS, M. (1936). *J. Bact.*, **31**, 489.
BAYLISS, M. and HALVORSON, H. O. (1935). *J. Bact.*, **29**, 9.
BEAN, H. S. and BERRY, H. (1950). *J. Pharm. Pharmacol.*, **2**, 484.
BEAN, H. S. and BERRY, H. (1951). *J. Pharm. Pharmacol.*, **3**, 639.
BEAN, H. S. and BERRY, H. (1953). *J. Pharm. Pharmacol.*, **5**, 632.
BECK, A. C. (1933). *Amer. J. Obstet. Gynec.*, **26**, 885.
BERRY, H. and BEAN, H. S. (1950). *J. Pharm., Pharmacol.*, **2**, 473.
BERRY, H. and STENLAKE, J. B. (1942). *Pharm. J.*, **148**, 112.
BILLING, EVE (1955). *J. gen. Microbiol.*, **13**, 252.
BIRKHAUG, K. E. (1931). *J. infect. Dis.*, **48**, 212.
BLICKE, F. F. and STOCKHAUS, R. P. (1933). *J. Amer. pharm. Ass. (Sci.)*, **22**, 1090.
CADE, A. R. (1944). *Soap*, **20(2)**, 111.
CARTER, D. V., CHARLTON, P. T., FENTON, A. H. and LESSEL, B. (1958). *J. Pharm. Pharmacol.*, **10**, 149T.
CHICK, HARRIETTE (1908). *J. Hyg., Camb.*, **8**, 92.
COATES, L. V., DRAIN, D. J., KERRIDGE, K. A., MACREA, F. JUNE, and TATTERSALL, K. (1957). *J. Pharm. Pharmacol.*, **9**, 855.
COLEBROOK, L. and MAXTED, W. R. (1933). *J. Obstet. Gynace., Brit. Emp.*, **60**, 966.
COOPER, E. A. (1948). *J. Soc. chem. Ind.*, **67**, 69.
COULTHARD, C. E. (1931). *Brit. J. exp. Path.*, **12**, 331.
COULTHARD, C. E., MARSHALL, J. and PYMAN, F. L. (1930). *J. chem. Soc.*, p. 280.
COULTHARD, C. E. and SYKES, G. (1936). *Pharm. J.*, **137**, 79.
DAGLEY, S., DAWES, E. A. and MORRISON, G. A. (1950). *J. Bact.*, **60**, 369.
DAVIS, B. D. (1950). *Nature, Lond.*, **166**, 1120.
DAVIES, G. E., FRANCIS, J., MARTIN, A. R., ROSE, F. L. and SWAIN, G. (1954). *Brit. J. Pharmacol.*, **9**, 192.
DOHME, A. R. L., COX, E. H. and MILLER, E. (1926). *J. Amer. chem. Soc.*, **48**, 1688.
EMMONS, C. W. (1933). *Arch. Dermatol. Syphylol.*, **28**, 15.
ERLANDSON, A. L. and LAWRENCE, C. A. (1953). *Science*, **118**, 274.
FAULKNER, G. H. (1944). *Biochem. J.*, **38**, 370.
FINCH, W. E. (1953). *Pharm. J.*, **170**, 59.
FINCH, W. E. (1958). *Pharm. J.*, **181**, 491.
FROBISHER, M. (1927). *J. Bact.*, **13**, 163.
FROBISHER, M., SOMMERMEYER, L. and BLACKWELL, M. J. (1953). *Appl. Microbiol.*, **1**, 187.
FROST, H. E. (1961). *Lancet*, ii, 877.
GALE, E. F. and TAYLOR, E. SHIRLEY (1947). *J. gen. Microbiol.*, **1**, 77.
GEMMELL, J. (1952). *Mfg Chem.*, **24**, 143.
GEMMELL, J. (1953). *Soap*, **29(3)**, 95.
GERSHENFELD, L. and PERLSTEIN, D. (1939). *Amer. J. Pharm.*, **111**, 227.
GERSHENFELD, L., GREENE, A. and WITLIN, B. (1951). *J. Amer. pharm. Ass. (Sci.)*, **40**, 457.
GIBSON, J. (1936). *Chem. & Ind.*, **55**, 107.

GRÜN, L. (1959). *Medizinische*, no. 13, p. 595.
GUMP, W. S. and CADE, A. R. (1952). *Soap*, **28**(12), 52.
GUMP, W. S. and CADE, A. R. (1953a). *Soap*, **29**(11), 91.
GUMP, W. S. and CADE, A. R. (1953b). *Mfg Chem.*, **24**, 143.
HARRIS, S. E. and CHRISTIANSEN, W. G. (1934). *J. Amer. pharm. Ass. (Sci.)*, **23**, 530.
HEINEMANN, B. (1944). *J. lab. clin. Med.*, **29**, 254.
HOGG, G. F. and LITTLE, B. H. (1935). *Soap*, **11**(6), 125.
HOPPER, S. H. and WOOD, K. M. (1958). *J. Amer. pharm. Ass. (Sci.)*, **47**, 317.
HURST, A., STUTTARD, L. W. and WOODROFFE, R. C. S. (1960). *J. Hyg., Camb.*, **58**, 159.
KLARMANN, E. G., GATES, L. W. and SHTERNOV, V. A. (1931). *J. Amer. chem. Soc.*, **53**, 3397.
KLARMANN, E. G., GATES, L. W. and SHTERNOV, V. A. (1932). *J. Amer. chem. Soc.*, **54**, 298, 1204.
KLARMANN, E. G., GATES, L. W., SHTERNOV, V. A. and COX, P. H. (1933). *J. Amer. chem. Soc.*, **55**, 4657.
KLARMANN, E. G. and SHTERNOV, V. A. (1936). *Ind. engng Chem. (Anal.)*, **8**, 369.
KLARMANN, E. G. and SHTERNOV, V. A. (1941). *Soap*, **17**(1), 23.
KLARMANN, E. G., SHTERNOV, V. A. and GATES, L. W. (1933). *J. Amer chem. Soc.*, **55**, 2576.
KLARMANN, E. G., SHTERNOV, V. A. and GATES, L. W. (1934). *J. lab. clin. Med.*, **20**, 40.
KLARMANN, E. G., SHTERNOV, V. A. and VON WOWERN, J. (1929). *J. Bact.*, **17**, 423.
KUNZ, E. C. and GUMP, W. S. (1942). Brit. Pat. 545, 648.
LAWRENCE, C. A. (1960). *J. Amer. pharm. Ass. (Sci.)*, **49**, 731.
LEHN and FINK, INC. (1932). Brit. Pat. 422, 219.
LEHN and FINK, INC. (1936). Brit. Pat. 484, 228.
LECOQ, R., LANDRIN, P. and SOLOMIDÈS, J. (1949). *Compt. rend. Acad. Sci.*, **228**, 1385.
LENNON, W. J., FURIA, T. E. and ZUSSMAN, H. W. (1960). *Soap*, **36**(3), 51.
LOWBURY, E. J. L. (1951). *Brit. J. ind. Med.*, **8**, 22.
LOWBURY, E. J. L. and LILLEY, H. A. (1960). *Brit. Med. J.*, i, 1445.
LUBSEN, N., BOISSEVAIN, W. and FASS, HANNA (1961). *Lancet*, i, 921.
McCULLOCH, E. C. (1945). *Disinfection and Sterilization:* Kimpton, London.
McCULLOCH, E. C. and COSTIGAN, STELLA M. (1936). *J. infect. Dis.*, **59**, 281.
MacDONALD, ETTA M. (1942). *J. Amer. pharm. Ass. (Pract.)*, **3**, 181.
MARSH, P. B. and BUTLER, MARY L. (1946). *Ind. engng Chem.*, **38**, 701.
MILLER, CATHERINE R. and ELSON, W. D. (1949). *J. Bact.*, **57**, 47.
MOILLIET, J. L. and COLLIE, B. (1951). *Surface Activity:* Spon, London.
MORTON, H. E. (1950). *Ann. N.Y. Acad. Sci.*, **53**, 191.
MYERS, G. E., MacKENZIE, W. C. and WARD, K. A. (1956). *Canad. J. Microbiol.*, **2**, 87.
NASH, T. and HIRCH, ANN (1954). *J. appl. Chem.*, **4**, 458.
NIEDERL, J. B., NIEDERL, V., SHAPIRO, S. and McGREAL, M. E. (1937). *J. Amer. chem. Soc.*, **59**, 1113.
NORDGREN, G. (1939). *Acta path. microbiol. scand.*, Suppl. 40.
ORDAL, E. J. (1941). *Proc. Soc. exp. Biol., N.Y.*, **47**, 387.
ORDAL, E. J., WILSON, J. L. and BORG, A. F. (1941). *J. Bact.*, **42**, 117.
PANZARELLA, F. P. and DEXTER, D. D. (1961). *Soap*, **37**(12), 73.
PEPPER, R. E. and CHANDLER, VELMA L. (1963). *Appl. Microbiol.*, **11**, 384.
PILLSBURY, D. M., LIVINGOOD, C. S. and NICHOLS, A. C. (1942). *Arch. Dermatol. Syphylol.*, **45**, 61.
PRICE, P. B. (1939). *Arch. Surg.*, **38**, 528.
PRICE, P. B. (1951). *Drug Stds*, **19**, 161.
PRICE, P. B. and BONNETT, A. (1948). *Surgery*, **24**, 542.
RAPPS, N. F. (1933). *J. Soc. chem. Ind.*, **52**, 175T.
READ, R. R. and MILLER, E. (1932). *J. Amer. chem. Soc.*, **54**, 1195.
REDDISH, G. F. (1941). *Soap*, **17**(9), 88.
RICHARDSON, E. M. and REID, E. F. (1940). *J. Amer. chem. Soc.*, **62**, 413.
RITTENBURY, M. S. and HENCH, M. E. (1965). *Ann. Surg.*, **161**, 127.
ROBERTSON, O. H., APPEL, E. M., PUCK, T. T., LEMON, H. M. and RITTER, M. H. (1948). *J. infect. Dis.*, **83**, 124.
ROMAN, D. P., BARNETT, E. H. and BALSKE, R. J. (1958). *Soap*, **34**(1), 35.

SABALITSCHKA, T. (1924). *Pharm. Monat.*, **5**, 235.
SALLE, A. J. and GUEST, H. L. (1944). *Proc. Soc. exp. Biol., N.Y.*, **55**, 26.
SCOTT, J. C. (1961). *Lancet*, **i**, 1292.
SCHAFFER, J. M. and TILLEY, F. W. (1926). *J. Bact.*, **12**, 307.
SCHAFFER, J. M. and TILLEY, F. W. (1927). *J. Bact.*, **14**, 259.
SEASTONE, C. V. (1947). *Surg. Gynec. Obstet.*, **84**, 355.
SHUMARD, R. S., BEAVER, D. J. and HUNTER, M. C. (1953). *Soap*, **29**(1), 34.
SMITH, C. R. (1947). *Publ. Hlth Rep., Wash.*, **62**, 1285.
SMYLIE, H. G., WEBSTER, C. V. and BRUCE, MARION L. (1959). *Brit. med. J.*, **ii**, 606.
SNYDER, R. W. and CHEATLE, ESTHER L. (1965). *Amer. J. hosp. Pharm.*, **22**, 321.
SOKOL, H. (1952). *Drug Stds*, **20**, 89.
STONEHILL, A. A., KROP, S. and BORICK, P. M. (1963). *Amer. J. hosp. Pharm.*, **20**, 458.
STORY, P. (1950). *Brit. med. J.*, **ii**, 1128.
STUART, L. S. and POHLE, W. D. (1941). *Soap*, **17**(2), 34; **17**(3), 34.
SUTER, C. M. (1941). *Chem. Rev.*, **28**, 269.
SUTER, C. M. and WESTON, A. W. (1939). *J. Amer. chem. Soc.*, **61**, 232.
SYKES, G. (1939). *J. Hyg., Camb.*, **39**, 463.
TANNER, F. W. and WILSON, FERNE L. (1943). *Proc. Soc. exp. Biol., N.Y.*, **52**, 138.
TEZUKA, E. (1940). *Jap. J. exp. Med.*, **18**, 387; via *Brit. Chem. Abs.*, *AIII* (1941), p. 1063.
TILLEY, F. W., MACDONALD, A. D. and SCHAFFER, J. M. (1931). *J. agric. Res.*, **42**, 653.
TILLEY, F. W. and SCHAFFER, J. M. (1925). *J. infect. Dis.*, **37**, 359.
TILLEY, F. W. and SCHAFFER, J. M. (1926). *J. Bact.*, **12**, 303.
TILLEY, F. W. and SCHAFFER, J. M. (1930). *J. agric. Res.*, **41**, 737.
TRAUB, E. F., NEWHALL, C. A. and FULLER, J. R. (1944). *Surg. Gynec. Obstet.*, **79**, 205.
WALKER, J. E. (1926). *J. infect. Dis.*, **38**, 127.
WALTER, G. and GUMP, W. S. (1963). *Soap*, **39**(7), 55.
WEATHERALL, J. A. C. and WINNER, H. I. (1963). *J. Hyg., Camb.*, **61**, 443.
WITHELL, E. R. (1942). *Quart. J. Pharm.*, **15**, 301.
WOLF, P. A. and WESTVEER, W. M. (1952). *Arch. Biochem. Biophys.*, **40**, 306.
WOODWARD, G. J., KINGERY, L. B. and WILLIAMS, R. J. (1934). *J. lab. clin. Med.*, **19**, 1216.
WRIGHT, ELEANOR S. and SHTERNOV, V. A. (1958). *Soap*, **34**(9), 95.
WRIGHT, ELEANOR S. and MUNDY, R. M. (1958). *Appl. Microbiol.*, **6**, 381.
ZONDEK, N. (1942). *Nature, Lond.*, **149**, 334.

CHAPTER 13

DYES

THE triphenylmethane dyes and the acridine compounds have been established as valuable antibacterial substances mainly in the treatment of wounds and burns since their first introduction into medicine a year or two before the First World War, but the more recent advent of the sulphonamides and antibiotics has now largely displaced them. For this reason little investigational work has been made on them during the last ten years or so.

The antiseptic dyes are all characterized by their outstanding powers of bacteriostasis, even at quite high dilutions, and by their selective activity against the Gram-positive group of organisms. This selectivity is so pronounced in some compounds, *e.g.* Brilliant Green and Crystal Violet, that they can be incorporated in various nutrient media for diagnostic selective purposes. Bacteriostasis is brought about by their interference in some way with the reproductive mechanism of the cell, which prolongs the lag phase and leads to its ultimate death. Thus, although the dyes are primarily bacteriostatic in their action, they are also slowly lethal.

Triphenylmethane dyes

The triphenylmethane dyes of principal bacteriological interest are Malachite Green, Brilliant Green and Crystal Violet; the last is also known as Methyl Violet or, in its crude form, as Gentian Violet. All of these compounds are amino derivatives of triphenylmethane, the first two being diamino compounds and the last a triamino compound.

Methylene Blue was actually one of the first dyes to be used medicinally in urinary and intestinal antisepsis, but now it is only of minor interest.

Mode of action

The antibacterial properties of the dyes were first recognized by Churchman (1912), who found them to be mainly bacteriostatic in their action and postulated that this arose through their affinities for certain of the bacterial protoplasmic substances. In other words, he inferred that they act as protoplasmic poisons. Stearn and Stearn (1924, 1926) extended this idea and developed the further hypothesis that the action is due to the dye radicals entering into combination with the amphoteric constituents of the cell to form unionized complexes, the basic dyes combining with the acidic groups and the acidic dyes with the basic groups. Whilst this seems to be a reasonable extension to Churchman's theory, Fischer and Muñoz (1947) pointed out certain anomalies which occur with the acidic dyes and also drew attention to the apparent difference in the mode of action of the alkylated and non-alkylated dyes. On these and other grounds, therefore, they were not disposed to conclude any further than that "In our opinion a modernized form of Churchman's hypothesis may be accepted, namely, that triphenylmethane dyes act by blocking some important biological mechanisms, possibly connected with oxidation processes." This theory may or may not be associated with the idea that the dyes poise the oxidation-reduction potential at levels above those at which the organisms are able to grow (Dubos, 1929; Ingraham, 1933; Rahn, 1945).

Relationship between constitution and activity. Numerous investigations have been made into the effects of various substituents on the activities of the triphenylmethane dyes, all of which have been effectively summarized by Fischer and Muñoz (1947) as follows:

(*i*) the triphenylmethane compounds are more active than are the diphenylmethanes;

(*ii*) the presence of amino groups is essential. It is not necessary, however, to substitute in each phenyl radical; two such substitutions are as effective as three;

(*iii*) methylation of the amino groups increases activity substantially. Ethylation is even more advantageous, but phenylation has a reducing effect;

(*iv*) conversion of one amino group into a quaternary ammonium radical greatly diminishes activity.

On this basis the most active compounds should be the tetramethyl or tetraethyl derivatives of the diamino compounds, or the hexamethyl or hexaethyl derivatives of the triamino compounds, and this is in fact the case. Malachite Green (tetramethyldiaminotriphenylmethane), Brilliant Green (the tetraethyldiamino compound), and Crystal Violet (the hexamethyl-triamino compound) are all highly active.

Uses and activities of the medicinal dyes

Brilliant Green inhibits the growth of staphylococci and streptococci in broth at concentrations between 1 in 750,000 and 1 in 5,000,000 and the Gram-negative organisms between 1 in 100,000 and 1 in 500,000. Similarly, Crystal Violet inhibits the cocci in the range 1 in 200,000 to 1 in 300,000, but ten times these concentrations are needed to inhibit *Escherichia coli.* Crystal Violet is also fungistatic and it is used against mycotic skin affections. According to Gomez-Vega (1935) a 1 in 10,000 solution is lethal to *Monilia* and *Torula* spp. within 30 minutes, and 1 in 1,000,000 will inhibit their growth, but other species, *e.g. Trichophyton* and *Epidermophyton*, are somewhat more resistant.

Serum and other body fluids substantially reduce the activities of the dyes so that much higher concentrations have to be used in clinical practice. Thus a 0·5 per cent solution of Crystal Violet or a 0·05 to 0·1 per cent solution of Brilliant Green in water or in hypertonic saline is recommended for treating infected wounds or burns or skin affections, but for skin disinfection and in gynaecology it is more usual to employ the B.P.C. Paint of Brilliant Green and Crystal Violet. This is a solution in water of equal parts of the two dyes each at a concentration of 0·5 per cent.

The greater activities of the dyes against the Gram-positive organisms has been put to good use by incorporating them in culture media for the selective culture of the Gram-negative types for certain diagnostic purposes. And not only are they useful for this selectivity but also for differentiating between certain types of the Gram-positive organisms, and even between pathogenic and non-pathogenic strains of *Staphylococcus aureus* (Chapman and Berens, 1935). Compound Paint of Crystal Violet B.P.C., or the so-called triple dye paint, is also used for application to burns, and this contains 0·229 per cent of Brilliant Green, 0·229 per cent of Crystal Violet and 0·114 per cent of Proflavine Hemisulphate.

The acridines

Interest in the acridines dates from the end of the nineteenth century when Ehrlich produced his trypaflavine for the treatment of trypanosomal infections, but it was not until after Browning had discovered the antibacterial properties of the aminoacridines in 1913 that they became acknowledged as important antiseptic compounds. One outstanding characteristic is their sustained, and sometimes enhanced, activity in the presence of serum (Browning and Gilmour, 1913). This was, and still is, unique amongst the antiseptics and immediately focused attention on their clinical potentialities. They were used extensively in the chemotherapeutic treatment of wounds and burns during both World Wars, and they still have applications in this field. Of later years, the chemistry and biological activities of the acridines have been the subject of several investigations, the majority of which have come from Albert and his school, and a "critical and orderly summary" of the subject has recently been presented by Albert (1951) in his book *The Acridines.**

It was early established that the complete acridine nucleus is essential for high antibacterial activity in this type of compound and that the presence of one or more amino groups is especially beneficial. For this reason, bacteriological interests have always been centred on the aminoacridines.

---

* Confusion has arisen in the past in interpreting the investigations of various workers due to the different systems of numbering used. The most generally accepted system, and the one used in the present context, is as follows:

Mode of action

The acridines differ from the phenols in almost every aspect of their mode and mechanism of action on the bacterial cell. They are powerfully bacteriostatic and only slowly bactericidal, they are selective in their activities against the different types of organism, and the effect of various substituent radicals is often quite different from that found with the phenols. They lack fungistatic properties.

Mechanism of bacteriostasis. Several studies have been made, notably by McIlwain (1941) and by Hinshelwood and his school (*e.g.* Davies, Hinshelwood and Pryce, 1944; Peacocke and Hinshelwood, 1948; Caldwell and Hinshelwood, 1950), of the mechanism of the antibacterial action of the acridines, from which it is now becoming clear that it is a result of their interference with an enzyme or other metabolic centre essential to the reproduction of the cell. It is not associated with the suppression of the respiratory enzymes, since there is no correlation between the order of this occurrence and of inhibition of growth (Ferguson and Thorne, 1946), but appears to be closely involved with the prevention of a fundamental oxidative process. According to the evidence of Caldwell and Hinshelwood (1950), this process is concerned in the synthesis of one of the ribose complexes, probably deoxyribose.

Significance of ionization. It has long been known that the acridines are more active in alkaline solutions than in acid ones but the significance of this in terms of their mode of action was not appreciated until after Albert and his colleagues had begun their investigations. These investigations, which involved the preparation and examination of 107 acridine compounds, were published in a series of papers between 1941 and 1948 (*see* list of references, p. 361). They led to the firm conclusions that: (*i*) the acridines are actively bacteriostatic only in their ionized form, (*ii*) ionization must be cationic and not anionic or zwitterionic, and (*iii*) the degree of ionization must be 50 per cent or more at pH 7·3 and 37°. Furthermore, they tended to confirm the postulate that the mechanism is one of competition and displacement of hydrogen ions or hydrogen carriers from vitally important enzyme centres of the cell (McIlwain, 1941). These are now thought to be anions of specific nucleoproteins (Albert, 1951).

'Dimensional factor'. A further characteristic which governs the activity of the acridines is the so-called 'dimensional factor', or the shape and size of the acridine molecule in relation to that of the bacterial receptor molecule. The receptor molecules are known to be partly planar in structure, and it now appears that for an acridine to enter into full combination a certain minimum area of its molecule must also be planar. If this area is not present then a steric hindrance is set up and the acridine is unable to exert its anticipated bacteriostatic effect. Such a situation arises with 5-amino-1:2:3:4-tetrahydroacridine, which although highly ionized does not have an adequately flat surface and so is almost devoid of antibacterial activity (Albert, 1951).

In terms of relative size, if the molecule is unnecessarily large, even though it has a large planar area, its opportunities of contact with the bacterial receptor are reduced, and sometimes may even be blocked, and this again results in low activity. The low activities of the compounds whose molecules consist of two acridine nuclei linked in one way or another are probably accounted for in this way.

Continuing this line of thought, it can also be seen how the dimensional factor may also be used to explain in part the varying sensitivities of different bacterial species to the same acridine compound. The individual species are known to vary in their characteristics because of their differing contents of proteins and other substances, and this is not the least evident in their different ribonucleic acids contents. Because of this, it is reasonable to assume that the individual sensitive nuclei may also vary, so that the area and accessibility of one may be quite different from that of another. If this is so, then the apparent affinity of the acridine ion for this area will be subject to variation and this becomes evident in the different activities of the acridines on Gram-positive and Gram-negative bacteria.

Other mechanisms. Whilst the degree of ionization and the dimensional factor are the most significant in determining the bacteriostatic power of the acridines, they are not always exclusive. Other factors may come into play, and the two which appear to be the most important are chelation and oxidation-reduction characteristics. Lipophilic properties and surface activity generally have no influence, although micelle formation, which is evident in some compounds, may have a bearing, at least with some organisms.

The idea that the acridines owe their activity to their ability to displace hydrogen carriers from active centres in the bacterial cell led to the suggestion that activity may be associated with the oxidation-reduction characteristics of the compounds, and Breyer, Buchanan and Duewell (1944) found such a relationship. They examined a small number of acridines and found that the three most active compounds, 5-amino-, 2:8-diamino-, and 2-amino-acridine, had reduction potentials of -0.916, -0.731 and -0.468 volt respectively at pH 7·3 whilst the less active ones had values of about -0.3 volt. From this they concluded that a reduction potential of less than -0.4 volt was necessary for high activity. Although this was a reasonable deduction on the evidence available, certain anomalies were observed by other workers, and so doubt was thrown upon its validity. Albert (1951) in particular raised the point that a reduction potential of -0.3 volt is much too low for an acridine to be converted into a hydrogen acceptor and so become a feebly ionized dihydro analogue with diminished activity. About the same time, however, Kaye (1950) showed that electro-reduction, as measured by polarimetric methods, takes place in two stages, the first of which yields "a free radical, apparently of great stability", and he was able to relate bacteriostatic activity to the nature of this first step of reduction. If this can be confirmed with a wider range of compounds, then the relationship between oxidation-reduction potential and activity is reinstated. But this still leaves Albert's contention unanswered.

Chelation, the other major factor which contributes to enhanced activity, is effective by virtue of the ability to abstract essential trace metals from the bacterial cell. The loss of these metals interferes with the vital metabolism of the cell and results in the death of the cell. Chelation occurs with acridines

TABLE 44

Relative bacteriostatic activities of aminoacridines

Acridine	Inhibitory index
Unsubstituted	6
1-Amino-	4
2-Amino-	21
3-Amino-	8
4-Amino-	9
5-Amino- (Aminacrine) . .	25
1:5-Diamino-	22
2:5-Diamino-	17
3:5-Diamino-	18
4:5-Diamino–	18
2:6-Diamino-	26
2:7-Diamino-	26
2:8-Diamino- (Proflavine) . .	22
2:9-Diamino-	9
1:9-Diamino-	0
3:7-Diamino-	9

hydroxylated in the 1-position, and good examples are found with 1-hydroxy-acridine and 1-hydroxy-5-aminoacridine (Albert *et al.*, 1945; Albert *et al.*, 1947; Albert and Goldacre, 1948).

Effect of substituent radicals. The activity of an acridine is profoundly affected by the nature and positioning of any radical or radicals which may be added to its nucleus. These substituents must always be small in size because of the need to preserve a planar structure in the molecule, but they can be added in more than one position. In order to be able to determine the significance of these additions it is necessary to have some means of comparing activities under a number of conditions, and Albert and his colleagues chose the minimum concentrations of each compound in serum broth capable of inhibiting five chosen test organisms, *Clostridium welchii*, *Staph. aureus*, *Streptococcus pyogenes*, *E. coli* and *Proteus*. The inhibitory concentration for each organism was given a number in the series 0 to 8, the larger numbers indicating the greater activities, and the sum of these numbers constitutes the 'inhibitory index' of the compound. This index is used in Tables 44 and 45, the data for which are abstracted from more detailed information given by Albert (1951).

The most significant of the substituent radicals is the amino group, and the effect of adding one or two such groups in various positions is indicated in Table 44. With regard to other substituent radicals, chlorination sometimes increases and sometimes decreases activity, and the introduction of a hydroxyl group is advantageous provided it is placed in the 1-position when the molecule then has chelating properties. The nitro group, in spite of its acidic nature and consequent tendency to reduce basicity and ionization, also enhances activity, and the nitroamino compounds are amongst the most active of the acridines. The presumed reason for this anomalous finding is that the nitroaminoacridines, along with other nitro compounds form "a distinct class of antiseptics which function through exerting an oxidizing

TABLE 45

Relative bacteriostatic activities of some substituted acridines

Acridine	Inhibitory index
1-Methyl-	2
5-Methyl-	3
1-Methoxy-	3
1-Hydroxy-	12
2-Hydroxy-	6
5-Hydroxy-	5
2-Amino-5-chloro-	1
2-Amino-8-chloro-	13
3-Amino-8-chloro-	0
5-Amino-1-chloro-	20
5-Amino-2-chloro-	26
5-Amino-1-nitro-	24
5-Amino-2-nitro-	30
5-Amino-4-nitro-	27
5-Amino-1-methyl-	27
5-Amino-2-methyl-	21
5-Amino-1-ethyl-	22
5-Amino-1-methoxy-	22
5-Amino-2-methoxy-	25
5-Amino-1:3-dimethyl-	24
5-Amino-1:9-dimethyl-	27
2:8-Diamino-1:9-dimethyl-	30
2:8-Diamino-3:7-dimethyl-	21
3-Amino-10-methylacridinium bromide	3
5-Amino-10-methylacridinium chloride	23
2:8-Diamino-10-methylacridinium chloride	22

action and forming possibly toxic hydroxylamines" (Albert, 1951). The methyl group also enhances activity provided it is introduced into the 1-position, and dimethylation is sometimes even more effective, but this again depends on the positioning and sometimes makes for greater selectivity. Thus, 1:9-dimethyl-5-aminoacridine has a better all-round activity than 5-aminoacridine, but the 1:3-dimethyl compound, whilst being more effective against the Gram-positive types, is relatively inactive against the Gram-negative ones. The inhibitory indexes of a number of these compounds is given in Table 45.

Little can be said of the effect of other substituent radicals because of the few examined, but active compounds have been obtained with methoxy, ethoxy, and phenyl substituent radicals, although they are not as generally effective as those mentioned above.

Selectivity. All of the acridines are selective in their activity against the different types of organism, showing greater efficacy against the nutritionally more exacting species, such as *Clostridium*, *Streptococcus* and *Brucella*, and to a less extent *Staphylococcus*, than against the less exacting species such as *Escherichia*, *Pseudomonas* and *Proteus*. This parallels to some extent the Gram-staining properties of the different organisms, although there are several exceptions. Thus, selectivity and Gram-staining, whilst not showing an exact relationship, are evidently associated in some way, and this would appear to be through the ribonucleic acid content of the cells. The staining characteristics of bacteria are known to depend on the presence of certain ribonucleates, and the selective antibacterial activities of the acridines can also be correlated with the different nucleic acid metabolisms of the various organisms (*cf.* p. 10).

Resistance. It is possible for bacteria to acquire resistance to acridines, but the mechanisms by which they achieve this are not entirely clear. Hinshelwood (1949) was firmly of the opinion that it is due to induced adaptation, but a series of investigations by Yudkin and his colleagues (Thornley and Yudkin, 1959; Sinai and Yudkin, 1959*a*, *b*) using proflavine and *E. coli* as the examples lead them to be even more convinced that it is mainly due to mutation and selection, the change being due to changes in the deoxyribonucleic acids complex. Even one subculture in a weak proflavine solution (3 or 5 μg per ml) produced a considerable increase in the numbers of resistant organisms and there was only a partial reversion to the original after many further subcultures in normal media. The increase in resistance was so great that at the third-step mutation it was 100-fold that of the original culture. This mutation of *E. coli* does not occur to the same extent with *Klebsiella pneumoniae* (*Aerobacter aerogenes*) but there is some selection: neither is there any incontrovertible evidence for adaptation, as suggested by Baskett (1952). The issue on these points may have been clouded in earlier work by the fact that it is possible to transform cultures – *E. coli* at least, although there is no reason why it should be so restricted – by adding deoxyribonucleic acid-containing extracts from resistant organisms (Sinai and Yudkin, 1959*b*).

Some useful acridines and their activities

The first acridine to be prepared as an antibacterial agent was Acriflavine, and an excellent review of the history of its uses in clinical medicine was made by Browning (1943). Acriflavine was thought at first to be 2:8-diamino-10-methylacridinium chloride, but it was subsequently shown (Gailliot, 1934; Hall and Powell, 1934) to be a mixture of about two parts of that compound to one part of 2:8-diaminoacridine (proflavine) dihydrochloride. Acriflavine, although it is still widely used, fell into disrepute for a while, mainly because of its high acidity and high tissue toxicity. The toxicity was found to be due to the 2:8-diamino-10-methylacridinium component, and so largely on the recommendation of Garrod (1940) and the clinical evidence of Russell and Falconer (1940, 1941) it began to be replaced by proflavine. Proflavine is used in two water-soluble forms, the acid sulphate and the neutral sulphate, or hemisulphate. It has the same activity as Acriflavine (Berry, 1941*a*; Albert *et al.*, 1945), and there is ample clinical proof of its efficacy in the treatment of wounds infected with Gram-positive and Gram-negative bacteria, as well as with *Cl. welchii*. Proflavine Hemisulphate and Aminacrine Hydrochloride, or 5-aminoacridine hydrochloride, each has a monograph in the British Pharmacopoeia, and Acriflavine now appears in the

TABLE 46

Antibacterial properties of the commoner acridines

Substance	Dilution (1 in —) inhibiting growth of				
	Cl. welchii	*Staph. aureus*	*Strep. pyogenes*	*E. coli*	*Prot. vulgaris*
5-Aminoacridine (Aminacrine)	320,000	40,000	160,000	40,000	40,000
2:7-Diaminoacridine	320,000	40,000	160,000	80,000	40,000
2:8-Diaminoacridine (Proflavine)	320,000	40,000	160,000	20,000	10,000
2:8-Diamino-10-methylacridinium chloride (Euflavine)	320,000	20,000	640,000	20,000	5,000
5-Amino-1-methyl acridine (Methylaminoacridine)	320,000	80,000	320,000	40,000	40,000

Note. Acriflavine behaves in much the same way as Proflavine.

British Pharmaceutical Codex. Neutral Acriflavine is also known unofficially as Euflavine.

Other acridine derivatives subsequently produced for clinical use are 2:7-diaminoacridine and 5-aminoacridine. The latter was first prepared and described by Albert, Rubbo and Goldacre (1941), and is particularly valuable because of its non-staining properties and its almost neutral reaction. Both compounds are highly active both *in vitro* and *in vivo*, and the 2:7-diamino derivative is less toxic and interferes less in wound healing than either the 5-amino derivative or Proflavine (Mitchell and Buttle, 1943; Ungar and Robinson, 1943, 1944). 2:7-Diaminoacridine, otherwise known as Diflavine, was first described by Albert and Linnell (1936) and its biological properties have been reported by various workers, including Albert *et al.* (1938), Russell and Falconer (1941), and Ungar and Robinson (1944). In spite of its favourable properties, it has a number of disadvantages, including that of leaving an intense red stain, and its clinical uses do not seem to have been pursued intensively.

According to Albert *et al.* (1945), the 1-methyl derivative of 5-aminoacridine possesses a rather greater activity than does 5-aminoacridine itself.

Furthermore it is more soluble and more easily tolerated systemically. It should, therefore, be another useful clinical compound in the acridine armoury, and trials in Australia have given consistently good results (Rubbo and Albert, 1946). In a series of *in vitro* tests against eleven different types of Gram-positive and Gram-negative organisms it was found to be bacteriostatic at concentrations in the range of from 1 in 130,000 to 1 in 300,000, whereas the 5-aminoacridine was effective in the range 1 in 100,000 to 1 in 160,000.

The bacteriostatic activities of the commoner acridines in 10 per cent serum broth are given in Table 46. They are taken from papers by Rubbo, Albert and Maxwell (1942), Albert *et al.* (1945) and Albert and Goldacre (1948), and were obtained with organisms freshly isolated from wounds. In presenting these results it was stated that there was but little variation in resistance between strains of the same species, but others have found fairly substantial variations. Thus, Berry (1941b) found his cultures of *E. coli* to be inhibited by proflavine at 1 in 40,000, but *Staph. aureus* was obviously more resistant and was not inhibited until a concentration of 1 in 20,000 had been reached. The author also found the inhibitory concentration of Acriflavine to be subject to variation according to the test conditions and the cultures used. In ordinary nutrient broth the inhibitory range for *E. coli* was between 1 in 50,000 and 1 in 100,000 and for *Staph. aureus* between 1 in 100,000 and 1 in 200,000, whereas in 20 per cent serum broth the comparative figures for *E. coli* were from 1 in 50,000 to 1 in 200,000 and for *Staph. aureus* from 1 in 100,000 to 1 in 200,000 with an occasional value as high as 1 in 300,000.

The acridines as a whole have relatively little effect on the *Pseudomonas* group of bacteria, against which concentrations substantially greater than 1 in 5,000 are needed to inhibit growth, and they are practically devoid of any antifungal activity, in fact, certain common moulds will actually grow in a 2 per cent solution of proflavine or acriflavine. They inhibit or inactivate some of the viruses and allied bodies.

Uses of acridines

As stated earlier, the acridines are used far less extensively than hitherto, largely on account of the introduction of the newer antiseptics, including the antibiotics. Their applications are mainly in the treatment of infected wounds and burns, although they have also been administered systemically, with limited success, in cases of septicaemia and *E. coli* infections. The concentration normally used in wound therapy is 1 in 1,000 in saline, but for ophthalmic use and bladder irrigation or urethral injection it is usually only 1 in 4,000. Proflavine in its undiluted powder form has been applied successfully to open wounds (Mitchell and Buttle, 1942) although others have noted that it can cause necrosis and hinder healing. One interesting feature of the acridines is that although they are quickly adsorbed by cotton materials such as gauze and lint they retain their full antibacterial properties, hence this is a convenient way of applying the acridines. After adsorption they are gradually eluted again into water or saline, so that an impregnated gauze actually acts as a depot of supply to any surface or wound with which it is in moist contact.

The various acridine ointments and creams can all be shown to have bacteriostatic properties, but this cannot be said of all of the emulsions. Some years ago it was demonstrated in the author's laboratory that the water-in-oil emulsions, including the B.P.C. 1934 formulation containing beeswax and liquid paraffin, was completely devoid of any activity either

TABLE 47

Bacteriostatic properties of Flavazole

Organism	Minimum bacteriostatic concentration (1 in —) at 37° of		
	Flavazole	Proflavine	Sulphathiazole
Cl. welchii.	160,000	160,000	500,000
Cl. septique	640,000	640,000	250,000
Staph. aureus	320,000	160,000	160,000
Strep. pyogenes	1,280,000	640,000	320,000
E. coli	40,000	40,000	20,000
Ps. pyocyanea	50,000	5,000	2,500
Proteus	160,000	40,000	2,500

in vitro or *in vivo*, but those in water-miscible bases or in oil-in-water emulsions were satisfactory.

More recently, Fenton and Warren (1962) have confirmed this with proflavine cream, at the same time extending their observations to include other salts besides the hemisulphate. They obtained maximum activity from a water-in-oil emulsion with the valerate, and from this concluded that "the hydrophile-lipophile balance conveyed to the salt by the acid is the main factor which determines the rate of release [of the antiseptic]."

An interesting acridine derivative which came to the fore during the later years of the Second World War is the preparation known as Flavazole. This is a compound made from equimolecular mixtures of proflavine base and sulphathiazole. It has all of the advantages of the two component substances and in addition has considerably enhanced activity against *Ps. pyocyanea* and *Proteus*. The minimum bacteriostatic concentration of this compound against a number of bacteria is shown in Table 47. It was first described by McIntosh, Robinson and Selbie (1945) who found that it could be safely employed in cleaning up wound infections from which bacteria disappeared in a few days. Later, it was found valuable in controlling experimental gasgangrene (McIntosh and Selbie, 1946) and a 1 in 2,000 solution was used effectively in treating infection of the bladder (Guttmann, 1947).

REFERENCES

ALBERT, A. (1951). *The Acridines:* Arnold, London.
ALBERT, A., FRANCIS, A. E., GARROD, L. P. and LINNELL, W. H. (1938). *Brit. J. exp. Path.*, **19**, 41.
ALBERT, A. and GOLDACRE, R. (1948). *Nature, Lond.*, **161**, 95.
ALBERT, A. and LINNELL, W. H. (1936). *J. chem. Soc.*, p. 1614.
ALBERT, A., RUBBO, S. D. and GOLDACRE, R. (1941). *Nature, Lond.*, **147**, 332.
ALBERT, A., RUBBO, S. D., GOLDACRE, R. J. and BALFOUR, B. G. (1947). *Brit. J. exp. Path.*, **28**, 69.
ALBERT, A., RUBBO, S. D., GOLDACRE, R. J., DAVEY, M. E. and STONE, J. D. (1945). *Brit. J. exp. Path.*, **26**, 160.
BASKETT, A. C. (1952). *Proc. Roy. Soc., B*, **139**, 251.
BERRY, H. (1941a). *Quart. J. Pharm.*, **14**, 149.
BERRY, H. (1941b). *Quart. J. Pharm.*, **14**, 363.
BREYER, B., BUCHANAN, G. S. and DUEWELL, H. (1944). *J. chem. Soc.*, p. 360.
BROWNING, C. H. (1943). *Brit. med. J.*, i, 341.
BROWNING, C. H. and GILMOUR, W. (1913). *J. Path. Bact.*, **18**, 144.
CHAPMAN, G. H. and BERENS, C. (1935). *J. Bact.*, **29**, 437.
CHURCHMAN, J. W. (1912). *J. exp. Med.*, **16**, 221.
CALDWELL, P. C. and HINSHELWOOD, C. N. (1950). *J. chem. Soc.*, p. 1415.
DAVIES, D. S., HINSHELWOOD, C. N. and PRYCE, J. M. (1944). *Trans. Faraday Soc.*, **40** 397.
DUBOS, R. J. (1929). *J. exp., Med*, **49**, 575.
FENTON, A. H. and WARREN, MARY (1962). *Pharm. J.*, **188**, 5.
FERGUSON, T. B. and THORNE, S. D. (1946). *Brit. J. Pharmacol.*, **86**, 258.
FISCHER, E. and MUÑOZ, R. (1947). *J. Bact.*, **53**, 381.
GAILLIOT, M. (1934). *Quart. J. Pharm.*, **7**, 63.
GARROD, L. P. (1940). *Proc. roy. Soc. Med.*, **33**, 497.
GOMEZ-VEGA, PAULINA (1935). *Arch. Dermatol. Syphylol.*, **32**, 49.
GUTTMANN, L. (1947). *Proc. roy. Soc. Med.*, **40**, 219.
HALL, G. F. and POWELL, A. D. (1934). *Quart. J. Pharm.*, **7**, 522.
HINSHELWOOD, C. N. (1949). *Symp. Soc. exp. Biol.*, N.Y., **3**, 243.
INGRAHAM, MARY A. (1933). *J. Bact.*, **26**, 573.
KAYE, R. C. (1950). *J. Pharm. Pharmacol.*, **2**, 902.
MCILWAIN, H. (1941). *Biochem. J.*, **35**, 1311.
MCINTOSH, J., ROBINSON, R. H. M. and SELBIE, F. R. (1945). *Lancet*, **249**, 97.
MCINTOSH, J. and SELBIE, F. R. (1946). *Brit. J. exp. Path.*, **27**, 46.
MITCHELL, G. A. G. and BUTTLE, G. A. H. (1942). *Lancet*, **243**, 416.
MITCHELL, G. A. G. and BUTTLE, G. A. H. (1943). *Lancet*, **245**, 287.
PEACOCKE, A. R. and HINSHELWOOD, C. N. (1948). *J. chem. Soc.*, pp. 1235, 2290.
RAHN, O. (1945). *Biodynamica*, **5**, 1.
RUBBO, S. D. and ALBERT, A. (1946). *Lancet*, **250**, 439.
RUBBO, S. D., ALBERT, A. and MAXWELL, M. (1942). *Brit. J. exp. Path.*, **23**, 69.
RUSSELL, DOROTHY S. and FALCONER, M. A. (1940). *Brit. med. J.*, i, 631; *Proc. roy. Soc. Med.*, **33**, 494.
RUSSELL, DOROTHY S. and FALCONER, M. A. (1941). *Brit. med. J.*, i, 378.
SINAI, J. and YUDKIN, J. (1959a). *J. gen. Microbiol.*, **20**, 373, 384.
SINAI, J. and YUDKIN, J. (1959b). *J. gen. Microbiol.*, **20**, 400.
STEARN, ESTHER W. and STEARN, A. E. (1924). *J. Bact.*, **9**, 463, 479, 491.
STEARN, ESTHER W. and STEARN, A. E. (1926). *J. Bact.*, **11**, 345.
THORNLEY, MARGARET J. nad YUDKIN, J. (1959). *J. gen. Microbiol.*, **20**, 355, 365.
UNGAR, J. and ROBINSON, F. A. (1943). *Lancet*, **245**, 285.
UNGAR, J. and ROBINSON, F. A. (1944). *Brit. J. Pharmacol.*, **80**, 217.

CHAPTER 14

SURFACE ACTIVE COMPOUNDS

SURFACE ACTIVE COMPOUNDS are to be found amongst the cationic, the nonionic, the anionic, and the amphoteric substances but from the angle of disinfection, the cationic group containing the quaternary ammonium compounds is by far the largest and most important. The amphoteric compounds are as yet of only minor significance, in the process of being developed: the nonionic and anionic groups, the latter comprising the soaps and considered in an earlier chapter, show little or no antibacterial activity.

Quaternary ammonium compounds

The quaternary ammonium compounds constitute the groups variously known as the "cationic detergents", "cationic wetting agents" or "surface-active cationic germicides", but in spite of their high surface activities they are, in fact, poor detergents, particularly at the concentration they are used as germicides, but relatively good wetting agents. They are popularly known as "quaternaries", "q.a.c's" or "quats", but the last is an ugly and dissonant term and its use is to be discouraged.

Quaternary ammonium bases and their salts were first synthesized about the turn of the century and the original observations on their germicidal properties were made by Jacobs and his colleagues some years later (1916*a*, *b*, *c*) when they studied the relationship between chemical structure and bactericidal activity in the hexamethylenetetramine series. The potentialities of this class of compounds were not realized, however, until after Domagk's investigations in 1935. Since then they have emerged into great prominence, largely because of certain claims made in the United States for their performances as germicides – claims since proved to be grossly exaggerated – and many hundreds of the type have been made and examined. One bibliography, for instance, compiled as early as 1952 contains over 500 references and it is estimated that since Domagk's initial publication over 1,000 publications on the subject have appeared in various journals. An excellent monograph, itself carrying 550 references, was published by Lawrence (1950) in which special emphasis was placed on the chemistry and biology of the quaternaries. They are also discussed by Moillet, Collie and Black (1961) in their book on *Surface Activity* mainly from the aspect of their physical and chemical properties and their technical applications.

In spite of the surge of activity in the synthetic field, less than a dozen of the compounds come into regular use. The most prominent of these, along with their trade names, are listed in Table 48. Cetrimide was admitted

362

into the British Pharmacopoeia, 1951 Addendum; a monograph on Domiphen Bromide appears in the British Pharmaceutical Codex, 1954; Benzalkonium Chloride was admitted to the United States Pharmacopeia, 13th Edition, and the United States New and Nonofficial Remedies, 1949, mentions Ceepryn, Phemerol and Zephiran.

The quaternaries undoubtedly have their place in the field of antisepsis and disinfection, but their performance characteristics should not be over-rated. To this end it is most important, as will be seen later, to select the right

TABLE 48

Some of the quaternary ammonium compounds and their trade names

Chemical name	Trade name
Cetyltrimethylammonium bromide	Cetrimide, CTAB, Cetavlon
Cetylpyridinium bromide *or* chloride . . .	Ceepryn, Fixanol C .
Tetradecylpyridinium bromide . . .	Fixanol V.R., Vantoc B .
Alkyldimethylbenzylammonium chloride . . .	Roccal, Zephiran, Zephirol, Benzalkonium Chloride
β-Phenoxyethyldimethyldodecylammonium bromide .	Domiphen Bromide, Bradosol
Di(*n*-octyl)dimethylammonium bromide . .	Diometam
p-tert-Octylphenoxyethoxyethyldimethylbenzyl-ammonium chloride	Phemerol, Hyamine 1622, Octaphen
N-(Acylcolaminoformylmethyl)pyridinium chloride	Emulsept

conditions for any laboratory evaluation, otherwise they will be either underestimated or grossly overestimated.

Chemical and physical properties

Constitution and activity. The quaternaries basically are organically substituted ammonium compounds in which the nitrogen atom has a cova-lence. of 5. They are therefore a class of amine, and have the general formula:

$$\left[\begin{matrix} R_1 & R_2 \\ & N \\ R_4 & R_3 \end{matrix} \right]^{+} X^{-}$$

in which X is a halide, sulphate or similar radical, and the substituents R_1, R_2, R_3 and R_4 each represents an alkyl, aralkyl or heterocyclic radical of a given size or chain length. Three of the radicals may be linked through the nitrogen atom to a cyclic amine, pyridine or similar structure.

Obviously within the definition an almost unlimited variety of compounds of different constitution and structure is possible. Each such compound, whilst possessing the general properties of the group, exhibits its own specific characteristics in terms of antibacterial and other activities; hence the frantic search, conducted mainly in the United States, in the hope of finding one member with outstanding properties.

Disinfection and sterilization

This search was initiated by Domagk (1935) who on examining the long-chain quaternary ammonium compounds found notable germicidal activity only when at least one of the four radicals had a carbon chain in the range C_8 to C_{18}. These compounds were apparently lethal at quite high dilutions to both vegetative bacteria and their spores, and some of them also appeared to retain their activities in the presence of serum better than did many other antiseptics – hence another reason for the early interest displayed in them.

Since Domagk's discovery the many compounds prepared and examined include (a) further homologues in the alkyl and aralkyl series, (b) those with two long-chain alkyl radical substituents, (c) cyclic amines of the pyridine, picoline and lutidine type incorporating a nitrogen atom in the ring, (d) compounds containing unsaturated and aromatic linkages in the long-chain group, and (e) a few compounds with certain substituted chlorine or nitro groups. The majority of these compounds have more or less the same properties and none has proved really outstanding.

Of the aliphatic single long-chain series, the typical compound is the $C_{16}H_{33}$ member, cetyltrimethylammonium bromide (Cetrimide), and this was the one recommended by Barnes (1942) for hospital disinfection. Of the group containing a simple ring structure the benzalkonium or alkyldimethylbenzylammonium chlorides, whose characteristics were first described by Dunn (1936), are typical. In an investigation of a long series of quaternaries derived from aliphatic and cyclic amines Shelton and his colleagues (1946) also found optimum activity to reside in those carrying a cetyl ($C_{16}H_{33}$) radical, and from them was selected cetylpyridinium chloride (Ceepryn), a compound which had already been described by Blubaugh *et al.* (1940, 1941). Again, Epstein, Harris and Katzmann (1943) examined a series in which oxygen was introduced into the alkyl chains in the form of carboxyl and amide linkages and from these selected the *N*-(acylcolaminoformylmethyl) pyridinium member. About the same time Rawlings, Sweet and Joslyn (1943) were looking at the properties of a series containing a variety of alkyl, aryl, cycloalkyl and aralkyl radicals, from which Hyamine 1622 (*p-tert*-octylphenoxyethoxyethyldimethylbenzylammonium chloride) was developed.

Yet another series was reported on more recently by Scott and Wolf (1962). They compared the group derived from the reaction of hexamine (hexamethylenetetramine) and halohydrocarbons. Although chemically they are described as quaternaries they are different from the normal members of the family in that they act by the slow release of formaldehyde. They can inhibit bacterial growth at concentrations down to 50 parts per million but they are only weakly bactericidal. Uses have been found for them in cutting oils, latex paints and adhesives (*see* Chapter 17).

Surface activity. When a quaternary ammonium compound dissolves in water it ionizes as a cationic compound, the long-chain nitrogen substituted part of the molecule carrying the positive charge. This group is always lipophilic and because of this it bestows high surface activity on the compound together with an ability to lower surface tension. Certain anomalies have been observed, however (Adam and Shute, 1938), and these have been attributed to micelle formation. This might explain the phenomenon of 'wild plusses' frequently encountered in testing these compounds, although other ideas have been put forward (see below). Surface tension, therefore, cannot be directly associated with germicidal activity, but it must play a significant part. The principal virtue of surface activity in relation to disinfection seems to be that it brings the compound into more effective contact with the bacterial cell and consequently there is an increase in local concentration around the cell (Albert, 1942; Hoogerheide, 1945). The same phenomenon has been observed with phenol and its homologues and with other compounds.

Mechanism of antibacterial activity

The bactericidal action of the quaternaries has been variously attributed to the inactivation of enzymes, denaturation of essential cell proteins and disruption of the cell membrane. The differentiation between enzyme inactivation and protein denaturation in this context is a very fine one. There is insufficient of quaternary in a lethal solution to cause a general denaturation of the proteins, but some selective action in this direction is feasible, and it is most likely that the enzyme proteins, being probably the most sensitive in the cell, would be the first to succumb. This argument could also explain the observed differential activities of the quaternaries between the Gram-positive and Gram-negative bacteria.

There is ample evidence of the destructive effect of various detergent substances on bacterial cells causing them to undergo cytolytic damage resulting in the leakage of cell constituents into the surrounding fluid. Hotchkiss (1946) demonstrated it, and so did Gale and Taylor (1946, 1947), who observed increases in cell permeabilities leading to their ultimate rupture and the release of lysine and glutamic acid. Salton (1951) also measured the uptake of cetrimide by bacteria, and Salton, Horne and Cosslett (1951) demonstrated by electron microscopy first a contraction of the cytoplasm followed by a complete stripping off of the cell wall.

But in spite of these evidences it does not seem that cell disruption can be the real, or even contributory, cause of death: enzyme inactivations are much more closely associated, although still somewhat circumstantially. Baker, Harrison and Miller (1941), for instance, found the loss of viability to be roughly paralleled by the suppression of respiratory and glycolytic activity in a bacterial population, although cessation of oxygen uptake frequently preceded actual death. A much closer correlation was found by Roberts and Rahn (1946) who demonstrated complete inactivation of the cell dehydrogenase systems by lethal concentrations of quaternaries. More particularly Knox *et al.* (1949) showed a close relationship between repression of certain metabolic processes and loss of viability of *Escherichia coli* but at the same time emphasized the selective nature of this disturbance. In a like manner Kravitz *et al.* (1958) studied the loss of viability of *Chromobacterium prodigiosum* in relation to lysis and loss of oxidative enzyme activity and found a much closer, though not quantitative, parallelism with the latter: this followed their earlier observations (Stedman, Kravitz and King, 1957), and those of Dawson, Lominski and Stern (1953), that death takes place with concentrations of quaternaries far below those causing cell damage. On balance, then, it seems that death occurs as a result of enzyme inactivation, the particular enzymes concerned being the energy producing ones such as the glucose, succinate and pyruvate systems.

The phenomenon of bacteriostasis exhibited by the quaternaries has probably a more simple explanation, and almost certainly involves reversible reactions of one type or another – reversible inactivation of enzymes or reversible interferences with other cell mechanisms – in which the time factor must be highly significant. All investigators have shown that if treated bacteria are left in a state of bacteriostasis for too long a period their capcity to recover is lost, even when they are placed in favourable cultural conditions. In this respect it should be noted that recovery from inhibition by quaternaries seems to be slower than with most disinfectants, presumably because of the intensely adsorbed layers on the cell which are not easily removed by simple dilutions or by physical means. Chemical removal by one or more of the inactivating agents (*see* p. 372) is the only satisfactory way.

Range of antimicrobial activities

Selective action. Generally speaking, the quaternary ammonium compounds are more selectively active against Gram-positive organisms than against the Gram-negative types, although the differences sometimes may not be very great. *Pseudomonas pyocyanea* is the most resistant amongst the Gram-negative types. There is no doubt that the Gram-negative organisms respond differently from the Gram-positive, as evidenced by the losses of different cell constituents as a result of increased permeability (Gale and Taylor, 1947; Salton, 1951), and one postulate put forward to explain this is related to possible differences in the type and content of phospholipids in the two groups of organism (Baker, Harrison and Miller, 1941). Some reported activities of cetrimide, Ceepryn and Zephirol against some of the more common bacteria are collected in Table 49.

In spite of reports to the contrary (Work and Work, 1948) bacteria can quite readily adapt themselves to become resistant to the quaternaries (Chaplin, 1952) in the same way as they do to the antibiotics and sulphonamides. The tolerance of *Pseudomonas aeruginosa* has been raised sevenfold from 100 to 700 parts per million after nine transfers in a liquid medium, and ultimately to 2,000 parts per million (MacGregor and Elliker, 1958). The addition of ethylenediaminetetracetic acid (EDTA) immediately restores the sensitivity of the organisms, thus indicating that increased resistance is due to enhancement in impermeability of the cell. Adaptation takes place more readily at pH 6·8 than at higher values (pH 7·4 and 7·7), and apparently more readily in the Gram-negative bacteria than in the Gram-positive ones, but this may be a false impression due simply to the higher activities of the

TABLE 49

Some reported bactericidal concentrations of three quaternary ammonium compounds

Organism	Lethal concentrations (1 in —) of		
	Cetrimide	Ceepryn	Zephirol
Staph. aureus . .	20,000 35,000 218,000	83,000 218,000	18,000 20,000 38,000 50,000 200,000
Strep. pyogenes . .	20,000	42,000 127,000	40,000
E. coli . . .	3,000 27,500 30,000	66,000 67,000	12,000 27,000
Salm. typhi . . .	13,000	15,000 48,000 62,000	10,000 20,000
Ps. pyocyanea . .	3,500 5,000		2,500
Proteus vulgaris . .	7,500	34,000	1,300

Note. These figures have been collected from various published sources; they were obtained therefore with different testing techniques.

quaternaries against the Gram-positive organisms (Fischer and Larose, 1952).

That the quaternaries are ineffective as lethal agents against *Mycobacterium tuberculosis* and other acid-fast organisms has been proved by Smith *et al.* (1950). Several, however, effectively inhibit their growth (Freedlander, 1940; Quisno and Foter, 1946). The lack of lethal activity is probably explained by the high lipoid content of the tubercle bacillus.

Sporicidal activity. In spite of earlier statements to the contrary, the quaternaries cannot be considered to be effectively sporicidal. There are claims in the literature that one part in several thousands is lethal in a matter of a few minutes to the spores *Bacillus subtilis*, *Bacillus anthracis*, and *Clostridium welchii*, but such claims all arose from a lack of appreciation of the consequences of the high surface activities of the quaternaries. Handled properly it has been shown (Kivela, Mallmann and Churchill, 1948) that spores of *B. subtilis* apparently killed by quaternaries can be revived by repeated washing processes, and Davies (1949), using a recovery medium containing a quaternary inactivator, demonstrated clearly that 1 per cent solutions of cetrimide, Zephiran, Phemerol or Ceepryn have no action at all upon the spores of *B. subtilis* and five other sporing bacilli in 3 days, although they were all apparently killed within 1 hour in the absence of an inactivator. Even heating to 95° in a 1 in 20 solution for 30 minutes is not completely effective (Curran and Evans, 1950).

Antifungal activity. Fungicidal and fungistatic activities at quite high dilutions have been claimed by a number of investigators, but again these earlier reports are unreliable. At a more realistic level Quisno and Foter (1946) found cetylpyridinium chloride to be lethal at 37° to species of *Candida, Trichophyton, Cryptococcus* and *Microsporon* at concentrations between about 1 in 30,000 and 1 in 60,000, and Dunn (1936) found concentrations of the order of 1 in 10,000 to 1 in 40,000 of alkyldimethylbenzylammonium chloride to be lethal in 10 minutes at 20° also to a variety of pathogenic types. Others who have reported on the fungicidal activities of the quaternaries include Knight and Frazier (1945), Jones *et al.* (1950) and Mason, Brown and Minga (1951). By way of complete contrast, Klarmann and Wright (1954) expressed the firm opinion that they are not really fungicidal and that the official A.O.A.C. test gives misleading results. Again, it is a matter of choice of conditions and of a suitable inactivator.

Antiviral activity. The viruses in general are rather more resistant than are the bacteria and fungi. Because of this, quaternary ammonium compounds have been used as a means of preparing vaccines and suspensions of organisms free from viable bacteria (*e.g.* Maier, 1939; Ducor, 1947). The concentrations necessary to inactivate the influenza virus in a few minutes are of the order of 1 in 500 to 1 in 8,000 (Klein and Stevens, 1945), but not all quaternaries show activity. Other workers (*see* Lawrence, 1950) have reported on their activity – or lack of activity – against the viruses of encephalomyelitis, vaccinia, poliomyelitis, Newcastle disease and the bacteriophages.

Toxicity. In relation to the concentrations used for the various purposes of disinfection the quaternaries are relatively non-toxic. Nevertheless, the opinion has been expressed in some quarters that certain of the group, particularly those with cyclic structures within the molecule, might possess carcinogenic properties if taken continuously in small doses such as might happen if drinking or eating utensils are incompletely rinsed after being disinfected with a quaternary. There seems to be little experimental evidence, however, to support this suspicion which is probably founded on the fact that fatalities have occurred in animals when they have been given large doses of quaternaries in their diet. For instance, 400 mgm of cetylpyridinium chloride per kilogram body weight has proved lethal to rabbits, but 100 mgm

administered daily for periods up to 4 weeks produced no significant patho-
logical changes (Warren *et al.*, 1942). In humans, dilutions of 1 in 5,000 of
several quaternaries in water have been tolerated for long periods (Shelanski,
1950), but they are much more toxic when administered by injection and high
concentrations can cause severe skin reactions and oedema. Down to quite
low concentrations they are haemolytic.

Factors affecting antibacterial activities

   Organic matter. In common with most other disinfectants, the antibacterial activities of the quaternaries are markedly suppressed in the presence of organic matter of any sort. Quisno and Foter (1946), for example,
found that on adding 10 per cent of ox serum the lethal concentration of
cetrimide was increased from 1 in 66,000 to 1 in 1,000 against *E. coli* and
from 1 in 127,000 to 1 in 17,000 against *Streptococcus pyogenes*, and losses
with other quaternaries of 95 per cent and more with serum, milk and other
organic material have frequently been reported. Almost certainly these
losses are due to the direct action of the quaternary with the added protein,
which combine in approximately equal weight ratios (Valko, 1946), thus
giving rise to their denaturation and frequent precipitation.

   Adsorption phenomena. Adsorption plays an important part in the process
of disinfection by quaternaries – exhibiting both good and bad features.
Being surface active, they all are readily adsorbed on any surface. Materials
such as filter paper, charcoal and any precipitated particulate matter can
remove quaternaries substantially from solution, and even agar is active
in the same direction (Sherwood, 1942; Quisno, Gibby and Foter, 1946*a*).
Glass and metal surfaces also adsorb quaternaries, so that the container
in which any solution is placed inevitably removes some of the substance
from the solution. In some respects the effect of this is salutary, for it
means that in practical disinfection all surfaces so treated are left with a
residual layer of the compound which continues to exert its antibacterial
effect. In other respects the effect is disadvantageous, because in testing
solutions of the quaternaries, one has always to be alert to the carry-over
effects when solutions are handled in pipettes, test tubes and the like; it also
poses the problem of cleansing laboratory glassware after use.

   Because bacteria themselves are particulate, they also act as adsorbents,
and this must be the first stage before the actual process of disinfection can
begin. It is this phenomenon, unappreciated at first, which gave rise to the
earlier false beliefs concerning the very high lethal activities of the quaternaries. The reason is not difficult to understand: when a bacterial cell,
treated with a sub-lethal concentration of any disinfectant, is subcultured
into a recovery medium, it carries with it an adsorbed aliquot of the disinfectant. Most disinfectants are diluted out by this procedure, but because
of their high surface activities the quaternaries are not so eluted, and so,
although the overall concentration of the quaternary in a solution may be

well diluted below its inhibitory level, the concentration in the immediate vicinity of the cell remains unchanged. The quaternary, therefore, continues to exert its inhibitory effect and the cell is unable to recover and proliferate, the net result being the impression that the organism has been killed. A further consequence of the phenomenon of adsorption is that it gives rise to clumping of the cells (McCulloch, 1947; McCulloch, Hauge and Migaki, 1948), and to their adherence to the walls of the tube (Klarmann and Wright, 1946). The effects of these phenomena on the technique of testing will be discussed later, but it can be said here that clumping can readily be used to explain the few persistent survivors which always occur in tests with the quaternaries by assuming that they are organisms actually within the clumps and are, therefore, not reached by the disinfectant.

Compatibilities and incompatibilities. As well as being affected by organic matter of biological origin, the quaternary ammonium compounds exhibit quite definite incompatibilities with certain other groups of compounds. In particular they are completely inactivated by anionic compounds, including the soaps (Domagk, 1935), and by compounds such as sodium lauryl sulphate (Valko and DuBois, 1944) as well as by several non-ionic compounds such as Lubrol W (Davies, 1949) and Tween 80 (Quisno, Foter and Rubenkoenig, 1947). Incompatibilities are found with phospholipids, and several substances of this type are used as inactivators when testing the quaternaries. With fatty substances generally, they orientate themselves in layers with the hydrophobic end of the molecule directed towards the inner fat surface and the hydrophilic, germicidal end towards the outside. This explains the peculiar effects observed in disinfecting the skin with quaternaries (Rahn and van Eseltine, 1947).

Mention must also be made of the adverse effect of certain metallic ions, a point of some importance when quaternaries are diluted with tap water before use. Calcium and magnesium ions are particularly detrimental (Ridenour and Armbruster, 1948); so are ferric ions (Armbruster and Ridenour, 1949) and some forms of aluminium, but to a much less extent. According to the Mueller and Seeley (1951) the metallic ions reduce activity according to their valencies, trivalent ions exerting a greater effect than divalent ones, and so on.

From the work of Klimek (1955) and Klimek and Bailey (1956) it is not the quaternary which is affected but the organism itself which is rendered more resistant as the result of cultivation or pretreatment with such ions. Water with 600 parts per million of calcium hardness can certainly increase the killing time of *E. coli* from less than 30 seconds to more than 120 seconds, but this has been shown to be an artifact since it can be demonstrated only when certain types of peptone are in the culture medium. In fact, only four peptones out of fourteen tested produced the effect, and it did not occur if liver extracts or similar biological nutrients were present. Likewise, there was no effect at all if the testing procedure was adjusted so that initially all of the hardness was in the quaternary solution and so came into contact with the bacteria at the same time as did the quaternary, and not before.

Klimek and Bailey also found no response with iron salts up to 5 parts per million or with aluminium in alkaline solution. Some 'natural' waters also extended the killing time slightly, but a much greater effect was noted with 'Allport' synthetic dirty water containing 4,000 parts per million of solids. To meet the metal effect in practical disinfection, it has been suggested that the concentration of the quaternary be suitably increased or that a sequestering agent be added.

Acidity decreases the efficiencies of many quaternaries to such an extent that at pH 3 their germicidal activities almost disappear (Gershenfeld and Milanik, 1941; Gershenfeld and Perlstein, 1941), although Ceepryn is said to be an exception (Quisno and Foter, 1946). To quote but one example, the concentrations of Roccal at different pH values giving a 99·99 per cent kill in 5 minutes are reported to be (Mueller and Seeley, 1951):

pH	3	5	7	9	10
Concentration killing in 5 min .	100	30	15	10	8 p.p.m.

Needless to say, temperature also affects activities as it does other disinfectants. The temperature coefficients of the different quaternaries seem to vary somewhat, but broadly speaking it would appear that only about half the concentration is necessary to produce the same killing effect at 37° as at 20°.

Testing quaternary ammonium compounds

A vast literature on the testing of the quaternaries has accumulated over the years, most of which has been directed either to adapting existing techniques to attain more practicable results or to developing new techniques of special application, including methods for field and semi-field studies. Most of these methods, as applicable both to disinfectants in general and to quaternaries in particular, have already been discussed in detail in Chapter 3. It is the intention is this section therefore to consider only the particular problems associated with testing the quaternaries and the safeguards necessary to overcome them.

In summary, the problems arise from the following points:

(1) the quaternaries are bacteriostatic at dilutions far greater than those at which they are lethal;

(2) the bacteriostatic 'carry-over' of a quaternary cannot be eliminated by simple dilution as is the case with most other disinfectants;

(3) an active chemical antidote must be added before the residual bacteriostatic effect is removed;

(4) the quaternaries in general are more active against the Gram-positive bacteria than against the Gram-negative ones, and they are devoid of sporicidal action;

(5) organic matter, especially that of a particulate, insoluble nature, very considerably reduces the efficacies of the quaternaries;

(6) surfaces of different types – glass, metal, rubber, wood, etc. – can exert quite different influences;

(7) the high surface activities of the quaternaries often cause 'clumping' in a bacterial population, thus leading to the protection of some of the cells from the disinfectant action as well as to an apparent reduction in the numbers surviving if estimated by clonal development.

This is a formidable but essential list, but there is still one other important point – the quaternaries, like many other disinfecting agents, should never be assessed against phenol, neither should any attempt be made to award a phenol coefficient. This has already been iterated and reiterated in several contexts in other chapters, but it cannot be overemphasized.

Inactivating and antidotal substances. Although organic matter is known to reduce the activities of the quaternaries the effect is more often than not only partial. Some of the richer culture media containing serum or milk are amongst the best, but ordinary nutrient broth is far from effective, hence the need to use a positive antidotal substance for testing purposes. Agar also brings about a partial reduction in activity (Sherwood, 1942) by virtue of its power of absorption, the saturation point corresponding to the critical micellar concentration and therefore differing for each type of quaternary (Groves and Turner, 1959). The phospholipids are antagonistic (Baker, Harrison and Miller, 1941) and several nonionic compounds have also been examined, sodium lauryl sulphate being amongst those suggested (Valko and DuBois, 1944). Perhaps in the same category can be included ox-gall, which when used in a concentration of 5 per cent in a culture medium, allowed growth of staphylococci at quaternary concentrations up to 1 in 400 (Klarmann and Wright, 1948).

Of all the suggestions put forward, Suramine U.S.P. (Naphuride or Bayer 205) and lecithin with either Tween 80 (a sorbitan mono-oleate) or Lubrol W (a fatty alcohol-ethylene oxide condensate) as the dispersing agent have proved the most satisfactory. Lawrence (1948) was the first to suggest Suramine Sodium, selected as the most effective of a series of high molecular weight naphthalene sulphonates, but it has not proved as acceptable as the lecithin-Tween mixture. The latter was first put forward by Quisno, Gibby and Foter (1946b), who recommended the addition of 0·07 per cent of lecithin and 0·5 per cent of Tween 80 to normal beef extract-peptone broth. This medium is incorporated in the 'Use-Dilution Confirmation' tests of the U.S. Association of Official Agricultural Chemists (Stuart, Ortenzio and Friedl, 1953).

Specific test methods. It is well recognized that the quaternary surface active agents cause bacterial cells both to clump into large masses and also to migrate and adhere to the walls of their container. The second point is not considered important from a testing point of view because the cells can easily be removed by gentle shaking (Davies, 1949), but the situation with regard to clumping is quite different. According to McCulloch (1947) it is the partial cause of quaternaries reducing so quickly the viable count of a bacterial population. The effect is to reduce the apparent number of potentially viable bacterial particles in the suspension and so reduce the probability that one such particle is picked up by the loop. When this occurs, it gives rise to 'wild plusses' which are so characteristic of these tests.

Using a similar argument, Klarmann and Wright (1946) had earlier proposed a semi-micro test method in which the volumes of disinfectant and of culture, namely 0·5 and 0·03 ml respectively, are sufficiently small for the whole amount, instead of the usual single loopful, to be cultured to assess the survivors. This is done by adding a large volume of nutrient broth (20 ml or more) to quench the action after the appropriate exposure time. The method is similar to that of Berry and Bean as described on p. 63. It certainly overcomes the normal errors due to sampling but it still leaves the difficulties associated with the initial mixing of such small volumes of disinfectant and culture and it also leaves a comparatively large volume of quaternary solution to be inactivated. More importantly it does nothing to solve the clumping problem. For these reasons Davies (1949) put forward a test method which (*a*) allows a sufficiently large sample to be cultured to ensure a proportion of clumped bacteria to be included, (*b*) provides a means of breaking up the clumps, (*c*) neutralizes the carry-over of quaternary, and (*d*) gives an actual count of surviving cells. Nine ml volumes of serial dilutions of the quaternary are inoculated with 1 ml of a suspension of a *Staph. aureus* culture on agar. At the end of the disinfecting period the mixture is stirred and 1 ml pipetted into 5 ml of a 1 per cent solution of Lubrol W in a small screw-capped bottle containing beads. The bottle is shaken to break up clumps and then allowed to stand for a few minutes, after which appropriate ten-fold dilutions are plated on agar. By this means, the bactericidal activity can be assessed at any desired killing level. The method is obviously sufficiently flexible to allow other organisms to be used and to allow organic matter in any form to be introduced.

Uses of quaternaries

Because of their particular characteristics the quaternaries have proved most useful in the field of surgery, where they are used principally for preoperative skin disinfection, and in the food industries, where they are used to disinfect food utensils, drinking glasses and dairy equipment. In addition, they have found applications, although much less extensively, as preservatives in the paper and textile industries and also in preventing putrefaction in certain materials of biological origin and in horticulture. They have been suggested (Fair *et al.*, 1945) for the emergency sterilization of highly polluted drinking waters under conditions where chlorine disinfection would be inadvisable because of the high organic content of the water and the consequent large dose of chlorine which would have to be used and which would leave a residual taste. But there are several good arguments against this.

One of the most serious of the limitations in the use of the quaternaries is the lack of activity of some of them against the pseudomonads, including *Ps. pyocyanea*. This was first noted by Lowbury (1951) and later by Robinson (1957) who actually isolated the organisms from a 1 per cent solution of cetrimide. Further investigation showed the source of the infection to have been in the cork of the bottle and not in the solution itself, and it occurs because the solution is unable to kill the organisms on and in the cork. As a consequence, when the bottle is opened some of the contaminants are inevitably shed into the solution, and this presents a real hazard because some measurable time must elapse before the invaders are killed whereas the solution is naturally used immediately on opening (Anderson and Keynes, 1958). The difficulty can easily be overcome by using screw-capped containers.

A greater difficulty arises from the practice of soaking pledgets of cotton wool for the purpose of cleansing the skin area prior to an injection. Each piece of wool not only adsorbs some of the quaternary but also protects any contaminating organism it may be carrying, so that survival and growth, particularly of the resistant pseudomonads, might readily be expected. Such occurrences have been observed with benzalkonium chloride, sometimes with fatal results, by Lee and Fialkow (1961) by Knudsin and Walter (1957) and Malizia, Gangarosa and Goley (1960), the latter finding *Cloaca* contaminations through the similar use of gauzes and sponges.

In surgery and medicine. For surgical hand-disinfection or for the preparation of the skin prior to surgery a quaternary concentration of 1 in 1,000 is the generally recommended level, although the British Pharmaceutical Codex, 1963, recommends a 0·5 per cent solution of domiphen bromide for this purpose, the same concentration as earlier recommended for cetrimide (Barnes, 1942; Williams *et al.*, 1943). Numerous workers have reported them to be at least as valuable as iodine tincture, and other accepted skin disinfectants. In particular, Kramer and Sedwitz (1944) have used a 1 in 200 solution of Ceepryn in 18,000 operation cases without a single instance of infection. On the other hand septicaemias due to *Ps. pyocyanea* infections have been traced to the inefficacy of Zephiran (*Annotation*, 1958) – and this is not the only quaternary so impugned.

Limitations have been observed in the efficacies of quaternaries for skin disinfection (Miller *et al.*, 1943), in that they are said to deposit a film on the skin surface which lacks any disinfecting property on its inner surface. This is because of the oriented adsorption of the molecules on the skin which leaves the active portion of the molecule in the outer surface and so keeps the film sterile, but which directs the inactive portion inwards and so has no effect on the deeply seated bacteria (Rahn, 1946). Any swabbing test made under these conditions, therefore, can give a false impression of the high activity of the disinfectant. These phenomena probably explain why some workers have found the compounds highly efficient, whereas others have reported less encouraging results (*e.g.* Gardner and Seddon, 1946; Robinson, 1952).

Because the quaternaries are practically non-toxic and non-irritant at the concentrations normally used, they can be applied to the more delicate membrane areas, and so they have found application in urology, in obstetrics and in gynaecology. The concentrations recommended for this purpose are generally lower, being of the order of 0·2–0·05 per cent. They have also been recommended for the sterilization of surgical instruments, but words of warning are necessary in this connexion. First, the quaternaries are not active against bacterial spores; secondly, the immersion of instruments for prolonged periods in any aqueous solution will cause rusting, although this can be overcome to a certain extent by adding a small amount of sodium nitrite; thirdly, it is possible for organisms of the *Pseudomonas* group to grow in them on storage (see below).

Besides the irrigation of wounds, claims have been made for the efficacy of quaternaries in treating various skin infections, and they have also been used as preservatives in solutions for injection and ophthalmic solutions.

They have been incorporated in surgical dressings by dipping them in an appropriate dilution of the chosen compound. By this means, gauzes containing 0·1 per cent by weight of the quaternary, β-phenoxyethyldimethyldodecylammonium bromide, have been shown by plate diffusion tests to be active against a range of organisms (Kay, 1954). Bartlett (1949) recommended the use of quaternaries for treating hospital bed-linen, hospital uniforms and even in laundering babies' napkins. They have also been advocated as a means of disinfecting blankets in hospitals, and thereby as an aid in preventing cross-infections. The value of Fixanol C in this respect was commented upon favourably by Marsh and Rodway (1954), although Blowers and Wallace (1955) have raised objections to it on the grounds that it has an unpleasant odour, it stains the blankets and does not dissolve easily. They prefer to use Cirrasol OD, a brand of cetrimide. According to Steingold, Wood and Finch (1954) blankets can adsorb sufficient of a quaternary during laundering for them to retain an antibacterial effect against most organisms for several weeks, but Frisby (1957) is of the opinion that repeated treatments are necessary to keep the blankets clean. Even this may not be adequate, as shown by Rubbo, Stratford and Dixson (1960) and by a hospital board working party (*Report*, 1962), who found viable bacteria, including staphylococci, after the blankets had been in use for only a short time. The reason for failure seems to be that generally there is not enough moisture available for the dust-borne bacteria to make contact with the quaternary, and so it is unable to exert its lethal action.

In the food industries. Quite early in the history of the development of the quaternaries, Krog and Marshall (1940) advocated their use for disinfecting eating and drinking utensils as a result of tests with a 1 in 5,000 dilution of

Zephiran, and subsequent investigations by other workers have substantiated these findings. Several mixtures with various compounds have been employed to enhance the detergent properties of the solutions. Various polyphosphates and nonionic compounds have been used, but Guiteras and Shapiro (1946) warned against including any highly alkaline compounds, pointing out that emulsifying detergents and not saponifying ones must be used, since the latter all antagonize the antibacterial activities of the quaternaries. In this connexion, Davis and Resuggan (1946) found a mixture of sodium carbonate and sodium metasilicate to be highly satisfactory in disinfecting drinking glasses. They preferred this in place of sodium phosphate which reduced the activity of the quaternary used (Diometam).

The quaternaries are used extensively, especially in the United States, for the disinfection, or, as they say in America, the sanitization, of food processing plants and of barbers' equipment, in the brewing industries, in the bottling of beverages, in the handling of shell foods, including eggs, and in canteens, restaurants and licensed premises for the treatment of crockery, cutlery and all drinking utensils (Lawrence, 1950; Resuggan, 1951). The particular virtues claimed for the compounds are that they are odourless, non-staining, practically tasteless and their action is rapid. The concentrations generally used seem to range between 1 in 5,000 and 1 in 2,000 although both weaker and stronger concentrations, 1 in 10,000 and 1 in 1,000 or even 1 in 400, have been recommended for certain specific purposes. It must be remembered, however, that the quaternaries are not highly efficient against *E. coli* or the *Pseudomonas* species.

An antiseptic hand cream containing a benzalkonium homologue (Wedderburn, 1960) has been strongly recommended by the medical profession (*Editorial*, 1960).

In dairying. One of the biggest uses for the quaternaries is in dairy disinfection, a field in which they are now acknowledged and authorized in Great Britain, provided the particular formulation is approved by the authorities and is at least equivalent in activity to the standard hypochlorite solution as assessed in the official Hoy Can test.

Since their introduction into this field there have been many publications on the subject, both in terms of laboratory experiments and findings, and of field trials. Much of this literature has been concerned with discussions on the relative merits of the quaternaries against hypochlorite in dairy disinfection, and many of the protagonists claim to have demonstrated the superiority of the quaternaries, but such claims are very tenuous. They are based partly on the allegation that solutions of the quaternaries are less rapidly exhausted than are the hypochlorites, but this also is highly questionable. The initial excitement in the field seems to have faded during the past few years, but for those interested in the controversy the monographs by Lawrence (1950) and Resuggan (1951) and several articles appearing in *Soap and Sanitary Chemicals* from 1947 onwards will be found informative.

The amphoteric compounds

In 1952 a new group of surface active agents, the higher molecular weight amino acids, appeared in the disinfectants field. These compounds have the general formula $R \cdot NHCH_2 \cdot COOH$, where R is usually an alkyl radical but can also be an acyl one; the group can also include the aminoethyl substituents of aminoacetic acid. They are all amphoteric in character, combining detergency in their anionic group with bactericidal power in their cationic moiety. Because of their chemical structure they are alleged not to be inactivated

TABLE 50

The bactericidal activities of surface-active amino acids

Formula	Compound	Time to kill *Staph. aureus*	pH for optimum activity
$NH \diagdown^{C_{12}H_{23}}_{CH_2 \cdot COOH}$	dodecyl-glycine	10 min	3
$NH \diagdown^{C_2H_4NH \cdot C_{12}H_{23}}_{CH_2 \cdot COOH}$	dodecyl-aminoethyl-glycine	5 min	6–6·5
$NH \diagdown^{C_2H_4NH \cdot C_2H_4NH \cdot C_{12}H_{23}}_{CH_2 \cdot COOH}$	dodecyl-di(amino-ethyl)-glycine	1 min	9–9·5

Tests were made with a 0·05 % solution in each case.

by proteins as are the quaternary ammonium compounds (Schmitz, 1952), and it is this property which had attracted interest and which gives them a superiority over the quaternaries. They are, however, sensitive to soaps and to other anionic and nonionic detergent compounds. They form micelles in aqueous solution, as do the quaternaries, but at lower concentrations, their critical micellar concentrations being in the range 0·2–0·4 gm per litre against 1–2 gm per litre for the quaternaries.

The compounds are marketed under the trade name "Tego". Tego 103S and 51 both contain dodecyldi-(aminoethyl)-glycine hydrochloride and Tegolan is an emulsion of the monoaminopropyl-aminobutyric acid derivative. Other preparations, *e.g.* Tego 103G and 51B, are based on mixtures of compounds with alkyl radicals of slightly different chain lengths.

Germicidal activities. Information on the bactericidal and fungicidal properties of these compounds is not very extensive and such as is available appears to stem mainly from one source. According to Schmitz and Harris (1958) activity increases as the number of nitrogen groups in the surface-active ion is increased. Thus, dodecylglycine is only about one-tenth as active, on a time basis, as is dodecyldi-(aminoethyl)-glycine (Table 50).

Increase in the number of nitrogen groups also increases the pH value at which optimum activity occurs, the values for the three compounds listed in Table 50 being approximately 3·0, 6–6·5 and 9–9·5 respectively. Mixtures of the compounds would, therefore, extend the range of bactericidal activity over a wide pH scale.

On the scant evidence available, the compounds within a given nitrogen group number, at least as far as the Tego types are concerned, do not appear to differ greatly in their activities, but this is perhaps not surprising since they are obviously selected ones. In 1 per cent solution they are claimed to be lethal at room temperature in 1–3 minutes to the staphylococci, coliforms and salmonellae, and to *Proteus* spp. and *Ps. pyocyanea* in 2–5 minutes. They are also said to kill pathogenic fungi such as *Epidermophyton* and *Trichophyton*, as well as the *Rickettsia*, in 3–5 minutes (*see*, for example, Neu, 1954).

Tests made by the author with Tego 51, 103G and 103S showed that dilutions of 1 in 500 in water were lethal to *Staph. aureus*, *Strep. pyogenes*, *E. coli* and *Ps. pyocyanea* in 1–3 minutes and that dilutions of 1 in 1,000 were effective in 4–10 minutes. When the dilutions were made in whole milk, however, the equivalent lethal dilution fell to 1 in 25; 1 in 50 was without action. In the presence of whole blood the lethal concentration fell further to about 1 in 10. This is contrary to the claim made by Schmitz (1952).

Uses. Because of their freedom from toxicity and their allegedly sustained activities in the presence of organic matter the amphoteric bactericides have found their main uses in skin disinfection, in the disinfection of instruments and other general hospital applications and in dairying. According to the trade literature a dilution of 1 in 20 of the di(ethylamino)-glycine derivative will sterilize instruments in 30 minutes if used hot and a 1 per cent solution is recommended for disinfecting the hands, with similar or weaker dilutions for other surgical purposes. The 51 compound appears to be specially designed for dairy disinfection and again a 1 per cent solution is specified for disinfecting the hands and milking equipment, with a 3 per cent solution for treating the udders.

In the author's hands, 1 per cent solutions of these compounds were not particularly effective as skin disinfectants, but Frisby (1959, 1961) reported on them favourably in hospital practice. He found substantial reductions in the bacterial counts of the skin of surgeons and nurses after using a 1 per cent solution of Tegolan (only 4 swabs taken from 51 subjects yielded any growth), and other preparations of the type when used as sprays etc. virtually eliminated staphylococci and *Cl. welchii* from floor sweepings.

REFERENCES

ADAM, N. K. and SHUTE, H. L. (1938). *Trans. Faraday Soc.*, **34**, 758.
ALBERT, A. (1942). *Lancet*, **243**, 633.
ANDERSON, K. and KEYNES, RUTH (1958). *Brit. med. J.*, ii, 274.
Annotation (1958). *Lancet*, ii, 306.

ARMBRUSTER, E. H. and RIDENOUR, G. M. (1949). *Soap*, **25**(1), 103.
BAKER, ZELMA, HARRISON, R. W. and MILLER, B. F. (1941). *J. exp. Med.*, **73**, 249; **74**, 611.
BARNES, J. M. (1942). *Lancet*, **242**, 531.
BARTLETT, P. G. (1949). *Soap*, **25**(3), 139.
BLOWERS, R. and WALLACE, K. R. (1955). *Lancet*, **268**, 1250.
BLUBAUGH, L. V., BOTTS, C. W. and GEOWE, E. G. (1940). *J. Bact.*, **39**, 51.
BLUBAUGH, L. V., BOTTS, C. W., GEOWE, E. G. and HELWIG, H. L. (1941). *J. Bact.*, **41** 34.
CHAPLIN, C. E. (1952). *J. Bact.*, **63**, 453; **64**, 805.
CURRAN, H. R. and EVANS, F. R. (1950). *J. dairy Sci.*, **33**, 1.
DAVIES, G. E. (1949). *J. Hyg., Camb.*, **47**, 271.
DAVIS, J. G. and RESUGGAN, J. C. L. (1946). *Proc. Soc. appl. Bact.*, **9**, 20.
DAWSON, I. M., LOMINSKI, I. and STERN, H. (1953). *J. Path. Bact.*, **66**, 513.
DOMAGK, G. (1935). *Deut. med. Woch.*, **61**, 829.
DUCOR, D. H. (1947). *Publ. Hlth Rep., Wash.*, **62**, 565.
DUNN, C. G. (1936). *Proc. Soc. exp. Biol., N.Y.*, **35**, 427.
Editorial (1960). *Brit. med. J.*, ii, 1792.
EPSTEIN, A. K., HARRIS, B. R. and KATZMANN, M. (1943). *Proc. Soc. exp. Biol., N.Y.*, **53**, 238.
FAIR, G. M., CHANG, S. L., TAYLOR, M. P. and WINEMAN, M. A. (1945). *Amer. J. publ. Hlth*, **35**, 228.
FISCHER, R. and LAROSE, P. (1952). *Nature, Lond.*, **170**, 715.
FREEDLANDER, B. L. (1940). *Proc. Soc. exp. Biol., N.Y.*, **44**, 51.
FRISBY, B. R. (1957). *Brit. med. J.*, ii, 506.
FRISBY, B. R. (1959). *Lancet*, ii, 57.
FRISBY, B. R. (1961). *Lancet*, ii, 829.
GALE, E. F. and TAYLOR, E. SHIRLEY (1946). *Nature, Lond.*, **157**, 549.
GALE, E. F. and TAYLOR, E. SHIRLEY (1947). *J. gen. Microbiol.*, **1**, 77.
GARDNER, A. D. and SEDDON, H. J. (1946). *Lancet*, **250**, 683.
GERSHENFELD, L. and MILANIK, V. E. (1941). *Amer. J. Pharm.*, **113**, 306.
GERSHENFELD, L. and PERLSTEIN, D. (1941). *Amer. J. Pharm.*, **113**, 89.
GROVES, M. J. and TURNER, H. A. (1959). *J. Pharm. Pharmacol.*, **11**, 169T.
GUITERAS, A. F. and SHAPIRO, REBECCA L. (1946). *J. Bact.*, **52**, 635.
HOOGERHEIDE, J. C. (1945). *J. Bact.*, **49**, 277.
HOTCHKISS, R. D. (1946). *Ann. N.Y. Acad. Sci.*, **46**, 479.
JACOBS, W. A. (1916*a*). *J. exp. Med.*, **23**, 563.
JACOBS, W. A., HEIDELBERGER, M. and AMOSS, H. L. (1916*b*). *J. exp. Med.*, **23**, 569.
JACOBS, W. A., HEIDELBERGER, M. and BULL, C. G. (1916*c*). *J. exp. Med.*, **23**, 577.
JONES, R. L., MADINAVEITIA, J., METCALFE, T. P. and SEXTON, W. A. (1950). *Biochem. J.*, **47**, 110.
KAY, E. (1954). M.Sc. Thesis, London University.
KIVELA, E. W., MALLMANN, W. L. and CHURCHILL, E. S. (1948). *J. Bact.*, **55**, 565.
KLARMANN, E. G. and WRIGHT, ELEANOR S. (1946). *Soap*, **22**(1), 125.
KLARMANN, E. G. and WRIGHT, ELEANOR S. (1948). *Soap*, **24**(3), 155.
KLARMANN, E. G. and WRIGHT, ELEANOR S. (1954). *Amer. J. Pharm.*, **126**, 267.
KLEIN, M. and STEVENS, D. A. (1945). *J. Immunol.*, **50**, 265.
KLIMEK, J. W. (1955). *Soap*, **31**(5), 207.
KLIMEK, J. W. and BAILEY, J. N. (1956). *Appl. Microbiol.*, **4**, 53.
KNIGHT, S. G. and FRAZIER, W. C. (1945). *J. Bact.*, **50**, 505.
KNOX, W. E., AUERBACH, V. H., ZARUDNAYA, K. and SPIRTES, M. (1949). *J. Bact.*, **58**, 443.
KNUDSIN, R. B. and WALTER, C. W. (1957). *Arch. Surg.*, **75**, 1036.
KRAMER, G. B. and SEDWITZ, S. H. (1944). *Amer. J. Surg.*, **63**, 240.
KRAVITZ, E., STEDMAN, R. C., ANMUTH, M. and HARDING, T. (1958). *Amer. J. Pharm.*, **130**, 301.
KROG, A. J. and MARSHALL, C. G. (1940). *Amer. J. publ. Hlth*, **30**, 341.
LAWRENCE, C. A. (1948). *J. Amer. pharm. Ass. (Sci.)*, **37**, 57.
LAWRENCE, C. A. (1950). *Surface Active Quaternary Ammonium Germicides:* Academic Press, Inc., N.Y.

LEE, J. C. and FIALKOW, P. J. (1961). *J. Amer. med. Ass.*, **177**, 708.

LOWBURY, E. J. L. (1951). *Brit. J. ind. Med.*, **8**, 22.

McCULLOCH, E. C. (1947). *Science*, **105**, 480.

McCULLOCH, E. C., HAUGE, S. and MIGAKI, H. (1948). *J. Amer. vet. med. Ass.*, **112**, 283; *Amer. J. publ. Hlth*, **38**, 493.

MacGREGOR, D. R. and ELLIKER, P. R. (1958). *Canad. J. Microbiol.*, **4**, 499.

MAIER, E. (1939). *J. Bact.*, **38**, 33.

MALIZIA, W. F., GANGAROSA, E. J. and GOLEY, A. F. (1960). *New Eng. J. Med.*, **263**, 800.

MARSH, F. and RODWAY, HELEN E. (1954). *Lancet*, **266**, 125.

MASON, C. T., BROWN, R. W., MINGA, A. E. (1951). *Phytopath.*, **41**, 164.

MILLER, B. F., ABRAMS, R., HUBER, D. A. and KLEIN, M. (1943). *Proc. Soc. exp. Biol.*, *N.Y.*, **54**, 174.

MOILLIET, J. L., COLLIE, B. and BLACK, W. (1961). *Surface Activity: the Physical Chemistry, Technical Applications, and Chemical Constitution of Synthetic Surface-active Agents*: Spon, London.

MUELLER, W. S. and SEELEY, D. B. (1951). *Soap*, **27**(11), 131.

NEU, R. (1954). *Mfg Chem.*, **25**, 10.

QUISNO, R. A. and FOTER, M. J. (1946). *J. Bact.*, **52**, 111.

QUISNO, R. A., FOTER, M. J. and RUBENKOENIG, H. L. (1947). *Soap*, **23**(6), 145.

QUISNO, R. A., GIBBY, I. W. and FOTER, M. J. (1946a). *J. Bact.*, **51**, 602.

QUISNO, R. A., GIBBY, I. W. and FOTER, M. J. (1946b). *Amer. J. Pharm.*, **118**, 320.

RAHN, O. (1946). *Proc. Soc. exp. Biol.*, *N.Y.*, **62**, 2.

RAHN, O. and ESELTINE, W. P. VAN (1947). *Ann. Rev. Microbiol.*, **1**, 173.

RAWLINGS, A. L., SWEET, L. A. and JOSLYN, D. A. (1943). *J. Amer. pharm. Ass.* (*Sci.*), **32**, 11.

Report by a Newcastle Regional Hospital Board Working Party (1962). *J. Hyg., Camb.*, **60**, 85.

RESUGGAN, J. C. L. (1951). *Quaternary Ammonium Compounds in Chemical Sterilization*: United Trade Press, London.

RIDENOUR, G. M. and ARMBRUSTER, E. H. (1948). *Amer. J. publ. Hlth*, **38**, 504.

ROBERTS, MARTHA H. and RAHN, O. (1946). *J. Bact.*, **52**, 639.

ROBINSON, C. R. (1952). *Lancet*, **262**, 163.

ROBINSON, G. L. (1957). *Brit. med. J.*, **i**, 1242.

RUBBO, S. D., STRATFORD, B. C. and DIXSON, SHIRLEY (1960). *Med. J. Australia*, **2**, 330.

SALTON, M. R. J. (1951). *J. gen. Microbiol.*, **5**, 391.

SALTON, M. R. J., HORNE, R. W. and COSSLETT, V. E. (1951). *J. gen. Microbiol.*, **5**, 405.

SCHMITZ, A. (1952). *Milchwiss*, **7**, 250.

SCHMITZ, A. and HARRIS, S. W. (1958). *Mfg Chem.*, **29**, 51.

SCOTT, C. R. and WOLF, P. A. (1962). *Appl. Microbiol.*, **10**, 211.

SHELANSKI, H. A. (1950). *Soap*, **26**(8), 123.

SHELTON, R. S., CAMPEN, M. G. VAN, TILFORD, C. H., LANG, H. C., NISONGER, L., BAUDELIN, F. J. and RUBENKOENIG, H. L. (1946). *J. Amer. chem. Soc.*, **68**, 753, 755, 757.

SHERWOOD, M. B. (1942). *J. Bact.*, **43**, 778.

SMITH, C. R., NISHIHAR, H., GOLDEN, F., HOYT, A., GUSS, C. O. and KLOETZEL, M. C. (1950). *Publ. Hlth Rep., Wash.*, **65**, 1588.

STEDMAN, R. L., KRAVITZ, E. and KING, J. D. (1957). *J. Bact.*, **73**, 655.

STEINGOLD, L., WOOD, J. H. F. and FINCH, W. E. (1954). *J. appl. Bact.*, **17**, 159.

STUART, L. S., ORTENZIO, L. F. and FRIEDL, J. L. (1953). *J. Ass. off. agric. Chem.*, **36**, 446.

VALKO, E. I. (1946). *Ann. N.Y. Acad. Sci.*, **46**, 451.

VALKO, E. I. and DuBOIS, A. S. (1944). *J. Bact.*, **47**, 15.

WARREN, M. R., BECKER, T. J., MARSH, D. G. and SHELTON, R. S. (1942). *Brit. J. Pharmacol.*, **74**, 401.

WEDDERBURN, DOREEN L. (1960). *Brit. J. ind. Med.*, **17**, 125.

WILLIAMS, R., CLAYTON-COOPER, BARBARA, DUNCAN, J. McK. and MILES, ELLEN M. (1943). *Lancet*, **244**, 522.

WORK, T. S. and WORK, ELISABETH (1948). *The Basis of Chemotherapy*, p. 253: Oliver and Boyd, London.

CHAPTER 15

THE HALOGENS

SINCE early in the nineteenth century, and particularly in the last sixty years or so, an extensive literature has been accumulated on almost every aspect of the germicidal properties of the halogens, with chlorine and iodine attracting particular attention: bromine and fluorine have not received the same attention because their usefulness is more limited. Bromine is strongly irritant and unpleasant to handle and it has no advantages over chlorine as a disinfectant. It is, therefore, never used for such purposes. Fluorine, in the form of hydrofluoric acid or the fluorides, has been used as a preservative against mould infections and also for disinfecting against certain virus infections, but this is about the limit of its usefulness. It is of interest to note that of the halides, the fluorides are the only ones possessing anti-microbial activities; the chlorides, bromides and iodides are inert, apart from any effect they may exert in strong solution by osmosis.

Chlorine

One of the earliest records of the use of chlorine as a disinfectant was in 1791 when it was employed in the gaseous state as a fumigant in hospitals. During the early part of the last century it was found useful for disinfecting water and for treating sewage, and this remains one of its major functions today, chlorine gas and the hypochlorites being employed for the purpose. Other large-scale uses for chlorine are in the disinfection of dairy equipment, of beer glasses and other drinking utensils, and in dishwashing. It also has applications in medicine for the treatment of infected wounds, and in the more domestic sphere for personal hygiene and for disinfecting such articles as babies' milk bottles for which comparatively large quantities are used.

Active compounds of chlorine

Hypochlorites. The hypochlorites were the first compounds of active chlorine to be made, the first one actually being the potassium salt. It was prepared by Berthollet in 1789 under the name of Eau de Javelle, but it has now little more than historic interest, having been displaced by the sodium and calcium salts. Calcium hypochlorite is made by allowing chlorine gas to react with slaked lime either in the solid state or in aqueous suspension, the latter being known in the trade as lime bleach liquor. When freshly prepared, chlorinated lime, or bleaching powder, may contain up to 39 per cent of available chlorine, but it is unstable under normal storage conditions, and is particularly sensitive to moisture and heat. Chlorinated Lime of the

British Pharmacopoeia contains not less than 30 per cent of available chlorine. A particularly potent liquid preparation said to contain as much as 70 per cent of available chlorine is now supplied specially for treating swimming-pool waters and sewage effluents.

Sodium hypochlorite in solution contains up to 20 per cent of available chlorine, but other weaker preparations are sold under numerous trade names for general household disinfection and for personal hygiene. These contain only about 1 per cent of available chlorine, and are usually stabilized in some way, often by adding calcium hypochlorite. Dakin's Solution, a standard product of the British Pharmacopoeia, is a solution of calcium hypochlorite with sodium carbonate and boric acid with an available chlorine content between 0·5 and 0·55 per cent. It is intended exclusively for surgical purposes. It is non-irritant and is fairly stable, although subject to a slow loss of chlorine, especially if exposed to light.

The stability of all of the hypochlorites in solution is affected by temperature, concentration and pH value, of which the last is the most important. Solutions rendered slightly alkaline to about pH 9·5 are the most stable, and it is for this reason that a mixture of sodium and calcium hypochlorites, as indicated above, is frequently used. Solutions of high available chlorine content are less stable than weaker ones. Regardless of strength, they should all be stored cool and in a dark place.

The inorganic chloramines. The simple chloramines in contrast to the more complex organic ones (see below), are formed by the direct action of chlorine with ammonia. Their application is exclusive to the treatment of water and sewage, their particular value being that they are more stable and have a more sustained reactivity than free chlorine or the hypochlorites. The course of the reaction between chlorine and ammonia is somewhat complex and varies according to the initial proportions of the two reagents, the pH value of the mixture and time of their interaction. Allen and Brooks (1952) have summarized it as follows:

$$NH_4^+ + HOCl = NH_2Cl + H_2O + H^+$$
$$2NH_2Cl + HOCl = N_2 + 3HCl + H_2O$$
$$NH_2Cl + HOCl = NHCl_2 + H_2O$$
$$NHCl_2 + HOCl = NCl_3 + H_2O$$

In general the formation of the more highly substituted derivatives appears to be favoured by low pH values and a high chlorine-nitrogen ratio. The significance of these simple chloramines in water and sewage treatment is discussed later.

The organic chlorine-releasing compounds. Besides the hypochlorites and inorganic chloramines there are organic compounds which also release chlorine and so can be used as disinfectants. Probably the best known of the group are Chloramine-T, Dichloramine-T, Halazone and Azochloramide, but others of more recent date include chlorinated derivatives of methylhydantoin and of isocyanuric acid.

Their advantages over the simpler chloramines and hypochlorites are that generally they release their chlorine less readily and so exert a more prolonged bactericidal effect, and they are less irritant and toxic – hence their special,

TABLE 51

The organic chlorine compounds

Common name	Chemical name	Configuration
Chloramine-T	Sodium *p*-toluenesulphonchloro-amide	CH_3⟨ ⟩$SO_2Na:NCl \cdot 3H_2O$
Dichloramine-T	*p*-Toluenesulphondichloroamide	CH_3⟨ ⟩$SO_2 \cdot NCl_2$
Halazone	*p*-Sulphondichloroamidobenzoic acid	$COOH$⟨ ⟩$SO_2 \cdot NCl_2$
Azochloramide	*N : N*-Dichloroazodicarbonamidine	$\begin{smallmatrix} NH_2 \\ \diagdown \\ NCl^{\diagup} \end{smallmatrix} C \cdot N : N \cdot C \begin{smallmatrix} \diagup NH_2 \\ \diagdown NCl \end{smallmatrix}$
ACL	Dichloroisocyanuric acid	$\begin{array}{c} NCl\!-\!CO \\ \diagup \quad \diagdown \\ CO \qquad NH \\ \diagdown \quad \diagup \\ NCl\!-\!CO \end{array}$
ACL 85	Trichloroisocyanuric acid	$\begin{array}{c} NCl\!-\!CO \\ \diagup \quad \diagdown \\ CO \qquad NCl \\ \diagdown \quad \diagup \\ NCl\!-\!CO \end{array}$
Halane	1 : 3-Dichloro-5 : 5-dimethylhy-dantoin	$\begin{array}{c} CO\!-\!\!-\!NCl \quad CH_3 \\ \mid \qquad\qquad \diagdown C \\ \mid \qquad\qquad \diagup \diagdown \\ NCl\!-\!\!-\!CO \quad CH_3 \end{array}$

but not exclusive, use in surgery and medicine. They are also much more stable in the solid state and in solution.

The two derivatives of isocyanuric acid, the dichloro and trichloro compounds, have about 72 and 90 per cent respectively of available chlorine. These two compounds have the advantage over the other organic chlorine-releasing compounds that they are only comparatively slightly affected in their activities by changes in pH value, the ratio between pH 6 and 10 varying with the available chlorine concentration but always being less than 2

(Ortenzio and Stuart, 1959). Because of the low solubilities of these compounds their sodium salts are generally used.

1:3-Dichloro-5:5-dimethylhydantoin is relatively insoluble in water and so a technical grade of about 25 per cent purity is employed. This gives an available chlorine content of about 16 per cent. It behaves quite differently from the isocyanurates in that it is more active on the acid side of pH 7, although the level above which it begins to lose its "hypochlorite equivalent" value varies a little with concentration. In this respect it is similar to Chloramine-T.

The chloramine group of compounds has been known to chemists for a long time, but their germicidal values were not recognized until after the publication of the now classical work of Dakin and his colleagues (Dakin, 1915; Dakin and Cohen, 1916; Dakin, Cohen and Kenyon, 1916 and Dakin and Dunham, 1917). Chloramine-T, or Chloramine of the British Pharmacopoeia, is a white crystalline powder, smelling of chlorine, and containing about 12·5 per cent of combined chlorine, that is, about 25 per cent of available chlorine. Although it is specified in the B.P. as the sodium salt of *p*-toluenesulphonchloroamide the mixed *ortho* and *para* isomers actually have about the same antibacterial activity. It is soluble in about seven parts of water to give a solution which is stable to both light and moderate heat, but at the same time it is advisable to keep it cool and in the dark. Because of its non-irritant properties, it is valuable for treating external infections of the body, although it has been largely supplanted by the more modern sulphonamides and antibiotics.

Dichloramine-T, or *p*-toluenesulphondichloroamide (Dakin *et al.*, 1916) has the very high chlorine content of about 29·5 per cent, but is rather less reactive than Chloramine-T. On this account its antibacterial activity is even more sustained. Because of the low water solubility of Dichloramine-T, its uses have been confined to its application in medicine where it has proved valuable for treating infected wounds (Dakin *et al.*, 1917). It is always applied as a solution in a chlorinated oil solvent; Chlorcosane, a chlorinated paraffin wax, is often used. It has the advantage over many other wound antiseptics that although it dissolves dead tissues, it does not coagulate proteins, but its position today is much the same as that of Chloramine-T in that it has been largely superseded by the more modern antiseptics.

Azochloramide is another of the chlorine compounds which exerts a mild and prolonged action against bacteria. It is the trade name for the substance, $N:N$-dichloroazodicarbonamidine. Azochloramide is said to potentiate the activities of the sulphonamides, and so mixtures with sulphathiazole have been recommended for treating infected wounds.

The bactericidal properties of Halazone, or *p*-sulphondichloroamido-benzoic acid, were first described by Dakin and Dunham (1917) who found it to be a most suitable agent for disinfecting drinking water in small amounts. It was used during the First World War for this purpose, largely because it could easily be dispensed in tablet form, and it is still sold in this form today. Each tablet contains 0·004 gm of Halazone, stabilized with small amounts of sodium chloride and sodium carbonate, and this is sufficient to treat 1 quart of normal water; a larger amount is necessary if the water is heavily polluted. At this concentration, equivalent to 1 part of Halazone in 300,000 parts of water, the Halazone is scarcely detectable by taste, and organisms such as *Escherichia coli*, *Salmonella typhi* and *Vibrio cholerae* are easily killed within 30 minutes. Halazone solutions are most stable if the pH value is at least 10. This does not affect the disinfecting power of the solution after appropriate dilution, and waters so treated can be kept in suitable containers for several weeks without any decline in their bacteriological quality.

Available chlorine

Although these compounds are germicidal by virtue of their available chlorine content, such an assay is not a true criterion of their germicidal activities. It measures only the total amount of chlorine available to enter into a reaction, whereas germicidal activity depends also on the rate of release of chlorine, a capacity which depends upon a number of external factors, including pH value, and which the normal chemical assay is unable to determine.

The technique normally employed for determining available chlorine is by the starch-iodine titration method. In this reaction each atom of iodine displaced is assumed to be equivalent to one atom of chlorine, but a glance at any typical reaction shows this to be fallacious. Taking sodium hypochlorite as the example, the reaction is

$$NaOCl + 2KI + 2HCl = NaCl + 2KCl + H_2O + I_2,$$

from which it is seen that each molecule of sodium hypochlorite, containing only one atom of chlorine, liberates actually two atoms of iodine from the potassium iodide. This fallacy in assessing available chlorine is universally recognized and accepted, but it underlines the importance of differentiating between the available chlorine and the combined chlorine content of a substance.

The disinfecting action of chlorine

Mechanism of disinfection. The intense chemical reactivity of chlorine is undoubtedly the reason for its outstanding characteristic as a rapid and effective germicide even at quite high dilutions. Several attempts have been made to compare the relative activities of the hypochlorites, which are the most reactive, and the chloramines, which are less intensely reactive but more sustained in their lethal effect, but, bearing in mind their different reaction characteristics and also their different sensitivities to external influences such as pH value and the presence of traces of organic matter, such comparisons seem to be invidious. There is no doubt, however, that in order to obtain the same high rates of kill, higher concentrations of the chloramines than of hypochlorites are necessary.

Curiously enough, comparatively little work seems to have been published on the death rates of organisms under the influence of chlorine. Bactericidal powers are almost universally expressed in terms of the minimum concentration producing a kill of 99 per cent or greater in a given time. From the information available, however, the shape of the disinfection curve depends, as with other types of germicide, on whether the killing rate is fast or slow. If it is fast, then a straight-line relationship appears to hold, whereas if it is slow, the initial lag in killing becomes more pronounced. This is well illustrated in Charlton and Levine's (1935) and Rudolph and Levine's (1941) curves showing the effect of temperature and pH value on the germicidal efficiencies of hypochlorite and Chloramine-T against *Bacillus metiens*, and in Allen and Brooks' (1952) similar findings with chloraminoacetic acid against *E. coli*. On the other hand Weber and Levine (1944) found that whereas chlorine gave at first a marked lag followed by progressively increasing death rates of *B. metiens*, Chloramine gave a steady rate throughout the disinfection period, this again is almost certainly a concentration-rate of reaction phenomenon.

Without doubt, chlorine is a bactericidal agent and possesses little, if any, bacteriostatic activity. Isolated claims have been made that in some cases it is only bacteriostatic (Mudge and Smith, 1935), but the speed of disinfection and the route of its attack on the bacterial cell lend no support to this suggestion and tend to confirm that its action is wholly bactericidal.

The lethal action is the result of the direct action of the chlorine on some vital constituent of the cell such as its protoplasm or enzyme system, although here again, suggestions have been made that oxygen plays some part. Rahn (1945) has suggested that the killing curve is non-logarithmic and so the lethal action must be due to a non-progressive reaction such as the destruction of the cell surface, and McCulloch (1945) has stated "The cell membrane appears to be particularly susceptible to chlorination. Chlorinated bacteria may disintegrate." But the mode of attack has not yet been clearly elucidated.

The prevalent theory is that the attack is through hypochlorous acid in its undissociated form. Whilst this may be finally proved true, Allen (1950), reviewing the published evidence, has drawn attention to certain deficiencies which still need to be met and has stated "More data on a wide variety of organisms are required before this conclusion can be generally accepted." The theory is based, first, on the now generally agreed concept that chlorine and all of its active compounds, whatever their type, are hydrolysed in solution to some extent to give hypochlorous acid, and, secondly, that bactericidal activity can be associated with the concentration of undissociated molecules of hypochlorous acid. With the inorganic compounds, the presence of hypochlorous acid is unquestioned, and its significance in the lethal process stems from the observed fact that bactericidal activity is influenced greatly by pH value, there being a progressive, but not always a regular, diminution in activity as the pH value is increased. Since the dissociation of hypochlorous acid with changes in pH value follows a similar path, the two facts appear to be linked together.

If the theory is true then maximum bactericidal activity should occur at pH 5, the level at which the dissociation of hypochlorous acid is at the minimum. But evidence on this seems to be lacking, there being apparently only one set of recorded values at pH values below 5, and that with the more complex Dichloramine and Halazone systems. Again, doubts have been cast against the validity of the theory because the observed changes in bactericidal

TABLE 52

Bactericidal efficiency of hypochlorite solution at different pH values against B. metiens (B. cereus) *spores*
(Rudolph and Levine, 1941)

pH	Time to kill 99% of the spores
10·0	121 minutes
9·35	35·5 minutes
9·0	19·5 minutes
8·0	5 minutes
6·0	2·5 minutes

Concentration of available chlorine—
25 p.p.m.

activity are not directly connected with changes in pH value. But again it is not pH value with which we are concerned, but the dissociation of hypochlorous acid, and the situation in this respect becomes more clear if killing times are plotted against concentrations of undissociated acid at different pH values: on a log-log scale it yields a linear response (Marks, Wyss and Strandskov, 1945).

With the organic compounds, the situation is rather more complex because of the greater obscurity of the reactions involving the release of hypochlorous acid. According to Marks, Wyss and Strandskov (1945), the germicidal properties of the chloramines can be due to the action of the chloramine molecules direct or to the hydrolytic hypochlorous acid formed from them. Since the latter substance possesses much the greater activity and is effective at very low concentrations, they argue that its presence, even in trace quantities, is a major factor in determining the disinfecting power of the chloramines. They then state "This is one reason why pH is such an important factor in the application of compounds of this type. The pH of the solution determines the fraction of the hypochlorous acid in the non-ionized form to which the activity may be attributed."

Effect of pH value. The effect of pH value on the activities of chlorine and its compounds had been observed in the early 1920s, but only in a somewhat empirical fashion. The first systematic studies came from Tilley and Chapin (1930) followed by those of Levine and his colleagues (Charlton and Levine, 1935; Rudolph and Levine, 1941) and others. In every case bacterial spores

TABLE 53

Bactericidal efficiency of hypochlorite solutions at different pH values against anthrax spores

(after Tilley and Chapin, 1930)

pH	Available chlorine (p.p.m.)	Spore survivals after				
		15 min	30 min	45 min	1 hr	2 hr
10	100	+	+	+	+	+
9	50	+	+	−	−	−
	40	+	+	+	−	−
	30	+	+	+	+	−
8	10	+	−	−	−	−
7	10	+	−	−	−	−
6	4	−	−	−	−	−
	3	+	+	+	+	+
5	3	+	−	−	−	−
	2	+	+	+	+	+
4	2	+	+	−	−	−
	1	+	+	+	+	+

TABLE 54

Effect of pH on the bactericidal activity of hypochlorite against B. metiens (B. cereus) *spores*

pH	Available chlorine (p.p.m.)	Time to kill 99% of the spores
11·3	1000	70 minutes
10·4	100	64 minutes
10·0	500	31 minutes
10·0	100	63·5 minutes
8·2	20	5 minutes
8·0	25	5 minutes
7·3	1000	less than 20 seconds
6·0	25	2·5 minutes
6·0	4	less than 15 minutes

were found necessary because the death rates with all vegetative types were much too high to yield any reliable comparative figures, but the methods differed. Tilley and Chapin chose anthrax spores and determined the concentrations of available chlorine to produce a total kill at fixed time periods: Rudolph and Levine used the spores of *B. metiens* and made their comparisons on the basis of the times needed for a fixed chlorine concentration to effect a

99 per cent kill. Their findings are summarized in Tables 52 and 53 and they are amply supported in other reports by various workers as quoted in Table 54, as well as by Brazis *et al.* (1958) who found 1·9 mg of chlorine per litre (1·9 parts per million) at pH 6·2 to be equivalent to 450 mg per litre at pH 10·5 in killing the spores of *B. globigii* and *B. anthracis* in 90 minutes. The change in

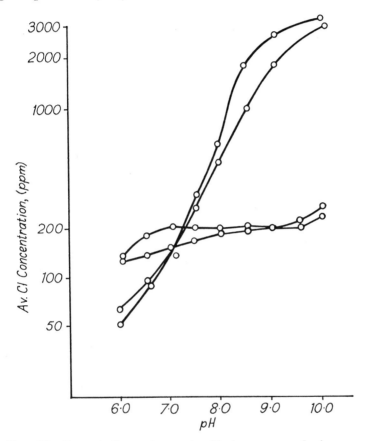

FIG. 18. *Concentrations of organic chlorine compounds in ppm available chlorine having germicidal activity equivalent to hypochlorite solution providing* 200 *ppm available chlorine at pH* 8.5 (Ortenzio and Stuart, 1959).

activity over a relatively small pH range is almost dramatic, and it will be seen from Tilley and Chapin's figures (Table 53) that in some respects pH value is more important than chlorine concentration: for example, 2 parts per million of available chlorine is lethal within 45 minutes at pH 4 but ineffective in 2 hours at pH 5, and it is equal in activity to 50 parts per million at pH 9 and over 100 parts at pH 10.

On surfaces the same rules seem to apply when spore-forming bacteria are involved, but not with vegetative types, as observed by Neave and Hoy (1941) and Cousins and Wolf (1946) in the disinfection of *Staphylococcus aureus* dried in milk films on metal surfaces, as well as by Chaplin and Johns (1949) with similar organisms dried on glass surfaces. Here, no differences in activity were apparent until the pH value was raised to 11 or more. The reason for these differences, as postulated by Cousins and Wolf (1946) and Cox and Whitehead (1949), probably lies in the fact that the protein present in the milk films reacts with the hypochlorite to form more stable chloramine

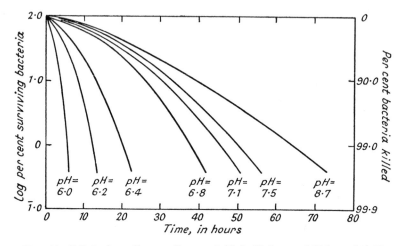

Fig. 19. *Effect of reaction on the germicidal efficiency of Chloramine-T*
(Charlton and Levine, 1935)
Available chlorine 2,000 p.p.m.; temperature 25°

compounds and that these are adequate to kill the more sensitive vegetative cells but not the resistant spores.

The organic chlorine-releasing compounds are also sensitive to pH changes but the pattern of response varies with the types of compound. The chlorinated isocyanuric acids seem to differ only slightly in their activities over the pH range 6·0 to 10·0, but the chloramines and dichlorodimethylhydantoin are very sensitive and can vary as much as five hundred or a thousand-fold over the same pH range (Ortenzio and Stuart, 1959). Fig. 18 illustrates the two types of curve obtained by these compounds. They represent the concentrations estimated to be equivalent to 200 parts per million of available chlorine in hypochlorite at pH 8·5, and they range from about 50 parts per million at pH 6 to 3,000 parts at pH 10 for Chloramine-T and the hydantoin compounds (the steep curves) but only from about 120 to 200 parts for the isocyanuric acids (the shallow curves). The shapes of the curves do not alter substantially when assessments are made against the standard hypochlorite at the lower concentrations of 100 and 50 parts per million, but they occur at somewhat lower levels, as might be expected, except in the case of Chlor-amine-T and the chlorinated hydantoin which are not significantly different at the higher pH values and still require about 3,000 parts of available chlorine to kill at pH 10.

These observations were made by the Chambers modification (1956) of the official test used in the United States for determining the 'Available Chlorine Germicidal Equivalent Concentration' as set out in the *Official Methods of Analysis* (1955). The details of this method are given in the chapter

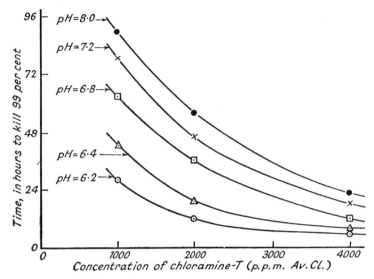

FIG. 20. *Lethal action of Chloramine-T at various concentrations and pH values* (Charlton and Levine, 1935)

on testing disinfectants (p. 68). By its nature it is a more exacting test, involving as it does the incremental additions of small volumes of a test culture, and so of small amounts of organic matter, therefore, the ratios of activities found at different pH values might be expected to be much greater than those obtained from simpler tests. Thus, at the other end of the scale, Wattie and Butterfield (1944) and Butterfield and Wattie (1946) using much lower and fixed concentrations of only 1·2 and 1·5 parts per million for dis-infecting Gram-negative organisms in water recorded only two- to four-fold increases in killing times when the pH value was raised from 6·0 to about 8·0, and Weber (1950) concluded that whereas 250 parts per million of available chlorine in Chloramine-T were adequate to sterilize "at a reaction not greater than about pH 7", 500 to 1,000 parts were required "at a reaction not more alkaline than pH 7·5." Similar results from Charlton and Levine's work (1935) are illustrated in Figs. 19 and 20.

These findings are not quite in line with those of Weber and Levine (1944) or of Marks, Wyss and Strandskov (1945), both of whom obtained optimum efficiencies of the chloramines *between* pH 6·0 and 8·0. Marks, Wyss and Strandskov's findings, with solutions of Dichloramine-T and Halazone containing 5 parts per million of available chlorine, reproduced in Table 55, show unmistakably a point of optimum activity at pH 7·0. The explanation offered by them is that as the pH value is raised from 3 upwards the hydrolysis of the chloramine compound is progressively enhanced to release more hypochlorous acid. At the same time, however, with each increase in pH

TABLE 55

Effect of pH on the sporicidal activity of Dichloramine-T and Halazone
(Marks, Wyss and Strandskov, 1945)

pH	Time in minutes for 99% kill with	
	Dichloramine-T	Halazone
3	87	35
4	72	33
5	60	26
6	24	13
7	16	9
8	42	43
9	—	60

Concentration = 5 p.p.m. available chlorine
Temperature = 25°
Test organism = *B. metiens* (*B. cereus*)

value from 6·0 onwards the free hypochlorous acid becomes more ionized. The net result is first an increase in killing rate up to about pH 7·0, due to the increasing concentration of free hypochlorous acid, followed by a continuous decrease beyond this value, due to the enhanced ionization of the freed acid.

Effect of concentration. Comparatively few investigations appear to have been made on the activity of chlorine in relation to its concentration, but from what has been said in the preceding pages it is of minor importance compared with the influence of pH. Weber and Levine (1944) have stated that by doubling the concentration of available chlorine the killing time for bacterial spores is reduced by about 50 per cent for hypochlorite and about 40 per cent for chloramine, and a similar value of 40–60 per cent was found by Charlton and Levine (1935) for Chloramine-T (*see* Fig. 20). This gives a value for the concentration exponent, n, in the formula $C^n t = K$ of about 1, and this lies in the middle of the range 0·5–1·5 calculated by Allen (1950) from data published by a number of other workers. Thus chlorine is in the class of disinfectants which is only a little affected by dilution.

Effect of temperature. Studies of the effect of temperature on the bactericidal activities of the chlorine compounds show that, as expected, they increase as the temperature is increased. The rate varies with the different chlorine compounds, being more marked with the chloramines than with hypochlorite, and higher in solutions at higher pH values. Typical figures given by Butterfield and Wattie (1946) for the disinfection of water indicate a temperature coefficient between 2–5° and 20–25° of about 2 at pH 7–8 but of 5 or more at pH 10 for hypochlorite; for chloramine it is about 5 at pH 7 and 20 or more at pH 9·5.

Against bacterial spores Rudolph and Levine (1941) obtained a coefficient of about 2 for each 10° over the range 20° to 50°, and a similar figure over the range 4° to 22° was found by Brazis *et al.* (1958). The actual times recorded by Rudolph and Levine to effect a 99 per cent kill with a hypochlorite solution containing 25 parts of available chlorine were 121 minutes at 20°, 65 minutes at 30°, 38·7 minutes at 35° and 9·3 minutes at 50°. With Chloramine-T, Charlton and Levine (1935) recorded decreases in killing times of 82 per cent at pH 6 and 71 per cent at pH 8·7 for every 10° rise in temperature.

Effect of organic matter. The bactericidal efficiency of chlorine is inevitably depressed in the presence of organic matter, and even quite small amounts of such material can be significant. For this reason chlorine should not be used as the disinfectant where large amounts of organic material may be involved. The outstanding exception to this is in the treatment of sewage and waste waters, and to a less extent in the disinfection of wounds, where, in fact, either deliberately or adventitiously the chloramines are involved. These compounds, as already indicated, are less susceptible to the adverse influences of other organic matter and so retain their activities better under these conditions.

Chlorine does not react, of course, with every type of organic compound. It does not generally react with carbohydrates, with the exception of laevulose, and there are many other compounds against which it is inert, including methyl and ethyl alcohols, glycerol, starch and sodium oleate, palmitate and acetate (Guiteras and Schmelkes, 1934; Allen and Brooks, 1952). In general, it is more reactive with nitrogenous substances, and so the extent of the loss of activity depends not only on the concentration of the organic matter present but also on its 'chlorine demand'. But this is not the whole of the story. In most cases, the product of the reaction with organic substances deprives the chlorine of its antibacterial properties, but if there are amino groups present, such as in amino acids and proteins, the reaction product is an N-chloro, or a chloramino, derivative, and here the chlorine retains its activity, albeit at a reduced level. This accounts for some unexpected results reported in the earlier literature, such as the disappearance of anthrax spores from chlorinated tannery wastes even in the apparent absence of residual chlorine (Tilley and Chapin, 1930), and the continued lethal effect of only 130 parts per million of available chlorine in the presence of solid chicken faeces (McCulloch, 1945).

Organic compounds are not the only substances with which chlorine reacts. It loses its bactericidal power in the presence of sulphides, thiosulphates and ferrous salts, and this is important in considering the disinfection of sewage in particular. Chlorine also reacts with thiocyanates, which are present in some industrial effluents, but in this case the product has an activity almost equivalent to that of chloramine (Allen and Brooks, 1949). Finally it is adsorbed by certain types of suspended matter, again an important point in sewage treatment.

Effects of ammonia and amino compounds. The reactions of ammonia and amino compounds with chlorine merit particular attention because of their importance in relation to the disinfection of water and of sewage. As indicated

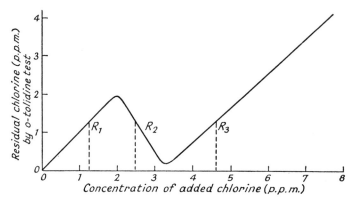

FIG. 21. *A typical break-point curve for chlorine and ammonia*

on page 382, the course of the reactions is complex and depends in part on the relative concentrations of the two substances present. When increasing amounts of chlorine are added to water containing ammonia and the concentration of added chlorine is plotted against the 'residual chlorine' (as determined by the *o*-tolidine test), the resultant graph gives a 'break-point' curve. A typical example of this is illustrated in Fig. 21. According to Allen and Brooks (1952) the three phases of the curve represent progressively: (*i*) the initial direct reaction of the chlorine with the ammonia to form the chloramines (mainly monochloramine); (*ii*) their gradual decomposition as the concentration of added chlorine is increased beyond a certain level, and finally (*iii*) the formation beyond the break-point of the ultimate chloramine, nitrogen trichloride, with the appearance of increasing amounts of free chlorine. It follows from the shape of the curve that a given concentration of 'residual chlorine' may result from the addition of three quite different amounts of chlorine; such a state is obtained, for example, at points R_1, R_2 and R_3 in Fig. 21. Whilst the 'residual chlorines' may be the same, it does not mean that the bactericidal activities are the same. At points R_1 and R_2, and in fact anywhere along the first two phases of the graph prior to the break-point, the chlorine is present as chloramines, and so the disinfecting powers of the solutions are relatively slow and persistent. At points along the third phase of the graph beyond the break-point, *e.g.* at R_3, there is always free chlorine present, and so the rate of destruction of bacteria is rapid. Allen and Brooks quote an example of this in which the concentration of residual chlorine at points R_1, R_2 and R_3 were practically the same at 24·9, 22·4 and 22·5 parts per million respectively, but the killing times for *B. metiens* spores were 83, 88 and 2·7 minutes.

Somewhat similar reactions take place with the amino acids and proteins, resulting in the formation of the appropriate *N*-chloro compounds. Of necessity this reaction is more complex than with simple ammonia, but it still gives the typical break-point curve. The characteristics of the curve are different from that with ammonia, not only because of the greater variability of the reactions concerned, but also because of varying stabilities of the products of the reaction.

The significance and virtues of the chlorine-ammonia reaction in relation to the disinfection of water are several. If a small amount of ammonia or an ammonium salt is added to water and it is then chlorinated to just beyond the break-point there is an initial free chlorine content which is sufficient to effect a rapid disinfection of the water. After this initial stage, the chloramine takes over in a preservative role, and by its sustained bactericidal action ensures it being maintained in a bacteriologically clean state and kept so at least until after it reaches the consumer. Moreover chloramine is tasteless at the levels employed, and it is also deodorant, so that not only does it not flavour the water as does chlorine but it also helps to remove the taint of phenols which are often present in small quantities in water and are said to be detectable in the chlorinated state at concentrations as low as one part in several hundred millions.

Similar advantages also obtain in the chlorination of sewage, but here the natural ammonia and amino acids content is sufficient without adding further ammonia.

Chlorine disinfection in practice

In water treatment. Although the hypochlorites were used originally for the disinfection of water supplies, and they are still so used in small installations, they have been largely superseded in big municipal undertakings by chlorine gas. Chlorine dioxide has also been considered, its main advantage over chlorine being that it removes objectionable tastes (Vincent, MacMahon and Synan, 1946; Ridenour and Armbruster, 1949), but it is not used extensively.

The concentration of chlorine employed varies according to the acidity, or alkalinity, and chemical purity of the water. In good quality waters less than 0·5 part per million is adequate, while as much as 20 parts per million may be necessary if the water is heavily contaminated. Generally, a residual chlorine content, after satisfying the normal chlorine demand of the water, of

0·2–0·4 part per million is sufficient to give a margin of safety. Butterfield (1948) says that under optimum conditions of pH and temperature (pH 7·0 and 20°–25°) as little as 0·04 part per million of free chlorine will sterilize water in 1 minute; the level will vary according to conditions and according to the relative susceptibilities of different organisms. *Salm. typhi*, for instance, is said to be more resistant than *E. coli* at pH 6·5–7·0, but less resistant at more alkaline pH values (Wattie and Butterfield, 1944).

Disinfection by the chloramine treatment is gaining wider acceptance, particularly in the United States. Progress in this country is less rapid, and less necessary, because the quality of the initial raw water is better. There is, therefore, less justification for the more complex treatment, since with good quality water ordinary chlorine treatment retains its effective residual concentrations for an adequate time without the need for stabilization. Where the ammonia-chlorine process is practised, the preammoniation technique is usually followed, that is, ammonia is added before the chlorine, since by this means the added chlorine can exert its rapid lethal action before it is absorbed by the ammonia to give the less vigorously active chloramines (Hoather, 1949). The amount of ammonia added varies according to the quality of the initial raw water, but in any case, break-point chlorination is the rule.

Prechlorination and superchlorination are also popular in certain areas. The purpose of prechlorination, or chlorination before filtration, is to avoid overloading filtration plants and so to extend their useful life; it was practised extensively during the Second World War. Superchlorination is used for rapid disinfection and also as a means of removing objectionable tastes. The procedure in this case is to add an initial concentration of free chlorine up to about 10 parts per million, and then after a short contact period to neutralize the majority of it by treating with sodium sulphite or activated carbon.

Earlier reports indicated that chlorination was of little value in dealing with virus infections, but they have now been disproved. They arose because of the failure to take into account the normal chlorine demand of the test system. One or 2 parts per million of free chlorine will rapidly inactivate the poliomyelitis virus (*Lancet*, 1949), and so superchlorination is an absolutely safe treatment. Likewise the viabilities of the viruses of the hepatitis, adeno, Coxsackie and ECHO groups, although varying in their resistances, are all reduced by over 99 per cent within 30 minutes by concentrations of 0·2–2 parts per million (Kabler *et al.*, 1961). Chloramine is much less effective.

In swimming baths. When chlorination is used for disinfecting swimming-bath water, it is required that the residual chlorine shall be maintained within the range 0·2–0·5 part per million. Chloramine treatment is an obvious advantage in this case, because it provides a reservoir of available chlorine, whilst at the same time not manifesting any of its irritant and objectionable side-effects. Chloramine-T has also been found effective for the same purpose (Thompson, 1949).

With an available chlorine control of not less than 0·4 part per million it is said that swimming-pool water can be maintained at the same level of bacteriological purity as drinking water. Whilst this may be true in a general sense, it would seem doubtful in the particular, if only because of the ease with which organisms in mucus and the like can be transmitted from one person to another before the chlorine has been able to deal fully with the infection. There is also the question of the transmission of virus infections.

In sewage. Chlorination of sewage is practised much more widely in the United States than in Great Britain. In the United States the sewage is usually much weaker and is discharged into larger rivers so that the deleterious effect of the residual chlorine on the river life is much less marked than in the more concentrated and smaller British systems. Nevertheless, with increasing population densities and the limited disposal facilities, safe chemical treatment is becoming more and more essential. The purpose of chlorination is threefold: to remove offensive odours, to eliminate pathogens which are inevitably present in all domestic and hospital sewage, and to prevent undue putrefaction before the sewage reaches the treatment works. It will also delay septicity after discharge to an estuary or near a bathing beach.

Much of the chlorine initially introduced is immediately lost for disinfection purposes due to the chlorine demand of the many organic and inorganic constituents of the sewage, but a proportion of it is taken up in the formation of the chloramines and N-chloro compounds and these constitute the effective germicidal agents. Cyanogen chloride, derived from thiocyanates in certain types of sewage effluents, is also an effective bactericide (Allen and Brooks, 1949). The chlorine demand naturally varies according to the concentration of the sewage and the nature of its make-up, but broadly speaking it ranges between about 10 and 20 parts per million. Rather curiously, the demand increases with the period of contact; for example, a demand of 15 parts after 15 minutes can rise to 20 parts after 6 hours and 30 parts after 46 hours (Allen, 1961). Hence the need for a really adequate chlorination if an effective disinfection is to be achieved. Low doses produce a temporary reduction in the bacterial count and some deodorization, but the cells surviving the early stages of the treatment are liable to proliferate at some later period. They are not likely, however, to reach very high counts because the protozoa which also survive the treatment are a controlling factor in restricting bacterial growth (Allen and Brooks, 1949). The surviving bacteria are mainly Gram-negative, non-sporing types, including *Proteus* spp. and the pseudomonads.

In dairying. Chlorine has a wide application in the disinfection of dairy equipment, for which purpose hypochlorite solutions are mainly used. The presence of residual milk films depletes the effectiveness of the chlorine, and so it is standard practice to use a considerable excess to meet this depletion. The Regulations for England and Wales require a detergent wash with a

14

hypochlorite solution containing 250–300 parts per million of available chlorine with 0·25 per cent of soda ash added, followed by a rinse with a weaker chlorine solution.

In spite of the high concentrations of chlorine applied, failures in disinfection treatments are not unknown. They arise from two causes: (*i*) the high resistance of naturally occurring infection in milk compared with that of laboratory strains, an example of which is found with *Streptococcus agalactiae*, said to be ten times more resistant in milk than laboratory maintained cultures (Taylor and Hoy, 1954); and (*ii*) the physical state of the equipment being disinfected. Neave and Hoy (1941) noted that milk cans which were old and had become scratched and rusted were much more difficult to disinfect than new cans, an occurrence which they later attributed to the physical protection given to the organisms by the uneven and hidden films of milk fats and solids in the broken metal surfaces (Hoy and Neave, 1955). Losses of as much as 50 per cent of the total added available chlorine from an initial solution containing 200 parts per million were recorded, and this markedly reduced the disinfecting efficiency compared with that found in new cans.

Trichloroisocyanuric acid has been formulated into a "detergent-sterilizer" using polyphosphate, metasilicate, etc. with up to 2 per cent of various other compounds. Hydrated substances should be avoided as they considerably reduce the stabilities of the mixtures (Petrie and Roman, 1958).

Chloramine-T is not universally considered to be a suitable disinfectant for dairy equipment because of the time required for adequate disinfection, although it is accepted in some countries.

For food and drinking utensils. In restaurants and public houses where there is a rapid turnover of dishes, glasses and cutlery there is an obvious obligation to eliminate as far as possible the transmission of bacterial infection from one user to the next. The normal washing process itself, if properly applied, will do much, but it is not always adequate, and something more positive is needed. The time factor here is important, because more often than not it is only possible to give a short rinse with a disinfectant. The hypochlorites, then, are particularly suitable, although care and control are needed to see that they are not used beyond the point of exhaustion.

When speed of action is not a primary consideration and a disinfection period of a few minutes can be allowed, the chloramines are satisfactory. This applies particularly to sink washing in contrast to mechanical washing where the cycle of operations includes a hot water treatment at 80° (175°F) or more. With sink washing it is never possible to work with temperatures exceeding about 50°, and under these conditions, a short treatment with a chloramine-detergent solution is advantageous. The United States Ordinance and Code for Restaurants, 1948, allows the use of hypochlorite solution containing 50 parts per million of available chlorine with an exposure time of two minutes in lieu of a hot water treatment; chloramine solutions may also be used provided they have equivalent bactericidal strength to the prescribed hypochlorite solution. The activity of chloramine is not adversely affected by detergents such as Teepol, Sulphonated Lorol and some soaps, in fact it appears to be enhanced in some cases, and on this basis the author has found immersion in 0·1 per cent solution of a mixture of 4 parts of Chloramine-T, 4 parts of Teepol, and 1 part of salt for only 30 seconds to be satisfactory for dealing with the majority of vegetative organisms carried on dried films of milk or serum on crockery and glassware.

The treatment of babies' bottles calls for particular mention because of the special and increasing attention now being given to the subject, and the hypochlorites again are ideal for such a purpose. The concentration recommended is 250–300 parts of available chlorine per million, the same as is used in dairying, but in this case the treatment time can be prolonged. A useful drill to follow after each feed is to rinse out the bottle and teats, using a brush to remove fats and solid matter if necessary, then immerse them in the hypochlorite, if possible until the time of the next feed. A clean rinse leaves the bottle ready for immediate use.

In addition to the disinfection of food utensils, chlorine has certain applications in the treatment of foods. It has been used for disinfecting shell fish, notorious as carriers of *Salmonella* and other infective organisms if harvested from polluted waters, and in the prevention of bacterial decay in some other foods. Some consider it to be better than the tetracyclines for preserving chicken carcases but it still has its disadvantages. Dixon and Pooley (1961), for instance, reported that an immersion for 10 minutes in a solution containing 200 parts of chlorine per million would eliminate the salmonellae if the total initial count were less than 1,000 organisms; with higher counts there was only a partial reduction.

For washing eggs, hypochlorites used at 200 parts per million will eliminate completely artificially induced contaminations of *Salm. typhimurium*: they were the best of eight commercial egg-washing preparations tested by Bierer *et al.* (1961). In similar circumstances, Chloramine-T has been found effective in treating the surfaces of incubator eggs to prevent salmonella infections in the newly hatched chick (Lancaster, Gordon and Tucker, 1952).

In medicine. As indicated earlier, the chlorine preparations are valuable agents in treating wound infections. Dakin's solution was developed particularly for use in the Carrel-Dakin irrigation technique, but Chloramine-T is probably more suitable as a general skin and wound disinfectant because of its greater sustained activity. Even in the presence of serum, a 1 in 1,250 solution is lethal to organisms such as *Staphylococcus*, *Streptococcus* and *Pseudomonas* types (Dakin, Cohen and Kenyon, 1916), and solutions ranging between 0·1 and 1 per cent in water are used effectively against various skin and eye infections, as well as for gargles and douches. It is also applied as an ointment.

Colebrook (1930) found Chloramine-T to be especially valuable as a disinfectant for the hands and gloves in preventing the transfer of streptococcal infections in childbirth and midwifery. Of several antiseptics examined, only iodine, 0·5–1 per cent, and Chloramine-T, 1–2 per cent, were reliably effective in killing these organisms.

Iodine

General properties

Iodine has been used for various purposes in medicine for nearly 150 years, but its appreciation as a germicide is of rather shorter duration. It was early employed in the treatment of wound infections and as an injection against anthrax, but it is only about 50 years ago that it was first used for skin disinfection.

Iodine is a solid at normal temperatures, but it has a high vapour pressure, and so sublimes readily. It is only slightly soluble in water, and its solubility is enhanced by the presence of iodide ions; it is readily soluble in alcohol. Solutions of iodine are normally brown in colour and they stain badly, but non-staining preparations are available, amongst which is the B.P.C. solution in arachis oil and liquid paraffin. So-called colourless iodine preparations are also made. Iodophors, or preparations of iodine solubilized with surface active agents, have attracted attention recently in the United States, and a number of organic derivatives of iodine has been found active (*see* page 403).

The 'official' solutions of iodine are Weak Solution of Iodine, B.P., Lugol's Solution, B.P. and Mandl's Paint, B.P.C. The American counterparts of these solutions, not always of identical concentrations, are found in the various United States Pharmacopeia and National Formulary monographs. The Weak Solution contains 2·5 per cent of iodine and 2·5 per cent of potassium iodide in 90 per cent alcohol and is the preparation most used for skin disinfection. Lugol's Solution is an aqueous solution containing 5 per cent of iodine and 10 per cent of potassium iodide and is sometimes preferred to the alcoholic solution because it is less irritant. Mandl's Paint, containing 1·5 per cent of iodine and 3 per cent of potassium iodide, is a weaker aqueous solution used for painting on the more delicate skin membranes.

There are many references in the medical literature to the use of iodine for the treatment of skin infections, for application to the mucous membranes, to root canals of the teeth and to the eye, and for the preoperative preparation of the skin. Numerous investigations by tissue culture techniques and on the skins and membranes of humans and animals have shown it to be relatively non-toxic, nevertheless, it can be harsh and irritant on some skins and can cause severe blistering if carelessly handled. For this reason, and because of its staining properties, it has tended to fall into disuse. In the face of the more modern preparations there is today not much glamour in iodine as a skin disinfectant, but it still remains a remarkably active agent for this purpose.

Germicidal properties

Activity against bacteria. Iodine is a highly reactive element and it is this reactivity which makes it an effective germicide. Two of its outstanding characteristics are its lack of selectivity against different bacteria, all types being killed at about the same level of concentration, and its exclusive bactericidal, rather than bacteriostatic, action (Gershenfeld and Patterson, 1945; Salle and Catlin, 1947). Several assessments of its phenol coefficient have been made, but bearing in mind the uses and activities of iodine such assessments are meaningless and so not worth quoting.

The reactivity of iodine is similar to that of chlorine, but unlike chlorine its disinfecting action is the result of the direct intervention of free iodine molecules (Nyiri and DuBois, 1931) which combine with the protein substances of the cell. Hypoiodous acid does not take any part, except possibly at high pH values (Wyss and Strandskov, 1945), and so presumably the major reaction is one of direct halogenation.

In the presence of iodides there is always a certain amount of periodide, or triiodide, formed through the simple reaction

$$I_2 + I^- \rightleftharpoons I_3^-$$

and this has only a low activity against both bacterial spores (Wyss and Strandskov, 1945) and vegetative cells (Carroll, 1955). A large excess of added iodide must therefore be avoided otherwise nearly all of the free iodine will be taken up into periodide, thus reducing its availability for germicidal purposes and so reducing the overall activity of the solution. From Wyss and Strandskov's figures, the addition of 100 parts by weight of potassium iodide can extend the killing time of a solution of iodine from 4 minutes to 39 minutes, and 1,000 parts can increase it to 220 minutes; the normal ratio of 2 parts of iodide has only little effect.

Effect of concentration. With solutions at the concentrations normally used the lethal action of iodine is rapid against all organisms. From various reports in the literature, the minimum concentration of iodine lethal to vegetative bacteria at time intervals up to 10 minutes falls in the range 1 in 7,500 to 1 in 20,000, although Carroll (1955), has put it at a much lower level, finding 2 parts per million to be lethal to *E. coli* in 10 minutes and 33 parts in 1 minute. These differences are probably due to the methods of testing employed and to the amount of organic matter, in the form of nutrient broth, added with a culture to the medication mixture. The significance of this is seen in an observation made by Gershenfeld and Witlin (1949a) who found that "One cc of 2 per cent iodine was inactivated by 40 cc of sterile F.D.A. broth."

Effect of organic matter. The foregoing statement indicates the marked depressant effect of organic matter on the activity of iodine, a point which has received attention by several investigators. Salle and Catlin (1947), for instance, found that the minimum concentration lethal to *Staph. aureus* in

10 minutes at 37° was increased from 1 in 20,000 to 1 in 2,500 on adding 10 per cent of horse serum, and Gershenfeld and Witlin (1949b) found that a 1 in 5,000 dilution in the presence of 5 per cent of human plasma was lethal to a number of organisms at 37° but not at 24°. In Dakin's (1915) hands, rather higher concentrations were necessary to kill *Staph. aureus*, the level being reduced from 1 in 3,500 to 1 in 1,700 by adding serum, and in the author's laboratory, *Staph. aureus*, *E. coli* and *Streptococcus pyogenes* in the presence of 10 per cent of whole blood were killed in 1 minute at 37° by a dilution of 1 in 800, but not 1 in 1,600.

In the concentrations normally used for skin disinfection the effect of organic matter is negligible because the lethal times are always measured in seconds (Gardner and Seddon, 1946; Gardner, 1948; Story, 1952). The same applies to organisms dried on surfaces, but in this case the killing times are extended from 20–100 seconds for unprotected organisms to 5 minutes or more for those dried with 50 per cent of human plasma (Gershenfeld, Greene and Witlin, 1951).

Effect of pH value. It is generally accepted that the germicidal activity of iodine is not sensitive to pH changes, but this appears to be true only for the more concentrated solutions used for surgical disinfection. With the weaker concentrations such as are used in the disinfection of food utensils and in water treatment there is a marked reduction in activity as the pH value is moved to the alkaline side, and this is reflected in the 'phenol coefficient' of iodine, which, according to Gershenfeld and Fox (1948), is only one-quarter the value at pH 9·55 as at pH 4·93. Wyss and Strandskov (1945) also found killing times against bacterial spores to be increased with pH value, a period of 2·3 minutes in the pH range 6·0–8·0 being increased to 4·5 minutes at pH 8·5 and 11 minutes at pH 9·0. This phenomenon they attributed to the hydrolysis equilibrium of iodine with water being shifted towards the production of increased amounts of hypoiodous acid under the more alkaline conditions.

Activity against spores. Iodine is almost equally effective against both spores and vegetative bacteria, provided the cells are in suspension. From the experiments of Wyss and Strandskov (1945) a solution containing 40 parts per million will kill 99 per cent of the spores of *B. metiens* in periods ranging from 2·2 to 5 minutes but according to Allawala and Riegelman (1953) much higher levels or longer times are required. They found that to kill the same spores in 5·1 minutes a concentration as high as 288 parts per million (28·8 mg in 100 ml) was required; alternately, 35 parts per million took 33 minutes to kill.

When the spores are on moist or dry surfaces the action is apparently quite different, and even with a standard 2 per cent solution in water sterilizing times for *B. subtilis*, *B. anthracis*, *B. mesentericus*, *B. megatherium* and *Cl. tetani* ranging between 90 minutes and over 5½ hours have been recorded (Gershenfeld and Witlin, 1949a). The shortest killing times occurred with organisms treated wet on metal surfaces, and the longest when they were dried on metal or absorbed on filter paper.

Activity against viruses. Iodine is also active at high dilutions against viruses. Solutions as weak as $0.0005N$ (approximately 60 parts per million) will inactivate washed influenza virus particles (Knight and Stanley, 1944), but ten times that concentration may be necessary if they are suspended in allantoic fluid (Dunham and MacNeal, 1944). In water, Chang and Morris (1953) say that a few parts per million will inactivate the poliomyelitis virus in 5–10 minutes, but according to Gershenfeld (1955) as much as 125–375 parts are needed to accomplish the same inactivation in 1 minute.

Activity against fungi. Opinions on the actual lethal concentrations of iodine against the fungi vary somewhat, but it is acknowledged to be an effective fungistatic and fungicidal agent. Most of the investigations reported have been carried out from the clinical aspect using pathogenic fungi, and the concentrations reported lethal to organisms such as *Monilia, Trichophyton, Epidermophyton* and *Torula* have ranged between 1 in less than 1,000 (Gomez-Vega, 1935) and 1 in 85,000 (Schamberg, Brown and Harkins, 1931); Emmons (1933) claimed 'phenol coefficients' against *Trichophyton* and *Monilia* of 3,100 and 3,600.

Iodine-impregnated wrapping paper has been tried for preserving fruit against destruction by mould growths.

Compounds of iodine

Iodoform. Iodoform, CHI_3, is probably the oldest known compound of iodine used for antiseptic purposes. It has a characteristic 'hospital' smell, but it appears to be devoid of antibacterial properties *in vitro*. *In vivo* it is said to release iodine slowly when in contact with body secretions, and if this is true it could account for its antiseptic activity. It was left out of the British Pharmacopoeia, 1953.

Iodine trichloride. This compound is described by Mackie (1928) as a highly active substance, a 1 per cent solution in water being lethal to bacterial spores within a few minutes. Even when embedded in material such as catgut the most resistant of them succumbed within 30 minutes. A 1 per cent solution is marketed as a disinfectant for external application.

Iodonium compounds. This group of compounds has the general formula R_2IX, where R is an organic radical, and X can be either an organic or an inorganic anion. In such a structure the iodine occurs as a trivalent ion. It is not present in the free state, since it does not react with thiosulphates. The compounds, all of which are strongly basic, are both bacteriostatic and bactericidal, and they possess antifungal properties.

Of several such compounds examined by Gershenfeld and Witlin (1948), they found that "Only bis-*p*-chlorophenyliodonium sulphate in saturated aqueous solution (even when diluted 1:4) displayed bactericidal efficiency against *M. pyogenes* var. *aureus* at 37°C within 1 minute", and the same

compound in "saturated alcohol-acetone solution . . . was capable of killing
. . . *B. subtilis* spores (4 day-old culture) within 4 hours at 37°C but was
devoid of killing effect within 240 hours at 25°C." In terms of bacteriostasis,
diphenyliodonium chloride showed the greatest over-all activity, followed
by bis-*p*-bromophenyliodonium iodide, the effective concentrations against
a range of bacteria being generally below 0·01 mg per ml. Curiously enough,
Salm. typhi was the most resistant in both cases, and the bacteriostatic levels
were beyond the normal saturation concentrations in water.

Diphenyliodonium chloride is marketed in an aqueous solution under
the trade name of Katiodin. In the author's experience, this is not a very
active preparation, although it is claimed to be sporicidal. The solution is
highly bacteriostatic, but when applied neat it did not kill the spores of
B. subtilis in 4 days, and vegetative types required up to 60 minutes.

Iodophores. The iodophores are not strictly compounds of iodine; they
are mixtures of iodine with surface active agents which act as carriers and
solubilizers for the iodine. They possess in general all the germicidal characteristics of iodine and there is always close relationship between colour and
activity. They have low vapour pressures and an almost complete lack of
odour; they have low irritant properties and are non-staining. Anionic,
cationic and nonionic agents can be used as solubilizers, but generally the
more stable preparations are obtained with nonionic substances. Not all of
the nonionics are suitable; some are not iodine carriers and others are not
sufficiently water soluble. Commercial products are made with compounds
such as polyvinylpyrrolidone, polyethoxyethanol derivatives and various
quaternary ammonium compounds, and they go under trade names such as
Wescodyne, Povidone-Iodine, Betadine, Virac, etc. This list does not, of
course, limit the types of compound available or the trade names used; it
only gives examples.

Because the iodine in these compounds is brought into solution with a
solubilizer other than the iodide ion there is no loss of iodine by its conversion
to the inactive triiodide ion (*see* p. 401), and this probably accounts for the
activities of the iodophores being allegedly higher than those of the simpler
iodine solutions. Gershenfeld and Witlin (1955), for instance, found that
whereas standard iodine-iodide solutions would kill *Staph. aureus* and *Salm.
typhi* in 5 minutes at concentrations down to 25 parts of iodine per million,
two commercial iodophores were effective down to as little as 6 parts per
million. There is, however, frequently some apparent loss of activity because
of the partitioning of the iodine between the micelle structure of the surface
active agent and the water phase, and the work of Allawala and Riegelman
(1953) "clearly indicates that the 99% killing time is proportional to the
equilibrium thermodynamic activity of iodine as represented by the free
iodine concentrations of water . . . and is not necessarily dependent upon
the total amount of that agent."

The iodophores exhibit maximum activity and stability in acid solutions at pH 3–4 and so for practical purposes the addition of phosphoric acid is recommended. Such a solution diluted to contain only 1 part of iodine per million is reported to be 99·9 per cent effective against staphylococci and *E. coli* in 1 minute; at 5 parts per million it gave no survivors in 15 seconds.

According to Brost and Krupin (1957) the activities of the iodophores are independent of the iodine-surfactant ratio and vary only with the iodine content. Excess of the surface active agent, that is a ratio of more than 10:1, is necessary only if detergency as well as disinfection is required, as in dairying. One can well imagine, however, that the ratio might vary with the type of surface active agent used.

There seems to be a considerable diversion of opinion concerning the minimum lethal concentration of the iodophores. It has already been stated above that 5 parts per million will kill in 15 seconds and 6 parts per million in 5 minutes; in addition Lawrence, Carpenter and Naylor-Foote (1957) reported that 25–50 parts per million were lethal to *Staph. aureus, Proteus* spp. and pseudomonads in 10 minutes, and under similar conditions the author found that as much as 100 parts or more were needed. These differences may have arisen as a result of using preparations of different composition and from different sources, but they could also be attributed to the varying testing methods employed, and this is best illustrated in some experimental results quoted by Gershenfeld and Witlin (1955) and Lawrence, Carpenter and Naylor-Foote (1957). According to the latter, the addition of 5 per cent of serum will bring about a four- to twenty-fold reduction in activity; according to the former, considerable differences occur by simply changing the amount of culture used in a test. Thus, by reducing the volume of inoculum from 0·2 to 0·05 ml the minimum lethal concentration can be reduced from 6 to 2 parts per million.

Besides being lethal to vegetative bacteria, the iodophores are active against tubercle bacilli (Wright and Shternov, 1950; Lawrence, Carpenter and Naylor-Foote, 1957) and they are also sporicidal, fungicidal and virucidal. The susceptibilities of the moulds and tubercle bacilli appear to be about the same as those of the vegetative bacteria, but for bacterial spores somewhat higher concentrations seem to be needed.

On the evidence available there does not appear to be much difference in the resistances of spores in suspension and those dried on surfaces. Bartlett and Schmidt (1957) quoted lethal times of 6 hours for suspension of *B. subtilis* and *Cl. welchii*, and 10–12 hours for *Cl. tetani* with a solution containing 500 parts of iodine per million. Similarly, the author found a commercial iodophore diluted to contain 1,000 parts of iodine per million to be lethal to mixed bacterial spores in about 6 hours, and Lawrence *et al.* (1957) were able to kill *B. subtilis* spores dried on silk sutures with a 1 in 1,000 solution in 2–6 hours. In contrast, Gershenfeld (1962) had to use an undiluted preparation containing 1 per cent of iodine to kill *B. subtilis, Cl. welchii* and

Cl. tetani spores within $2\frac{1}{2}$ hours when dried on metal blades. This preparation, along with iodine itself, was the only solution capable of killing spores under these conditions with any speed, seven others requiring over 24 hours. Against the Newcastle disease virus suspended in allantoic fluid Bartlett and Schmidt (1957) claim that 25 parts per million are effective in 30 seconds and that 50 parts per million will inactivate the poliomyelitis virus in 5 minutes.

Other compounds. A group of other iodine derivatives are being used as antiprotozoal agents in the treatment of amoeba and trichomonad infections. They are all quinoline compounds and are administered either orally or topically. They are marketed under an embarrassing variety of trade names and some of them are listed in the Pharmacopeia of the United States.

Iodine disinfection in practice

In skin disinfection. Iodine is still accepted as one of the most efficient of the germicides for the preoperative preparation of the skin, and generally an aqueous solution is preferred before an alcoholic tincture because of its less irritant properties. The references to its application in this field are too numerous to recite in detail, but they cover practically all forms of surgical treatment, including operations for the removal of cataracts and for the correction of uterine prolapse. It is also used in administering injections and for removing blood and the body fluid samples, as well as in making skin grafts and in carrying out other aseptic surgical manipulations.

Gardner and Seddon (1946) and Gardner (1948) examined the efficiencies of a wide range of skin antiseptics by a simple patch swabbing technique, and found that "Virtual disinfection was achieved in 15–20 seconds with a single application of 2% iodine in 70% alcohol." This was the only solution which was consistently rapid in its action; other solutions, even though some contained alcohol, revealed "either a slower or an imperfect disinfecting power." This opinion was reiterated by Story (1952) in a comparison of aqueous solutions of iodine with solutions of quaternary ammonium compounds. Using a novel testing technique in which small areas of skin enclosed in glass cylinders were infected with various organisms and then subjected to swabbing with the disinfectant, he found a 1 per cent solution of iodine to be the only solution giving virtual sterilization within 30 seconds.

By hand washing tests, Frisch, Davies and Krippaehne (1958) found an iodophore to be the most effective of the several preparations they examined, and only slightly inferior to alcohol. But there were always a few organisms left, as was also found by Blatt and Maloney (1961) in their *in vivo* tests. However, in this connexion it should be remembered that the hand washing technique is much more critical than are swabbing tests on limited areas of the skin, and so the inferiority of the iodophores against straight iodine solutions may be more apparent than real.

Generally a 2 per cent solution in water or in alcoholic tincture is used for skin disinfection, although much weaker ones are often employed for irrigating wounds and for preoperational hand disinfection. A novel preparation which has been found effective in treating deep wound infections is Heliogenin (Ryan *et al.*, 1949). It consists of a mixture of Chloramine-T, potassium iodide, glucose and sodium phosphate and combines the virtues of chlorine in the Chloramine-T with those of iodine, which is slowly released from the mixture in the presence of water.

As emphasized in the chapter on testing antiseptics, a good skin disinfectant should not only show immediate antibacterial activity, but it should also retain this activity and from tests carried out by the technique described on page 95, iodine possesses this property. According to the results obtained, 0·5 per cent solutions in alcohol or water applied by swabbing to the skin and allowing to dry are still lethal to *Staph. aureus* 2 hours after the application. The same can also be said of the iodophores even when diluted to contain only 0·1 per cent of iodine.

For disinfecting surgical and domestic equipment. Iodine has been recommended for the emergency sterilization of various types of surgical equipment, especially rubber and plastic apparatus and knife blades. Immersion for a short period in solutions containing up to 2 per cent of iodine have been used, and weaker solutions have been employed for the temporary storage of non-rusting materials. Iodophores can also be used for the same purposes, and in particular they have been found valuable for disinfecting rectal catheters. Immersion for only 5 minutes in a solution containing 75 parts of iodine per million is adequate for artificially infected units, but for those in clinical use 60 minutes are needed (Maher, Rogers and Peterson, 1961).

Particular attention has been given to the disinfection of clinical thermometers from the point of view of transferring respiratory infections, and Gershenfeld, Greene and Witlin (1951) found a 2 per cent aqueous solution or a 2 per cent tincture (the U.S.P. XIV formula) to be always superior to the various alcohols commonly used; the aqueous solution was preferred to the tincture. *Strep. pyogenes, Staph. aureus, E. coli* and other organisms, after drying on to thermometer stems, were all killed at 20° in periods varying between 20 and 120 seconds, but when the organisms were dried from 50 per cent citrated plasma as long as 5 minutes were required to kill. In this respect the iodophores at 200 parts per million are about as effective as 70 per cent alcohol. Both were about 95 per cent effective in disinfecting thermometers, taken straight from the wards and dried for 3–4 hours, after a 15 minutes treatment (Wright and Mundy, 1958).

Gershenfeld and Witlin (1951) also recommended weak iodine solutions for disinfecting eating and drinking utensils. From an investigation of the efficacy of solutions ranging in strength between 200 and 0·5 parts of iodine per million of water they found that "dishes, cups, glassware, knives, forks and spoons after scraping and a preliminary 10 second spray rinse in water (between 130° and 170°F) were sanitized by dipping in iodine solutions for

1, 10, 20, 30 and 60 second intervals (100 and 200 p.p.m.)" and that such solutions give "a greater safety throughout the 8-hour working day" because there is still free active iodine at the end of that period.

For sterilizing catgut and sutures. Catgut and other surgical sutures are amongst the most difficult of materials to sterilize because of the destructive effect of either dry or moist heat on some types and the problem of penetration of chemical sterilizing agents. Sporicidal action is, of course, essential, and the treatment must extend beyond simply the surface of the material. For this purpose, iodine was used for many years, and, in a report to the Scottish Board of Health, Mackie (1928) found a 1 per cent solution in water to be an entirely satisfactory sterilizing agent, although as long as 7 days at normal temperatures were required to kill the most resistant spores of *B. mesentericus* embedded in the gut; the anaerobic spores, *Cl. tetani* and *Cl. welchii*, were killed in a matter of hours. Reference has already been made (p. 405) to the use of iodophores for this purpose.

In dairy disinfection. Although iodine is, for obvious reasons, not suitable for disinfecting dairy equipment the iodophores are now used widely in this field. The concentration generally employed seems to be 50 parts of iodine per million with phosphoric acid added to reduce the pH value below 4 and so increase the activity of the solution. Used properly such a solution measures up to the standard hypochlorite in the Hoy Can test and in field trials, although Cousins, Hoy and Clegg (1959) have indicated that 100 parts per million of a proprietory iodophore are desirable—25 parts were certainly inferior to the standard 300 parts of chlorine. The same ratio of 3 : 1 of chlorine to iodophore was also obtained in a short period suspension test in the presence of 10 per cent of milk. Iodophores, being in acid solution, will also dissolve and prevent milk stone (Davis and Howe, 1962).

In water treatment. Because iodine retains its activity over a wider range of pH values than does chlorine, it has been advocated for the sterilization of drinking water, especially under emergency conditions, and for the treatment of swimming-bath water. Chang and Morris (1953) recommended a concentration of 8 parts per million, chosen because at such a level it is lethal to most water-borne pathogenic organisms, including amoebae and viruses, in about 10 minutes at normal temperatures, or rather longer at lower temperatures; later, Chang (1958) put the level at 4 parts per million with a contact time of 15–20 minutes. These concentrations appear to be high in comparison with the findings of Chambers *et al.* (1952), but it must be borne in mind that the treatment was intended for waters of unknown and doubtful quality and the iodine was introduced in tablet form as tetraglycine hydroperiodide (Morris *et al.*, 1953). Chambers assessed the minimum concentrations lethal in 1 minute against a range of organisms of intestinal origin and found that whereas 4·5 per million were necessary in cold water at pH 9·1, 0·6 part was adequate at pH 6·5 and in the ambient temperature range of 20°–26°. *Alkaligenes faecalis* is said to be the most difficult of the bacteria to deal with in swimming baths, being about six times more resistant than the coliforms, salmonellae and shigellas (Marshall, Wolford and Faber, 1961).

REFERENCES

ALLAWALA, N. A. and RIEGELMAN, S. (1953). *J. Amer. pharm. Ass. (Sci.)*, **42**, 396.
ALLEN, L. A. (1950). *J. Inst. Water Engrs*, **4**, 502.
ALLEN, L. A. and BROOKS, EILEEN (1949). *J. Hyg., Camb.*, **47**, 320.
ALLEN, L. A. and BROOKS, EILEEN (1952). *Proc. Soc. appl. Bact.*, **15**, 155.
ALLEN, L. A. (1961). Effluent and Water Treatment Convenstion, London: Thunderbird Enterprises, London.
BARTLETT, F. G. and SCHMIDT, W. (1957). *Appl. Microbiol.*, **5**, 355.
BIERER, B. W., VALENTINE, H. D., BARNETT, B. D. and RHODES, W. H. (1961). *Poultry Sci.*, **40**, 148.
BLATT, R. and MALONEY, J. V. (1961). *Surg. Gynec. Obstet.*, **113**, 699.
BRAZIS, A. R., LESLIE, J. E., KABLER, R. W. and WOODWARD, R. L. (1958) *Appl. Microbiol.*, **6**, 338.
BROST, G. A. and KRUPIN, F. (1957). *Soap*, **33**(8), 93.
BUTTERFIELD, C. T. (1948). *Publ. Hlth Rep., Wash.*, **63**, 934.
BUTTERFIELD, C. T. and WATTIE, E. (1946). *Publ. Hlth Rep., Wash.*, **61**, 157.
CARROLL, B. (1955). *J. Bact.*, **69**, 413.
CHAMBERS, C. W., KABLER, R. W., MOLONEY, G. and BRYANT, A. (1952). *Soap*, **28**(10), 149.
CHAMBERS, C. W. (1956). *J. milk food Technol.*, **19**, 183.
CHANG, S. L. (1958). *J. Amer. pharm. Ass. (Sci.)*, **47**, 417.
CHANG, S. L. and MORRIS, J. C. (1953). *Ind. engng Chem.*, **45**, 1009.
CHAPLIN, C. E. and JOHNS, C. K. (1949). *J. Dairy Res.*, **16**, 322.
CHARLTON, D. B. and LEVINE, M. (1935). *J. Bact.*, **30**, 163.
COLEBROOK, L. (1930). *Ministry of Health Interim Report of Departmental Committee on Maternal Mortality and Morbidity:* H.M.S.O., London.
COUSINS, CHRISTINA M. and WOLF, J. (1946). *Proc. Soc. appl. Bact.*, p. 15.
COUSINS, CHRISTINA M., HOY, W. A. and CLEGG, L. F. L. (1959). *Internat. Dairy Congr., London*, **3**, 1807.
COX, G. A. and WHITEHEAD, H. R. (1949). *J. Dairy Res.*, **16**, 327.
DAKIN, H. D. (1915). *Brit. med. J.*, ii, 308.
DAKIN, H. D. and COHEN, J. B .(1916). *Proc. roy. Soc. Med.*, **89**, 232.
DAKIN, H. D., COHEN, J. B., DAUFRESNE, H. and KENYON, J. (1916). *Proc. Roy.Soc. B.* **89**, 232.
DAKIN, H. D., COHEN, J. B. and KENYON, J. (1916). *Brit. med. J.*, i, 160.
DAKIN, H. D. and DUNHAM, E. K. (1917). *Brit. med. J.*, i, 682.
DAKIN, H. D., LEE, W. E., SWEET, J. E., HENDRIX, B. M. and LE CONTE, R. G. (1917) *J. Amer. med. Ass.*, **69**, 27.
DAVIS, J. G. and HOWE, G. ANNE (1962). *J. appl. Bact.*, **24**, ii.
DIXON, J. M. S. and POOLEY, F. E. (1961). *J. Hyg., Camb.*, **59**, 343.
DUNHAM, C. G. and MACNEAL, W. J. (1944). *J. Immunol.*, **49**, 123.
EMMONS, C. W. (1933). *Arch. Dermatol. Syphylol.*, **28**, 15.
FRISCH, A. W., DAVIES, G. H. and KRIPPAEHNE, W. (1958). *Surg. Gynec. Obstet.*, **107**, 442.
GARDNER, A. D. (1948). *Lancet*, **255**, 760.
GARDNER, A. D. and SEDDON, H. J. (1946). *Lancet*, **250**, 683.
GERSHENFELD, L. (1955). *J. Amer. pharm. Ass. (Sci.)*, **44**, 177.
GERSHENFELD, L. (1962). *Amer. J. Pharm.*, **132**, 78.
GERSHENFELD, L. and FOX, D. (1948). *Amer. J. Pharm.*, **120**, 279.
GERSHENFELD, L., GREENE, A. and WITLIN, B. (1951). *J. Amer. pharm. Ass. (Sci.)*, **40**, 457.
GERSHENFELD, L. and PATTERSON, G. W. (1945). *Amer. J. Pharm.*, **117**, 5.
GERSHENFELD, L. and WITLIN, B. (1948). *Amer. J. Pharm.*, **120**, 158, 170.

GERSHENFELD, L. and WITLIN, B. (1949a). *Amer. J. Pharm.*, **121**, 95.
GERSHENFELD, L. and WITLIN, B. (1949b). *J. Amer. pharm. Ass. (Sci.)*, **38**, 411
GERSHENFELD, L. and WITLIN, B. (1951). *Amer. J. Pharm.*, **123**, 87.
GERSHENFELD, L. and WITLIN, B. (1955). *Soap*, **31**(12), 189.
GOMEZ-VEGA, PAULINA (1935). *Arch. Dermatol. Syphylol.*, **32**, 49.
GUITERAS, A. F. and SCHMELKES, F. C. (1934). *J. biol. Chem.*, **107**, 235.
HOATHER, R. C. (1949). *J. Inst. Water Engrs*, **3**, 507.
HOY, W. A. and NEAVE, F. K. (1955). *J. appl. Bact.*, **18**, 66.
KABLER, P. W., CLARKE, N. A., BERG, G. and CHANG, S. L. (1961). *Publ. Hlth Rep., Wash.*, **76**, 565.
KNIGHT, C. A. and STANLEY, W. M. (1944). *J. exp. Med.*, **79**, 291.
LANCASTER, J. E., GORDON, R. F. and TUCKER, J. (1952). *Brit. vet. J.*, **11**, 418.
Lancet, editorial (1949). **256**, 1056.
LAWRENCE, C. A., CARPENTER, C. M. and NAYLOR-FOOTE, A. W. C. (1957). *J. Amer. pharm. Ass. (Sci.)*, **46**, 500.
McCULLOCH, E. C. (1945). *Disinfection and Sterilization:* Kimpton, London.
MACKIE, T. J. (1928). *An Inquiry into Post-Operative Tetanus* – a Report to the Scottish Board of Health: H.M.S.O., London.
MAHER, J. T., ROGERS, M. R. and PETTERSON, D. W. (1961). *Appl. Microbiol.*, **9**, 273.
MARKS, H. C., WYSS, O. and STRANDSKOV, FREDE B. (1945). *J. Bact.*, **49**, 299.
MARSHALL, J. D., WOLFORD, CLAIRE B. and FABER, J. B. (1961). *Publ. Hlth Rep., Wash.*, **76**, 529.
MORRIS, J. C., CHANG, S. L., FAIR, G. M. and CONANT, G. H. (1953). *Ind. engng Chem.*, **45**, 1013.
MUDGE, C. S. and SMITH, F. R. (1935). *Amer. J. publ. Hlth*, **25**, 442.
NEAVE, F. K. and HOY, W. A. (1941). *Proc. Soc. appl. Bact.*, p. 37.
NYIRI, W. and DuBOIS, L. (1931). *J. Amer. pharm. Ass. (Sci.)*, **20**, 546.
Official Methods of Analysis (1955). 8th Ed., p. 93: Association of Official Agricultural Chemists, Washington, D.C.
ORTENZIO, L. F. and STUART, L. S. (1959). *J. Ass. off. agric. Chem.*, **42**, 630.
PETRIE, E. M. and ROMANS, D. P. (1958). *Soap*, **34**(8), 99.
RAHN, O. (1945). *Biodynamica*, **5**, 1.
RIDENOUR, G. M. and ARMBRUSTER, E. H. (1949). *J. Amer. Water Wks. Ass.*, **41**, 537.
RUDOLPH, A. S. and LEVINE, M. (1941). *Iowa Engng Exp. Sta. Bull. No.* 150.
RYAN, A. J., STONE, F. M., RAMSEY, E. B. and JOHNSTON, E. (1949). *Amer. J. Surg.*, **78**, 446.
SALLE, A. J. and CATLIN, B. W. (1947). *J. Amer. pharm. Ass. (Sci.)*, **36**, 129.
SCHAMBERG, J. F., BROWN, H. and HARKINS, M. J. (1931). *Arch. Dermatol. Syphylol.*, **24**, 1033.
STORY, P. (1952). *Brit. med. J.*, ii, 1128.
TAYLOR, MARGARET E. and HOY, W. A. (1954). *J. appl. Bact.*, **17**, ii.
THOMPSON, F. (1949). *Lancet*, **257**, 350.
TILLEY, F. W. and CHAPIN, R. M. (1930). *J. Bact.*, **19**, 295.
VINCENT, G. P., MacMAHON, J. D. and SYNAN, J. F. (1946). *Amer. J. publ. Hlth*, **36**, 1035.
WATTIE, E. and BUTTERFIELD, C. T. (1944). *Publ. Hlth Rep., Wash.*, **59**, 1661.
WEBER, G. R. (1950). *Publ. Hlth. Rep., Wash.*, **65**, 503.
WEBER, G. R. and LEVINE, M. (1944). *Amer. J. publ. Hlth*, **34**, 719.
WRIGHT, ELEANOR S. and MUNDY, A. (1958). *Appl. Microbiol.*, **6**, 381.
WYSS, O. and STRANDSKOV, FREDE B. (1945). *Arch. Biochem.*, **6**, 261.

CHAPTER 16

HEAVY METALS

ALL of the heavy metals possess antimicrobial properties to some degree, but most of them are only weakly bactericidal. The outstandingly active ones are the salts and organic complexes of mercury, tin and silver, and to a less extent copper, and these are in a class of their own. The mercury, tin and silver compounds are both antibacterial and antifungal, but the copper compounds are employed mainly for their antifungal properties.

The mode of action appears to be the same for all metals, but the concentrations at which it becomes operative vary considerably. It is a function of their ability to enter into combination with the proteins, and more specifically the enzymes, of the bacterial cell, and depends upon the presence of free metal-containing ions. It is independent of the molecular concentration of the salt. The actual concentrations at which the different metals exhibit antimicrobial activity range from parts in millions in the case of mercury and silver up to 10 per cent and greater in the case of aluminium, cobalt and some other metals. The heavy metals are generally more effective than those with low atomic weights, but there appears to be no connexion with their valency or position in the Periodic Table.

Several of the metals are essential for the growth and metabolism of micro-organisms, and these are found mainly amongst those of low atomic weight, such as sodium, potassium, calcium and magnesium, although others of higher atomic weight, such as copper, cobalt, zinc, molybdenum and vanadium, are equally important for some bacteria. There is no evidence that mercury and silver, the most potent of the antimicrobial metals, can exert a salutary influence at any level. The amounts of the metals required for stimulation are in all cases quite small, but the concentrations of their solutions differ considerably, and organisms can generally tolerate concentrations much greater than the metabolic optimum. Each metal, however, has a limiting concentration of tolerance beyond which it becomes increasingly toxic, exhibiting first inhibitory, and finally lethal, properties. The limit of tolerance depends to some extent on the presence of other metals, on the form in which the metal is present and on certain other factors, and toxicity appears to be associated with astringency.

The foregoing observations show that many of the metals can act in a dual role. At low concentrations they function as cell stimulants, and at higher concentrations they reverse this function and become growth antagonists and cell poisons. The contrast between mercury and silver and the other metals in this respect is interesting, but it may be an artifact; it may be linked with the extremely low concentrations at which these two metals are actively antagonistic.

Mercury compounds

Mercury and its salts have been used during many centuries for the treatment of certain diseases and skin affections, but the first demonstration of its antibacterial value was made by Koch in his classical experiments on the disinfection of anthrax spores with mercuric chloride. Now, we not only have the inorganic mercurials but also a large number of organic derivatives, many of which are highly active as antibacterial and antifungal agents. The organic derivatives were produced at the end of the First World War in response to the need for a preparation for use in medicine which had all the antibacterial properties of the inorganic mercurials, whilst at the same time being non-toxic and non-irritant. Several such compounds are now available commercially. Most of them have relatively low solubilities in water. They ionize in solution to give organo-mercuric cations, with no free mercury ions, and this accounts for their low toxicities and other favourable properties. Care is needed, however, in interpreting this toxicity. It applies only to acute toxicity; in chronic toxicity the organic mercurials are much more toxic than the inorganic ones (Fitzhugh *et al.*, 1950).

There is a voluminous literature on the bacteriology and chemotherapy of the mercurials in general, and of the organic compounds in particular, but their use today is practically limited to two fields, as local antiseptics for topical application and as preservatives for pharmaceutical products and industrial materials. They are all lethal to vegetative forms and to mould spores, but they are primarily bacteriostatic and fungistatic, and are effective in these capacities at extreme dilutions. For this reason the mercurials cannot be recommended as sterilizing agents, although they are sometimes used for disinfecting surgical equipment.

Much confusion was at first created concerning the true lethal properties of the mercurials because of the lack of appreciation of their bacteriostatic powers and of their variable activities in different media. The situation was not resolved until after the discovery of a number of antidotal substances capable of neutralizing the effect of the mercury. All of these substances are sulphur-containing compounds, and include glutathione, cysteine and thioglycollic acid as well as the soluble sulphides.

Organic matter, and particularly plasma and whole blood, also seriously depress, and may even abolish, the activities of the mercurials. In this respect the organic derivatives are said to be less affected than the inorganic ones, but in either case the extent of the loss depends upon the concentration of the mercurial and the amount of organic matter present.

Lack of sporicidal activity is one of the principal disadvantages of the mercurials. Over the years, many claims have been made that they can kill such organisms in the space of a few minutes, but even as early as the late 1920s Mackie (1928) and Bulloch (1929) showed that they could not sterilize catgut by this means, and amongst the most convincing later proofs are those of Scott (1937) and of Brewer (1939). Scott showed that Merthiolate, Metaphen and phenylmercuric nitrate required 3 days, and often much longer, to sterilize several species of the genus *Clostridium*, and Brewer showed that even at relatively high concentrations none of the mercurials could be relied upon to kill *Bacillus anthracis* or several of the *Clostridium* species in 24 hours.

Mode of action

The antibacterial action of the mercurials has long been attributed to the ability of their ions to combine with and precipitate the cell proteins. As with many other agents, the proteins involved are probably associated with the enzyme system of the organism because enzymes are known to be reversibly inactivated by heavy metals, and this fits the case of the mercurials very well. In an excellent review of the subject, Fildes (1940) shows that the mechanism of the action is one of interference with an essential metabolite of the R–SH type and that it can be prevented or antagonized by adding any other –SH compound. Glutathione was the substance particularly investigated, although cysteine, thioglycollic acid and the inorganic sulphides also function in the same role, and they were thought to be effective by virtue of their ability to attract the mercury ions away from the bacterial –SH compound. The validity of this argument is confirmed by the fact that these compounds are effective in quantities close to their theoretical stoichiometric amounts (Cook and Steel, 1959).

Activated charcoal is also a mercury antidote (McCulloch, 1945), but the action in this case is obviously not a chemical one. It is rather the result of a preferential adsorption phenomenon, and indicates that the mercury-protein combination can only be a loose one. Moreover, since it is impossible for charcoal particles to enter the bacterial cell, it shows also that the reaction or combination resulting in the antibacterial action must take place at the cell surface. The easy reversibility of the action by chemical agents supports this contention.

Action on spores. If these postulates on the mechanism of the antibacterial action of the mercurials are accepted, they also provide a basis for explaining the lack of sporicidal activity. A bacterial spore consists, in effect, of a relatively thick and impervious envelope with a complete complement of essential enzymes inside. When exposed to a mercurial disinfectant the mercury ions are adsorbed on the surface, and may even coat it entirely, but they never penetrate beyond the envelope. The enzymes are, therefore, entirely protected and the vital mechanism of the cell remains inviolate. In the absence of other interfering factors, this state of stasis can be maintained for an indefinite period, and it only needs the removal of the mercury coating and the presence of favourable nutritive conditions to allow the spore to germinate normally.

Activities of mercury compounds

Inorganic compounds. The chloride, cyanide and oxycyanide, and the potasssium-mercuric iodide complex, are the most active of the inorganic mercury compounds. They do not manifest selectivity against any particular group of bacteria, but they are not reliably sporicidal. Mercurous chloride, or

TABLE 56

'*Lethal*' activities of mercury compounds
(after Birkhaug, 1933)

Compound	Dilution (1 in —) 'lethal' to			
	Staph. aureus	*Strep. pyogenes*	*E. coli*	*B. subtilis*
Mercuric chloride . . .	16,000	32,000	10,000	12,000
Mercurochrome . . .	160	320	180	300
Merthiolate	120,000	112,000	32,000	24,000
Phenylmercuric nitrate . .	192,000	144,000	48,000	65,000

calomel, *per se* has little or no antibacterial power, although it is used for packing deep wounds, where it exerts a gentle antiseptic action by reason of its slow oxidation to the active mercuric salt.

Mercuric chloride will inhibit the growth of *Staphylococcus aureus* in nutrient broth at concentrations of about 1 in 50,000 to 1 in 100,000. It will also inhibit *Escherichia coli* at 1 in 100,000 to 1 in 400,000, and *Aspergillus niger* at about 1 in 10,000, but in 20 per cent serum these values are all reduced to about 1 in 10,000 to 1 in 25,000. A 1 in 1,000 solution in 50 per cent serum will kill mixed cultures of *Staphylococcus* and *Streptococcus* in 2–4 hours, and a 1 in 200 solution is lethal in whole blood within 5 minutes. The activity of mercuric chloride is enhanced under acid conditions (Vaichulis and Arnold, 1935) and there is some evidence of synergism with wetting and surface tension reducing agents. The influenza and vaccinia viruses are rapidly inactivated by a dilution of 1 in 1,000 (Dunham and MacNeal, 1943).

Organic compounds. The organic mercurials are of much later origin than the inorganic ones, having been introduced only since the end of the First World War. With the exception of Mercurochrome, they are much more effective as antibacterial agents than are the inorganic salts, but they tend to exhibit greater selectivity and specificity, and they still lack sporicidal power.

Very many organic mercury compounds have been described and patented in recent years, and a few of them have achieved some distinction as antiseptics and preservatives. The most interesting of these are Mercurochrome,

Merthiolate and the phenylmercuric salts. It is of little value to quote the phenol coefficients of these compounds as a measure of their activities, because all of the published figures seem to have been obtained without due regard to their bacteriostatic effects, but the so-called "killing" dilutions as obtained by Birkhaug (1933) are quoted in Table 56 to give some indication of their relative antibacterial properties; they also show the tendency of the organic compounds towards specificity.

Mercurochrome, the sodium salt of dibromohydroxymercuric fluorescein, was the first of the organic mercurials to be made for antiseptic purposes (Young, White and Swartz, 1919). It is the least active of all of the mercury compounds, requiring concentrations of the order of 1 in 200 to 1 in 400 before it will kill vegetative bacteria with any rapidity. It is bacteriostatic in broth at concentrations of about 1 in 10,000 to 1 in 25,000 and is active against the pathogenic fungi at 1 in 10,000 in the light but not at 1 in 500 in the dark (Gomez-Vega, 1935). A 2 per cent solution is needed to inactivate the fowl pox virus (McCulloch, 1945).

Serum again markedly depletes its action, and in whole blood renders it practically inert. In 50 per cent serum dilutions of 1 in 30 to 1 in 70 are needed to kill most organisms in 10 minutes; at 1 in 1,000 it will kill *Staph. aureus* and *Strep. pyogenes* in 24 but not in 8 hours. Its total loss of activity in whole blood, attributable to the presence of glutathione and similar sulphur-containing substances, explains why even a 2 per cent solution in blood broth still allows the growth of *Strep. pyogenes* (Morton, North and Engley, 1948), and why it, and other mercurials, does not reliably eliminate the virulence of this organism (Brewer, 1950), or of *Clostridium tetani* (Engley, 1950), in infectivity tests.

The antiseptic properties of Merthiolate, the sodium salt of ethylmercuri-thiosalicylic acid, were first described by Jamieson and Powell (1931), who found it to be a highly effective germicide with low toxicity. It has a high solubility in water and body fluids, and is free from any tendency to coagulate proteins. A 1 in 1,000 solution is alkaline in reaction, having a pH value of nearly 10·0. By the United States Food and Drug Administration technique, a 1 in 3,000 solution is lethal to *Salmonella typhi* in 5 minutes, and a 1 in 4,000 solution is similarly lethal to *Staph. aureus* (Nye, 1937). A 1 in 10,000 solution will kill the spores of *Trichophyton* in 5 minutes, but a 1 in 1,000 solution is not effective against the virus of encephalitis (Rogers, 1951). The very high phenol coefficient values claimed in the literature are fictitious.

Phenylmercuric nitrate, acetate and borate have identical biological activities in terms of their phenylmercuric ion content, and they differ from each other only in their solubilities. The acetate is the most soluble compound of the group and for this reason it is sometimes preferred in place of the nitrate. According to the British Pharmaceutical Codex, it is soluble in cold water at 1 in 600, although Hopf (1953) gives it as 0·47 per cent (1 in 210).

The nitrate is only soluble to the extent of 1 in 1,500. Both are much more soluble in hot water.

Whatever the type of compound, the activity resides primarily in the phenylmercuric radical, although the acid radical also contributes to some extent through the different properties it confers on the molecule. According to Hopf (1953) a sequestering radical, such as the ethylenediamine tetra-acetate, is most striking in this respect in that it produces a much lower level of activity than do the chelating, colloid-forming or ionizing radicals. Again, the oxyphenylmono-, di- and tri-mercuric salts are all inferior in their activities to the simpler phenylmercuric salts (Keil, 1959), and so for these reasons the acetate, borate and nitrate have come into almost exclusive use. Goldberg, Shapero and Wilder (1950), however, expressed a preference for a colloid-forming compound, the dinaphthylmethane disulphonate, alias methylenebis-(2-naphthyl-3-sulphate), which they found to be three times more active than the acetate.

At dilutions down to 1 in 300,000 phenylmercuric nitrate will inhibit the growth of *E. coli*, and with *Staph. aureus* they can be extended to 1 in 10,000,000; if only small inocula are used these dilutions can be extended as far as 1 in 2,500,000 and 1 in 307,000,000 (Stark and Montgomery, 1935). In contrast, a 1 in 1,500 solution is not reliably lethal to pathogenic spores (Brewer, 1939). Dilutions of 1 in 500,000 to 1 in 1,000,000 inhibit the growth of the common moulds. Organic matter seriously affects the activity of phenylmercuric nitrate so that in 20 per cent serum broth the effective inhibitory dilutions are reduced to 1 in 50,000 for *E. coli* and 1 in 250,000 for *Staph. aureus*. At 1 in 2,000 in 50 per cent serum it will kill *Staph. aureus* in 2 hours or less but at 1 in 5,000 it requires 4 hours or longer.

Uses of the mercurials

The main uses of the inorganic mercury compounds are in preserving industrial materials, in skin disinfection and in other aspects of antisepsis, although in many cases their place has been taken by the more active and less toxic organic compounds. Mercuric chloride is a valuable agent for preserving materials such as timber, paper, board and leather as well as for controlling fungal infections in seeds, bulbs and tubers. As a skin disinfectant it is considered to be too slow and unreliable (Gardner, 1948) but a lotion and an ointment containing 1 per cent of mercuric chloride are used for treating skin affections. The nitrate is also used in ointments. Such ointments are often found to be irritant.

Both mercuric cyanide and oxycyanide have limited applications as antiseptics, their advantage over the chloride being that they are rather less toxic and much less irritant. The cyanide is relatively little used, but the oxycyanide containing about 15 per cent of mercuric oxide and 85 per cent of mercuric cyanide was given a monograph in the British Pharmacopoeia,

1953, and it now appears in the British Pharmaceutical Codex. It is more active than the chloride or cyanide, and does not precipitate proteins.

Solutions of 1 in 1,000 to 1 in 10,000 are used in treating conjunctivitis, as eye lotions, as gargles, for application to wounds and for antiseptic irrigations. In disinfection they are useful for treating surgical instruments, catheters and other equipment, which might otherwise be damaged by heat treatment, and for this purpose 0·5 per cent solutions are recommended. The equipment must be washed clean before immersion in the solution, and the disinfecting period must not be less than 15 minutes; Hayes (1949) found that a 0·4 per cent solution of mercuric cyanide sometimes took over 60 minutes to kill some strains of *Staph. aureus*, but the Gram-negative species were more easily susceptible.

Of the organic compounds, Mercurochrome is reasonably effective as a skin disinfectant, for which a 2 per cent solution in 55 per cent alcohol and 10 per cent acetone is commonly used, but for general antiseptic purposes serious doubts have been raised against its reliability because of its loss of activity in serum and blood. Brewer (1948), however, has attempted to explain the whole position away by laying emphasis on the residual infectivity of the organisms after treatment and not on their viability, and has stated: "the treatment of pathogenic bacteria with a 1 per cent solution of 'Mercurochrome' impairs the infectivity of these bacteria to such an extent that the chance of infection is practically eliminated." From the practical standpoint, this rationalization may be true, but Brewer's own results, quoted above, show that infectivity is only impaired and not abolished.

Merthiolate has also been used for skin disinfection, but its main value today is as a preservative in biological products of low protein content, but not for sera and similar products of high protein content. It is particularly suitable for use in vaccines, and for this purpose a concentration of 1 in 10,000 is used.

Of the phenylmercuric compounds, the nitrate, acetate and borate can be used almost interchangeably, although the nitrate is preferred for most medicinal purposes. They are all relatively non-toxic and non-irritant and non-corrosive and have equivalent high antibacterial activities. Phenylmercuric nitrate is used widely as the bactericide in many preparations administered by injection, for which purpose a 0·001 per cent concentration is officially recommended in the British Pharmacopoeia and in the Pharmacopeia of the United States. For the 'heat-plus-bactericide' sterilization process (*see* p. 139) the concentration is raised to 0·002 per cent. It must be used with circumspection in any preparation containing a chloride because of the extremely low solubility of phenylmercuric chloride – it is only soluble to the extent of about 1 in 24,000. The low initial concentration also means that the loss by absorption in the rubber closure of a multidose container can be significant.

A 1 in 1,500 to 1 in 3,000 solution can be used for skin disinfection, but for irrigation and douching much lower concentrations of 1 in 15,000 to 1 in 24,000 are employed. It is also an effective fungicide, and a 1 in 30,000 solution can be used for treating vaginal infections; an ointment containing 0·1 per cent of phenylmercuric nitrate is also useful in treating mycotic skin infections.

Phenylmercuric borate has been used in a tincture containing 43 per cent of alcohol, 4·6 per cent of acetone and 1 per cent each of boric acid and sodium acid phosphate for skin disinfection and for treating superficial wounds (McCulloch, 1945). The colloidal dinaphthylmethylenedisulphonate, under the trade name of Penotrane, is also used in aqueous solution, creams, tinctures etc. in the same role and for treating fungal infections of the skin and of the vagina.

Both the acetate and nitrate are suitable as industrial preservatives. They are acceptable fungicides for leather, and they have been described as the most effective preservatives in the pulp and paper industry.

Ethylmercuric phosphate, ethylmercuric chloride and tolylmercuric acetate have also been found useful in the control of fungal infections in seeds and in various industrial materials. Tolylmercuric acetate has the same order of activity as the phenyl derivative, but it is only soluble to the extent of about 1 in 250,000.

Silver and its compounds

The disinfecting power of silver has been known virtually since Babylonian times and silver containers were provided for transporting water for the personal use of the Great Kings of Persia. Silver compounds have been employed medicinally for several centuries in the treatment of various maladies and diseases, but their function as antibacterial agents was not really recognized until the latter half of the nineteenth century.

Both metallic silver and its compounds are bacteriostatic in extreme dilution – sometimes they would seem to have almost homoeopathic properties – and for this reason, as with the mercurials, it is difficult to assess their true germicidal powers. There is little doubt, however, that silver is a protoplasmic poison and that in whatever form it is initially present the antibacterial action arises from the production of silver ions which enter into combination with the bacterial proteins. According to some workers the action does not stop at this stage, but the silver proteinate so formed continues to exert a sustained, though mild, antiseptic action through the subsequent gradual release of silver ions. The process is, therefore, more or less a continuous one. There is no effective antidote for silver as there is for mercury, but serum by its nature depresses its activity considerably.

Oligodynamic silver

Metallic silver itself has bactericidal powers and this is known as oligodynamic activity. The term was coined some sixty years ago by von Nägeli to describe the lethal properties of any metal which exhibits bactericidal properties at minute concentrations. It is not exclusive to silver, although it is most closely associated with this metal, but occurs with copper, brass and tin, as well as with cobalt, nickel, zinc, and mercury. The first three are capable of destroying coliforms, staphylococci and typhoid bacilli in water, but the last four are only mildly active. Since about 1870 an extensive literature, mainly of German origin, has accumulated on the mode of action and uses of the oligodynamic metals generally, and it has been fully reviewed more recently by Romans (1954). The following pages present only a brief summary of the present knowledge of the subject.

There does not appear to be any substantial relationship between the oligodynamic activities of metals and their valency or position in the Periodic Table, neither is there much correlation between activity and the Gram-staining response of organisms, although on balance the Gram-positive types are probably slightly more resistant.

Mode of action. Numerous attempts have been made to explain the oligodynamic action of metals, and of silver in particular, but the most generally accepted idea is that it is due to the micro-solubility of the metal in water and the production of active metal ions. The ions so formed are adsorbed by the bacteria, and protein coagulation follows. The many investigations published by different workers between about 1900 and 1930 have broadly confirmed this, but opinions concerning the exact mechanism of the action vary in detail. In several instances the activity of metallic silver has been found to be the same as that of its salts at the same ionic concentration. Other investigators have been unable to confirm this relationship, finding generally that metallic silver is less active than its salts, and so have deduced either that the ion formed from the metal must be a more complex entity or that the mode of attack of metallic silver on the bacterial cell is different from that of the salts and may involve the formation of a less reactive silver-protein complex as an intermediate.

Whatever the detailed mechanism of the action may be, it is now certain that the *pure* metal is inactive. A trace of impurity is essential, and this can take the form of a trace of oxide on the metal surface, another metal, or a small amount of an added salt such as sodium chloride. In the presence of other metals or added salts some potentiation of activity often occurs.

Activities and uses. As well as possessing antibacterial properties metallic silver is also non-toxic, and so it has several practical applications as an antiseptic. Adsorbed on various surfaces it is used for the disinfection of water, and colloidal suspensions have proved valuable in the therapy of certain skin and membrane infections. It is also considered to be as good as hypochlorite for sterilizing bottles (Dachs, 1962).

For water disinfection one of the earliest and best known preparations is that known under the trade-name of Katadyn, a product first introduced by Krause in Germany in 1928. It is described as a spongy preparation of metallic silver, although it can also be obtained as a coating on sand or impregnated on filter material. It always contains a small amount of another added metal such as palladium or gold which potentiates the activity of the silver.

Published estimates of the lethal properties of Katadyn silver vary considerably, ionic concentrations as low as 0·006 part per million and as high as 0·5 part per million having been reported as killing *E. coli* in periods ranging from 2 to 24 hours. The concentration needed undoubtedly varies according to the number of organisms present, and the temperature; below about 20° the rate of disinfection is markedly reduced. Organic matter, especially if present in colloidal form such as in milk, and certain inorganic impurities in water also affect adversely the efficacy of Katadyn. Pathogenic organisms are said to be rather more susceptible than normal water-borne organisms, but bacterial spores, moulds and protozoa are highly resistant. Spores of *Bacillus mesentericus* have been reported to survive more than 5 weeks in 300 ml of water containing 200 gm of Katadyn sand carrying 20 gm of silver.

The Katadyn process for the disinfection of water by metallic silver is not the only such process available. Others have also been used, including various electrolytic methods. They all depend on the ultimate production of silver ions and involve setting up a potential between two plates immersed in the water. The plates can be both silver, as is used in the 'Electro-Katadyn' process, or they can be one of silver and one of another metal, and small amounts of salts may be added to enhance the disinfecting effect. The Electro-Katadyn process has been used mainly for treating swimming-bath water, but reports on its efficacy have been conflicting.

For clinical purposes oligodynamic silver can be applied as a colloidal suspension, as a lotion, in an ointment base or adsorbed on powders or dressings, and it has been mixed with various 'potentiating' substances such as silver oxide, manganese dioxide and gold. Many of these preparations have been covered by patent specifications, and they are variously applied in dentistry and in the treatment of burns and skin infections. That preparations of this type are antiseptic under clinical conditions was proved by Romans (1954) who showed that pieces of skin from experimental animals treated with O-Silver, "an aqueous solution containing oligodynamic silver", when placed on an agar plate gave substantial zones of inhibition of *Staph. aureus*, *E. coli* and *Pseudomonas pyocyanea*.

Silver salts

As well as metallic silver and its oxide, the salts of silver which have been used for antiseptic purposes include the nitrate, citrate, lactate, picrate, chloride and proteinates. The first four compounds are easily soluble and are crystalloids by nature, but the chloride, which is inevitably present under most conditions of application because of its low solubility, and the proteinates are colloids. All of these compounds are given monographs in the various Pharmacopoeias of the world.

Soluble silver salts. The soluble salts of silver exhibit some selectivity against the different groups of organism, being rather more effective against the Gram-negative types than against the Gram-positive ones. Silver nitrate is lethal to *Staph. aureus* in 10 minutes at 37° at a dilution of 1 in 80, but against *Salm. typhi* the much lower concentration of 1 in 1,250 is effective. It will inhibit the growth of bacteria at dilutions of 1 in 30,000

TABLE 57

Lethal dilutions of silver salts

Compound	Dilution lethal in 10 min at 37°	
	Staph. aureus	*Salm. typhi*
Silver nitrate . . .	1 in 80	1 in 1,250
Silver citrate . . .	1 in 600	1 in 4,500
Silver lactate . . .	1 in 110	1 in 690
Silver-protein (strong) . .	1 in 15	1 in 175
Silver-protein (mild) . .	1 in <12	1 in 70

or greater, and moulds at 1 in 20,000; and in 50 per cent serum it is slowly lethal over a period of hours at 1 in 1,000, or sometimes even at 1 in 5,000. Silver lactate has broadly the same activity as silver nitrate, but silver citrate is considerably more effective, especially against *Staph. aureus* (Salle *et al.*, 1939).

Silver nitrate is used in medicine in 1 to 5 per cent solutions as a throat paint, as a lotion and in eye-drops, but it is extremely irritant and corrosive. Ammoniacal silver nitrate is used in dental surgery for instillation into teeth cavities. Silver lactate can also be used for similar purposes and concentrations of 1 in 200 to 1 in 500 are usually employed. The citrate is completely non-irritant and so can be applied to open wounds and the more delicate membranes. In the past the picrate was also popular, being applied either as a 1 or 2 per cent solution, as a powder by insufflation or in pessary form for treating fungal infections of the vagina.

A preparation containing silver nitrate, ammonium thiocyanate and propylene glycol has been used in hospital disinfection for treating floors, walls, etc., and as the bactericide in air filters (Hudson, Sanger and Sproul, 1959).

Colloidal silver preparations. Colloidal preparations of the oxide, chloride, iodide and the proteinates, besides the metal itself, have various uses in medicine, being employed mainly for the treatment of infections of the eye, of the respiratory membranes and of the genito-urinary tract. Relatively high concentrations of these compounds have to be used in practice, and their action is mainly bacteriostatic. More effective in this field is the methylenebis-(2-naphthyl-3-sulphonate) which is rather more active than the other silver salts and does not lose its activity in the presence of serum (Goldberg, Shapero and Wilder, 1950).

Copper compounds

Copper compounds are used mainly in industry as preservatives against fungal spoilage and this aspect is considered in Chapter 17: they have no applications outside this field. They are nearly all strongly bacteriostatic and to some extent bactericidal, and they have weak virucidal properties. Both inorganic and organic salts are used, but there is a tendency nowadays to prefer the organic compounds because of their higher activities and their more suitable physical properties. They include the naphthenate, oleate, pentachlorophenate and the 8-quinolinate (the 8-hydroxyquinoline compound). Compounds with sequestering agents are to be avoided because, like the mercury compounds, they are the least active (Biederman and Muller, 1951).

Dilutions of 1 in 10,000 or greater of copper sulphate are inhibitory to many of the bacteria and moulds, although the author has found *Cladosporium* and *Penicillium* species growing in Benedict's solution containing 6·9 per cent of copper sulphate. The staphylococci are known to be particularly sensitive to traces of copper in normal culture media (O'Meara and Macsween, 1936, 1937), but this sensitivity depends upon a number of environmental factors. The addition of copper chloride equivalent to 10 mg of copper per litre to a peptone or casein medium does not reduce the nutrient properties of the medium, but on heating the same solution in an autoclave it becomes strongly inhibitory to *Staph. aureus*. If, however, the heating is carried out in a sealed container there is no such inhibition. The mechanism of this bacteriostasis remains enigmatic, it has been linked with the formation of copper sulphide, which in spite of its almost complete insolubility and non-reactivity is highly bacteriostatic (Woiwod, 1954).

The bactericidal properties of the different copper salts vary considerably and are not consistent with different types of organism. According to Sprowls and Poe (1943*a*) copper chloride is the most active, being lethal in 10 minutes to *Salm. typhi* at 1 in 300 and to *Staph. aureus* at 1 in 7. The comparative figures for the sulphate were 1 in 40 and 1 in 5, and for the nitrate 1 in 50 and 1 in 6.

Tin compounds

Of recent years several organic tin compounds, "organotins", have attracted attention both as bactericides and as fungicides. In the stannous and stannic states tin has very little activity; it is only when coupled with organic radicals that its antimicrobial properties become manifest. The compounds concerned can be of the type $RSnX_3$, R_2SnX_2, R_3SnX or R_4Sn, where R is an organic radical linked directly to the tin atom by C—Sn bond and X is an inorganic, or organic, radical not so linked.

In an investigation mainly into the antifungal properties of a series of such compounds, van der Kerk and Luijten (1954) found that the R_3SnX molecule was the most active, and that in the alkyl series the optimum

TABLE 58

The antifungal properties of organic tin compounds
(after van der Kerk and Luijten, 1954)

Compound	Range of fungistatic* concentrations (p.p.m.)
Ethyltin trichloride	>1,000
Diethyltin dichloride	100–500
Triethyltin chloride	0·5–5
Tetraethyltin	50–1,000
Trimethyltin acetate	20–200
Triethyltin acetate	1–5
Tri-*n*-propyltin acetate	0·1–1
Tri-*n*-butyltin acetate	0·1–0·5
Tri-*n*-hexyltin acetate	1–100
Triphenyltin acetate	0·5–2
Triethyltin hydroxide	0·2–5
,, benzoate	2–10
,, acetate	1–5
,, cyanide	2–10
,, phenoxide	0·5–2
,, toluene-*p*-sulphonamide	1–5

* Fungi tested were *Penicillium italicum, Aspergillus niger, Rhizopus nigricans* and *Botrytis alii.*

rested generally in the butyl (C_4) radical. Therefore, the most active of the compounds are the tri-*n*-butyltin salts. The radical X has some influence, but it is only comparatively small, and activities tend to fall, but again only slightly, as the pH value is reduced below about 7. Much of this work was confirmed by Zedler and Beiter (1962) using bacteria as well as moulds. They found that optimum activity against the staphylococci was exhibited by the tri-*n*-amyl compound, which inhibited down to 1 part per million, and that the pseudomonads were best inhibited by the triethyl compound which was active down to 16 parts per million. On the other hand, Grün and Fricker (1963) claimed the tripropyl compounds to be more effective against Gram-negative bacteria in general, by a factor of up to 60.

The organic tin compounds have found a place as disinfectants in hospital practice, where they have been used in formulations for sprays, for treating walls, floors and other surfaces and in the laundries (Hudson, Sanger and Sproul, 1959; Rees, 1963) but their principal values lie in the preservation of wood, paints and textiles as well as in the treatment of industrial waters; these are discussed in the chapter on preservatives (Chapter 17).

Other metal salts

Many others of the heavy metal salts exert inhibitory and lethal properties against micro-organisms, but their activities are far less than those of the metals discussed above, although organogermanium and organolead compounds are said to have substantial antimicrobial properties (Sijpesteijn, Rijkens and Luijten, 1962). Sprowls and Poe (1943*b*) examined the

TABLE 59

Effect of metal salts on the bactericidal power of iodine

Iodine solution	Concentration of iodine lethal in 10 min at 37° to	
	Staph. aureus	*Salm. typhi*
In water	1 in 20,000	1 in 17,500
With 1:3,000 o/r solution . .	1 in 80,000	1 in 60,000
With 1:100 o/r solution . .	1 in 450,000	

Note. The o/r solution was an equimolar mixture of manganous and ferric sulphates.

bactericidal powers of a number of metallic salts in solution and found them to be always more effective against the Gram-negative bacteria than against the Gram-positive ones. Salts of iron and tin were lethal to *Salm. typhi* in 10 minutes at concentrations of from 1 in 200 to 1 in 500, but against *Staph. aureus* the equivalent concentrations were from 1 in 10 to 1 in 70. Salts of aluminium, cobalt, lead, nickel and zinc were not effective until concentrations of 12 per cent and sometimes over 30 per cent were used.

Certain of the metallic ions are mutually antagonistic in their antibacterial effects. MacLeod and Snell (1950) showed that zinc is toxic to several bacterial species, but that its toxicity to *Lactobacillus arabinosus* could be removed by adding manganese, an essential growth element, or magnesium, calcium or strontium; the same did not apply to *Leuconostoc mesenteroides*. Similarly, Abelson and Aldous (1950) found that magnesium will markedly reduce the toxicities of cadmium, cobalt, nickel and zinc to *E. coli*, *Aspergillus niger* and other organisms.

Activity can be induced in some metals by mixing them in suitable proportions to produce oxidation-reduction systems. Thus a mixture of ferrous and ferric chlorides has a pronounced bactericidal effect on *Salm. typhi* and *Staph. aureus*, whereas the two salts separately have very little action (Guest and Salle, 1942), and the same effect is found with salts of manganese, tin and iron in various oxidation-reduction combinations. This idea can also be extended to certain well-known active germicides such as iodine and the phenols. The enhanced activity induced in an iodine solution by adding an equimolar mixture of manganous and ferric sulphates is illustrated in Table 59 (Salle, 1945). Similarly the enhanced activity induced in phenol and cresol solutions, first by adding ferric chloride and then ferrous chloride to create a second system, are given in Table 60 (Salle and Guest, 1944).

Some compounds exert a selective action against certain groups of

TABLE 60

Effect of metal salts on the bactericidal power of phenol and cresol

Germicide	Added salts	Concentration of germicide lethal to *Staph. aureus* in 10 min at 37°
Phenol	Nil	1 in 100
Phenol 1·25 gm	FeCl$_3$ cryst. 3·6 gm	1 in 1,500
Phenol 1.25 gm	*(FeCl$_3$ cryst. 10·8 gm) (FeCl$_2$ 1·7 gm)	1 in 4,500
Cresol	Nil	1 in 300
Cresol 1·45 gm	FeCl$_3$ cryst. 3·6 gm	1 in 4,000
Cresol 1·45 gm	*(FeCl$_3$ cryst. 10·8 gm) (FeCl$_2$ 1·7 gm)	1 in 12,000

* The additional FeCl$_3$ cryst. and the FeCl$_2$ provide a second oxidation-reduction system.

bacteria and use is made of this in culture media for diagnostic purposes. Thus, tellurite is added to suppress the growth of Gram-negative organisms in the diagnosis of pyogenic infections, and selenite and bismuth sulphite are used in enrichment media for the typhoid-paratyphoid bacilli.

REFERENCES

ABELSON, P. H. and ALDOUS, ELAINE (1950). *J. Bact.*, **60**, 401.
BIEDERMAN, W. and MULLER, E. (1951). *Phytopath. Z.*, **18**, 307.
BIRKHAUG, K. E. (1933). *J. infect. Dis.*, **53**, 250.
BREWER, J. H. (1939). *J. Amer. med. Ass.*, **112**, 2009.
BREWER, J. H. (1948). *J. Amer. med. Ass.*, **137**, 858.
BREWER, J. H. (1950). *Ann. N.Y. Acad. Sci.*, **53**, 211.
BULLOCH, W. (1929). *The Disinfection and Preparation of Catgut for Surgical Purposes.* Med. Res. Counc. Spec. Rep. Ser. No. 138: H.M.S.O., London.
COOK, A. M. and STEEL, K. J. (1959). *J. Pharm. Pharmacol.*, **7**, 152.
DACHS, E. (1962). *Brauwiss.*, **15**, 3.
DUNHAM, W. B. and MACNEAL, W. J. (1943). *J. lab. clin. Med.*, **28**, 947.
ENGLEY, F. B. (1950). *Ann. N.Y. Acad. Sci.*, **53**, 197.
FILDES, P. (1940). *Brit. J. exp. Path.*, **21**, 67.
FITZHUGH, O. G., NELSON, A. A., LANG, E. P. and KUNZE, F. M. (1950). *Arch. ind. Hyg.*, **2**, 433.
GARDNER, A. D. (1948). *Lancet*, **255**, 760.
GOLDBERG, A. A., SHAPERO, M. and WILDER, E. (1950). *J. Pharm. Pharmacol.*, **2**, 20.
GOMEZ-VEGA, PAULINA (1935). *Arch. Dermatol. Syphylol.*, **32**, 49.

GRÜN, L. and FRICKER, H. H. (1963). *Tin and its Uses*, No. 61, p. 8.

GUEST, H. L. and SALLE, A. J. (1942). *Proc. Soc. exp. Biol., N.Y.,* **51**, 272.

HAYES, W. (1949). *Brit. J. Urol.,* **21**, 198.

HOPF, P. P. (1953). *Mfg Chem.,* **24**, 444.

HUDSON, P. B., SANGER, G. and SPROUL, EDITH E. (1959). *J. Amer. med. Ass.,* **169**, 1549.

JAMIESON, W. A. and POWELL, H. M. (1931). *Amer. J. Hyg.,* **14**, 218.

KEIL, R. (1959). *Die Pharmazie,* **14**, 76.

McCULLOCH, E. C. (1945). *Disinfection and Sterilization:* Kimpton, London.

MacLEOD, R. A. and SNELL, E. E. (1950). *J. Bact.,* **59**, 783.

MACKIE, T. J. (1928). *An Inquiry into Post-operative Tetanus* – A Report to the Scottish Board of Health: H.M.S.O., London.

MORTON, H. E., NORTH, L. L. and ENGLEY, F. B. (1948). *J. Amer. med. Ass.,* **136**, 37.

NYE, R. N. (1937). *J. Amer. med. Ass.,* **108**, 280.

O'MEARA, R. A. Q. and MACSWEEN, J. C. (1936). *J. Path. Bact.,* **43**, 373.

O'MEARA, R. A. Q. and MACSWEEN, J. C. (1937). *J. Path. Bact.,* **44**, 225.

POWELL, H. M. (1948). *J. Amer. med. Ass.,* **137**, 862.

REES, G. (1963). *Tin and its Uses*, No. 60, p. 1.

ROGERS, N. G. (1951). *J. lab. clin. Med.,* **38**, 483.

ROMANS, I. B. (1954). *Antiseptics, Disinfectants, Fungicides and Chemical and Physical Sterilization*, p. 388: Kimpton, London.

SALLE, A. J. (1945). *Proc. Soc. exp. Biol., N.Y.,* **58**, 149.

SALLE, A. J. and GUEST, H. L. (1944). *Proc. Soc. exp. Biol., N.Y.,* **55**, 26.

SALLE, A. J., McOMIE, W. A., SECHMEISTER, I. L. and FOORD, D. C. (1939). *J. Bact.,* **37**, 637.

SCOTT, J. P. (1937). *J. infect. Dis.,* **61**, 103.

SIJPESTEIJN, A. K., RIJKENS, F. and LUIJTEN, J. G. A. (1962). *Antonie van Leewenhoek J. Microbiol. Serol.,* **28**, 346.

SPROWLS, J. B. and POE, C. F. (1943a). *J. Amer. pharm. Ass. (Sci.),* **32**, 41.

SPROWLS, J. B. and POE, C. F. (1943b). *J. Amer. pharm. Ass. (Sci.),* **32**, 33.

STARK, O. K. and MONTGOMERY, MARJORIE (1935). *J. Bact.,* **29**, 6.

VAICHULIS, J. A. and ARNOLD, L. (1935). *Surg. Gynec. Obstet.,* **62**, 333.

VAN DER KERK, G. J. M. and LUIJTEN, J. G. A. (1954). *J. appl. Chem.,* **4**, 314.

WOIWOD, A. J. (1954). *J. gen. Microbiol.,* **10**, 509.

YOUNG, H. H., WHITE, E. C. and SWARTZ, E. O. (1919). *J. Amer. med. Ass.,* **73**, 1483.

ZEDLER, R. J. and BEITER, C. B. (1962). *Soap,* **38**(3), 75.

PART VI

Preservation and Preservatives

CHAPTER 17

PRESERVATION AND PRESERVATIVES

THE PREVENTION of microbial spoilage by physical or chemical means represents the practice of disinfection in its true and original sense. It is a subject to which more and more attention is being given because of its increasing importance in the economic life and health of the community. It is an ancient practice dating back to the early history of man, and it is interesting to recall how many of the methods still survive; methods which originally must have been applied in ignorance of the causes of spoilage but which gave these early people the results they wanted and subsequently have stood the test of time right to the present day.

Thousands of years ago salting and smoking were standard methods for preserving meats; aromatic oils were employed to protect parchments; methods of embalming were practised with complete success and use was made of the preservative action of drying. The value of heat has also long been established, but the value of cold seems to have been less appreciated, although not unnoticed, probably because the principles of refrigeration are a comparatively recent discovery. Similarly, the beneficial effects of sunlight were early recognized, but for obvious reasons nothing was known of the other forms of radiation treatment.

Preservation today is applied to the storage of meat, fish and vegetables, in the preparation of canned and bottled foods and in the processing of various natural and manufactured industrial materials such as wood, paper, board, concrete, textiles and paints. Preservatives are also added to many toilet, cosmetic and pharmaceutical preparations, and their use in solutions and suspensions administered parenterally is of special significance.

In the following pages it is intended first to discuss the various physical methods of preservation and their applications, and then to consider the complementary aspects of chemical preservation.

General principles

Most materials, whether natural, processed or manufactured, are either nutrient in themselves or they carry sufficient of nutrient substances to render them easily subject to microbial invasion. Even those materials which might appear to be devoid of such substances are not entirely immune, because in nature both bacteria and moulds appear to have remarkable capacities for adaptation; moreover, they only require micro quantities of nutrients to allow of substantial growth. Consequently they are found invading and colonizing in most unexpected places: the lens mountings in optical systems can carry enough materials to allow of substantial growths of moulds, likewise so-called distilled waters can sometimes support surprisingly large microbial populations: moulds can adapt themselves to grow in standard solutions of mineral acids, and the count of water-borne bacteria in suspensions of aluminium or magnesium hydroxide can rise to many thousands in a few days even though the pH value is about 10.

Preservation can be effected either by depriving the invading organisms of their basic nutritional requirements or by interfering with their normal metabolic processes and thus preventing their multiplication. From what has been said in the preceding paragraph it is difficult, if not impossible, to fulfil the first requirements, and so resort has to be made in nearly all cases to the second. This is, in fact, the fundamental of all methods of preservation, and it is achieved by adjusting the physical environment beyond the normal limits of tolerance of the cell, as by dehydration, osmosis or pH variation, or by actual physical or chemical attack on the cell.

As frequently underlined in earlier chapters in other contexts, it is always the hardier types or members which are the cause of trouble – the weaker or less adaptable ones tend to fade out naturally – and so the problem of preservation resolves itself into suppressing those organisms, by family, genus or species, able to persist and flourish in the conditions in which they find themselves. The degree of suppression necessary depends largely on the nature of the materials to be preserved. With most industrial materials it suffices simply to prevent growth, but with foods and pharmaceutical products something more is required. Here the conditions are such that a more varied range of organisms can flourish, some of which may be a source of danger to the health of the community. Hence the treatment must be such as will render the potential pathogens completely harmless and reduce all other organisms to a practicable minimum.

With the medicaments intended for parenteral administration the problem is somewhat different. These products are prepared sterile and the purpose of the preservative is to control the occasional contamination which may gain access during handling. It should, therefore, at least prevent the growth of all organisms and be lethal to the more commonly occurring ones.

As a general rule the chemical methods of preservation are more suitable for treating industrial materials and pharmaceutical and cosmetic preparations. For reasons of toxicity and flavour they have only very restricted applications in the food industries where the physical methods are usually more appropriate and acceptable.

Preservation by physical means

Foods and food products

The physical methods of preservation as applied in the food industries comprise principally heating, chilling, freezing, dehydration and radiation treatments. Through their agencies the world-wide distribution of these essential commodities is being greatly facilitated and at the same time they are helping to improve the presentation besides bringing about a number of changes and extensions in our general diet. Canned foods are now commonplace items in the domestic larder, pasteurized milk is on the doorstep every morning, packets of frozen vegetables are available in the stores, refrigeration is enabling meats and vegetables to be transported long distances with safety, dried egg and milk products have been processed commercially for some years, and now dehydrated meats, fish, soups and vegetables are making their appearance. Much attention is also being paid to packaging, especially in relation to the newer forms of film packs, and its influence on the storage of foods, and a short symposium on the subject was published in the *Journal of Applied Bacteriology* in 1962.

Heat as a sterilizing agent is discussed fully in Chapter 5 and so there remains to consider only the role of pasteurization in relation to preservation. Similarly, the effect of cold on micro-organisms is dealt with in Chapter 9, so there is little to add to the information already given. Dehydration and radiation treatments have likewise been discussed in earlier chapters, but here some further points are worthy of consideration. Finally, certain aspects of osmosis and acidity justify a mention.

Pasteurization. Pasteurization is most generally thought of as a means of improving the keeping quality of milk and ensuring its safety against infection with pathogenic organisms, especially the tubercle bacillus, but the process was first discovered by Pasteur during his investigations into the prevention of spoilage in French wines. It was later used by him to stop undesirable fermentations in beer, and its application to milk was a subsequent adaptation. It is now used in various forms with other liquid foods and beverages; it is not applicable to solid foods. It has been the concern of many authors in many books and journals, particularly those dealing with milk and dairying, and so it is considered here only briefly.

Pasteurization is not a sterilization process; its purpose is only to destroy the more heat-sensitive organisms which could be a source of danger or cause undesirable spoilage. It owes its origin to the discovery by Pasteur that a mild heating to 50° or 60° would prevent completely the spoilage of wines. In beers and wines it kills off the unwanted wild yeasts and bacteria causing abnormal fermentations – 95 per cent or more, depending on the actual treatment applied – and at the same time kills most of the pathogenic organisms of the coli-aerogenes group, including *Salmonella typhi*, as well as *Brucella abortus*, *Corynebacterium diphtheriae*, the streptococci (except the thermoduric types) and *Mycobacterium tuberculosis*. The thermoduric and thermophilic organisms, including bacterial spores, are unaffected.

The time-temperature equivalents producing the same degree of bacterial destruction in milk were worked out by Wilson (1942) and are given in Table 61, and it is on this information that the two officially accepted methods of milk pasteurization are based. The first, the 'holding' process, consists of heating the milk to 61·7° (143°F) and holding for at least 30 minutes; the second, or the 'flash' process, probably better referred to as a 'high temperature–short time' (H.T.S.T.) process, consists of heating to 71·1° (160°F) and holding for 15 seconds. The former must be carried out batchwise, whereas the latter is a continuous flow method. Both are equally satisfactory methods of treatment provided the plant is properly designed and handled, but various preferences have been expressed for one or the other owing to the different opinions prevalent concerning the influence of temperature and

TABLE 61

Time-temperature equivalents for pasteurizing milk
(after Wilson, 1942)

Temperature		Time to pasteurize
°C	°F	
60	140·0	63 min
62	143·6	25 min
63	145·4	16 min
64	147·2	10 min
65	149·0	6 min
66	150·8	4 min
70	158·0	38 sec
72	161·6	15 sec
74	165·2	6 sec
76	168·8	2·4 sec
80	176·0	0·4 sec

duration of heating on the cream-line of the milk, a matter of no little importance to the industry. There is also the question of the recovery and regrowth of the surviving bacteria. Treatment at the higher temperatures favour the subsequent growth of the lactic bacteria, but lower temperatures for longer times tend to encourage other organisms of the micrococcus group, etc. For these reasons, even higher temperatures for shorter times have been suggested but they have not been received enthusiastically. 82–83° (180–185°F) for 2 seconds only is said to destroy all the vegetative bacteria and 99 per cent of the spore formers, but it can also alter the flavour of the milk.

The efficacy of the treatment is controlled either by direct plate counts or, in the case of milk, by the more rapid phosphatase test. The latter test is particularly applicable to milk because the rate of destruction of the enzyme concerned parallels closely the rate of kill of tubercle bacilli by heat during the pasteurization process. But there are reservations on this point.

Wines and beers are effectively pasteurized with much less heating than is required for milk because of their acidity and alcoholic content which affect significantly the process. In general, lower temperatures are used, in the range of 44° to 56°, and the time of heating does not exceed 15 minutes.

Somewhat allied to pasteurization is the process euphemistically known as 'commercial sterilization'. This is a heat treatment which does not guarantee to give a sterile product but leaves only an occasional survivor of the more resistant type. It is applied to canned fruits, meats and condensed milk, and leaves the product in such a state that it will neither spoil on storage nor endanger the health of the consumer. Quite commonly thermophilic organisms and spore-forming aerobes and anaerobes are found in foods so treated, but their condition appears to be such that they are unable to multiply; growth, however, does take place when the can is opened and the organisms transferred to normal laboratory culture media. Two classical examples of this, quoted by Jones and Pearce (1954), are (*i*) the survival of six strains of aerobic spore-formers in a can of roasted veal 113 years old, and (*ii*) the survival of *Clostridium sporogenes*, artificially infected into chopped pork, after heat sterilization and subsequent incubation at 37° for 57 days. In both cases the cans were whole, the meat was sound and edible and there was no evidence of any spoilage, but the organisms grew out when they were cultured in the laboratory.

'Commercial sterilization' is sometimes known as ultra-pasteurization, and is widely applied in the processing of milk. It extends the keeping quality better than does ordinary pasteurization and it is not as damaging as absolute sterilization to its taste and appearance. The treatment destroys all of the vegetative bacteria and most of the sporing ones, leaving only a few of the most resistant cells to survive, and by this means a high proportion of bottles of milk can be kept even at 37° for several days without showing signs of curdling. The time-temperature combinations employed range between 45 minutes at 100° to 35 minutes at 110°, the more usual being 35 minutes at 106·5°. This heating is normally preceded by a homogenization treatment and it can be applied as a continuous flow method. The efficacy of the process is subject to a seasonal variation, the incidence of resistant spores being higher in the winter months than during the summer (Ridgway, 1954). This is most probably due to the greater access of spores into the raw milk from dusty hay and fodder during the period when the cattle are kept indoors. Ultra-high temperatures up to 149° for a few seconds by a heat-exchange process have also been tried, but they affected the flavour of the milk (Capstick, 1954).

Dehydration. Although the preservation of foods by drying has been practised since time immemorial, the method earliest employed, that of exposure to the atmosphere with or without the aid of a certain amount of heat, had obviously severe limitations, and under the influence of military and other considerations greatly improved methods with wider applications have been evolved. These include roller drying and spray drying for milk, eggs and other liquid foods, of which accounts of earlier work have been given by Crossley and Johnson (1942) and Haines and Elliot (1944); partial cooking followed by tunnel drying for fish (Shewan, 1945) and vegetables (Rishbeth,

1947), vacuum drying for fish (Woodbine, Reid and Scorer, 1953) and other products, and more recently with the improvements in high vacuum techniques for the freeze drying of a variety of foods. We are not concerned here with the details of these processes; that is outside the scope of this volume, but we are concerned with the fate of the micro-organisms on or in the foods both during and after the treatment, as were also each of the authors quoted above and several others such as Hawley and Benjamin (1955). The great danger is that food poisoning organisms such as *Clostridium botulinum* and those of the *Salmonella* and *Staphylococcus* groups are capable not only of surviving but of considerable multiplication during the drying process thus causing the food to become heavily infected. It can occur with any of the processes named, except that of freeze drying which is safe as soon as the material has been chilled and frozen, and in order to minimize the danger Haines and Elliot (1944) recommended that the drying should never be carried out at a temperature below 50°.

Whichever process is adopted, an adequate degree of dehydration is essential and, equally important, the subsequent storage conditions must be such as will prevent the re-entry of moisture, otherwise spoilage will certainly occur in time. The actual amount of moisture permitted differs for each of the foods but it is never more than a few per cent. It must also be borne in mind that at such low moisture levels all materials have hygroscopic tendencies, therefore the relative humidity is an important factor during storage.

In terms of relative humidity, feeding stuffs can be stored safely for short periods up to a few months if the level is kept below 73 per cent, but for long term storage it must be reduced to 65 per cent or less (Snow, Crichton and Wright, 1944). The same order of humidity is critical in preventing the growth of yeasts on sweetmeats (Pouncy and Summers, 1939). For preserves and purées the equivalent relative humidity varies with their solids content and their nature. With a tomato purée containing 38–40 per cent of solids the critical humidity level is about 95 per cent, but on adding 8 per cent of salt it falls to 85–87 per cent (Vas, 1957). Similarly, for jams with a total solids content of 60 per cent the critical relative humidity to prevent mould and yeast growth is around 85 per cent, and when the solids are raised to 63–65 per cent it falls to 80 per cent.

Packaging and storage conditions. It is appropriate to consider now the influence of packaging and storage conditions on the preservation of foods, because they are the most closely associated with drying. They are not confined, however, to this aspect; they are also involved with meats, bacon, fruit and vegetables prepared in other ways. The factors concerned are temperature, relative humidity, the gaseous atmosphere and the correlated oxidation–reduction potential.

The influence of temperature is fairly self-evident. Cool storage is an obvious advantage and temperatures in the range of normal growth of contaminating organisms should be avoided. But trouble can occur, both with artificially dried foods and with naturally dry materials such as grain, if the temperature is uneven and fluctuating. This is because under such conditions there is a tendency for moisture to drift and concentrate at one side or at the top of the material in its container and so set up local conditions more favourable to growth. The same can occur with plastic film packs where local accumulations of free water, arising from irregular temperature changes in the pack or from water absorption by the film, provide focal points for the initiation of surface spoilage (Hannan, 1962).

Moisture content is, of course, very much dependent on relative humidity, since for each humidity level there is an equilibrium moisture content of the material associated with it. Bacteria universally require near-saturation conditions before they will grow, but moulds are much more tolerant and will flourish sometimes in quite low humidity conditions. For raw meat bacterial growth is inhibited, according to Scott (1957), at equilibrium relative humidities below 95 per cent – Ingram (1962) gave 98·5 per cent – but in cured meats resistances appear to be rather greater so that the limiting values given by these two workers are 80–90 per cent and 90–95 per cent respectively. A slight degree of dryness on a meat surface would appear, therefore, to delay spoilage; but there are reservations to this general statement (Ingram, 1962).

In packaged meats, where the oxygen tension is lower and more anaerobic conditions obtain, the situation is again rather different and from reports quoted by Ingram (1962) the limiting humidity level for both salmonellae and staphylococci is about 4 per cent lower.

The same arguments also apply to fruits and vegetables but the problems are different. Here (Tomkins, 1962), the natural water content of the fresh products induces a relative humidity in a sealed container of 96–98 per cent, and this induces fungal and bacterial rotting. On the other hand excessive loss of moisture reduces the storage life for other reasons, and so a balanced level of humidity is required. This is obtained by having holes in the package.

Passing reference was made in a preceding paragraph to the effect of oxygen tension on the storage of packaged foods. It is an important factor, the significance of which has been brought to the fore by the introduction of film, and particularly vacuum, packaging. The intention of these new packs is to improve the quality of the foodstuff, and this it does in certain directions, but at the same time it brings its own microbiological problems, for during the storage period there is a much longer time for any new microbial situation to establish itself.

Raw meats are usually packed in oxygen-permeable film in order to maintain their characteristic redness, but for cured meats, and bacon in particular, the reverse is the rule and vacuum packs with impermeable film are used (Ingram, 1962). The physical characteristics of the film are, therefore, important, and the water vapour and oxygen permeabilities of some materials are given in Table 62. Quite frequently, as pointed out by Hannan

(1962), these two properties run similarly, although one notable exception is polyethylene which has a low permeability to water vapour but a high oxygen permeability.

Within each package is an enclosed ecological system. The micro-organisms originally present continue to grow and so alter the gaseous atmosphere, reducing the oxygen tension and increasing the carbon dioxide content. At normal oxygen levels the pseudomonads and micrococci are the

TABLE 62

Typical permeabilities to water vapour and oxygen of
packaging materials
(Hannan, 1962)

Material	Permeability to	
	Water vapour†	Oxygen‡
Cellulose, grade { PT	500	{ <1 when dry 3 at 50% R.H. 5,000 at 100% R.H.
QSAT	150–350	2,000 at 100% R.H.
MSAT	3	1·5 at 50% R.H.
MXXT	1·5	<1 at 50% R.H.
Low density polyethylene	5	3,000–10,000
High density polyethylene	1·5	500–3,000
Polypropylene	1·5	1,500
Polyvinyl chloride**	10	200
Polyvinylidene chloride co-polymer	0·5	3
Rubber hydrochloride**	2–80	100–5,000
Cellulose acetate**	500	—
Polystyrene	50	4,000
Polyester	10	50
Nylon { 6	15	25
11	5	300

* The figures, which refer to materials approximately 0·001 in. thick, are based partly on data given in the literature and partly on practical observations on a limited number of samples: they indicate only the probable order of magnitude and not the detailed performance which can be expected from materials from different sources of supply.
† Results given as g/m²/24 hr at 25° and 75% RH.
‡ Results given as ml/m²/24 hr at 20°.
** The precise permeability is markedly dependent on the plasticizer concentration.

dominant organisms, but at reduced oxygen tensions these tend to fade out and on bacon (Cavett, 1962) and raw meats (Ingram, 1962) their place is taken by other groups to be ultimately dominated by the lactic acid bacteria. This is somewhat dependent on temperature, however; at elevated tempera-tures the lactic bacteria can be replaced on bacon by coagulase-negative staphylococci (Cavett, 1962).

Carbon dioxide acts in a converse manner to that of oxygen; above certain concentrations it inhibits the growth of bacteria, although it is dis-tinctly selective in this direction, whilst moulds are sensitive and yeasts are comparatively resistant. The effect of carbon dioxide in an enclosed pack can, therefore, vary considerably, but it does account in part for the dominance of the lactobacilli which are known to be resistant. In fruit packages the build up of carbon dioxide to a level between 7 per cent and 30 per cent, depending on the type of fruit concerned, can be beneficial to the storage life (Tomkins, 1962).

Osmosis. High osmotic pressure is always inimical to microbial growth, and particularly to bacteria. Forty per cent glucose and 60 per cent sucrose solutions are actually lethal to staphylococci (Nunheimer and Fabian, 1940). Moulds and yeasts are much less susceptible and certain types will grow, or can adapt and grow, in quite strong sugar solutions. Moulds can easily disfigure the surface of jams and preserves, although they do not penetrate deeply, and spoilage in syrups, honey and other products with high sugar contents is almost invariably due to the presence of osmophilic yeasts. In the author's experience, as well as that of Ingram (1950), even concentrated orange juice is not immune from this type of infection, in spite of the fact that it contains up to 70 per cent of sugar and has a pH value of 3 or less.

Similar effects are observed with salts and brines, but the concentrations at which they begin to exert their influence are much lower than with sugars. Moreover, there is a greater diversity of resistances between the bacteria, and even within the genus *Staphylococcus* there are halophilic, halotolerant (able to grow in salt concentrations up to 15 per cent) and nonhalotolerant species (Pohja, 1960). The halophilic types in general are not common, being found mainly in curing factories where brines are used containing up to 26 per cent of salt, but they are important in this branch of food preservation and a symposium on the subject was held in Cambridge in 1958 (*Report*, 1958).

The halotolerant bacteria are much more widespread, and, in fact, many strains can be preserved in salt solutions. Starting with washed cells suspended in 1 per cent saline, which apparently evaporated during storage to give final concentrations up to 8 or 9 per cent, Chance (1963) found that *Klebsiella pneumoniae, Coryn. diphtheriae* and several *Streptococcus* species would survive at room temperature for 21 months, and *E. coli, Pseudomonas pyocyanea* and *Staphylococcus* species for 4 years. This was, of course, survival without growth, there being no nutrient present to encourage growth.

The moulds and yeasts are also resistant, and there are records of their growth in strong brines containing up to 30 per cent of salt.

The inhibitory effect of high salt concentrations cannot be attributed wholly to their osmotic influence (Spiegelberger, 1944). It is also bound up with factors such as the presence of protein material, the ratios of other inorganic substances in the solution, pH value and temperature, each of which comes into play more significantly with salts than with sugar solutions. The various interrelationships of these factors have been studied by many investigators, especially those concerned with food microbiology, and they have been fully reviewed by Baumgartner (1946).

Acidity. The effect of acids in preventing the growth of micro-organisms is due both to hydrogen ion concentration and to the nature of the acid radical. The mineral acids rely wholly on hydrogen ion concentration, but the organic acids owe their action mainly to the undissociated molecules. For these reasons it is not possible to specify exact limiting pH values, but generally speaking bacteria will not grow at pH values below about 4·5 or above 8·5. There are many exceptions to this generalization, notably amongst the lactic bacteria and certain other saprophytic types, but they do not include any of the pathogens. In contrast to the bacteria, moulds and yeasts are distinctly acidophilic and can sometimes grow under quite acid conditions. The extreme example of this is the occasional appearance of mould growth in N sulphuric acid.

From a range of acids which included hydrochloric, acetic, citric, lactic, malic and tartaric, Levine and Fellers (1940) found acetic acid to be the most effective. Its activity was "in almost direct proportion to the amount present", and not to the final pH value, and in their opinion it and certain other organic acids "appear to have a toxicity in excess of that which could possibly be due to the pH alone." When used to adjust the acidity of nutrient broth, it inhibited bacteria at pH 4·9, *Saccharomyces cerevisiae* at pH 3·9 and *Aspergillus niger* at pH 4·1. Nunheimer and Fabian (1940) likewise found acetic acid to be the most effective of the acids against the food-poisoning staphylococci; it inhibited them below pH 4·59 and killed them below pH 4·37. These observations show why vinegars, pickles, mayonnaises and similar acid products are always so well preserved.

Acid conditions not only exert a preservative action *per se* but they also influence considerably the efficacy of other chemical preservatives. Phenolic substances are always more active at acid pH values by virtue of their nonionic state in these conditions. Benzoic acid and the esters of *p*-hydroxy-benzoic acid also respond in the same way being some two or three times more active at pH 3 than at pH 6 (Entrekin, 1961). Other compounds which respond in a similar way include mercuric chloride, sorbic acid, salicylanilide and dehydroacetic acid; cetrimide, hexachlorophane and hexylresorcinol are not affected.

Acidity also reduces considerably the resistance of spores to heat. Coulthard (1939) proved that heavy inocula of even the most resistant types could be sterilized at pH 2·25 by heating to only 80° for 1 hour, and he ventured to suggest that the same heating "would probably be efficient in practice at pH values below 5·0." This latter observation is in agreement with the general opinion of food microbiologists who consider a pH value of 4·5 to be the threshold value below which pressure sterilization is not necessary to kill off even *Cl. botulinum*, the most formidable of the food-poisoning bacteria. Actually the effect of moderate changes in pH value around the neutral point on bacterial resistance appears to be indeterminate but on the acid side below about pH 5 there is often a sudden change in resistance with quite a small reduction in pH value (*see* Baumgartner, 1946).

Radiation treatment. Of recent years much attention has been given to the preservation of foods by irradiation with gamma rays and cathode rays. Ultraviolet irradiation has also been considered, but it has obvious limitations in that it only reaches unprotected organisms exposed on immediately accessible surfaces. Obviously complete sterilization is the ideal target, but in the majority of cases the dose required is so high that it damages the appearance and organoleptic properties of the food. This is not surprising because protein is one of the main constituents of foods as well as of bacteria and there is no reason why radiations should be selective in their attack. A compromise treatment has, therefore, to be adopted, one which will destroy a sufficiently large proportion of the organisms on the food to extend its safe storage by a reasonable period but which at the same time will not affect its palatability and general acceptability. For this reason a large concentration of effort in many parts of the world is being centred on "radiopasteurization" as applied to red and white meats, fish including shellfish, soft fruits, liquid and dried egg, vegetables, milk and grain.

As indicated in Chapter 6, the majority of bacterial cells are killed by comparatively small radiation doses, leaving only the most resistant to survive. For absolute sterilization, doses as high as 4–5×10^6 rad may be necessary, but one-fiftieth of this amount can destroy a sufficiently high proportion of organisms to allow the storage life to be extended five- or tenfold and thus make it a practicable means of preservation. In fact, most of the investigations are being made with doses ranging between 50,000 and 500,000 rad, at which levels most of the vegetative bacteria are totally destroyed, and the overall reduction in microbial activity is of the order of 99·9 per cent or greater. Thus, it can be used for destroying salmonella infections in egg and staphylococci on fish or bacon, but it cannot deal adequately with *Cl. botulinum* in meat products where a total kill is essential. For further discussion on these points, the reader is referred to Chapter 6.

There is no acquired radioactivity by such treatment, but it does bring in its train other problems. The fact that there is a small residuum of viable bacteria often means that the type of ultimate spoilage differs from that normally encountered because the nature and balance of the bacterial flora in the food is different before and after treatment: this aspect is fully discussed in Chapter 6. Again, radiopasteurization is not as effective against enzymes as against bacteria, so that in spite of the near-sterilization of the food, destructive enzymic action mainly of the catheptic oxidative and phosphorylating type, can proceed unabated. Similarly, film and other sealed packs introduce their own problems: with some meat packs the oxidation-reduction potential gradually reduces to -300 mv, but after irradiation it rises slowly to a level of about 300–400 mv.

Industrial materials

By their nature, constitution and construction, the majority of industrial materials cannot be preserved by physical methods. Heat, radiations, acidity, etc. are plainly not applicable under the normal conditions of usage of such materials, and the only direction in which any attempt at control can be made is that of humidity and moisture.

Humidity. Most industrial materials are subject to spoilage through fungi rather than bacteria or yeasts, and so the influence of humidity is considerable. The actual limiting humidity and moisture content to prevent fungal growth cannot be specified because it depends greatly on the nature of the materials concerned; it appears to be associated with hygroscopicity, the more hygroscopic materials being more susceptible to mould growth and so requiring lower humidities before growth is arrested. Well known examples of fungal spoilage are found industrially in damp areas of premises caused by steam condensation and domestically on damp walls of houses and the so-called dry rot of floor boards. All of these are the result of maintaining an atmosphere of constant high humidity and they can be prevented by proper ventilation, thus reducing the humidity level to something near ambient.

The natural fibres of cotton, wool and jute are very susceptible to mould growth and so humidity control is highly important. According to Block (1953) no growth will occur on cotton if the relative humidity is below 92 per cent, whereas the comparative value for wool is about 80 per cent, for wood about 76 per cent and for leather even lower. These figures do not coincide with those of Burgess (1954) who stated that 70–75 per cent humidity would allow growth on cotton, 82 per cent would allow growth on jute and 94 per cent on wool. The actual value depends to some extent on the 'cleanliness' of the fibres used and also on temperature, and these factors might account for the differences quoted above. A good example of the influence of temperature is seen with glue-bonded cork such as is used for liners in bottle closures. With this material a humidity of 66 per cent or less is sufficient to prevent growth at 20°, but at 30° it must be reduced to not greater than 56 per cent (Everton and Bashford, 1952).

Preservation with chemicals

Foods

The substances which may be added as preservatives in foods are severely restricted by law. In Great Britain they are confined to benzoic acid and its sodium salt, sulphur dioxide and certain sulphites. However, substances such as salt, sugars, lactic acid, acetic acid, glycerol, alcohol, herbs, spices and essential oils, which are present naturally in many foods and have a long tradition of usage, are not considered to be preservatives in law and so may be used freely. Likewise sodium nitrate is permitted in limited amounts, but only with bacon, ham and cooked meats. All other additives, including boric acid and the borates, are considered to be adulterants and their use may lead to prosecution under the law. In Canada the permitted choice is a little wider and includes propionic and sorbic acids and sodium diacetate, and in the United States penicillin and chlortetracycline are also included.

Both benzoic acid and sulphur dioxide are, of course, much more effective in acid conditions than in neutral or alkaline ones, and so they are used mainly with acid foods. Benzoic acid is used exclusively with fruit juices and wines, and the maximum permitted addition varies with the different types of beverage from 120 to 600 parts per million. Sulphur dioxide is used much more extensively with dried fruits, fruit pulps and juices, wines, preserves, meats and various dehydrated foods, and the amounts range between 70 and 3,000 parts per million.

Very many compounds have been examined for their efficacy as food preservatives, but the majority have proved too chronically toxic or have not measured up to other essential physiological and biochemical criteria such as have been discussed by Banfield (1952). Those which have received most attention include derivatives of benzoic acid such as salicylic acid and the *p*-hydroxybenzoates, derivatives of acetic acid such as dehydroacetic and chloroacetic acids, boron compounds, fluorides, formaldehyde, ethylene oxide, diphenyl derivatives, quaternary ammonium compounds and propionic and sorbic acids, not forgetting the antibiotics. Of these compounds, the esters of *p*-hydroxybenzoic acid have shown most promise. Banfield (1952) expressed a preference for them rather than for benzoic acid because of their greater activities at neutral pH values – a performance subsequently underlined by many other workers – and they are used extensively on the Continent, particularly in Germany. Of the remainder, the boron compounds, the fluorides, salicylic acid and formaldehyde are now discredited because of their chronic toxicity or other undesirable properties, whilst the others have limited useful applications. Thus, treatment with ethylene oxide gas will effectively prevent fungal infections on citrus, pome and dried fruits, and impregnation of wrapping papers with diphenyl compounds will also retard mould growth. Likewise, propionic and sorbic acids will prevent mould and 'rope' in bread, and so will dehydroacetic acid in flour (Mossel and de Bruin, 1950) but this has proved too toxic to be of practical application. Investigations with sorbic acid derivatives are proceeding actively.

Antibiotics are comparative newcomers in the field of food preservation, but already they are presenting a number of public health problems, the most prominent of which are the development of allergies and the sensitization of persons through their continuous intake in small amounts and the evolution of antibiotic-resistant strains of micro-organisms (Banfield, 1952; Ingram and Barnes, 1955). The principal antibiotics so far examined are penicillin, streptomycin, aureomycin, subtilin, nisin, neomycin and chloramphenicol. These have been variously tested in tinned and raw meats, vegetables, custard fillings, milk and cheese, and the two most promising are penicillin and aureomycin, although nisin has been used effectively in preventing spoilage in cheese and shows promise with other foods (Hawley, 1955, 1957). Penicillin will effectively improve the keeping quality of milk (Foley and Byrne, 1950; Rowlands, 1951) and aureomycin is most useful in preventing the bacterial spoilage of poultry, fish and meat. Aureomycin is now permitted in the United States for preserving poultry; it is usually added to the iced wash water after evisceration. Sensitization does not arise with either of these antibiotics because penicillin is not very stable in aqueous solution and aureomycin is destroyed during cooking.

For preserving citrus fruits against fungal decay, induced mainly by *Penicillium digitatum*, a dip or wash in a 0·5 per cent solution of sodium *o*-phenylphenate at low temperature is frequently employed, but more recently 2-aminobutane (*sec*-butylamine), as a 0·5 per cent solution in water, or a 2 per cent emulsion in a water-wax base, has been found more effective, as well as being less injurious to the fruit (Eckert and Kolbezen, 1962).

Industrial materials

The laboratory assessment of chemical preservatives for industrial materials is a difficult matter by *in vitro* methods, and frequently the only resort is to '*in vivo*' determinations. The antifungal and antibacterial properties of the compounds themselves can easily be measured in the laboratory but the situation becomes much more complex when they are incorporated in textiles or applied to wood and subjected to weathering, the usual temperature fluctuations and the different microbial flora and other variables encountered in nature. For this reason soil burial tests are often applied as a means of assessing '*in vivo*' activity. In these tests, the treated material is buried in an infected soil and examined at intervals to assess the amount of destruction which may have occurred: the assessment should always be related to the performance of a known preservative. Weathering tests under natural or artificial conditions are also applied. Thus, by using a combination of several different tests, a fair measure of the performance characteristics of a preservative can be determined – at least it eliminates the least suitable compounds.

Textiles. Much damage can be caused to textiles due to mildew and rot on storage and this is of very high economic importance. Deterioration can also arise from similar causes during manufacture, but this can be prevented at certain stages by acidification or by adding sodium silicofluoride. One of the most widely used antifungal preservatives for finished cotton materials is salicylanilide, or Shirlan, so named because it was introduced by the Shirley Institute following the work of Fargher, Galloway and Probert (1930). This compound has little bacteriostatic action but it is reliably fungistatic when incorporated into cotton yarn at the rate of 0·1 per cent by weight. It is also equally useful for preserving wool against mould infection. Many other phenolic substances have been examined in comparison with salicylanilide, but none has proved superior. Amongst those which have shown the most promise are pentachlorophenol, mercaptobenzthiazole and *o*-phenylphenol (2-hydroxydiphenyl); in addition, dichlorophene, or di-hydroxydichlorodiphenylmethane, has received high praise in the United States.

Copper compounds are used extensively for the preservation of nets, tent canvas, sandbags and similar materials, where the blue coloration is of no importance. Along with other metal compounds, they are both fungistatic and bacteriostatic. Armstrong (1941) advocated using one of the copper soaps, such as copper naphthenate, oleate or stearate, or cuprammonium, for preserving sandbags. He found the minimum safe concentration of copper in the cotton to be 0·35 per cent by weight, at which level the preservative value was equivalent to that of 25 per cent of creosote. The actual amounts of the various compounds recommended were 0·8–1 per cent of the copper soaps and 1–1·5 per cent of cuprammonium. Marsh *et al.* (1944) confirmed the value of copper by soil burial tests and selected copper naphthenate as outstandingly the best. This compound was also the choice of Block (1949) who found that it was the most resistant to leaching, cotton duck so treated retaining the majority of the added copper even after two years' weathering.

Unfortunately, copper naphthenate is not always suitable in all circumstances because apart from its colour it also has a penetrating odour, and in such cases it can be replaced by some other salt such as the chromate, 8-hydroxyquinoline (also known as copper 8-quinolinate), oleate, stearate, rosinate or pentachlorophenate. The pentachlorophenate, although a more effective preservative than the naphthenate, is little used because of its deep reddish colour and low solubility in ordinary solvents. Copper 8-hydroxy-quinoline, the most recent of the copper preservatives, also has a low solubility, but it has a comparably high activity, less than 1 part per million being effectively fungistatic in broth, and so it has reasonable potentialities. Copper chromate, although found to be exceedingly valuable as a cotton preservative and superior to the other salts (Armstrong, 1941; Block, 1949), does not seem to have attracted any further attention.

An interesting feature of the copper compounds, and indeed of those of other metals, is that binary mixtures are more effective than the single salts, mainly because they mutually retard the rate of leaching. Thus, the efficacies of copper and zinc naphthenates are much enhanced by adding mercuric or phenylmercuric naphthenate (Bayley and Weatherburn, 1947). Similar results are obtained with several other metals, and some ternary mixtures are even superior to the binary ones.

Metals other than copper have also been examined for their preservative value. Silver compounds are actually superior to copper, but they are not a practical proposition because of their high cost. Zinc naphthenate is sometimes used, although this is no more active than naphthenic acid (Marsh *et al.*,

1944). With the exception of the 2:2'-dinaphthylmethane-3:3'-disulphonate the arylmercuric salts have proved disappointing in field trials (Hopf and Race, 1949). The virtue of this compound is that it gives a colloidal solution which breaks irreversibly on the cloth fibres, and so gives a more permanent protection. The organic tin compounds are more recent introductions into the field, with particular emphasis on tri-*n*-butyltin salts.

Wood. The damage caused to wood by fungal attack during its useful life is of enormous importance, affecting as it does so many aspects of our industrial and economic life, and many investigations have been carried out on the problem over many years. These investigations have resulted in very many patents being taken out in Great Britain, in the United States and elsewhere in the world.

It has long been accepted that if sufficiently dry conditions can be maintained, then there is no problem. But often the environment is far from satisfactory in this respect, and so chemical methods of preservation have to be sought. One of the earliest of wood preservatives was creosote, and this still has many useful applications. For many purposes, however, it is unsuitable, and of recent years copper compounds have tended to take its place. Others which have had a degree of success include pentachlorophenol, zinc compounds, mercury compounds, arsenic compounds including thioarsenites, and various resins some of which have been chlorinated.

Paper and board. The preservation of paper and board from microbial spoilage is a problem similar to that for textiles, and broadly speaking the same measures are adopted. The need for preservation arises mainly from the conditions of high humidity which often obtain with these materials when they are used for packaging and wrapping purposes. Under such conditions moulds can develop freely, using the glues, waxes and starches in the paper as nutrients, and causing discoloration and weakening of the fibre structure. Bacteria are rarely involved, except when the moisture level is unusually high; the main offending organisms are species of *Chaetomium, Penicillium* and *Aspergillus.*

The most common proofing agents are copper or zinc naphthenate, phenylmercuric compounds, pentachlorophenol, *o*-phenylphenol and dichlorophene. Each can be incorporated into the paper whilst it is still in the pulp stage or it can be impregnated into the sheet either before drying or into the finished product. Impregnation involves the use of suitable solvents and may result in an uneven distribution of the preservative; incorporation into the pulp gives a more even product but introduces problems of effluent disposal.

The mercury compounds, although useful for preserving industrial papers and boards, are obviously unsuitable in this context where foods are concerned. In such cases less toxic substances must be employed, of which the most common are the diphenyl compounds. *o*-Phenylphenol itself is effective, but Tomkins (1963) finds certain of its esters even more so, namely those of acetic, propionic and butyric acids but not of benzoic, caproic or methoxy-acetic acids. These active compounds are incorporated in wrapping papers at the rate of 40–50 mg per 100 sq in. of paper, and at this level they will extend the storage life of citrus fruits at all temperatures substantially. Storage life of 6 days at 20° under normal conditions can be extended to 11 days using *o*-phenylphenol-treated paper and to over 27 days with *o*-phenyl-phenyl acetate. (Tomkins, 1963). Dichloro- and dibromo-methylhydantoin and dichloroisocyanuric acid have also been used for the same purpose (Eckert and Kolbezen, 1962) as well as 2:4:5-trichlorophenoxytrichloro-methane (Spenser and Wilkinson, 1958).

As with all industrial materials, the methods employed for testing for mould resistance are somewhat empirical, but a technique which gives reasonably reproducible results has been described by Howard (1954). It is an adaptation of an early one by Thom, and consists essentially of placing a piece of the test paper or board, 5 cm square, on the surface of a petri-plate containing Czapek's agar at pH 4·2, spraying with a mixed suspension of mould spores, incubating for 14 days at 25° and inspecting at intervals for mould growth. The amount of growth is assessed according to a predetermined scale and from it the relative efficiency of the preservative determined.

Paints. The preservation of paints is a twofold problem. It involves the protection first of the liquid material during storage, when bacteria are the most likely cause of trouble; secondly, it involves the final finished surface, when moulds are the most common invaders. The preservation of liquid paints concerns only the casein and glue-based water paints which are parti-cularly susceptible to bacterial growth; it does not apply to the non-aqueous oil paints. Sometimes the spoilage is accompanied by gas production so that, apart from any changes occurring in the physical characteristics of the paint, it is not uncommon for cans to blow up. Such spoilage can be prevented by simply adding a preservative such as *p*-chloro-*m*-cresol, pentachlorophenol or one of the phenylmercuric compounds.

The protection of a paint surface from discoloration, disfiguration and even flaking as a result of mould growth is a more difficult matter, and it is not made easier by the extreme thinness of the paint film which limits severely the amount of preservative that can be used. The organisms most likely to cause damage are species of *Penicillium, Aspergillus, Cladosporium* and *Pullularia,* and the extent to which they can establish themselves on a finished surface depends very much on the nature of the paint. The invading organisms obtain most of their nutriment from the plaster, wood or other substratum on which the paint is applied, although a small amount un-doubtedly comes from the paint itself, so that a hard film with a gloss finish is naturally more resistant than a soft matt one in that it is less permeable and so acts as a more effective barrier against the diffusion of the nutrients and access by the mould mycelium. Moreover, a gloss surface is not only less likely to collect and hold dust and dirt but it is also less susceptible to the influence of humidity and moisture.

Very many compounds with known antifungal properties have been examined for their ability to protect paint surfaces but none has proved entirely satisfactory at the maximum concentration normally acceptable in paint, *i.e.* 1 per cent, and so the search continues. The choice of compounds is somewhat restricted, for not only must they be active at as low a concentration as possible and possess the physical properties as outlined below, but also they must not affect the viscosity of the paint or the setting and hardening properties of the film. The compounds which have proved most effective include salicylanilide, pentachlorophenol, *p*-chloro-*m*-cresol, copper 8-hydroxyquinoline and the phenylmercuric derivatives. Of these, the copper and mercury compounds are the most efficient, but unfortunately copper is not always practicable because of the colour it imparts to the paint, and mercury is not acceptable because of its potential toxicity, particularly when the paint is applied by spraying. Zinc compounds have only poor activities, although zinc oxide, a normal constituent of paint pigment, is one of the best antifungal agents, provided it is there in sufficient quantity; titanium dioxide, also used as a paint pigment, does not possess this property.

In spite of its unpromising prospect, paraformaldehyde has been incorporated with effect in gloss paints and in resin floor seals (Kingston, Lidwell and Noble, 1962). The counts on such surfaces were reduced in 24 hours by up to 99 per cent and remained so for six months. Such a preparation, therefore, affords a long-term, self-disinfecting period, but the authors warn that "it is rash to assume that such treatments would have any useful effect in reducing the spread of disease" and "may not be of any great practical importance."

In assessing the antifungal properties of paint films and surfaces, the nature of the paint, the thickness of the film, the amount of moisture, the influence of light and the effect of weathering are all important variables, but probably the most significant is the substratum on which the paint is applied. The most common substrata are metals, wood, board, plaster, asbestos and concrete, and they all differ in the amount of nutrient materials they carry. Even the different types of plaster vary in this respect (Findlay, 1940) and soft woods are notably more susceptible to infection than are hard woods. Such differences naturally affect the apparent resistance of a paint to infection and so, in the absence of an agreed standard for testing, it is not surprising that conflicting reports have appeared on the efficacy of different preservatives in the various paint formulations.

The tests applied to paints to assess their mould resistance may be grouped into (*i*) laboratory tests, with or without artificial weathering conditions, (*ii*) panel tests, and (*iii*) field patch tests. Laboratory tests are valuable first-stage assessments, because they give results quickly and so save much otherwise wasted time with preparations which are manifestly unsatisfactory. One of the simplest of such tests is to apply the paint to paper strips, allow to dry and mature, lay on the surface of a nutrient agar plate and inoculate with streaks of various mould spores. After incubating for a week or so at 25° or at room temperature, the extent of inhibition of growth is assessed and from this the efficacy of the paint can be deduced (*see* Plate 1). Unfortunately, this type of test can give misleading results, because it depends on diffusion of the antifungal agent into the agar, and this is a quality often not desirable, because it indicates that the preservative may easily be eluted from the paint film.

A more suitable laboratory test is one using wood blocks or compressed wood pulp such as has been suggested by Findlay (1940) and by Galloway (1954). In each of these techniques the wood is pretreated with added nutrients such as malt and gelatin; this is in order to obtain results more rapidly. A technique similar to these has been used by the author, the procedure in this case being to spray pieces of either soft wood or hardboard, about 4 in. by 12 in., several times with a suspension of mixed mould spores in glucose broth and allow them to dry overnight. Each piece then is divided into three sections, and two coats of paint are applied to each section. After drying and hardening for three days, the panels are reinfected, again by spraying, and then incubated in a sealed glass tank over water. Incubation for about one month at room temperature is sufficient to differentiate between a good and bad paint, as is clearly indicated in Plate 2.

This type of test is a drastic one in some respects in that the infection is a heavy one on both sides of the paint film, but in other respects it is deficient because it does not take into account the possible effects of weathering and ageing. The significance of this is illustrated in some findings published by Morris and Darlow (1959) on the bactericidal properties of paint films. These authors examined a range of compounds, many of which were readily soluble in water, after incorporating them at a concentration of 10 per cent (w/w) in the liquid paint. The freshly prepared and matured films showed some bactericidal activity, but it was completely removed by washing with gentle rubbing in water.

The effects of weathering and ageing can be assessed roughly by subjecting the test pieces to artificial 'weather' in a specially designed tank, but the more reliable method is by long-term trials with panel or patch tests.

Panel tests are made by treating large panels of wood or any other appropriate material with the test paint and then exposing them to natural weathering for periods of many months. They are examined at intervals during this period for mould growth and mould resistance. Patch tests are somewhat similar, except that they are carried out on walls, partitions, ceilings, etc., *in situ* and *in natura*. The paint is applied to selected areas known to be heavily infected with moulds and the areas are kept under observation for a predetermined length of time. Such tests are ideal in that they simulate exactly the conditions of usage, but they are lengthy and do not lend themselves to standardization.

Leather. Leather is essentially a protein material, and so in the raw state it is easily subject to bacterial attack. After tanning, however, it becomes resistant to bacterial attack, but is still susceptible to mould growth, and this tends to harden the leather and reduce its tensile strength.

The compound most widely used for preserving leather is *p*-nitrophenol, and the concentration employed depends upon the method of tanning. For chrome-tanned leather 0·1 per cent is adequate, but for vegetable-tanned leather 0·5 per cent is preferred. Other phenols have also been used, and these include β-naphthol, as recommended by the British Leather Manufacturers' Research Association, *p*-chloro-*m*-xylenol, salicylanilide, tetrachlorophenol and pentachlorophenol. The last mentioned compound has proved to be the most effective. Phenylmercuric compounds are also highly active, but they are not used in practice because of their potential toxicity if allowed to be in continuous contact with the skin.

Other industrial materials. Other materials for which some degree of preservation is desirable include rubber, plastics (by virtue of the added plasticizers which are sometimes nutrient), optical equipment, flood water in oil wells, cutting oils and masonry. Phenylmercuric salts and copper-8-quinolinate are most commonly used in rubbers and plastics, quaternary ammonium compounds are used in lens systems, mercurials and inorganic fluorides in masonry, and chlorinated phenols, quaternary ammonium compounds and dichlorodimethylhydantoin in cutting oils and well boring systems. In particular, quaternaries made from hexamine and halohydrocarbons have been recommended for the preservation of emulsions industrially (Scott and Wolf, 1962). These compounds are all readily soluble in water, and depend for their activity on the slow release of formaldehyde. Their individual inhibitory and lethal concentrations vary with the halohydrocarbon used. In agar, the inhibitory concentrations against bacteria and fungi range from about 10 to 500 parts per million.

Pharmaceutical and cosmetic preparations

The preservation of pharmaceutical preparations, including cosmetics, can be considered under two headings: (*i*) the protection from undue microbial contamination of preparations taken by mouth or applied externally, (*ii*) the prevention from infection of preparations administered by injection. They represent two different facets of the subject, the one being concerned only with preventing the growth of micro-organisms in a product and the other with maintaining its sterility, and so in some respects they require different treatments. One aspect in common, however, is the need to ensure the integrity of the preparation not only during storage but also whilst in the hands of the consumer. This means that the preservative chosen must be able to deal with, or otherwise render harmless, any contaminating organisms accidentally introduced during use. It is a point which is continually before those concerned with parenteral preparations but which is less appreciated in other contexts. It is, none the less, important in all cases. Micro-organisms of different types can grow sometimes under the most unexpected conditions, and each time a container is opened there is the distinct possibility of some bacteria, yeasts or moulds gaining access. Therefore, unless the conditions are sufficiently inimical to growth or an adequate preservative is present the product will ultimately be spoiled.

Preparations administered parenterally. Preparations for parenteral use are essentially sterile products, and the function of a preservative is to protect them from bacterial infection and so keep them safe for injection. Infections occur mainly in preparations dispensed in containers from which successive doses can be removed at intervals, and they arise through the accidental introduction of bacteria or moulds during the removal of the first doses. In the absence of an adequate preservative these organisms are liable to grow out, sometimes quite quickly, and so produce a heavy infection in the remainder of the injection. The consequences of such a happening can be disastrous, and the medical literature contains many reports of deaths following the administration of injections infected in this way. The matter is considered to be so serious that the British Pharmacopoeia requires that "When the container is sealed so as to permit the withdrawal of successive doses on different occasions, the solution or preparation of the drug contains sufficient of a suitable bactericide"; no bactericide is required in single-dose containers, although one is frequently added as a precautionary measure. Similar requirements are made in other pharmacopoeias.

Typical bactericides recommended in the B.P. are phenol 0·5 per cent, cresol 0·3 per cent, chlorocresol 0·1 per cent and phenylmercuric nitrate 0·001 per cent, and others which are commonly used include benzyl alcohol 1 per cent, phenylethyl alcohol 0·5 per cent, phenoxetol (β-phenoxyethyl alcohol) 1 per cent, cetrimide or one of the other quaternary ammonium compounds 0·01–0·02 per cent and various esters of p-hydroxybenzoic acid, notably a mixture of the methyl and propyl esters usually at 0·2 and 0·02 per cent respectively. Chlorbutol, 0·5 per cent, also featured in earlier editions of the B.P., but it has now been removed; other compounds which have been used include chlorhexidine, although this is more suitable in preparations for topical use, and dichlorobenzyl alcohol.

Until the British Pharmacopoeia, 1963, was published, such a solution was referred to as "a suitable bacteriostatic" but, in fact, they are all substantially bactericidal, being lethal to the commonly occurring non-sporing bacteria, and to some of the mould spores, in a matter of hours. This is an obvious essential property where solutions or suspensions for injection are concerned, and so the term "bactericide" is more appropriate and more accurately descriptive than the earlier "bacteriostatic": it is also semantically more correct!

As yet there is no approved method for determining what is "a suitable bactericide", although the British Pharmacopoeia, 1963, now states that "Any other substance used [other than those cited above] must have a bactericidal activity not less than that shown by 0·5 per cent w/v of Phenol", and it further stipulates that "[it] shall not interfere with the therapeutic efficiency of the drug or cause a turbidity"; attention is also drawn to its possible loss by absorption into the rubber closure of the container. The idea of using 0·5 per cent phenol solution as the standard was proposed in a report by the Ministry of Health Subcommittee on Bacteriostatics in 1957 (*Report*, 1957). The choice was fairly self-evident, since phenol is the best known and best tried of the bactericides, but in addition the Subcommittee proposed the method whereby any other bactericide should be compared. They suggested that two bacterial species were adequate, and chose *Staph. aureus* and *Ps. pyocyanea* as representing the most resistant of the Gram-positive and Gram-negative groups of bacteria and indicated that up to ten freshly isolated strains of each should be used to better ensure a high degree of resistance. They also suggested that the final concentration of the 24 hour cultures in the test solutions should be 10^6–10^7 viable cells per ml and that the tests should be made at a temperature of about 25°: care must also be taken to overcome any bacteriostatic carry-over, either by adequate dilution or by means of a suitable inactivator. A bactericide is considered satisfactory if it gives a rate of kill comparable with that of 0·5 per cent phenol and sterility of the test organisms in 24 hours. In making such determinations it is important to take into account the nature of the preparation with which the bactericide is to be used, and if possible to make the appropriate tests under those conditions. A suspension, for example, may absorb the bactericide and so reduce its efficacy, and pH value can also be important. If, of course, a preparation is sufficiently bactericidal *per se* there is no need to make a further addition, but such occasions are rare.

A similar scheme was also put forward for discussion by the author (Sykes, 1958), but there was one major difference. Moulds can sometimes be as troublesome in 'sterile' preparations as are bacteria and so a mixed suspension of the spores of several species of *Aspergillus, Cladosporium, Mucor* and *Penicillium* was included. On this basis a number of bactericides in common use were examined, with the results summarized in Table 63, and in so far as comparisons can be made (only phenol, cetrimide, phenylmercuric nitrate and the mixed parabens were common to both investigations) they did not differ significantly from those of the Subcommittee (*Report*, 1957). The only divergence was with phenylmercuric nitrate where the Subcommittee sometimes obtained survivors beyond 24 hours. Of particular interest in the author's findings are the high resistance of *Staph. aureus* compared with that of *Ps. pyocyanea*, and the inefficacy of phenol and cresol against mould spores. This defect is somewhat mitigated by the fact that the two compounds are effective inhibitors of mould growth.

The fact that a given solution will kill a series of test cultures under laboratory conditions does not mean that it is universally effective under all circumstances. No reference has yet been made to the spore-forming bacteria, for instance. These are certainly not killed by any of the bactericides named, but they are almost certainly prevented from germination from the spore state, and so their multiplication is thereby prevented. The same applies to

TABLE 63

Lethal properties of some bactericides

Bactericide	Lethal times (in hours) against		
	Staph. aureus	*Ps. pyocyanea*	Mould* spores
A. B.P. BACTERICIDES			
Phenol 0·5%	8–24	8	>24
Cresol 0·3%	2–4	1	>24
Chlorocresol 0·1% . . .	1	1	3
Phenylmercuric nitrate 0·001% . .	4	1–4	3
B. OTHER BACTERICIDES			
Benzyl alcohol 2%	1	1	>24
„ „ 1% . . .	6–24	6	N.A.
Dichlorobenzyl alcohol 0·1% . .	1–3	1	>24
Methyl paraben 0·2% . . .	8	24	N.A.
Propyl paraben 0·02% . . .	4	N.A.	N.A.
Mixed parabens 0·2% + 0·02% . .	4–8	8–24	>24
Cetrimide 0·01%	1	6–24	2
Chlorbutol 0·5%	8–24	2	>24

* Mixed spores from species of *Aspergillus, Cladosporium, Mucor* and *Penicillium*. N.A. = no significant action in 24 hours.

some extent to certain mould spores, which in nature can exhibit high resistances to chemical disinfectants. Several examples have been quoted in earlier chapters and in earlier sections of this chapter (*see*, for example, pages 437 and 438), and there is on record (Sykes and Hooper, 1954) at least one further example, this time of a *Cladosporium* species growing in an insulin solution containing 0·17 per cent of cresol. Certain of the pseudomonads, notably of the water-borne *fluorescens* type, can cause similar trouble, and some wild yeasts also can survive, and grow, in solutions which are otherwise adequately preserved – the author has encountered one such culture, an inoculum from which was largely killed by several of the bactericides but sufficient cells evidently survived to allow of ultimate growth to a few thousand viable cells per ml. In some ways these examples may be considered to be exceptions but they underline the importance of reliable aseptic manipulations at all stages in the handling of preparations for injection.

Yet a further essential attribute in "a suitable bactericide" is its low affinity for rubber. Many of the substances employed have an appreciable solubility in rubber and this means that during storage in a rubber-closed container the bactericide is slowly lost from the injection thus increasing the hazard of its possible subsequent contamination. The subject had been under investigation in the author's laboratory and elsewhere for some years, but it was some time (McGuire and Falk, 1937; Berry, 1953; Sykes, 1953; Wiener, 1955; Wing, 1955, 1956) before any quantitative evidence became available. McGuire and Falk demonstrated a 40 per cent loss of phenol from

TABLE 64

The partitioning of bactericides between rubber and water

Bactericides	Approximate distribution (%) between	
	Rubber	Water
Phenol	25	75
Cresol	33	67
Chlorocresol . . .	85	15
Chlorbutol	80–90	10–20
Benzyl alcohol . . .	15	85
Dichlorobenzyl alcohol .	90	10
Cetrimide	80–95	5–20
Phenylmercuric nitrate .	95	5
Methyl paraben . . .	10	90
Propyl paraben . . .	30–40	60–70

rubber-capped containers after 237 days at 37°, but subsequent investigations indicate that this is probably a low estimate. Berry, for instance, reported that vials of insulin containing originally 0·5 per cent of phenol are unprotected after 12 months' storage: he likewise showed an almost total loss of chlorocresol and presumed that "ultimately an equilibrium is set up between the phenol in the rubber and in the aqueous or oily solution". This was, in fact, proved by Wing with both phenol and chlorocresol, and shown to be a reversible process. He showed that the rate of uptake was rapid in the initial stages and fell away progressively as the equilibrium point was reached. The rate of absorption also increased with each rise in temperature, but the final amount of bactericide absorbed was rather smaller, that is, the partition coefficient, or ratio of amount of bactericide absorbed per g of rubber to amount per ml left in solution, was less. In Wing's experiments, saturation at 2° was not reached until after some 6–9 weeks, whereas at 37° it was substantially complete in about 3 or 4 days, and the partition coefficient of chlorocresol was "about 20 times greater than that of phenol".

Royce and Sykes (1957) and Sykes (1958) also determined the partitioning ratios of a number of bactericides and their results with phenol and chlorocresol were very similar to those of Wing, in spite of the rather different experimental conditions employed. In the author's experiments the ratio was always 1 g of rubber to each 3 ml of solution, and the results so obtained are recorded in Table 64. From these figures, methyl paraben and benzyl alcohol had the most favourable partition ratios followed by phenol and cresol, hence these are the most suitable as bactericides in rubber-closed containers. At the other end of the scale, and therefore least acceptable, are phenylmercuric nitrate, chlorbutol, chlorocresol and cetrimide. Again, in another series of comparisons, Lachman *et al.* (1962, 1963a,b) found the order of solubility, and therefore of preference, to be benzyl alcohol, methyl paraben, phenylethyl alcohol, *p*-chloro-*β*-phenylethyl alcohol and chlorbutol: an order not very different from that of the author's, so far as a comparison can be made.

As might be expected, differences are to be·found with the various types of rubber available. They were not so much in evidence with the three rubbers used by Royce and Sykes (1957), but Lachman *et al.* (1962) preferred a neoprene to a butyl or natural rubber, and when Wing (1955, 1956) examined some thirty different combinations of fillers, accelerators and vulcanizers he obtained some quite interesting results. In general the absorption was not greatly affected by variations in the chemical composition of the mix, but variations in the natural rubber resulted in differing absorbencies of the cured rubbers. These all gave partition coefficients at 37° ranging between 0·7 and 1·2 for phenol and between about 15 and 25 for chlorocresol. A precipitated silica filler, VN3, produced a large increase in absorption, and so did the plasticizer, "factice" (an oxidation product of linseed oil), but the accelerator, Santocure (a benzthiazole derivative), had the reverse effect. These resulted in extremes of partition coefficients of 0·31 and 1·70 for phenol and 7 and 47 for chlorocresol. Smaller differences were noted when the sulphur and the zinc oxide contents were varied.

Lachman *et al.* (1963b) also noted the effect of extractives leached from rubbers on the antibacterial properties of the preservative solutions. This is probably to be expected when compounds such as benzthiazole and thiuram disulphide derivatives are used as accelerators, etc., but it is difficult to see why they should wish to correct the "interference" except for purely analytical purposes.

Oily preparations for injection occupy a special position with regard to bactericides. If properly formulated and made they are devoid of water, and so no contaminating organism could grow in them, neither could a bactericide exert its action. A preservative, then, in such conditions is both unnecessary and useless: its only possible function could be to protect the injection from infection during use, and this is based on the assumption that any contamination which may be introduced will be carried on water droplets or in some other aqueous medium.

Of the bactericides already mentioned phenol is still the most widely used. It has a favourable partition coefficient in rubber and at the concentration prescribed it will kill small inocula of most vegetative bacteria in a matter of minutes but, as indicated in a preceding paragraph and in Table 63, it may require up to 24 hours to deal with heavy inocula. Its activity, along with that of cresol and chlorocresol, is influenced considerably by the acidity of the solution, so much so that at pH 3 a 0·2 per cent solution is equal in activity to a 0·5 per cent solution at pH 7 (Sykes and Hooper, 1954). It is not particularly fungicidal.

The esters of *p*-hydroxybenzoic acid have received much publicity ever since they were introduced into this field by Sabalitschka in 1924, and they have on more than one occasion been described as the nearest approach to the ideal pharmaceutical preservatives. They are more extensively popular in the United States than in Britain, where they are used mainly in preparations for topical use. They have the advantage over the phenols that they are neutral in solution, they are not reactive and are much less affected by changes in pH value. Their activities at pH 7 are only slightly lower than at pH 4, although between pH 6 and pH 3 Entrekin (1961) reported twofold differences for the methyl and ethyl esters and threefold ones for the propyl and butyl esters. At concentrations of 0·15 to 0·2 per cent the methyl ester will kill most vegetative bacteria within 24 hours, but it is of little value against moulds. The propyl ester, on the other hand, is not effective against bacteria but in 0·012 per cent solution it will inhibit moulds. For this reason it is more usual to use a mixture of the two esters, in the ratio of either 10:1 or 2:1, for which some of potentiation of activity is claimed.

Benzyl alcohol was not introduced as a bactericide until 1947. There is some uncertainty about the concentration needed, some suggesting a level as high as 2 per cent, but Gershenfeld (1952) considered 1 per cent to be satisfactory and Hartshorn (1953) observed that several preparations on the American market contain only 0·9 per cent. In the author's opinion 0·9 per cent of benzyl alcohol is about the threshold value. For this reason, a rather higher concentration is desirable, and this is supported by Klein, Millwood and Walther (1954) who warned against the dangers from *Ps. pyocyanea* infections in eye drops by permitting concentrations below 0·9 per cent. The dichloro compound is much more active, but it is of little value in rubber closed containers because of its high partition ratio.

Phenylethyl alcohol, *p*-chloro-*β*-phenylethyl alcohol and phenoxetol came to the fore because of their particular activities against Gram-negative bacteria. Berry (1944) described phenoxetol as a valuable agent in controlling *Ps. pyocyanea* infections, and found that a variety of bacteria were inhibited at 37° in broth by concentrations ranging between 0·3 and 0·8 per cent and killed in 20 minutes at 20° by concentrations of from 1·3 to 1·9 per cent. The concentration used for bacteriostatic purposes is usually 1 per cent. Phenylethyl alcohol was first introduced (Lilley and Brewer, 1953) as a means of isolating Gram-positive bacteria from mixed cultures.

The quaternary ammonium compounds have certain applications as bactericides, but they are limited by their high surface activity, their sensitivity to traces of organic matter and their relatively low inhibitory activities against Gram-negative bacteria. They are readily absorbed by rubbers.

Ophthalmic preparations. The dangers of bacterial infections in preparations used for the eyes can be almost as great as with those administered parenterally, and certainly the chances of contamination during use are much greater. For this reason, therefore, they should be dispensed as sterile solutions and due consideration should be given to their proper preservation. Not all solutions are susceptible to infection to the same degree; some of them are themselves mildly bacteriostatic or bactericidal and so they need no further protection, but others can be distinctly nutrient and these are the ones needing attention. The organisms causing most trouble are *Ps. pyocyanea*, *Proteus* and *Staph. aureus*, but others, including some of the so-called saprophytic types, have been suspected on various occasions, therefore any bactericide used must have a wide antibacterial 'spectrum'.

There is as yet no agreed ideal preservative for ophthalmic use, but the substances most favoured include phenylmercuric nitrate, quaternary ammonium compounds, the esters of *p*-hydroxybenzoic acid, phenylethyl alcohol and one or two of the antibiotics. Of these, phenylethyl alcohol has been strongly recommended because of its particular activity against *Ps. pyocyanea* (Goldstein, 1953; Brewer, Goldstein and McLaughlin, 1953). By the same argument, the quaternary ammonium compounds are the least attractive, although Lawrence (1955) considers benzalkonium chloride to be one of the most suitable, along with chlorbutol and phenylmercuric nitrate. Heller *et al.* (1955) agree with this, except that they have little use for chlorbutol or phenylethyl alcohol, and so more recently do Kohn, Gershenfield and Barr (1963). Quite properly they insist that the preservative added must be fairly rapidly lethal, and for this reason dismissed chlorbutol, 0·5 per cent; phenyethyl alcohol, 0·5 per cent; methyl and propyl paraben mixture, 0·2 and 0·04 per cent; phenylmercuric nitrate, 1 in 10,000; thiomersal, 1 in 5,000, and polymyxin, 2,000 units per ml as being much too slow, taking between 3 and 24 hours to kill inocula of *Pseudomonas* spp. Only benzalkonium at 1 in 5,000 was lethal in less than 1 hour, and these findings were confirmed by *in vivo* tests in the cornea of rabbits. Benzyl alcohol is also sometimes used, but at the concentration normally employed, 0·9 or 1 per cent, it is slightly irritant on first contact with the eye.

Preparations for external or oral use. With certain exceptions, namely, when they are to be applied to the broken skin or to the more delicate membranes, preparations for external or oral use do not have to be made sterile, although in some cases near-aseptic conditions may have to be established in order to keep the level of microbial contamination to a satisfactory minimum and prevent the transfer of infection from one batch of material to another. In every case, of course, scrupulous cleanliness and good house-keeping are taken as axiomatic. This is more difficult to achieve on the large manufacturing scale than in the laboratory and may involve the thorough disinfection of vessels, pipelines, pumps, filling machines, etc. with steam or by other suitable means. It may also require the use of pre-sterilized containers and closures and the completion of the manufacturing and filling processes with the very minimum of delay. With these precautions a product with a reasonably low level of contamination will result, so that the added preservative has a better chance of dealing with the few organisms unavoidably present. It is a curious fact that in some preparations a low level of infection can die out if filled without delay into its final containers, but not so if the infection is allowed to develop beyond a certain level. Sometimes difficulties can be overcome by reformulating to the exclusion of constituents which support microbial growth or give rise to fermentation.

Not all preparations are susceptible to the same types of contaminating organisms; in some, Gram-negative bacteria will grow most readily; in others, yeasts will proliferate; and so on. This, therefore, is one of the factors to be taken into account in making a choice of preservative. Other factors include the nature of the preparation, its alkalinity or acidity, and the compatibilities of its constituents with the proposed preservative.

The compounds most commonly used include benzoic acid, the p-hydroxy-benzoic esters, dehydroacetic acid, sorbic acid, ethyl vanillate, formaldehyde, alcohol, chloroform, chlorbutol, chlorocresol, quaternary ammonium compounds and phenylmercuric salts. Mention might also be made of the dichlorobenzyl alcohols (Carter *et al.*, 1958), hexachlorophane and chlorhexidine. Chloroform is, of course, present as a flavouring agent in many preparations given by mouth, and the concentrations employed, normally 0·15 to 0·25 per cent, are quite adequate to inhibit, and even to kill, bacteria and moulds. It is, however, easily lost by evaporation, and if the concentration is allowed to fall below about 0·1 per cent then bacterial growth may occur. With alcohol the level required to inhibit bacteria and moulds is about 7 per cent, but certain yeasts will resist concentrations up to about 12 per cent.

Benzoic acid at 0·2 per cent concentration is used mainly in preparations given orally, but in those applied externally, and particularly in cosmetic preparations, the esters of p-hydroxybenzoic acid are the more popular. The methyl and propyl esters are the usual choice, and they are added either separately or together at concentrations up to 0·2 per cent and 0·02 per cent respectively. The methyl ester is the more bacteriostatic and the propyl ester the more fungistatic. The hydroxybenzoic esters have the advantage over benzoic acid in that pH value has but little effect on their activities, whereas above about pH 6 benzoic acid is virtually inactive. Sorbic acid, dehydroacetic acid and the vanillic acid esters also behave in a similar way. Several other benzoate esters are also available, including the ethyl, butyl and benzyl compounds, each of which is claimed to possess special virtues; they can be obtained in several combination mixtures.

The phenylmercuric compounds are occasionally used at a concentration of about 0·002 per cent for preserving some lotions and creams, and cetrimide and other quaternary ammonium compounds are suitable for the same purposes at concentrations of about 0·02 per cent. The efficacies of both of these groups of compounds are depleted in preparations formulated as suspensions, and the quaternaries are also inactivated when anionic and certain nonionic substances are present.

Neither are these the only compounds to be so affected. Amongst others, the *p*-hydroxybenzoic acid esters are bound by nonionics such as the Tweens so that they are no longer available to exert their antimicrobial effects. This has been demonstrated by dialysis studies which showed that in a 5 per cent solution of Tween 80 only 22 per cent of methyl paraben and 4·5 per cent of the propyl ester remain unbound and so free to fulfil their preservative functions (Patel and Kostenbauder, 1958). In a like manner, the activities of hexachlorophane and bacitracin are also depleted, when measured by dilution methods. But here a word of warning is necessary concerning the method of assessment, because if an agar diffusion method is used there is an apparent increase in activity, due simply to the enhanced diffusion rate induced by the surface active agent (Beckett and Robinson, 1958).

With particular emphasis on the nonionic emulsifying agents used in cosmetics, this interference phenomenon was studied in some detail by de Navarre (1963). He examined some twenty preservatives and forty nonionics and concluded that "Practically all nonionics based on ethylene or propylene oxide condensates . . . inactivate all presently usable drug and cosmetic preservatives". The extent of the inactivation depended on the ratio of nonionic to preservative, its purity, the pH value and the presence of mineral salts: anionic agents sometimes prevented the interference. Gum tragacanth and methylcellulose can also affect adversely the activities of some preservatives (Eisman, Cooper and Jaconia, 1957; Tillman and Kuramoto, 1957). Finally, care is needed with plastic containers; some can absorb substantial amounts of preservatives.

REFERENCES

ARMSTRONG, H. E. (1941). *Chem. & Ind.*, **60**, 668.
BANFIELD, F. H. (1952). *Chem. & Ind.*, p. 114.
BAUMGARTNER, J. G. (1946). *Canned Foods – An Introduction to their Microbiology:* Churchill, London.
BAYLEY, C. F. and WEATHERBURN, MURIEL W. (1947). *Canad. J. Res., F.*, **25**, 209.
BECKETT, A. H. and ROBINSON, ANN E. (1958). *Soap, Perf. Cosm.*, **31**, 453.
BERRY, H. (1944). *Lancet*, **247**, 175.
BERRY, H. (1953). *J. Pharm., Pharmacol.*, **5**, 1008.
BLOCK, S. S. (1949). *Ind. engng Chem.*, **41**, 1783.
BLOCK, S. S. (1953). *Appl. Microbiol.*, **1**, 287.

BREWER, J. H., GOLDSTEIN, S. W. and McLAUGHLIN, C. B. (1953). *J. Amer. pharm. Ass. (Sci.)*, **42**, 574.
BURGESS, R. (1954). *J. appl. Bact.*, **17**, 230.
CARTER, D. V., CHARLTON, P. T., FENTON, A. H. and LESSEL, B. (1958). *J. Pharm. Pharmacol.*, **10**, 149T.
CAPSTICK, E. (1954). *Chem. & Ind.*, p. 1242.
CAVETT, J. J. (1962). *J. appl. Bact.*, **25**, 282.
CHANCE, H. L. (1963). *J. Bact.*, **85**, 719.
COULTHARD, C. E. (1939). *Pharm. J.*, **142**, 79.
CROSSLEY, E. L. and JOHNSON, W. A. (1942). *J. dairy Res.*, **13**, 5.
DE NAVARRE, M. G. (1963). *J. Soc. cosm. Chem.*, **8**, 68, 371.
ECKERT, J. W. and KOLBEZEN, M. J. (1962). *Nature, Lond.*, **194**, 888.
EISMAN, P. C., COOPER, J. and JACONIA, D. (1957). *J. Amer. pharm. Ass. (Sci.)*, **46**, 144.
ENTREKIN, D. N. (1961). *J. Pharm. Sci.*, **50**, 743.
EVERTON, J. R. and BASHFORD, T. E. (1952). *Proc. Soc. appl. Bact.*, **15**, 94.
FARGHER, R. G., GALLOWAY, L. D. and PROBERT, M. E. (1930). *Shirley Inst., Man.*, **9**, 37; *J. Text. Inst.*, **21**, 245T.
FINDLAY, W. P. K. (1940). *J. oil. col. Chem. Ass.*, **23**, 217.
FOLEY, E. J. and BYRNE, J. V. (1950). *J. Milk Tech.*, **13**, 170.
GALLOWAY, L. D. (1954). *J. appl. Bact.*, **17**, 207.
GERSHENFELD, L. (1952). *Amer. J. Pharm.*, **124**, 399.
GOLDSTEIN, S. W. (1953). *J. Amer. pharm. Ass. (Pract.)*, **14**, 498.
HAINES, R. B. and ELLIOT, E. M. L. (1944). *J. Hyg., Camb.*, **43**, 370.
HANNAN, R. S. (1962). *J. appl. Bact.*, **25**, 248.
HARTSHORN, E. A. (1953). *Amer. J. Pharm.*, **125**, 365.
HAWLEY, H. B. (1955). *J. appl. Bact.*, **18**, 388.
HAWLEY, H. B. (1957). *Food Mfg*, **32**, 370, 430.
HAWLEY, H. B. and BENJAMIN, MARGARET I. W. (1955). *J. appl. Bact.*, 18, 493.
HELLER, W. M., FOSS, N. E., SHAY, D. E. and ICHINOWSKI, C. T. (1955). *J. Amer. pharm. Ass. (Pract.)*, **16**, 29.
HOPF, P. P. and RACE, E. (1949). *Ind. engng Chem.*, **41**, 820.
HOWARD, E. (1954). *J. appl. Bact.*, **17**, 219.
INGRAM, M. (1950). *J. gen. Microbiol.*, **4**, ix.
INGRAM, M. and BARNES, ELLA M. (1955). *J. appl. Bact.*, **18**, 549.
INGRAM, M. (1962). *J. appl. Bact.*, **25**, 262.
JONES, O. and PEARCE, EVELYN (1954). *J. appl. Bact.*, **17**, 272.
KINGSTON, D., LIDWELL, O. M. and NOBLE, W. C. (1962). *Mon. Bull, Publ. Hlth Lab. Serv.*, **21**, 246.
KLEIN, M., MILLWOOD, E. G. and WALTHER, W. W. (1954). *J. Pharm. Pharmacol.*, **6**, 725.
KOHN, S. R. GERSHENFELD, L. and BARR, M. (1963). *J. pharm. Sci.*, **52**, 967.
LACHMAN, L., WEINSTEIN, S., HOPKINS, G., SLACK, S., EISMAN, P. and COOPER, J. (1962). *J. Pharm. Sci.*, **51**, 224.
LACHMAN, L., WEINSTEIN, S., URBANYI, T., EBERSOLD, E. and COOPER, J. (1963a). *J. Pharm. Sci.*, **52**, 241.
LACHMAN, L., URBANYI, T. and WEINSTEIN, S. (1963b). *J. Pharm. Sci.*, **52**, 244.
LAWRENCE, C. A. (1955). *Amer. J. Ophthal.*, **39**, 385.
LEVINE, A. S. and FELLERS, C. R. (1940). *J. Bact.*, **39**, 499; *J. Bact.*, **40**, 255.
LILLEY, B. D. and BREWER, J. H. (1953). *J. Amer. pharm. Ass. (Sci.)*, **42**, 6.
McGUIRE, GRACE and FALK, G. K. (1937). *J. lab. clin. Med.*, **22**, 641.
MARSH, P. B., GREATHOUSE, G. A., BOLLENBACKER, KATHERINA and BUTLER, MARY L. (1944). *Ind. engng Chem.*, **36**, 176.
MORRIS, E. J. and DARLOW, H. M. (1959). *J. appl. Bact.*, **22**, 64.
MOSSEL, D. A. A. and DE BRUIN, A. S. (1950). *Antonie van Leeuwenhoek J. Microbiol. Serol.*, **16**, 393.
NUNHEIMER, T. D. and FABIAN, F. W. (1940). *Amer. J. publ. Hlth*, **30**, 1040.
PATEL, N. K. and KOSTENBAUDER, H. B. (1958). *J. Amer. pharm. Ass. (Sci.)*, **47**, 289.
POHJA, M. S. (1960). *Suom. Maataloust. Seur. Julk.*, no. 96, p. 1.
POUNCY, A. E. and SUMMERS, B. C. L. (1939). *J. Soc. chem. Ind. (Trans.)*, **58**, 162.

Report (1957). *Bacteriostatics for Parenteral Injections of Procaine Penicillin:* Ministry of Health Bacteriostatics Subcommittee of the Conference on the Control of Antibiotics: Ministry of Health, London.

Report (1958). *Second International Symposium on Food Microbiology, Cambridge:* H.M.S.O., London.

RIDGWAY, J. D. (1954). *J. appl. Bact.,* **17,** 1.

RISHBETH, R. (1947). *J. Hyg., Camb.,* **45,** 35.

ROWLANDS, A. (1951). *Proc. Soc. appl. Bact.,* **14,** 7.

ROYCE, A. and SYKES, G. (1957). *J. Pharm. Pharmacol.,* **9,** 814.

SCOTT, C. B. and WOLF, P. A. (1962). *Appl. Microbiol.,* **10,** 211.

SCOTT, W. J. (1957). *Adv. food Res.,* **7,** 83.

SHEWAN, J. M. (1945). *J. Hyg., Camb.,* **44,** 193.

SNOW, D., CRICHTON, M. G. H. and WRIGHT, N. C. (1944). *Ann. appl. Biol.,* **31,** 102.

SPENSER, D. M. and WILKINSON, E. H. (1958). *Nature, Lond.,* **181,** 1603.

SPIEGELBERG, C. H. (1944). *J. Bact.,* **48,** 13.

SYKES, G. (1953). *J. Pharm. Pharmacol.,* **5,** 1018.

SYKES, G. and HOOPER, MARGARET C. (1954). *J. Pharm., Pharmacol.,* **6,** 552.

SYKES, G. (1958). *J. Pharm. Pharmacol.,* **10,** 40T.

TILLMAN, W. J. and KURAMOTO, R. (1957). *J. Amer. pharm. Ass. (Sci.),* **46,** 211.

TOMKINS, R. G. (1962). *J. appl. Bact.,* **25,** 290.

TOMKINS, R. G. (1963). *Nature, Lond.,* **193,** 669.

VAS, K. (1957). *Food Manufacture,* **32,** 71.

WIENER, S. (1955). *J. Pharm. Pharmacol.,* **7,** 118.

WILSON, G. S. (1942). *The Pasteurization of Milk:* Arnold, London.

WING, W. T. (1955). *J. Pharm. Pharmacol.,* **7,** 648.

WING, W. T. (1956). *J. Pharm. Pharmacol.,* **8,** 734, 738

WOODBINE, M., REID, E. M. and SCORER, EILEEN M. C. (1953). *Proc. Soc. appl. Bact.* **16,** 56.

AUTHOR INDEX

Numbers in *italics* indicate pages in reference lists.

Where an author is included in the text under *"et al.,"* only the appropriate
reference list page is given.

SUBJECT INDEX

Acetic acid in food preservation, 438, 441

Achromobacter-Alkaligenes bacteria, in radiation treated meats, 166
resistance, to ozone, 203
to ionizing radiations, 153

Acidity, effect of, in heat sterilization, 118
preservative action in foods, 438

Acids, growth of moulds in, 430
mode of lethal action, 28

Acridines, 352 (*see also* under individual compounds)
acquired resistance to, 357
action on bacterial enzymes, 11
constitution and activities, 29, 353, 355
dimensional factor, 353
mechanisms of bacteriostasis, 353
selective activities, 357
uses, in medicine, 359

Acriflavine, 357, 358

Actamer, 322
in soaps, 328

Adaptations in bacteria, to acridines, 359
mechanisms of, 12, 14
and resistance to disinfectants, 13

Agar diffusion and surface contact tests for antiseptics, 90, 91

Air, disinfectants in, methods of testing, 264
activities of, 269
disinfection of, by chemical means, 264, 267
effect of humidity, 269
'initial kill' phenomenon, 268
mechanism of, 267
by UV, 178
filters, sterilizing mechanism, 5, 273
sampling, methods and devices, 258
sterilization, 253
by compression, 283
by electrostatic precipitation, 284
by filtration, 273
with glycidaldehyde, 223
by heat, 282
methods of assessing, 256
with β-propiolactone, 221
by scrubbing, 285
by UV, 283

Air-borne organisms, viability, 254
effect of humidity, 254
effect of suspending medium, 256

Alcohol, activities, 343
as preservative, 456
for foods, 440
in instrument sterilization, 344
in skin disinfection, 344

Alcohols (*see also* under individual compounds)

Alcohols—*continued*
constitution and activities, 29, 342
mechanisms of lethal action, 25, 341
as preservatives, in injections, 449, 451, 454
in ophthalmic preparations, 455
temperature coefficients of, 22
as virucidal agents, 300, 301

Aminacrine, 355, 358

Amphoteric compounds, constitution and activities, 377
mode of action, 29
uses, in hospitals, 378
in skin disinfection, 378

Amyl-*m*-cresol, activities, 315
lethal properties of vapour, 225
uses in medicine, 326

Antibiotics, as preservatives, in foods, 441
in ophthalmic preparations, 455
in radiopasteurization, 167
stability to radiation sterilization, 167

Antifungal agents (*see also* under individual compounds)
for cutting oils, 448
for leather, 448
for paints, 441
for paper, 444
for rubber, 448
for textiles, 442
for wood, 444

Antifungal tests, for antiseptics, 85
for disinfectants, 85
in paints, 445, 446
in textiles, 442

Anthrax spores, death rate, 39
with mercuric chloride, 17
with phenol, 17
disinfection of, with chlorine, 388
with formaldehyde, 345
with dry heat, 115
with steam, 114
in early testing methods, 17, 39

Antiseptic, defined, 7

Antiseptic testing (*see also* under individual methods)
by agar diffusion methods, 90
by agar surface-contact methods, 91
for antifungal activity, 85
bactericidal tests, 84
bacteriostatic tests, 83
in blood, 88
on egg membranes, 89
and phagocyte toxicity, 89
on the skin, 93
by hand washing methods, 97
for retention of activity, 99

Antiseptics (*see also* under individual compounds)
ideals for, 81
oral, testing of, 100

Mutations in bacteria, mechanisms of, 13
and resistance to disinfection, 14
role of enzymes in, 13

Newcastle disease virus, inactivation of,
with ether and chloroform, 302
with ethylene oxide, 303
in testing virucides, 294
Nitrophenols, 325
as leather preservatives, 448

O-silver, 420
Oils (*see also* Essential oils)
effects of, on activities of phenols, 30
sterile filtration of, 198
survival of bacteria in, 340
Fligodynamic metals, 3, 418
Ophthalmic preparations, preservation of,
455
Oral antiseptics, testing, 100
Organic matter, effect of, on disinfectant
activity, 24 (*see also* under individual compounds etc.)
uses of, in testing antiseptics, 82, 83,
84
in testing disinfectants, 25, 51, 67
Organolead compounds, 424
Organotins, *see* Tin compounds
Osmosis, in bactericidal activity, 30, 31
and food preservation, 437
Oxidizing agents, mechanism of action, 27
Oxygen effect in radiation sterilization,
158
Ozone, effect of humidity, 205
effect of organic matter, 203
sensitivities of organisms to, 203
sterilization by, 203
uses of, in air disinfection, 272
in food preservation, 206
in water treatment, 206

Paints, preservation of, 445
Paper, preservation of, 416, 444
Parabens, as preservatives, in foods, 44
in injections, 449, 451, 454
in pharmaceuticals, 323
Pasteurization, by heat, of foods, 431
HTST processes, 432
susceptibilities of bacteria to, 431
time-temperature equivalents, 431
by radiations, *see* High energy ionizing radiations, Radiopasteurization
Pentachlorophenol, as preservative, in
leather, 448
in paints, 445, 446
in paper, 444
for textiles, 443
for wood, 444

Permanganate, early uses, 4
mechanisms of action, 27
Phagocyte toxicity tests on antiseptics, 89
Pharmaceutical products (*see also* under
individual materials, processes etc.)
preservation of, 323, 375, 416, 455, 457
sterilization of, by radiations, 167
Phenol, adaptation of bacterial resistance
to, 12
dilution coefficient of, 23
effect of oils, fats, alcohols, 30
effect of surface tension on, 29, 31
enhancement of activity by iron salts,
424
potentiation of activity of, 29, 31
as preservative in injections, 449, 450
as standard in disinfectant testing,
41, 45, 51, 53, 54, 57, 60
vapour, activities, 225
in virus disinfection, 299, 300
Phenol coefficient tests (*see also* under
individual methods)
defects in, 21, 56
fluctuations on, 48, 57
interpretation of results, 44
limits of error in, 57
types of, 45
Phenol-soaps (*see also* Coal tar disinfectants)
activities, 30, 326, 327, 338
Phenols, (*see also* individual compounds)
alkyl, 314
potentiation of activities, 316
constitution and activities, 29, 311
effect of organic matter, 312, 321
effect of membrane permeability,
30, 31
effect of solvents and solutes, 313
diphenyl derivatives, 319
in disinfectant fluids, 331
effect of, on bacterial enzymes, 11
effect of soaps on, 30, 320, 322, 337
in 'germicidal' soaps, 327
mode of action, 28, 312
nitro derivatives, 325
polyhydric, 318
temperature coefficients of, 22
as virus inactivators, 300
Phenoxetol, 449, 454
Phenylethyl alcohol, as preservative in
pharmaceuticals, 445, 451, 454, 455
Phenylmercuric salts, 415
in medicine and surgery, 417
as preservatives for industrial materials, 416
as preservatives in pharmaceuticals,
416, 449, 453, 455
as skin disinfectants, 416
o-Phenylphenol, *see* Diphenyl
pHisoHex, 322
Phosphatase test in milk, 432
Photoreactivation of bacteria, after UV,
178
Pine oil disinfectants, 337
Poliomyelitis virus, inactivation of, 292
by chlorine, 304

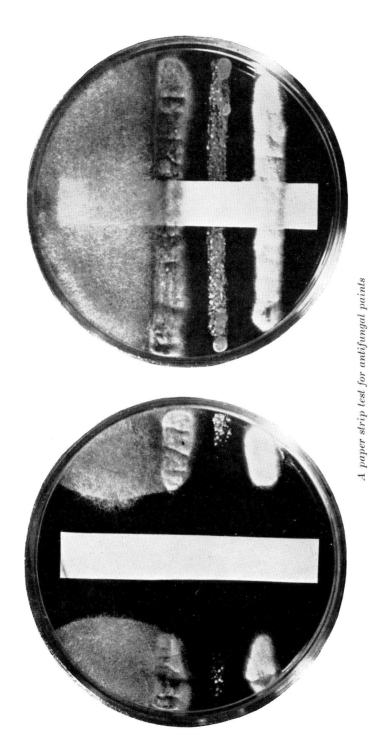

A paper strip test for antifungal paints

The plate was inoculated with four saprophytic moulds. The sample on the left is satisfactory, and that on the right unsatisfactory.

(*See* pp. 77 and 446–447)

PLATE 1

A laboratory panel test for antifungal paints

Three samples on each panel. The dark areas are all patches of mould growth. (*See* pp. 77 and 447)

PLATE 2